CORBAN
C O L L E G E

9000 Deer Park Drive S.E., Salem, Oregon 97301 / (503) 581-8600

THE NEW AMERICAN COMMENTARY

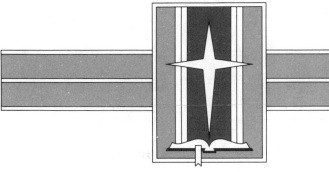

An Exegetical and Theological
Exposition of Holy Scripture

THE NEW AMERICAN COMMENTARY

Volume
22

MATTHEW

Craig L. Blomberg

BROADMAN PRESS
NASHVILLE, TENNESSEE   1992

Library of Congress Cataloging-in-Publication Data

Blomberg, Craig.
  Matthew / Craig L. Blomberg.
    p. cm. — (The New American commentary ; v. 22)
  Includes indexes.
  ISBN 0-8054-0122-9
  1. Bible. N.T. Matthew—Commentaries. I. Title. II. Series.
BS2575.3.B6   1992
226.2′077—dc20

To Bear Valley Church

and all its members and staff
who have modeled many of the lessons of the Gospel of Matthew
who have shown me how today's church can make a difference
and who have supported me and one another in difficult times

Editors' Preface

God's Word does not change. God's world, however, changes in every generation. These changes, in addition to new findings by scholars and a new variety of challenges to the gospel message, call for the church in each generation to interpret and apply God's Word for God's people. Thus, THE NEW AMERICAN COMMENTARY is introduced to bridge the twentieth and twenty-first centuries. This new series has been designed primarily to enable pastors, teachers, and students to read the Bible with clarity and proclaim it with power.

In one sense THE NEW AMERICAN COMMENTARY is not new, for it represents the continuation of a heritage rich in biblical and theological exposition. The title of this forty-volume set points to the continuity of this series with an important commentary project published at the end of the nineteenth century called AN AMERICAN COMMENTARY, edited by Alvah Hovey. The older series included, among other significant contributions, the outstanding volume on Matthew by John A. Broadus, from whom the publisher of the new series, Broadman Press, partly derives its name. The former series was authored and edited by scholars committed to the infallibility of Scripture, making it a solid foundation for the present project. In line with this heritage, all NAC authors affirm the divine inspiration, inerrancy, complete truthfulness, and full authority of the Bible. The perspective of the NAC is unapologetically confessional and rooted in the evangelical tradition.

Since a commentary is a fundamental tool for the expositor or teacher who seeks to interpret and apply Scripture in the church or classroom, the NAC focuses on communicating the theological structure and content of each biblical book. The writers seek to illuminate both the historical meaning and contemporary significance of Holy Scripture.

In its attempt to make a unique contribution to the Christian community, the NAC focuses on two concerns. First, the commentary emphasizes how each section of a book fits together so that the reader becomes aware of the theological unity of each book and of Scripture as a whole. The writers, however, remain aware of the Bible's inherently rich variety. Second, the NAC is produced with the conviction that the Bible primarily belongs to the church.

We believe that scholarship and the academy provide an indispensable foundation for biblical understanding and the service of Christ, but the editors and authors of this series have attempted to communicate the findings of their research in a manner that will build up the whole body of Christ. Thus, the commentary concentrates on theological exegesis, while providing practical, applicable exposition.

THE NEW AMERICAN COMMENTARY's theological focus enables the reader to see the parts as well as the whole of Scripture. The biblical books vary in content, context, literary type, and style. In addition to this rich variety, the editors and authors recognize that the doctrinal emphasis and use of the biblical books differs in various places, contexts, and cultures among God's people. These factors, as well as other concerns, have led the editors to give freedom to the writers to wrestle with the issues raised by the scholarly community surrounding each book and to determine the appropriate shape and length of the introductory materials. Moreover, each writer has developed the structure of the commentary in a way best suited for expounding the basic structure and the meaning of the biblical books for our day. Generally, discussions relating to contemporary scholarship and technical points of grammar and syntax appear in the footnotes and not in the text of the commentary. This format allows pastors and interested laypersons, scholars and teachers, and serious college and seminary students to profit from the commentary at various levels. This approach has been employed because we believe that all Christians have the privilege and responsibility to read and seek to understand the Bible for themselves.

Consistent with the desire to produce a readable, up-to-date commentary, the editors selected the *New International Version* as the standard translation for the commentary series. The selection was made primarily because of the NIV's faithfulness to the original languages and its beautiful and readable style. The authors, however, have been given the liberty to differ at places from the NIV as they develop their own translations from the Greek and Hebrew texts.

The NAC reflects the vision and leadership of those who provide oversight for Broadman Press, who in 1987 called for a new commentary series that would evidence a commitment to the inerrancy of Scripture and a faithfulness to the classic Christian tradition. While the commentary adopts an "American" name, it should be noted some writers represent countries outside the United States, giving the commentary an international perspective. The diverse group of writers includes scholars, teachers, and administrators from almost twenty different colleges and seminaries, as well as pastors, missionaries, and a layperson.

The editors and writers hope that THE NEW AMERICAN COMMENTARY will be helpful and instructive for pastors and teachers, scholars and students, for men and women in the churches who study and teach God's Word in various settings. We trust that for editors, authors, and readers alike, the commentary will be used to build up the church, encourage obedience, and bring renewal to God's people. Above all, we pray that the NAC will bring glory and honor to our Lord, who has graciously redeemed us and faithfully revealed himself to us in his Holy Word.

SOLI DEO GLORIA
The Editors

Author's Preface

Until the 1980s, Matthew was not well served by commentaries. Each of the other Gospels had a larger number available from which to select, whether popular or expositional or critical in nature. The past decade has seen this gap dramatically filled. More than half of the nearly thirty commentaries which I regularly employed as part of my background reading for this work were published in the last decade. For Evangelicals, Carson and France should remain standards for years to come. For creative systematic theology organized in the sequence of a biblical text, Bruner's two volumes offer many challenging insights. For comprehensive discussions from a moderately critical perspective, the two multivolume series by Allison and Davies and by Luz, currently in progress, should render further detailed treatments unnecessary for some time.

In fact, I am convinced that most of the new commentary series being planned for the 1990s, at least on the *New* Testament, are superfluous and distract researchers from more important projects to which they should be devoting their attention. Publishers' motives often seem primarily to center on duplicating or outdoing what the "competition" is offering. I am convinced, however, that *The New American Commentary* has the potential to be a significant exception to these trends. Its unique balance of theological exposition and application, based on solid scholarship yet presented in a relatively limited and readable format, holds promise of offering busy pastors and teachers a more usable resource than many of the more massive volumes available and a more accurate resource than many of the devotional or homiletical works in the current market. I hope that I can approximate the high standard achieved by the initial volumes of the NAC which have preceded mine.

For this reason, I have focused primarily on what might be called a cautious evangelical redaction criticism. The most important consideration in the theological exposition of a Gospel is to determine what a given Evangelist wants to stress. God inspired four accounts of the life of Jesus, not one, apparently because he wanted his church to understand the significance of the foundational events for their faith from numerous perspectives. Yet conservative scholarship has typically blurred the distinctions between the four Gospels in its quest to outline and defend a harmony of the life of Christ. More liberal scholarship has understandably reacted against this tendency but has often swung the pendulum too far in the opposite direction, pitting one Gospel against another rather than viewing the canonical diversity as complementary rather than contradictory. Robert Gundry's unique work was hailed as the first thoroughgoing evangelical redaction-critical commentary on Matthew, but it actually focused much more on Matthew's linguistic and stylistic features than on his theology, and it proposed idiosyncratic understandings of Matthew's interpretive methods which have not caught on in either evangelical or liberal circles.

I have approached Matthew's text *not* by *presupposing* some view of inerrancy but on the basis of my previous study of historical convention in the ancient world (see the commentary introduction under "Historicity and Genre"). Following the standard canons of historiography of the day, I find no reason for viewing any part of Matthew as "errant," and I am convinced that the differences between Gospel parallels can be plausibly harmonized. But commentators and preachers ought not to be overly distracted by these issues. The important question at each point in the exposition of a Gospel is why the Evangelist phrased his account in the unique form in which it appears. If, for example, I want to preach on the miracle of Jesus' feeding the five thousand, I ought to become familiar with the distinctive concerns of Matthew, Mark, Luke, and John and then choose *one* of the four versions of that story to expound because it best matches the message I believe God wants me to give to my audience. Or, if I am preaching or teaching consecutively through a Gospel, I ought to ask at each stage what it is that my particular Gospel writer wants to stress which I would miss if I only had the other three, and then I must make sure those themes are emphasized in my message.

Sometimes, however, the distinctives between parallels are too minor to find much by this method. In other instances, one Gospel presents material not paralleled elsewhere. So the Gospel expositor must learn to think vertically (down the pages of a single narrative) as well as horizontally (across the columns of a synopsis). In my opinion, the single greatest deficiency of most Gospel commentaries is their failure to reflect in detail on why one Evangelist ordered his material in the sequence he did. Obviously, chronology is not the main motive. Too frequently the Gospels differ in order of passages, and even when they remain the same, so many other things happened in Jesus' life (John 20:30; 21:25) that it is still crucial to ask why these particular events were chosen for permanent record. The answer regularly lies in the arena of thematic or topical groupings which greatly illuminate the author's original purposes.

To be sure, commentators run the risk of perceiving patterns which were not originally intended. But my study has convinced me that Matthew (like the other Gospels) regularly juxtaposes discrete sections of his text for significant, theological reasons which we do well to try to recover. Readers will have to decide for themselves at which points my outline of the Gospel is plausible. That outline is probably the single most distinctive feature of my work. My concern with Matthew's narrative flow may therefore be the commentary's greatest justification for taking its place alongside the plethora of other works on this Gospel as well as the area in which from time to time I am most likely to be wrong!

In other aspects of the book, I am aware of how much I am indebted to previously published works even where my documentation is not more ample. Still, I have tried to include more footnotes than some volumes in this series, focusing particularly on scholarly books and articles on Matthew in which interested readers can pursue topics which cannot be explored at length in the commentary. Other issues, such as the *Traditionsgeschichte* of a certain passage or the history of interpretation of a given text, have for the most part been omitted due to the scope of this series.

I am most grateful to the editors of Broadman Press for this opportunity to comment on Matthew's Gospel. I have long been fascinated with Matthew's work. But my scholarly career began by focusing on Luke, largely due to the initiatives of my doctoral supervisor. My two dominant concerns in those days revolved around Luke's parables and issues of the historical reliability of Jesus' teaching. Each of these interests, in turn, issued in full-length books dealing with the Gospels more generally. My teaching responsibilities, however, found me focusing primarily on Mark as the basis for "Life of Christ" and "Survey of the Gospels" courses, first at the undergraduate and then at the graduate level. So I was delighted, in preparation for this commentary, to have the chance to branch out even further to explore in some depth what is perhaps my favorite Gospel.

I am equally thrilled to be participating in what has the potential for being a landmark series for Southern Baptists. Although we hope to reach a wide readership, it is highly likely that Baptist pastors, students, and teachers will comprise the largest single segment of our audience. I am currently teaching outside the Convention (in a Conservative Baptist Seminary) and ministering in a church which, while jointly Southern Baptist and Conservative Baptist, in ethos resembles neither! But both of my ordinations, first as a deacon and then to the gospel ministry, come from a Southern Baptist church, and my first college-level teaching position was in an SBC school. So I hope that my periodic applications of Matthew to contemporary Christian living may prove relevant to distinctively Southern Baptist concerns while also addressing a much wider audience.

Many individuals merit heartfelt thanks for reading and reacting to this book in manuscript form. These include my editor, David Dockery; my friend and professional peer, Scot McKnight; my informal advisor on English style, Phyllis Klein; my father, John Blomberg, representing the "educated layperson"; and my devoted wife, Fran, who pored over my work day after day despite the many more exciting things she could have been doing. Rebecca Barnes and Ruth Miksell spent countless hours transcribing at times virtually unintelligible dictation and hand-printed text into typescript. The faculty and trustees of Denver Seminary graciously granted me a sabbatical term in 1990 which enabled me to complete the first draft of the book. I am also grateful to my students who honed my thoughts on Matthew as this manuscript was "under construction," and particularly to eight who read and commented on the entire work in its penultimate form—Goran Anic, David Campbell, Bruce Cross, Mike Ediger, Lance Hartman, Anahid Katchian, Deb Marshall, and Bill Mullen.

In 1988, not long after I first accepted the invitation to begin working on this project, I had to undergo surgery to repair a detached retina in my right eye. In 1991, shortly before submitting the final draft of this manuscript, I underwent follow-up procedures to remove cataracts that had been growing on that eye since shortly after the original operation. God has been most gracious in making both of these treatments, to date, successful and in sustaining me through many difficult days in between. I am particularly conscious and appreciative of the skills of my retinal surgeon, Dr. Kevin Brady, and of my ophthalmologist, Dr. Allan Berg, without which this commentary would never have been produced. May they continue to give sight to many.

Abbreviations

Bible Books

Gen
Exod
Lev
Num
Deut
Josh
Judg
Ruth
1, 2 Sam
1, 2 Kgs
1, 2 Chr
Ezra
Neh
Esth
Job
Ps (*pl.* Pss)
Prov
Eccl
Song of Songs

Isa
Jer
Lam
Ezek
Dan
Hos
Joel
Amos
Obad
Jonah
Mic
Nah
Hab
Zeph
Hag
Zech
Mal
Matt
Mark

Luke
John
Acts
Rom
1, 2 Cor
Gal
Eph
Phil
Col
1, 2 Thess
1, 2 Tim
Titus
Phlm
Heb
Jas
1, 2 Pet
1, 2, 3 John
Jude
Rev

Commonly Used Sources

AB   *Anchor Bible*
AC   An American Commentary
Adv. Haer. Against Heresies
AJTh   *Asia Journal of Theology*
Ann.   *Annals*
Ant.   *Antiquities*
ATR   *Anglican Theological Review*

AusBR	*Australian Biblical Review*
AUSS	*Andrews University Seminary Studies*
BAGD	W. Bauer, W. F. Arndt, F. W. Gingrich, and F. Danker, *Greek-English Lexicon of the New Testament*
BARev	*Biblical Archaeology Review*
b. B. Bat.	Babylonian Talmud *Baba Batra*
b. Ber.	Babylonian Talmud *Berakot*
BCBC	*Believers Church Bible Commentary*
BDF	F. Blass, A. Debrunner, R. W. Funk, *A Greek Grammar of the New Testament*
b. Hag.	Babylonian Talmud *Hagiga*
Bib	*Biblica*
b. Pesah.	Babylonian Talmud *Pesahim*
BJRL	*Bulletin of the John Rylands Library*
BSac	*Bibliotheca Sacra*
b. Sanh.	Babylonian Talmud *Sanhedrin*
BT	*The Bible Translator*
b. Taᶜan.	Babylonian Talmud *Taᶜanit*
BTB	*Biblical Theology Bulletin*
b. Yoma	Babylonian Talmud *Yoma*
BZ	*Biblische Zeitschrift*
CBAA	Catholic Biblical Association of America
CBQ	*Catholic Biblical Quarterly*
CSR	*Christian Scholars' Review*
CTQ	*Concordia Theological Quarterly*
CTR	*Criswell Theological Review*
Dial.	*Dialog with Trypho*
Did.	*Didache*
Dio Cass	*Dio Cassius Cocceianus*
DNTT	*Dictionary of New Testament Theology*
DownRev	*Downside Review*
EBC	Expositor's Bible Commentary
EKK	Evangelisch-katholischer Kommentar zum Neuen Testament
ETR	*Etudes théologiques et religieuses*
ETS	Evangelical Theological Society
EvQ	*Evangelical Quarterly*
Exp	*Expositor*
ExpTim	*Expository Times*
Flacc.	*In Flaccum*
FNT	*Filologia Neotestamentaria*
GNBC	Good News Bible Commentary
GTJ	*Grace Theological Journal*
H.E.	*Church History*

HeyJ	*Heythrop Journal*
Hist.	*History*
HNTC	Harper's NT Commentaries
HTK	Herders theologischer Kommentar zum Neuen Testament
HTR	*Harvard Theological Review*
HUCA	*Hebrew Union College Annual*
IBS	*Irish Biblical Studies*
ICC	International Critical Commentary
IDB	*Interpreter's Dictionary of the Bible*
Int	*Interpretation*
ISBE	*International Standard Bible Encyclopedia*, Revised
JAAR	*Journal of the American Academy of Religion*
JANES	*Journal of Ancient Near Eastern Studies*
JBL	*Journal of Biblical Literature*
JES	*Journal of Ecumenical Studies*
JETS	*Journal of the Evangelical Theological Society*
JR	*Journal of Religion*
JRH	*Journal of Religious History*
JSNT	*Journal for the Study of the New Testament*
JTS	*Journal of Theological Studies*
J.W.	*Jewish War*
LXX	Septuagint
Mak.	*Makkot*
m. Git	Mishna *Gittin*
m. Hag.	Mishna *Hagiga*
MT	Masoretic Text
NAC	New American Commentary
NCB	New Century Bible
NIC	New International Commentary
Neot	*Neotestamentica*
NovT	*Novum Testamentum*
NTS	*New Testament Studies*
PEQ	*Palestine Exploration Quarterly*
PRS	*Perspectives in Religious Studies*
RB	*Revue biblique*
RestQ	*Restoration Quarterly*
RevExp	*Review and Expositor*
RevQ	*Revue de Qumran*
RNT	Regensburger Neues Testament
RTR	*Reformed Theological Review*
SEAJT	*Southeast Asia Journal of Theology*
SJT	*Scottish Journal of Theology*
SNTU	*Studien zum Neuen Testament und seiner Umwelt*

SVTQ	*St. Vladimir's Theological Quarterly*
SWJT	*Southwestern Journal of Theology*
TDNT	G. Kittel and G. Friedrich, eds., *Theological Dictionary of the New Testament*
Tg. Isa	*Targum of Isaiah*
Theol	*Theology*
ThT	*Theology Today*
T. Levi	*Testament of Levi*
TNTC	Tyndale New Testament Commentaries
TrinJ	*Trinity Journal*
TS	*Theological Studies*
TynBul	*Tyndale Bulletin*
TZ	*Theologische Zeitschrift*
UBS	United Bible Societies
UBSGNT	United Bible Societies' *Greek New Testament*
USQR	*Union Seminary Quarterly Review*
VE	*Vox Evangelica*
WBC	Word Biblical Commentary
WTJ	*Westminster Theological Journal*
ZDPV	*Zeitschrift des deutschen Palästina-Vereins*
ZNW	*Zeitschrift für die neutestamentliche Wissenschaft*
ZTK	*Zeitschrift für Theologie und Kirche*

Contents

Matthew

————————— **INTRODUCTION** —————————

Although it is sustaining challenges from many fronts, Christianity continues to be the religion that claims more adherents than any other in the world. At the center of the Christian faith is the life and work of Jesus of Nazareth. Without the teachings and mighty deeds of this first-century Jew, the Christian religion would never have been born. The four Gospels in the New Testament tell the story of the very birth and foundation of Christianity. Of the four, Matthew was usually the most popular in the first several centuries of the church's history. It contains the greatest quantity of Jesus' teaching, including his most famous sermon (the Sermon on the Mount; chaps. 5–7), which in turn includes some of his most well-known teachings (e.g., the Beatitudes, Lord's Prayer, and Golden Rule).

Matthew also contains the greatest number of links with Judaism and the Old Testament. It probably was placed first in the collection of Gospels, when they were initially brought together in the second century and viewed as on a par with the already existing Hebrew Scriptures, precisely for that reason. Matthew demonstrates that Jesus and his church were the fulfillment of all God's promises to Israel. This Gospel remains treasured in Christian circles today, from its famous "Christmas story" in chaps. 1–2, through many of Jesus' most beloved parables (chap. 13), to the poignant account of his passion and crucifixion (chaps. 26–27), followed by the dramatic sequel of the resurrection (chap. 28). Perhaps no more significant challenge faces those who would call themselves Jesus' followers than the challenge of obedience to the closing charge of the Gospel—to make disciples in every part of the world (28:19).

Introductions to commentaries on books of the Bible usually begin with a discussion of author, date, audience, and place of composition and then move on to topics such as theology and outline. Because so little is known with certainty about the setting of the Gospel of Matthew, I have chosen to begin inductively, with structure and theology, and then to use the results of those discussions to help inform decisions about authorship, date, and the like. I have also chosen to write a relatively brief introduction for several reasons. First, *The New American Commentary* series is aimed above all at preachers and teachers in churches; busy pastors and laypersons seldom have time for or interest in wading through lengthy commentary introductions. Second, several excellent, up-to-date, and thorough introductions to Matthew are available elsewhere.[1] R. T. France, who has written the most detailed of these works, very closely approximates my own conclusions, except on structure (and very occasionally elsewhere); so I perhaps may be forgiven for referring the reader to it for a more thorough defense of the views we have in common and for a more extensive bibliography.[2]

A. Structure

Most readers of the Gospels naturally assume that these accounts of Jesus' ministry unfold chronologically. Most commentaries on Matthew develop their outlines along chronological lines. Many see Matthew's Gospel as a collection of discrete passages about what Jesus said and did at different stages in his life and in different locations without trying to group those episodes into any larger thematic sections. Since the early part of the twentieth century, however, it has been common to point out that Matthew, unlike the other Gospels, presents five major blocks of discourses of Jesus (we might call them "sermons") in chaps. 5–7; 10; 13;

---

[1] From an evangelical perspective, see D. A. Carson, "Matthew," in *EBC*, vol. 8, ed. F. E. Gaebelein (Grand Rapids: Zondervan, 1984), 3-57. From a more eclectic perspective, see D. C. Allison and W. D. Davies, *A Critical and Exegetical Commentary on the Gospel according to Saint Matthew*, ICC, vol. 1 (Edinburgh: T & T Clark, 1988), 1-148. For a good survey of relatively recent studies, see G. Stanton, "The Origin and Purpose of Matthew's Gospel: Matthean Scholarship from 1945 to 1980," in *Aufstieg und Niedergang der römischen Welt*, Teil 2: Principat, 25.3, ed. W. Hasse (Berlin: de Gruyter, 1985), 1889-1951.

[2] R. T. France, *Matthew: Evangelist and Teacher* (Grand Rapids: Zondervan, 1989).

18; and 23–25. Matthew makes plain that these are important sections for his outline by including a summary statement at the end of each (8:1; 11:1; 13:53; 19:1; 26:1), which unites the sayings material of each discourse and moves the narrative along to a new segment.

B. W. Bacon proposed that Matthew wanted to present Jesus as a new Moses, giving his followers a new Law or Pentateuch, just as the Old Testament presents five books of Moses—the Torah.[3] Of course, five sermons in and of themselves hardly prove Matthew is imitating the Pentateuch, and few contemporary scholars follow Bacon on this point. But many are persuaded by the idea of Jesus as a new Moses or Lawgiver and see the blocks of discourse as key to developing Matthew's outline.[4] Closer analysis, however, suggests that Matthew is actually contrasting Jesus and the law more than he is paralleling them (see "Theology").

A second prominent approach to Matthew's structure, particularly associated with J. Kingsbury, finds the major subdivisions indicated by the twice-used formula "From that time on Jesus began to" in 4:17 and 16:21. Matthew 1:1–4:16 then becomes the Gospel's introduction; 4:17–16:20, its body; and 16:21–28:20, the conclusion.[5] These three sections fit these labels well, inasmuch as they present, respectively, events prior to Jesus' public ministry, representative samplings of his major teachings and miracles, and the climactic development of his life—the road to the cross. These divisions seem more promising than Bacon's, but often they are presented without adequate recognition of the importance of the "sermons." Several attempts have been made to combine the strengths of both of these approaches, often finding some kind of chiasmus or inverted parallelism (ABB'A,' ABCB'A,' etc.) as the key to Matthew's outline.[6] Yet these parallels inevitably prove vague and break down at crucial points. Other proposals seem even more idiosyncratic and have garnered few followers.[7]

There is of course no reason why Matthew must have had a detailed outline in view as he wrote. Many writers in the ancient Middle East were far less preoccupied with exhibiting a linear development of thought than are we in the contemporary Western world. Still, a careful analysis of Matthew's juxtaposition of passages regularly suggests that they are grouped as they are for specific reasons. And the frequency with which

[3]B. W. Bacon, "The Five Books of Matthew against the Jews," *Exp* 15 (1918): 56-66.

[4]See W. D. Davies, *The Setting of the Sermon on the Mount* (Cambridge: University Press, 1963).

[5]See J. D. Kingsbury, *Matthew: Structure, Christology, Kingdom* (Philadelphia: Fortress, 1975); D. R. Bauer, *The Structure of Matthew's Gospel* (Sheffield: Almond, 1989).

[6]See C. H. Lohr, "Oral Techniques in the Gospel of Matthew," *CBQ* 23 (1961): 403-35; P. F. Ellis, *Matthew: His Mind and His Message* (Collegeville, Ill.: Liturgical, 1975); H. J. B. Combrink, "The Structure of the Gospel of Matthew as Narrative," *TynBul* 34 (1983): 61-90.

[7]See the thorough survey in Bauer, *Structure*, 21-55.

parallel passages appear in different places or sequences in the other Gospels, particularly Mark and Luke, suggests that many of those juxtapositions are not first of all chronologically motivated.[8] In view of the historical and biographical styles of Matthew's day, it is wise *not* to assume that two consecutive stories occurred one after the other unless one of the passages specifically declares that they did or unless the second passage refers to the first in a way that logically requires the stories to have occurred in that order.[9] And even when we may reasonably assume a chronological sequence, Matthew's motivation for skipping over intervening events is often that he sees thematic links between the passages he includes (see particularly the introductory sections to the commentary on 8:1–9:35; 11:1–12:50; 13:53–16:20).

I wish to propose an outline of Matthew, therefore, that combines the strengths of Bacon and Kingsbury but moves beyond them as well. The three main sections of the Gospel will be 1:1–4:16 (introduction), 4:17–16:20 (development), and 16:21–28:20 (climax). Thus far I agree with Kingsbury. All the episodes of 1:1–4:16 present events prior to the actual beginning of Christ's ministry; with 4:17 his great Galilean ministry gets underway. From 4:17–16:20 Jesus teaches and preaches, heals and works miracles, gains increasing popularity and arouses growing animosity, and consistently forces people to raise the question of his identity, which is climactically and correctly answered by Simon Peter in 16:13-20. But despite the lack of scene change, the tone and content of 16:21-28 could scarcely introduce a more abrupt about-face. From this passage through the end of the Gospel all attention is centered on the road to the cross, with its glorious sequel, the resurrection.

Having begun with Kingsbury, however, I turn immediately to Bacon for my second level of subdivisions. From 4:17–25:46 these subsections form pairs of discourse (sermonic material) and narrative (nonsermonic material). The two members of each pair address similar themes, though not always the ones identified by Bacon. Matthew 1:1–4:16 contains no discourses, though it also divides neatly into two: the so-called infancy narratives (chaps. 1–2) and the preparation for Jesus' adult ministry (3:1–4:16). But beginning with 4:17, the pattern unfolds relatively plainly. The Sermon on the Mount (chaps. 5–7) combines with two chapters of Jesus' miracles, primarily healings (8:1–9:35), to illustrate Jesus' unique authority. The sermon on mission (chap. 10) predicts rising opposition to the

---

[8]Readers who have never consulted a synopsis or harmony of the Gospels should do so in order to see just how widespread this phenomenon is. One of the best is K. Aland, *Synopsis of the Four Gospels* (New York: UBS, 1976 [Greek-English], 1979 [English only]).

[9]A point regularly noted in the history of interpretation from at least as early as Augustine (cf. J. D. Woodbridge, *Biblical Authority* [Grand Rapids: Zondervan, 1982], 42) but often neglected by the casual reader.

message of Jesus and the Twelve, which chaps. 11–12 illustrate both implicitly and explicitly. The chapter of parables (13:1-52) predicts further polarization and explains some of its rationale; God is judging those who refuse to respond favorably to Jesus. Matthew 13:53–16:20 illustrates that growing polarization, which leads Jesus to successively harsher interchanges with the Jewish leaders but also to increasingly favorable response in Gentile territory as well as among his Jewish disciples, who are prepared to confess him as Christ and Son of God.

Combining Bacon and Kingsbury means that the sequence of discourse and narrative would be inverted from 16:21 on, and that fits what we find. Matthew 16:21–17:27 introduces Jesus' first two passion predictions and related material; the community discourse of chap. 18 focuses on the humility that should characterize disciples, who themselves may have to follow Jesus' cross-bearing example. Matthew 19:1–22:46 depicts Jesus literally on the road to Jerusalem, arriving there and teaching in word and deed about God's impending judgment on that city. Chapters 23–25 expand that teaching into a full-fledged sermon and then expand that judgment to encompass all the world, which will be held accountable for how it responds to Christ and his emissaries. Chapters 26–28 form the concluding and climactic portion of the Gospel and, like the introductory chapters, divide conceptually into two clear, if more unequally proportioned, parts: Jesus' passion and death (chaps. 26–27) and his resurrection (chap. 28).

A three-level outline of Matthew's Gospel is given at the conclusion to the introduction.

B. Theology

1. Israel and the Gentiles

Outlines usually provide a window through which to view a biblical writer's distinctive theological emphases. Matthew proves no exception to the rule. When we analyze the topics that link together material in the various pairs of narrative and discourse, a unified plot emerges. Many of the scenes in the development of this plot have been profitably analyzed by an emerging body of literature on the Gospels that employs the various insights of modern literary criticism.[10] We are more interested here in the significance of the structure for the theology Matthew wishes to communicate. The most obvious thrust of the sequence of topics in the Gospel is that Matthew is tracing the events of Jesus' life in terms of a growing

---

[10]See R. A. Edwards, *Matthew's Story of Jesus* (Philadelphia: Fortress, 1985); J. D. Kingsbury, *Matthew as Story* (Philadelphia: Fortress, 1986); D. B. Howell, *Matthew's Inclusive Story* (Sheffield: JSOT, 1990).

hostility on the part of the Jewish leaders that increasingly leads Jesus himself to turn to the Gentiles and to anticipate a later, widespread ministry on the part of his disciples among them. Theologians often refer to the development of this theme as the tension between particularism and universalism in Matthew. Few have elevated it to the role of the most foundational or overarching theme of the book, but our structure suggests that it should be so identified. Above all, Matthew thus wants to demonstrate God's work in Jesus to bring the fulfillment of his promises to his chosen people, the Jews, and, through (or even in spite of) their reaction, to offer identical blessings and judgments to all humanity.

On the one hand, Matthew includes some of the most exclusive texts in all of the Gospels. Only he inserts Jesus' sayings in 10:5-6 and 15:24 about Jesus and his disciples going only to the lost sheep of the house of Israel. Only he anticipates a perennially incomplete Jewish mission (10:23). On the other hand, Matthew just as uniquely presents some of the most inclusive texts imaginable. Only he has Gentile Magi come and worship the Christ child (2:1-12). Only he speaks of Israel being judged and replaced by a new "people" (21:43). Only he includes the Great Commission, in which Jesus sends his followers to make disciples from every ethnic group on the face of the globe (28:19). Many scholars find these two strands of thought hopelessly contradictory and assume that Matthew is composed of conflicting traditions from different stages of early Christian history.[11] More plausible is the interpretation that sees Jesus as going first to the Jews and then also to the Gentiles. God's chosen people get first chance to respond to the gospel, but then Jesus and his disciples must expand their horizons to encompass all the earth. This is exactly the pattern Paul adopted throughout the Book of Acts (e.g., 13:46; 18:6; 19:9) and articulated in his Epistles (see Rom 1:16).[12]

With Israel's increasing rejection of Jesus comes God's increasing threats of judgment on Israel. The first signs of hostility appear among the Pharisees, in stark contrast to Jesus' immense popularity with the Jewish crowds (9:33-34). Soon, however, Jesus begins to indict this generation, which suggests a larger body of people opposing him (11:16; 12:39,45). Large numbers of the crowds continue to follow enthusiastically, but Jesus makes clear that most of them do not truly understand who he is (13:11-15). Even as late in his life as the Sunday before "Good Friday," the crowds acclaim him (21:1-11) but without grasping the nature of his

---

[11]See S. Brown, "The Matthean Community and the Gentile Mission," *NovT* 22 (1980): 193-221.

[12]See A. Levine, *The Social and Ethnic Dimensions of Matthean Social History* (Lewiston, N.Y.: Mellen, 1988); J. J. Scott, Jr., "Gentiles and the Ministry of Jesus: Further Observations on Matt 10:5-6; 15:21-28," *JETS* 33 (1990): 161-69.

messiahship—as Suffering Servant who must die before he can reign victoriously. Jesus' final interaction with the temple authorities (21:12–22:46), like his last major discourse (chaps. 23–25), therefore predicts God's judgment on the nation of Israel. Matthew 27:25 depicts some in the crowd who are crying out for the crucifixion as willing to accept responsibility for Jesus' death.[13]

Nevertheless, contrary to popular belief, Matthew does not maintain that God has rejected all of Israel for all of time. Matthew 23:39 and 24:30 seem to envision a day when Jews will once again turn to Jesus as Messiah. Matthew 27:25 does not, by itself, call for God's judgment to affect more than simply the particular people present and their immediate families. Matthew undoubtedly sees the destruction of the temple in A.D. 70 as God's judgment on the nation (23:37–24:20), but no text suggests that his punishment endures beyond that date. Rightly interpreted, 28:19 includes the Jews among the nations of the world to be evangelized. Matthew 10:23 may even suggest that Jewish mission always takes priority over Gentile mission (see commentary at each of these texts for further discussion).

But Jews living after the death of Christ must come to God through Jesus. So too Gentiles may now serve God by following Christ in discipleship. Both Jesus and the church in a sense become a new Israel. Jesus embodies all of the promises of the Old Testament; indeed, he is the goal of all of Scripture, as all of the law and the prophets are fulfilled in him (5:17). Where Israel failed, he remains faithful (4:1-11). Just as God gave Jacob twelve sons to found the twelve tribes of Israel, Jesus constitutes the new community of God's people with twelve apostles (10:1-4). These apostles will even judge the twelve tribes (19:28). And lest any professing believers grow smug at God's judgment of Israel, Matthew reports Jesus' warning that many seemingly "Christian" leaders will be damned on Judgment Day because their works demonstrate that in fact Christ never knew them (7:21-23). What is crucial is whether or not they have obeyed Christ by putting his words into practice (7:24-27).[14]

2. Christology

So who is this Jesus who can command absolute allegiance? Clearly Matthew views him as Teacher, not only because of the five extensive

---

[13]On the theme of the judgment of Israel in Matthew, see S. van Tilborg, *The Jewish Leaders in Matthew* (Leiden: Brill, 1972); D. R. A. Hare, *The Theme of Jewish Persecution of Christians in the Gospel according to St. Matthew* (Cambridge: University Press, 1967); D. Marguerat, *Le jugement dans l'Évangile de Matthieu* (Geneva: Labor et Fides, 1981).

[14]On Jesus as the new Israel in Matthew, see W. Kynes, *A Christology of Solidarity: Jesus as the Representative of His People in Matthew* (Lanham: University Press of America, 1991); on the church as a new Israel, cf. K. Tagawa, "People and Community in the Gospel of Matthew," *NTS* 16 (1969/70): 149-62.

sermons but because of the prominence of ethical instruction throughout the Gospel (contrast Mark, who has a higher percentage of narrative and miracle material). P. Minear has appropriately entitled Matthew "The Teacher's Gospel," thinking also that it was written by a teacher especially for teachers.[15] Yet none of Jesus' disciples except for Judas ever call Jesus *didaskalos* (*Teacher*) or *Rabbi* (26:25,49). Those who do are always his opponents or the uncommitted (cf. also 8:19; 12:38; 19:16; 22:16,24,36). "Teacher" is not inaccurate as a title, simply inadequate. What is more, Jesus strongly discourages his followers from using the title among themselves because of the abuses to which it can lead (23:8-12).

One of the most distinctive titles for Jesus in Matthew is *Son of David*. It occurs nine times, eight of which are unparalleled in any of the other Gospels, whereas Mark uses it only three times and Luke four. No other document in the New Testament employs the title at all, though Rom 1:3 comes close to this idea. "Son of David" fits the Jewish orientation of Matthew and reflects the messianic tradition of a king from the lineage of David who would rule Israel. To that extent it is synonymous with *Christ* and *King of the Jews* (Pilate's unique concern regarding Jesus, 27:11). "Son of David" is apparently more adequate than "Teacher," inasmuch as it is often found on the lips of those who request healing from Jesus and believe that he can provide it (e.g., 9:27; 15:22; 20:30). Strikingly, these people are often those whom the religious authorities despise as outcasts yet equally those who display better insight into Jesus than their leaders, who should know better.[16] But "Son of David," like "Christ," could conjure up the image of merely a triumphal, human conqueror and healer (cf. 22:41-45), so Jesus himself shies away from these terms. When finally confronted directly by Caiaphas about his self-understanding, he supplies merely a qualified affirmation of the title "Christ" and then redefines it in terms of the heavenly Son of Man (26:64).

Matthew's *Son of Man* references generally parallel the range of usage elsewhere in the Gospels—the human Jesus, the one who must suffer, and the exalted figure of Dan 7:13-14. But Matthew may show a slight preference for the last of these three usages.[17] Here is the title Jesus most prefers to use for himself, no doubt because it did not come with a well-established tradition of misconceptions. He could thus invest it with his own interpretation.[18] And contrary to the popular view of many Chris-

---

[15]P. S. Minear, *Matthew: The Teacher's Gospel* (New York: Pilgrim, 1982).

[16]See J. M. Gibbs, "Purpose and Pattern in Matthew's Use of the Title 'Son of David,'" *NTS* 10 (1963/64): 446-64; W. R. G. Loader, "Son of David, Blindness, Possession, and Duality in Matthew," *CBQ* 44 (1982): 570-85.

[17]France, *Matthew: Evangelist and Teacher*, 291.

[18]F. F. Bruce, "The Background to the Son of Man Sayings," in *Christ the Lord*, ed. H. H. Rowdon (Leicester: InterVarsity, 1982), 50-70.

tians, that interpretation makes "Son of Man" more a title of exaltation, somewhat synonymous with the typical understanding of "Son of God," rather than a mere affirmation of Jesus' true humanity.[19]

Kingsbury has vigorously defended *Son of God* as the key Christological title for Matthew.[20] Matthew includes it at strategic points in his narrative: at Jesus' birth (2:15), temptations (4:3,6), recognition by the disciples (14:33; 16:16), and passion and death (26:63; 27:40,43). Yet it is not at all clear that it dominates Matthew's entire story, even throughout large sections in which it is absent, as Kingsbury alleges.[21] Still, it remains important and, like "Christ" and "Son of David," carries a built-in ambiguity in light of its Jewish and Greco-Roman backgrounds. In Jesus' day various speakers no doubt employed it to mean nothing more than *messiah* (most notably Caiaphas) or a great man who became a god after his death (most notably the centurion at the cross). But Matthew and his readers will consistently view "Son of God" as a testimony to Jesus' unique relationship with his Father and probably even to his deity.[22]

Perhaps the most significant title of all for Matthew is that which addresses Jesus as *Lord*. Again ambiguities are associated with the original context of Jesus' life, when *kyrios* may often have reflected an underlying Hebraic *adonai* ("lord" as in *master*; NIV's frequent use of "sir" is a bit weak). But Matthew and his readers will see at least some of the references as virtually equivalent to *Yahweh*. "Lord" is the correct term for a disciple to use, particularly when in need of a miracle that only one who has divine power can supply (e.g., 8:2,6,25; 9:28).[23]

Other titles (e.g., *Servant* or *Wisdom*) may or may not be as significant for Matthew as some have thought. But R. T. France is surely correct in stressing that Matthew ultimately portrays Jesus as "the man who fits no formula" but whose authority and power (28:18), declarations of forgiveness (9:2), reception of worship (14:33), and demands for allegiance (10:37-39) all depict him as one "in the place of God," or in Matthew's own language, "Immanuel, God with us."[24] Not surprisingly, references to Jesus as *God with us* bracket the entire Gospel (1:23 and 28:20).

---

[19]See S. Kim, *"The 'Son of Man'" as the Son of God* (Tübingen: Mohr, 1983).

[20]Kingsbury, *Structure*; cf. idem, "The Figure of Jesus in Matthew's Story: A Literary-Critical Probe," *JSNT* 21 (1984): 3-36.

[21]Cf. the important critique by D. Hill, "The Figure of Jesus in Matthew's Story: A Response to Professor Kingsbury's Literary-Critical Probe," *JSNT* 21 (1984): 37-52.

[22]Cf. and contrast D. J. Verseput, "The Role and Meaning of the 'Son of God' Title in Matthew's Gospel," *NTS* 33 (1987): 532-56; and R. L. Mowery, "Subtle Differences: The Matthean 'Son of God' References," *NovT* 32 (1990): 193-200.

[23]See G. Bornkamm, G. Barth, and H. Held, *Tradition and Interpretation in Matthew* (Philadelphia: Westminster, 1963), 41-43. On Jesus' miracles in Matthew, cf. B. Gerhardsson, *The Mighty Acts of Jesus according to Matthew* (Lund: Gleerup, 1979).

[24]France, *Matthew: Evangelist and Teacher*, 306-12.

3. The Fulfillment of Scripture

Matthew's twin interests in God's dealings with the Jews and the person of Jesus intertwine in a third key theme that regularly punctuates the Gospel narrative: Jesus' person and ministry so fulfill the purposes of all the Old Testament that he alone now has the authority to dictate how his followers must obey those Scriptures in the new age he has inaugurated.

First, Matthew repeatedly cites Old Testament passages, over half of them not found in any other Gospel, which he introduces with a "fulfillment formula" to show how Jesus has accomplished that to which those texts ultimately pointed. Five of these unique references appear in the first two chapters alone (1:22-23; 2:5-6,15,17,23), setting the tone for the whole Gospel, even though the frequency of citations subsides (but cf. 8:17; 12:18-21; 13:35) until the passion narrative (in which references and allusions to Ps 22 dominate). These unparalleled citations deviate more from the LXX than do those Matthew shares with Mark or Luke and often reflect a better translation of the original Hebrew.[25] At the same time, Matthew frequently does not operate with a direct prediction-fulfillment scheme but employs typology to demonstrate recurring patterns of God's activity in salvation history. Only Matthew refers to Jesus' baptism as fulfilling "all righteousness" (3:15). Only Matthew has Jesus declare that he has not come to abolish the law but to fulfill it (5:17).

Second, particularly in view of 5:17 and the theme of fulfillment, many commentators have argued that Matthew demonstrates a very conservative view toward the law or at least has preserved (perhaps in tension with his own emphases) the older traditions of a Torah-observant, Jewish-Christian community.[26] Neither of these options seems at all probable. When one reads on in 5:17-48, it becomes clear that "fulfill" is not the opposite of "abolish," as if it were equivalent to something like "preserve intact." Rather, Jesus demonstrates a sovereign authority to interpret, tran-

---

[25]The Septuagint (LXX) was a Greek translation of the Old Testament, produced ca. 200 B.C., probably at least two hundred years after the completion of the latest of the original Hebrew Scriptures. When the LXX differs from the Hebrew texts, it is usually assumed to reflect a later, inferior reading, though occasionally it may preserve in translation earlier, more authentic tradition than has survived in any existing Hebrew manuscript, the oldest of which also date to ca. 200 B.C. (from the Dead Sea Scrolls collection). Numerous studies have investigated Matthew's OT quotations and their "text type" at length. See K. Stendahl, *The School of St. Matthew and Its Use of the Old Testament* (Philadelphia: Fortress, 1968); R. H. Gundry, *The Use of the Old Testament in St. Matthew's Gospel* (Leiden: Brill, 1967); G. M. Soarés Prabhu, *The Formula Quotations in the Infancy Narratives of St. Matthew's Gospel* (Rome: Biblical Institute Press, 1976).

[26]The most extreme example, which seeks to place Matthew's Jesus entirely *within* Pharisaic Judaism, is P. Sigal, *The Halakah of Jesus of Nazareth according to the Gospel of Matthew* (Lanham: University Press of America, 1986).

scend, and even change the way the law does or does not apply to his followers. By the time we reach the Great Commission, it is obedience to all of *Jesus'* commands that constitutes discipleship, not Torah-observance (28:19).[27]

Third, and closely related, is Matthew's insistence that Jesus is "greater than" all three major Old Testament categories of national leaders—prophet, priest, and king (12:1-8,39-42). He is thus no new Moses (see above) but one far greater than Moses. He does not promulgate a new law but the gospel, which far transcends the righteousness of the scribes and Pharisees (5:20), even at their best moments of well-motivated, genuine obedience to the Torah.

Fourth, what thus is involved in fulfillment is the salvation historical shift between the old and new ages, prevalent in Jewish thinking. But instead of completely ushering in the kingdom era, Jesus has merely inaugurated the new covenant (see 26:28), with its full consummation yet awaiting Christ's return (see 25:31-46). Nevertheless, this Gospel makes plain that the kingdom has at least partially arrived (3:2; 4:17; 10:7; 11:12). No text phrases it more starkly than 11:11, which relegates John the Baptist to a lesser status than everyone in the kingdom age because he failed to live to see its inauguration with the death, resurrection, and exaltation of the Christ.[28]

Matthew, hence, combines the principles of both "historicizing" and "transparency" as he recounts his narrative.[29] "Transparency" means that Jesus' followers represent Christians in Matthew's community and, indeed, in any church; what applies to the one group of Christ's followers should apply to all. There is no justification, for example, for restricting the Great Commission to the apostles. To a certain extent Christ's opponents may also be portrayed in ways that enable Matthew's audience to recognize and respond to the opposition they faced in the Jewish community of their day. At the same time, many items in the Gospel may not carry over because of the shift in ages. "Historicizing" may be taken (less radically than it sometimes is) as the inclusion of those features of Matthew's Gospel which appear simply because they happened and were

---

[27]See J. P. Meier, *Law and History in Matthew's Gospel* (Rome: Biblical Institute Press, 1976); R. J. Banks, "Matthew's Understanding of the Law: Authenticity and Interpretation in Matthew 5:17-20," *JBL* 93 (1974): 226-42; D. J. Moo, "Jesus and the Authority of the Mosaic Law," *JSNT* 20 (1984): 3-49.

[28]On John the Baptist in Matthew, see J. P. Meier, "John the Baptist in Matthew's Gospel," *JBL* 99 (1980): 383-405.

[29]The terms, often pitted against each other, are classically debated in the studies of G. Strecker, "The Concept of History in Matthew," and U. Luz, "The Disciples in the Gospel according to Matthew," respectively, in G. N. Stanton, ed., *The Interpretation of Matthew* (Philadelphia: Fortress, 1983), 67-84, 98-128.

important, even though no direct analogies may be drawn to the people in and around Matthew's church. So, for example, the fact that Jesus told the Pharisees and scribes that they should have tithed, but without neglecting the weightier matters of the law (23:23), does not automatically mean that Christians should tithe. Tithing was commanded under the Old Testament. So as long as the age of the law remained in force, God's faithful had to tithe. But the question of whether tithing remains mandatory after Christ's death and resurrection will have to be settled on the basis of other texts.

4. Discipleship and the Church

Matthew's fourth and final principal area of theological concern follows from the third. Requirements for discipleship and the constitution of the community of Jesus' followers that became the church dominate Matthew's Gospel as they do no other. To begin with, it is often alleged that Matthew paints a much more positive picture of the disciples than does Mark.[30] To a certain extent, this claim proves valid. Matthew often tones down or omits Mark's "messianic secret" motif. Matthew 14:33 even has the disciples worshiping Jesus as Son of God, where the Markan parallel leaves them with hardened hearts and without understanding (Mark 6:52). In the story of the storm-stilling, Matthew has Jesus berate the disciples for their lack of faith before the miracle (8:26) rather than afterwards, as in Mark 4:40, when the rebuke seems that much more embarrassing. Unlike Mark 4:1-34, Matthew's "parable chapter" (13:1-52) frequently has the disciples understanding Jesus (see v. 51), even if not always right away.

Still, numerous passages continue to portray the disciples in a much more negative light. Matthew's unique and characteristic *oligopistoi* ("you of little faith") in 8:26; 14:31; and 16:8 does not emphasize what faith the disciples may have but rebukes them for how small a quantity it is—not even that of a grain of mustard seed (17:20). Despite a more positive reaction to the miracles, Matthew's focus in those stories is fundamentally Christological, not "mathetological" (focused on the disciples). And in 13:36; 15:15-16; and 16:9,11, the disciples' lack of understanding remains as painfully obvious as anywhere in Mark.[31]

An examination of various categories of disciples within Matthew reinforces this pattern of not overly emphasizing their capabilities. Matthew is

---

[30]See Bornkamm, Barth, Held, *Matthew*, 52-57; R. H. Gundry, *Matthew: A Commentary on His Literary and Theological Art* (Grand Rapids: Eerdmans, 1982), 626.

[31]For the various points in this paragraph, cf. G. Theissen, *The Miracle Stories of the Early Christian Tradition* (Philadelphia: Fortress, 1983), 137-38; and P. F. Feiler, "The Stilling of the Storm in Matthew: A Response to Günther Bornkamm," *JETS* 26 (1983): 399-406.

the Gospel from which the Roman doctrine of the papacy is often derived (see 16:16-19) and is frequently said to exalt Peter more than does Mark, Luke, or John. A more careful look suggests precisely the opposite. The five times in which Matthew, unlike Mark or Luke, inserts references to Peter in chaps. 14–18 consistently wind up describing him in a negative or embarrassing fashion (14:28-31; 15:15-16; 16:16-23 [see vv. 21-23]; 17:24-27 [this is arguably the only neutral text]; and 18:21-22). And Peter ends up denying Jesus just as clearly in Matthew as elsewhere (26:69-75). But, like the rest of the eleven, he is reinstated (28:16-20). Matthew is not trying to denigrate Peter per se but to encourage his readers that they too can overcome failure as Peter did. Still, he may also be trying to play down an overexaltation of Peter already creeping into the church to which he writes.[32] What is true of Peter is true of the Twelve. Peter gets the "keys of the kingdom" to bind and loose (16:19), but so do the rest of the disciples (18:18).[33]

The terms *wise men, prophets,* and *scribes* ("teachers of the law") may suggest different categories of Christian leaders in Matthew's church, though first of all they refer to various kinds of faithful people of God under Old Testament arrangements (10:40-42; 13:52; 23:34). But if such distinctions exist, they must be minimized. Members of Matthew's community must not address each other as "Rabbi," "Father," or "Teacher" but exalt Christ alone (23:8-12). All believers are "brothers" (28:10). In sociological terms the church must be more egalitarian than hierarchical. What is more, Jesus reserves a special place in his heart for "the little ones," which may refer to the entire community but probably focuses specifically on the marginalized and powerless within that community (see chap. 18).[34]

Jesus thus anticipates his followers' living in community and begins to make provisions for the maintenance of that body of believers. Chapter 18 may be thought of as the foundational manifesto,[35] but chap. 16 has already predicted the establishment of Christ's church. Of the four Evangelists, only Matthew uses the word *ekklēsia* ("church") and only in these two chapters (16:18; 18:17 [2X]). Only Matthew gives rules for exclusion from that community (18:15-20), and only Matthew gives Jesus' commission to scour the ends of the earth in order to bring new members into it (28:19-20).

---

[32]See A. Stock, "Is Matthew's Presentation of Peter Ironic?" *BTB* 17 (1987): 64-69.

[33]Cf. J. D. Kingsbury, "The Figure of Peter in Matthew's Gospel as a Theological Problem," *JBL* 98 (1979): 67-83.

[34]On the various members of Matthew's church, see E. Schweizer, "Matthew's Church," in Stanton, *Matthew,* 129-55.

[35]On which see W. G. Thompson, *Matthew's Advice to a Divided Community* (Rome: Biblical Institute Press, 1970).

Finally, Matthew stresses discipleship as following Jesus so as to obey the sum total of God's commandments as interpreted by and fulfilled in Christ. To have what John calls "eternal life" and Luke calls "salvation" requires "doing the will of God" (7:21; 12:46-50). Matthew's Jesus can, with Paul, speak of saving "faith" (9:22,28; 15:28), often in the context of physical healing but suggesting that spiritual wholeness accompanied the restoration of health. But, as with James, true faith for Matthew demonstrates itself in good works that reflect obedience to Jesus' commandments. In Matthew discipleship combines grace and demand (cf. 8:10-13; 9:14-27, esp. vv. 18-22) in a way that avoids the twin heresies of workless faith and works-righteousness.[36] Matthew is just as concerned to oppose lawlessness as to combat legalistic self-righteousness (e.g., 7:13-27 with 5:17–6:18), though attempts to pinpoint a specific group of "antinomians" in Matthew's audience must be judged unsuccessful.[37]

C. Purpose and Audience

A rather fruitless debate often rages about the purpose of a given book of Scripture. There is no reason why a writer, inspired or otherwise, has to have one and only one purpose in writing. Suggestions for Matthew's Gospel have usually involved apologetic designs to try to convince non-Christian Jews of the truth of the gospel, catechetical purposes (instructions for Christian living, perhaps administered to initiates into the community), encouragement to the church's witness in a hostile world, and deepening Christian faith by supplying more details about Jesus' words and works.[38] All of these proposals make good sense and may well form part of Matthew's intention. But in light of his structure and theological emphases, perhaps pride of place attaches to the first of these purposes— apologetics in interaction with Jews.

To what kind of church under what circumstances would such a Gospel be addressed? The text itself never says; we are left to make reasonable inferences from its contents. It is usually assumed that all of the Gospels are first of all addressed to Christian communities (even, as with Luke, when one individual is more directly in view), since from the earliest days of Christian testimony that is where these documents are read. Suggestions about the church to which Matthew presumably is writing usually try to relate the circumstances of that body of believers to the larger Jewish world. Has the church in this community not yet broken

---

[36]Cf. B. Przybylski, *Righteousness in Matthew and His World of Thought* (Cambridge: University Press, 1980); R. Mohrlang, *Matthew and Paul: A Comparison of Ethical Perspectives* (Cambridge: University Press, 1984); M. J. Wilkins, *The Concept of Disciple in Matthew* (Leiden: Brill, 1988).

[37]On which see J. E. Davison, "*Anomia* and the Question of an Antinomian Polemic in Matthew," *JBL* 104 (1985): 617-35.

[38]Cf. Carson, "Matthew," 25.

from the synagogue, thus accounting for the heavily Jewish flavor and potentially strong apologetic value? Or is Matthew's audience largely Gentile, with the rupture between Christians and Jews in the relatively distant past? In this scenario the reason for the scriptural emphasis and Jewish themes could well be to demonstrate to Gentile Christians how to reappropriate their Jewish heritage in a context in which the church is tempted to jettison it altogether.[39]

The amount and depth of the hostility between Jesus and his disciples on the one hand and unbelieving Jews on the other, which Matthew takes pains to emphasize throughout his narrative, makes both of these hypotheses improbable. Had the church not already broken from the synagogue, it is not likely that Matthew would go out of his way to emphasize God's judgment on the Jews and the sins of their leaders, indeed, of a large number of people in the nation as a whole. Were the rupture with Judaism well in the past, it is also unlikely that Matthew's tone would reflect such hostility. A third, mediating perspective seems more likely: Matthew's church has recently been severed from the synagogue; but its predominantly Jewish members remain in frequent, vigorous, and sometimes polemical dialogue with their non-Christian Jewish families and friends. G. Stanton helpfully imagines this scenario as the church interacting with "the synagogue across the street."[40] Ideologically, interpersonally, and perhaps even geographically, these Jews and Christians remain in close proximity. Most likely some Jews are sharply condemning these "apostate" Jewish Christians who, in their opinion, have defected from God's truth, while many Jewish Christians are still struggling persistently to win their loved ones to Christ. More often than not exchanges become pointed, leading Matthew to the kind of rhetoric reflected in his narrative. The Gospel then reinforces Christian faith and encourages Matthew's audience to stand fast in their allegiance to Christ despite the hostilities they incur as a result. But it also gives them more "apologetic ammunition" as they seek to win others to their convictions and loyalties.

What kind of rupture has occurred? A substantial scholarly consensus associates the Gospel of Matthew with a setting following the fairly formal and widespread rejection of Christians by Jews from about the mid-80s of the first century onward. Often this rupture is linked with the so-called *birkat ha-minim* (*the blessing* [as a euphemism for curse] *on the heretics*), which many believe became a common addition to the eighteen benedictions regularly recited as part of the synagogue liturgy. But recent research is increasingly questioning just how widespread or formal such

---

[39]For a survey of these views and a defense of the position adopted in the next paragraph, see G. N. Stanton, "The Gospel of Matthew and Judaism," *BJRL* 66 (1984): 264-84.

[40]See ibid., 266; cf. also from a sociological perspective, J. A. Overman, *Matthew's Gospel and Formative Judaism* (Minneapolis: Fortress, 1990).

rejection ever was, indeed, if such a prayer were ever ritualized; and nothing in the text of Matthew demands that hostilities have been triggered by official promulgation.[41] While we cannot rule out a post-85 setting, nothing demands this identification.

Once this is recognized, the door is opened to almost any setting in which Jews and Christians regularly associated and discussed their differences. The pages of Acts are sprinkled with examples of antagonism between Jews and Christians, particularly associated with Paul's ministry, as his synagogue appearances invariably led to expulsion and his turning to the Gentiles. But Luke makes it clear that Paul and his converts continued to evangelize the Jews even after he left the synagogues (Acts 19:10 and possibly 18:8), so the situation envisaged for Matthew is quite plausible in many parts of the Roman Empire from a very early period in Christian history.

External evidence does not help us narrow down the location of Matthew's congregation. Very little Christian tradition from the first several centuries of church history makes any claims about the whereabouts of Matthew when he wrote or the audience to which he penned this Gospel. What little evidence does emerge supports some place in Palestine or Judea, possibly Jerusalem. Scribal notations at the end of three manuscripts (K, 126, 174) from the eighth, ninth, and eleventh centuries locate Matthew's audience in Palestine; but it is hard to know if this represents reliable information or a logical inference. Irenaeus, around the beginning of the third century, declared that Matthew wrote his Gospel "among the Hebrews" (*Adv. Haer.* 3.1.1), which could imply Palestine but might also refer to any Jewish-Christian congregation in the Diaspora. A century later Eusebius taught that Matthew wrote to the Hebrews "when he was on the point of going also to other nations" (*H.E.* 3.24.5-6), but this citation carries the same built-in ambiguity. By the early fifth century, Jerome would specify that Matthew composed his work "in Judea, for the sake of those who had come to faith out of the circumcision" (*De vir. ill.* 3), but the larger context of this quote suggests that Jerome may be referring to the apocryphal "Gospel of the Hebrews," which seems to have been a revision and/or corruption of the original Matthew for various sectarian purposes within Jewish Christianity, arising no earlier than the mid-second century.[42]

---

[41]See R. Kimelman, "*Birkat Ha-Minim* and the Lack of Evidence for an Anti-Christian Jewish Prayer in Late Antiquity," in *Jewish and Christian Self-Definition*, vol. 2, ed. E. P. Sanders, A. J. Baumgarten, and A. Mendelson (Philadelphia: Fortress, 1981), 226-44.

[42]Allison and Davies, *Matthew* 1:38-47, survey the options and various scholars who defend each. For a thorough discussion of the extant sources for Ebionite or later, sectarian Jewish Christianity, see R. A. Pritz, *Nazarene Jewish Christianity* (Leiden: Brill, 1988).

Modern scholarship has offered many other suggestions, most notably Caesarea Maritimis, the Transjordan, Phoenicia, Alexandria, and Edessa. At least a plurality of commentators, however, would tentatively place Matthew's community in Syria and most probably in Antioch, home to a large Jewish community and a sizable Jewish-Christian congregation from at least the time of Acts 11:19-30 (no later than A.D. 46) and lasting well into the second century.[43] Interesting incidental evidence might support this identification: e.g., the claim that only in Antioch did a *statēr* exactly equal two *didrachma* as in 17:24-27 (though this claim has recently been challenged).[44] Fortunately it does not matter much for the interpretation of the book whether we opt for Antioch and Syria or Jerusalem and Palestine. Either way we have an apparently Jewish-Christian author (see comments under "Author") addressing a Christian audience with distinctively Jewish-Christian concerns.

D. Sources

The most common modern reconstruction of the relationship among the Synoptic Gospels (Matthew, Mark, and Luke) identifies Mark as the earliest of the three, with Matthew and Luke both utilizing Mark's Gospel extensively as one of their sources. Slightly less entrenched but still commanding a widespread majority following is the "Q" hypothesis, in which Matthew and Luke each utilized a second source, no longer extant, and hence labeled Q, probably from the German word for *source* (*Quelle*). Q then accounts for much of the material, predominantly sayings of Jesus, which Matthew and Luke have in common but which is lacking in Mark. Less secure still is the "M" hypothesis, in which Matthew relied on a third source, also no longer extant, to account for much or all of his otherwise unparalleled material.[45]

Dissenting voices demand increasing attention. Largely through the efforts of W. Farmer, the so-called Griesbach hypothesis (named after an eighteenth-century advocate) has experienced something of a revival. In this view Mark is the latest of the Synoptics, conflating and abridging Matthew and Luke.[46] Ancient tradition, followed widely in Roman Christianity because of the influence of Augustine (early fifth century—see esp. his *De con. ev.* 1.2.4), consistently placed Matthew first, followed by

---

[43]Cf. further R. R. Hahn, "Judaism and Jewish Christianity in Antioch: Charisma and Conflict in the First Century," *JRH* 14 (1987): 341-60.

[44]The classic defense of Antioch as home for Matthew's audience appears in B. H. Streeter, *The Four Gospels: A Study of Origins* (London: Macmillan, 1924), 500-23. His argument concerning the *stater* has been challenged by U. Luz, *Matthew 1-7: A Commentary* (Minneapolis: Augsburg, 1989), 91, n. 184.

[45]The classic case again appears in Streeter, *Gospels, passim.*

[46]See W. R. Farmer, *The Synoptic Problem* (New York: Macmillan, 1964).

Mark and then Luke. Only a very few scholars, but often many laypeople, assume independence among these three Evangelists.[47]

Some literary interrelationship is virtually certain. Luke himself speaks of relying on previous written accounts (Luke 1:1-4), making it probable that other Gospel writers did so too. The amount and nature of verbal parallelism among the three in Greek translation (not the language in which Jesus originally spoke most of his sayings) all but proves that one or two Evangelists in part relied on the works of the others. None of these affirmations call into question the inspiration of the Scriptures; they merely specify how God chose to inspire these particular authors—through their work, in part at least, as historians and compilers of traditions.

Of the various solutions to the so-called Synoptic problem, the one that places Mark earliest, with canonical Matthew and Luke dependent on Mark, remains the most plausible.[48] Mark is the most vivid, his rough grammar is smoothed out by Matthew and Luke, potentially embarrassing or misleading details are reworded (cf., e.g., Matt 19:16-17 with Mark 10:17-18), and individual passages are more often than not abbreviated. Very little material appears in Mark that is not duplicated in Matthew. Were Matthew written before Mark, there would have been virtually no need for Mark to write. Rarely do Matthew and Luke simultaneously agree with each other against Mark in a passage found in all three Gospels. A high incidence of Aramaisms appears in Mark, and there seems to be no other explanation for Mark's omission of the material Matthew and Luke have in common save that he wrote first. Perhaps most importantly, Matthew's theological and stylistic tendencies, when it is assumed he used and edited Mark, fall into recognizable and coherent patterns (see "Theology"). The rival hypotheses (particularly Griesbach) that place Mark after Matthew have yet to show that Mark demonstrates equally coherent and consistent patterns.[49]

The Q-hypothesis is more shaky but still probable, though Q may have to be thought of as a collection of documents, of oral traditions, or as some combination of the two.[50] Direct dependence of Matthew on Luke

---

[47]See J. M. Rist, *On the Independence of Matthew and Mark* (Cambridge: University Press, 1978).

[48]For detailed defenses see R. H. Stein, *The Synoptic Problem* (Grand Rapids: Baker, 1987), 29-157; D. Guthrie, *New Testament Introduction*, rev. ed. (Downers Grove: Inter-Varsity, 1990), 136-208.

[49]The recent work by C. S. Mann (*Mark*, AB [Garden City: Doubleday, 1986]) was the first full-length commentary to adopt the Griesbach hypothesis. After an inordinately long introduction, the exegetical sections, which would demonstrate if this hypothesis were viable, proved painfully brief and wholly incapable of sustaining the premises on which they were built.

[50]For current assessment see H. C. Bigg, "The Present State of the Q Hypothesis," *VE* 18 (1988): 63-73.

or vice versa seems to be ruled out by Matthew's consistently more Semitic style combined with Luke's seemingly earlier order. For example, it seems inconceivable that Luke should have broken up Matthew's five main sermons and scattered his parallels all over his Gospel, but it makes good sense to see Matthew thematically compiling previously independently circulating traditions. What is more, the generally greater variation between Q parallels than between Mark and Matthew or between Mark and Luke suggests that both Matthew and Luke have variously edited a common source. The apparent theological homogeneity of typical reconstructions of Q further suggests that this symbol does indeed reflect some unified body of traditions known to both Matthew and Luke.

M is least demonstrable of all, and if Matthew was written by the apostle of that name, this symbol need represent nothing more than that apostle's own memory. Still, it is not impossible that Matthew had access to shorter collections of Jesus' teachings and deeds which he incorporated into his narrative along with items from Mark and Q. Various studies continue to analyze the distinctive vocabulary of M and to postulate the nature of the M community, but usually they do so at the cost of pitting one part of Matthew against another as the product of unresolved conflicts among various stages of early Christian tradition.[51]

But whereas the internal evidence of the Greek text of Matthew strongly suggests dependence on Mark, early Christian traditions consistently attributed the oldest Gospel to Matthew. Yet they equally maintained consistently that Matthew wrote his Gospel in a Hebraic language (Hebrew or Aramaic). The oldest of these testimonies is ascribed to Papias (ca. A.D. 100–150), though preserved only as a quotation in Eusebius (*H.E.* 3.39.14-16), which is usually translated roughly as, "Matthew composed his Gospel in the Hebrew language, and everyone translated as they were able." Several key words in this sentence, however, might be rendered quite differently. *Dialektos* ("language") has been taken to mean *style* so that Papias's remarks could be applied to canonical Greek Matthew without postulating a lost Aramaic original.[52] But this is an extremely rare meaning for the term and not a likely interpretation. Others translate *hermēneuō* ("translate") as "interpret," a common meaning but not as likely in a context that seems to be contrasting Hebrew and

---

[51]On the former see J. H. Friedrich, "Wortstatistik als Methode am Beispiel der Frage einer Sonderquelle im Matthäusevangelium," *ZNW* 76 (1985): 29-42. On the latter see S. H. Brooks, *Matthew's Community: The Evidence of His Special Sayings Material* (Sheffield: JSOT, 1987); H. Klein, "Jüdenchristliche Frömmigkeit im Sondergut des Matthäus," *NTS* 35 (1989): 466-74.

[52]See J. Kürzinger, "Das Papiaszeugnis und die Erstgestalt des Matthäusevangeliums," *BZ* 4 (1960): 19-38; idem, "Irenäus und sein Zeugnis zur Sprache des Matthäusevangeliums," *NTS* 10 (1963): 108-15.

Greek texts. Most significant is the debate over the meaning of *logia*, which does not naturally mean *Gospel* but *sayings*. Perhaps Papias is claiming that Matthew wrote down in Aramaic or Hebrew something less than a full-fledged Gospel but a collection of Jesus' sayings (conceivably something like what modern scholars have labeled Q).[53] Then either he or a later Christian reviser supplemented this source with other materials and turned it into the Greek form of Matthew we now know.

Largely because canonical Matthew does not betray very much evidence of having been translated literally from a Semitic tongue, most modern scholarship is inclined to discount the value of Papias's testimony however it is interpreted. But there is no reason that a new revision or edition of the Gospel would have had to have been produced so woodenly as to constantly disclose its cross-cultural origin. Jewish authors like Josephus, writing in Greek while at times translating Hebrew materials, often leave no linguistic clues to betray their Semitic sources. Various studies have suggested that Papias was more reliable than many have credited him with being.[54] Tellingly, numerous ancient Christian sources preserve the same tradition (cf. further Irenaeus, *Adv. Haer.* 3.1.1; Eusebius, *H.E.* 5.10.3; Origen, *Comm. in Jn.* 6.17; Epiphanius, *Panar.* 30.13.1-30.22.4). Though some or all of these may simply be following Papias, the widespread nature of this tradition, coupled with the lack of competing or conflicting traditions, suggests that we ought to take it more seriously. A fourteenth-century Hebrew manuscript of Matthew shows some evidence of being not just a translation of our canonical Greek text but of reflecting certain independent renderings of a Hebrew original; it is not inconceivable that it preserves traces of what Matthew originally wrote.[55]

All this suggests that perhaps the solution to the Synoptic problem is not as simple as most of the major theories would have us believe. Perhaps the apostle Matthew wrote a first draft of Jesus' teachings, possibly also including certain narratives, which either he or someone else later revised in light of Mark. This would account for those occasional pas-

---

[53]See T. W. Manson, *The Sayings of Jesus* (London: SCM, 1949), 16-20; M. Black, "The Use of Rhetorical Terminology in Papias in Mark and Matthew," *JSNT* 37 (1989): 31-41. France (*Matthew: Evangelist and Teacher*, 58) protests that Papias's previous use of λογία refers to an entire Gospel (Mark), but his evidence seems to point in the opposite direction. In the phrase "an ordered collection of the Lord's λογία," it is the "collection" that refers to the entire document, whereas the λογία seem to refer to its constituent elements.

[54]Cf. further R. Glover, "Patristic Quotations and Gospel Sources," *NTS* 31 (1985): 234-51; A. C. Perumalil, "Are Not Papias and Irenaeus Competent to Report on the Gospels?" *ExpTim* 91 (1980): 332-37.

[55]See G. Howard, *The Gospel of Matthew according to a Primitive Hebrew Text* (Macon: Mercer University Press, 1987).

sages in Matthew for which a case can be made that Mark's version is later than Matthew's (e.g., 16:13-20; 19:1-12), without calling into question the larger hypothesis of Markan priority. Concerning the question of why this "original Matthew" was not preserved, the answer is that it was—at least in much of the Q + M material of the canonical Gospel. There would have been no need to save the earlier draft once the fuller, more complete account was available.

E. Date

The Gospel of Matthew as we know it was almost certainly written before A.D. 100. It is clearly quoted by Ignatius (e.g., in *Smyrn.* 1.1), writing in approximately 110–115, and probably alluded to in the *Didache*, which may date to some time in the late 90s.[56] If Matthew's final text did not necessarily appear after any formal, empirewide rupture between synagogue and church, then the major reason modern scholars have dated Matthew late (after ca. A.D. 85) vanishes. If Matthew depends on Mark, it must obviously be later than Mark, but the dating of Mark is equally uncertain. Most would place Mark under the Neronian persecution in the mid- to late-60s, but the evidence is highly inferential.[57] Older scholarship frequently dated Luke-Acts to ca. 62, since that is when Luke's story ends (with Paul in house arrest in Rome awaiting the outcome of his appeal to Caesar). But if Luke too depends on Mark, then Mark would have to be earlier than 62. On the other hand, there may be theological reasons why Luke would have wanted to end his story on a relatively triumphant note with Paul still alive in Rome, even if he wrote much later with full knowledge of the outcome of Paul's appeal (implied by Acts 20:25?). He would have demonstrated the spread of the gospel from sectarian beginnings in Jerusalem to empirewide influence in Rome and arrived at a good place to close off the first stage in a history of the early church.

Certain details in Matthew have often been said to betray the Evangelist's knowledge of the fall of Jerusalem and the destruction of the temple in A.D. 70 (most notably 22:7 and 23:37–24:20). But, at best, these passages reflect Jesus' predictions of that destruction. Unless one refuses to believe in the possibility of predictive prophecy (an unjustifiable, antisupernaturalist presupposition), this argument too collapses. Still, these texts could reflect Matthew's post-70 paraphrase of Jesus' genuine prophecy, making clear for

---

[56]For a survey of the citations of and allusions to Matthew in second- or near-second-century sources, see E. Massaux, *The Influence of the Gospel of Saint Matthew on Christian Literature before Saint Irenaeus* (Macon: Mercer University Press, 1991).

[57]Gundry, *Matthew*, 601, notes that there is less evidence for dating Mark than for dating Matthew, so the former can scarcely be allowed to control the latter.

Matthew's audience its fulfillment in recent events. Scholars further debate just how closely these details correspond to what actually did happen in Jerusalem in 70 and therefore whether or not they would represent after-the-fact reflections.

Various items in this Gospel have also been said to prove a pre-70 origin.[58] Why would Matthew (and only he) include references to the temple tax (17:24-27), offerings (5:23-24) and ritual (23:16-22), or to Sabbath keeping in Judea (24:20) in an era (after 70) in which none of these was practiced any longer? Why would he, throughout his Gospel, distinctively emphasize the antagonism of the Sadducees (and of Jerusalem more generally) when neither this sect nor this center of Judaism persisted after the war with Rome? One answer, of course, is that they had value both historically and as examples for his community despite its changed circumstances.

External evidence proves scarcely more conclusive than internal evidence. Only Irenaeus (again in *Adv. Haer.* 3.1.1.) and Eusebius, quoting this passage (*H.E.* 5.8.2), record any traditions about the time of Matthew's writing, "While Peter and Paul were preaching the gospel and founding the church in Rome." This would require a date at least by the mid-60s, assuming the reliability of strong early church tradition that both of these apostles were martyred under Nero in this decade. But recall that Irenaeus and Eusebius may be speaking of a Hebrew sayings collection. In that event, even if we accept the trustworthiness of their testimony, we learn nothing about the time of completion of Greek Matthew.

Considerations of authorship prove equally indecisive. We have no secure traditions about how long the apostle Matthew lived or when he died. Nor does a possible provenance in Palestine or Syria enable us to narrow the time span. We must conclude, with D. A. Carson, that any date between 40 and 100 fits the data.[59] But perhaps a very slight preponderance of weight favors a date from ca. 58–69. J. J. Ensminger postulates a Sadducean persecution of Christians at least in both Jerusalem and Rome between A.D. 58–65;[60] this would fit Matthew's increased, hostile interest in the Sadducees, accommodate the admittedly sparse external tradition, and correspond to a commonly held date throughout the history of scholarship (even if widely rejected outside of more conservative circles today). But we dare not be dogmatic; the evidence is simply too slim to come to any secure conclusion.

---

[58]See ibid., 599-609.

[59]Carson, "Matthew," 21.

[60]J. J. Ensminger, "The Sadducean Persecution of the Christians in Rome and Jerusalem, A.D. 58 to 65," *SWJT* 30.3 (1988): 9-13.

F. Author

Strictly speaking, this Gospel, like all four canonical Gospels, is anonymous. The titles, "The Gospel according to X," are almost certainly not original. It is doubtful that four early Christians would all choose this identical wording and far more probable that the documents were given these headings in order to distinguish one from the other only when they were first combined into a fourfold collection. The diversity of ways in which these titles are phrased among the existing manuscripts ("According to Matthew," "The Gospel according to Matthew," "The Gospel according to Matthew beginning with God," "The Holy Gospel according to Matthew," "From the [Gospel] according to Matthew") reinforces this supposition.[61] Probably these headings were first added some time in the late first or early second century. But apart from these ascriptions, nothing in the actual text of the Gospel ever specifically discloses its author.

All of the evidence surveyed so far ("Structure," "Theology," etc.) allows for authorship by the apostle Matthew, but none of that evidence demands it. Canonical Matthew is written in relatively good Greek, better, for example, than Mark, but not quite as polished as that of the native Greek writer, Luke. Given the amount of Hellenization that had infiltrated Galilee by the first century, and given the regular contacts with Gentiles that a toll collector would have had, the apostle Matthew would have become a reasonably cosmopolitan Jew, quite capable of this kind of writing. But if he wrote only an Aramaic precursor to the Gospel, then any Gentile Christian could have been responsible for Greek Matthew as well, though interestingly the tide of scholarship is again strongly returning to a Jewish Christian as the author of the final form of this Gospel, even if many remain reluctant to identify the apostle as the specific Jewish Christian, Matthew.[62]

It is often alleged that the apostle Matthew would scarcely have consulted, much less extensively relied on, canonical Mark, written by one who was not even a follower of Jesus during most of his ministry. But early church tradition regularly associates Mark with Peter. If Matthew recognized Mark's Gospel as in some sense reflecting Peter's "memoirs," he would have had many reasons to consult and follow it: Peter was one of the inner core of three disciples who experienced certain things Matthew

---

[61]For the Greek titles and manuscripts in which they occur, see Allison and Davies, *Matthew*, 129, n. 90.

[62]Cf. the chart of scholarly opinions in ibid., 10-11. Allison and Davies examine the evidence at length (7-58), with numerous charts displaying Matthew's use of the OT (34-57) to defend the Jewish-Christian origin of the author. For even more exhaustive analysis of Matthew's vocabulary and style, see W. Schenk, *Die Sprache des Matthäus* (Göttingen: Vandenhoeck und Ruprecht, 1987).

did not (cf. e.g., Matt 17:1; 26:37), by the 60s Peter was probably the most prominent apostle in Christian circles, and it is always helpful and interesting to see how others have already tackled a project one wishes to undertake.[63] A second main reason for dissociating "Matthew" from the apostle by that name involves this Gospel's alleged distance from Judaism: it apparently ignores the distinctions between Pharisees and Sadducees by grouping them together (e.g., 3:7; 16:1) and often refers to Jewish places with the third person plural pronoun "their" (e.g., 4:23; 12:9; 13:54) as if its author were not himself Jewish. But the grouping of Pharisees and Sadducees remains rare and suggests only an occasional joint foray against a common enemy, while the use of "their" (particularly with synagogues) needs only reflect Matthew's stronger commitment to Christianity now that the synagogue and church have separated. Other charges of anachronisms or ignorance of things Jewish have been ably refuted.[64]

Some have inferred from references like 13:52 that Matthew himself was a scribe (or even a rabbi), either before or after becoming a Christian, and that he therefore could not also have been a toll collector.[65] This does not follow. In fact, if he were a Christian scribe or teacher, his previous experience with an occupation that required writing and record keeping might even have helped better prepare him for his later responsibilities. When all the evidence is amassed, there appears no conclusive proof for the apostle Matthew as author but no particularly cogent reason to deny this uniform early church tradition. Were the Gospel not written by him, the church surely chose a rather strange individual (in light of his unscrupulous past by Jewish standards) as a candidate for authorship. Without any ancient traditions to the contrary, Matthew remains the most plausible choice for author. This author, at least of an original draft of this book (or one of its major sources), seems quite probably to have been the converted toll collector, also named Levi, who became one of Jesus' twelve apostles (cf. 10:3; 9:9-13; Mark 2:14-17).

But again we present these conclusions tentatively. Little depends on them. Neither inspiration nor apostolic authority depends on apostolic authorship (cf. Mark and Luke), and the church was capable of preserving accurate information outside of apostolic circles (Luke 1:1-4). Indeed, few of the conclusions offered in this introduction "bias" the subsequent commentary. Different assessments concerning audience, sources, date, or author should not prevent one from benefiting from our analysis of the

---

[63]Cf. France, *Matthew: Evangelist and Teacher*, 73-74.

[64]Cf. D. A. Carson, "The Jewish Leaders in Matthew's Gospel: A Reappraisal," *JETS* 25 (1982): 161-74.

[65]See, respectively, O. L. Cope, *A Scribe Trained for the Kingdom of Heaven* (Washington: CBAA, 1976); E. von Dobschütz, "Matthew as Rabbi and Catechist," in Stanton, *Interpretation*, 19-29.

meaning and significance of the text itself. But there is one final introductory area that does determine crucial directions of the commentary proper; to it we now turn.

G. Historicity and Genre

Though it may not look like it to the average layperson, this commentary is quite brief. Detailed historical and theological commentaries on an individual Gospel usually run more than 1,000 pages and often require two or three volumes to bind them. That quantity of space is needed if one is to do justice to all of the kinds of questions scholars ask of the text and to interact with the wealth of literature already in existence. The scope of this series does not permit such leisurely examination of all the issues; many worthy topics must be excluded. Because the primary purpose of this series is "theological exposition," one of the major concerns of many studies I only rarely address is the history of the tradition. On what sources does an individual passage rest? How were those sources modified over the course of time? How did Matthew further edit his material to produce the form of the passage we now have? How historically reliable is the final product? How closely do the sayings of Jesus conform to his *ipsissima verba* ("actual words") or *ipsissima vox* ("actual voice"—paraphrase rather than exact quotation)? For the most part, all of these questions have had to be laid to one side. Hopefully readers who share quite different convictions from my own regarding the kinds of answers I would give to those questions may nevertheless profit from the exposition of the final form of the Gospel. But it is only fitting that I indicate here the kind of approach I would defend in detail were space to allow it.

None of the Gospels is a history or biography of Jesus according to modern standards of precision in reporting, accuracy in quotation, or nature of materials included and excluded. Nevertheless, Matthew, like the other three Gospels and particularly Mark and Luke, measures up quite well when compared with ancient Jewish and Greco-Roman histories and biographies.[66] In antiquity, historical and ideological concerns were regularly intertwined. Standards of objectivity, while important, did not require the kind of distancing from one's subject matter or compartmentalization of reporting and interpretation that modern-day counterparts demand. Although numerous proposals have tried to label the Gospels, and Matthew in particular, as representing some largely nonhis-

---

[66]P. L. Shuler, *A Genre for the Gospels: The Biographical Character of Matthew* (Philadelphia: Fortress, 1982), though it is not clear Matthew is as narrowly an "encomium" or laudatory biography as Shuler alleges. More general but more accurate is D. E. Aune, *The New Testament in Its Literary Environment* (Philadelphia: Westminster, 1987), 17-76.

torical or nonbiographical genres, the fairest assessment of the evidence points in the opposite direction.[67] Once all due allowances are made for literary conventions in antiquity, Matthew's Gospel may properly be labeled as historical and biographical and the appropriate principles of historiography applied to it.[68] Among other things, this means that his testimony will be compared and contrasted with other historical evidence about the topics at hand. Possibilities of harmonization must be explored but not forced.[69] And if Matthew stands up reasonably well where he can be tested against other evidence, he must be given the benefit of the doubt where he cannot be tested. Put another way, the burden of proof resides with the skeptic and not with the believer.[70]

In light of my numerous published works defending in detail my conviction that Matthew, like Mark and Luke, is historically reliable, as defined by the standards of his day,[71] I forbear from re-presenting all the evidence here. I remain convinced that we may learn from Matthew's Gospel not only what he believed about the life and ministry of Jesus but also what any sympathetic observer of the events narrated would have agreed happened and therefore what all sincere seekers after truth should believe about Jesus. In a pluralistic age this conviction is not popular; in some circles it is scathingly ridiculed or viciously attacked. Such ridicule and attack cannot alter the fact that the Christian church for nearly two thousand years has overwhelmingly affirmed the trustworthiness of the Gospels' testimony to the uniqueness of Jesus in a way that disallows the sentimental notion that one can choose to reject him in favor of other religious masters or principles and still find God or eternal life. Matthew's Gospel concludes with the ringing call for believers to evangelize all the nations, based on the absolute, universal, and divine sovereignty of Jesus, thus assuming that no other religion adequately satisfies the deepest of human needs either for this life or the life to come (28:18-20).

---

[67]Most recently and most notably, cf. Gundry, *Matthew*, *passim*, for the view that Matthew is an often unhistorical "midrash" on Mark and Q. The best refutations of this theory appear in D. A. Carson, "Gundry on Matthew: A Critical Review," *TrinJ* n.s. 3 (1982): 71-91; D. J. Moo, "Matthew and Midrash: An Evaluation of Robert H. Gundry's Approach," *JETS* 26 (1983): 31-39; and S. Cunningham and D. Bock, "Is Matthew Midrash?" *BibSac* 144 (1987): 157-80.

[68]Cf. C. L. Blomberg, "New Testament Genre Criticism for the 1990s," *Themelios* 15 (1990): 40-49, and the literature there cited.

[69]*Idem*, "The Legitimacy and Limits of Harmonization," in *Hermeneutics, Authority, and Canon*, ed. D. A. Carson and J. D. Woodbridge (Grand Rapids: Zondervan, 1986), 139-74.

[70]S. C. Goetz and C. L. Blomberg, "The Burden of Proof," *JSNT* 11 (1981): 39-63.

[71]In addition to the works cited earlier in notes 68-70, see C. Blomberg, *The Historical Reliability of the Gospels* (Downers Grove: InterVarsity, 1987). Cf. also *Gospel Perspectives*, 6 vols., ed. R. T. France, D. Wenham, and C. Blomberg (Sheffield: JSOT, 1980-86).

This Great Commission, like the rest of Matthew, defines evangelism as making disciples for Jesus who are baptized and who obey all of his commandments. Matthew knows no salvation apart from Christ's lordship (see "Theology"). A Christian world view should not expect all humanity to agree with these bold claims. Matthew himself repeatedly predicts that many will reject them but that they do so at their own peril (cf. 8:12; 10:33; 13:40-42; 25:41-46). But we do have the right to request that anyone who claims to be Christian should affirm them; anything less represents so great a rupture with both Scripture and historic Christian tradition that it should apply a different label to itself. Sadly, Matthew's Gospel also recognizes that not everyone will comply with this request (7:21-27; 25:1-13). The tragic fate that awaits such persons should prevent any of us from usurping God's role in prematurely judging them (cf. 7:1-5).[72] I leave the readers of the commentary to determine for themselves what they will do with Matthew's Jesus. But commentators who are concerned with the original intention of the text must alert their readers to the fact that Matthew himself is passionately convinced that the only valid response to his Gospel is to follow Jesus in the lifelong commitment of discipleship.

---

[72]Particularly well balanced in his approach to these topics is L. Newbigin, *The Gospel in a Pluralist Society* (Grand Rapids: Eerdmans, 1989).

─────────────── OUTLINE OF THE BOOK ───────────────

I. Introduction to Jesus' Ministry (1:1–4:16)
   A. Jesus' Origin (1:1–2:23)
      1. Heading (1:1)
      2. Genealogy (1:2-17)
      3. The Virginal Conception: God Becomes Human (1:18-25)
      4. Bethlehem: Herod versus the Magi (2:1-12)
      5. The New Exodus from Egypt (2:13-15)
      6. Ramah: Weeping for Dead Children (2:16-21)
      7. Nazareth: Coming Home to Obscurity (2:19-23)
   B. Jesus' Preparation for Ministry (3:1–4:16)
      1. John the Baptist: The Prophetic Forerunner to the Messiah (3:1-12)
      2. John and Jesus: The Messiah's Baptism (3:13-17)
      3. Jesus Alone: The Messiah's Temptation (4:1-11)
      4. Jesus Settles in Capernaum (4:12-16)
II. The Development of Jesus' Ministry (4:17–16:20)
   A. Jesus' Authority in Preaching and Healing (4:17–9:35)
      1. Introduction (4:17-25)
      2. Paradigmatic Preaching: The Sermon on the Mount (5:1–7:29)
      3. Paradigmatic Healing (8:1–9:35)
   B. Rising Opposition to Jesus' Mission (9:36–12:50)
      1. Opposition Predicted for the Disciples' Mission (9:36–10:42)
      2. Opposition Experienced in Christ's Mission (11:1–12:50)
   C. Progressive Polarization of Response to Jesus (13:1–16:20)
      1. The Polarization Explained: Kingdom Parables (13:1-52)
      2. The Polarization Enacted: From Jew to Gentile (13:53–16:20)
III. The Climax of Jesus' Ministry (16:21–28:20)
   A. Focus on Coming Death and Resurrection (16:21–18:35)
      1. Implications for Discipleship: Correcting Misunderstandings (16:21–17:27)
      2. Implications for the Church: Humility and Forgiveness (18:1-35)
   B. The Road to Jerusalem: Impending Judgment on Israel (19:1–25:46)
      1. True Discipleship versus Harsher Condemnation for the Jewish Leaders (19:1–22:46)
      2. Judgment on the Temple but Also on the Nations (23:1–25:46)
   C. Jesus' Ultimate Destiny (26:1–28:20)
      1. Passion and Crucifixion (26:1–27:66)
      2. Resurrection! (28:1-20)

──────────── *SECTION OUTLINE* ────────────

I. INTRODUCTION TO JESUS' MINISTRY (1:1–4:16)
   A. Jesus' Origin (1:1–2:23)
      1. Heading (1:1)
      2. Genealogy (1:2-17)
      3. The Virginal Conception: God Becomes Human (1:18-25)
      4. Bethlehem: Herod versus the Magi (2:1-12)
      5. The New Exodus from Egypt (2:13-15)
      6. Ramah. Weeping for Dead Children (2:16 21)
      7. Nazareth: Coming Home to Obscurity (2:19-23)
   B. Jesus' Preparation for Ministry (3:1–4:16)
      1. John the Baptist: The Prophetic Forerunner to Messiah (3:1-12)
         a. His Ministry (3:1-6)
         b. His Message (3:7-12)
      2. John and Jesus: The Messiah's Baptism (3:13-17)
      3. Jesus Alone: The Messiah's Temptation (4:1-11)
      4. Jesus Settles in Capernaum (4:12-16)

────── **I. INTRODUCTION TO JESUS' MINISTRY (1:1–4:16)** ──────

The Gospel of Matthew divides into three main sections: 1:1–4:16;
4:17–16:20; and 16:21–28:20. These three sections correspond to the
three main stages of Matthew's portrayal of Jesus' ministry: introduction,
development, and climax. The contents of each of these three sections are
clearly distinct (see "Structure" in the Introduction), and Matthew marks
the major new thematic divisions of his narrative with the words "from
that time on Jesus began to" in both 4:17 and 16:21.

Matthew 1:1–4:16 divides neatly in half. Chapters 1–2 describe events
surrounding Jesus' birth, while 3:1–4:16 deals with events of his adult
life just preceding the beginning of his formal ministry.

A. Jesus' Origin (1:1–2:23)

Chapters 1–2 are usually referred to as Matthew's birth narratives; but,
in fact, Jesus' birth is never described. Only a selection of events before
and after his birth appears. When we compare these chapters with Luke
1–2, we realize that Matthew is highly selective in describing events surrounding the beginning of Jesus' life. Actually, very little of Luke's more
detailed nativity story reappears in Matthew.

Three major unifying themes account for what Matthew chose to include in chaps. 1–2. The most obvious is the theme of the fulfillment of Scripture. Five times Matthew quotes the Old Testament (1:23; 2:6,15,18,23). Only that which serves to illustrate how Jesus' origins fulfilled these various Old Testament prophecies appears in these two chapters. Second, Matthew focuses on who Jesus is and what key locations were involved in his birth. Chapter 1 portrays Jesus as the Christ, the son of David, the son of Abraham, and Immanuel; chap. 2 describes the significance of Jesus in Bethlehem, Egypt, and Nazareth.[1] Third, Matthew develops a contrast between the illegitimate King Herod and the legitimate King Jesus.

1. Heading (1:1)

[1]A record of the genealogy of Jesus Christ the son of David, the son of Abraham:

1:1 The opening verse of Matthew's Gospel introduces its main character and describes his identity in very Jewish terms. The first phrase, "a record of the genealogy" (*biblos geneseōs*), would more literally be translated "a book of the genesis" (or origin). This phrase has therefore been taken to refer to the entire Gospel or to all of 1:1–4:16, but *genesis* is not a natural description of the contents of the whole book or of the events of Jesus' adult life. The NIV understandably limits this heading to the genealogy that follows, but *genesis* reappears in 1:18 with reference to Jesus' conception. In the LXX comparable phrases regularly refer both to genealogies and to the narrative material that follows them, but they do not generally refer to entire biblical books (see Gen 5:1a as the introduction to 5:1–9:29). The best interpretation of the opening words of Matthew thus views them as a heading for all of chaps. 1–2. They therefore carry the sense of *an account of the origin*.

Key Matthean titles for Jesus also appear here in the opening verse. "Christ" is the Greek translation of the Hebrew *Meshiach* (Messiah), meaning *Anointed One*. There was a great diversity of Jewish messianic expectation in the first century and previous eras, but one common thread involved liberation of Israel from its enemies.[2] "Son of David" points to the Messiah's necessary lineage and royal role (see 2 Sam 7:11b-16). The classic intertestamental illustration of the messianic Son of David appears in *Pss Sol* 17:21–18:7—a righteous warrior-king who establishes God's rule in Israel.[3] "Son of Abraham" traces Jesus' lineage back to the found-

---

[1]See K. Stendahl, "Quis et Unde? An Analysis of Matthew 1–2," in *Judentum, Urchristentum, Kirche*, ed. W. Eltester (Berlin: Töpelman, 1960), 94-105.

[2]See R. A. Horsley, *The Liberation of Christmas* (New York: Crossroad, 1989).

[3]On the royal role of the Messiah in Matthew, see esp. B. M. Nolan, *The Royal Son of God* (Fribourg: Editions Universitaires, 1979).

ing father of the nation of Israel, thus ensuring his Jewish pedigree from the earliest stage of his people's history. But echoes are probably also to be heard here of God's promises to Abraham that his offspring would bless all the peoples of the earth (Gen 12:1-3). "Son of Abraham" also carried messianic overtones as well in at least some intertestamental Jewish circles (e.g., *T. Levi* 8:15).

Already in this title verse, key themes of chaps. 1–2 are presented in a nutshell. Matthew's names for Jesus present him as the fulfillment of the hopes and prophecies of Israel but also as one who will extend God's blessings to Gentiles. His birth marks a new epoch in human history.

2. Genealogy (1:2-17)

The first main portion of the account of Jesus' origin presents his genealogy in order to validate Matthew's claims that Jesus is the son of Abraham and of David. The genealogy divides into three sections, as v. 17 makes clear. The times of Abraham, of David, and of the Babylonian exile mark the beginnings of these three periods. The genealogy culminates in the arrival of the Christ (vv. 16-17). Thus all three titles of v. 1 reappear as central elements in the genealogy. The Babylonian exile appears centrally as well, perhaps because Jesus is seen as the climax of the restoration of the nation of Israel from exile.

David, however, is the central figure throughout the genealogy. When one adds up the numerical values of the Hebrew consonants in his name (*DVD*), one arrives at the number fourteen (4+6+4). This *gematria*, as ancient Hebrew numerical equivalents to words are termed, probably accounts for the centrality of the number fourteen in Matthew's genealogy. Each of the three sections contains fourteen generations (v. 17), and David's name itself is the fourteenth entry. The actual number of generations in the three parts to the genealogy are thirteen, fourteen, and thirteen, respectively; but ancient counting often alternated between inclusive and exclusive reckoning. Such variation was thus well within standard literary convention of the day (for a good rabbinic parallel, see *m. ʾAbot* 5:1-6). When one compares the genealogy with Luke's account (Luke 3:23-37) and with various Old Testament narratives, it is clear that Matthew has omitted several names to achieve this literary symmetry. But the verb consistently translated in the NIV "was the father of" (more literally *begat*) could also mean *was the ancestor of*. Other differences from Luke are more difficult to explain. Two major proposals concern the divergence of names in the two genealogies: (1) Luke presents Mary's genealogy, while Matthew relates Joseph's; (2) Luke has Jesus' actual human ancestry through Joseph, while Matthew gives his legal ancestry by which he was the legitimate successor to the throne of David. Knowing which of these solutions is more likely probably is impossible unless new evidence turns up.[4]

> [2]Abraham was the father of Isaac,
> Isaac the father of Jacob,
> Jacob the father of Judah and his brothers,
> [3]Judah the father of Perez and Zerah,
> whose mother was Tamar,
> Perez the father of Hezron,
> Hezron the father of Ram,
> [4]Ram the father of Amminadab,
> Amminadab the father of Nahshon,
> Nahshon the father of Salmon,
> [5]Salmon the father of Boaz,
> whose mother was Rahab,
> Boaz the father of Obed,
> whose mother was Ruth,
> Obed the father of Jesse,
> [6]and Jesse the father of King David.
> David was the father of Solomon,
> whose mother had been Uriah's wife,
> [7]Solomon the father of Rehoboam,
> Rehoboam the father of Abijah,
> Abijah the father of Asa,
> [8]Asa the father of Jehoshaphat,
> Jehoshaphat the father of Jehoram,
> Jehoram the father of Uzziah,
> [9]Uzziah the father of Jotham,
> Jotham the father of Ahaz,
> Ahaz the father of Hezekiah,
> [10]Hezekiah the father of Manasseh,
> Manasseh the father of Amon,
> Amon the father of Josiah,
> [11]and Josiah the father of Jeconiah and his brothers at the time of the exile to Babylon.
> [12]After the exile to Babylon:
> Jeconiah was the father of Shealtiel,
> Shealtiel the father of Zerubbabel,
> [13]Zerubbabel the father of Abiud,
> Abiud the father of Eliakim,
> Eliakim the father of Azor,

---

[4]For the first view, see J. L. Nolland, *Luke 1–9:20*, WBC (Dallas: Word, 1990), 170; for the second, cf. J. G. Machen, *The Virgin Birth of Christ* (New York: Harper and Row, 1930), 202-9. The most detailed study of Matthew's and Luke's genealogies is J. Masson, *Jésus fils de David dans les généalogies de saint Matthieu et de saint Luc* (Paris: Tequi, 1981), which opts for a combination of (1) and (2) with Mary and Joseph sharing a common great-grandfather.

[14]Azor the father of Zadok,
Zadok the father of Akim,
Akim the father of Eliud,
[15]Eliud the father of Eleazar,
Eleazar the father of Matthan,
Matthan the father of Jacob,
[16]and Jacob the father of Joseph, the husband of Mary,
   of whom was born Jesus, who is called Christ.
[17]Thus there were fourteen generations in all from Abraham to David, fourteen from David to the exile to Babylon, and fourteen from the exile to the Christ.

1:2-17 Abraham, Isaac, Jacob, and Judah figure prominently in Gen 12–50. The other male names in vv. 2-6a correspond to 1 Chr 2.3-15. Solomon through Josiah (vv. 6b-11) all appear in 1 Chr 3:10-14 (recalling that Azariah is the same individual as Uzziah—cf., e.g., 2 Kgs 15:1-2 with 2 Chr 26:3—and that there are omissions in Matthew's list). In vv. 12-16 Jeconiah is a variant form of Jehoiachin, who with Shealtiel and Zerubbabel appear in 1 Chr 3:17-19. But there Zerubbabel is a nephew of Shealtiel, which may suggest that the latter died childless and that the line of succession passed to his brother's family. In Ezra 3:2, Zerubbabel is legally considered a son of Shealtiel. The rest of the names from Abiud to Jacob are unparalleled, but ancient Jews tried scrupulously to preserve their genealogies; so it is not implausible that Matthew had access to sources that have since been lost.

Deviations from the otherwise repetitive pattern of "X the father of Y" throughout these verses begin with the addition of "and his brothers" to the reference to Judah in v. 2. Obviously, it was natural to speak of all twelve of the sons of Jacob as founding fathers of the tribes of Israel. In v. 3 Zerah appears along with his twin brother Perez, a natural pairing (Gen 38:27-30). In v. 11 Jeconiah also appears with "his brothers," again a reference to the nation of Israel as a whole at the time of its deportation. Otherwise the most notable break in pattern in Matthew's genealogy involves the introduction of five women, both unnecessary and unusual in Jewish genealogies. These include Tamar (v. 3; cf. Gen 38), Rahab[5] (v. 5; cf. Josh 2), Ruth (v. 5; cf. Ruth 3), Bathsheba (v. 6; cf. 2 Sam 11)— referred to only as "Uriah's wife," perhaps to remind the reader of David's adulterous and murderous behavior—and Mary (v. 16).

Why are the first four of these women included? Suggestions have included viewing them as examples of sinners Jesus came to save, representative Gentiles to whom the Christian mission would be extended, or women who had illicit marriages and/or illegitimate children. The only

---

[5]That this is in fact the Rahab of the Joshua narrative is demonstrated by R. E. Brown, "*Rachab* in Mt 1,5 Probably Is Rahab of Jericho," *Bib* 63 (1982): 79-80.

factor that clearly applies to all four is that suspicions of illegitimacy surrounded their sexual activity and childbearing.[6] This suspicion of illegitimacy fits perfectly with that which surrounded Mary, which Matthew
immediately takes pains to refute (vv. 18-25). In fact, the grammar of
v. 16 makes clear that Joseph was not the human father of Jesus because
the pronoun "whom" is feminine and therefore can refer only to Mary as
a human parent of the Christ child.

Within the Gospels, Jewish polemic hinted (John 8:48) and in the early
centuries of the Christian era explicitly charged that Jesus was an illegitimate child. Matthew here strenuously denies the charge, but he also
points out that key members of the messianic genealogy were haunted by
similar suspicions (justified in at least the two cases of Tamar and Bathsheba and probably unjustified in the case of Ruth). Such suspicions, nevertheless, did not impugn the spiritual character of the individuals
involved. In fact, Jesus comes to save precisely such people. Already here
in the genealogy, Jesus is presented as the one who will ignore human
labels of legitimacy and illegitimacy to offer his gospel of salvation to all,
including the most despised and outcast of society. A question for the
church to ask itself in any age is how well it is visibly representing this
commitment to reach out to the oppressed and marginalized of society
with the good news of salvation in Christ.[7] At the same time, Matthew
inherently honors the five women of his genealogy simply by his inclusion of them. So it is not enough merely to minister to the oppressed; we
must find ways of exalting them and affirming their immense value in
God's eyes.

3. The Virginal Conception: God Becomes Human (1:18-25)

Having shown that Jesus has the correct scriptural pedigree to be the
Messiah, Matthew now narrates five ways in which the events surrounding his birth fulfill the Scriptures. The first of these is the most remarkable, miraculous, and controversial. Unfortunately these verses are often
studied in isolation from chap. 2. Matthew's use of Scripture here, in fact,
fits a consistent pattern throughout his opening chapters. He selects and
describes events in a way that calls to mind a certain Old Testament text
or theme. The correspondence is not exact enough to substantiate charges

---

[6]The most detailed study of these women appears in J. Schaberg, *The Illegitimacy of
Jesus* (San Francisco: Harper and Row, 1987), 33. Schaberg's case that Jesus was illegitimate is highly unlikely, but she has identified a theme of suspicion that united the references
to the five women in this genealogy.

[7]See esp. C. L. Blomberg, "The Liberation of Illegitimacy: Women and Rulers in Matthew 1-2," *BTB* 21 (1991): 145-50. More generally, on "Jesus and Women in Matthew," cf.
J. Kopas's article so entitled in *ThT* 47 (1990): 13-21.

that Matthew has fabricated history to create fulfillment of prophecy,[8] but he nevertheless tailors his narratives to bring out as many of the similarities between text and fulfillment as possible. This relationship, however, is not always straightforward. In two cases the Old Testament texts cited do not even have future tense verbs in them. Rather, Matthew is operating typologically. Old Testament events, viewed as of crucial significance in the history of salvation, are seen to display patterns of God's activity, which are being repeated in the events surrounding Jesus' birth. Such parallels can be attributed only to God.[9] A text that may well have had a previous historical referent is seen as being *completed* or *filled full*, a common meaning of the verb *plēroō* ("fulfill").[10] Much controversy in an often polarized and heated debate concerning Matthew's use of Isa 7:14 in v. 23 could be defused if these hermeneutical principles were recognized.

The term virgin *birth* is a misnomer. Neither Matthew nor Luke describes Jesus' birth at all but only his conception. The apocryphal *Protevangelium of James* 19:3, an important source for the traditional Catholic doctrine of Mary's perpetual virginity, is in fact the main source for the unscriptural notion that Mary's hymen was not broken at the time of delivery.

[18]This is how the birth of Jesus Christ came about: His mother Mary was pledged to be married to Joseph, but before they came together, she was found to be with child through the Holy Spirit. [19]Because Joseph her husband was a righteous man and did not want to expose her to public disgrace, he had in mind to divorce her quietly.

1:18-19 The situation described in these verses is Joseph's legal engagement to Mary. If typical Jewish custom were followed, she may well have been still a young teenager. Joseph may have been considerably older. Engagement in ancient Judaism was legally binding and required divorce if it were to be broken, but sexual relations and living together under one roof were not permitted until after the marriage ceremony. Joseph could therefore be spoken of already as Mary's husband, but Matthew emphasizes this was "before they came together."[11]

---

[8]See esp. R. T. France, "Scripture, Tradition and History in the Infancy Narratives of Matthew," in *Gospel Perspectives*, vol. 2, ed. R. T. France and D. Wenham (Sheffield: JSOT, 1981), 239-66.

[9]Cf. R. T. France, *The Gospel according to Matthew*, TNTC (Grand Rapids: Eerdmans, 1985), 40: Matthew's typology may be defined as "the recognition of a correspondence between New and Old Testament events [persons and institutions], based on a conviction of the unchanging character of the principles of God's working."

[10]R. Schippers, "πληρόω," *DNTT* 1:733-41.

[11]See the Mishnaic tractate *Kiddushin* for a whole series of related laws; for the most relevant selection of these and other Jewish traditions, see D. C. Allison and W. D. Davies, *A*

Matthew is clearly describing a supernatural conception here, but he uses remarkable restraint in that description (similarly Luke 1:35). Most non-Christian legends of virginal conceptions were quite different and much more detailed and/or crass.[12] Belief in this kind of conception obviously depends on one's approach to the supernatural more generally.[13] On the virginal conception in particular, it is often said that such a belief stems from prescientific superstition. But even the relatively primitive stage of first-century science was sufficiently advanced for people to know that in every other known instance it required a biological father as well as a biological mother to produce a human child. The Christian notion of a virginal conception was no more plausible in first-century Judaism than it is in the twentieth-century Western world, yet it has formed an integral part of Christian belief for two thousand years. Though Matthew expounds nothing of its significance here, the virginal conception has regularly been understood as a way by which Jesus could be both fully human and fully divine. His father, in essence, was God, through the work of the Holy Spirit; his mother was the fully human woman, Mary. As fully God, Jesus was able to pay the eternal penalty for our sins (v. 21) for which finite humanity could not atone. As fully human he could be our adequate representative and substitutionary sacrifice.

Joseph, however, knows nothing of this yet. When he discovers Mary's pregnancy, he naturally assumes that she has been unfaithful to him. He is called a "righteous" man, which for Matthew does not imply sinless perfection but regularly refers to one who is law-abiding, upright in character, and generally obedient and faithful to God's commandments.[14] Here Joseph's righteousness leads him to want to spare Mary the disgrace of public divorce and censure and the legal proceedings for a suspected adulteress (*m. Sota* 1:1,5).[15] Jewish laws typically required a man to divorce an adulterous wife (*m. Sota* 5:1), but Joseph proposes to divorce her "quietly," which is perhaps better translated "privately" (Goodspeed), in the sense of a settlement out of court.

Critical and Exegetical Commentary on the Gospel according to Saint Matthew, vol. 1, ICC (Edinburgh: T & T Clark, 1988), 199.

[12]See Machen, *Virgin Birth*, 280-379.

[13]On miracles in the Gospels, see esp. D. Wenham and C. Blomberg, *Gospel Perspectives*, vol. 6 (Sheffield: JSOT, 1986); and C. Blomberg, *The Historical Reliability of the Gospels* (Downers Grove: InterVarsity, 1987), 73-112, and the literature there cited.

[14]B. Przybylski, *Righteousness in Matthew and His World of Thought* (Cambridge: University Press, 1980), 99: "proper conduct before God"—not tied to the concepts of salvation or grace, as in Paul.

[15]On Joseph's choice as the most compassionate of his legal options, see A. Tosato, "Joseph, Being a Just Man (Matt 1:19)," *CBQ* 41 (1979): 547-51.

20But after he had considered this, an angel of the Lord appeared to him in a dream and said, "Joseph son of David, do not be afraid to take Mary home as your wife, because what is conceived in her is from the Holy Spirit. 21She will give birth to a son, and you are to give him the name Jesus, because he will save his people from their sins."

1:20-21 God quickly changes Joseph's plans. The first of several angelic visitors in Matt 1–2 appears. The angel comes in a dream, an important form of divine communication in the Old Testament and also in the chapters that frame this Gospel (compare 2:12-13,19,22; 27:19).[16] The angel explains to Joseph that Mary has not been unfaithful and that her child has been supernaturally conceived. He reminds Joseph of his messianic lineage by calling him "son of David." He commands Joseph not only not to divorce Mary but to go ahead and marry her. The child will therefore legally be Joseph's son and thus legally son of David.

Such a child will also obviously be very special. Part of this special role is now specified. He is to be named Jesus (Heb. *Yeshua*), which means *Yahweh is salvation* or "the Lord saves" (NIV marg.). His ministry will not first of all involve the physical liberation of Israel from its enemies but the spiritual salvation of God's people by removing the alienation from God which their sins have created. An echo of Ps 138:7 appears here.

22All this took place to fulfill what the Lord had said through the prophet: 23"The virgin will be with child and will give birth to a son, and they will call him Immanuel"—which means, "God with us."

1:22-23 Matthew now introduces his first Old Testament fulfillment quotation. Divine purposes are seen at work in the events that have just been prophesied. Matthew quotes Isa 7:14 in a form similar to that of the LXX. Isaiah's prophecy is viewed as God's word. "Immanuel" is translated for the benefit of those in Matthew's audience who could not understand the Hebrew.

The miraculous conception is itself not the primary focus of the quotation but understandably raises many important questions. What kind of woman was involved? How did Matthew understand the prophecy? Is such understanding legitimate? Discussion has tended to polarize around two extreme views. On the one hand, a majority of commentators assumes that Isaiah had only a *young woman of marriageable age* (Heb. *ᶜalmah*) in view and that he was referring only to a child of his day—e.g., Hezekiah as the royal son and heir to the throne of King Ahaz, or Maher-Shalal-Hash-Baz (cf. Isa 8:4,8), or some otherwise anonymous child

---

[16]On specific Old Testament background, see R. Gnuse, "Dream Genre in the Matthean Infancy Narratives," *NovT* 32 (1990): 97-120.

named Immanuel. That there was originally no reference to the virginity of this child's mother and that Matthew's use of the text goes beyond anything that can be fairly attributed to the original intentions of the prophecy then follows naturally.[17] Conservatives have tended to react by saying that ᶜalmah must be taken as a "virgin," that it refers only to a miraculous birth not previously fulfilled in any way, and that its only fulfillment was in the conception of Jesus.[18]

An understanding of prophetic foreshortening of time (the Old Testament prophets often predicted in one and the same context various events that would take place in entirely different future eras), multiple fulfillment of prophecy (partial fulfillments often preceded and foreshadowed later complete fulfillments), and Matthew's use of typology, along with a careful reading of the larger context of the Isaiah quote (7:1–9:7), offers a mediating and more convincing alternative.[19] The reference in Isa 7:15-16 to the short period of time in the promised child's life before the kings Ahaz dreads are destroyed seems to require at least a partial fulfillment of the prophecy in Isaiah's day. Nevertheless, the LXX translation of ᶜalmah as *parthenos* (both words often though not always mean "virgin," though the Greek term is less equivocal) shows that some Jews already two hundred years before Christ favored an interpretation in which this immediate fulfillment was not seen as exhausting Isaiah's prophecy. Further exegetical clues in Isaiah support the LXX's interpretation. Isaiah 8:4,8 seems to equate Immanuel with Maher-Shalal-Hash-Baz, but Isa 7:11; 8:18 suggests that this child will be a "sign," a term that regularly in Scripture refers to a more remarkable event than the simple birth of a child to a normally impregnated woman. By the time one reaches Isa 9:6, the prophet is speaking of a child, naturally taken as still referring to Immanuel, who is the "Mighty God." In no sense can this prophecy be taken as less than messianic or as fulfilled in a merely human figure. So it is best to see a partial, proleptic fulfillment of Isaiah's prophecy in his time, with the complete and more glorious fulfillment in Jesus' own birth.[20]

Notwithstanding the extensive discussion his reference to a "virgin" has triggered, Matthew's own focus lies elsewhere. The passage climaxes by claiming this child to be "Immanuel," meaning *God with us*. Verse 21 introduces the key Matthean theme of God's presence with his people, which is emphasized again at the end of his Gospel in 28:18-20. The

---

[17]See, e.g., J. D. W. Watts, *Isaiah 1–33*, WBC (Waco: Word, 1985), 98-104.

[18]See, e.g., E. J. Young, *The Book of Isaiah*, vol. 1, NIC (Grand Rapids: Eerdmans, 1965), 288-94.

[19]For an explanation of these and related concepts and for an excellent survey of interpretations of Isa 7:14, see J. T. Willis, *Isaiah* (Austin: Sweet, 1980), 158-68.

[20]Cf. esp. J. N. Oswalt, *The Book of Isaiah*, vol. 1, NIC (Grand Rapids: Eerdmans, 1986), 207-13.

church in every age should recognize here a clear affirmation of Jesus' deity and cling tightly to this doctrine as crucial for our salvation. At the same time, Matthew wants to emphasize that Jesus, as God, is "with us"; deity is immanent. Too often those who have rightly contended for Jesus' full deity have created a God to whom they do not feel close rather than one who became human in every way like them but without sin (Heb 4:15). As God "with us," Jesus enables us to come boldly before God's throne (Heb 4:16) when we accept the forgiveness of sins he made available (Matt 2:21) and develop an intimate relationship with him.

24When Joseph woke up, he did what the angel of the Lord had commanded him and took Mary home as his wife. 25But he had no union with her until she gave birth to a son. And he gave him the name Jesus.

1:24-25 In keeping with his "righteous" character (v. 19), Joseph obeys the Lord's directives (vv. 24-25b). Verse 25a goes beyond what the angel explicitly commands but further refutes any claim that might be made then or later that Joseph himself was Jesus' biological father. The grammatical construction translated "until" strongly suggests (but does not prove) that Mary and Joseph proceeded to have normal sexual relations after Jesus' birth.

4. Bethlehem: Herod versus the Magi (2:1-12)

The second of Matthew's five fulfillment quotations appears in 2:6. The quote comes primarily from Mic 5:2 and focuses on the role of Bethlehem in prophecy. All twelve verses in this section narrate events in Bethlehem and nearby Jerusalem. Yet the story is not about Jesus' birth but about subsequent events pitting the Magi against Herod. Despite their pagan background and powerful influence in the Babylonian or Persian courts, the Magi recognize and worship the Christ child for who he is. Despite his role as legally installed ruler of Israel and his professed conversion to Judaism, Herod rejects the newborn king and plots to destroy him. He fears that this young boy will threaten his royal position and authority. So we learn already at this early stage of the life of Jesus that the allegiances he will create will extend far beyond the boundaries of Judaism, while at the same time he will threaten and alienate many within those boundaries.

1After Jesus was born in Bethlehem in Judea, during the time of King Herod, Magi from the east came to Jerusalem 2and asked, "Where is the one who has been born king of the Jews? We saw his star in the east and have come to worship him."

2:1-2 How long after Jesus' birth these events take place is unknown. The birth itself is probably to be dated around the year 6 B.C. A comparison of vv. 7 and 16 suggests that perhaps one to two years have elapsed since Jesus' birth. Verse 11 describes Joseph and Mary now living in a house, so they obviously have left their temporary lodgings described in Luke 2:7. From other historical materials we know that Herod died in 4 B.C. (The calendrical confusion was caused by the switch from a Roman to a Christian calendar in the sixth century A.D., based on the faulty calculations of Dionysius Exiguus, who did not have accurate information about the time of Herod's death.)[21] Jesus' birth itself almost certainly did not occur on December 25. This date became attached to the celebration of Christmas later because it coincided with a Roman holiday known as Saturnalia, when Christians had time off work to worship. Perhaps Jesus was born in the spring when shepherds would have been watching their flocks by night because lambs might be born (Luke 2:8).

Herod the Great was a half-Jew, half-Idumean, who, through accommodation to the Romans, ascended to power as client-ruler of Israel in 37 B.C. He was known as a great builder of public works and a shrewd diplomat in his dealings with both Romans and Jews, but he laid oppressive taxes on and conscripted labor from the Israelites. As he grew older, he became increasingly paranoid about threats against his person and throne. He had numerous sons, wives, and others close to him put to death because he feared plots to overthrow him. After frequent disputes with Caesar Augustus, the emperor uttered his famous pun that he would rather be Herod's pig (*hys*) than his son (*huios*).[22]

The Magi were not kings but a combination of wise men and priests probably from Persia. They combined astronomical observation with astrological speculation. They played both political and religious roles and were figures of some prominence in their land.[23]

The Magi's question to Herod emphasizes the word "born." The grammatical construction makes it clear that they ask about who the child is who has legitimate claim to Israel's throne by virtue of his birth. Herod is thus viewed as a usurper to the throne. A new star in the sky was often believed to herald the birth of a significant person in the land over which the star shone. So the Magi's question is a natural inference from their observation. If "in the east" is the correct translation in v. 2, then this phrase modifies "we saw" not "his star." Otherwise the geography would

---

[21]Recent attempts to date Jesus' birth significantly later or earlier (e.g., by E. L. Martin, "The Nativity and Herod's Death," 85-92, and J. Vardaman, "Jesus' Life: A New Chronology," 35-82) prove unpersuasive. For these articles, as well as others that defend the consensus dating, see *Chronos, Kairos, Christos*, ed. J. Vardaman and E. M. Yamauchi (Winona Lake, Ind.: Eisenbrauns, 1989). Note also esp. Yamauchi's "The Episode of the Magi" (15-39) for the background and historicity of the Magi narrative.

[22]Most of our historical information concerning Herod comes from Josephus's *Antiquities*, Books 14-18.

[23]For further details see G. Delling, "μάγος," *TDNT* 4:356-59.

be confused. But the NIV margin "when it rose" is perhaps a more likely translation and would explain how the Magi's attention was called to this new celestial feature. The statement that these pagans "have come to worship" the Christ child is both remarkable and significant for what lies ahead.

[3]When King Herod heard this he was disturbed, and all Jerusalem with him. [4]When he had called together all the people's chief priests and teachers of the law, he asked them where the Christ was to be born. [5]"In Bethlehem in Judea," they replied, "for this is what the prophet has written:
[6]"'But you, Bethlehem, in the land of Judah,
are by no means least among the rulers of Judah;
for out of you will come a ruler
who will be the shepherd of my people Israel.'"

2:3-6 If Herod[24] were a true devotee of the Judaism of Scripture, he should have rejoiced greatly, but he does not. Instead, he views the new child as a mortal threat. "Disturbed" is too weak a translation of his reaction; "in turmoil" or even "terrified" (cf. Weymouth, "greatly agitated") would be more accurate. "All Jerusalem" probably refers primarily to the religious leaders of Israel who dominated the city, many of whom were also personally installed by Herod.[25] The rejection of Jesus by Jerusalem foreshadows his similar fate at the end of his life.

Verse 4 refers to the two key groups of religious leaders in Jerusalem. The "chief priests" headed the twenty-four main orders of priests who lived in and around the city. The scribes ("teachers of the law") had inherited the ancient profession of copying Scripture, but they had evolved into a class of teachers well trained in interpreting and applying the Old Testament as well.[26]

The newborn king is now equated with the Christ. "Messiah" and "King of the Jews" doubtless coalesced in the minds of many. Herod reveals his superficial knowledge of Scripture by having to ask the religious authorities where this Messiah is to be born. They supply the answer from Mic 5:2. Bethlehem was a small city approximately five miles south of Jerusalem.

---

[24]The Greek reads literally *the King Herod* (vs. *Herod the King* in v. 1). The latter is the more natural grammatical construction. The term "king" is used loosely to reflect the contrast between Herod and Jesus, though that was not a title that strictly applied to Herod. But having introduced two kings, when v. 3 resumes talking about *the* king, the particular one in view has to be specified.

[25]See Horsley, *Liberation*, 49-52.

[26]For more details on these and other divisions of the Jerusalem authorities, see esp. J. Jeremias, *Jerusalem in the Time of Jesus* (Philadelphia: Fortress, 1969), 147-221, esp. 160-81 on the religious hierarchy.

Here is as close to a straightforward prediction-fulfillment scheme as is found anywhere in Matthew. The context of the passage in Micah seems clearly messianic and was regularly so taken by pre-Christian Jews. The remainder of the verse which Matthew leaves unquoted ("whose origins are from of old, from ancient times") suggests more than a mere mortal is in view. Perhaps Micah even had in mind the child of Isa 7:14 and 9:6.[27] Certainly such a prophecy excludes many potential messianic aspirants and refutes the argument that Jesus claimed to be the Messiah simply by setting out to fulfill all of the Scriptures relevant to the office. He scarcely could have chosen his place of birth.

Matthew makes a key addition to Micah's wording, by inserting the word translated "by no means," to show that the fulfillment of this prophecy has transformed Bethlehem from a relatively insignificant town into a city of great honor. What seems at first glance to create a formal contradiction in fact involves an addition designed to make the text accurately reflect the altered situation. This combination of translation and commentary closely resembles that of the Jewish targums. Discerning Jewish readers would have known the wording of the original text and would have recognized that Matthew's addition was not a mistake in quoting the Scriptures but an interpretative explanation. Other changes to the text are minor and do not affect the overall meaning. Nevertheless, Matthew's rendering of the Old Testament is more paraphrastic here than in 1:23 and probably reflects his independent translation of the Hebrew rather than dependence on the LXX. This in fact is Matthew's consistent practice in citing Scripture when he is not following a previously written Gospel source.[28]

Matthew's quotation not only answers Herod's and the Magi's question regarding the place of the Christ child's birth while showing the city once despised as now honored, but it also adds another aspect to the work of the royal Messiah. He will not only rule but also "shepherd" the people of Israel. A shepherd as an image of a ruler of God's people appeared commonly in the Old Testament (see Ezek 34). It implies guidance, pastoral care, and a sense of compassion (see Mark 6:34). The final phrase of Matthew's quotation comes from 2 Sam 5:2, in which godly shepherding formed part of the role assigned to Israelite kings. What they often failed to carry out, the Messiah will now perform properly.

---

[27]Cf. R. L. Smith, *Micah-Malachi*, WBC (Waco: Word, 1984), 43-44; T. McComiskey, "Micah," in EBC, vol. 7, ed. F. E. Gaebelein (Grand Rapids: Zondervan, 1985), 427.

[28]For key studies of all of Matthew's quotations of Scripture, see R. H. Gundry, *The Use of the Old Testament in St. Matthew's Gospel* (Leiden: Brill, 1967); G. M. Soarés Prabhu, *The Formula Quotations in the Infancy Narrative of Matthew* (Rome: Biblical Institute Press, 1976). On the quotations just in chap. 2, see esp. R. T. France, "The Formula-Quotations of Matthew 2 and the Problem of Communication," *NTS* 27 (1981): 233-51.

⁷**Then Herod called the Magi secretly and found out from them the exact time the star had appeared. ⁸He sent them to Bethlehem and said, "Go and make a careful search for the child. As soon as you find him, report to me, so that I too may go and worship him."**

2:7-8 Comparing vv. 7 and 16 demonstrates Herod's evil plans. The end of v. 8 is therefore a bald-faced lie; Herod has no intentions of worshiping the child. Instead he makes his plans "secretly" even as Joseph had "quietly," i.e., in private (1:19). Both proposals were inappropriate. Joseph, however, was warned directly against his plan, while Herod receives no such warning. As a result, Herod is able to get his scheme underway.

⁹**After they had heard the king, they went on their way, and the star they had seen in the east went ahead of them until it stopped over the place where the child was. ¹⁰When they saw the star, they were overjoyed. ¹¹On coming to the house, they saw the child with his mother Mary, and they bowed down and worshiped him. Then they opened their treasures and presented him with gifts of gold and of incense and of myrrh. ¹²And having been warned in a dream not to go back to Herod, they returned to their country by another route.**

2:9-12 The Magi do not recognize Herod's purposes at first but are later warned in a dream just as Joseph had been (1:20-21). Like Joseph they obey God's words (v. 12). Meanwhile, the star guides them to Bethlehem.[29] This is the first time the star is actually said to move. The text leaves open the question of whether or not it had so moved previously. If it had not, this could explain why the Magi had managed to get only as far as Jerusalem. They may have seen the star above Israel and assumed that its ruler would be born in the capital. But regardless of how much the star had traveled, its motion here seems to require a supernatural event. Various attempts to link the star with different astronomical phenomena, especially for purposes of dating (e.g., a comet or a conjunction of planets), prove interesting but are probably irrelevant.[30]

What the Magi recognize as divine guidance fills them, literally, with *exceedingly great joy* (v. 10). They find the mother and child and prostrate themselves before him in worship. The gifts used to honor the new king were typically associated with royalty. Because Matthew has not yet introduced the theme of Jesus' death, it is not likely that he is implying it here, even though myrrh was a spice often used in embalming. Rather, all three

---

[29]The same ambiguity with the phrase "in the east" appears here as in v. 2. Translations of the two verses should be consistent.

[30]For examples of these, see D. A. Carson, "Matthew," in EBC, vol. 8, ed. F. E. Gaebelein (Grand Rapids: Zondervan, 1984), 85.

gifts honor the Christ child as King. Gold, then as now, was a precious metal prized for its beauty and value, an appropriate regal gift. Frankincense and myrrh were fragrant spices and perfumes equally appropriate for such adoration and worship.[31] Similar visits of Magi to royalty are described in other Greco-Roman literature of the time (Dio Cassius *Roman History* 63.7; Suetonius, *Nero* 13), but more significant here is the Jewish background. The Magi appear as Balaam's successors to witness the fulfillment of Num 24:17.[32]

Thus one born in obscurity is recognized by unlikely devotees as the future King of Israel. The child whose birth is shrouded in suspicions of illegitimacy (chap. 1) is in fact God's legitimate appointee. On the other hand, the legal rulers, both political and religious, by their clinging to positions of power and prestige, prove themselves to be illegitimate in God's eyes. Sadly, the church in many ages has perpetuated this pattern. Meanwhile, God often chooses to reveal himself to pagans, at times even in the midst of their religious practices, to lead them on to the full truth found only in Christ.

5. *The New Exodus from Egypt (2:13-15)*

[13]**When they had gone, an angel of the Lord appeared to Joseph in a dream. "Get up," he said, "take the child and his mother and escape to Egypt. Stay there until I tell you, for Herod is going to search for the child to kill him."**

2:13 The third fulfillment-quotation narrative introduces a third dream and the second interchange between Joseph and an angel (cf. 1:20; 2:12). "The child and his mother" reappear as in v. 11. Matthew does not call Jesus Joseph's child, perhaps to remind his readers of the virginal conception. Also "the child" is mentioned before "his mother." Jesus remains the central focus of the the the text. The angel tells Joseph to take his family and flee to Egypt because of Herod's murderous schemes.[33] These schemes will be described in more detail in v. 16. Egypt afforded a natural haven for first-century Jews. A large Jewish community had lived there for several centuries, and even from Old Testament times Egypt had often provided a refuge when danger threatened Israel (e.g., 1 Kgs 11:40; 2 Kgs 25:26; Zech 10:10).

---

[31]Interestingly, the text never refers to three Magi. Their number may or may not be implied by the fact that three gifts are brought. Also they are given no names, despite the later tradition that ascribed to them the names Gaspar, Melchior, and Balthasar.

[32]Allison and Davies, *Matthew*, 1:231.

[33]The motif of Jesus' withdrawal from hostility appears frequently in Matthew, but God's providence overrides any sense of defeat in retreat. Cf. D. Good, "The Verb Ἀναχωρέω in Matthew's Gospel," *NovT* 32 (1990): 1-12.

[14]So he got up, took the child and his mother during the night and left for Egypt, [15]where he stayed until the death of Herod. And so was fulfilled what the Lord had said through the prophet: "Out of Egypt I called my son."

2:14-15 Joseph apparently sensed an urgency to the angel's commands. The expression "is going to" in v. 13 is best rendered "is about to" or even "is on the verge of." The family leaves during the night under cover of darkness. They remain in Egypt until Herod's death (4 B.C.) when the angel tells them to return (v. 20). As before, the fulfillment quotation does not contradict the events of history, but neither does it fit them so closely as to substantiate charges that the narrative was created out of the quotation. The historical events described focus on the flight of Jesus and family; the quotation described their return. In its original context the Old Testament text cited (Hos 11:1) is not predictive prophecy but a recollection of God's love for his people Israel at the time of the exodus. Attempts to find a messianic title in Hosea's use of "son" seem contrived and unconvincing.[34] Most simply attribute Matthew's hermeneutic to some form of Jewish exegesis (e.g., midrash or pesher) which many today would recognize as illegitimate.

Better than either of these approaches is that which recognizes the exegesis as typological (and even more specifically that of analogical correspondence). Matthew sees striking parallels in the patterns of God's activities in history in ways he cannot attribute to coincidence. Just as God brought the nation of Israel out of Egypt to inaugurate his original covenant with them, so again God is bringing the Messiah, who fulfills the hopes of Israel, out of Egypt as he is about to inaugurate his new covenant.[35] This is the first of several instances in Matthew in which Jesus recapitulates the role of Israel as a whole.[36] The language of Jesus' sonship foreshadows Jesus' role as Son of God (or Immanuel) and recalls Old Testament texts that link Messiah with "the Son" (e.g., Pss 2:7; 89:26-27; 2 Sam 7:14; cf. Num 24:7-8, LXX, in which God himself brings the Messiah out of Egypt).[37]

---

[34]E.g., W. C. Kaiser, Jr., *The Uses of the Old Testament in the New Testament* (Chicago: Moody, 1985), 49.

[35]An excellent survey of approaches to Matthew's use of Hos 11:1, which agrees entirely with the conclusions adopted here, is T. L. Howard, "The Use of Hosea 11:1 in Matthew 2:15: An Alternative Solution," *BibSac* 143 (1986): 314-28. Cf. esp. p. 322: "As Matthew drew these correspondences he saw Jesus as the One who *actualizes* and *completes* all that God intended for the nation."

[36]See esp. W. Kynes, *A Christology of Solidarity: Jesus as the Representative of His People in Matthew* (Lanham: University Press of America, 1991).

[37]On the close link between "Son of God" and "Messiah" in Matthew, see esp. J. D. Kingsbury, *Matthew: Structure, Christology, Kingdom* (Philadelphia: Fortress, 1975). For cautions against overestimating this linkage, see D. Verseput, "The Role and Meaning of the 'Son of God' Title in Matthew's Gospel," *NovT* 33 (1987): 532-56.

6. Ramah: Weeping for Dead Children (2:16-21)

¹⁶**When Herod realized that he had been outwitted by the Magi, he was furious, and he gave orders to kill all the boys in Bethlehem and its vicinity who were two years old and under, in accordance with the time he had learned from the Magi. ¹⁷Then what was said through the prophet Jeremiah was fulfilled:**

¹⁸**"A voice is heard in Ramah,**
    weeping and great mourning,
  Rachel weeping for her children
    and refusing to be comforted,
  because they are no more."

2:16-18 Matthew now picks up the narrative thread he dropped at the end of v. 12. Herod behaves in keeping with his murderous and paranoiac personality. The massacre offers a classic example of overkill, but vv. 7,16b together suggest that Herod may have known that the child was already one to two years of age and wanted to make sure he did not miss him. It is often observed that there are no other historical documents substantiating Herod's "massacre of the innocents." But given the small size of Bethlehem and the rural nature of the surrounding region, there may have been as few as twenty children involved, and the killings would have represented a relatively minor incident in Herod's career, worthy of little notice by ancient historians who concentrated on great political and military exploits. The number could be even less if, as the grammar allows, the phrase "two years old and under" is translated "under two years old."[38]

The fourth fulfillment quotation harks back to Jer 31:15. In its original context, the passage depicted the lament of mothers in Israel bewailing their sons led off into exile. Already a sense of the recapitulation of history appeared in Jeremiah's time in that the mothers of Israel were personified as "Rachel," the mother in the days of the patriarchs whose sons Joseph and Benjamin had also been threatened with being "no more" (i.e., carried away into Egypt; cf. Gen 42:36). Now Matthew applies the passage to the mothers in first-century Israel in anguish over the babies Herod massacred. Ramah originally was located approximately five miles north of Jerusalem and would have been one of the first cities the exiles passed by as they headed north on their way out of Israel. First Samuel 10:2-3 associates Rachel's tomb with the same general area on the border of Judah and Benjamin.

---

[38]On the meaning and historical plausibility of this episode, see esp. R. T. France, "Herod and the Children of Bethlehem," *NovT* 21 (1979): 98-120.

7. Nazareth: Coming Home to Obscurity (2:19-23)

[19]After Herod died, an angel of the Lord appeared in a dream to Joseph in Egypt [20]and said, "Get up, take the child and his mother and go to the land of Israel, for those who were trying to take the child's life are dead."

2:19-20 Matthew now resumes the story of vv. 13-15. Angel and dream reappear for Joseph as before. The wording of the Lord's command begins exactly as in v. 13, but now Joseph and family are told to leave Egypt and return home to Israel. The immediate danger has passed with Herod's death. The plural "those who were trying to take the child's life" may include along with Herod some of his royal advisors.[39]

[21]So he got up, took the child and his mother and went to the land of Israel. [22]But when he heard that Archelaus was reigning in Judea in place of his father Herod, he was afraid to go there. Having been warned in a dream, he withdrew to the district of Galilee, [23]and he went and lived in a town called Nazareth. So was fulfilled what was said through the prophets: "He will be called a Nazarene."

2:21-23 The wording of the narrative echoes the angel's command and highlights Joseph's careful obedience. Now another potential threat appears on the horizon. After Herod the Great died, his kingdom was divided into four parts or tetrarchies. His oldest son Archelaus ruled in Judea and was notorious for his cruelty. Not long after his father's death, he too ordered a massacre (Josephus, *Ant.* 17.9.3). The Jews soon protested his cruel leadership, sending an embassy to Caesar in Rome. Augustus responded in A.D. 6 by removing Archelaus from power. Antipas, a second son of Herod, who ruled in Galilee to the north, was not perceived as such a threat. So Joseph, Mary, and Jesus go to Galilee rather than Judea to settle in the city in which they once lived.

Many commentators find a contradiction in these verses with Luke because Matthew seems to know nothing of Mary's and Joseph's original residence in Nazareth. But Matthew narrates only that which is relevant to his fulfillment quotations. He certainly says nothing that would exclude a previous residence in Galilee. Probably Mary and Joseph had intended to resettle in Bethlehem in their ancestral homeland and now have to change their plans and go north once again.[40] Joseph has yet another dream, and as in v. 12 it is a warning. The angel does not explicitly appear, though his presence may be presupposed.

---

[39]R. G. Bratcher, *A Translator's Guide to the Gospel of Matthew* (New York: UBS, 1981), 18.

[40]Similarly, commentators on Luke often remark that he leaves no place for Matthew's account of the flight into Egypt, but the vagueness of Luke 2:39 provides precisely such a location for inserting a trip to Egypt and back again.

The last of the five fulfillment quotations in Matt 1–2 poses a unique problem. No such citation appears in the Old Testament. Matthew may be acknowledging this fact by using, for the first time here, the plural "prophets." In other words, he may be indicating that he is not quoting one specific text but summarizing a broader scriptural theme. What might this theme be? A common suggestion links Nazareth with the Hebrew *nezer*, which means *branch* and signifies *a king from David's line* (cf. e.g., Isa 11:1). Matthew would then be making a typical Hebrew play on words because "Nazareth" itself does not derive from *nezer*.

The second possibility, proposed at least as long ago as the days of Jerome (fourth century), is that "Nazarene" was a slang or idiomatic term for an individual from a very remote or obscure place (much like our contemporary words *hick* or *backwoodsman*). This interpretation would fit well with the attitude toward Nazareth reflected in John 1:46 and is perhaps to be preferred in light of the context of Matt 2. Matthew has pointed out the originally insignificant town in which Jesus was born, the ignominy of his flight to Egypt, and the grief of death surrounding his infancy. It would be appropriate if a reference to the obscure and despised city of his childhood appeared here. Old Testament precedent for the Messiah's obscurity culminates in Isa 52–53. A third explanation links "Nazarene" and "Nazirite." But Jesus was not a Nazirite, and the orthographical evidence for this linkage is lacking.[41]

Matthew 2:13-23 thus concludes the presentation in chaps. 1–2 of Jesus as the legitimate Messiah of Israel and the fulfillment of its Scriptures, including those which predicted that through Abraham's offspring all peoples would be blessed. But the second half of Matt 2 turns attention more to the hostility that arises against the Christ child, his flight into exile, and settlement in obscurity. Matthew foreshadows the similar reaction to Jesus which will characterize the final months of his life and which has recurred frequently throughout church history. True believers, moreover, often follow their Lord in suffering and persecution. Matthew reminds us that this is part of God's sovereign plan. But just as the larger context of Jer 31 (presupposed in the quotation in 2:18) focuses exclusively on the vindication and restoration of God's people, culminating in the establishment of his new covenant with them, so also suffering, rejection, and even death are never God's final word for either Christ or his disciples. But they often must precede exaltation.[42]

---

[41]The Greek literally reads Ναζωραῖος, but the ω/α spelling interchange is attested in Galilean Aramaic. So "Nazarene" (but not "Nazirite") is a legitimate derivation from this term. See H. P. Ruger, "ΝΑΖΑΡΕΘ/ΝΑΖΑΡΑ ΝΑΖΑΡΗΝΟΣ/ΝΑΖΩΡΑΙΟΣ," *ZNW* 72 (1981): 257-63.

[42]For a good summary of the theology of chaps. 1–2, see Schweizer, *Matthew*, 45. Allison and Davies (*Matthew*, 1:282) put it even more succinctly: "Jesus culminates Israel's history in chapter 1; in chapter 2 he repeats it."

An additional unifying feature of chap. 2 is the person of Herod, who is mentioned in each of the four subsections. Just as chap. 1 has defended Jesus against suspicions of illegitimacy, so chap. 2 clearly portrays Herod as the real usurper to the throne. He whose birth is hounded by charges of illegitimacy is in fact the truly legitimate king of Israel. Self-appointed leaders of God's people in every age must guard against making the same mistake that Herod did in not recognizing God's true messengers when they appear. Jesus comes to seek and to save all the lost. In so doing he brings justice for the oppressed and threatens those who continue to cling to humanly erected social barriers. There is no place in God's economy for discrimination against any kind of people. God's own Messiah appears in ignominious circumstances to identify with and liberate all those who would accept the gift of forgiveness which those in positions of power and privilege so often reject and despise.[43]

B. Jesus' Preparation for Ministry (3:1–4:16)

Matthew abruptly jumps from the events surrounding Jesus' birth to the time of his adult life. Apart from the one episode of Jesus teaching in the temple at age twelve (Luke 2:41-52), none of the canonical Gospels describes anything about his intervening years. Apparently, they provided few clues to his true identity or coming mission. In striking contrast, the apocryphal gospels fill Jesus' "hidden years" with all kinds of miraculous exploits, esoteric teaching, and exotic travels.

The events of chaps. 3–4 probably date from A.D. 27 and focus on God's preparation for the beginning of Jesus' public ministry. These necessary preliminaries include the emergence of the Messiah's prophetic forerunner (3:1-12), his baptism of Jesus (3:13-17), and the Messiah's temptation (4:1-11). Matthew 4:12-16 brings this period of preparation to a close with a characteristically Matthean fulfillment quotation and ushers in the second main section and largest portion of Matthew's Gospel (4:17–16:20). In fact, Matthew's predilection for Scripture quotations continues throughout this part of his introduction (3:3,17; 4:4,6,7,10,15-16), but only the first and last of these speak of fulfillment (3:3; 4:14). Matthew does not so focus the narrative in this second major portion of the first section of his Gospel to what is needed to show Jesus as the culmination of specific prophetic texts, as was the case in 1:18–2:23.

---

[43]Cf. Blomberg, "Liberation." The fullest introduction to Matthew's and Luke's infancy narratives is R. E. Brown, *The Birth of the Messiah* (Garden City: Doubleday, 1977). The best survey of scholarship is H. Hendrickx, *The Infancy Narratives* (San Francisco: Harper and Row, 1984).

1. John the Baptist: The Prophetic Forerunner to Messiah (3:1-12)

Popular Jewish expectation anticipated a messianic forerunner. Deuteronomy 18:18, speaking of the prophet like Moses to whom all Israel should listen, became a seminal text in the development of this expectation. Some expected a literal Elijah to return from heaven, based on Mal 4:5. John comes fitting no one stereotype but fulfilling a variety of prophetic roles and themes. More about his ministry will appear in 11:2-19 (in other Gospels, cf. Luke 1:11-17 and John 1:19-34; 3:22-36). Interesting extracanonical confirmation of the main contours of John's message and ministry appears in Josephus as well (*Ant.* 18.5.2).[44]

¹In those days John the Baptist came, preaching in the Desert of Judea ²and saying, "Repent, for the kingdom of heaven is near." ³This is he who was spoken of through the prophet Isaiah:
"A voice of one calling in the desert,
'Prepare the way for the Lord,
make straight paths for him.'"

a. His Ministry (3:1-6). **3:1-3** Matthew first introduces what John was about and shows how he fulfilled Scripture. "In those days" (v. 1) refers to the days of Christ's life; otherwise there is approximately a thirty-year gap from the preceding chapter. The exact date depends on establishing the year of the crucifixion (probably A.D. 30, though A.D. 33 is also possible) and then subtracting the three to four years of Jesus' ministry that preceded his death (cf. references to annual Passovers in John 2:13; [5:1?]; 6:4; 13:1). Jesus' age at the start of his ministry ("about thirty years," Luke 3:23) fits better with the earlier date for his death. That it was the fifteenth year of Tiberius's reign (Luke 3:1) fits somewhat better with the later date, though without ruling out the earlier one. The forty-six years since the beginning of the rebuilding of the temple (John 2:20) might point very precisely to A.D. 28, in which case John's preparation for Jesus' ministry probably began in the preceding year.[45]

Matthew introduces John as he came to be known—as one who baptized people. He calls him a preacher or, more literally, one who *speaks as a herald*. John proclaimed God's message as a prophetic spokesman in the desert of Judea, the wilderness area to the south of Jerusalem. Reminiscent

---

[44]For detailed study of all of the John the Baptist traditions, see R. L. Webb, *John the Baptizer and Prophet: A Socio-Historical Study* (Sheffield: JSOT, 1991). On Matthew's distinctive emphases concerning John, see J. P. Meier, "John the Baptist in Matthew's Gospel," *JBL* 99 (1980): 383-405.

[45]For more details supporting the earlier dates for Jesus' ministry, see G. B. Caird, "The Chronology of the New Testament," *IDB* 1:599-603. The best defense of the later dates is H. Hoehner, *Chronological Aspects of the Life of Christ* (Grand Rapids: Zondervan, 1977).

perhaps of Israel's wandering in the wilderness prior to their entry into the promised land, John too prepared the way for One who would reconstitute God's people. Jesus himself would also have his time in the wilderness shortly (4:1-11).

John's message called for repentance from sin. He thus anticipated the Messiah's mission as described in 1:21. *Repentance* in Greek traditionally implied a change of mind or attitude, but under Old Testament influence it took on the sense of a change of action as well. This combination means that John was asking his hearers "to change their way of life as a result of a complete change of thought and attitude with regard to sin and righteousness."[46] So radical an appeal stemmed from the belief that a new epoch of world history was dawning. The verb translated "is near" (*engizō*) means more precisely to *draw near*. Much debate has centered around whether the kingdom is so near as to be actually present or simply imminent. Probably we are to see an overlapping of ages here,[47] but the perfect tense suggests the meaning *has drawn near* and points to the present as the decisive moment of the kingdom's arrival.

The "kingdom of heaven" is a circumlocution for the *kingdom of God*, reflecting pious Jewish avoidance of the divine name. The expression appears only in Matthew, but it occurs thirty-three times and is largely interchangeable with "kingdom of God," as 19:23-24 makes clear. "Kingdom of heaven" perhaps refers also to the fact that all power and authority in heaven are given to Jesus.[48] Older dispensationalist attempts to drive a wedge between these two expressions have now been largely and rightly abandoned.[49] John's one-sentence command here in v. 2 will be repeated verbatim by Jesus in 4:17 as a summary of his message as well.

A vast literature discusses the concept of the kingdom in the Gospels.[50] New Testament occurrences of *basileia*, under the influence of the Hebrew *malkuth*, most commonly refer to *God's reign* or *kingly rule*. Specifically, "the kingdom" depicts the irruption of God's power into history in a new and dramatic way with the advent of Messiah Jesus. Much

---

[46]J. P. Louw and E. A. Nida, *Greek-English Lexicon of the New Testament* (New York: UBS, 1988), 510.

[47]See G. R. Beasley-Murray, *Jesus and the Kingdom of God* (Grand Rapids: Eerdmans, 1986), 72-73.

[48]E. Schweizer, *The Good News according to Matthew* (Atlanta: John Knox, 1975), 47.

[49]See S. D. Toussaint, *Behold the King: A Study of Matthew* (Portland: Multnomah, 1980), 65-68.

[50]See I. H. Marshall, "The Hope of a New Age: The Kingdom of God in the New Testament," *Themelios* 11 (1985): 5-15. For a brief survey and the most up-to-date history of modern interpretation of the kingdom, see W. Willis, ed., *The Kingdom of God in 20th-Century Interpretation* (Peabody, Mass.: Hendrickson, 1987). For an anthology of some of the most significant modern treatments of this subject, see B. D. Chilton, ed., *The Kingdom of God in the Teaching of Jesus* (Philadelphia: Fortress, 1984).

Jewish thought of the day, though highly diverse, equated the arrival of the kingdom with the completion of God's plans for his people in a physically visible, materially prosperous, and powerful geopolitical entity. The kingdom continues to be so viewed by some who deny its presence with Jesus' first advent. Such an approach often leads to the notion that because most of the Jews rejected Jesus' call to repentance he withdrew his offer of the kingdom and postponed its arrival until his second coming.[51] Others delete all future aspects, "de-apocalypticizing" the kingdom and turning it into a form of existence in human history which illustrates new possibilities of relationships among people.[52]

A large consensus and a vast array of scriptural data support a two-pronged focus in which the kingdom is both present and future (both in Jesus' day and our own)—contrast, e.g., Matt 12:28; Luke 7:22-23; 17:20-21 with Matt 6:10; Luke 13:28-29; Mark 9:47.[53] The kingdom is not currently a geographical entity, but it manifests itself in space and time in the community of those who accept the message John and Jesus proclaimed and who begin to work out God's purposes on earth—personally, socially, and institutionally. Thus to declare that the kingdom is at hand "means that the decisive establishment or manifestation of the divine sovereignty has drawn so near to men that they are now confronted with the possibility and the ineluctable necessity of repentance and conversion."[54] More comprehensively:

> The kingdom sums up God's plan to create a new human life by making possible a new kind of community among people, families, and groups. [It combines] the possibility of a personal relationship to Jesus with man's responsibility to manage wisely the whole of nature; the expectation that real change is possible here and now; a realistic assessment of the strength of opposition to God's intentions; the creation of new human relationships and the eventual liberation by God of the whole nature from corruption.[55]

Verse 3 presents John the Baptist as the fulfillment of Isa 40:3. The quotation reproduces the LXX almost verbatim. In Isaiah the speaker remains unidentified. He could be viewed individually as a specific

---

[51]As in the standard dispensationalist interpretation; see, e.g., J. F. Walvoord, *Matthew: Thy Kingdom Come* (Chicago: Moody, 1974), *passim*. From a very different perspective, cf. also the conclusions of C. Sullivan, *Rethinking Realized Eschatology* (Macon: Mercer, 1988).

[52]Cf., e.g., J. D. Crossan, *In Parables: The Challenge of the Historical Jesus* (New York: Harper and Row, 1973), 27; M. J. Borg, *Conflict, Holiness, and Politics in the Teachings of Jesus* (New York: Edwin Mellen, 1984), 248-63.

[53]See esp. Beasley-Murray, *Jesus*; G. E. Ladd, *The Presence of the Future* (Grand Rapids: Eerdmans, 1974).

[54]D. Hill, *The Gospel of Matthew*, NCB (London: Oliphants, 1972), 90.

[55]A. Kirk, *The Good News of the Kingdom Coming* (Downers Grove: InterVarsity, 1983), 47.

prophet or corporately as all of the people of Israel (so Qumran; cf. 1QS 8:14). The larger context of Isa 40–66 discloses that the prophecy depicts part of Israel's end-time restoration. The messianic era, the millennial kingdom, and eventually the new heavens and the new earth often blend together in characteristic prophetic foreshortening. John is thus heralding the beginning of the full restoration and blessing of God's people. Just as roads were often repaired in the ancient world in preparation for royalty traveling on them, so John calls his listeners to rebuild highways of holiness (cf. Isa 35:8), i.e., to return to moral living in preparation for God's coming in Jesus.

[4]John's clothes were made of camel's hair, and he had a leather belt around his waist. His food was locusts and wild honey. [5]People went out to him from Jerusalem and all Judea and the whole region of the Jordan. [6]Confessing their sins, they were baptized by him in the Jordan River.

3:4-6 Matthew describes John's dress as much like that of the prophet Elijah of old (2 Kgs 1:8). His diet resembles that of desert dwellers of the day. Both clothing and food point to an austerity and asceticism appropriate to his stern calls for repentance. John is apparently a charismatic figure who attracts crowds from many nearby places. His welcome reception provides a striking contrast with 2:3, though hostilities will resume in v. 7, confirming that it is primarily the official Jewish leaders who reject God's new revelation. The crowds who come and repent make public their change of heart by acknowledging their failure to meet God's standards and by resolving to change their ways. They visibly demonstrate the seriousness of their pledge with the rite of water baptism. The Greek imperfect tense (literally, *were being baptized*) suggests that John's ministry lasts for a significant period of time.

Jews seem regularly to have practiced water baptism by immersion for adult proselytes from pagan backgrounds as an initiation into Judaism. Qumran commanded ritual bathing daily to symbolize repeated cleansing from sin.[56] But John's call for a one-time-only baptism for those who had been born as Jews was unprecedented. John thus insisted that one's ancestry was not adequate to ensure one's relationship with God. As has often been put somewhat colloquially, "God has no grandchildren." Our parents' religious affiliations afford no substitute for our own personal commitment (cf. v. 9). Once people made that commitment, however, and solemnized it in baptism, there is no evidence that John permitted them to be rebaptized when they became followers of Jesus. John's baptism

---

[56]K. Pusey, "Jewish Proselyte Baptism," *ExpTim* 95 (1984): 141-45; W. S. La Sor, "Discovering What Jewish Miqva'ot Can Tell Us about Christian Baptism," *BARev* 13.1 (1987): 52-59.

foreshadowed Christian baptism.[57] Christians ought therefore never to require people who have been immersed as believers to be rebaptized. On the other hand, they ought never to denounce fellow Christians who seek immersion as believers after having only undergone some ritual with water-sprinkling in their infancy. To call this practice "rebaptism" entirely ignores the point Baptists have historically made, namely, that the sprinkling of infants is not a true baptism, irrespective of what it may be called and the sincerity of those who practice it.

Baptizing in the river suggests that the people were either immersed or had water poured over them. The best historical evidence suggests immersion was more likely. The most common meaning of the verbs *baptō* and *baptizō* points in this direction as well, though there are instances in which the terms also refer to a more superficial dipping (e.g., Rev 19:13). In general the New Testament evidence concerning baptism strongly supports immersion for believers,[58] even if the history of the church is littered with sad examples of individuals and movements that have proved overly divisive on this issue.[59]

b. HIS MESSAGE (3:7-12).   Illustrations of the implications of repentance and of the nearness of the kingdom now follow.

7But when he saw many of the Pharisees and Sadducees coming to where he was baptizing, he said to them: "You brood of vipers! Who warned you to flee from the coming wrath? 8Produce fruit in keeping with repentance. 9And do not think you can say to yourselves, 'We have Abraham as our father.' I tell you that out of these stones God can raise up children for Abraham. 10The ax is already at the root of the trees, and every tree that does not produce good fruit will be cut down and thrown into the fire."

3:7-10   Two new groups of Jewish leaders appear on the scene. The Pharisees and Sadducees represent two of the three main religious sects (along with the Essenes) described in some detail by Josephus (*J.W.* 2.8.2-14). Today we probably would consider them a cross between political parties and religious factions. Of the Sadducees we know little else than what Josephus tells us. Their name derives perhaps from David's

---

[57]W. B. Badke, "Was Jesus a Disciple of John?" *EvQ* 62 (1990): 195-204; U. Luz, *Matthew 1-7: A Commentary*, EKK (Minneapolis: Augsburg, 1989), 169.

[58]See esp. G. R. Beasley-Murray, *Baptism in the New Testament* (London: Macmillan, 1962).

[59]To be commended for its suggestions concerning Christians who disagree on the doctrine of baptism is D. Bridge and D. Phypers, *The Water That Divides* (Downers Grove: InterVarsity, 1977). G. W. Bromiley (*Children of Promise* [Grand Rapids: Eerdmans, 1979]) offers one of the stronger cases for infant baptism, but P. K. Jewett (*Infant Baptism and the Covenant of Grace* [Grand Rapids: Eerdmans, 1978]) provides an excellent defense of believers' baptism from within the same Reformed tradition from which Bromiley writes.

priest Zadok. They were political liberals and religious conservatives, a small aristocratic and priestly sect that had made its peace with the Roman government. They believed only in the written Scriptures as divinely inspired and would believe no doctrine that could not be derived from the five books of Moses. Hence, they rejected angels and the resurrection of the dead.

The Pharisees (the name perhaps coming from Heb. *Perushim*, meaning *separatists*) were a larger more popular group of teachers of the law. They tended toward political conservatism and religious liberalism. They had developed the oral law as a "fence around the Torah," which included detailed interpretations, applications, and amplifications of the written Scriptures to enable people to obey them properly. They continued to view Rome as illegitimate in preventing Israel from enjoying its divinely ordained blessings of freedom and peace in the land. The Pharisees were generally liked and respected by the ordinary people. They were by no means uniformly hypocritical, as Christians have often wrongly assumed on the basis of the New Testament references to a small number of particularly notorious Pharisees. The Talmud, in fact, describes seven classes of Pharisees, though only one of these seven proves particularly exemplary (*b. Sota* 22b).

The Pharisees and Sadducees apparently began to organize themselves at approximately the same time in the second century B.C. Together they probably comprised no more than 5 percent of the populace. Here they are linked as representatives of the official leadership of Judaism. Most of the Jewish supreme court, the Sanhedrin, belonged to one of these two groups. Many commentators characterize Matthew's failure to distinguish between them as a historical anachronism, but diverse factions will often unite against a common opponent.[60]

Here John perceives some kind of hypocrisy that leads him to unleash a verbal attack against these particular Pharisees and Sadducees. He follows his accusation (v. 7) with a command (v. 8). He then anticipates their objection (v. 9) and responds with a stern warning (v. 10). Their hypocrisy presumably involves their pretending to support his ministry. The NIV correctly translates "coming to where he was baptizing" (literally, *coming to the baptism*) rather than "coming for baptism" (NASB). "Brood" is more literally *offspring*. By calling them "vipers," John refers to their shrewdness and to the danger they pose to others. Possibly an

---

[60]See esp. D. A. Carson, "Jewish Leaders in Matthew's Gospel: A Reappraisal," *JETS* 25 (1982): 161-74. The most recent detailed treatment of these Jewish leaders, reflecting a newer sociological approach, is A. J. Saldarini, *Pharisees, Scribes, and Sadducees in Palestinian Society* (Wilmington: Glazier, 1988). Also cf. J. Polhill, *Acts*, NAC (Nashville: Broadman, 1992), 470.

indirect allusion to the evil caused by the original serpent (Gen 3) appears as well. The last line of v. 7 therefore oozes with sarcasm. John knows full well that the Jewish leaders are not fleeing from the coming wrath. This wrath forms part of the full arrival of the kingdom, which will lead to judgment of God's enemies as well as blessing for his followers. God's wrath does not reflect "the emotion of anger but that part of his divine holiness that actively repudiates that which is unholy in his creatures."[61]

Verse 8 provides the key to one of Matthew's crucial themes—righteousness by good deeds. But Matthew does not contradict Paul's doctrine of justification by faith.[62] Rather, true faith or repentance will produce a life-style and behavior that demonstrate the reality of a changed heart. In v. 9 John again reminds his listeners that they dare not trust in their ancestral credentials or believe that they alone are legitimate candidates for inclusion in the people of God. Matthew's two-pronged emphasis, introduced in chaps. 1–2, thus continues: the messianic age brings new people into God's kingdom and excludes others who thought themselves secure. The Messiah is the true Son of Abraham (1:1-2); apart from him there is no salvation. The reference to "these stones" probably reflects an original Aramaic wordplay between children (*běnayyā*) and stones (*’abnayyā*) and was no doubt inspired by the characteristically rocky ground that covers Israel.

As at the end of v. 7, v. 10 again predicts imminent judgment for those who reject John's call to repentance. The fire, as v. 12 makes clear, stands for eternal punishment. One must not think of any lesser judgment as in view. A "fruitless" Christian is no Christian at all (cf. Jas 2:14-26). Christians in every age must heed John's warning to the Pharisees and Sadducees. Too often in the history of the church, people have trusted in living in a "Christian" country, being raised in a Christian family, holding membership or even office in a local church, and even in verbal claims to have repented and to have trusted in Christ. Yet without the evidence of a changed life and perseverance in belief, all such grounds of trust prove futile. One cannot determine the number of truly saved people in any given church by simply counting those who have responded to altar calls, received baptism, or become church members.[63]

---

[61]R. H. Mounce, *Matthew*, GNC (San Francisco: Harper and Row, 1985), 22.

[62]The fullest, though sometimes one-sided treatment of the relationship between the ethics of the two authors is R. Mohrlang, *Matthew and Paul* (Cambridge: University Press, 1984).

[63]Cf. G. T. Montague, *Companion God: A Cross-Cultural Commentary on the Gospel of Matthew* (New York: Paulist, 1989), 36: "The greatest obstacle to genuine repentance is found in those who somewhere got just enough religion to be inoculated against its further demands."

[11]"I baptize you with water for repentance. But after me will come one who is more powerful than I, whose sandals I am not fit to carry. He will baptize you with the Holy Spirit and with fire. [12]His winnowing fork is in his hand, and he will clear his threshing floor, gathering his wheat into the barn and burning up the chaff with unquenchable fire."

3:11-12 John now compares himself with Jesus. The coming one (v. 11) is probably a messianic title and may stem from texts like Pss 118:26 and 40:7.[64] John views himself as of lower status than a slave, one of whose most menial tasks was to carry the usually dirty sandals of his master. If John's audience should think him impressive, one far more powerful will soon appear. Both John and Jesus will preach repentance and use water baptism as the outward sign of an inward change (cf. John 4:1-2), but only Jesus will baptize with the Holy Spirit and fire. The phrase "after me" refers to one who follows after a leader. Jesus will come in the guise of a disciple of John, but his ministry will soon far outstrip that of the one who baptizes him.

The phrase "for repentance" could suggest that one must be baptized to be saved, but this interpretation founders on New Testament teaching elsewhere (e.g., Acts 3:19; Rom 3:23-24; Eph 2:8-9). Interestingly, even Josephus recognizes this (*Ant.* 18.5.2) when he writes that John taught that his followers "must not employ [baptism] to gain pardon for whatever sins they committed, but as a consecration of the body implying that the soul was already thoroughly cleansed." A venerable tradition of Baptist interpreters has seen the "for" (*eis*) as actually meaning *because* here,[65] but more recent grammatical analysis makes this unlikely. Probably the term simply should be taken as *in reference to*.[66] Baptism in reference to repentance thus distinguishes John's baptism from other religions' ritual washings which do not symbolize turning away from sin.

The expression baptism "with/in the Holy Spirit" appears six other times in the New Testament. Five of these texts refer to this very saying of John (Mark 1:8; Luke 3:16; John 1:33; Acts 1:5; 11:16). Acts 1–2 demonstrates that John's prediction was fulfilled at Pentecost. The sixth reference appears in 1 Cor 12:13, where it is clear that all Christians receive Spirit-baptism. The phrase therefore refers to a ritual that depicts a believer's initiation into the body of Christ by the indwelling Holy Spirit, who never departs following true conversion and regeneration. Baptism of the Spirit must not be confused with the "filling of the Spirit," which recurs repeatedly to empower believers to proclaim God's word

---

[64]Allison and Davies, *Matthew*, 1:313-14.

[65]See esp. H. E. Dana and J. R. Mantey, *A Manual Grammar of the Greek New Testament* (London: Macmillan, 1927), 104.

[66]M. J. Harris, "Appendix," in *DNTT* 3:1208.

boldly (Acts 2:4; 4:8,31; 9:17; 13:9).[67] Here is further reason why one cannot be a Christian without having a changed life; the indwelling Spirit guarantees that the process of sanctification will begin (cf. Rom 6–8).

If baptism with the Holy Spirit refers to the conversion of believers, baptism with fire would naturally be associated with the fiery judgment of unbelievers described in vv. 10 and 12. Yet the actual grammatical construction in Greek suggests that v. 11 refers to only one baptism, that which combines the Holy Spirit and fire.[68] For believers this would most likely refer to the Holy Spirit's purifying and refining activity, but the same convicting power when spurned by unbelievers leads ultimately to judgment.[69] Verse 12 expands the judgment metaphor of v. 10. John uses the image of a farmer separating valuable wheat from worthless chaff by throwing the grain into the air and allowing the two constituent elements to separate in the wind. The wheat, like believers, is preserved and safeguarded; the chaff, like unbelievers, is destroyed.[70]

There exists a certain tension between the imagery of fire and the other major biblical (and Matthean) image for eternal punishment, namely, outer darkness. Fire and total darkness cannot literally coexist. But even as metaphors, each graphically depicts the pain and separation from God that characterizes damnation.[71] The adjective "unquenchable" (literally, *fireproof* [Greek *asbestos*]) implies that fuel will always remain to keep the fire burning and speaks against the doctrine of annihilationism (the idea that unbelievers simply cease conscious existence upon death). Matthew's main focus, however, remains not on the nature of hell but on the inevitable twofold division of all people based on their response to John's and Jesus' call to repentance (cf. 13:36-43).

---

[67]See especially J. D. G. Dunn, *Baptism in the Holy Spirit* (Philadelphia: Westminster, 1970). The response by H. M. Ervin (*Conversion-Initiation and the Baptism in the Holy Spirit* [Peabody, Mass.: Hendrickson, 1984]) points out a few problems and ambiguities in Dunn's arguments but otherwise fails to overturn his general thesis. See R. B. Gardner (*Matthew*, BCBC [Scottdale, Penn.: Herald, 1991], 66-69) for a good discussion of the meaning of baptism in this context. Also cf. D. S. Dockery, "Baptism," *Dictionary of Jesus and the Gospels*, ed. S. McKnight et al. (Downers Grove: InterVarsity, 1992).

[68]The Greek employs one preposition to govern two nouns functioning as a compound object (ἐν πνεύματι ἁγίῳ καὶ πυρί)—*with the Holy Spirit and fire* (contra NIV's repetition of "with")—most naturally suggesting one baptism with two aspects to it.

[69]Cf. J. L. Nolland, *Luke 1–9:20*, WBC (Dallas: Word, 1990), 153: "In both Spirit and fire [appear] the means of eschatological purgation experienced by the penitent as purification in the refiner's fire and by the godless as destruction by wind and fire."

[70]R. L. Webb ("The Activity of John the Baptist's Expected Figure at the Threshing Floor [Matthew 3.12 = Luke 3.17]," *JSNT* 43 [1991]: 103-11) believes the winnowing has already occurred in the Spirit-filled ministry of John, so that "wind" here should rather be translated "Spirit."

[71]Cf. G. E. Ladd, *A Theology of the New Testament* (Grand Rapids: Zondervan, 1974), 196.

2. John and Jesus: The Messiah's Baptism (3:13-17)

The paths of the two main characters of chap. 3 now intersect. John will climax his ministry of baptism by baptizing Jesus. Then John's role will decrease, as Jesus' ministry gains momentum (cf. John 3:30).

¹³Then Jesus came from Galilee to the Jordan to be baptized by John. ¹⁴But John tried to deter him, saying, "I need to be baptized by you, and do you come to me?"

¹⁵Jesus replied, "Let it be so now; it is proper for us for us to do this to fulfill all righteousness." Then John consented.

3:13-14 In chap. 2 Matthew leaves Jesus as a child in Galilee. Now Jesus has grown up and comes south to Judea. Because baptism implies that a person has repented, John balks at baptizing Jesus. Matthew does not explicitly enunciate the doctrine of Christ's sinlessness, but he seems to hint at it. In v. 11 John has already disclosed his "inferiority complex" in the presence of the Messiah. He now acknowledges his own sinfulness in comparison with Jesus and how the tables ought rightfully to be turned. Jesus should be baptizing John.

3:15 Jesus' somewhat ambiguous reply seems to acknowledge the force of John's logic but nevertheless requests baptism for different reasons. Jesus has not come to confess any sin but "to fulfill all righteousness." He has previously fulfilled specific prophecies as well as more general scriptural themes. Now he wishes to obey all the moral demands of God's will.[72] "To fulfill all righteousness" means *to complete everything that forms part of a relationship of obedience to God*. In so doing, Jesus identifies with and endorses John's ministry as divinely ordained and his message as one to be heeded.

¹⁶As soon as Jesus was baptized, he went up out of the water. At that moment heaven was opened, and he saw the Spirit of God descending like a dove and lighting on him. ¹⁷And a voice from heaven said, "This is my Son, whom I love; with him I am well pleased."

3:16-17 Matthew does not describe Jesus' baptism itself but rather what happens immediately afterwards. As Jesus comes up out of the river, God places his stamp of approval on him in two ways. First, the Holy Spirit descends "like" a dove, which suggests that no actual bird appeared but that some visible manifestation of the Spirit led observers to recognize that God was revealing himself through those attributes regularly

---

[72] Cf. esp. J. P. Meier, *Law and History in Matthew's Gospel* (Rome: Biblical Institute Press, 1976), 76-80.

associated with a dove—e.g., superintending over creation (cf. Gen 1:2), offering peace (as in Gen 8:10), gentleness in contrast to the judgment of vv. 7-12, or as "the loving character of divine life itself."[73] The second sign of approval is "a voice from heaven." The heavenly voice is often linked with the Hebrew idea of the *bath qol* ("daughter of the voice"), the way in which Jews in intertestamental times believed God spoke with them after the cessation of prophecy. More likely the voice is a sign that divine communication with Israel is resuming.[74]

The heavenly voice cites excerpts of Ps 2:7 and Isa 42:1. Both texts were taken as messianic by important segments of pre-Christian Judaism (see 4QFlor 10-14 and *Tg. Isa* 42:1, respectively). Together they point out Jesus' role as both divine Son and Suffering Servant, a crucial combination for interpreting Jesus' self-understanding and mission. An incipient trinitarianism appears with the conjunction of God, Son, and Spirit in this narrative. Nothing suggests that Jesus began a relationship with the Holy Spirit only at this point. Matthew 2:15 makes clear that Matthew views Jesus as God's Son at least from infancy, while 1:23 views him as "God with us" from birth. Rather, as in the royal enthronement context of Ps 2, what appears here is a formal installment and commissioning.[75] Now one understands better why Jesus' baptism was "proper" or *appropriate* (v. 15). God is initiating Jesus into the public phase of his ministry on earth.

Chapter 3 forms the first part of Matthew's narrative, which is closely paralleled in the other Synoptic Gospels. Only minor differences with Mark and Luke appear in vv. 1-12, but a major addition arises in vv. 13-17 with the inclusion of two unparalleled verses (vv. 14-15). In them Matthew continues to highlight his theme of fulfillment. Jesus is the one in whom the hopes of Israel coalesce, but God's promises must be appropriated by personal discipleship. If the Jewish leaders reject him, others will respond more positively.

3. Jesus Alone: The Messiah's Temptation (4:1-11)

One might expect the main, central period of Jesus' public ministry to unfold at once, but one more crucial preparatory event must occur. Jesus could well have perverted the nature of his messianic sonship and bypassed the way of the cross in favor of some more glamorous political or military role as liberator of Israel. But refusing to die for the sins of the world would have given the devil rather than God the victory. So Jesus'

---

[73]C. H. Talbert, *Reading Luke* (New York: Crossroad, 1986), 40.

[74]L. Sabourin, *L'Évangile selon saint Matthieu et ses principaux parallèles* (Rome: Biblical Institute Press, 1978), 39.

[75]See H. N. Ridderbos (*Matthew*, BSC [Grand Rapids: Zondervan, 1987], 59-60) for a helpful refutation of the view that this text teaches adoptionism—the idea that Jesus became God's (adopted) Son only after his baptism.

resolve to fulfill God's plans for him must be tested and proved right at the outset of his ministry.

¹Then Jesus was led by the Spirit into the desert to be tempted by the devil. ²After fasting forty days and forty nights, he was hungry.

4:1-2 It is no coincidence that Jesus' temptation immediately follows his baptism. Many of God's people have had similar experiences. Right after conversion or some other significant spiritual event, precisely when a certain level of victory or maturity seems to have been attained, temptations resume more strongly than ever (cf. Elijah in 1 Kgs 19:1-18 and Paul in Rom 7·14-25).[76]

An important interplay between the work of the Spirit and that of the devil appears here. The same Spirit who has anointed Jesus in 3:16 now leads him to the place of temptation but does not himself cause the temptation, which is attributed instead to the devil. By this phrasing, Matthew warns against two common errors—blaming God for temptation and crediting the devil with power to act independently of God. In the New Testament, God is always so dissociated from evil that he is never directly responsible for tempting humans (Jas 1:13). Yet the devil is never portrayed as an enemy equal with but opposite to God; he always remains bound by what God permits.

"Devil" in Greek means *accuser*, as does "Satan" in Hebrew (v. 10). Scripture teaches that he was a created being, an archangel, and the leader of the rebellious angels who became forever opposed to God and whose ultimate doom Christ's death ensured (e.g., Job 1–2; Zech 3:1-2; 1 Chr 21:1; Luke 10:18; Rev 20). The desert location again recalls the wanderings of the Israelites in the wilderness. Jesus will succeed as the true representative and fulfillment of Israel where Israel had failed (Deut 8:2). *Peirazō* can mean both *to test* and *to tempt* (NIV). As something the devil does, it must here be taken as *to tempt*, in the sense of *to try to entice to sin*. But what the devil sees as a temptation, God may simultaneously use as a more positive test to prove Jesus' faithfulness.[77]

Jews commonly practiced fasting in order to spend more time in prayer and to develop greater spiritual receptivity.[78] Here the devil uses the result of Jesus' fasting—hunger—as an entrée for his temptations. The

---

[76]Cf. F. D. Bruner, *The Christbook* (Waco: Word, 1987), 100: "There is no dominically instituted rite of confirmation in the Gospels except temptation."

[77]Cf. Allison and Davies, *Matthew*, 1:360. Genesis 50:20 offers the classic scriptural paradigm of God's good intentions being worked out through free, evil human choices.

[78]The particular kind of fasting here is not described. Sometimes Jews went without food but were permitted to drink. Sometimes they went without one or both during the day but were permitted one or both during nighttime hours. More generally, cf. J. F. Wimmer, *Fasting in the New Testament* (New York: Paulist, 1982).

"forty days and forty nights" offer another significant parallel with the forty years of Israel's wanderings. Matthew's wording does not preclude earlier hunger on the part of Jesus or earlier temptations by Satan (cf. Luke 4:2).

³The tempter came to him and said, "If you are the Son of God, tell these stones to become bread."
⁴Jesus answered, "It is written: 'Man does not live on bread alone, but on every word that comes from the mouth of God.'"

4:3-4 Matthew now refers to the devil by his function. "The tempter" addresses Jesus with the same title God applied to him at his baptism (3:17). The first-class conditional clause, "If you are the Son of God," does not imply any doubt on the devil's part (cf. Jas 2:19). Rather, what is in doubt is what type of Son Jesus will be. If stones can become children of Abraham (3:9) or provide water for the Israelites (Exod 17:1-7), then they can surely satisfy Jesus' hunger.

Jesus, however, replies by quoting Deut 8:3. In fact, for each of the three temptations he will refute the devil with Scripture, always from Deuteronomy, continuing the link with the Israelites' desert experience. In this instance the text he cites originally underscored God's provision of manna as an alternative to the Israelites' reliance on their own abilities to feed themselves. The principle applies equally well to Jesus' situation and to any other context in which people are tempted to give physical needs priority over spiritual needs.

⁵Then the devil took him to the holy city and had him stand on the highest point of the temple. ⁶"If you are the Son of God," he said, "throw yourself down. For it is written:
   "'He will command his angels concerning you,
     and they will lift you up in their hands,
   so that you will not strike your foot against a stone.'"
⁷Jesus answered him, "It is also written: 'Do not put the Lord your God to the test.'"

4:5-7 The second temptation[79] brings Jesus to the holy city, Jerusalem. "The highest point" is the *wing* or *portico*, not "pinnacle" (NASB). *Portico* refers to the flat-topped corner of Solomon's porch on the southeast corner of the temple complex overlooking the Kidron Valley. This time the devil asks Jesus to demonstrate miraculously God's ability to preserve his life. The devil again knows that Jesus has the power to do this, and he cites Ps 91:11-12 to justify it. There God promises all who

---

[79]Matthew's order is probably more chronological (cf. τότε—["then"] in v. 5) and Luke's more thematic (Luke 4:1-13), in which the temple episode appears last as a climax in keeping with Luke's distinctive emphasis on Jesus' relationship with the temple.

"dwell in the shelter of the Most High" (Ps 91:1) safeguarding and protection. The devil's mistake is to confuse the psalmist's stumbling so as to
fall with Jesus' deliberately jumping off.[80] We must not test God's faithfulness to his word by manufacturing situations in which we try to force
him to act in certain ways. We dare not deliberately put our lives in danger as some kind of fleece. Jesus thus replies by quoting Deut 6:16 on not
testing God. The original context alluded to Israel's rebellion against the
Lord at Massah (again harking back to Exod 17:1-7).

**[8]Again, the devil took him to a very high mountain and showed him all the
kingdoms of the world and their splendor. [9]"All this I will give you," he said,
"If you will bow down and worship me."**
**[10]Jesus said to him, "Away from me, Satan! For it is written: 'Worship the
Lord your God, and serve him only.'"**
[11]Then the devil left him, and angels came and attended him.

4:8-10 After having tempted Jesus to satisfy a legitimate bodily
appetite in an illegitimate way and then to use his supernatural power to
rebel against God even while seeming to demonstrate great faith, Satan
now makes the most brazen offer of all. He will give Jesus all the kingdoms of the world in return for worship.[81] Ironically, Jesus would receive
this glory anyway after his death and resurrection; but here the devil tries
to seduce him with instant power, authority, and wealth apart from the
way of the cross. Satan regularly tempts Christians in the same way—
with the success syndrome, empire building, or alleged guarantees of
health and wealth. But the devil's price is damning. He requires nothing
short of selling one's soul in worshiping him, which leads inexorably to
eternal judgment. Whatever joy and power he can offer vanishes with
death. Jesus rightly rejects the devil's offer and quotes Deuteronomy for a
third time (Deut 6:13). Only one is worthy of worship, the One who
redeemed Israel from Egypt, the Lord God Yahweh himself. Jesus' insistence on worshiping God alone makes the characteristic Matthean theme

---

[80]Cf. Nolland, *Luke*, 181: "According to the Devil's theory there should be no martyrs!"

[81]The action of v. 8b, of course, could not have literally occurred, since no mountain in
the world offers a view of the entire globe. Nothing in Scripture suggests the devil has the
power to alter this situation. So probably some type of visionary experience is in view here.
This in turn makes it at least plausible that v. 8a and perhaps also v. 5 (cf. Ezek 8:3) were
visionary as well, inasmuch as walking all the way to the temple would have been extremely
hard and climbing a high mountain impossible in Jesus' weakened condition unless he drew
on the very supernatural power to which he otherwise refused here to appeal. But the temptations would have been no less real for being to a certain measure subjective (cf. Mounce,
Matthew, 27). This interpretation is at least as old as Theodore of Mopsuestia and other
Antiochene theologians of the fourth century (generally the most literal interpreters of the
Patristic period). It was endorsed by Calvin and is well defended today by Ridderbos, *Matthew*, 64-65.

of worshiping Jesus (e.g., 2:2; 8:2; 9:18; 14:33; 15:25; 20:20; 28:17) all the more significant as evidence for his divinity.

4:11 With this rebuke the devil departs, but he will resume similar temptations at the beginning of the next key stage of Jesus' life (16:21-23). The very help Jesus had rejected when it would have put God to the test now makes itself available as angels arrive to serve him. They apparently stay for some time, since Matthew uses the imperfect tense (*diēkonoun, were serving*) to describe their ministry. Jesus has passed the test, recovers from his fast, and is ready to begin his public ministry.[82]

Interesting parallels emerge between Jesus' three temptations and those of Eve and Adam in the garden (Gen 3:6—"good for food," "pleasing to the eye," "desirable for gaining wisdom"). Both of these triads seem to parallel John's epitome of human temptation: "the lust of the flesh and the lust of the eyes and the pride of life" (1 John 2:16, RSV). Jesus' temptations therefore illustrate the precious truth that he was indeed tempted in every way common to human experience (Heb 2:17-18; 4:15). This does not mean that he underwent every conceivable temptation but that he experienced every major kind. Someone who appreciates the insidious lure of one addictive drug, for example, need not be tempted by every other drug in order to empathize with those temptations. But the three temptations Matt 4:1-11 presents encompass a remarkable amount of human experience. We are tempted to gauge life by human comforts and consumerism, to misuse spiritual gifts and power for our own glory and benefit rather than serving others, and to seize power by shortcuts, such as equating a particular political agenda with God's will.

Jesus experienced temptation more strongly than anyone else because he never gave in and sinned. The temptation always remained before him. Whether or not Jesus could have sinned is a question that has historically divided Christians. Some argue that it was impossible even in his human nature for him to have sinned. Others believe that in order for him to be truly human he had to have a sinful nature, but that unlike the rest of humanity he never yielded to that nature in committing a sinful action. A mediating and more convincing alternative is that Jesus could have sinned but never did and that like Adam and Eve before the fall he had a sinless human nature. It is difficult to see how he could have been tempted in every way as we have been without at least the possibility of sinning. That very possibility makes his ability to sympathize with us all the more

---

[82]Interestingly, the Greek behind 3:15 ("then [John] consented") and 4:11 ("then [the devil] left him") is identical. Though the verb ἀφίησιν is used in two different ways, the two passages are parallel in that both John and the devil, wittingly or unwittingly, were trying to deter Jesus' appointed course but failed.

precious.[83] Of course, we should not associate that possibility of sinning with his divine nature but only with his human nature; God cannot sin. And some have argued from this that Jesus' divine nature overruled the possibility of his sinning in his human nature. But the historic Christian doctrine of the union of Christ's natures has regularly viewed him as relinquishing the independent exercise of his divine attributes, so this argument collapses.

These debates of course go far beyond the text of Matthew, whose key point is that Jesus did remain obedient to God and died for our sins rather than meeting other, triumphalist messianic expectations of his day. Even Hebrews merely stresses his ability to relate to our experience of life. Yet many Christians find it difficult to believe that Jesus can identify with them when they are severely tempted or that he can forgive them when they commit some heinous sin, especially when it happens over and over. No area offers a better test for how biblical one's understanding of Christ's temptation is than that of sexuality. Do we seriously envisage Christ as being tempted to lust or commit sexual sin so that he can sympathize with our sexual temptations and sins? If not, our Jesus is not the one of Scripture![84]

4. Jesus Settles in Capernaum (4:12-16)

[12]When Jesus heard that John had been put in prison, he returned to Galilee. [13]Leaving Nazareth, he went and lived in Capernaum, which was by the lake in the area of Zebulun and Naphtali— [14]to fulfill what was said through the prophet Isaiah:
[15]"Land of Zebulun and land of Naphtali,
     the way to the sea, along the Jordan,
     Galilee of the Gentiles—
[16]the people living in darkness
     have seen a great light;
  on those living in the land of the shadow of death
     a light has dawned."

4:12-16 In a style reminiscent of 1:18–2:23, this second section of Matthew's introduction (3:1–4:16) closes with a brief narrative that centers around an Old Testament fulfillment quotation (Isa 9:1-2). Verse 12 alludes to the fate of John the Baptist, which chap. 11 will describe in

---

[83]See especially M. Erickson, *Christian Theology*, vol. 2 (Grand Rapids: Baker, 1984), 720.

[84]For an introduction to the temptations of Christ more generally but with specific reference to Matthew 4:1-11, see C. L. Blomberg, "The Temptations of Jesus," *ISBE* 4:784-86. The fullest modern study of this passage is B. Gerhardsson, *The Testing of God's Son* (Lund: Gleerup, 1966), though the parallels drawn with the three elements of loving God in Deut 6:5 seem remote.

more detail. After John's imprisonment, Jesus has no more reason to stay in Judea and so returns home to Galilee. But he now settles in a new town. Capernaum was larger and more significant than Nazareth and strategic in its lakeside setting on the northwest shore of the Sea of Galilee. Here too Matthew sees the fulfillment of prophecy. Zebulun and Naphtali were the Old Testament territories closest to contemporary Galilee.

The phrases "way to the sea" and "along the Jordan" (literally, *beyond the Jordan*) probably reflect the perspective of foreigners from the northeast heading through Israel to the Mediterranean (as with the Assyrians' invasion that Isaiah consistently predicted). From Isaiah's day on, many foreigners had lived in Galilee; in the first century more than half the population was Gentile. So Matthew no doubt sees here a foreshadowing of Christian ministry to those who were not Jews (cf. Luke 2:32, echoing Isa 42:6 and 49:6). But the word for the "people" living in darkness is *laos*, which most commonly refers to Israel. Jesus will preach first to Jews before his followers move out to other ethnic groups. "Light" versus "darkness," as consistently in Scripture, refers to the knowledge of or obedience to God versus the ignorance of or disobedience to his revelation. Jesus illuminates God's purposes and brings liberation from oppression (Isa 9:4).[85] In John 8:12 he calls himself "the light of the world."

We thus come to the end of the first major section of this Gospel (1:1–4:16). Matthew has shown Jesus as the royal Messiah who fulfilled Scripture. He has foreshadowed Jesus' rejection and the hostility that would arise against him from among his own people. He has depicted Jesus as the Coming One, prophesied by John the Baptist, who will combine the Old Testament roles of Son and Servant and who will not use his power to circumvent the way of the cross. With this introduction to Jesus' person and mission, the ministry for which he was baptized and commissioned can now begin.

---

[85]As in chaps. 1–2, the text of this Scripture quotation resembles the LXX less closely than when Matthew's quotations are paralleled in another Gospel (as, e.g., in the previous three quotations from Deuteronomy).

── **II. THE DEVELOPMENT OF JESUS' MINISTRY (4:17–16:20)** ──

Matthew brackets the main section of his Gospel with two uses of "from that time on, Jesus began to" (4:17; 16:21). Matthew 16:21 will mark the turning point in Jesus' career, from which time on all events lead toward his death and resurrection. Matthew 4:17 introduces the largest of the three main divisions of the Gospel. Here Matthew begins to alternate large blocks of discourse and narrative. Each block combines accounts that are sometimes chronological and sometimes thematic in arrangement. Chapters 5–9 sum up the essence of Jesus' preaching (chaps. 5–7) and healing (chaps. 8–9) ministries. Chapters 10–12 focus on responses to the disciples (chap. 10) and to Jesus (chaps. 11–12). Matthew 13:1–16:20 highlights the growing polarization of that response, which triggers Jesus' teaching in parables (13:1-52) and mission to the Gentiles (13:53–16:20).

A. Jesus' Authority in Preaching and Healing (4:17–9:35)

Matthew 4:23-25 and 9:35 form a framework that surrounds the first pair of discourse and narrative in the body of Matthew's work. In almost identical language these texts refer to Jesus' widespread ministry of teaching and preaching, which the Sermon on the Mount classically epitomizes, and his healings, which the collection of ten miracles in chaps. 8–9 amply illustrate.

1. Introduction (4:17-25)

Matthew introduces Jesus' public ministry with a summary of the message of his preaching and teaching, examples of the call of his first disciples, and a summary of his ministry to the crowds, with a particular focus on healing. Preaching and healing sum up Matthew's distinctive epitome of the ministry of Jesus and his disciples (4:23; cf. 9:35; 10:7-8),[1] and each makes people confront the question of Jesus' identity. Calling Peter, Andrew, James, and John anticipates Matthew's intense interest in discipleship. A focus on Christology and discipleship accounts for a substantial portion of what appears in 4:16–16:20.

[17]From that time on Jesus began to preach, "Repent, for the kingdom of heaven is near."

a. HEADING: SUMMARY OF JESUS' PREACHING (4:17). **4:17** This verse repeats 3:2 verbatim (see commentary there). However else Jesus and John differed (cf. 11:16-19), the core of their message was identical. Both were God's spokesmen proclaiming the arrival of the kingdom in the person of the Messiah. Although Jesus' ministry began to establish God's reign, his role will not be universally acknowledged until he returns.

[18]As Jesus was walking beside the Sea of Galilee, he saw two brothers, Simon called Peter and his brother Andrew. They were casting a net into the lake, for they were fishermen. [19]"Come, follow me," Jesus said, "and I will make you fishers of men." [20]At once they left their nets and followed him.

b. BEGINNING: EXAMPLES OF CALLING DISCIPLES (4:18-22). **4:18-20** As Jesus is walking about the vicinity of his new home in Capernaum, perhaps in conscious imitation of the peripatetic ministries of many rabbis and philosophers of the day, he finds two brothers who are fishermen and commands them to become his disciples. A disciple was an adherent or follower of a master, an intimate companion in some common endeavor, often learning and promoting a particular ideology. Matthew can use the term to refer just to the twelve apostles (10:1) or clearly to a member of a larger group (8:21), but usually it refers to an unspecified number of followers who are more devoted to Jesus than the large crowds that often "follow" as well.[2] Here Jesus, possibly imitating Elijah's call of Elisha (1 Kgs 19:19-21) inverts the standard procedure whereby a would-be disciple came and asked to follow a master of his choice. Simon and Andrew have already encountered Jesus when Andrew was a disciple of John (John 1:35-41), so Jesus' call is not as abrupt as might otherwise be imagined. Matthew nevertheless emphasizes their decisive response.

John 1:42 explains Matthew's expression "Simon called Peter" and makes a prediction that finds its fulfillment in Matt 16:18. "Follow me" in v. 19 is literally *come after me*, in the same sense as "the one coming after

---

[1]Cf. M. Green, *Matthew for Today* (Dallas: Word, 1989), 67: "Wherever the church is truly carrying out the work of the Kingdom, [the] strands of challenging preaching, clear teaching and healing (of physical disease, inner hurts and grip by dark forces) will be seen."

[2]M. J. Wilkins, *The Concept of Disciple in Matthew's Gospel* (Leiden: Brill, 1988).

me" in 3:11. "Followed" in v. 20 (from *akoloutheō*) is a key word for
Matthew and often, though not always, implies discipleship. Jesus makes
a play on words based on Simon and Andrew's occupation. Like all analogies, all possible points of comparison must not be pressed. Jesus is not
implying that being a "fisher of men" involves anything seductive, deceitful, or harmful. Rather, he is pointing out that just as fishermen try to
gather fish from the sea, his disciples too will be trying to gather together
other individuals who are willing to follow Jesus in radical obedience.[3]

**²¹Going on from there, he saw two other brothers, James son of Zebedee
and his brother John. They were in a boat with their father Zebedee, preparing their nets. Jesus called them, ²²and immediately they left the boat and
their father and followed him.**

4:21-22 The pattern of call and response is repeated with the second
pair of fishermen brothers. Peter, James, and John will form the inner
core of Jesus' followers—his three closest disciples (cf. 17:1 and 26:37).
The reference to Zebedee appears because the two sons will leave their
father and the family business they shared for full-time itinerant companionship with Jesus. Jesus elsewhere will stress the priorities of God above
those of family (10:37). No information appears here about whether or
not James and John had previously heard of Jesus. Matthew focuses
solely on the immediacy of their response on this occasion ("at once" in
v. 20 and "immediately" in v. 22 reflect the identical Greek *eutheōs*).
When Jesus calls a person to discipleship, there is no excuse for delay or
disobedience.

**²³Jesus went throughout Galilee, teaching in their synagogues, preaching
the good news of the kingdom, and healing every disease and sickness among
the people. ²⁴News about him spread all over Syria, and people brought to
him all who were ill with various diseases, those suffering severe pain, the
demon-possessed, those having seizures, and the paralyzed, and he healed
them. ²⁵Large crowds from Galilee, the Decapolis, Jerusalem, Judea and the
region across the Jordan followed him.**

c. SUMMARY OF JESUS' PUBLIC MINISTRY (4:23-25). **4:23-25** Matthew
leaves the private lakeside setting. As Jesus' public ministry gets underway, he travels throughout Galilee, preaching spontaneously to open-air
crowds and making guest appearances in local synagogues (cf. Luke
4:16-17 for details). The message he preaches (v. 17) is "good news."
From this term (*euangelion*) comes the English word *gospel*, which would
become so linked with Jesus' message in Christian circles as to become a

---

[3]Cf. U. Luz, "The Disciples in the Gospel according to Matthew," in G. N. Stanton, ed.,
The Interpretation of Matthew (Philadelphia: Fortress, 1983), 199-200.

title for books about his life as well as a characterization of the message he proclaimed. Jesus heals many, not as an ordinary physician, as will become clear, but by drawing on supernatural power. A report of these miracles goes out to all of the nearby territories both inside and outside of Israel, except for Samaria.[4]

Matthew enumerates several categories of maladies that Jesus cures. Examples of all of these will subsequently be illustrated.[5] The most striking on the list is demon possession, which Matthew carefully distinguishes from ordinary diseases, including epilepsy ("those having seizures"). Contrary to what many today believe, the ancient world regularly and carefully distinguished between afflictions ascribed to demons and other forms of illness.[6] Demon possession was viewed as a unique situation in which an evil spirit actually took control of an individual, acting and speaking through that person in at least partial independence of his or her own volition and consciousness. Almost everyone in ancient societies believed in the reality of demon possession, and striking examples of it remain common enough today so as to be deniable only through severe naturalistic prejudice.[7] Jesus' miracle working understandably attracts crowds, but those in the crowds will need to be instructed on what true discipleship involves if they are to become genuine followers.

---

[4]See A. Sand (*Das Evangelium nach Matthäus*, RNT [Regensburg: Pustet, 1986], 88-95) for a detailed excursus on the possible theological implications of the various territories, concluding that all, indiscriminately, who accept Jesus as Messiah are the "renewed people of Israel" (93).

[5]In light of this fact, "all" of v. 23 probably means *all kinds*, not *every sick individual*. Cf. John 5:1-15, in which Jesus singles out for healing only one person in a large crowd of sick people. The second "all" in v. 24 therefore probably has a similar meaning, given the unlikelihood of every single ill person of all these regions actually being brought to Jesus.

[6]See esp. E. Yamauchi, "Magic or Miracle? Disease, Demons and Exorcisms," in *Gospel Perspectives*, ed. D. Wenham and C. Blomberg, vol. 6 (Sheffield: JSOT, 1986), 89-183.

[7]See esp. J. Richards, *But Deliver Us from Evil* (New York: Seabury, 1974); J. W. Montgomery, ed., *Demon Possession* (Minneapolis: Bethany, 1976).

───────── *SECTION OUTLINE CONTINUED* ─────────

2. Paradigmatic Preaching: The Sermon on the Mount (5:1–7:29)
    a. Introduction (5:1-16)
        (1) Setting (5:1-2)
        (2) Kingdom Blessings (5:3-12)
        (3) Salt and Light (5:13-16)
    b. Thesis: Greater Righteousness (5:17-48)
        (1) Statement (5:17-20)
        (2) Illustrations (5:21-48)
            (a) On Murder (5:21-26)
            (b) On Adultery (5:27-30)
            (c) On Divorce (5:31-32)
            (d) On Oaths (5:33-37)
            (e) On Retaliation (5:38-42)
            (f) On Loving Enemies (5:43-48)
    c. True versus Hypocritical Piety (6:1-18)
        (1) Heading (6:1)
        (2) Almsgiving (6:2-4)
        (3) Prayer (6:5-15)
        (4) Fasting (6:16-18)
    d. Wealth and Worry: Money versus Real Riches (6:19-34)
        (1) Two Masters (6:19-24)
        (2) The Futility of Worry (6:25-34)
    e. How to Treat Others (7:1-12)
        (1) On Judging Others (7:1-6)
        (2) God's Generosity (7:7-11)
        (3) The Golden Rule (7:12)
    f. Conclusion: Only Two Ways (7:13-27)
        (1) The Narrow versus the Wide Gate/Road (7:13-14)
        (2) Good versus Bad Fruit (7:15-23)
        (3) Wise versus Foolish Builders (7:24-27)
    g. Response (7:28-29)

2. Paradigmatic Preaching: The Sermon on the Mount (5:1–7:29)

Perhaps no other religious discourse in the history of humanity has attracted the attention which has been devoted to the Sermon on the Mount. Philosophers and activists from many non-Christian perspectives who have refused to worship Jesus nevertheless have admired his ethic. In the twentieth century, Mohandas Gandhi was the sermon's most famous non-Christian devotee. The literature on the sermon is vast.[1] One recent survey has itemized thirty-six different interpretations.[2] Only eight of the most significant and influential approaches can be listed here.

1. Since at least medieval times, many have seen two levels of ethics in Jesus' teaching, with the sermon reflecting the stricter requirements for those who would pursue a higher level of righteousness, as, e.g., among clergy and monastic orders.

2. In Luther's widely influential approach, the sermon functions as the law does for Paul—God's impossible moral demands disclose the depths of our sinfulness and drive us to our knees in repentance.

3. Many Anabaptists applied the sermon's ethics in an extremely literal fashion to the civil sphere and endorsed full-fledged pacifism.

4. Protestant liberals have seen the sermon as a paradigm for the social gospel and a call to the church to usher in the kingdom of God on earth (a view also adopted in secular form by Karl Marx).

5. Existentialists have rejected taking any of the sermon's ethics as absolute but view them rather as a profound challenge to personal decisions to live in the consciousness of human finitude and divine encounter.

6. Albert Schweitzer's interim ethic also relativized the sermon by finding in it a unique urgency that remained only as long as the first disciples, like Jesus, mistakenly believed that he would return in their lifetime.

7. Dispensationalism has classically limited the sermon's ethic to the future millennial kingdom which Jesus offered to the Jews but which they rejected so that it was postponed until after his second coming.[3]

All of these approaches contain elements of truth, but none seems fully satisfactory. Nothing in the sermon suggests that Jesus' commands are

---

[1]For bibliography and a history of interpretation through the midseventies, see W. S. Kissinger, *The Sermon on the Mount: A History of Interpretation and Bibliography* (Metuchen, N.J.: Scarecrow, 1975). A wealth of background material appears in W. D. Davies, *The Setting of the Sermon on the Mount* (Cambridge: University Press, 1964). The best detailed exegesis is that of R. Guelich, *The Sermon on the Mount: A Foundation for Understanding* (Waco: Word, 1982). The two best popular expositions are J. R. W. Stott, *Christian Counter-Culture* (Downers Grove: InterVarsity, 1978), and D. A. Carson, *The Sermon on the Mount* (Grand Rapids: Baker, 1978); also cf. D. S. Dockery and D. E. Garland, *Seeking the Kingdom: The Sermon on the Mount Made Practical* (Wheaton: Harold Shaw, 1992). A classic series of evangelical sermons appears in printed form as D. M. Lloyd-Jones, *Studies in the Sermon on the Mount* (Grand Rapids: Eerdmans, 1959).

[2]C. Bauman, *The Sermon on the Mount: The Modern Quest for Its Meaning* (Macon: Mercer, 1985).

[3]Many contemporary dispensationalists have abandoned this view in favor of view 8. Cf. esp. C. Blaising, "Development of Dispensationalism by Contemporary Dispensationalists," *BibSac* 145 (1988): 254-80; R. L. Saucy, "The Presence of the Kingdom and the Life of the Church," *BibSac* 145 (1988): 30-46.

limited only to a certain group of his followers. They are in fact expressly addressed to all "disciples" (v. 1), those who have already repented and are seeking further instruction. Commands for disciples are not self-evidently limited to personal relationships nor clearly applicable to governments. Questions of pacifism versus just war or of the extent of church/state interaction are legitimate but not directly addressed. Nor does anything in the sermon suggest that Jesus' commands here are more or less absolute than any of the rest of his ethic, or that his teaching can be restricted either to present norms or future possibilities. The type of society requiring commands against murder, adultery, divorce, and so on can hardly be described as millennial, but that does not mean that Jesus' vision is fully realizable in this age. Finally, it is impossible to separate Jesus' ethic from allegiance to his person, as Marx and Gandhi tried, or to find any consistent form of application if one follows pure existentialism.

8. Inaugurated eschatology thus seems most in keeping with Jesus' teaching on the kingdom more generally. Inaugurated eschatology recognizes an "already/not yet" tension in which the sermon's ethic remains the ideal or goal for all Christians in every age but which will never be fully realized until the consummation of the kingdom at Christ's return.

We can expect the Spirit to empower us to make substantial strides in obedience, even as we recognize that our sinfulness will prevent us from ever coming close to attaining God's standards.[4] The metaphors of salt and light in 5:13-16, moreover, suggest that Jesus is first of all addressing the community of his followers, rather than the individual or the state, so that the church should comprise the primary arena of their application. The sermon thus forms the manifesto by which the new community Jesus is forming should live. But the church must try to permeate society with these ideals, albeit in a persuasive rather than coercive fashion.[5]

The Sermon on the Mount is very carefully structured.[6] The nine Beatitudes (5:3-12) and the salt and light metaphors (5:13-16) form the sermon's introduction. Matthew 5:17-20 provides the thesis statement of the greater righteousness required of Jesus' disciples. Matthew 5:21-48 contrasts Jesus' teaching with the law by means of six antitheses. Matthew 6:1-18 contrasts true and hypocritical piety by means of three examples. Matthew 6:19-34 turns to social issues, with various commands regarding

---

[4]See esp. R. A. Guelich, "Interpreting the Sermon on the Mount" (117-30); J. D. Kingsbury, "The Place, Structure and Meaning of the Sermon on the Mount within Matthew" (131-43), and L. S. Cahill, "The Ethical Implications of the Sermon on the Mount" (144-56), all in *Int* 41 (1987).

[5]Cf. esp. R. Lischer, "The Sermon on the Mount as Radical Pastoral Care," *Int* 41 (1987): 157-69; cf. C. L. Blomberg, "How the Church Can Turn the Other Cheek and Still Be Political," *Southern Baptist Public Affairs* 2.1 (1990): 10-12.

[6]D. C. Allison, Jr., "The Structure of the Sermon on the Mount," *JBL* 106 (1987): 423-45.

money and true riches. Matthew 7:1-12 gives three further commands on how to treat others. Matthew 7:13-27 concludes the sermon with three illustrations of the only two possible responses to Jesus' message.

Form and redaction criticism have regularly viewed this arrangement of material, like that of the other four major discourses of Jesus in Matthew, as a composite product, a collection of shorter sayings of Jesus from various original contexts. The parallels in Luke, which are much briefer and scattered about his Gospel, seem to support this view. It is consonant with ancient practice and was endorsed already in Reformation times by John Calvin.[7] But 7:28 seems to suggest that Matthew believed Jesus spoke the sermon on one particular occasion. Such a sermon in fact would have had to have been far longer than the few brief minutes it would take to read Matt 5–7 aloud. Much ancient writing excerpted and epitomized longer materials, and a detailed study of Jesus' final discourse in Matthew (chaps. 24–25) suggests that this is precisely the approach the Gospel writers have adopted there.[8] A similar process may therefore have led to the Sermon on the Mount as we know it. After all, Luke arranges much of his material thematically, and many of the shorter sayings common to Matthew and Luke could well have been repeated by Jesus on many different occasions.

Jesus seems to have delivered this sermon after a considerable amount of ministry in Galilee (4:23-25). Events that actually appear later in Matthew may already have occurred, most notably Jesus' gathering all twelve of his disciples (cf. Luke 6:12-16). If Matthew and Luke are both excerpting from longer originals, there is no reason not to see Luke's Sermon on the Plain (6:17-49) as comprising teaching Jesus gave on this same occasion.

¹Now when he saw the crowds, he went up on a mountainside and sat down. His disciples came to him, ²and he began to teach them, saying:

a. INTRODUCTION (5:1-16). *(1) Setting (5:1-2).* **5:1-2** The reference to the crowds in v. 1 calls to mind the crowds of 4:25, but 4:23-25 is a more general summary of major portions of Jesus' Galilean ministry. Matthew 5:1 refers to a specific occasion, so we must not assume the crowds are identical in both passages. Jesus goes up onto a mountainside just as Moses did at Sinai to receive the Ten Commandments. Many have seen Matthew's portrait of Jesus, therefore, as one of a new Moses or new

---

[7]For a detailed reconstruction of a tradition-history of these discrete elements, see esp. H. D. Betz, *Essays on the Sermon on the Mount* (Philadelphia: Fortress, 1985), although Betz often unnecessarily assumes that the various traditions actually contradict each other.

[8]See D. Wenham, *The Rediscovery of Jesus' Eschatological Discourse* (Sheffield: JSOT, 1984).

lawgiver. As subsequent exposition will make clear, however, Jesus is not proclaiming a new law but announcing what he believes is the legitimate interpretation of God's will as contained in the already-existing Torah.[9] The Greek reads literally *the mountain*, but Matthew uses this expression (*to oros*; "a mountainside") elsewhere to refer more generally to *the hill country* that dominated the skyline surrounding Capernaum (14:23; 15:29).[10] So we cannot determine exactly where Jesus delivered his message.

The traditional site on the northeast shore of Galilee, known as the Mount of Beatitudes, at least gives a good acoustical illustration of how a speaker could address a large crowd on a plateau in the hills overlooking the lakeside and be heard by thousands at once. Luke refers to Jesus' speaking on a "level place," but since Jesus has been in the mountains (cf. 6:12 with 6:17), Luke scarcely contradicts Matthew. Both writers envisage a plateau in a hilly area. Sitting was the common posture for teaching. "His disciples" seems to presume that he has already called more than the four described in 4:18-22. Matthew does not give the names of all twelve until 10:2-4, but 10:1 makes clear they had already been called. As noted above, identifying the disciples as Jesus' audience is crucial for recognizing the ethics of the sermon as applying to those already committed to Jesus as a group of his followers trying to live together in community.[11] But great crowds also form an important part of Jesus' audience. They too will learn what genuine discipleship involves as they consider the possibility of commitment to Jesus.

(2) Kingdom Blessings (5:3-12).[12] The Beatitudes, as they have traditionally been called from the Latin word for "blessings," are a common biblical form in both Testaments (e.g., Ps 1:1; Prov 3:13; Dan 12:12; Matt 11:6; Acts 20:35; Rev 1:3). The word "blessed" refers to those who are and/or will be *happy, fortunate*, or as those who are "to be congratulated"[13] because of God's response to their behavior or situation. An important change in tenses separates vv. 3 and 10 from vv. 4-9. In the first and last Beatitudes, Jesus declares God's kingdom to be present for those who are blessed. In the intervening verses he refers to future consolation.

---

[9]Cf. P. Lapide, *The Sermon on the Mount: Utopia or Program for Action?* (Maryknoll: Orbis, 1986), 14.

[10]Cf. L. Sabourin, *L'Évangile selon Saint Matthieu et ses principaux paralleles* (Rome: Biblical Institute Press, 1978), 53.

[11]See esp. R. A. Guelich, "The Matthean Beatitudes: 'Entrance-Requirements' or Eschatological Blessings?" *JBL* 95 (1976): 415-34.

[12]The fullest treatment of the Beatitudes is J. Dupont, *Les béatitudes* (Paris: Gabalda, 1969-73); the best popular exposition appears in H. W. Robinson, *The Christian Salt and Light Company* (Grand Rapids: Discovery House, 1988).

[13]R. T. France, *Matthew: Evangelist and Teacher* (Grand Rapids: Zondervan, 1989), 108.

Partial recompense may come in this age, but complete fulfillment of Jesus' promises often requires waiting for the age to come. Numerous passive voice verbs function as divine passives; e.g., "they will be comforted" means *God will comfort them* (v. 4). The Beatitudes form an appropriate introduction to Jesus' sermon as they remind his disciples that God blesses them before he makes demands on them (the body of the sermon). The same sequence appeared at Sinai. God redeemed his people from Egypt and reminded them of his blessings before giving them his law.

Matthew records eight blessings followed by a generalizing summary, whereas Luke presents four blessings, the summary, and four parallel woes. Most scholars assume that only those sayings found in both Gospels are authentic and that each Evangelist has created and embellished his sources. But the structure of a collection of blessings and curses in 2 Enoch 52:11-12 along with the recently translated Dead Sea document 4Q525, which also presents a large number of parallel Beatitudes,[14] suggests that both Matthew and Luke might be excerpting from an original set of eight Beatitudes and eight woes.

3 "Blessed are the poor in spirit,
for theirs is the kingdom of heaven.

5:3 "Poor in spirit," as a virtue, must refer not to a poor quality of faith but to the acknowledgment of one's spiritual powerlessness and bankruptcy apart from Christ (cf. Goodspeed, "Those who feel their spiritual need"). Blessing the spiritually poor provides an important qualification of Luke's more absolute use of "poor" (Luke 6:20). No contradiction appears here because an important strand of Jewish thought had developed a close equation between poverty and piety in the use of the Hebrew term *anawim* (as, e.g., in Isa 61:1, which probably underlies this passage).[15] In other words, both Matthew and Luke picture "those who because of sustained economic privation and social stress have confidence only in God."[16] This interpretation coincides with Paul's observation in Corinth that most who were becoming Christians came from the poorer classes of society (1 Cor 1:26-29). It is consistent with the experience of

---

[14]Cf. E. Puech, "4Q525 et les péricopes des béatitudes en ben Sira et *Matthieu*," *RB* 98 (1991): 80-106.

[15]See E. Schweizer, *The Good News according to Matthew* (Richmond: John Knox, 1975), 86, for numerous other references. F. D. Bruner (*The Christbook* [Waco: Word, 1987], 135) comments: "If we say that 'blessed are the poor in spirit' means 'blessed are the rich too, if they act humbly,' we have spiritualized the text. On the other hand, if we say 'blessed are the poor' means 'poor people are happy people,' we have secularized the text. . . . Jesus said something incorporating Matthew's spirituality and Luke's sociality, with the best of each."

[16]Carson, *Sermon on the Mount*, 131.

a majority of Jesus' own followers who came from the poor *am-ha-aretz* ("people of the land"), and it fits in with the fact that in many periods of world history including our own, the gospel has spread fastest among those who have had the fewest possessions to stand in the way of whole-hearted commitment to God. As previous discussion of the kingdom showed (see 3:2), part of the church's mission is to try to improve the socioeconomic lot of the poorest of this world. But fallen humanity will never create social utopia; the truth of Rom 8:18 must remain important consolation for many people.[17]

⁴Blessed are those who mourn,
for they will be comforted.

5:4 "Mourn" remains unqualified and parallels Luke's "weep" (Luke 6:21). In light of v. 3 and a probable allusion to Isa 61:2-3, however, we should again think of both spiritual and social concerns. Mourning includes grief caused by both personal sin and loss and social evil and oppression. God will comfort now in part and fully in the future. That Christian mourning does not outweigh happiness as the more dominant characteristic of the Christian life remains clear from Matt 9:15.

⁵Blessed are the meek,
for they will inherit the earth.

5:5 A "meek" person is not the "wallflower" we often think of when we use the word but one who is *humble, gentle*, and *not aggressive.* Nevertheless, in the ancient Greco-Roman world, such humility was no more valued than in our world today. Inheriting the earth as future compensation suggests that the meekness in view also included a lack of earthly possessions. Most poor people in Israel did not own their own land and were subject to the whims of oppressive landlords (Jas 5:1-6). The future reward echoes Ps 37:11 but generalizes the promise of inheriting the land of Israel to include all of the earth. Christian hope does not look forward to inhabiting a particular country but to ruling with Christ over all the globe and ultimately to enjoying an entirely re-created earth and heavens (Rev 20–22).

⁶Blessed are those who hunger and thirst for righteousness,
for they will be filled.

5:6 "Hunger and thirst for righteousness" explains Luke's "hunger" (Luke 6:21). For the poor, "righteousness" would include having their

---

[17]A study of the Beatitudes that generally balances well spiritual and social concerns is M. H. Crosby, *Spirituality of the Beatitudes: Matthew's Challenge for First-World Christians* (Maryknoll: Orbis, 1981).

basic needs for food met, but it goes on to include a desire to see God's standards established and obeyed in every area of life. Again, God promises that his purposes will be accomplished and that his justice will eventually reign (cf. Isa 55:1).

7Blessed are the merciful,
for they will be shown mercy.

5:7 "Merciful" embraces the characteristics of being generous, forgiving others, having compassion for the suffering, and providing healing of every kind. The link between our mercy and God's mercy anticipates 6:12,14-15. Like vv. 3-6 this Beatitude echoes a key prophetic theme (cf. Mic 6:8). In light of Exod 34:6, mercy may be God's most fundamental attribute.

8Blessed are the pure in heart,
for they will see God.

5:8 Purity in heart refers to moral uprightness and not just ritual cleanliness. The Pauline theme of the impossibility of perfect purity in this life should not be imported here. Rather, as with "righteousness" in general for Matthew, what Jesus requires of his disciples is a life-style characterized by pleasing God (see comments under 1:18-19). The "pure in heart" exhibit a single-minded devotion to God that stems from the internal cleansing created by following Jesus. Holiness is a prerequisite for entering God's presence. The pure in heart pass this test, so they will see God and experience intimate fellowship with him. This Beatitude closely parallels Ps 24:3-4.

9Blessed are the peacemakers,
for they will be called sons of God.

5:9 As with the "merciful" of v. 7, "peacemakers" focus on interpersonal relationships. Those who work for *shalôm* (wholeness and harmony rather than strife and discord in all aspects of life) and who reconcile others to God and each other will "be called sons of God." Others will identify them as God's true ambassadors, as those who are being conformed to his likeness. Matthew 10:34 reminds us that such attempts at peacemaking in this age are often thwarted, but this gives us no excuse to become warmongers.

10Blessed are those who are persecuted because of righteousness,
for theirs is the kingdom of heaven.

5:10 All of these characteristics which Jesus labels as blessed are usually not welcomed in the world at large. Hostility may well arise against Jesus' followers, but even persecuted people are seen by Christ as

fortunate. This persecution, however, must be the result of righteous living and not due to individual sin or tactlessness (cf. 1 Pet 3:14; 4:14-15).
What is even more tragic is when one Christian persecutes another, allegedly "because of righteousness," when the persecution actually stems
from too narrow a definition of Christian belief or behavior.[18]

[11]**"Blessed are you when people insult you, persecute you and falsely say
all kinds of evil against you because of me. [12]Rejoice and be glad, because
great is your reward in heaven, for in the same way they persecuted the
prophets who were before you.**

5:11-12 These verses repeat, amplify, and personalize v. 10 by shifting from third-person to second-person address. "Falsely" is missing
from a few of the earliest manuscripts (most notably D, the Latin and Syriac versions) but probably belongs in the original text[19] and is in any
event a correct interpretation. "Because of me" provides another key
qualification. As in v. 10, the only persecution that is blessed is that
which stems from allegiance to Jesus and living in conformity with his
standards. Because this life is just a fraction of all eternity, we can and
must rejoice even in persecution. The joy commanded here, as elsewhere
in Scripture (esp. Jas 1:2), is not an emotion but an attitude.

"Reward" (more literally *wages*) is more a promise of "future recompense for a present condition of persecution and reproach" than a reward
for piety.[20] There is no comparison here between those with a lesser
reward and a greater reward. So the reward should be thought of as
heaven itself and not some particular status in the life to come. Jesus
offers a poignant reminder that the great men and women of Old Testament times often suffered a similar fate. The prophet Jeremiah provides
the classic example. The same is true of Christian history. When we
suffer, we must avoid the trap of thinking that we are the only ones who
have ever experienced such problems.

The upshot of the Beatitudes is a complete inversion of the attitude
popularly known in our culture as "machismo." In fact, this attitude is not
limited to a particular culture but characterizes humanity's self-centered,
self-arrogating pride which invariably seeks personal security and survival above the good of others.[21] We are enabled to invert these natural,
worldly values only when we recognize that God will in turn invert our

---

[18]Guelich (*Sermon on the Mount*, 75) notes the synonymous parallelism between vv. 3
and 10, so that part of being poor in spirit is to be persecuted for righteousness' sake and
vice versa.

[19]See M. W. Holmes, "The Text of Matthew 5.11," *NTS* 32 (1986): 283-86.

[20]W. C. Allen, *A Critical and Exegetical Commentary on the Gospel according to St.
Matthew*, ICC (Edinburgh: T & T Clark, 1907), 42.

[21]This theme characterizes the innovative study by A. Kodjak, *A Structural Analysis of
the Sermon on the Mount* (Berlin: de Gruyter, 1986).

marginalized status and grant eternal compensation. This is not to promote works-righteousness; Jesus is addressing those already professing discipleship (5:1). But, like James among the Epistles, Matthew is the one Gospel to emphasize most the changed life that must flow from commitment to Christ.

13"You are the salt of the earth. But if the salt loses its saltiness, how can it be made salty again? It is no longer good for anything, except to be thrown out and trampled by men.
14"You are the light of the world. A city on a hill cannot be hidden.

(3) Salt and Light (5:13-16).   **5:13-14**   In light of the countercultural perspectives enunciated in the Beatitudes, it would be easy to assume that Jesus was calling his followers to a separatistic or quasimonastic lifestyle. Here Jesus proclaims precisely the opposite. Christians must permeate society as agents of redemption. Of the numerous things to which salt could refer in antiquity,[22] its use as a preservative in food was probably its most basic function. Jesus thus calls his disciples to arrest corruption and prevent moral decay in their world. One must avoid assuming that all possible uses of salt were in view here. We may today think of salt primarily as a spice giving flavor; but given the amount of salt needed to preserve meat without refrigeration, it is not likely that many ancient Jews considered salt primarily as enhancing taste. "Loses its saltiness" reads more literally "is defiled." This is not the scientifically impossible notion of salt becoming flavorless but rather the common problem in the ancient world of salt being mixed with various impure substances and therefore becoming worthless as a preservative.

"To be thrown out and trampled by men" neither affirms nor denies anything about "eternal security." Rather, as Luke 14:35 makes even clearer, this phrase refers to the world's response to Christians if they do not function as they should. Believers who fail to arrest corruption become worthless as agents of change and redemption. Christianity may make its peace with the world and avoid persecution, but it is thereby rendered impotent to fulfill its divinely ordained role. It will thus ultimately be rejected even by those with whom it has sought compromise.[23]

15Neither do people light a lamp and put it under a bowl. Instead they put it on its stand, and it gives light to everyone in the house. 16In the same way,

---

[22]See Allison and Davies, *Matthew* 1:472-73, for no less than eleven possibilities.

[23]H. Hobbs (*An Exposition of the Gospel of Matthew* [Grand Rapids: Baker, 1965], 63) observes: "Thus their lives become insipid. This is here the case of lost opportunity. Talents unused are talents lost. . . . Life simply passes them by. They receive only scorn as the world tramples them under its feet as it rushes on to corruption, despair, and loss."

let your light shine before men, that they may see your good deeds and praise your Father in heaven.

5:15-16 Of the various possible uses of light, Jesus obviously has in mind the bringing of illumination through the revelation of God's will for his people. Since Jesus is the Light of the world (John 8:12; 9:5), so also his followers should reflect that light. Like lights from a city illuminating the dark countryside or a lamp inside a house providing light for all within it, Christians must let their good works shine before the rest of the world so that others may praise God. The good works are most naturally seen as the "fruits in keeping with repentance" of 3:8. This verse does not contradict 6:1 because there the motive for good behavior in public is self-glorification rather than bringing glory to God.

Both metaphors of salt and light raise important questions about Christian involvement in society regarding all forms of separatism or withdrawal. We are not called to control secular power structures; neither are we promised that we can Christianize the legislation and values of the world. But we must remain active preservative agents, indeed irritants, in calling the world to heed God's standards. We dare not form isolated Christian enclaves to which the world pays no attention.

b. THESIS: GREATER RIGHTEOUSNESS (5:17-48). Jesus' sermon has thus far proved sufficiently radical so as to raise the question of his role regarding the Old Testament law.

¹⁷"Do not think that I have come to abolish the Law or the Prophets; I have not come to abolish them but to fulfill them. ¹⁸I tell you the truth, until heaven and earth disappear, not the smallest letter, not the least stroke of a pen, will by any means disappear from the Law until everything is accomplished.

(1) Statement (5:17-20). **5:17** Now Christ makes clear that he is not contradicting the law, but neither is he preserving it unchanged. He comes "to fulfill" it, i.e., he will bring the law to its intended goal. This is what the Pharisees and scribes have missed, who therefore need a greater conformity to God's standards (v. 20). Both the Law and the Prophets together (v. 17) and the Law by itself (v. 18) were standard Jewish ways of referring to the entire Hebrew Scriptures (our Old Testament).

Fulfillment of Scripture, as throughout chaps. 1–4, refers to the bringing to fruition of its complete meaning. Here Jesus views his role as that of fulfilling all of the Old Testament. This claim has massive hermeneutical implications and challenges both classic Reformed and Dispensationalist perspectives. It is inadequate to say either that none of the Old Testament applies unless it is explicitly reaffirmed in the New or that all of the Old Testament applies unless it is explicitly revoked in the New. Rather, all of the Old Testament remains normative and relevant for Jesus' followers (2 Tim 3:16), but none of it can rightly be interpreted until one understands how it has been fulfilled in Christ. Every Old Testament text must be viewed in light of Jesus' person and ministry and the changes introduced by the new covenant he inaugurated.[24] Nor is there any evidence here for the common Christian division of the law into moral, civil, and ceremonial categories or for elevating the Ten Commandments above others. This is not to say that the law cannot or should not be subdivided, but valid divisions will probably require greater thematic nuance and sophistication.[25]

5:18 Verse 18 reaffirms the absolute authority of all of the Scriptures down to the smallest components of individual words.[26] They will endure for all time but with the important qualification "until everything is accomplished." With the coming of Christ, many aspects of the law are brought to complete fruition (e.g., the need for sacrifices, on which see Hebrews). In other instances certain requirements of the law endure until Christ's coming again (e.g., classically, love of neighbor and God).[27] In short, Christian application of the Old Testament must always take into account both the continuities and the discontinuities with the New Testament.[28] Given this hermeneutic, correct teaching and practice of all

[24]See esp. D. A. Dorsey, "The Law of Moses and the Christian: A Compromise," *JETS* 34 (1991): 321-34. Cf. L. Sabourin, *Matthieu*, 64-65; G. Strecker, *The Sermon on the Mount: An Exegetical Commentary* (Nashville: Abingdon, 1985), 54.

[25]Cf., e.g., C. J. H. Wright, *An Eye for an Eye* (Downers Grove: InterVarsity, 1983), 151-59. Wright treats five discrete categories of law: criminal, civil, family, cultic, and charitable. Some of these in turn need subdivisions that are treated distinctly. Cultic laws, e.g., include sacrifices, dietary restrictions, Sabbaths and other festivals, circumcision, and so on.

[26]The Greek refers to the ἰῶτα, the smallest letter of the alphabet and to *one horn* of a letter, apparently referring to a small, curved stroke. The underlying Hebrew/Aramaic probably had in mind the ʾ (also transliterated into English as an *i*) and the small strokes distinguishing similar Hebrew letters (e.g., ר and ד). A logical corollary of this authority is inerrancy, for which one of the most helpful and accurate definitions appears in P. D. Feinberg, "The Meaning of Inerrancy, in *Inerrancy*, ed. N. L. Geisler (Grand Rapids: Zondervan, 1979), 294: "Inerrancy means that when all facts are known, the Scriptures in their original autographs and properly interpreted will be shown to be wholly true in everything they affirm, whether that has to do with doctrine or morality or with the social, physical, or life sciences." On the relation between the authority, inspiration, and inerrancy of Scripture, see D. A. Carson and J. D. Woodbridge, eds., *Scripture and Truth* (Grand Rapids: Zondervan, 1983); idem, *Hermeneutics, Authority and Canon* (Grand Rapids: Zondervan, 1986); and D. A. Garrett and R. R. Melick, Jr., eds., *Authority and Interpretation: A Baptist Perspective* (Grand Rapids: Baker, 1987).

[27]Cf. esp. H. N. Ridderbos, *Matthew*, BSC (Grand Rapids: Zondervan, 1987), 100.

[28]For detailed justification of the various points of these last two paragraphs, see esp. the studies of R. Banks, "Matthew's Understanding of the Law: Authenticity and Interpretation in Matthew 5:17-20," *JBL* 93 (1974): 226-42; J. P. Meier, *Law and History in Matthew's Gospel* (Rome: Biblical Institute Press, 1976), *passim*. Since G. Barth ("Matthew's Understanding

"these commandments" (v. 19, almost certainly referring back to the Old Testament law just mentioned) are crucial. Jesus will give six illustrations of such correct interpretation shortly (vv. 21-48).

¹⁹Anyone who breaks one of the least of these commandments and teaches others to do the same will be called least in the kingdom of heaven, but whoever practices and teaches these commands will be called great in the kingdom of heaven. ²⁰For I tell you that unless your righteousness surpasses that of the Pharisees and the teachers of the law, you will certainly not enter the kingdom of heaven.

5:19 "Breaks" (*lysē*) involves a word play with "abolish" in v. 17 (*katalysai*) and is better rendered "sets aside" (as no longer applicable). The "least of these commandments" reflects a typical Jewish view of a hierarchy or ranking of God's priorities in the Torah, which Jesus himself elsewhere endorses (e.g., 23:23) even as he challenges some of the Pharisees' and scribes' priorities. Even worse is their practice, as teachers, of not only misconstruing God's will but also leading others astray. But here Jesus is concerned most with his disciples as teachers, as he contrasts greatness and obscurity *within* the kingdom. Variation of ranking within the community of God's people is best taken as referring to those whom God will truly honor in the present age. It is not as clear whether Jesus intends such ranking to include varying status in eternity, an idea that 20:1-16 seems to rule out.[29]

5:20 Jesus next introduces a new category of individuals, those who are not currently in the kingdom at all. He mentions the Pharisees and scribes precisely because they were a paradigm of the greatest righteousness imaginable within Judaism. Here he does not challenge their scrupulous attention to the law; but as the subsequent antitheses will illustrate, he simply observes that now, with the coming of a new age, more is required to be in fellowship with God and in conformity to his will.[30] People must follow Jesus in discipleship, which for the most part these Jewish leaders refuse to do. Harking back to vv. 6 and 10, Jesus thus introduces the thesis statement that unifies his entire sermon. Christian discipleship requires a greater righteousness.

---

of the Law," in G. Bornkamm, G. Barth, and H. J. Held, *Tradition and Interpretation in Matthew* [Philadelphia: Westminster, 1963], 58-164), the prevailing consensus has wrongly viewed Matthew's Jesus as quite conservative with respect to the Torah. An extreme, recent illustration of this trend is P. Sigal, *The Halakah of Jesus of Nazareth according to the Gospel of Matthew* (Lanham, Md.: University Press of America, 1986).

[29]Cf. Ridderbos, *Matthew*, 101.

[30]On "entering the kingdom," see esp. J. Marcus, "Entering into the Kingly Power of God," *JBL* 107 (1988): 663-75.

(2) Illustrations (5:21-48). In these six antitheses Jesus illustrates the greater righteousness he demands of his disciples. With each example he contrasts what was said in the Torah and in its traditional interpretations with his more stringent requirements. In the process, however, he contravenes the letter of several of the Old Testament laws, not because he is abolishing them but because he is establishing a new covenant in which God's law is internalized in a way that prevents it from being fully encapsulated in a list of rules and that precludes perfect obedience (cf. Heb 8:7-13). Even more fundamental to the six illustrations is Jesus' role as sovereign interpreter of the law, as he himself fulfills it (v. 17). He alone, therefore, has the authority to declare how each part of the law will apply to his followers.[31]

21"You have heard that it was said to the people long ago, 'Do not murder, and anyone who murders will be subject to judgment.' 22But I tell you that anyone who is angry with his brother will be subject to judgment. Again, anyone who says to his brother, 'Raca,' is answerable to the Sanhedrin. But anyone who says, 'You fool!' will be in danger of the fire of hell.

(a) On Murder (5:21-26). **5:21-22** Jesus cites what was spoken "to the people long ago," an expression that could also be rendered "in ancient times" or "by people long ago." In any event, he refers to the Sixth Commandment of the Decalogue given on Mount Sinai (Exod 20:13). "Murder" is the correct rendering since the underlying Hebrew (*ratsach*, sometimes translated "kill") did not include killing in self-defense, wars ordered by Yahweh, capital punishment following due process of law, or accidental manslaughter. "Subject to" could also be rendered "liable." Christ refers to one who currently stands condemned and is therefore in danger of judgment, but judgment is not inevitable if the proper remedy is sought. Like Moses, Jesus condemns murder, but he goes on to claim that harboring wrath in one's heart is also sinful and deserving of punishment (he doesn't say it is as bad!).

A strong manuscript tradition (D, L, W, f^1, f^{13}, etc.) adds the phrase "without cause" following the word "brother." This phrase is usually viewed as a later textual addition,[32] but it nevertheless gives the correct interpretation. There is a righteous indignation against sin (as esp. with Jesus versus the money changers in the temple—21:12-17), and God himself is properly wrathful (cf. 18:34; 22:7). But it is unusual for human

---

[31]For a good survey of various approaches to the use of the law in Jesus' teaching and for an articulation of the view espoused here, see D. J. Moo, "Jesus and the Authority of the Mosaic Law," *JSNT* 20 (1984): 3-49.

[32]But see D. A. Black, "Jesus on Anger: The Text of Matthew 5:22a Revisited," *NovT* 30 (1988): 1-8.

anger to be free from mixed motives and not be in some sense self-avenging. "Brother" in Matthew, when not referring to a biological sibling, consistently means *a fellow member of the religious community* and usually refers to Jesus' disciples (cf. 5:44; 7:3-5; 12:49-50; 18:15,21,35; 23:8; 25:40; 28:10). Jesus does not thereby imply that it is all right to be angry against those who are not believers; rather, he applies his injunction first of all to those against whom anger is most inappropriate. That is to say, it is particularly bad for Christians to get angry at other Christians who have themselves also been spared God's wrath. Restraining one's wrath against a fellow believer is a virtue still desperately needed today.

Jesus illustrates his point that not just murder but also anger is sinful in two additional, parallel ways. First, he considers those who accost their fellow believers with the epithet "Raca" (a quasi-swear word in Aramaic). The expression probably meant something like *empty-headed*.[33] So too those who call someone a "fool" commit a sin. This word (*mōros*) carries overtones of immorality and godlessness as well as idiocy. As with the commands against anger, both of these prohibitions against the use of insulting names undoubtedly carried the implicit qualification of "where unjustified," since Jesus himself uses the term *mōros* in 23:17,19 (in direct address) and in 7:26 (in indirect address) when the label is accurate. Some have seen an increasing severity of judgment as Jesus progresses from the terms "judgment" to "the Sanhedrin" (the Jewish supreme court) to Gehenna ("fire of hell")—a reference to the valley south of Jerusalem in which children were slaughtered in Old Testament times and traditionally associated with a perpetually burning garbage dump in later centuries. But given the close parallelism among the first clauses of each illustration, the entire sentences should probably be taken as largely synonymous. All three metaphorically refer to the danger of eternal judgment.

23"Therefore, if you are offering your gift at the altar and there remember that your brother has something against you, 24leave your gift there in front of the altar. First go and be reconciled to your brother; then come and offer your gift.

5:23-24 Jesus' listeners therefore urgently need to escape this judgment by dealing decisively with sin. Jesus drives home his point with two dramatic illustrations. First, he envisages a worshiper who is called to place interpersonal reconciliation above correct ritual. Of course, we cannot guarantee that another person will agree to be reconciled with us, but we should make every effort "as far as it depends on" us (Rom 12:18).

---

[33]See T. Sorg, "ῥακά," *DNTT* 1:417-18.

"Has something against you" probably implies a "just claim"[34] and also suggests that we ought not bring up our grievances with others that they do not yet know about but that we deal with situations in which others remain upset with us. How many of our churches would or should be temporarily emptied if these commands were taken seriously? But Jesus remains concerned that we still offer correct worship. The Christian sacrifice is first of all one of trusting in Christ, but true discipleship will necessarily lead to reconciliation with fellow believers. Neither one without the other can save a person (cf. 1 John 1:8-9 with 2:9).

25 "Settle matters quickly with your adversary who is taking you to court. Do it while you are still with him on the way, or he may hand you over to the judge, and the judge may hand you over to the officer, and you may be thrown into prison. 26I tell you the truth, you will not get out until you have paid the last penny.

5:25-26 Jesus' second illustration of the urgency of reconciliation pictures an out-of-court settlement between fellow litigants. These verses offer good advice at the literal level of legal proceedings, but in light of vv. 21-22 they obviously refer primarily to the spiritual goal of averting God's wrath on Judgment Day before it is too late to change one's destiny. As a metaphor with one central point of comparison, the details of vv. 25-26 must not be allegorized. No spiritual counterparts to the adversary and officer appear, nor does v. 26 support the traditional Roman Catholic doctrine of purgatory, as if one could ever pay enough to get out of hell.[35] "The last penny" is a *kodrantēs*, which was 1/64 of the standard minimum daily wage (a denarius) and the second smallest Roman coin in first-century currency.

27 "You have heard that it was said, 'Do not commit adultery.' 28But I tell you that anyone who looks at a woman lustfully has already committed adultery with her in his heart.

(b) On Adultery (5:27-30). **5:27-28** Jesus moves on from the Sixth to the Seventh Commandment (Exod 20:14). "Adultery" usually referred to sexual relations by a married person with a partner other than his or her spouse, but v. 28 makes clear that Jesus is not limiting his commandments to married people but speaking of sexual sin in general. The grammar of v. 28a leads to two possible translations. Jesus could be speaking of one who "looks at a woman with the intention of committing adultery"[36] or to one who "looks at a woman for the purpose of getting

---

[34]D. Hill, *The Gospel of Matthew*, NCB (London: Oliphants, 1972), 122.

[35]"Or he may" in v. 25 is more literally "so that he does not." Once one is delivered to the judge, the sequence of events described here is irrevocable.

[36]R. G. Bratcher, *A Translator's Guide to the Gospel of Matthew* (New York: UBS, 1981), 47.

her to lust after him."[37] Either way, the present tense participle *blepōn* refers to one who continues to look rather than just casting a passing glance, and in either case the mere viewing or mental imagining of a naked body is not under consideration. Instead Jesus is condemning lustful thoughts and actions—those involving an actual *desire* (the most literal translation of the verb *epithymeō*) to have sexual relations with someone other than one's spouse. Yet despite the danger of overapplying this verse, an even greater danger is that of underapplying it. Adultery among Christians today is a scandal, yet it almost never occurs without precipitation. Christians must recognize those thoughts and actions which, long before any overt sexual sin, make the possibility of giving in to temptation more likely, and they must take dramatic action to avoid them.[38]

[29]If your right eye causes you to sin, gouge it out and throw it away. It is better for you to lose one part of your body than for your whole body to be thrown into hell. [30]And if your right hand causes you to sin, cut it off and throw it away. It is better for you to lose one part of your body than for your whole body to go into hell.

5:29-30 As in vv. 23-26, Jesus illustrates this decisive action with two metaphorical illustrations. Eyes and hands are primary offenders in sexual sin, but vv. 29-30 may be applied more broadly as well.[39] Literal self-mutilation is not Christ's objective. It is quite possible to be blind or crippled and still lust. Rather, as is characteristic of Jesus' figurative and hyperbolic style, he commands us to take drastic measures to avoid temptations to sexual sin—to remove from ourselves anyone or anything that could *lead us into scandal* ("causes you to sin").[40] The "right" eye and hand refer to those viewed in antiquity as more valuable. Again, eternal judgment appears as the punishment for those who fail to heed Jesus' words. Sin that is not dealt with leads inexorably to judgment. Jesus is not implying, however, that sexual sin cannot be forgiven when there is true repentance.

---

[37]The first αὐτήν is more naturally taken as the subject of the infinitive ἐπιθυμῆσαι since this verb usually takes its direct object in the genitive. See K. Haacker, "Der Rechtsatz Jesu zum Thema Ehebruch," *BZ* 21 (1977): 113-16; but see BDF 171 (1) for occasional exceptions.

[38]Cf. esp. the balanced statement of F. Stagg ("Matthew," in *The Broadman Bible Commentary*, vol. 8, ed. C. J. Allen [Nashville: Broadman, 1969], 109): "The New Testament does not equate temptation with sin . . . sin begins at the point of consent not with the temptation itself and not first in the overt act."

[39]W. Deming ("Mark 9.42-10.12, Matthew 5.27-32 and *B. Nid.* 13b: A First Century Discussion of Male Sexuality," *NTS* 36 [1990]: 130-41) thinks primarily of masturbation and pederasty, but this is probably too limited.

[40]Greek σκάνδαλον. For its meaning in the various contexts in Matthew in which it occurs, see esp. J. Mateos, "Análisis semántico de los lexemas σκανδαλίζω y σκάνδαλον," *FNT* 2 (1989): 57-92.

If translated as in the NIV, these paragraphs do not specifically refer to a woman lusting after a man, only a man after a woman; but given the reciprocity of Jesus' teaching elsewhere (see, e.g., v. 32 immediately below), it is clearly implied. Nevertheless, men may well sin more often than women in this particular way because male sexual arousal comes primarily through sight. Jesus' teaching, like much of the antipornography movement today, is greatly liberating for women.

31"It has been said, 'Anyone who divorces his wife must give her a certificate of divorce.' 32But I tell you that anyone who divorces his wife, except for marital unfaithfulness, causes her to become an adulteress, and anyone who marries the divorced woman commits adultery.

(c) On Divorce (5:31-32).   **5:31-32**   The third antithesis follows naturally, inasmuch as sexual sin often leads to divorce. Again Jesus requires a more exacting standard of his followers than was prevalent in the Judaism of his day. In the Old Testament divorce was legislated but never banned. Deuteronomy 24:1-4 formed a central part of that legislation, and Jesus alludes to v. 1 here. In the first century two slightly older contemporaries of Jesus, the Pharisees Shammai and Hillel, vigorously debated the legitimate grounds for divorce. Hillel permitted a man to put away his wife for "any good cause" (which could be as minor an issue as frequently burning his food!), while Shammai limited it to "adultery" (*m. Giṭ.* 9:10).

"Marital unfaithfulness" here translates *porneia*, a broader term for sexual sin of all kinds. Many have therefore attempted to distinguish it from adultery in this text on the grounds that Jesus would otherwise not differ from Shammai and because Matthew did not use one of the regular words for adultery (e.g., *moicheia*) as he did in translating Jesus' words in vv. 27-28. Other alternatives have therefore become popular—most notably that Jesus was referring to the discovery of premarital unfaithfulness or prohibiting certain marriages among close relatives that would have been defined as incestuous. Others argue that "except" means *except for a consideration of*, so that Jesus is not ruling one way or the other on divorce for adultery. Many scholars attribute Matthew's exception clause to a later redactional change. D. A. Carson gives a good, brief survey of the various exegetical options here and an excellent defense of the NIV rendering.[41] Objections to that rendering overlook the point that Jewish law *required* divorce in the case of adultery (*m. Yebam.* 2:8; *m. Soṭa* 5:1),[42] whereas Christianity never does. Even with the exception, Jesus is stricter than Shammai. Jesus never commands divorce but only permits it

---

[41]Carson, "Matthew," 413-18.

[42]For further rabbinic background, see also M. Bockmuehl, "Matthew 5.32; 19.9 in the Light of Pre-Rabbinic Halakhah," *NTS* 35 (1989): 291-95.

if all attempts at reconciliation have failed because he recognizes that the adultery has already undermined one of the most fundamental elements of a marriage—sexual exclusivity. *Porneia* (rather than *moicheia*) is used probably because it was the term more commonly used to describe female rather than male infidelity.[43] Jesus follows social convention by phrasing his example from the perspective of the man who has been defrauded, but v. 32b makes plain that, in radical opposition to prevailing mores, he considers a man's infidelity as equally grievous.

Ancient Jews (like Greeks and Romans) almost universally agreed that lawful divorce granted a person the right to remarry. So Jesus' words would almost certainly have been taken as permission for remarriage when divorce was permitted, i.e., after marital unfaithfulness. In other cases divorce causes adultery. The phrase "causes her to become an adulteress," however, is misleading. The Greek does not use the noun "adulteress" but the verb *makes her commit adultery*. There is no indication here that a second marriage, even following an illegitimate divorce, is seen as permanently adulterous. Divorced Christians who have remarried should not commit the sin of a second divorce to try to resume relations with a previous spouse (see again Deut 24:1-4) but should begin afresh to observe God's standards by remaining faithful to their current partners. What is more, it was probably not the taking of a new husband that made the wife commit adultery, since some divorced women remained unmarried. Jesus maintains that the divorce *itself* creates adultery—metaphorically, not literally—through infidelity to the lifelong, covenantal nature of marriage (cf. the characteristic Old Testament use of "adultery" to refer to breaking one's commitments to God—e.g., Hos 2:4; Jer 5:7; Ezek 16:32).[44]

All of these views, of course, are hotly debated in Christian circles today.[45] Other issues, including some of contemporary application, will be treated under 19:1-12; but it is worth noting here that just as vv. 22 and 28 do not prohibit all forms of anger or sexual desire, and just as the exceptions to Jesus' commands there are more implicit than explicit, so also v. 32 most likely does not reflect a consideration of every conceivable legitimate or illegitimate ground for divorce. Instead Jesus is responding to a specific debate in first-century Judaism. At least Paul seems to have recognized Jesus' words as not comprehensive, since in

---

[43]J. B. Bauer, "Bemerkungen zu den matthäischen Unzuchtsklauseln (Mt. 5,32; 19,9)," in *Begegnung mit dem Wort*, ed. J. Zmijewski and E. Nellessen (Bonn: Hanstein, 1980), 26-27.

[44]See esp. W. F. Luck, *Divorce and Remarriage* (San Francisco: Harper and Row, 1987), 247-51.

[45]Cf. esp. H. W. House, ed., *Divorce and Remarriage: Four Christian Views* (Downers Grove: InterVarsity, 1990).

1 Cor 7:15 he introduces a second legitimate ground for divorce that Jesus never mentioned.[46]

33"Again, you have heard that it was said to the people long ago, 'Do not break your oath, but keep the oaths you have made to the Lord.' 34But I tell you, Do not swear at all: either by heaven, for it is God's throne; 35or by the earth, for it is his footstool; or by Jerusalem, for it is the city of the Great King. 36And do not swear by your head, for you cannot make even one hair white or black. 37Simply let your 'Yes' be 'Yes,' and your 'No,' 'No'; anything beyond this comes from the evil one.

(d) On Oaths (5:33-37). **5:33-37**   The theme of greater righteousness continues, but Jesus' examples move outside the Decalogue. As with his teaching on divorce, he again forbids what the Old Testament permitted. "Do not break your oath" alludes to Lev 19:12 and Num 30:2 and would more commonly be translated "do not swear falsely" or "do not perjure yourself." To "swear" (v. 34) does not mean to curse or use bad words but to affirm the truth of a statement while calling on God to judge oneself if it is in fact untrue. Again qualifications are implicit. There are oaths which are consistent with God's character and demands even in the New Testament (e.g., 2 Cor 1:18; Gal 1:20), but given the casuistry (an elaborate hierarchy of laws) of first-century Judaism on oaths (cf. the entire Mishnaic tractate *Shebuoth*), Jesus declares that it would be best to avoid them altogether. The situation described is one in which many Jews viewed swearing by "heaven," "earth," "Jerusalem," or "one's head" as less binding than swearing "by God." Jesus stresses that each of these items belongs to God in an important way (cf. Isa 66:1) so that the conventional Jewish distinctions are spurious. Even one's head, which might be thought to be uniquely under an individual's control, has divinely predetermined features, such as hair coloring (temporary dyeing is not in view here!). Rather, Jesus' followers should be people whose words are so characterized by integrity that others need no formal assurance of their truthfulness in order to trust them. On this topic cf. further the comments under 23:16-22.

38"You have heard that it was said, 'Eye for eye, and tooth for tooth.' 39But I tell you, Do not resist an evil person. If someone strikes you on the right cheek, turn to him the other also. 40And if someone wants to sue you and take your tunic, let him have your cloak as well. 41If someone forces you to go one mile, go with him two miles. 42Give to the one who asks you, and do not turn away from the one who wants to borrow from you.

---

[46]On the various issues raised here, cf. further C. L. Blomberg, "Marriage, Divorce, Remarriage and Celibacy: An Exegesis of Matt. 19:3-12," *TrinJ* n.s. 11 (1990): 161-96; D. Atkinson, *To Have and to Hold* (Grand Rapids: Eerdmans, 1981).

(e) On Retaliation (5:38-42). **5:38-42** Jesus next alludes to Exod 21:24 and Deut 19:21. Again he formally abrogates an Old Testament command in order to intensify and internalize its application. This law originally prohibited the formal exaction of an overly severe punishment that did not fit a crime as well as informal, self-appointed vigilante action. Now Jesus teaches the principle that Christian kindness should transcend even straightforward tit-for-tat retribution. None of the commands of vv. 39-42 can easily be considered absolute; all must be read against the historical background of first-century Judaism.[47] Nevertheless, in light of prevailing ethical thought Jesus contrasts radically with most others of his day in stressing the need to decisively break the natural chain of evil action and reaction that characterizes human relationships.[48]

Antistēnai ("resist") in v. 39 was often used in a legal context (cf. Isa 50:8)[49] and in light of v. 40 is probably to be taken that way here. Jesus' teaching then parallels 1 Cor 6:7 against not taking fellow believers to court, though it could be translated somewhat more broadly as "do not take revenge on someone who wrongs you" (GNB). We must nevertheless definitely resist evil in certain contexts (cf. Jas 4:7; 1 Pet 5:9). Striking a person on the right cheek suggests a backhanded slap from a typically right-handed aggressor and was a characteristic Jewish form of insult. Jesus tells us not to trade such insults even if it means receiving more. In no sense does v. 39 require Christians to subject themselves or others to physical danger or abuse, nor does it bear directly on the pacifism-just war debate. Verse 40 is clearly limited to a legal context. One must be willing to give as collateral an outer garment—more than what the law could require, which was merely an inner garment (cf. Exod 22:26-27). *Coat* and *shirt* reflect contemporary parallels to "cloak" and "tunic," though both of the latter looked more like long robes. Verse 41 continues the legal motif by referring to Roman conscription of private citizens to help carry military equipment for soldiers as they traveled.

Each of these commands requires Jesus' followers to act more generously than what the letter of the law demanded. "Going the extra mile" has rightly become a proverbial expression and captures the essence of all of Jesus' illustrations. Not only must disciples reject all behavior motivated only by a desire for retaliation, but they also must positively work for the good of those with whom they would otherwise be at odds. In

---

[47]See esp. R. A. Horsley, "Ethics and Exegesis: 'Love Your Enemies' and the Doctrine of Non-Violence," *JAAR* 54 (1986): 3-31; and cf. Blomberg, "Church."

[48]J. L. Nolland, *Luke 1–9:20*, WBC (Dallas: Word, 1990), 294-304, includes excellent comparative ethical material and incisive analysis.

[49]Cf. the three definitions of J. P. Louw and E. A. Nida, eds., (*Greek-English Lexicon of the New Testament* [New York: UBS, 1988], 495): *to resist by actively opposing pressure or power; to fight back against; to oppose in return.*

v. 42 Jesus calls his followers to give to those who ask and not turn from those who would borrow. He presumes that the needs are genuine and commands us not to ignore them, but he does not specifically mandate how best we can help. As Augustine rightly noted, the text says "give to everyone that asks," not "give everything to him that asks" (*De Sermone Domine en Monte* 67). Compare Jesus' response to the request made of him in Luke 12:13-15. It is also crucial to note that "a willingness to forego one's personal rights and to allow oneself to be insulted and imposed upon is not incompatible with a firm stand for matters of principle and for the rights of others (cf. Paul's attitude in Acts 16:37; 22:25; 25:8-12)."[50] Verses 39-42 thus comprise a "focal instance" of nonretaliation; specific, extreme commands attract our attention to a key ethical theme that must be variously applied as circumstances change.[51]

43"You have heard that it was said, 'Love your neighbor and hate your enemy.' 44But I tell you: Love your enemies and pray for those who persecute you, 45that you may be sons of your Father in heaven. He causes his sun to rise on the evil and the good, and sends rain on the righteous and the unrighteous. 46If you love those who love you, what reward will you get? Are not even the tax collectors doing that? 47And if you greet only your brothers, what are you doing more than others? Do not even pagans do that?
48Be perfect, therefore, as your heavenly Father is perfect.

(f) On Loving Enemies (5:43-48). **5:43-47** This final antithesis is the first to begin with a quotation not entirely from Scripture. "Love your neighbor" comes from Lev 19:18, but "hate your enemy" appears nowhere in the Old Testament. Commentators debate whether or not this latter command is a legitimate inference from texts like Deut 23:3-6; 25:17-19; or Ps 139:21, but hatred of enemies was common enough in subsequent generations so as to fit under the category of something Jesus' audience had "heard that it was said" (cf. the attitude combatted in Luke 10:25,37 and expressed in 1QS 1:4,10). Again Jesus opposes the traditional teaching and enunciates a more demanding ethic. Christians must love their enemies (v. 44). Otherwise they are no different than tax collectors and pagans, two groups classically despised by orthodox Jews—the first for working for Rome in collecting tribute from Israel and the second because of their false religion (v. 46). Almost all people look after their own. The true test of genuine Christianity is how believers treat those whom they are naturally

---

[50]R. T. France, *The Gospel according to Matthew*, TNTC (Grand Rapids: Eerdmans, 1985), 126.
[51]R. C. Tannehill, "The 'Focal Instance' as a Form of New Testament Speech: A Study of Matthew 5:39b-42," *JR* 50 (1970): 372-85. On this approach to Jesus' ethics more generally, cf. esp. A. E. Harvey, *Strenuous Commands: The Ethic of Jesus* (Philadelphia: Trinity, 1990).

inclined to hate or who mistreat or persecute them. Whatever emotions may be involved, "love" here refers to "generous, warm, costly self-sacrifice for another's good."[52] "Greet" (v. 47) refers to more than a simple hello, namely, heartfelt "expressions of desire for the other person's welfare."[53] People who so love and greet their enemies and pray for their persecutors thus prove themselves to be those, as in v. 9, who are growing in conformity to the likeness of their Heavenly Father (v. 45).

Jesus' followers must thus demonstrate a higher moral standard than the average unbeliever. A second rationale for loving one's enemies is that God loves them too. Among other ways, he demonstrates that love through common grace for all humanity in his good provisions in nature (the sun shining and rain falling, v. 45). "What reward will you get?" (v. 46) parallels "What are you doing more than others?" (v. 47), suggesting not the idea of compensation for doing good but the recurrent theme of the believer's distinctiveness.

5:48 The paragraph begun in v. 43 closes with a command that may equally summarize all six antitheses. "Perfect" here is better translated as "mature, whole," i.e., loving without limits (probably reflecting an underlying Aramaic *tamim*). Jesus is not frustrating his hearers with an unachievable ideal but challenging them to grow in obedience to God's will—to become more like him. J. Walvoord rightly observes, "While sinless perfection is impossible, godliness, in its biblical concept, is attainable."[54] But such godliness cannot be comprehensively formulated in a set of rules; the ethics of the sermon are suggestive, not exhaustive.[55] The parallel passage in Luke (6:36) uses synecdoche (the use of a part for the whole) to capture the essence of God's image in which we are being renewed, namely, mercy (cf. Exod 34:6-7a). Even as God sets higher standards in his new covenant than in the law, he reveals himself as more forgiving of our failures.[56]

---

[52]Carson, "Matthew," 158.

[53]R. H. Gundry, *Matthew: A Commentary on His Literary and Theological Art* (Grand Rapids: Eerdmans, 1982), 99.

[54]J. Walvoord, *Matthew: Thy Kingdom Come* (Chicago: Moody, 1974), 51.

[55]See S. Westerholm, *Jesus and Scribal Authority* (Lund: Gleerup, 1978), 113, for good comments on not applying Jesus' teaching as a new law.

[56]U. Luz, *Matthew 1-7: A Commentary*, EKK (Minneapolis: Augsburg, 1989), 349-51, has a profound summary of the significance of Jesus' exacting demands, particularly with respect to enemy-love. For example, "such unconditional signs of God's yes to the human being cannot and are not meant to answer the questions of the strategy to be applied in the struggle for social justice or concerning the survival of humankind. Their legitimacy and strength lie on a different level. . . . They are necessary in a fundamental sense and stand alongside of and *before* all realistic strategies of 'intelligent' love." For possible models of application to Christian living in community, see esp. S. Hauerwas and W. Willimon, *Resident Aliens* (Nashville: Abingdon, 1989).

c. True versus Hypocritical Piety (6:1-18). From illustrations of Jesus' teaching in relation to the law, Matthew now turns to Jesus' instruction on the manner in which persons should do God's will. Correct actions with improper motives still do not please God. The theme of internalizing God's standards continues, as Jesus stresses the importance of righteous behavior when no one but God is watching as over against public piety designed to elicit human praise rather than to glorify God. The three closely parallel examples of almsgiving, prayer, and fasting focus on three of the cardinal components of Jewish piety (see esp. Tob 12:8). The insertion of the Lord's Prayer makes the second section disproportionately longer than the other two. The theme of the entire sermon—the greater righteousness demanded of Jesus' disciples—clearly continues.

¹ **"Be careful not to do your 'acts of righteousness' before men, to be seen by them. If you do, you will have no reward from your Father in heaven.**

² **"So when you give to the needy, do not announce it with trumpets, as the hypocrites do in the synagogues and on the streets, to be honored by men. I tell you the truth, they have received their reward in full. ³But when you give to the needy, do not let your left hand know what your right hand is doing, ⁴so that your giving may be in secret. Then your Father, who sees what is done in secret, will reward you.**

(1) Heading (6:1). **6:1** The principle uniting all three illustrations appears first. Verse 1 does not contradict 5:16 because the motives in the two passages are entirely different. That which is done solely or primarily for personal honor or gain may accomplish its objective (v. 2b), but God will grant no further reward.

(2) Almsgiving (6:2-4). **6:2-4** In a society without social security or welfare, voluntary charity and donations for the destitute formed a key part of ancient Jewish life and remained an important virtue enjoined upon the righteous. But it was easy to abuse almsgiving by making it plain to others how generous the person was and thus receiving their adulation. It is not clear whether the trumpets "in the synagogues and on the streets" (v. 2) were literal or metaphorical (cf. our expression "blow your own horn"). The best guess may be that they refer to the noise and clang of throwing money into various collection receptacles.[57] But Jesus' point is unambiguous: his followers must not parade their piety or show off their good deeds. Such ostentation nullifies the possibility of any spiritual benefit for the almsgiver.

---

[57]See N. J. McEleney, "Does the Trumpet Sound or Resound? An Interpretation of Matthew 6:2," *ZNW* 76 (1985): 43-46.

The positive alternative Jesus commands is that we should give in such a way that there is no temptation for others to glorify the giver rather than God. Jesus' language again is figurative (v. 3 is literally possible only for those who undergo a lobotomy!) and does not imply that we must not keep track of giving or that we be irresponsible in stewardship of finances or refuse to disclose how we spend our money for the sake of demonstrating financial accountability. Jesus was simply explaining that the motive for charity must not be the desire for praise from others. In striking contrast stands the common approach to fund raising in many churches and Christian organizations in which lists of benefactors are published, often as an incentive for people to give. This kind of motive for giving or soliciting reflects hypocrisy (v. 2), pretending to honor God when in fact one is distracting attention from him. The reward humans can offer obviously refers to acclaim in this life, so the reward God will bestow or withhold (v. 4) probably also refers to spiritual benefit and growth in holiness in this life.

⁵ **"And when you pray, do not be like the hypocrites, for they love to pray standing in the synagogues and on the street corners to be seen by men. I tell you the truth, they have received their reward in full. ⁶But when you pray, go into your room, close the door and pray to your Father, who is unseen. Then your Father, who sees what is done in secret, will reward you. ⁷And when you pray, do not keep on babbling like pagans, for they think they will be heard because of their many words. ⁸Do not be like them, for your Father knows what you need before you ask him."**

(3) Prayer (6:5-15). **6:5-8** Verses 5-6 closely parallel vv. 2-4 but with respect to prayer. As with almsgiving, Jesus does not rule out all public behavior but stresses the private side of piety. Public prayer is very appropriate when practiced with right motives. But public orations should represent the overflow of a vibrant personal prayer life. What is more, prayer ought not to be used to gain plaudits, summarize a sermon, or communicate information to an audience but should reflect genuine conversation with God.[58]

Verses 7-8 add a second element to Jesus' teaching on prayer. We must not "babble" (an onomatopoeic word—*battalogeō*, literally, *to say batta*). In light of vv. 7b-8, this at least refers to a long-winded and probably flowery or rhetorical oration. "Vain repetitions" (KJV) should be taken as

---

[58]Cf. Ridderbos (*Matthew*, 124): "Since the presence of other people can so easily compromise the purity of this motive, prayer should always be as inconspicuous as possible." For an excellent, cross-cultural symposium on biblical and contemporary issues related to prayer, see D. A. Carson, ed., *Teach Us to Pray* (Grand Rapids: Baker, 1990). A good popular introduction to the theology of prayer is W. B. Hunter, *The God Who Hears* (Downers Grove: InterVarsity, 1986).

emphasizing "vain" and not "repetitions." The term may also refer to the uttering of nonsense syllables common to magical incantations in the pagan religions of Jesus' day. Verse 8 does not forbid prayer, as vv. 9-13 make clear, but calls for simplicity, directness, and sincerity in talking to God. Matthew 7:7-8 will urge persistence in prayer, but here we are reminded that God wants to give us good gifts; therefore, we need not badger him with our requests (cf. 7:11).[59] God knows our needs, but he has also chosen to grant some things only when his people pray (Jas 4:2).

9"This, then, is how you should pray:

'Our Father in heaven,
hallowed be your name,
10your kingdom come,
your will be done
on earth as it is in heaven.
11Give us today our daily bread.
12Forgive us our debts,
as we also have forgiven our debtors.
13And lead us not into temptation,
but deliver us from the evil one.'"

6:9-13 Jesus then gave his disciples the "Our Father," or the "Lord's Prayer." Actually, the "Lord's Prayer" is a better designation for John 17, whereas the model given here might be better entitled "The Disciples' Prayer." In light of vv. 7-8 it is highly ironic that this prayer has come to be repeated mechanically in many Christian traditions (already *Did.* 8:3 commanded Christians to recite it three times daily), accompanied by the notion that frequent repetition develops spirituality. Still, the prayer remains an excellent model; it is equally ironic that other Christian traditions have carefully avoided its use or recitation. The key word in v. 9a is "how." Verses 9b-13 illustrate key components and attitudes that Jesus' disciples should incorporate into their prayer lives. We may choose to pray these exact words thoughtfully and reflectively or to put into our own words similar concerns.[60] Close parallels appear in the standard Jew-

---

[59]Cf. Hobbs, *Matthew*, 73: "Prayer is not some battering ram by which we gain entrance to God's treasury. It is a receptacle by which we receive that which He already longs to give us." Cf. also the excellent selected comments on the virtue of Luther's simple, frequent, brief prayers, cited in Bruner, *Christbook*, 237.

[60]On the theology of the Lord's Prayer, see esp. J. M. Lochman, *The Lord's Prayer* (Grand Rapids: Eerdmans, 1990). For the distinctive Matthean form, see esp. B. Gerhardsson, "The Matthaen Version of the Lord's Prayer (Matt 6:9b-13): Some Observations," in *The New Testament Age*, ed. W. C. Weinrich (Macon, Ga.: Mercer University Press, 1984), 1:207-20. For implications for social ethics, see esp. M. H. Crosby, *Thy Will Be Done* (Maryknoll: Orbis, 1977).

ish Kaddish prayer and remind us that many Jews were not guilty of the hypocrisy warned against here.[61] The parallel in Luke 11:2-4 is usually seen as a more primitive version of the same account, though the direction of development could be reversed.[62] More likely the two reflect similar teachings of Jesus from two different occasions in his ministry.

The Greek "Father" (*pater*) probably translates the Aramaic *Abba* (cf. Mark 14:36). Use of this intimate term for God (almost equivalent to the English "Daddy") was virtually unparalleled in first-century Judaism. Christians should consider God as accessible as the most loving human parent. ("Father" should not be read as implying that God has gender or sexuality.) The phrase "in heaven" balances this intimacy with an affirmation of God's sovereignty and majesty. The use of the first-person plural pronouns throughout the prayer reminds us that our praying ought to reflect the corporate unity, desires, and needs of the entire church. The Lord's Prayer is not simply a private utterance. The intimacy Christians may have with their Heavenly Father is balanced also with insistence on reverence in the clause "hallowed be your name." "Name" refers to one's person, character, and authority. All that God stands for should be treated as holy and honored because of his utter perfection and goodness.

"Your kingdom come, your will be done on earth as it is in heaven" expresses the desire that the acknowledgment of God's reign and the accomplishment of his purposes take place in this world even as they already do in God's throne room. The first half of the prayer thus focuses exclusively on God and his agenda as believers adore, worship, and submit to his will before they introduce their own personal petitions.

The meaning of v. 11 depends largely on the very rare adjective *epiousios*. In addition to the traditional translation, "daily" bread, it could also mean bread *for tomorrow* (taken either as the next period of twenty-four hours or as the coming fullness of the kingdom)[63] or *necessary for existence*. The best lexical research suggests that the noneschatological interpretation of "bread for tomorrow" may be best.[64] Christians therefore should pray daily for the next day's provision of life's essentials as they recognize that all sustenance for one's life comes from God and that he makes no long-term future guarantees. The average affluent Westerner more than likely plans and prays for "annual bread" except perhaps in

---

[61]See Allen, *Matthew*, 60, for the text in translation. On a comparison of the prayer with Jewish thought more broadly, see J. J. Petuchowski and M. Brocke, eds., *The Lord's Prayer and Jewish Liturgy* (New York: Seabury, 1978).

[62]Sabourin, *Matthieu*, 78-79.

[63]For an influential interpretation of the Lord's Prayer as consistently eschatological in this sense, see J. Jeremias, *The Lord's Prayer* (Philadelphia: Fortress, 1964); R. E. Brown, "The Pater Noster as an Eschatological Prayer," *TS* 22 (1961): 175-208.

[64]See C. J. Hemer, "ἐπιούσιος," *JSNT* 22 (1984): 81-94.

times of extreme crisis. It is also worth noting that the prayer makes request for our needs and not our greed (cf. Jas 4:3).[65]

"Forgive us our debts" renders the Greek literally. Luke 11:4, however, refers to "sins," as does Matthew in vv. 14-15 (with the more specific *paraptōmata, trespasses* or *conscious transgressions*). Spiritual debts to God are first of all in view. Our plea for continued forgiveness as believers, requesting the restoration of fellowship with God following the alienation that sin produces, is predicated on our having forgiven those who have sinned against us. As v. 15 stresses, without this interpersonal reconciliation on the human level, neither can we be reconciled to God.

"Lead us not into temptation" does not imply "don't bring us to the place of temptation" or "don't allow us to be tempted." God's Spirit has already done both of these with Jesus (4:1). Nor does the clause imply "don't tempt us" because God has promised never to do that anyway (Jas 1:13).[66] Rather, in light of the probable Aramaic underlying Jesus' prayer, these words seem best taken as "don't let us succumb to temptation" (cf. Mark 14:38) or "don't abandon us to temptation."[67] We do of course periodically succumb to temptation but never because we have no alternative (1 Cor 10:13). So when we give in, we have only ourselves to blame. The second clause of v. 13 phrases the same plea positively, "Deliver us from evil" (or "from the evil one" [NIV marg.], from whom all evil ultimately comes). This parallelism renders less likely the alternate translation of the first clause as "do not bring us to the test" ("test" is an equally common rendering of *peirasmos*) either as times of trial in this life or as final judgment. If we are praying for rescue from the devil, he is more likely tempting than testing us (cf. under 4:1). God tests us in order to prove us and bring us to maturity (Jas 1:2-4; 1 Pet 1:6-9). Such tests should not be feared, nor should we pray for God to withhold them.[68]

Numerous late manuscripts add various forms of a conclusion to Jesus' prayer, probably based on 1 Chr 29:11-13, no doubt to give the prayer a "proper" doxology that it otherwise lacked. This well-known conclusion

---

[65]For further helpful background on "daily bread" in the ancient world, see E. M. Yamauchi, "The 'Daily Bread' Motif in Antiquity," *WTJ* 28 (1966): 145-56.

[66]With S. E. Porter ("Mt 6:13 and Lk 11:4: 'Lead Us Not into Temptation,'" *ExpTim* 101 [1990]: 359-62) it is undoubtedly valid to distinguish a final sense in which God does permit and therefore indirectly cause temptation from a more immediate cause-and-effect relationship, but it is not clear that this distinction solves the problems of the text at hand.

[67]See Allison and Davies, *Matthew,* 1:612-13, who cite *b. Ber.* 60b: "Bring me . . . not into the power of temptation." Cf. also E. Moore, "'Lead Us Not into Temptation,'" *ExpTim* 102 (1991): 171-72.

[68]Contra C. L. Blomberg, "Trial," in *ISBE* 4:904. A new approach to translating πειρασμός as "test" or "trial" appears in P. S. Cameron, "'Lead Us Not into Temptation'," *ExpTim* 101 (1990): 299-301, namely, "Do not judge us according to our deserts," but the linguistic basis for this rendering (נָסָה in Ps 26:2) is slender.

("for yours is the kingdom and the power and the glory forever. Amen.") appears in the NIV margin but almost certainly did not appear in Matthew's original text. It is absent, e.g., from אָ, B, D, f^1, various Latin and Coptic versions, and numerous church fathers. It nevertheless affords a very appropriate conclusion, and no one need campaign to do away with its use in churches today. Christians regularly and rightly utter many things in prayer that do not directly quote the autographs of Scripture.

14For if you forgive men when they sin against you, your heavenly Father will also forgive you. 15But if you do not forgive men their sins, your Father will not forgive your sins.

6:14-15 Verses 14-15 repeat in third-person form the thought of v. 12 and add the negative consequences of failure to forgive others. See the comments on v. 12 for more details, but note that Jesus is not claiming God's unwillingness to forgive recalcitrant sinners but disclosing their lack of capacity to receive such forgiveness.[69]

16 "When you fast, do not look somber as the hypocrites do, for they disfigure their faces to show men they are fasting. I tell you the truth, they have received their reward in full. 17But when you fast, put oil on your head and wash your face, 18so that it will not be obvious to men that you are fasting, but only to your Father, who is unseen; and your Father, who sees what is done in secret, will reward you."

(4) Fasting (6:16-18). **6:16-18** Jesus proceeds with the third example of a common element of Jewish piety. He himself has fasted for forty days (4:2-11). Pharisees typically fasted on Mondays and Thursdays, refraining from food but not from drink. In light of such texts as 9:14-17, fasting is more controversial in Christian circles than prayer or giving to the needy. Jesus apparently did not give this spiritual discipline a high priority, especially during his ministry, but he did anticipate that it would occur later (9:15). The only specific New Testament references to later Christian fasting come in contexts of seeking God's will in choosing church leaders (Acts 13:2-3; 14:23). As with almsgiving and prayer, those who fast must not advertise their piety by visible signs of suffering and deprivation.[70] Otherwise a person again gains accolades from people rather than from God. Instead people must groom themselves according to cultural norms in order to appear joyful and content. The same refrain

---

[69]C. F. D. Moule, "'. . . As We Forgive . . .'" in *Donum Gentilicum*, ed. E. Bammel, C. K. Barrett, and W. D. Davies (Oxford: Clarendon, 1978), 68-77.
[70]Cf. Gundry (*Matthew*, 111): "Ironically, the hypocrites made themselves unrecognizable (ἀφανίζουσιν) in trying to be recognized (φανῶσιν)."

of vv. 4b and 6b reappears for a third and final time (v. 18b) and rounds out this section of the sermon.

A. Plummer aptly summarizes vv. 1-18 as follows: "The light of a Christian character will shine before men and win glory for God without the artificial aid of public advertisement. Ostentatious religion may have its reward here, but it receives none from God."[71] Christians who judge successful ministries by external statistics such as attendance figures, membership, baptisms, and offerings should seriously rethink their criteria in light of Jesus' words here. God judges the greatness of his servants by searching their hearts, examining their inner attitudes, and seeing deeds done in secret. Doubtless, his evaluations of who most honors him will invert a substantial majority of his people's evaluations.

d. WEALTH AND WORRY: MONEY VERSUS REAL RICHES (6:19-34). The fourth section of Jesus' sermon collects a group of teachings that are not as obviously parallel as the Beatitudes, the antitheses, or his teaching on almsgiving, prayer, and fasting. A clear theme nevertheless unites these verses, contrasting earthly and spiritual treasures. This section links with 5:3-6:18 by warning that even when a person's behavior and attitudes are correct, the greater righteousness demanded of disciples is not present unless God and not money is served. Matthew 6:19-34 also links naturally with 6:1-18 by continuing the contrast between seeking human reward and desiring to please God.

19"Do not store up for yourselves treasures on earth, where moth and rust destroy, and where thieves break in and steal. 20But store up for yourselves treasures in heaven, where moth and rust do not destroy, and where thieves do not break in and steal. 21For where your treasure is, there your heart will be also."

(1) Two Masters (6:19-24). **6:19-21** Jesus commands his followers not to accumulate possessions they do not use for his work. Wealth in the ancient world, as often still today, regularly consisted of precious metals and cloth. Owners thus worried about attacks of moth and rust.[72] Both were common in the hot, sandy Palestinian climate. The danger of theft applies to almost all kinds of valuables in every time and place. Rather than accumulating material wealth, people should work for spiritual riches invulnerable to loss and death (cf. Luke 12:15-21).[73] Even if

---

[71]A. Plummer, *An Exegetical Commentary on the Gospel according to St. Matthew*, (London: E. Stock, 1909), 90.

[72]"Rust" is literally "eating," as perhaps in the corrosion of metal but also the gnawing of clothing by vermin. R. H. Mounce, *Matthew*, GNC (San Francisco: Harper and Row, 1985), 56, states that the rendering "rust" was introduced into English by Tyndale.

[73]On the definition of "treasure," see Louw and Nida, *Greek-English Lexicon*, 1:621, "That which is of exceptional value and kept safe."

people succeed in safeguarding all their earthly riches, they cannot control how long they will live. Spiritual treasure should be defined as broadly as possible—as everything that believers can take with them beyond the grave—e.g., holiness of character, obedience to all of God's commandments, souls won for Christ, and disciples nurtured in the faith. In this context, however, storing up treasures focuses particularly on the compassionate use of material resources to meet others' physical and spiritual needs, in keeping with the priorities of God's kingdom (vv. 25-34; cf. Luke 16:8-13).

Against the potential objection that material prosperity has no effect on one's spiritual condition, v. 21 adds that one's affections are inherently drawn to one's treasure. This does not imply that rich people cannot be Christians, although the first centuries of Christianity knew only a small number of them. It does imply that riches bring grave dangers, not least of which is the extra anxiety of having to protect one's possessions. To avoid those dangers, rich Christians must be characterized by generosity in giving and meticulous stewardship in using money for the Lord's work. F. W. Beare rightly notes that without some accumulation of capital, no new ventures can be easily undertaken: "The words assume that the treasures are hoarded; they are prized for their own sake, not put to work to create jobs and produce goods."[74] Nevertheless, most all people who are able to save and invest experience the temptation drastically to overestimate their genuine needs and/or to try to secure their futures against all calamity. Meanwhile, the truly destitute of the world continue to grow poorer.[75]

22"The eye is the lamp of the body. If your eyes are good, your whole body will be full of light. 23But if your eyes are bad, your whole body will be full of darkness. If then the light within you is darkness, how great is that darkness!"

6:22-23 Just as the "heart" (v. 21) forms the center of one's affections and commitments, the "eyes" enable the whole person to see. Good[76] and bad eyes probably parallel a good and bad heart and thus refer, respectively, to storing up treasures in heaven versus storing them up on earth. Verses 22-23 therefore restate the truth of the previous paragraph, that the way people handle their finances affects every other part of

---

[74]F. W. Beare, *The Gospel according to Matthew* (San Francisco: Harper and Row, 1981), 182.

[75]Two excellent treatments of wealth and poverty in the Gospels are D. P. Seccombe, *Possessions and the Poor in Luke-Acts* (Linz: SNTU, 1982); and T. E. Schmidt, *Hostility to Wealth in the Synoptic Gospels* (Sheffield: JSOT, 1987).

[76]"Good" is actually the more specific word ἁπλοῦς,'" implying *single-minded devotion* and/or *generosity*.

their lives, either for good or for bad. And if that which should lead to good actually causes evil, then the person is truly perverse (v. 23b).

²⁴ **"No one can serve two masters. Either he will hate the one and love the other, or he will be devoted to the one and despise the other. You cannot serve both God and Money."**

6:24   Against those who might protest that they can accumulate both spiritual and earthly treasures, Jesus replies that they have only two options. They must choose between competing loyalties. "Master" suggests a slaveowner who required total allegiance. People could not serve two masters in the way in which people today often work two jobs. "Money" is more literally *mammon*, referring to all of a person's material resources. Of course, many people do try to cherish both God and mammon, but ultimately only one will be chosen. The other will be "hated," even if only by neglect. "Love" and "hate" in Semitic thought are often roughly equivalent to *choose* and *not choose*.

Many perceptive observers have sensed that the greatest danger to Western Christianity is not, as is sometimes alleged, prevailing ideologies such as Marxism, Islam, the New Age movement or humanism but rather the all-pervasive materialism of our affluent culture. We try so hard to create heaven on earth and to throw in Christianity when convenient as another small addition to the so-called good life. Jesus proclaims that unless we are willing to serve him wholeheartedly in every area of life, but particularly with our material resources, we cannot claim to be serving him at all (cf. under 8:18-22).[77]

²⁵ **"Therefore I tell you, do not worry about your life, what you will eat or drink; or about your body, what you will wear. Is not life more important than food, and the body more important than clothes? ²⁶Look at the birds of the air; they do not sow or reap or store away in barns, and yet your heavenly Father feeds them. Are you not much more valuable than they? ²⁷Who of you by worrying can add a single hour to his life?**
²⁸ **"And why do you worry about clothes? See how the lilies of the field grow. They do not labor or spin. ²⁹Yet I tell you that not even Solomon in all his splendor was dressed like one of these. ³⁰If that is how God clothes the grass of the field, which is here today and tomorrow is thrown into the fire, will he not much more clothe you, O you of little faith? ³¹So do not worry, saying, 'What shall we eat?' or 'What shall we drink?' or 'What shall we wear?' ³²For the pagans run after all these things, and your heavenly Father knows that you need them. ³³But seek first his kingdom and his righteousness, and all these things will be given to you as well. ³⁴Therefore do not worry**

---

[77]Cf. esp. G. A. Getz, *A Biblical Theology of Material Possessions* (Chicago: Moody, 1990); R. J. Sider, *Rich Christians in an Age of Hunger*, rev. (Dallas: Word, 1990).

about tomorrow, for tomorrow will worry about itself. Each day has enough
trouble of its own."

(2) The Futility of Worry (6:25-34). **6:25-34** If, on the other hand,
we put trust in God first, God will take care of the rest of life. This renders worry unnecessary. "Worry" is the key word of this entire section,
since it occurs six times (vv. 25,27-28,31,34 [2x]). The KJV's "take no
thought" is definitely misleading here. Christians must plan for the future,
but they need not be anxious. Jesus illustrates his point by discussing the
basic provisions of food and clothing.

First, he focuses on the need for food. Birds in their wild state provide
a good example because they are tirelessly industrious. Jesus is not dis-
couraging hard work to provide for our needs. Yet despite their constant
efforts, birds remain far more dependent on the "whims" of nature (which
Jesus views as God's provisions) than are people. We who have so much
more opportunity to use creation for our own ends ought to worry even
less than birds.

Two additional rationales for Jesus' instruction follow. First, we are
more valuable in God's eyes because we are the only creatures made in
his image.[78] Second, worry doesn't accomplish anything anyway, at least
not in terms of enabling us to live longer. The NIV marginal note "single
cubit to his height" is a somewhat more natural translation of the Greek
than "single hour to his life," but it does not fit as well into the context.
Adding a foot and one half to one's height is not the trifling amount Jesus'
flow of thought seems to demand, and stature does not fit the context of
provisions of food and clothing nearly as well as longevity.

To illustrate God's provision of clothing, Jesus next directs attention to
"the lilies of the field" (perhaps a reference to wild flowers and grasses
more generally). "See how" is better translated "learn carefully from"
(*katamathete*). Uncultivated vegetation does much less to provide for itself
than do birds, yet God adorns it with beauty that at times surpasses the
greatest splendor of human raiment (on Solomon's wealth, cf. 1 Kgs 4:20-
34; 7:1-51; 10:14-29). "Labor" (toiling in the field) and spinning (sewing
clothing at home) probably refer, respectively, to the characteristic occu-
pations of men and women in ancient rural culture. Yet plants prove even
more fragile than birds and more short-lived than humans. People even
picked plants and used them as fuel for the ovens in which they baked
bread.[79] If God lavishes such concern over the rest of his creation, how
much more does he love us! Again, Jesus uses the characteristically

---

[78]We cannot help thinking of the perverse inversion of God's values among people who
campaign more for animal rights than for human rights (including especially those of unborn
humans).

[79]Bratcher, *Matthew*, 68.

Jewish type of reasoning—from the lesser to the greater. If the logic of his argument be granted, then worry can only result from a lack of genuine belief in God's goodness and mercy. R. Mounce says, "Worry is practical atheism and an affront to God."[80] Anxiety characterized pagan religions, which were dominated by fears of a capricious and despotic deity who constantly had to be appeased.[81] In its modern, irreligious garb, pagan anxiety displays a great preoccupation with physical exercise and diet without a corresponding concern for spiritual growth and nutrition.[82] Verse 32a recalls the logic of 5:47; v. 32b parallels and recalls 6:8b.

Verse 33 brings this paragraph to its climax. When priorities regarding treasures in heaven and on earth are right, God will provide for fundamental human needs. Seeking first the righteousness of the kingdom implies obedience to all of Jesus' commands and shows that the thesis of 5:20 continues to be advanced. Of course, the major problem with the promise "all these things [food, drink, clothing] will be given to you" is the contrary experience of many Christians throughout history who have suffered deprivation and even starvation. One possible solution to this problem is to reserve all guarantees for the age to come. "Will be given" does not specify when God will provide. To be sure, the fullness of the kingdom will eradicate all suffering for God's people, but it is hard to see why Jesus would rule out worry in the present age if his promise applies only to a distant future. And if God's kingdom has already been inaugurated, then believers should expect to receive in this age the firstfruits of its material blessings. Hence, v. 33b is probably to be interpreted in light of Luke 12:33 and Mark 10:30a, which presuppose the sharing of goods within the Christian community.[83] When God's people corporately seek first his priorities, they will by definition take care of the needy in their fellowships. When one considers that over 50 percent of all believers now live in the Two-Thirds World and that a substantial majority of those believers live below what we would consider the poverty line, a huge challenge to First-World Christianity emerges. Without a doubt, most individual and church budgets need drastic realignment in terms of what

---

[80]Mounce, *Matthew*, 58. Cf. M. Green, *Matthew*, 35-36.

[81]An excellent introduction to the pagan religions of the biblical world is J. Finegan, *Myth and Mystery* (Grand Rapids: Baker, 1989).

[82]In this context also, Schweizer, *Matthew*, 165, raises the provocative question of the motivation and legitimacy of human efforts to prolong life artificially when allowing death to take its natural course might be far more humane.

[83]Cf. R. A. Guelich (*Mark 1–8:26*, WBC [Dallas: Word, 1989], 373): "Part of the presence of the Kingdom is indeed material blessings. Therefore, we can hardly live under God's reign, receive his blessings, and not use them to help alleviate the evil of hunger and need elsewhere."

Christians spend on themselves versus what they spend on others (cf. 2 Cor 8:13-15).[84]

In v. 34 Jesus returns full circle to the beginning of his discussion (v. 25), encouraging daily dependence on God (cf. also v. 11). As if to underscore that v. 33 will never be implemented absolutely in this age, he reminds his audience of the daily *evil* (a more literal rendering than NIV "trouble") that persists. But there are enough non-Christian sources of evil for believers (most notably the persecutions predicted in 5:10-11) that Christian self-centeredness ought never compound the problems of fellow believers who live in poverty.

e. HOW TO TREAT OTHERS (7:1-12). This section seems more loosely tied together than 5:3–6:34. Certainly, the demanding nature of the greater righteousness required of Jesus' disciples means that they have plenty to do just to take stock of their own spiritual progress. Christians scarcely can afford to be judgmental. Verses 1-6 seem to be united by the theme of how believers treat each other, specifically in judging or not judging one another, while vv. 7-11 illustrate how God treats his people. Verse 12 rounds out this section and probably summarizes the body of the sermon as a whole, with its classic statement of ideal interpersonal behavior.[85]

[1] "Do not judge, or you too will be judged. [2]For in the same way you judge others, you will be judged, and with the measure you use, it will be measured to you.

(1) On Judging Others (7:1-6). **7:1-2** "Judge" (*krinō*) can imply *to analyze* or *evaluate* as well as *to condemn* or *avenge*. The former senses are clearly commanded of believers (e.g., 1 Cor 5:5; 1 John 4:1), but the latter are reserved for God. Even on those occasions when we render a negative evaluation of others, our purposes should be constructive and not retributive. So Jesus is here commanding his followers not to be characterized by judgmental attitudes (cf. Williams, "Stop criticizing others"). The immediate practical rationale for his command is that others, including God, may treat us in the same manner we treat them. Verse 2 provides the premise for v. 12.[86]

[3] "Why do you look at the speck of sawdust in your brother's eye and pay no attention to the plank in your own eye? [4]How can you say to your brother,

---

[84]T. E. Schmidt ("Burden, Barrier, Blasphemy: Wealth in Matt 6:33, Luke 14:33, and Luke 16:15," *TrinJ* n.s. 9 [1988]: 188): "To stand still because the end is so far away is to miss the point of discipleship as a journey. Most of us could travel a considerable distance on that road before anyone suspected us of extreme obedience."

[85]Cf. Ridderbos, *Matthew*, 143, who identifies 7:1-12 as about righteousness in relation to one's neighbor and a further explication of 5:13-16.

[86]On the connection of v. 1 to vv. 2-6, see J. D. M. Derrett, "Christ and Reproof (Matthew 7.1-5/Luke 6.37-42)," *NTS* 34 (1988): 271-81.

'Let me take the speck out of your eye,' when all the time there is a plank in your own eye? ⁵You hypocrite, first take the plank out of your own eye, and then you will see clearly to remove the speck from your brother's eye.

7:3-5 Jesus now illustrates the foolishness of most judgmentalism with the hyperbole of the speck and the plank. He is clearly not concerned about literal pieces of foreign matter in people's eyes but about his followers' moral failures. How often we criticize others when we have far more serious shortcomings in our own lives. Such behavior offers another example of hypocrisy (recall 6:2,5,16), especially when we treat fellow believers this way, whose sins God has already forgiven. But v. 5 makes clear that vv. 3-4 do not absolve us of responsibility to our brothers and sisters in Christ. Rather, once we have dealt with our own sins, we are then in a position gently and lovingly to confront and try to restore others who have erred (cf. Gal 6:1).

⁶"Do not give dogs what is sacred; do not throw your pearls to pigs. If you do, they may trample them under their feet, and then turn and tear you to pieces.

7:6 Verse 6 seems cryptic and unconnected to the immediate context, but it probably further qualifies the command against judging.[87] One must try to discern whether presenting to others that which is holy will elicit nothing but abuse or profanity. In these instances restraint is required. "Do not give dogs what is sacred" and "do not throw your pearls to pigs" are obviously parallel in meaning, so it is natural to assume that both dogs and pigs are the subjects of the verbs "trample," "turn," and "tear" in the second half of the verse. But the verse may form a chiasmus. After all, pigs are more likely to trample than dogs, while dogs more normally tear things in pieces than do pigs (cf. GNB: "Do not give what is holy to dogs—they will only turn and attack you. Do not throw your pearls in front of pigs—they will only trample them underfoot").[88]

The dogs described here are wild scavengers. The pigs best represent unclean animals for Jews. Both are natural opposites to what is holy or, like pearls, of great value. Both "dogs" and "pigs" were regularly used as pejorative epithets for Gentiles within ancient Judaism. Jesus is using the

---

[87]For a survey of interpretations, see T. J. Bennett, "Matthew 7:6—A New Interpretation," *WTJ* 49 (1987): 371-86, although it is not clear that Bennett's alternative—that Jesus is referring to what others, and not necessarily he himself, consider to be holy or profane—improves any on the more established interpretations. Frequent proposals regarding development from the underlying Aramaic have taken most current form in S. Llewelyn, "Mt 7:6a: Mistranslation or Interpretation," *NovT* 31 (1989): 97-103.

[88]See esp. H. von Lips, "Schweine füttert Man, Hunde nicht—ein Versuch, das Rätsel von Matthäus 7,6 zu lösen," *ZNW* 79 (1988): 165-86.

terms equally pejoratively but in the more general sense of those who are ungodly (cf. 2 Pet 2:22 for the same combination). Certainly for him these would include those who heaped scorn upon his message, which ironically occurred most commonly among his fellow Jews and among the more conservative religious teachers and leaders (cf. Ps 22:16).[89] The number of parallels in modern Christianity to this phenomenon remain frightening. Jesus is obviously not telling his followers not to preach to certain kinds of people, but he does recognize that after sustained rejection and reproach, it is appropriate to move on to others (cf. Paul's regular practice in Acts—e.g., 13:46; 18:6; 19:9). Bruner's additional applications prove equally incisive:

> There is a form of evangelism that urges Christians to use every opportun
> ity to share the gospel. Unfortunately, insensitive evangelism often proves
> harmful not only to the obdurate whose heart is hardened by the undifferen-
> tiating evangelist, but harmful also to the gospel that is force-fed. . . . Ag-
> gressive evangelism gets converts and counts them, but we are never able to
> count those turned away from the gospel for the numbers of the offended
> are never tallied.[90]

The cultic language of "what is sacred," probably referring to consecrated food, has from as early as the end of the first century suggested the bread and wine of the Lord's Supper (cf. *Did.* 9:5). Here, however, it is not clear why dogs would spurn food and turn on the one offering it, but it is completely understandable if something other than food was offered to animals expecting to satisfy their hunger.

7 "Ask and it will be given to you; seek and you will find; knock and the door will be opened to you. 8For everyone who asks receives; he who seeks finds; and to him who knocks, the door will be opened.

9 "Which of you, if his son asks for bread, will give him a stone? 10Or if he asks for a fish, will give him a snake? 11If you, then, though you are evil, know how to give good gifts to your children, how much more will your Father in heaven give good gifts to those who ask him!

(2) God's Generosity (7:7-11). **7:7-11** In anticipating but going beyond the principle of v. 12, Jesus tells how God treats people at least as well as and often even better than they treat each other. Verses 7-11 may also link back with the rest of the sermon in that they show people how to get the help they need to obey all that Jesus has previously commanded. We must ask, seek, and knock—petitioning God with an expectant attitude. As Heavenly Father, God will respond with "good gifts," just as otherwise

---

[89]Cf. Gundry, *Matthew*, 122-23, who takes the animals as referring to those from among God's people who turn on the righteous in persecution.

[90]Bruner, *Christbook*, 275-76.

sinful human fathers usually do. Isaiah 49:15 uses the image of a mother to convey the same truth about God's care and is aware of exceptions in the human realm which do not apply to God. Strikingly, Jesus dissociates himself from sinful humanity by using the second-person form of address ("though *you* are evil," v. 11).

The rhetorical questions of vv. 9-10 imply a negative answer and are based on the similarities in appearance between small loaves of bread and stones and between certain eel-like fish and snakes. No loving parent would try to trick his or her children into thinking their requests had been granted by such deceptive substitutions. "How much more" logic prevails again. Even if human parents did occasionally prove untrustworthy (and far too often they do), God would never so mistreat his children. He always gives good things. "Give" is the key word throughout vv. 7-11, appearing five times as well as linking back with v. 6. The "good gifts" God gives include everything that pertains to seeking first his kingdom and its righteousness (6:33).[91] They do not necessarily correspond to everything for which we ask. The commands of vv. 7-8 are in the present tense, suggesting persistent prayer over a period of time. "It" in v. 7 is somewhat misleading. The word does not refer to any particular thing requested but forms part of a divine passive construction that means *ask and God will give you [what he deems best].*

Jesus also presupposes that his listeners will recall his teaching in the Lord's prayer in which one insists that God's will be done (6:7-8). Those who today claim that in certain contexts it is unscriptural to pray "if it is the Lord's will"[92] are both heretical and dangerous. Often our prayers are not answered as originally desired because we do not share God's perspective in knowing what is ultimately a good gift for us. We are especially tempted to think of the values of this world (e.g., health and wealth) rather than spiritual values. Not surprisingly, the parallel passage in Luke uses synecdoche to replace "good gifts" with "the Holy Spirit" (Luke 11:13)—the preeminent example of a good and perfect gift coming down from above.[93]

[12]So in everything, do to others what you would have them do to you, for this sums up the Law and the Prophets.

(3) The Golden Rule (7:12). **7:12** In view of God's generosity to us, treating others in the manner we would like ourselves to be treated is

---

[91]Sand, *Matthäus*, 148.

[92]Cf., e.g., K. Hagin, as quoted in B. Barron, *The Health and Wealth Gospel* (Downers Grove: InterVarsity, 1987), 103-4.

[93]Luke also replaces the bread/stone comparison with an egg/scorpion comparison. In light of the almost verbatim parallelism between the three clauses of Matt 7:7-8 and Luke 11:9-10, it is natural to assume that Matthew and Luke have each selected two elements of an originally tripartite illustration here too.

the least we can do. "As you would have them" does not imply "in order that they might," as some have mistakenly thought.[94] Verse 12 embraces an impressive amount of scriptural teaching, including, as Jesus says, the "Law and the Prophets" (the Old Testament).[95] This epigram has become known as the Golden Rule because of its central role in Christian ethics. Jesus assumes no pathological deviations in which one would desire to harm oneself, and he presupposes the perspective of disciples who seek what is God's desire rather than self-aggrandizement.

Many parallels to this "rule" appear in the history of religion. Of those closest in time and milieu to Jesus, see especially Tob 4:15, Hillel in b. Sabb. 31a, and Did. 1:2.[96] Most of these parallels phrase the rule negatively (sometimes called the "silver rule"), implying, "Don't do to others what you don't want them to do to you." It is not clear how significant this difference is, but Jesus' positive phrasing does remind us of the principle that we can never fully carry out Christ's commands. As Mounce explains: "In its negative form, the Golden Rule could be satisfied by doing nothing. The positive form moves us to action on behalf of others."[97] But from a Christian perspective even negative commands imply positive action. Thus, e.g., in the first antithesis (5:21-26) even if we succeed in not murdering and in not hating or verbally abusing others, we still have not completely obeyed until we earnestly seek others' well-being. With its reference to "the Law and the Prophets," 7:12 ties back in with 5:17 and provides a frame to bracket the body of the sermon.

f. CONCLUSION: ONLY TWO WAYS (7:13-27). The rest of the Sermon on the Mount adds no new commandments but encourages obedience to those already given while warning against disobedience. By three illustrations, Jesus makes plain that there are ultimately only two categories of people in the world, despite the endless gradations we might otherwise perceive. He utilizes a "two-ways" genre well-known from other Jewish literature (e.g., Deut 30:15-20; 2 Esdr 7:1-16; cf. also Did. 1:1–6:7). These three illustrations contrast those who select the narrow rather than the wide gate and road (vv. 13-14), those who bear good rather than bad fruit (vv. 15-23), and those who build their homes on solid rock rather than shifting sand (vv. 24-27). In each case the first category refers to those who hear, obey, and are saved; the second, to those who only hear and so are destroyed. In each case eternal life and judgment are at stake.

---

[94] As, e.g., P. Ricoeur, "The Golden Rule: Exegetical and Theological Perplexities," NTS 36 (1990): 392-97.

[95] "Sums up" is literally "is" but could also be translated "fulfill" (Carson, "Matthew," 188).

[96] For a full list of parallels, see V. P. Furnish, The Love Commandment in the New Testament (Nashville: Abingdon, 1972), 63.

[97] Mounce, Matthew, 63.

13 "Enter through the narrow gate. For wide is the gate and broad is the road that leads to destruction, and many enter through it. **14**But small is the gate and narrow the road that leads to life, and only a few find it.

(1) The Narrow versus the Wide Gate/Road (7:13-14). **7:13-14** These verses provide an important balance to 24:14. The fulfillment of the Great Commission does not imply that a majority will respond with genuine faith. The percentage of true believers in places and times in which being "Christian" is popular is perhaps not that different from the percentage of Christians in times of persecution, when few dare to profess who are not deeply committed. "Wide" versus "narrow" may refer not only to the majority versus the minority but also to relative levels of difficulty or ease. "Narrow" in v. 14 comes from the verb *thlibō*, meaning *to experience trouble or difficulty*, while "broad" in v. 13 can have overtones of *prosperous*.[98]

15 "Watch out for false prophets. They come to you in sheep's clothing, but inwardly they are ferocious wolves. **16**By their fruit you will recognize them. Do people pick grapes from thornbushes, or figs from thistles? **17**Likewise every good tree bears good fruit, but a bad tree bears bad fruit. **18**A good tree cannot bear bad fruit, and a bad tree cannot bear good fruit. **19**Every tree that does not bear good fruit is cut down and thrown into the fire. **20**Thus, by their fruit you will recognize them.
21 "Not everyone who says to me, 'Lord, Lord,' will enter the kingdom of heaven, but only he who does the will of my Father who is in heaven. **22**Many will say to me on that day, 'Lord, Lord, did we not prophesy in your name, and in your name drive out demons and perform many miracles?' **23**Then I will tell them plainly, 'I never knew you. Away from me, you evildoers!'

(2) Good versus Bad Fruit (7:15-23). **7:15-23** Jesus now explicitly addresses the situation in which greater numbers profess Christ than actually follow him. He describes some of the pretenders as "false prophets," those who claim to be God's spokespersons but are not. Yet, like wolves in sheep's clothing, they give all external appearances of promoting authentic Christianity in both word and work.[99] "Prophets," as in the Old Testament, refer to those who either foretell or "forthtell" God's word.[100]

Verses 21-22 enumerate some of the ways in which individuals can masquerade as Christians. They may verbally affirm that Jesus is their

---

[98] A. H. M'Neile, *The Gospel according to St. Matthew* (London: Macmillan, 1915), 94.

[99] For possible first-century Jewish and Christian examples of these, see D. Hill, "False Prophets and Charismatics: Structure and Interpretation in Matthew 7,15-23," *Bib* 57 (1976): 327-48. It is not as clear, however, with Hill, that the false prophets and "charismatics" refer to two separate groups of individuals.

[100] To date, the definitive study of NT prophecy in its milieu is D. E. Aune, *Prophecy in Early Christianity and the Ancient Mediterranean World* (Grand Rapids: Eerdmans, 1983).

Master, perhaps even with great joy and enthusiasm, but such claims must issue in lives of obedience (an important qualification of Rom 10:10-13). Some may be preachers. Others perform exorcisms (see comments under 8:28-34), and some work various kinds of miracles (see comments under chaps. 8–9 *passim*). We are reminded that signs and wonders can come from sources other than God, including both the demonic world and human manufacture (cf. Acts 19:13-16; Rev 13:13-14). According to Allison and Davies, "The call to righteousness encompasses personal virtue, private devotion, and unselfish social behavior; and to these things seemingly supernatural powers are incidental."[101] It also is interesting that prophecy, exorcisms, and miracle workings all characterize "charismatic" activity, which has a tendency, by no means universal, to substitute enthusiasm and the spectacular for more unglamorous obedience in the midst of suffering. But these external demonstrations prove nothing. The question is whether one's heart has been cleansed inwardly (v. 15) or whether apparent acts of ministry still serve only self, *rapaciously* (Greek *harpages*; NIV "ferocious") using others for one's own ends (cf. Acts 20:29-30).

At the same time, v. 16 suggests that outward behavior may enable one to distinguish between true and false Christians. Like inspecting vegetation, which inevitably discloses fruit in keeping with its species and state of health, so also one can look for good or bad (literally, *rotten or worthless*) spiritual fruit (vv. 17-20). Verse 21 further equates this fruit with doing "the will of my Father who is in heaven," precisely what the Sermon on the Mount is elaborating. Of course, any individual action can prove insincere, but those who have detailed opportunities to scrutinize both the private and public behavior of people who claim to be Jesus' followers (and particularly who can watch how those people respond after sinning) will have the best chance of evaluating the genuineness of professed commitments to Christ. It is worth emphasizing, however, that one can never know with absolute certainty the spiritual state of any other individual.

Judgment for those who were masquerading as disciples leads to eternal separation from Christ. The metaphor of cutting down and burning the plant that bears no good fruit (v. 19) echoes verbatim the second half of 3:10. Verse 23 repeats this theme of God's judgment in a way that makes clear that true Christians cannot lose their salvation. Jesus addresses those he rejects by declaring, "I never knew you." Perhaps these people fooled many on earth, but Jesus knows that they never had a saving relationship with him.[102]

---

[101] Allison and Davies, *Matthew* 1:729.

[102] Allison and Davies (*Matthew* 1:717) refer to this expression as a formula of renunciation equivalent to "I never recognized you as one of my own."

24 "Therefore everyone who hears these words of mine and puts them into practice is like a wise man who built his house on the rock. 25The rain came down, the streams rose, and the winds blew and beat against that house; yet it did not fall, because it had its foundation on the rock. 26But everyone who hears these words of mine and does not put them into practice is like a foolish man who built his house on sand. 27The rain came down, the streams rose, and the winds blew and beat against that house, and it fell with a great crash."

(3) Wise versus Foolish Builders (7:24-27). **7:24-27** It is not enough simply to hear Jesus' call or even to respond with some temporary flurry of good deeds. Rather, we must build a solid foundation that combines authentic commitment to Christ with persevering obedience. Jesus graphically illustrates his point with a parable (on which see comments under chap. 13). The wise person living in the Palestinian desert would erect a dwelling on a secure rock to protect the house from the flash floods that sudden storms created. The foolish person would build directly on the sand and would have no protection against the devastation of the elements.[103] So too Judgment Day will come like a flood to disclose which spiritual structures will endure. Preliminary crises may also reveal authentic and inauthentic spirituality. In fact, often only in times of crisis can one's faith be truly proven. This parable concludes Jesus' "two ways" discussion and forms a fitting conclusion to the sermon as a whole by making plain that there is no valid reason for refusing Christ's appeal. As R. T. France states succinctly, "The teaching of the Sermon on the Mount is not to be admired but to be obeyed."[104]

28When Jesus had finished saying these things, the crowds were amazed at his teaching, 29because he taught as one who had authority, and not as their teachers of the law.

g. RESPONSE (7:28-29). **7:28-29** Jesus' words have now ended ("finished," from *teleō*, suggests the derivative sense of *fulfillment*). Not surprisingly, the crowds marvel and contrast Jesus' teaching with that of the scribes. For them the difference was one of authority. Of course the scribes and Pharisees were religious authorities, but their right to speak was always based on their ability to quote Scripture or subsequent Jewish teachers and tradition. Strikingly, Jesus quotes Scripture in his sermon only to reinterpret it, he cites no human authorities or tradition, and he

---

[103]Luke 6:47-49 seems to have contemporized or contextualized the parable for a more Hellenistic audience familiar with houses built on basements. The changes of imagery do not alter the meaning of the passage as a whole; rather, they help to preserve it in a new setting. Cf. S. J. Kistemaker, *The Parables of Jesus* (Grand Rapids: Baker, 1980), 7-8.

[104]France, *Matthew*, 146.

speaks with directness and confidence that he himself is bringing God's message for a new era in human history. Such preaching reflects either the height of presumption and heresy or the fact that he was a true spokesman for God, whom we dare not ignore.

─────────── *SECTION OUTLINE CONTINUED* ───────────

3. Paradigmatic Healing (8:1–9:35)
   a. Jesus Heals the Outcasts in Israel (8:1-17)
     (1) Touching the Leper: Response to Bodily "Uncleanness" (8:1-4)
     (2) Rewarding the Centurion: Response to Ethnic "Uncleanness" (8:5-13)
     (3) Healing Peter's Mother-in-Law: Response to Gender "Uncleanness" (8:14-15)
     (4) Summary and Conclusion (8:16-17)
   b. Jesus Demonstrates His Divine Authority and Demands Decisive Discipleship (8:18–9:17)
     (1) The Demands of Discipleship: Inadequate Responses (8:18-22)
       (a) A Scribe's Overeagerness (8:18-20)
       (b) A Would-Be Disciple's Undereagerness (8:21-22)
     (2) Divine Authority over Satan's Realm (8:23–9:8)
       (a) Stilling the Storm: Response to Disaster (8:23-27)
       (b) Exorcising the Gadarene Demoniac: Response to Demons (8:28–9:1)
       (c) Healing the Paralytic: Response to Disease (9:2-8)
     (3) The Demands of Discipleship: Adequate Responses (9:9-17)
       (a) Matthew Becomes a Disciple (9:9-13)
       (b) John's Disciples Question Jesus (9:14-17)
   c. Jesus Continues to Heal: Hints of Hostility Loom Ahead (9:18-35)
     (1) Stopping a Hemorrhage and Awakening the Dead: Positive Publicity (9:18-26)
     (2) Giving Sight to the Blind: Hints of Danger (9:27-31)
     (3) Giving Speech to the Mute: Sharp Division (9:32-34)
     (4) Conclusion (9:35)

3. Paradigmatic Healing (8:1–9:35)

Matthew sets the stage for chaps. 4–9 with his summary of Jesus' ministry of teaching, preaching, and healing in 4:23. The Sermon on the Mount (chaps. 5–7) has beautifully illustrated his teaching and preaching; now Matthew turns to Jesus' healing. Matthew 9:35 forms an inclusio (a framing device in which a passage begins and ends with similar statements or concepts) with 4:23 by repeating verbatim how Jesus was "teaching in their synagogues, preaching the good news of the kingdom, and healing every disease and sickness." Matthew 9:36 echoes 5:1 and should thus be viewed as introducing the next sermon of Jesus (10:5). This leaves 8:1–9:35 as a major unit of material. Here Matthew presents nine miracle stories (containing ten actual miracles plus summaries of several others). These accounts are arranged into three groups of three stories each. All but one of the miracles involve physical healings of various individuals. The lone exception, the stilling of the storm, is probably to be seen as a kind of exorcism (see comments under 8:23-27) and thus a "healing" of nature appropriate for this collection of miracles. In between the three triads appear two pairs of passages dealing with discipleship. The first pair (8:18-22) seems clearly to introduce the narrative that follows (8:23-27). The second pair (9:9-17) is not as clearly tied to either the preceding or subsequent narrative but probably is meant to tie back in with the previous passage (9:2-8).

These two chapters thus subdivide into: three healings of illness, focusing on Jesus' ministry to social outcasts (8:1-17); negative and positive paradigms of discipleship, framing three dramatic miracles of Jesus which point to his divine nature and sovereignty over Satan's realm (8:18-9:17); and three more accounts of healings, illustrating the growing polarization of responses to the person of Christ (9:18-35).[1] Most of the passages in Matt 8–9 are paralleled in either Mark or Luke or both, but they often appear in quite different contexts, suggesting that one or more of the Gospel writers were arranging their material more thematically than chronologically. This is certainly true of Matthew; explicitly chronological connections between passages appear only half of the time in these two chapters (in the Greek, only in 8:23,28; 9:18,27,32). On the whole question of the supernatural world view assumed here, see comments under 1:18-25 and the literature there cited.[2]

a. Jesus Heals the Outcasts in Israel (8:1-17).   In this section Jesus touches a leper, who was ritually unclean due to his bodily disease. He rewards and praises the faith of a Gentile centurion who was an outcast among Jews due to his ethnic background. He heals and cares for a woman, who was usually treated as a second-class citizen due to her gender. In each case Jesus ignores cultural taboos and lavishes compassion upon the ostracized. These three passages summarize the wider healing

---

[1]Cf. esp. B. F. Drewes, "The Composition of Matthew 8–9," *SEAJT* 12 (1971): 92-101; L. Sabourin, *L'Évangile selon saint Matthieu et ses principaux parallèles* (Rome: Biblical Institute Press, 1978), 101.

[2]For good theological treatments of these chapters and of Matthew's views of healing miracles more generally, see, respectively, J. D. Kingsbury, "Observations on the 'Miracle Chapters of Matthew 8–9,'" *CBQ* 40 (1978): 559-73; J. P. Heil, "Significant Aspects of the Healing Miracles in Matthew," *CBQ* 41 (1979): 274-87. For an excellent popular exposition of Matt 8–9, see D. A. Carson, *When Jesus Confronts the World* (Grand Rapids: Baker, 1987).

ministry of Jesus. Characteristically, Matthew finds the fulfillment of Scripture in Jesus' actions.

¹When he came down from the mountainside, large crowds followed him. ²A man with leprosy came and knelt before him and said, "Lord, if you are willing, you can make me clean."

(1) Touching the Leper: Response to Bodily "Uncleanness" (8:1-4).
8:1 Verse 1 can be taken as the end of the section containing the Sermon on the Mount. It creates closure with 5:1 by referring to the crowds and by describing Jesus' coming down from the mountain he had previously ascended. But *kai idou* ("and behold"—untranslated in NIV) in v. 2 creates a closer link between 8:1 and 2, and the main verb of v. 1 ("followed") provides a fitting introduction to the second of the two key concerns of 8:1–9:35: Christology (who is this Jesus?) and discipleship (how do we respond to him?).

8:2 The reader is struck immediately by the sudden appearance of a leper, one who epitomized physical and ritual uncleanness. Lepers were ostracized from society and lived in "colonies." They still exist in many parts of the world today, but the closest counterparts with which most people are familiar may be AIDS victims.[3] The leper introduced in v. 2 displays a great audacity to mingle with such a large crowd, in apparent defiance of Lev 13:46,[4] but he certainly treats Jesus with great respect. First, he kneels (a posture appropriate for adoration), then he calls Jesus "Lord," which by Matthew's time regularly referred to Christ's divinity.[5] The leper himself did not likely worship Jesus or acknowledge him as God in the way Christians later would, but Matthew no doubt saw these gestures as appropriately foreshadowing more explicit discipleship. The leper reveals an astonishing confidence in Jesus' power ("you can"), especially in light of the Jewish belief that cures of lepers were as difficult as resurrections from the dead (based originally on 2 Kgs 5:7). At the same time, the leper defers to Jesus' sovereignty ("if you are willing"). These twin thrusts are crucial in all Christian prayers for healing.

³Jesus reached out his hand and touched the man. "I am willing," he said. "Be clean!" Immediately he was cured of his leprosy. ⁴Then Jesus said to him,

---

[3] G. T. Montague, *Companion God: A Cross-Cultural Commentary on the Gospel of Matthew* (New York: Paulist, 1989), 110.

[4] The entire chapter of Lev 13 gives laws regarding lepers, though this term, as also in Matthew, embraced a wide variety of infectious skin diseases. So it is not certain whether this man was afflicted with what we today technically know as "Hansen's disease."

[5] Even the term "came before" (from προσέρχομαι) is a key word for Matthew, describing others who approach Jesus with requests and employing a cultic term with overtones of worship. See J. R. Edwards, "The use of προσέρχεσθαι in the Gospel of Matthew," *JBL* 106 (1987): 65-74.

"See that you don't tell anyone. But go, show yourself to the priest and offer the gift Moses commanded, as a testimony to them."

8:3 Jesus declares that he is willing and cures the man. In so doing, he extends his hand to touch him. This gesture proves at least as shocking as the leper's original approach and request. Matthew's readers will soon learn that it was unnecessary for Jesus to touch the man in order to heal him (see vv. 5-13), so obviously he is making a point by means of an action that others could easily interpret as breaking the law (by defiling himself; cf. Lev 5:3). Whether or not he actually did defile himself is debated (since his touch made clean the unclean) but largely irrelevant. Jesus' gesture made clear that he was not concerned with others' taboos and dramatically demonstrated that God's love extends to even the most outcast of society. The cleansing, which was even more significant ritually than physically, was instantaneous. No one could fairly doubt that a miracle had occurred.

8:4 Here appears the first of several occasions in Matthew (and the other Gospels) in which Jesus commands silence in a context in which one would have expected him to encourage people to proclaim his deeds. The motif has often been referred to as the "messianic secret," especially since the seminal work of W. Wrede nearly a century ago. Wrede believed that these injunctions to silence were later additions of the early church designed to account for how it came to believe in Jesus as the Messiah, when in fact he had never made such claims or done anything to justify such recognition.[6] It is increasingly being acknowledged, however, that there is no one, unified messianic secret motif in the Gospels and several different reasons why Jesus commands people to silence in various settings.[7] Here perhaps nothing more is implied by Jesus' words than that the newly cleansed leper should not be distracted from his responsibility to follow the procedures of the law (as set forth in Lev 14:1-32). He could easily have been so overjoyed, telling everyone what had happened, that he would not have obeyed God's commandments. Until Jesus' death and resurrection, the sacrificial laws remained God's will for his people; Jesus never encouraged anyone to contravene them during his lifetime.

The leper will bear witness to his healing, however, precisely by making it public when he appears before the priest. "As a testimony to them" should not be taken as a sign of Matthew's conservatism regarding the law,

---

[6]See W. Wrede, *The Messianic Secret* (London: J. Clarke, 1971 [German orig. 1901]). For a history of response to Wrede, see esp. C. M. Tuckett, ed., *The Messianic Secret* (Philadelphia: Fortress, 1983).

[7]See esp. H. Räisänen, *Das "Messiasgeheimnis" im Markusevangelium* (Helsinki: Finnischen Exegetischen Gesellschaft, 1973); J. D. G. Dunn, "The Messianic Secret in Mark," *TynBul* 21 (1970): 92-117.

as if the phrase meant *to prove to others that Jesus was not a law breaker.* Rather, Jesus implies that the man should testify to what he has done for him. Jesus' healings will disclose his unparalleled authority over sickness, matching the unique authority his preaching and teaching has already illustrated (7:28-29).[8] The identical phrase recurs in 10:18 and 24:14, where the testimony clearly refers to the good news of Jesus himself. In Mark 6:11 it even carries the sense of *a testimony against them*, and there may be slight overtones of such hostility here too.[9] Jesus does what the religious leaders cannot do and in a way that often alienates them.

[5]When Jesus had entered Capernaum, a centurion came to him, asking for help. [6]"Lord," he said, "my servant lies at home paralyzed and in terrible suffering."

(2) Rewarding the Centurion: Response to Ethnic "Uncleanness" (8:5-13). **8:5-6** A second petitioner approaches Jesus as he is returning home to Capernaum. Again the identity of the supplicant is crucial. The centurion would have been a Gentile, the commander of a division of the occupying imperial troops, theoretically one hundred in number.[10] Orthodox Jews would have considered the centurion unclean because of his race and despised him all the more as a symbol of Roman subjugation. But, like the leper, the centurion approaches Jesus with remarkable respect. He submissively calls him "Lord." He demonstrates unusual concern for the great suffering of one who is merely his "servant" (cf. Luke 7:2). Matthew specifies that the servant is a paralytic to illustrate Jesus' healing of paralytics, referred to more generally in 4:24. The Lukan parallel describes two other groups of individuals who speak with Jesus on behalf of the centurion (Luke 7:3-6). Luke is probably more literal at this point and Matthew more dramatic (cf. his additions in vv. 11-12). Both renderings are legitimate and draw attention to the centurion's faith rather than his personal presence.[11]

[7]Jesus said to him, "I will go and heal him."

---

[8]See esp. R. T. France, *The Gospel according to Matthew*, TNTC (Grand Rapids: Eerdmans, 1985), 153; R. J. Banks, *Jesus and the Law in the Synoptic Tradition* (Cambridge: University Press, 1975), 103-4.

[9]Cf. H. N. Ridderbos, *Matthew*, BSC (Grand Rapids: Zondervan, 1987), 160; R. A. Guelich, *Mark 1–8:26*, WBC (Dallas: Word, 1989), 76-77.

[10]For a concise introduction to the Roman military structure, see E. Ferguson, *Backgrounds of Early Christianity* (Grand Rapids: Eerdmans, 1987), 38-42.

[11]We too often use similar literary devices. A news report declares, "The President announced today" when in fact only his press secretary ever spoke to anyone. On the lack of contradiction between these accounts, see C. L. Blomberg, *The Historical Reliability of the Gospels* (Downers Grove: InterVarsity, 1987), 134. Matthew also avoids portraying the Jewish leaders in a positive light, a consistent feature of his Gospel, by omitting reference to them here.

8:7 Jesus again affirms his willingness to help. The verb "heal" (*therapeuō*) is the same term found in the summary statements of 4:23 and 9:35. Some view Jesus' words here as a question (Will I go and heal him?)[12] because of the emphatic use of "I" and because of the many parallels between this passage and 15:21-28, in which Jesus again tries to provoke a Gentile to a confession of faith by at first seeming to rebuff her. But 15:21-28 contains no actual questions, and Luke 7:6 assumes that Jesus has promised to come and help. An emphatic "I" is equally appropriate for a forceful statement, and in this context Matthew seems to be stressing Jesus' authority and control in each new encounter so as to make a question less appropriate. Still, it may be true that Jesus said what he did in anticipation of a response he could then praise.

8The centurion replied, "Lord, I do not deserve to have you come under my roof. But just say the word, and my servant will be healed. 9For I myself am a man under authority, with soldiers under me. I tell this one, 'Go,' and he goes; and that one, 'Come,' and he comes. I say to my servant, 'Do this,' and he does it."

8:8-9 No one else, however, would have anticipated the centurion's response. These verses disclose an astonishing attitude for an authoritative commander of military forces. The man repeats the title "Lord." He admits his unworthiness ("I do not deserve"), using a statement identical in the Greek to that used by John the Baptist in 3:11 ("I am not fit"). He emphatically positions the word "my" in the Greek sentence to emphasize his subordination. He recognizes the barriers of ritual uncleanliness that would have prevented a Jew from entering his home, and he amazingly believes in Jesus' ability to cure his servant from a distance merely by a word of command. Such healing was virtually unprecedented in ancient Judaism, and Matthew has not prepared his readers to expect it. But the centurion bases his belief on his own experience with the military. Just as he can command others to carry out the orders he himself has been given and can expect their instant and complete obedience, so also he believes that Jesus, under God's authority, gives orders for illnesses to be cured instantaneously. "Authority" is obviously the key term again in these verses.

10When Jesus heard this, he was astonished and said to those following him, "I tell you the truth, I have not found anyone in Israel with such great faith. 11I say to you that many will come from the east and the west, and will take their places at the feast with Abraham, Isaac and Jacob in the kingdom

---

[12]See esp. H. J. Held, "Matthew as Interpreter of the Miracle Stories," in G. Bornkamm, G. Barth, and H. J. Held, *Tradition and Interpretation in Matthew* (Philadelphia: Westminster, 1963), 194-95.

of heaven. [12]But the subjects of the kingdom will be thrown outside, into the darkness, where there will be weeping and gnashing of teeth."

[13]Then Jesus said to the centurion, "Go! It will be done just as you believed it would." And his servant was healed at that very hour.

8:10-12 Jesus marvels at the centurion's faith. He uses the man's words as a lesson for those "following" him (the verb of discipleship). As in vv. 1-4 the focus of the passage thus goes beyond the healing itself. Verses 11-12 are unparalleled in Mark and Luke (John's similar story in John 4:46-54 is probably a different episode altogether)[13] and provide both the distinctive and the core elements of the passage for Matthew. The centurion is a paradigm of many outside Judaism ("from the east and the west"—cf. Ps 107:3) who will become Jesus' followers. Jesus thus points forward to a time beyond his earthly ministry when Gentiles will flock to the faith.

More sobering is his observation that even as newcomers arrive, many from within Judaism ("subjects of the kingdom"), who by ancestry believe themselves still part of God's covenant,[14] will discover that they are not in the kingdom at all but painfully and eternally excluded from God's presence. Darkness here is the opposite of the light of God in Christ (cf. 4:15-16). The refrain "weeping and gnashing of teeth" highlights the agony of this separation and recurs regularly as a Matthean distinctive (13:42,50; 22:13; 24:51; 25:30).[15]

Happily, those who do respond positively to Jesus in this age, from whatever ethnic background, will join the faithful Israelites of previous generations (classically represented by Abraham, Isaac, and Jacob) to enjoy eternal fellowship with God. Jesus characterizes that bliss as taking "their places at the feast," the messianic banquet image depicting the intimate fellowship among God's people in the age to come (cf. Isa 25:6-9; 65:13-14). The contrast between faith and faithlessness thus stands out even more than the miracle Jesus works. "Such great faith" does not refer to a particular quantity but to a quality of faith, which is both Christological in focus and universal in scope. Those who claim to be Christians can also be excluded from the kingdom if they lack either of these two elements. Those who deny people of certain races, classes, or creeds access to God's message and ministry in this life may find themselves excluded from his presence in the next. As Bruner provocatively warns, "Hell is

---

[13]See esp. L. Morris, *The Gospel according to John*, NIC (Grand Rapids: Eerdmans, 1971), 288.

[14]Cf. A. H. M'Neile, *The Gospel according to St. Matthew* (London: Macmillan, 1915), 105: "All Jews who trust in their Judaism."

[15]On the imagery of these metaphors, see esp. E. Schweizer, *The Good News according to Matthew* (Richmond: John Knox, 1975), 215-16.

not a doctrine used to frighten unbelievers; it is a doctrine used to warn those who think themselves believers."[16]

8:13 Matthew concludes the passage by narrating the miracle almost as an afterthought. Jesus' healing nevertheless verifies the appropriateness of the man's faith, and it occurs at a time and in a way which confirms that supernatural power has been at work.

[14]When Jesus came into Peter's house, he saw Peter's mother-in-law lying in bed with a fever. [15]He touched her hand and the fever left her, and she got up and began to wait on him.

(3) Healing Peter's Mother-in-Law: Response to Gender "Unclean-ness" (8:14-15)   **8:14-15** The third episode in this first series of healing miracles is also the shortest. From the details of v. 14, one may infer that Peter was married and that Jesus may well have been living with Peter's extended family from the time he had left Nazareth. But the only point that concerns Matthew is Jesus' compassion for yet a third category of people who were viewed as second-class citizens within Judaism, namely, women. We also see Jesus' ability to heal a third kind of illness, in this case a fever. As with the leper, he heals with a touch, and touching women in this fashion was banned by at least some Jewish traditions.[17] As with both previous healings, the cure takes place at once. Peter's mother-in-law responds by getting up and *continuing to serve* (the more literal rendering of the Greek imperfect tense) the one who healed her. Her action need imply nothing more than proper etiquette as a hostess. But the verb *diakoneō* regularly came to refer to Christian service, and the distinctive "him" (versus "them" of Mark 1:31; Luke 4:39) may suggest that the woman was beginning a life of discipleship at this point.

Many in the church today need to recover more of the biblical witness concerning God's dealings with women. He is an equal opportunity dispenser both of his grace and of contexts to serve him. Nevertheless, the lesson of this passage is not specific enough either to rule out or to require certain role differentiations between men and women.[18]

---

[16]F. D. Bruner, *The Christbook* (Waco: Word, 1987), 306.

[17]See D. Hill, *The Gospel of Matthew*, NCB (London: Oliphants, 1972), 160. Cf. *b. Ber.* 61a.

[18]The literature on women's roles in home and church is enormous. Most helpful with respect to women in Jesus' ministry is B. Witherington III, *Women in the Ministry of Jesus* (Cambridge: University Press, 1984). Very balanced in its exegesis of a broader set of passages is D. S. Dockery, "The Role of Women in Worship and Ministry: Some Hermeneutical Questions," *CTR* 1 (1987): 363-86. Full of practical insights for Christian living is R. and B. Allen, *Liberated Traditionalism: Men and Women in Balance* (Portland: Multnomah, 1985). The most comprehensive discussion of the issues is the volume produced by the Council on Biblical Manhood and Womanhood, uniformly advocating a "complementarian" perspective (*Recovering Biblical Manhood and Womanhood*, ed. J. Piper and W. Grudem [Wheaton:

16When evening came, many who were demon-possessed were brought to him, and he drove out the spirits with a word and healed all the sick. **17**This was to fulfill what was spoken through the prophet Isaiah:
"He took up our infirmities
   and carried our diseases."

(4) Summary and Conclusion (8:16-17). **8:16-17** From Mark 1:21,29 we learn that Jesus healed Peter's mother-in-law on a Sabbath. Jesus has done privately that which would later incur public hostility (e.g., Matt 12:9-14). Matthew is not concerned to note the day of the week here, but the information from Mark explains why the "many" who bring their sick (v. 16) wait until sunset—the end of the Sabbath when normal activity could resume. At this time Jesus exorcises demons and heals large numbers of people. Matthew uses language designed to recall 4:24. Jesus heals "with a word," demonstrating the simplicity and directness already illustrated in vv. 5-13.

As was frequently the case in chaps. 1–4, Matthew uniquely includes a fulfillment quotation of the Old Testament (Isa 53:4). This quote comes from one of the "suffering servant" passages of Isaiah, which early Christianity consistently saw as pointing to the Messiah's atonement for sin (cf. 1 Pet 2:24).[19] Matthew's language closely follows the MT ("He Himself has born our griefs/illnesses, and as for our sufferings, He has loaded Himself with them") against the LXX ("this man bears our sins and suffers anguish for our sake"),[20] although it is probable that Isaiah had both sin and sickness in view in his original prophecy.[21]

From this text, among others, neoorthodoxy has developed its doctrine of Jesus' vicarious humanity, i.e., that Christ's life as well as his death

---

Crossway, 1991]). The egalitarian or evangelical feminist group to which they respond (Christians for Biblical Equality) has not yet produced a correspondingly comprehensive treatment, but excellent representatives of their perspective include A. B. Spencer, *Beyond the Curse: Women Called to Ministry* (Nashville: Nelson, 1985); A. Mickelsen, ed., *Women, Authority and the Bible* (Downers Grove: InterVarsity, 1986); and G. Bilezikian, *Beyond Sex Roles* (Grand Rapids: Baker, 1985).

[19]Despite many protests to the contrary, there seems to be good evidence that this text was viewed as messianic in at least some pre-Christian Jewish circles. See J. Jeremias, "παῖς θεοῦ in Later Judaism in the Period after the LXX," *TDNT* 5:677-717.

[20]Translations according to G. L. Archer and G. C. Chirichigno, *Old Testament Quotations in the New Testament* (Chicago: Moody, 1983), 121.

[21]Cf. R. H. Gundry, *Matthew: A Commentary on His Literary and Theological Art* (Grand Rapids: Eerdmans, 1982), 150: "The healings anticipate the passion in that they begin to roll back the effects of the sins for which Jesus came to die." Some think Isaiah spoke only of sins, but physical well-being was also thought to characterize the messianic age (Isa 29:18; 32:3-4; 35:5-6). "We therefore do well to follow Matthew's literalism."

helped atone for sin.[22] Matthew, however, focuses more on the cures of disease than on forgiveness of sin. Charismatics have regularly appealed to this verse in maintaining that there is healing for physical maladies in the atonement. Inasmuch as the healings consistently function as pointers to God's in-breaking kingdom, one should expect the present blessings of God's reign at times to include miraculous recovery from illness.[23] But to require such healing of God this side of eternity loses sight of the future aspect of the kingdom. Only in the world to come will sickness and death be banished altogether from believers' lives. Claims that so far all who were sick in Jesus' presence seem to have been cured must be balanced with the data of John 5:1-15, in which Christ selected only one of many sick people to receive healing. Nor is it adequate to reply that the others didn't ask to be made well, because the man Jesus chose to heal didn't ask either. Jesus frequently worked miracles to create faith where it was not already present (e.g., Mark 4:35-41; 5:1-20), even while refraining from such activity in similar situations elsewhere (e.g., Mark 6:1-6a; 8:11-13). There is physical healing in the atonement for this age, but it is up to God in Christ to choose when and how to dispense it. Perfect healing, like the believer's resurrection body, ultimately awaits Christ's return.[24]

Yet even this discussion about atonement introduces elements not clearly in Matthew's mind at this point. It may be, after presenting three cases of Jesus' potentially defiling himself ritually, that he simply wishes to underline how Jesus was willing to become unclean in order to make others clean. The physical removal of the virus or bacteria would thus prove less significant than the spiritual removal of man-made distinctions that ostracize certain kinds of people from the love of God and from fellow humans.[25]

b. JESUS DEMONSTRATES HIS DIVINE AUTHORITY AND DEMANDS DECISIVE DISCIPLESHIP (8:18–9:17). Matthew's second group of three miracles proves highly dramatic. Each carefully focuses the Christological question. These three miracles are framed by exacting demands for discipleship, once

---

[22]Cf., most recently, *Christ in Our Place: The Humanity of God in Christ for the Reconciliation of the World*, ed. T. Hunt and D. Thimell (Allison Park, Pa.: Pickwick, 1989).

[23]Cf., from philosophical, exegetical, and experiential perspectives, respectively, C. Brown, *Miracles and the Critical Mind* (Grand Rapids: Eerdmans, 1984); L. Sabourin, *The Divine Miracles Discussed and Defended* (Rome: Catholic Book Agency, 1977); and J. Wimber with K. Springer, *Power Evangelism* (San Francisco: Harper & Row, 1986).

[24]See esp. D. J. Moo, "Divine Healing in the Health and Wealth Gospel," *TrinJ* n.s. 9 (1988): 191-209; D. A. Carson, "Matthew," in *EBC*, vol. 8, ed. F. E. Gaebelein (Grand Rapids: Zondervan, 1984), 207.

[25]Cf. esp. D. Patte, *The Gospel according to Matthew: A Structural Commentary* (Philadelphia: Fortress, 1987), 117.

with illustrations of inadequate reactions, the other with much more adequate response.

(1) The Demands of Discipleship: Inadequate Responses (8:18-22). The scene and theme shift. As will happen repeatedly, Jesus tries to escape the crowds (cf. 12:15; 14:13; 15:21). Later he will flee hostility; here he is probably just seeking physical rest (cf. his deep sleep through the subsequent storm, v. 24) and spiritual refreshment (cf. Luke 6:12—following a previous frenzy of healings).

18When Jesus saw the crowd around him, he gave orders to cross to the other side of the lake. 19Then a teacher of the law came to him and said, "Teacher, I will follow you wherever you go."

20Jesus replied, "Foxes have holes and birds of the air have nests, but the Son of Man has no place to lay his head."

(a) A Scribe's Overeagerness (8:18-20). **8:18-20** Jesus commands an unspecified group of individuals, most likely the Twelve, to get boats ready to cross to the east side of the Sea of Galilee. Before he can leave, two other people express their desire to follow Jesus across the lake. The first man stands out because he is called a scribe ("teacher of the law"). So far in Matthew scribes, like Pharisees, have been objects only of denunciation. So one expects this scribe to illustrate inadequate discipleship, and Matthew includes nothing to discourage this expectation.[26] The man addresses Jesus as "teacher" (*didaskale*), a title given to Christ in Matthew only by those who do not fully believe in him (cf. 12:38; 19:16; 22:16,24,36). The title is accurate but not adequate. The scribe professes absolute allegiance, but Jesus realizes that the man doesn't know what such a commitment would actually involve. He describes his itinerant ministry as even more austere than the lives of birds and foxes. Of course, Jesus had a home in Capernaum even if it was a borrowed one, but he was often not there to use it. At a deeper level Jesus' disciples must recognize that no location on earth affords a true home. Our citizenship is in heaven (Phil 3:20), and life on earth is lived as "strangers [sojourners, exiles] in the world" (1 Pet 1:1).

Verse 20 contains the first reference in Matthew to Jesus as "Son of Man." There is a vast literature on the origin, meaning, and authenticity of this title.[27] Three categories of "Son of Man" sayings in the Gospels are

---

[26]Contra J. Kiilunen, "Der nachfolgewillige Schriftgelehrte: Matthäus 8.19-20 im Verständnis des Evangelisten," *NTS* 37 (1991): 268-79.

[27]For the best recent representatives of important diverse viewpoints, see M. Casey, *Son of Man: The Interpretation and Influence of Daniel 7* (London: SPCK, 1979); B. Lindars, *Jesus Son of Man* (Grand Rapids: Eerdmans, 1984); and C. Caragounis, *The Son of Man* (Tübingen: Mohr, 1986).

generally recognized: those that present him in his earthly role, those that highlight his suffering, and those that point to his glory. Although it is widely disputed, the probable background for the title remains Dan 7:13-14. Thus the term actually focuses on the exaltation and preexistence of Jesus, who was present in God's heavenly throne room and given everlasting authority over all the world. In general "Son of Man" focuses more on Christ's divinity than on his humanity.[28] Still, the title is ambiguous enough to sustain more than one meaning per passage and for Jesus to have invested it with distinctive significance in various contexts.[29] Here the expression may function simply as a circumlocution for "I" or "someone like me." Here too appears a sharp and poignant contrast between Jesus' authority to work the kinds of miracles Matthew has already narrated and his choice to deny himself normal creaturely comforts. As a result, Jesus cannot promise those who wish to "go on the road" with him as many material provisions as they might prefer.[30] Potential disciples often long for the glory associated with following Jesus and forget the deprivation that may often precede it.[31]

[21]Another disciple said to him, "Lord, first let me go and bury my father." [22]But Jesus told him, "Follow me, and let the dead bury their own dead."

(b) A Would-Be Disciple's Undereagerness (8:21-22). **8:21** Matthew describes the second would-be follower as "another disciple." This seems to imply that the scribe had also been some kind of disciple, yet at this stage in Matthew's narrative, before the Twelve have formally been presented (10:1-4), the term "disciple" must be taken more loosely as anyone who follows along with Jesus and shows some kind of interest in him. Matthew again wishes to illustrate the inadequacy of this man's response. His attitude does not demonstrate sufficient commitment. If the first man was overeager, this one is undereager. Jesus had to remind the scribe that sacrifices would be necessary. He must warn this "disciple" that distractions cannot be countenanced. The man is not ready to follow quite yet. "Bury my father" implies at the very least that the man wishes to postpone discipleship until after a funeral and the mandatory months of mourning that followed. Quite possibly he is saying much more: the

---

[28]See esp. S. Kim, *The Son of Man as the Son of God* (Grand Rapids: Eerdmans, 1985); W. Horbury, "The Messianic Associations of 'The Son of Man'," *JTS* 36 (1985): 34-55.

[29]See esp. F. F. Bruce, "The Background to the Son of Man Sayings," in *Christ the Lord*, ed. H. H. Rowdon (Leicester: InterVarsity, 1982), 50-70.

[30]See esp. M. Casey, "The Jackals and the Son of Man (Matt. 8.20 // Luke 9.58)," *JSNT* 23 (1985): 3-22.

[31]Cf. R. H. Mounce (*Matthew*, GNC [San Francisco: Harper and Row, 1985], 75): "Miracles create enthusiasts who need to learn the difficulties connected with discipleship before they start on the journey."

expression may well have been an idiom for *let me wait until my father is dead*.[32] The man perhaps fears that his family will object. At any rate, other priorities come before discipleship.

8:22 Jesus can brook no such excuses but requires an immediate response. A future opportunity may not come. Let the spiritually dead (or perhaps even the physically dead, if Jesus is employing biting sarcasm here) worry about the affairs of this life and ceremonies for the physically dead. Ironically, the expense of most Christian funerals continues to burden those who grieve their loved ones while lavishing care upon corpses oblivious to such affection. Even more ironically, many who are alive postpone their response to the direct call of Jesus because of more pressing human allegiances.[33] D. A. Carson insightfully observes, "Little has done more to harm the witness of the Christian church than the practice of filling its ranks with every volunteer who is willing to make a little profession, talk fluently of experience, but display little of perseverance."[34]

Taken together, Jesus' responses to these two men could hardly reflect a sharper break from Judaism or a more stringent call to count the cost of discipleship (cf. Luke 14:28-32).[35] Some have imagined that one or both of these would-be disciples became genuine followers of Christ,[36] but Matthew does not describe their actions to Jesus' rebukes. And without specifying any positive response, he seems to imply that they refused Jesus' terms. At any rate, what Matthew does include uniformly warns against inadequate response to Jesus' call.[37]

(2) Divine Authority over Satan's Realm (8:23–9:8). The three miracles in 8:23–9:8 illustrate Jesus' power over disaster, demons, and disease. The storm stilling contains a rebuke of the elements that resembles an exorcism (8:26). The exorcism of the two Gadarenes clearly van-

---

[32]See esp. K. Bailey, *Through Peasant Eyes: More Lucan Parables* (Grand Rapids: Eerdmans, 1980), 26-27. B. R. McCane ("'Let the Dead Bury Their Own Dead': Secondary Burial and Matt 8:21-22," *HTR* 83 [1990]: 31-43) thinks that the practice of reburying the bones of a deceased person in an ossuary is in view here, so that the man may be asking for up to nearly a year's reprieve before he can follow Jesus.

[33]Cf. Bailey, *Peasant Eyes*, 31-32: "Loyalty to Jesus and the kingdom he inaugurates is more important than loyalty to the cultural norms of your society or parental authority."

[34]Carson, *When Jesus Confronts*, 43.

[35]For a full-length treatment of the theme of Jesus' itinerant ministry, taking its starting point from these verses, see M. Hengel, *The Charismatic Leader and His Followers* (New York: Crossroad, 1981).

[36]See esp. J. D. Kingsbury, "On Following Jesus: The 'Eager' Scribe and the 'Reluctant' Disciple (Matthew 8.18-22)," *NTS* 34 (1988): 45-59.

[37]Cf. Luke 9:61-62 for additional details that support this interpretation. Note also that Luke again has three examples from which Matthew has apparently excerpted two.

quishes Satan's minions. And the paralytic's malady is linked to his sin—further enslavement to the devil's realm.

23Then he got into the boat and his disciples followed him. 24Without warning, a furious storm came up on the lake, so that the waves swept over the boat. But Jesus was sleeping. 25The disciples went and woke him, saying, "Lord, save us! We're going to drown!"

(a) Stilling the Storm: Response to Disaster (8:23-27). **8:23-25** Verse 23 resumes the story line of v. 18. The words "disciples" and "followed" link back with v. 21 and vv. 19 and 22, respectively. The two dialogues with the would-be disciples and the stilling of the storm narrative belong together. True disciples do model appropriate detachment from home and family, which in this case involves physical separation for a time. As commonly happened, a sudden squall arises on the Sea of Galilee. Matthew, however, calls the storm a seismos (literally, earthquake), a term used for apocalyptic upheavals (cf. 24:7; 27:54; 28:2), often with preternatural overtones. This seems to be no ordinary storm but one in which Satan is attacking. The boat is in danger of being swamped, and lives are at risk. Amazingly, Jesus remains so calm that he continues to sleep. The disciples rouse him and beg for help. "Save" and perish ("drown") refer first of all to the disciples' physical lives, but by Matthew's time they have become the standard terms for spiritual salvation and destruction. Matthew may well intend a double entendre here.[38]

26He replied, "You of little faith, why are you so afraid?" Then he got up and rebuked the winds and the waves, and it was completely calm.
27The men were amazed and asked, "What kind of man is this? Even the winds and the waves obey him!"

8:26 Despite their acknowledgment of dependence on him and use of the address "Lord" (v. 25, a positive title for Jesus throughout Matthew), Jesus rebukes their "little faith." Matthew places Jesus' rebuke before the miracle, while Mark reverses the sequence (Mark 4:40). Yet even though Matthew's narrative reads more naturally, it is hard to believe that he is trying to present the disciples in a more positive light.[39] "Little faith" simply stresses their lack of faith; it scarcely improves on Mark's "no faith."[40] The "rebuke" of the elements employs the same term (*epitimaō*) used elsewhere

---

[38]Cf. F. W. Beare (*The Gospel according to Matthew* [San Francisco: Harper and Row, 1981], 215), who notes that "Lord, save" may have been a liturgical form in Matthew's church like the later "Lord, have mercy" (*Kyrie eleison*).

[39]As often held since the seminal study of G. Bornkamm, "The Stilling of the Storm in Matthew," in Bornkamm, Barth, and Held, *Tradition and Interpretation*, 52-57.

[40]Cf. further Blomberg, *Historical Reliability*, 115-16.

in exorcism stories (Mark 1:25; 9:25; Luke 4:41). Jesus demonstrates power over the destructive forces of nature, which remain under the devil's sway. As with his healings, Jesus' "cure" takes effect immediately.

8:27 Astoundingly, Jesus has demonstrated the identical sovereignty over wind and waves attributed to Yahweh in the Old Testament (cf. Jonah 1–2; Pss 104:7; 107:23-32).[41] Such power can do far more than just heal sickness. Miracles over "nature" remain much rarer in Jewish and Christian history. Quite understandably, the disciples wonder aloud about the identity of the man, bringing the narrative to its Christological climax. Jesus' nature miracles in general (and rescue miracles in particular)[42] should lead men and women to worship.[43] The disciples' fear (Mark 4:41; Luke 8:25), which could imply terror and/or awe, is entirely compatible with their amazement here.

Contemporary applications of this miracle almost universally "demythologize" the narrative (deriving a naturalistic lesson from a supernatural event), so that it becomes a lesson about Jesus "stilling the storms" of our lives. Matthew did not likely have such an application in mind. There are implications for discipleship here, to be sure; we must turn to Jesus as the one to trust in all circumstances of life. But the focus of this passage remains squarely Christological—on who Christ is, not on what he will do for us.[44] One who has this kind of power can be no less than God himself, worthy of worship, irrespective of when and how he chooses to use that power in our lives. Sometimes he leaves storms unstilled for good and godly ends (cf. 2 Cor 12:7-8).

28When he arrived at the other side in the region of the Gadarenes, two demon-possessed men coming from the tombs met him. They were so violent that no one could pass that way. 29"What do you want with us, Son of God?" they shouted. "Have you come here to torture us before the appointed time?"

(b) Exorcising the Gadarene Demoniac: Response to Demons (8:28–9:1). **8:28-29** Jesus and company arrive on the eastern shores of the Sea of Galilee. Gadara was the name of a city substantially inland, as well as of the province whose boundary abutted the lake. Mark and Luke speak instead of Gerasa, a different city in the same province. Probably the town in view was Khersa, close to the shore. The various renderings

---

[41]Cf. P. J. Achtemeier, "Person and Deed: Jesus and the Storm-Tossed Sea," *Int* 16 (1962): 169-76.

[42]For a form-critical classification of Jesus' miracles, see esp. G. Theissen, *The Miracle Stories of the Early Christian Tradition* (Philadelphia: Fortress, 1983).

[43]See esp. C. L. Blomberg, "The Miracles as Parables," in *Gospel Perspectives*, vol. 6, ed. D. Wenham and C. Blomberg (Sheffield: JSOT, 1986), 340-42.

[44]See esp. P. F. Feiler, "The Stilling of the Storm in Matthew: A Response to Günther Bornkamm," *JETS* 26 (1983): 399-406.

and subsequent textual variants then resulted from confusion by later Greek translators and copyists.[45] Here Matthew offers his first full-length narrative illustrating Jesus' ministry of exorcism, already summarized in 4:24 and 8:16. As in both those verses, and consistently in antiquity, demon possession is distinguished from illness in general though sometimes seen as the cause of a particular malaise. *Demonization* (a more literal rendering of *daimonizomenos*) involves the indwelling of unseen evil spirits in a way that prevents an individual from fully controlling his or her own actions (see comments under 4:23-25). Exorcists abounded in ancient Judaism and Greco-Roman religions; but Jesus displayed a unique directness, immediacy, and effectiveness.[46]

Only Matthew speaks of two demoniacs, but he does not thereby contradict Mark and Luke. Neither of the other Evangelists refers to "only" one. Perhaps one of the two dominated the conversation. But Matthew elsewhere includes two characters, where parallel accounts have one (9:27; 20:30); so he may be uniquely concerned to follow the principle of Deut 19:15, that a testimony be confirmed by two or three witnesses.

The tombs (more properly "burial caves," GNB) epitomized uncleanness, forming an appropriate abode for the devils. Satan regularly dwells in that which is most profane. The violence of the demoniacs kept them from the rest of civilization. Mark 5:5 shows that their violence threatened themselves as well. Their cry, "What do you want with us?" employs an idiom that might better be translated "What have you to do with us?" or perhaps even "Don't bother us!"[47] Like Satan at Jesus' temptation, they acknowledge him as Son of God and recognize their eventual doom, but they nevertheless use his name in an attempt to ward him off (cf. Mark 5:7, which reads literally, "I adjure you by God," and 5:9, in which Jesus himself demands to know their name as part of the process of gaining mastery over them). In other words, the demons are not concerned to confess Jesus' identity but are trying to use his name to exorcise him. When they fail, Jesus in turn casts them out. To the demons his arrival seems premature; Judgment Day has not come. They overlook the "already" of the "already-not yet" equation. The end times were breaking into human history with Jesus' exorcisms, demonstrating the inauguration of God's kingdom (cf. 12:28), even if he still granted the demons limited freedom for a time.

---

[45]See Blomberg, *Historical Reliability*, 149-50, and the literature there cited, for more detailed explanation. There is no contradiction here.

[46]On parallels and differences between Jesus' exorcisms and those of others, see esp. G. Twelftree, "Εἰ δὲ . . . ἐγὼ εκβάλλω τὰ δαιμόνια . . . ," in *Gospel Perspectives* 6:361-400.

[47]See R. G. Bratcher, *A Translator's Guide to the Gospel of Matthew* (New York: UBS, 1981), 94.

30Some distance from them a large herd of pigs was feeding. 31The demons begged Jesus, "If you drive us out, send us into the herd of pigs."

32He said to them, "Go!" So they came out and went into the pigs, and the whole herd rushed down the steep bank into the lake and died in the water.

8:30-31 When the demons recognize that Jesus will cast them out ("if you drive us out" is a first-class condition almost equivalent to *when you drive us out*) but will delay their total destruction, they request a new home. Swine, like tombs, defiled Jews but afforded appropriate refuge for evil spirits.

8:32 Jesus accedes to the demons' request. "Go!" is more literally, *You may go*, granting permission. Against many interpretations, it seems that the pigs' drowning surprises neither Jesus nor the demons. They continue their destructive activity by throwing the swine off the rocky cliffs on the eastern shores of Galilee. Nothing else in the Bible suggests that angels or demons can die, so Matthew must mean only that "the whole herd" of pigs perished.[48] Jesus permits the demons to continue to live, but they may no longer torment these particular men.[49] The destruction of the herd of swine also convinces those men of the decisiveness of their liberation.

Readers concerned about the destruction of animal life and the loss of the farmers' livelihood exhibit a contemporary sentimentality not shared by a Jewish audience who knew these pig farmers should not have been raising animals whose meat was forbidden to eat.[50] Human sanity and salvation, moreover, must always take priority over financial prosperity.

33Those tending the pigs ran off, went into the town and reported all this, including what had happened to the demon-possessed men. 34Then the whole town went out to meet Jesus. And when they saw him, they pleaded with him to leave their region.

8:33-34 The farmers naturally spread the word about what has happened and, like the nearby townsfolk, are distressed. The meeting in v. 34 provides closure with v. 28 and rounds out the story. Jesus should have been welcomed, but the Gadarenes dwell only on the loss of their pigs and fear the power that could vanquish Satan so dramatically. The Christological question is again posed starkly, but these people are unwilling to face it. A man with Jesus' power must be divine and holy, but sinful

---

[48]The grammar seems to suggest otherwise, since "herd" is singular but "died" is plural (as if the "demons" were the subject of the verb). More likely, Matthew is thinking of the herd as a collection of individual animals that died (Carson, "Matthew," 219).

[49]See Ridderbos, *Matthew*, 177.

[50]Beare (*Matthew*, 219) notes that a typical Jewish audience would not have seen this as a calamity but as an occasion for merriment.

humans recoil in the presence of holiness because it points out their own shortcomings all the more glaringly.[51]

¹Jesus stepped into a boat, crossed over and came to his own town.

9:1 The passage ends with Jesus returning across the lake to his current home in Capernaum (cf. 4:13). Matthew 9:1 is often assumed to introduce the next miracle story rather than to conclude the account of Jesus in Gadara, but the varying locations of the healing of the paralytic in Mark and Luke (Mark 2:1-12; Luke 5:17-26) suggest that Matthew is arranging material topically here and that the events of 9:2 do not necessarily follow those of 9:1.[52]

²Some men brought to him a paralytic, lying on a mat. When Jesus saw their faith, he said to the paralytic, "Take heart, son; your sins are forgiven." ³At this, some of the teachers of the law said to themselves, "This fellow is blaspheming!"

(c) Healing the Paralytic: Response to Disease (9:2-8). **9:2** Jesus once again encounters a paralytic (recall 4:24; 8:6). The sick man is brought on a stretcherlike cot by an otherwise unidentified group of individuals. "Their" faith most naturally refers to those bringing the paralytic. The spiritual state of the sick man remains unspecified. "Son" implies nothing about the man's age or relationship to Jesus except that he was younger than Christ. Jesus surprisingly refers not to the man's physical condition but to his spiritual state, and he takes the initiative to declare the man's sins forgiven without any prompting from the sick man himself. Onlookers would assume that Jesus was linking the man's handicap to some sin, a common Jewish presumption (cf. John 9:2), which may or may not have been true in this case.

9:3 The scribes mutter *among themselves* (more likely than NIV "to themselves"). These Jewish leaders interpret Jesus' declaration of forgiveness as a blasphemous usurping of divine prerogative (Isa 43:25). "This fellow" refers to Jesus disparagingly.

⁴Knowing their thoughts, Jesus said, "Why do you entertain evil thoughts in your hearts? ⁵Which is easier: to say, 'Your sins are forgiven,' or to say, 'Get up and walk'? ⁶But so that you may know that the Son of Man has

---

[51]Cf. A. Plummer (*An Exegetical Commentary on the Gospel according to St. Matthew* [London: E. Stock, 1909], 134): "Fear in the presence of the supernatural is common in man; and dislike of the presence of greater holiness is specially natural in those who know that their own lives are quite out of harmony with heaven."

[52]Cf. Carson, "Matthew," 220-21, for detailed explanation and diagrams of the chronologies implied by the various Evangelists at this point.

authority on earth to forgive sins. . . . " Then he said to the paralytic, "Get up, take your mat and go home." [7]And the man got up and went home. [8]When the crowd saw this, they were filled with awe; and they praised God, who had given such authority to men.

9:4-8 Jesus recognizes their objection. "Knowing their thoughts" does not preclude their having voiced them, and it neither demands nor rules out supernatural insight. Jesus simply stresses that their objections issued from evil hearts (cf. 7:15-20). Their internal disposition is rebelling against God's will. To justify his behavior, Jesus asks whether it is easier to pronounce a person forgiven or healed. Whichever might be easier to *do*, it was obviously easier to "say" that someone's sins were forgiven without fear of contradiction. So to prove his authority for making the easier claim, he performs the harder task (the typically Semitic from-the-lesser-to-the-greater logic). So clear is his reasoning for Matthew's original audience that the quotation is broken off midsentence. At once Jesus commands the paralytic to walk and carry his mat back home, and the man does so. Jesus' claim is thus vindicated. A key Son of man reference appears here too. As in 8:20, it need mean nothing more than "I," but "on earth" suggests that Jesus is contrasting his present life with his heavenly preexistence and that Dan 7:13-14 is again in the background.

The crowd is afraid (cf. 8:27 and parallels), probably combining terror and awe, and glorifies God, always an appropriate response to great works performed by his servants. The key Matthean distinctive appears in 9:8, "who had given such authority to men." The plural may be rhetorical and not refer to anyone other than Jesus. Still, many have assumed that Matthew was foreshadowing Christ's delegation of his authority to his followers (16:19; 18:19).[53] In any event, Matthew's focus remains Christological. Jesus continues to appear as one with divine authority. Just as Jesus exercised Yahweh's sovereignty over wind and waves and demonstrated his superiority over Satan's minions, so now he displays the very authority of God to forgive sins.

(3) The Demands of Discipleship: Adequate Responses (9:9-17). The second group of three miracles should have made plain Christ's nature. So it is possible to return again to a call for discipleship in hopes of more adequate responses than those of 8:18-22. This is precisely what happens with the call of Levi (9:9-13) and the little parables of the bridegroom, garments, and wineskins (9:14-17). Each of these pronouncement stories (short episodes culminating in a key pronouncement from Jesus) presents a proper response to Jesus in light of criticism from representatives of the Pharisees and John the Baptist.

---

[53]France, *Matthew*, 166.

Inasmuch as 8:18-22 introduced the triad of miracles that followed, and given the close temporal connection between 9:17 and 18, it is possible that 9:9-34 is meant to form the last major section of 8:1–9:35. But no obvious thematic parallels appear to connect vv. 9-17 and 18-34, whereas vv. 9-17 do fit well with the healing of the paralytic (vv. 2-8) as a series of controversy or conflict stories.[54] After Jesus' declaration of forgiveness for the paralytic, his calling of a notorious sinner follows naturally.

[9]As Jesus went on from there, he saw a man named Matthew sitting at the tax collector's booth. "Follow me," he told him, and Matthew got up and followed him.

(a) Matthew Becomes a Disciple (9:9-13). **9:9** Jesus leaves the site of his last healing, somewhere in Capernaum, and heads for the toll booths on the edge of town. Matthew's station was probably located on the landing stage of the lake, where commercial ships would arrive from territory outside the rule of Herod Antipas.[55] The "tax" Matthew collected then would more specifically have been *customs duties.*

Only Matthew uses the name "Matthew" here (but cf. Mark 3:18; Luke 6:15; Acts 1:13). Mark and Luke call this disciple Levi. It was common for first-century Jews to have two or three names. Sometimes more than one name was Jewish; more commonly one was Jewish and one Greek (cf. Saul-Paul). The name "Levi" harks back to the third son of Jacob (Gen 29:34). "Matthew" comes from the Aramaic for *gift of God.* Why only Matthew uses the name is uncertain. Perhaps it was the name he came to be more known by in his later ministry. It was at least the easier of the two names to pronounce in Greek transliteration. Jesus extends his call to Matthew in words that echo 4:19,21 and 8:22. Matthew responds as immediately as did Andrew, James, Peter, and John. Matthew gives no indication of what prior exposure, if any, he had to Jesus' person and teaching.

[10]While Jesus was having dinner at Matthew's house, many tax collectors and "sinners" came and ate with him and his disciples. [11]When the Pharisees saw this, they asked his disciples, "Why does your teacher eat with tax collectors and 'sinners'?"

9:10-11 On some later occasion, Matthew throws a party for Jesus (cf. Luke 5:29, in which the antecedent of "his" is less ambiguous than in

---

[54]In the Markan parallels (2:1-22) it is clear the healing of the paralytic; the call of Levi; and the little parables of bridegroom, garments, and wineskins go together as part of a larger collection of pronouncement or controversy stories. See esp. J. Dewey, *Markan Public Debate* (Chico, Cal.: Scholars, 1980).

[55]M'Neile, *Matthew*, 117.

the Greek of Matthew). Many of his colleagues—fellow tax collectors and other "sinners"—join him. The NIV puts "sinners" in quotation marks because first-century Judaism used the term in at least two specialized senses: (1) *Am-ha-aretz* ("the people of the land"), i.e., the vast majority of Jews who did not follow the stricter sectarian regulations of the Pharisees; and (2) particularly grievous sinners—the most criminal and disreputable types of people in society. Here "sinners" carries this second sense, since Jesus and his disciples themselves were *am-ha-aretz* and would have provoked no objection simply by eating with their own kind.[56] The combination of "tax collectors" with "sinners," "prostitutes" or "Gentiles" ("pagan[s]") recurs throughout the Gospels (Matt 11:19; 18:17; 21:31-32; Luke 15:1). Such references became idiomatic, demonstrating how unwelcome the tax collectors were to the Pharisees. Various factors in different times and places fueled this hostility, including the tax collectors' support for the levies of the Roman government, making some view them as traitors to their country. They also regularly defiled themselves by contact with Gentiles and often were dishonest and unscrupulous—charging more than they were required to so they could keep the additional profits for themselves.[57]

The Pharisees' criticism may well have occurred later. They would not likely have attended such a party, but word in the close-knit communities of ancient Judaism would have spread at once, though it is possible they might have been watching not too far outside Matthew's home. "Saw," however, does not necessarily imply literal vision. It is interesting that they pose their objection as a question for Jesus' disciples, perhaps due to a reluctance to address Jesus directly in deference to his role as teacher and miracle worker. This pattern of questioning will recur (e.g., 17:24), and it will change (e.g., 21:23–22:40).

[12]On hearing this, Jesus said, "It is not the healthy who need a doctor, but the sick. [13]But go and learn what this means: 'I desire mercy, not sacrifice.' For I have not come to call the righteous, but sinners."

9:12-13 Whether the disciples are in Jesus' company or report the Pharisees' question to him, Jesus replies with what may already have become a well-known proverb. Jesus has already illustrated that proverb with physical healings (recall 8:16), but now he centers attention on spiritual health and sickness. "Righteous" and "sinners" here refer to the

---

[56]R. Guelich, *Mark 1-8:26*, WBC (Dallas: Word, 1989), 102.

[57]Cf. esp. J. R. Donahue, "Tax Collectors and Sinners," *CBQ* 33 (1971): 39-61. Cf. also the qualifications, though overstated, of F. Herrenbrück, "Zum Vorwurf der Kollaboration des Zöllners mit Rom," *ZNW* 78 (1987): 186-99.

"respectable" and "outcasts" of society (cf. GNB). Some see Jesus' statement here as ironic, believing that he would not have called the Pharisees "righteous," but he simply may be accepting their self-perceptions for the sake of discussion.[58] It is also worth noting that the passage does not even directly link the Pharisees with the "righteous."

Characteristically, only Matthew has Jesus quote the Old Testament (Hos 6:6). "Not *X* but *Y*" is a Semitic idiom for "more *Y* than *X*." Hosea did not abolish the sacrificial cult but graphically emphasized the priority of interpersonal relationships over religious ritual.[59] On mercy see under 5:7. Jesus introduces the quote with the command "go and learn," a standard charge from rabbis to their disciples. Jesus is dealing the Pharisees a double rebuke by treating them first as learners rather than teachers and second as beginners who have yet to learn Scripture correctly. His logic is impeccable; the Pharisees have no reply. "I have come" hints at his prior existence in heaven, from which he was sent.

Jesus' fraternizing with disreputable people remains a scandal in the predominantly middle class, suburban, Western church. Many of us, like the Pharisees, at best ignore the outcasts of our society and at worst continue to discriminate against them.[60] We do well to consider substantially increasing our spiritual, evangelistic, and social outreach to minorities, the homeless, prostitutes, addicts and pushers, gays and lesbians, AIDS victims, and the like, as well as to the more hidden outcasts such as divorcees, single parents, the elderly, white-collar alcoholics, and so on. We must get to know them as intimately as Jesus did—only close and trusted friends shared table fellowship over meals. We dare not join with sinners in their sinning, but we may well have to go places with them and encounter the world's wickedness in ways that the contemporary Pharisees in our churches will decry.[61]

[14]Then John's disciples came and asked him, "How is it that we and the Pharisees fast, but your disciples do not fast?"

[15]Jesus answered, "How can the guests of the bridegroom mourn while he is with them? The time will come when the bridegroom will be taken from them; then they will fast.

---

[58]Cf. France (*Matthew*, 168): "*Righteous* is not entirely ironical: in their sense of the word they *were* 'righteous' (cf. Phil. 3:6), but it is precisely the adequacy of such righteousness that Jesus constantly calls in question."

[59]On the use of this verse in Matthew, see esp. D. Hill, "On the Use and Meaning of Hosea VI.6 in Matthew's Gospel," *NTS* 24 (1977-78): 107-19.

[60]Cf. F. Stagg, "Matthew," in *The Broadman Bible Commentary*, vol. 8, ed. C. J. Allen (Nashville: Broadman, 1969), 129: "Strange it is that Jesus' followers, like the Pharisees, are often more exclusive than their Master."

[61]Cf. A. Campolo, *The Kingdom of God Is a Party* (Dallas: Word, 1990).

(b) John's Disciples Question Jesus (9:14-17). **9:14** The flip side of
the objection to Jesus' partying with the disreputable is the complaint that
he does not fast. Here John's disciples pose the question, seemingly sid-
ing with the Pharisees. This surprises us because John has prepared the
way for Jesus and sternly criticized the Jewish leaders (3:7-10), but
John's message and ministry style also contrast with Jesus' (see comments
under 11:16-19). Preparation for the Messiah's coming required repentance and a certain austerity, but now the time for joy has arrived. Neither
the Pharisees nor John's disciples were wrong in fasting as a prelude to
the reception of spiritual blessings, but now those blessings are present.
Jesus' inauguration of the kingdom stimulates celebration and rejoicing,
as at wedding festivities.

  9:15 Hence Jesus' reply—he is the "bridegroom" who is "with them"
(cf. the meaning of Immanuel in 1:23). The bridegroom was a key Jewish
metaphor for God (see Hos 2:16-23).[62] This intimation of Jesus' divinity
further connects this passage to the previous three miracles.[63] Jesus' disciples may also recall John the Baptist's own use of the metaphor for
Jesus (John 3:29). The "guests" (literally, *sons*—in the Hebraic sense of
companions) refer to Jesus' followers. *Apairō* (*to take from*) seems to
imply a violent removal, perhaps alluding to Isa 53:8 and probably foreshadowing Jesus' crucifixion. Then fasting and mourning will be appropriate, even if short-lived (recall comments under 6:16-18). Jesus'
imagery is more allegorical than realistic because bridegrooms are not
usually mourned or removed.

  **16"No one sews a patch of unshrunk cloth on an old garment, for the patch
will pull away from the garment, making the tear worse. 17Neither do men
pour new wine into old wineskins. If they do, the skins will burst, the wine
will run out and the wineskins will be ruined. No, they pour new wine into
new wineskins, and both are preserved."**

  9:16-17 Jesus reinforces the point of the parable of the bridegroom
with two further illustrations of the incompatibility of the old and new
ages. One cannot put an unshrunk patch on an already-shrunk garment;
for when it is washed, the patch will shrink, pulling at the garment and
tearing it further.[64] Nor can wine that has not yet fermented—bubbling,

---

  [62]Cf. further P. B. Payne, "Jesus' Implicit Claim to Deity in His Parables," *TrinJ* n.s. 2
(1981): 3-23, esp. 11-12.
  [63]Beare (*Matthew*, 229) notes that v. 15 "makes the highest Christological claim
imaginable."
  [64]On the specific details of the grammar and imagery of this little parable, see esp. M. G.
Steinhauser, "The Patch of Unshrunk Cloth (Mt 9:16)," *ExpTim* 87 (1976): 312-13, esp. 313:
"No one puts a patch of unshrunk cloth on to an old cloak; because the patch of unshrunk
cloth draws the overlapping section of the unshrunk cloth from the cloak and the tear
becomes worse."

expanding, and emitting gas—be put into old, brittle containers, or they will explode. One needs new containers that are more flexible. So too the new age Jesus inaugurates brings new practices appropriate to the changed circumstances, most notably in this context the joy of celebration rather than the sorrow of fasting. "Both" at the end of v. 17 refers to both "wine" and "wineskins" (the two nearest antecedents),[65] not to the old and the new, despite the popular view that sees Matthew redacting his sources in a more conservative direction to make Jesus say that the old is preserved by means of the new.

All Christians would do well to reflect on whether their demeanor, lifestyle, and words convey to others, especially the unsaved, this joy of salvation and the lively presence of Jesus or whether they communicate, even unwittingly, a dour, judgmental attitude that is quicker to point out the wrongs of others. We must also consider, even as the *message* of the gospel remains unchanged, whether the *methods* of evangelism, preaching, church growth, music, and worship, once effective in different circumstances, have turned counterproductive and need to be replaced by new methods that will more effectively win and minister to the current generation.[66]

c. JESUS CONTINUES TO HEAL: HINTS OF HOSTILITY LOOM AHEAD (9:18-35). Now follows the last in the series of three groups of three healing narratives. New categories of healing appear, which will be cited in 11:5. The first of these three accounts actually sandwiches two miracles together. Explicit references to the faith of those healed appear in vv. 22 and 28-29, recalling similar statements in 8:10 and 9:2. Verse 33 contains the strongest statement to date of the crowds' positive response to Jesus' healing, but v. 34 immediately follows with the strongest statement to date of the Jewish leaders' opposition. A polarization is beginning which Matthew will develop more explicitly as his Gospel unfolds. And a progression may be discerned within these three passages—from a completely positive response in 9:26, to hints of possible trouble in 9:30-31, to overt hostility in 9:34.

[18]While he was saying this, a ruler came and knelt before him and said, "My daughter has just died. But come and put your hand on her, and she will live." [19]Jesus got up and went with him, and so did his disciples.

(1) Stopping a Hemorrhage and Awakening the Dead: Positive Publicity (9:18-26). **9:18-19** Jesus next encounters a "ruler." Mark and Luke add his name (Jairus) and explain that he is a ruler of the synagogue (Mark

---

[65]See Carson, "Matthew," 227-28.
[66]Cf. H. Snyder, *The Problem of Wineskins: Church Structure in a Technological Age* (Downers Grove: InterVarsity, 1975).

5:22; Luke 8:41), i.e., a layman who is responsible for the order and progress of worship. Substantial ruins of a second-century synagogue built on the foundations of the one from Jesus' day still stand on the ancient site of Capernaum. Excavations have unearthed a large house adjacent to it, quite possibly the "parsonage," which could therefore have been Jairus's home. Only Matthew describes how Jairus "knelt"—his characteristic word for worship. As consistently throughout his Gospel (and esp. with miracle stories), Matthew abbreviates Mark, this time to such an extent that he seems to contradict the parallel accounts (Mark 5:21-43; Luke 8:40-56). Instead of coming to plead with Jesus while his daughter is still alive, Jairus apparently arrives only after her death. Yet to call this a contradiction is anachronistically to impose on an ancient text modern standards of precision in story telling.[67] What is more, in a world without modern medical monitors to establish the precise moment of expiry, there is not nearly so much difference between Matthew's *arti eteleutēsen* in v. 18 (which could fairly be translated "just came to the point of death"; cf. Heb 11:22) and *eschatos echei* in Mark 5:23 (which could also be rendered "is dying").[68] What is important is not the precise moment of death but Jairus's astonishing faith. On any interpretation, this influential religious leader believes that Jesus can miraculously reclaim his daughter's life. The faith to which Jesus will explicitly point in v. 22 is implicitly present here already. As before (8:7), Jesus and his troupe go at once to help.

[20]Just then a woman who had been subject to bleeding for twelve years came up behind him and touched the edge of his cloak. [21]She said to herself, "If I only touch his cloak, I will be healed."

9:20-21 This time, however, an obstacle intrudes in their path—another needy person. A woman has been "bleeding" for twelve years, i.e., hemorrhaging in between her normal menstrual flows. To have survived that length of time shows that her life is probably not threatened at this particular moment but also points to the incorrigibility of the illness. Like the girl who is dying, this woman would be viewed as ritually unclean, an even greater stigma than her physical problem (cf. Lev 15:19-33 and the entire Mishnaic tractate *Zabim*). The reader wonders if Jesus deliberately delays his journey to Jairus's home so as to be able to perform not just a healing but a restoration of life (as with Lazarus in John 11:6), but Matthew leaves no clues. Instead he shifts his focus immediately to this second woman, who also believes in Jesus' power to heal. Her faith seems mixed with superstition because she believes that she

---

[67]Cf. Blomberg, *Historical Reliability*, 134-36, and the literature there cited.

[68]See B. M. Newman, *A Concise Greek-English Dictionary of the New Testament*, s.v. τελευτάω (180) and ἐσχάτως (74).

merely needs to touch the edge of Jesus' garment (literally, the *fringe* or *tassel* of his prayer shawl; cf. Num 15:38-39; Deut 22:12).[69] Matthew eliminates the events of Mark 5:30-33 which seem to reinforce this magical element.

22 Jesus turned and saw her. "Take heart, daughter," he said, "your faith has healed you." And the woman was healed from that moment.
23 When Jesus entered the ruler's house and saw the flute players and the noisy crowd, 24 he said, "Go away. The girl is not dead but asleep." But they laughed at him. 25 After the crowd had been put outside, he went in and took the girl by the hand, and she got up. 26 News of this spread through all that region.

9:22 All three Synoptic Gospels make it plain that even if Jesus did accommodate the woman's superstitious beliefs in some way, her faith alone brought about the conditions that made healing possible. "Take heart" parallels Jesus' words in 9:2 and calms the woman's fears (which are explained more completely in Mark 5:33). Verse 21 represents a third-class conditional clause (one that introduces a measure of doubt into the woman's statement). Praiseworthy faith does not doubt God's ability to act, but it does not presume to know how he will choose to act. The word for "healed" in vv. 21-22 is more literally *saved*. The NIV rendering fits the situation in the life of Jesus, but Matthew's church undoubtedly could see implications for the woman's spiritual state as well. "From that moment" suggests an instantaneous cure and that the woman remained healthy for a considerable time afterwards.

9:23-26 Jesus may now complete his trip to Jairus's home. The "flute players" and "noisy" (literally, *in an uproar*) crowd prove that at least by now the girl is definitely believed to be dead. Loud mourning and wailing characterized Jewish wakes. Even the poorest people were required to hire at least two flute players and one wailing woman to perform these services (*m. Ketub.* 4:4). The crowd views Jesus' claim that the girl was not dead as ludicrous; death was seen as every bit as irreversible then as now. "Sleep" implies that Jesus views the girl's death as not permanent. Elsewhere in Scripture sleep is often a euphemism for death (e.g., Matt 27:52; Acts 13:36; 1 Cor 11:30; 15:20,51; 1 Thess 4:14), but that of course would make no sense here.

Nevertheless, Jesus succeeds in getting the crowd to leave the young girl's house. "Put outside" seems too mild a term for *ekballō*, which can be translated *throw out* or even *exorcise!* Jesus evicts the mourners probably to regain some calm and decorum inside. Mark 5:40 indicates that he brings the girl's family into her room, possibly restricting onlookers to

---

[69]But cf. M. Hutter, "Ein altorientalischer Bittgestus in Mt 9, 20-22," *ZNW* 75 (1984): 133-35, who argues that the woman's gesture was an established manner of asking for help.

those who had faith.[70] Jesus takes the girl's hand and lifts her up, bringing her to life again. *Korasion* may refer to a "girl" near the age of puberty; Mark 5:42 says she was twelve years old. *Egeirō* ("got up") means *to raise up*, both in the sense of getting out of bed and coming back to life. This "reawakening" is arguably Jesus' greatest miracle to date, though he will perform two more revivifications, one with Lazarus, after four days of death (John 11; cf. the son of the Nain widow in Luke 7:11-17). Old Testament precedent for such miracles appears in the ministries of Elijah and Elisha (see 1 Kgs 17:20-24; 2 Kgs 4:17-37).[71] The news understandably spreads like wildfire. Matthew omits Jesus' injunction to silence (Mark 5:43), though it will reappear shortly (v. 30). As the blind men did in vv. 30-31, the astonished crowd pays no attention to his command; one could scarcely expect them to heed it.

27As Jesus went on from there, two blind men followed him, calling out, "Have mercy on us, Son of David!"

28When he had gone indoors, the blind men came to him, and he asked them, "Do you believe that I am able to do this?"

"Yes, Lord," they replied.

29Then he touched their eyes and said, "According to your faith will it be done to you"; 30and their sight was restored. Jesus warned them sternly, "See that no one knows about this." 31But they went out and spread the news about him all over that region.

(2) Giving Sight to the Blind: Hints of Danger (9:27-31). **9:27** Matthew illustrates yet another category of illness Jesus can overcome. Isaiah 35:5-6 predicts the healing of the blind and deaf mutes in the messianic age. This passage is unparalleled in Mark and Luke but closely parallel to Matt 20:29-34, which is paralleled in the other Synoptics. Matthew's account here is thus often viewed as a "doublet," created by Matthew to reinforce the theme of the more well-attested episode. But Jesus frequently healed the blind (11:5); it would be natural for Matthew as a storyteller to use similar wording where events were similar, and there are significant differences between 9:27-31 and 20:29-34. So the two accounts should be taken to reflect distinct events in Jesus' ministry. The blind men appeal for Jesus' compassion by addressing him with the uniquely Jewish title "Son of David" (see comments under 1:1). It is interesting, though, that in Matthew such recognition comes primarily

---

[70]Or with Bruner (*Christbook*, 346): "As often as possible Jesus wants healing to be unpublic."

[71]We cannot yet speak of full-fledged "resurrections" here, i.e., being raised to live forever. Presumably all these individuals did die normal deaths again at a later date. Cf. esp. M. J. Harris, "The Dead Are Restored to Life: Miracles of Revivification in the Gospels," in *Gospel Perspectives*, 6:295-326.

from blind people and Gentiles (viewed by many as spiritually blind).[72] Matthew's twin themes of Jesus' rejection by official Judaism and acceptance by outcasts (see comments under 2:1-12) reappear here and set the stage for an increasing polarization of response to Christ.

9:28 As in vv. 23-25, Jesus performs a healing in private, away from the crowds. As in v. 22, he initiates a conversation designed to stretch the faith of these men. As he has in 8:2, Matthew centers attention on Jesus' "ability" to heal.

9:29-31 "According to your faith" means *in response to* not *in proportion to their faith*. The blind men receive their sight. At this point Matthew retains the messianic secret motif (or at least Jesus' injunction to silence), which is probably explained by and prepares the reader for the hostility Jesus will experience in v. 34. But his warning goes unheeded, and, as in v. 26, the news spreads. "Warned . . . sternly," from *embrimaomai*, could almost be rendered *snorted* and suggests an emotional outburst, probably stemming from "the intensity of Jesus' desire to avoid winning an inadequate or falsely based loyalty."[73]

32While they were going out, a man who was demon-possessed and could not talk was brought to Jesus. **33**And when the demon was driven out, the man who had been mute spoke. The crowd was amazed and said, "Nothing like this has ever been seen in Israel."

34But the Pharisees said, "It is by the prince of demons that he drives out demons."

(3) Giving Speech to the Mute: Sharp Division (9:32-34). **9:32-33** The third miracle in this final series of healings involves a demonization causing a particular malady. *Kophos* ("A man who . . . could not talk") can refer to one who is either deaf or dumb or both. As noted under 4:24, such language does not imply that all similar illnesses were believed to be caused by demon possession. The passage is another uniquely Matthean "doublet" of similar material (cf. 12:22-24) but again most likely reflects a separate incident from the life of Christ. As at the end of the first series of miracles (8:14-17), this final narrative is so abbreviated as to focus more on Matthew's conclusion than on the miracle itself. This particular kind of exorcism leads the crowd to marvel at the uniqueness of Jesus' authority (v. 33b). For Matthew this marveling could just as easily refer to all of the miracles of chaps. 8–9 and could be parallel to the crowd's

---

[72]See esp. J. M. Gibbs, "Purpose and Pattern in Matthew's Use of the Title 'Son of David,'" *NTS* 10 (1963-64): 446-64.

[73]Hill, *Matthew*, 180-81. Cf. also A. Sand, *Das Evangelium nach Matthäus*, RNT (Regensburg: Pustet, 1986), 204, who sees the rationale as one of avoiding turning the person of Jesus into a spectacle instead of service for a suffering people.

marveling at Jesus' authoritative teaching after his Sermon on the Mount (7:28-29).

9:34 An ominous countercharge mars Jesus' reception. This charge will be elaborated and Jesus will respond to it in 12:24-37. Lines are beginning to be drawn. The majority still side with Christ at least superficially. By the end of Matthew's Gospel, the majority will oppose him. Two possible relationships between faith and miracles have been illustrated. Sometimes faith can produce a miracle. Sometimes a miracle can produce faith. Verse 34 proves that no one can predict what will happen in any given situation.

35Jesus went through all the towns and villages, teaching in their synagogues, preaching the good news of the kingdom and healing every disease and sickness.

(4) Conclusion (9:35). **9:35** Matthew rounds off this section of healing narratives with a statement that closely echoes 4:23 and thus frames this larger unit of Jesus' teaching and healing. Both aspects of Jesus' ministry have had a widespread impact.

——————— *SECTION OUTLINE CONTINUED* ———————

B. Rising Opposition to Jesus' Mission (9:36–12:50)
  1. Opposition Predicted for the Disciples' Mission (9:36–10:42)
    a. Introduction (9:36–10:4)
      (1) The Need for Mission (9:36-38)
      (2) Commissioning the Twelve (10:1-4)
    b. The Immediate Charge (10:5-16)
    c. Future Prospects (10:17-42)
      (1) The Prospect of Future Hostility (10:17-25)
      (2) The Proper Reaction to Hostility: Fear God, Not People (10:26-31)
      (3) Only Two Options (10:32-42)
        (a) Acknowledging Jesus (10:32-33)
        (b) Putting God above Family (10:34-39)
        (c) Receiving God's Messengers (10:40-42)

B. Rising Opposition to Jesus' Mission (9:36–12:50)

The second paired discourse and narrative in Matthew feature Jesus' sermon on mission (9:36–10:42) and the beginnings of significant opposition to the ministry of Christ and his disciples (11:1–12:50). The sermon in chap. 10 points back to chaps. 5–9, as Jesus gives the disciples his authority to proclaim the gospel and heal people. But the sermon links even more closely with chaps. 11–12 by foreshadowing the increasingly hostile responses to Jesus and the disciples, which those chapters will stress. That hostility in turn stems largely from competing interpretations of the miracles Jesus has been performing and now commissions the disciples to continue (11:4-6,21-24; cf. 12:24,39-42).

1. Opposition Predicted for the Disciples' Mission (9:36–10:42)

Here begins the second of the five major discourses of Matthew's Gospel.[1] Jesus is commissioning the Twelve to go out two-by-two to continue his ministry of preaching/teaching and healing. The discourse is thus addressed exclusively to the disciples. After an introduction (9:36–10:4), which explains the need for mission (9:36-38) and formally lists the twelve apostles (10:1-4), the speech divides itself into two very different

---

[1] For helpful literary-critical analysis, see D. J. Weaver, *Matthew's Missionary Discourse* (Sheffield: JSOT, 1990).

sections. Matthew 10:5-15 clearly addresses the immediate historical circumstances, while vv. 17-42 refer largely to future events that will not
take place until after Jesus' death and resurrection. Verse 16 forms a
hinge between the two sections but probably is best taken as the end of
the first section. Unlike vv. 5-16, vv. 17-42 are not paralleled in this context in Mark or Luke, but various parallels do appear in Jesus' eschatological discourse (esp. Mark 13:9-13; Luke 21:12-17) and scattered about
Luke elsewhere (e.g., 12:2-9,51-53; 14:26-27), much as with Luke's parallels to the Sermon on the Mount. These features do not rule out the possibility that Matthew 10 reflects a unified discourse uttered on one
occasion by Jesus and abbreviated by Matthew. But the vague wording of
11:1 makes a theory of composite origins more plausible here than with
Matthew's other four major discourses of Jesus.[2]

**36When he saw the crowds, he had compassion on them, because they were
harassed and helpless, like sheep without a shepherd.**

a. INTRODUCTION (9:36–10:4). *(1) The Need for Mission (9:36-38).*
9:36   Despite Jesus' extensive ministry, many in Israel, no doubt even in
Galilee, remain unreached with his message. Jesus' human emotions reflect
a deep, *gut-level* "compassion" (a reasonable, idiomatic English equivalent
for a term [from Greek *splanchnos*] that could refer to bowels and kidneys)
for this sea of humanity. His compassion increases because Israel lacks
adequate leadership, despite the many who would claim to guide it. The
Twelve begin to fill that vacuum, foreshadowing the institution of the
church. The language of "sheep without a shepherd" echoes Num 27:17
and Ezek 34:5, in which the shepherd is most likely messianic (cf. Ezek
34:23). Similar sentiments will well up in Jesus again at the feeding of the
five thousand (Mark 6:34). As in the days of the prophets, the rightful leadership of Israel had abdicated its responsibility, as demonstrated by its
inability or unwillingness to recognize God's true spokesmen. "Harassed
and helpless" literally means *torn and thrown down* (cf. Berkeley, "man-
gled and thrown to the ground"). Predators, and possibly even unscrupulous shepherds (Zech 10:2-3; 11:16) have ravaged the sheep.[3] Verse 36
provides a stinging rebuke to the Pharisees, scribes, and Sadducees.

**37Then he said to his disciples, "The harvest is plentiful but the workers
are few. 38Ask the Lord of the harvest, therefore, to send out workers into his
harvest field."**

---

[2]D. A. Carson, "Matthew," in *EBC*, vol. 8, ed. F. E. Gaebelein (Grand Rapids: Zondervan, 1984), 240-43. Cf. R. E. Morosco, "Matthew's Formation of a Commissioning Type-
Scene out of the Story of Jesus' Commissioning of the Twelve," *JBL* 103 (1984): 539-56.

[3]R. T. France, *The Gospel according to Matthew*, TNTC (Grand Rapids: Eerdmans,
1985), 175.

9:37-38 Shifting the metaphor from flock to field, Jesus now envisions a vast crop of ripe grain in need of harvesters.[4] The unreached people of his world need more preachers and ministers of the gospel. Jesus can personally encounter only a small number, so he will commission his followers to begin to reach the rest. Even then many more will be needed (cf. his sending of the seventy-two in Luke 10:1-12). Verses 37-38 have rightfully led Christians in all ages to pray for, call, and send men and women into all kinds of ministries. The need remains as urgent as ever, with billions who have not heard the gospel or seen it implemented holistically. "Send out" (from *ekballō*—recall under 9:25) could also be translated *thrust out*, and it could even refer to workers already in the field who "need to have a fire lit under them to thrust them out of their comforts into the world of need."[5]

[1]He called his twelve disciples to him and gave them authority to drive out evil spirits and to heal every disease and sickness. [2]These are the names of the twelve apostles: first, Simon (who is called Peter) and his brother Andrew; James son of Zebedee, and his brother John; [3]Philip and Bartholomew; Thomas and Matthew the tax collector; James son of Alphaeus, and Thaddaeus; [4]Simon the Zealot and Judas Iscariot, who betrayed him.

(2) Commissioning the Twelve (10.1-4). **10:1** "His . . . disciples" suggests that the Twelve have already been chosen (see under 5:1), but to date they have apparently always accompanied Jesus. Now he is sending them out on their own in twos (Mark 6:7). Matthew pairs their names accordingly. This grouping no doubt enabled the disciples to support, protect, and empower each other better than if each went alone, and it perhaps was patterned after the law that required at least two witnesses (Deut 19:15). By not staying together as a larger group, the disciples also maximized their ability to reach large numbers of people. Timeless principles for discipleship and missions appear here.[6] The mission of the Twelve further provides incidental support for the careful preservation of the Jesus-tradition from these early days on, as the disciples, through repetition, would have begun to tell the story of Jesus in somewhat standardized form.[7] Verse 7 makes plain they will preach, but here Matthew

---

[4]B. Charette ("A Harvest for the People: An Interpretation of Matthew 9.37f," *JSNT* 38 [1990]: 29-35) argues that the Old Testament background points more to the subsequent blessings of the messianic age than to the actual in-gathering of God's people.

[5]F. D. Bruner, *The Christbook* (Waco: Word, 1987), 366.

[6]E.g., M. Green (*Matthew for Today* [Dallas: Word, 1989], 109-12): Mission is "crucial," "shared," "sustained," "complex," "strategic," "demanding," and "Jesus-shaped."

[7]See esp. H. Schürmann, "Die vorösterlichen Anfänge der Logientradition," in *Der historische Jesus und der kerygmatische Christus*, ed. H. Ristow and K. Matthiae (Berlin: Evangelische Verlagsanstalt, 1960), 342-70.

focuses on their mighty deeds. Jesus transfers the same miracle-working authority to his disciples on which he himself drew. Matthew again carefully distinguishes exorcisms and healings, and the end of v. 1 repeats verbatim the end of 9:35. Matthew 17:20 (cf. Mark 9:29), however, shows that the disciples cannot automatically draw on this power apart from faith and prayer.

10:2-4 Only here does Matthew label the Twelve "apostles," *those sent out on a mission*,[8] and he names them for his readers' benefit. He has previously introduced only five of them (4:18-22; 9:9-13).[9]

"Simon" comes from the Hebrew for *hearing*. He is also called Peter or Cephas, meaning *rock*, in Greek and Aramaic, respectively. The significance of his nickname appears in 16:16-19. The leader and frequent spokesman for the Twelve, he three times denied Jesus (cf. 26:69-75) but was later restored to fellowship (John 21:15-19). The first leader of the Jerusalem church, from Pentecost until his arrest and escape from prison (Acts 1–12), he subsequently ministered to churches in Asia, Pontus, Bithynia, Galatia, and Cappadocia (1 Pet 1:1), to which he wrote (or substantially influenced the composition of) 1 and 2 Peter. Reasonably strong Christian tradition places him in Rome at least by the early 60s, where he became the bishop of the church in that city (perhaps reflected already in 1 Pet 5:13). *Apocalypse of Peter* 37 narrates his martyrdom by upside-down crucifixion, probably in the late 60s.[10]

"Andrew" comes from the Greek for *manliness*. Like Peter, his brother, Andrew was originally a fisherman from Bethsaida (John 1:44). He was the first-known disciple of John the Baptist to begin to follow Christ (John 1:40).

"James" comes from the Hebrew *Jacob*, meaning *he who grasps the heel* (see Gen 25:26). Another Galilean fisherman and son of Zebedee (4:21-22), he was executed by Herod Agrippa I not later than A.D. 44 (Acts 12:2). He is therefore to be distinguished from the James who wrote

---

[8]Luke's technical use of the term "apostle" as equivalent to one of the Twelve (see Acts 1:12-26) is the most well known. But Paul used it in its broader sense for people like Andronicus and Junia (Rom 16:7), Epaphroditus (Phil 2:25), James, the Lord's brother (Gal 1:19), and Titus (2 Cor 8:23). The spiritual gift of apostleship (Eph 4:11) should probably thus be roughly equated with "missionary" or "church-planter." Cf. further E. von Eicken, H. Linder, D. Müller, and C. Brown, "ἀποστέλλω," in *DNTT* 1:126-37.

[9]On the details of what can be known about each apostle in Scripture, later history, and legend, see E. Hennecke, *New Testament Apocrypha*, vol. 2, ed. W. Schneemelcher (Philadelphia: Westminster, 1965), 23-578, esp. 45-66 and the entries under each man's name in *ISBE*.

[10]Cf. further C. P. Thiede, *Simon Peter: From Galilee to Rome* (Exeter: Paternoster, 1986); R. E. Brown, *et al.*, eds., *Peter in the New Testament* (Minneapolis: Augsburg, 1973); O. Cullmann, *Peter: Disciple, Apostle, Martyr* (Philadelphia: Westminster, 1962).

the epistle of that name and who was the leader of the church in Jerusalem after Peter's departure.

"John" in Hebrew means *the Lord is gracious*. He was James's brother. Like Peter and James, he formed part of the inner circle of the three disciples closest to Jesus (see comments under 4:21-22). The Fourth Gospel, three Epistles, and the Book of Revelation are all attributed to him, the last of these while he was exiled for his faith on the island of Patmos, probably under the emperor Domitian in the mid-90s. Strong, early church tradition associates his ministry with Ephesus, combating the Gnostic teacher Cerinthus. Reasonably strong, though sometimes conflicting tradition maintains that he was the only one of the Twelve not to die a martyr's death for his faith. He would thus have lived to quite an old age—at least into his eighties or nineties.

"Philip" comes from the Greek for *horse lover*. With Simon and Andrew, he was one of Jesus' earliest disciples. He too was from Bethsaida (John 1:43-48) and is to be distinguished from Philip the "deacon" of Acts 6:5 and 8:26-40.

"Bartholomew" comes from the Hebrew for *son of Talmai*. Probably he is the same person as Nathanael, Philip's companion in John 1:45-49. His home would then have been Cana (John 21:2). Matthew likewise groups Philip and Bartholomew together.

"Thomas" stems from the Hebrew for *twin* (John 11:16). He became famous for doubting the resurrection of Jesus until he personally saw and felt the Lord's risen body (John 20:24-28). Thomas's lack of understanding appears already in John 14:5. Possibly reliable later tradition associates him with the establishment of the church in India.

"Matthew" comes from the same Hebrew phrase as Nathanael (*God has given*). He was also called Levi, a converted tax collector, and had this Gospel attributed to him. For his call see comments under 9:9-13.

James, son of Alphaeus, is also called *ho mikros* in Mark 15:40 (*the small one* or "the younger"), presumably to distinguish him in age or size from James, son of Zebedee. Little else is known for sure about him.

Thaddaeus is also called Lebbaeus in some textual variants and Judas son of James in Luke 6:16. The first two are probably nicknames of devotion or endearment, coming from the Hebrew *taday* (*breast*) and *leb* (*heart*).

Simon, *ho Kananaios* (the Cananean—NIV "the Zealot"), was a man whose nickname meant *zealous one*, probably not yet in the sense of a member of the later, more formal political movement known as the Zealots but as one of the predecessors of that movement whose revolutionary aspirations for Israel against Rome perhaps led him to engage in terrorist activities against the government. Contra the NIV, only Luke actually uses the word "zealot" (*zēlōtēs*, Luke 6:15).

Judas Iscariot, infamous for betraying Jesus (26:47-50), was the treasurer for the Twelve (John 12:6). "Iscariot" is usually interpreted as Hebrew for *man of Kerioth*, the name of cities in both Judea and Moab, which could make Judas the only non-Galilean of the Twelve. Others take Iscariot as from a word for *assassin* or from a term meaning *false one*.[11] He ended his life by regretting his betrayal (27:1-10), hanging himself, and falling from the rope so that "all his bowels gushed out" (Acts 1:18-19, KJV).[12]

The number twelve would certainly have called to mind the twelve tribes of Israel and suggests that Jesus is constituting a community of followers, in conscious opposition to the current leadership of Israel, as the new recipients of God's revelation and grace. Only Matthew specifically calls Simon the "first," which fits a special prominence given to him in this Gospel (but see comments under 16:13-20). Only Matthew also reminds readers of his own background, perhaps specifically to recall 9:9-13.

⁵These twelve Jesus sent out with the following instructions: "Do not go among the Gentiles or enter any town of the Samaritans. ⁶Go rather to the lost sheep of Israel.

b. The Immediate Charge (10:5-16).   **10:5-6**   Only Matthew includes vv. 5-6, a distinctively particularist text. But these restrictions do not contradict the Great Commission (28:18-20). Even 10:18 anticipates the disciples going into Gentile territory. Instead, Jesus' commands fit the larger pattern of his own ministry prior to his death and match the missionary priority Paul himself maintained throughout Acts (e.g., 13:46; 18:6; 19:9; 28:25-28) and articulated in Rom 1:16 ("first for the Jew, and then for the Gentile").[13] It is not clear that even the end of Acts heralds a change in strategy,[14] and it is at least possible that God intended Israel to be the first mission field in every era of Christian history.[15] Even if this is not the case, it certainly does not justify relegating the Jews to the relatively low position in Christian missionary strategy they have usually been assigned.

---

[11]For a good discussion of these and still further suggestions, see S. T. Lachs, *A Rabbinic Commentary on the New Testament: The Gospels of Matthew, Mark and Luke* (Hoboken, N.J.: KTAV, 1987), 179.

[12]Historical and theological studies of Judas often try to account for his behavior with a variety of speculative hypotheses. One of the better, recent treatments is D. Roquefort, "Judas: une figure de la perversion," *ETR* 58 (1983): 501-13.

[13]So also J. J. Scott, "Gentiles and the Ministry of Jesus: Further Observations on Matt. 10:5-6; 15:21-28," *JETS* 33 (1990): 161-69. Cf. esp. A. Levine, *The Social and Ethnic Dimensions of Matthean Social History* (Lewiston, N.Y.: Mellen, 1988).

[14]See esp. R. C. Tannehill, "Rejection by Jews and Turning to Gentiles: The Pattern of Paul's Mission in Acts," in *Luke-Acts and the Jewish People: Eight Critical Perspectives*, ed. J. B. Tyson (Minneapolis: Augsburg, 1988), 83-101.

[15]See esp. Bruner, *Christbook*, 372.

The "lost sheep" of "Israel" (literally, *of the house of Israel*) does not refer to a portion of the nation but to all the people (see 9:36; cf. Jer 50:6).

[7]As you go, preach this message: 'The kingdom of heaven is near.' [8]Heal the sick, raise the dead, cleanse those who have leprosy, drive out demons.

10:7-8a Jesus previously commissioned the disciples to exorcise the demons and to heal the sick (v. 1). Now he tells them they must preach as well (v. 7). Their message remains identical to that of John the Baptist and Jesus (3:2; 4:17). Their miracle-working ministry is also restated and itemized. Jesus has already performed healings in each of these categories; all but the curing of lepers (probably a coincidental omission) will explicitly reappear in Acts through the ministries of various Christians (e.g., Acts 3:1-10; 8:7,13; 9:32-43; 14:8-10; 19:13-16; 20:7-12). Even though not all of the commands of vv. 5-16 remain normative today (most notably vv. 5-6 and 8b-10a), the fact that miraculous healings continue after Jesus' resurrection, coupled with the lack of exegetical support for views that see gifts of healings as ceasing at the end of the apostolic age, suggests that believers in all eras may expect supernatural healings from time to time.[16] Verse 8 has regularly been taken as support for modern medical missions as well; appropriate as these may be, they are not what Jesus envisions here.

Freely you have received, freely give. [9]Do not take along any gold or silver or copper in your belts; [10]take no bag for the journey, or extra tunic, or sandals or a staff; for the worker is worth his keep.

10:8b-10 The blessings associated with discipleship come solely by grace and must be similarly imparted (v. 8b). Dependence on benefactors is to be illustrated by traveling as simply as possible. All the resources the disciples need—money, travel provisions, and extra clothing—will be given to them (v. 11) by those who accept their ministry (vv. 9-10). The metal coins were carried in money belts. The "bag" was either a knapsack or beggar's bag. The "tunic" was the garment under one's cloak; the "staff," a walking stick. Paul appeals to the principle of v. 10b in 1 Tim 5:18 (and even refers to the parallel account in Luke 10:7 as "Scripture") to support his contention that congregations must generously support their full-time ministers. On the other hand, as v. 8b hints at here, and as texts such as 1 Cor 9:12b,15-18 make more explicit, there are times when Christian ministers should refuse remuneration for the sake of the gospel. When Christians accept money for ministry, they ought never view it as a wage but as a gift. D. A. Carson comments, "The church does not pay its

---

[16]See M. M. B. Turner, "Spiritual Gifts Then and Now," *VE* 15 (1985): 7-64; D. A. Carson, *Showing the Spirit* (Grand Rapids: Baker, 1987).

ministers; rather, it provides them with resources so that they are able to serve freely."[17]

There are scriptural paradigms for missionary and ministry activity that recognize dependence both on others' support and on one's own resources earned through a different trade (cf. 1 Cor 9:1-18; Phil 4:10-19). Neither may be made absolute. What is most likely to advance the gospel in an honorable way should be adopted in any given context. A serious danger of paid ministry is that preachers will tailor their message to suit their supporters. A key problem with "tentmaking" is a lack of accountability of ministers to those with whom they work. Luke 22:35-38 specifically revokes the commands to travel with great urgency and unprotected. But Matt 7:6 recalls the timeless principle that one should not remain ministering indefinitely to a hostile audience.

A famous so-called contradiction appears between v. 10 and its parallels (Mark 6:8-9; Luke 9:3). Did Jesus permit or prohibit a staff and sandals?[18] If Matthew's account is composite, this verse may have originally applied to the sending of the seventy-two (Luke 10:1-12), which likely included the Twelve, at which time Jesus' instructions differed slightly from those he gave just to the Twelve. That 9:37-38 and 10:10b find their only parallels in Luke 10:2 and 7b may support this reconstruction.[19] At any rate, all accounts agree on Jesus' central theme of the simplicity, austerity, and urgency of the mission. The point of Jesus' strictness is not to leave his disciples deprived and defenseless but dependent on others for their *nourishment* ("keep," v. 10) in every area of life.

11"Whatever town or village you enter, search for some worthy person there and stay at his house until you leave. 12As you enter the home, give it your greeting. 13If the home is deserving, let your peace rest on it; if it is not, let your peace return to you. 14If anyone will not welcome you or listen to your words, shake the dust off your feet when you leave that home or town. 15I tell you the truth, it will be more bearable for Sodom and Gomorrah on the day of judgment than for that town.

10:11-15 As they enter each new location, the disciples must look for those who are open to their message and ministry. Such people will provide the characteristic hospitality given to friends and respected people who traveled in the ancient Roman world (bed and board). Such hospitality proved vital, given the generally nefarious state of public lodging—

---

[17]D. A. Carson, *When Jesus Confronts the World* (Grand Rapids: Baker, 1987), 125.

[18]See B. Ahern, "Staff or No Staff," *CBQ* 5 (1943): 332-37, for a survey of various possible solutions.

[19]Cf. C. L. Blomberg, *The Historical Reliability of the Gospels* (Downers Grove: Inter-Varsity, 1987), 145-46; G. R. Osborne, "The Evangelical and Redaction Criticism," *JETS* 22 (1979): 314.

hotbeds of piracy and prostitution. "Worthy" in v. 11 is the same word translated "worth" in v. 10 and "deserving" in v. 13. In light of v. 14, the term must refer to the response of welcoming the disciples, not to any necessary merit or virtue in the individuals. The disciples must remain with such worthy people to avoid accusations of favoritism or the jealousies of competition among potential hosts. On the "greeting," see comments under 5:47. To give or return "peace" meant *to bless or retract a blessing from an individual or a household.* Shaking the dust off one's feet was a ritual of renunciation used by Jews when they returned to Israel from Gentile territories (cf. Paul's Christian modification of this practice in Acts 13:51). Rejecting the disciples' message is thus seen as a serious sin, indeed, worse even than the gross rebellion of Sodom and Gomorrah in Old Testament times (cf. Gen 18:20–19:28). The increasing culpability of such rejection probably stemmed from the fact that God's revelation in Christ was that much clearer and more immediate.[20] Verse 15 also suggests that there are degrees of eternal punishment (a doctrine taught more explicitly in Luke 12:47-48).

Treating an entire "home" (vv. 11-13) or "town" (vv. 14-15) on the basis of the actions of one person within it reflects the corporate solidarity common in much of antiquity and in many parts of the world today, in which the decisions of a key individual are owned by an entire community. Church growth specialists fearful of the genuineness of modern-day group responses are increasingly moderating such skepticism. The picture of the church as a household has also been profitably expounded.[21] Radical Western democratic individualism is a relatively new sociological phenomenon and often gets in the way of genuine discipleship, in which decisions affecting entire congregations should be made corporately and not so much by majority vote as by common consensus under the Spirit's guidance.

[16]I am sending you out like sheep among wolves. Therefore be as shrewd as snakes and as innocent as doves.

10:16 Jesus' conclusion ties back in with the reference to sheep in 9:36 and likens the disciples' opponents to those who would attack the flock. With incisive, proverbial language, Jesus calls the Twelve to exhibit great acumen without sinful compromise. "Innocent" literally

---

[20]Cf. E. Schweizer, *The Good News according to Matthew* (Richmond: John Knox, 1975), 240-41: "'Post-Christian' man is a different man from the heathen, to whom the Word of Jesus has not yet come"; i.e., he will be judged more severely. Cf. also H. N. Ridderbos (*Matthew*, BSC [Grand Rapids: Zondervan, 1987], 200): "No one can encounter Jesus without increasing his responsibility and, if he is unbelieving, his guilt."

[21]M. H. Crosby, *House of Disciples: Church, Economics, and Justice in Matthew* (Maryknoll: Orbis, 1988).

means *unmixed* and refers to purity of intention. Shrewdness and integrity form a crucial combination not often found in the Christian church. In fact, we more often invert the two, proving to be as guilty as serpents and as stupid as doves![22] High Christology appears in Jesus' claim that one's eternal destiny is based on one's response to him and his emissaries.

c. FUTURE PROSPECTS (10:17-42). With v. 17 Jesus shifts to predictions that were not fulfilled in the immediate mission of the Twelve. The events of vv. 17-22 took place only during the postresurrection ministry of the disciples. Verses 23-42 could be applied to both the immediate and distant future but seem to focus primarily on the experience of the later church age. Jesus' warnings predict the nature of coming persecutions (vv. 17-25), outline the implications of those persecutions (vv. 26-31), and restate the only two possible responses to his message (vv. 32-42), not unlike the concluding "Two Ways" section of the Sermon on the Mount (7:13-27).

[17]"**Be on your guard against men; they will hand you over to the local councils and flog you in their synagogues. [18]On my account you will be brought before governors and kings as witnesses to them and to the Gentiles. [19]But when they arrest you, do not worry about what to say or how to say it. At that time you will be given what to say, [20]for it will not be you speaking, but the Spirit of your Father speaking through you.**

(1) The Prospect of Future Hostility (10:17-25). **10:17-20** The worst rejection Jesus has so far predicted the disciples would receive is lack of a proper welcome. Now he warns of overt hostility. Although the disciples must remain innocent and pure (v. 16), they dare not be overly naive. Some will face arrest ("hand over" in v. 17 is the same verb as "betrayed" in v. 4), being brought before the Jewish courts ("councils" is literally *sanhedrins*, referring to the various local courts). Others will be flogged in the synagogues—the Jewish houses of worship. Yet persecution will not be limited to a Jewish milieu. Other run-ins with the law will bring disciples before Gentile officials ("kings" and "governors," v. 18) as well.[23] Such appearances before Jewish and Gentile authorities are amply illustrated in Acts (4:1-22; 5:17-41; 6:12–8:3; 12:1-19; 16:19-40; 21:27–28:31) and later church history.

---

[22]H. Hobbs, *An Exposition of the Gospel of Matthew* (Grand Rapids: Baker, 1965), 123: "Alone, [shrewdness] produces evil and [simplicity] results in gullibility. But together they produce the spirit which enabled the early Christians successfully to storm citadels of sin."

[23]"To them and to the Gentiles" in v. 18 does not mean the governors and kings are not Gentiles but carries the sense of "to them and to their peoples" or "subjects" (R. G. Bratcher, *A Translator's Guide to the Gospel of Matthew* [New York: UBS, 1981], 115).

Jesus views this persecution positively as an opportunity for the disciples to be "witnesses" to the truths of the gospel (cf. Phil 1:12-18).[24] Interrogation need not terrify Christians, even when their lives may be on the line. Relatively uneducated Christians would naturally have felt most inadequate when pitted against the professional prosecutors known for their rhetorical skill (cf. Tertullus in Acts 24:1-8). Jesus promises that the Holy Spirit will give these believers the right words and enable them to proclaim his word boldly (vv. 19-20)—closely parallel to the ministry of the Paraclete promised in John 14:15-31; 15:26–16:13 and illustrated by the regular testimony of the disciples when they are "filled with the Spirit" throughout Acts (see comments under Matt 3:11).

Using this verse as a proof text for avoiding careful study and preparation for normal preaching and teaching ministries clearly violates its context, although it does remind us that without the power of the Spirit human rhetoric accomplishes nothing of eternal value. The necessary balance between anxiety and apathy closely parallels Jesus' teaching on "worry" about food, drink, and clothing in 6:25-34.

[21]"Brother will betray brother to death, and a father his child; children will rebel against their parents and have them put to death. [22]All men will hate you because of me, but he who stands firm to the end will be saved. [23]When you are persecuted in one place, flee to another. I tell you the truth, you will not finish going through the cities of Israel before the Son of Man comes.

10:21-23   Hostility will come not only from civil and religious authorities but also from members of one's own household (v. 21). Here Jesus alludes to Mic 7:6. The "all men" of Matt 10:22 is more literally just *all* and probably refers to *all kinds* of people, i.e., even close relatives. It should not be taken to include other believers. As in 5:10-12, disciples are hated and rejected for their allegiance to Christ. Christians will be greatly tempted to apostatize, but perseverance will bring eternal life (v. 22b). "Saved" clearly cannot refer to the preservation of physical life since some believers are martyred for their faith. Jesus offers a sober reminder that the true colors of our faith may become visible only when our lives are on the line (as in the situation facing the readers of Hebrews; cf. also 1 Pet 1:7; Jas 1:2-4). The "end" most naturally refers to the end of the age but would also include the moment of death for those who do not live to see Christ return.[25]

---

[24]Cf. G. T. Montague, *Companion God: A Cross-Cultural Commentary on the Gospel of Matthew* (New York: Paulist, 1989), 130: "In countries today where Christianity is outlawed, more people learn about the gospel in the courtroom than on the street."

[25]The expression "to the end" is idiomatic for "completely, totally, entirely, wholly" (J. P. Louw and E. A. Nida, eds., *Greek-English Lexicon of the New Testament* [New York: UBS, 1988], 692), i.e., for the duration of the hostility however it may end.

The flip side of encouraging bold testimony under persecution when one has no alternative is the command to flee hostility whenever possible (v. 23a). Jesus calls his followers to bravery but not foolishness. Believers must not seek out persecution.[26] God's word can go forth powerfully through the unspoken testimony of martyrdom, but it is often better for people to remain alive to speak it aloud.

Verse 23b, a uniquely Matthean text, is often misinterpreted as if it appeared in the more limited context of the immediate mission of vv. 5-16. Then it is taken as a mistaken prediction of Jesus' second coming during the lifetime of the Twelve. In this context of postresurrection ministry, however, it is better viewed as a reference to the perpetually incomplete Jewish mission, in keeping with Matthew's emphasis on Israel's obduracy. Christ will return before his followers have fully evangelized the Jews. But they must keep at it throughout the entire church age.[27]

24"A student is not above his teacher, nor a servant above his master. [25]It is enough for the student to be like his teacher, and the servant like his master. If the head of the house has been called Beelzebub, how much more the members of his household!

10:24-25 Jesus links his assurance that the disciples will be persecuted with the treatment he is already beginning to receive, hostility that will culminate in his crucifixion. Verses 24-25a are simply false if generalized and applied out of context (cf. Jesus' own prediction that the disciples will do greater works than he, John 14:12). Verse 25b gives the correct application and recalls 9:34. "Beelzeboul" (NIV marg.) most likely meant *lord of the high abode*, i.e., of the home of pagan deities, which Jews believed were demons.[28] Hence some textual variants use "Beelzebub"—*lord of the flies*—the common Hebrew parody of Beelzeboul.[29] "How much more" implies *how much more certain* not *to what a*

---

[26]Cf. A. Plummer (*An Exegetical Commentary on the Gospel according to S. Matthew* [London: E. Stock, 1909], 152): "To stop and meet useless risks, because one of is afraid of being called a coward, is one of the subtlest forms of cowardice."

[27]For a more detailed articulation of this view, see J. M. McDermott, "Mt. 10:23 in Context," *BZ* 28 (1984): 230-40. For a brief overview of other alternatives, cf. Carson, "Matthew," 250-53. A detailed history of interpretation appears in M. Künzi, *Das Naherwartungslogion Matthäus 10.23: Geschichte seiner Auslegung* (Tübingen: Mohr, 1970). A helpful update is R. Bartnicki, "Das Trostwort an die Jünger in Mt 10,23," *TZ* 43 (1987): 311-17.

[28]O. Böcher, "βεέλζεβουλ" in *Exegetical Dictionary of the New Testament*, vol. 1, ed. H. Balz and G. Schneider (Grand Rapids: Eerdmans, 1990), 211.

[29]See F. W. Beare (*The Gospel according to Matthew* [San Francisco: Harper and Row, 1981], 278) for the textual evidence, which the NIV reading obscures.

greater extent. Even as they do not seek persecution and in fact actively shun it, all Christians can at times expect it. Promises of exemption from persecution offer false hope. People who have never experienced it probably have not sufficiently witnessed to their faith. But Jesus' words here must be balanced with the principles of 1 Tim 3:7 and 1 Pet 2:12; 3:15-16. To the extent that it is possible, Christians and their leaders should try to get along with and gain the respect of unbelievers in their communities.

[26] **"So do not be afraid of them. There is nothing concealed that will not be disclosed, or hidden that will not be made known.** [27] **What I tell you in the dark, speak in the daylight; what is whispered in your ear, proclaim from the roofs.**

[28] **Do not be afraid of those who kill the body but cannot kill the soul. Rather, be afraid of the One who can destroy both soul and body in hell.**

(2) The Proper Reaction to Hostility: Fear God, Not People (10:26-31). **10:26a** Verses 17-25 did not paint a pleasant picture. If Christians had to look forward only to a life of suffering and persecution, they might well despair or, more likely, abandon all Christian commitment (and rightly so—see 1 Cor 15:19). But the future holds much more for the believer. Judgment Day is coming when God will eternally compensate his people for their suffering and punish their enemies forever. Then the injustices of this world will disappear before the grandeur and glory of life in God's presence (Rom 8:18). So Jesus can confidently encourage his followers, "Do not be afraid." Matthew punctuates vv. 26-31 with this encouragement, repeating it again for emphasis in the middle (v. 28).

10:26b-27 Jesus describes the coming judgment as a time for disclosing all the secrets of individuals' lives. The sins people think they have committed with impunity (v. 26) will be revealed (cf. Luke 12:3). Indeed, the disciples will help out (v. 27) as they judge all unbelievers (1 Cor 6:2). Either or both of vv. 26-27 may also refer to the universal public declaration of the gospel, which will have previously received only a partial hearing.[30]

10:28 Physical death thus pales in comparison with the prospect of eternal punishment. "Body" and "soul" point to a fundamental dualism in human beings.[31] In this life, of course, body and soul are closely united, and God will eventually reunite them in the resurrection body. But Scripture

---

[30] J. Broadus, *Commentary on the Gospel of Matthew*, AC (Valley Forge: American Baptist Publication Society, 1886), 229.

[31] Cf. J. W. Cooper, *Body, Soul, and Life Everlasting* (Grand Rapids: Eerdmans, 1989), against the prevailing fashion that speaks of humans as indissoluble wholes. The "trichotomist" view, which separates a person into body, soul, and spirit, misses the fact that in Scripture "soul" and "spirit" are largely synonymous.

consistently teaches that the two are separated at death (see Luke 23:43; 2 Cor 5:1-10; Phil 1:23-24). "Kill," like "destroy," does not imply annihilation but eternal suffering, as the qualification "in hell" makes clear (on which, see comments under 5:27-30). The NIV rightly capitalizes "One" as referring to God and not the devil (cf. Jas 4:12).[32]

29Are not two sparrows sold for a penny? Yet not one of them will fall to the ground apart from the will of your Father. 30And even the very hairs of your head are all numbered. 31So don't be afraid; you are worth more than many sparrows.

10:29-31   To reassure the disciples of God's fatherly love, Jesus contrasts their great worth with the comparatively insignificant value of sparrows, a cheap marketplace item sold for 1/32 of the minimum daily wage ("penny" is literally an *assarion*, which equaled 1/16 of a denarius). So, too, God knows the very number of our hairs. If he is aware and in control of such minor details, "how much more" will he not care for his own people and vindicate them despite their present suffering? "The will of" in v. 29 does not appear in the Greek but is probably a correct interpolation,[33] although the parallelism with v. 30 could suggest the translation *apart from the knowledge of your Father*.[34] A clear perspective of a person's finitude, of God's coming justice, and of the expanse of eternity should encourage believers in the worst of circumstances and should instill terror in anyone who fails to take into account God's future plans for the universe.

(3) Only Two Options (10:32-42).   When we understand how the world will end, the only question that ultimately matters is whose side we are on come Judgment Day. Jesus contrasts the two alternatives in three ways: Are we genuinely serving Christ as Lord (vv. 32-33)? Do we love God more than the closest of human friends and relatives (vv. 34-39)? Have we given those who are God's true spokespersons an appropriate welcome (vv. 40-42)? As at the end of the Sermon on the Mount (7:24,26), Jesus closes this discourse by no longer addressing just the dis-

---

[32]On this verse in general, see I. H. Marshall, "Uncomfortable Words: VI. 'Fear Him Who Can Destroy Both Soul and Body in Hell' (Mt 10:28 RSV)," *ExpTim* 81 (1969-70): 276-80.

[33]B. Newman and P. Stine, *A Translator's Handbook on the Gospel of Matthew* (New York: UBS, 1988), 317. T. Hirunuma ("ἄνευ τοῦ πατρός: 'Without [of] the Father,'" *FNT* 3 [1990]: 53-62) argues that this meaning can be derived simply from the genitive without inferring an ellipsis.

[34]D. C. Allison, Jr., "Matthew 10:26-31 and the Problem of Evil," *SVTQ* (1988): 293-308; *idem*, "'The Hairs of Your Head Are All Numbered,'" *ExpTim* 101 (1990): 334-36. For a good survey and discussion of these and other options, see J. G. Cook, "The Sparrow's Fall in Mt. 10:29b," *ZNW* 79 (1988): 138-44.

ciples but "whoever" (vv. 32-33,39) and "anyone" (vv. 37-38,41-42). Jesus the healer and teacher is now the judge of all humanity.[35]

32"Whoever acknowledges me before men, I will also acknowledge him before my Father in heaven. 33But whoever disowns me before men, I will disown him before my Father in heaven.

(a) Acknowledging Jesus (10:32-33). **10:32** "Acknowledge" (*homologeō*) carries the sense of *confess* or *trust in*, i.e., to declare one's allegiance to Christ. In the context of persecution (recall vv. 17-25), such acknowledgment means remaining faithful to Jesus even if one must die for him. This kind of commitment is not likely to be faked. For all who so acknowledge him, Christ will in turn acknowledge them before God (note the earth-heaven contrast as in 6:1-18) so that they may receive eternal life (cf. Rev 3:5). Noteworthy in both v. 32 and v. 33 is Jesus' speaking of God as "my Father in heaven." Most often it has been "your father" (5:16,45,48; 6:1,4,6,8,14-15,18,26,32; 7:11; 10:20,29) or "our Father" (6:9). Only here and in 7:21 does he use "my Father." Note in both 7:21 and 10:32-33 the focus is on final judgment.

10:33 "Disown" (*arneomai*) can also mean *deny* or *reject*. The word does not necessarily imply some previous kind of profession, though, as in 7:22-23, some may cry out, "Lord, Lord." Such a person, Jesus proclaims, "has never belonged to Him."[36] In close parallelism with v. 32, v. 33 maintains that God will deny or reject those people who reject Jesus and that he will exclude them from eternal life. Striking and profound Christology emerges here, as often not found in the Gospels except in John. One who can make such claims must be none other than the one who declares: "I am the way and the truth and the life. No one comes to the Father except through me" (John 14:6). Nor does Jesus countenance any middle ground. Christians understandably ask questions about the fate of those who have not consciously accepted or rejected Jesus or who have not even had a chance to hear the gospel. There seems to be scriptural warrant both for excluding all who do not explicitly confess Christ and for accepting all who do not explicitly refuse him (cf., e.g., Matt 12:30 with Mark 9:40), but here such questions remain unaddressed.[37]

---

[35]D. Patte, *The Gospel according to Matthew: A Structural Commentary* (Philadelphia: Fortress, 1987), 153-54.

[36]Ridderbos, *Matthew*, 208.

[37]The former, however, seems better supported, and both views, of course, are to be distinguished from the popular modern heresy of universalism—the view that all people will one day be saved. It is also worth noting with F. Stagg ("Matthew," in *The Broadman Bible Commentary*, vol. 8, ed. C. J. Allen [Nashville: Broadman, 1969], 138) that "presumably there is a distinction between willful denial and human weakness which is not equal to the demands of a crisis situation," esp. in light of Peter's later experience.

34"Do not suppose that I have come to bring peace to the earth. I did not come to bring peace, but a sword. **35**For I have come to turn
"'a man against his father,
a daughter against her mother,
a daughter-in-law against her mother-in-law—**36**a man's enemies will be the members of his own household.'

(b) Putting God above Family (10:34-39). **10:34-36** The inferior text of Luke 2:14 in the KJV has led generations of people celebrating Christmas to promote the false notion that Christ brings "peace on earth, good will to men." Instead, Jesus promises *peace on earth to men of good will,* namely, to "those on whom his favor rests." To those who welcome him, he offers *eirēnē* ("peace"—from the Hebrew concept of *shālôm*). Such peace brings the wholeness of restored relationships with God (Rom 5:1) and interpersonal reconciliation within the community of believers (Eph 4:3). Jesus' peace does not preclude wars between nations, conflicts among unbelievers, or the persecution of Christians which Jesus has already predicted.[38] In fact, not only does Jesus not come to eradicate all human conflict but he actually promises hostility (v. 34). His ministry proved so confrontational that he either attracted people to himself or visibly repelled them. The "sword" of v. 34 is therefore metaphorical.[39]

Hostility against Christians results not from their making themselves obnoxious but from the sad fact that, despite the peacemaking principles of 1 Pet 2:12–3:22, sometimes the gospel so alienates unbelievers that they lash out against those who would love them for Christ's sake. "Turn . . . against" (v. 35) is a bit mild for a verb (*dichazō*) that refers to incitement to revolt and rejection of authority (i.e., *to sow discord*). The family members of vv. 35-36 represent the closest of human relationships. In each case Jesus implies that an unbeliever is initiating the hostility against a believing family member. Verse 36 generalizes to make plain that the hostility is not necessarily limited to the three pairs of relationships chosen. Verses 35-36 reiterate the language of v. 21 and allude even more extensively to Mic 7:6, a text that was applied to the messianic age in at least some Jewish circles (*b. Sanh.* 97a).

---

[38]Cf. Schweizer (*Matthew*, 251): "God's Kingdom has never been the peace of the false prophets who cry, 'Peace, peace!' while avarice and meanness lay waste the earth and transform God's good creation into its opposite (Jer 6:14; etc.); neither, however, is it the 'holy war' of the devout who take the field to conquer their oppressors with the mighty support of God."

[39]Hence, L. Sabourin (*L'Évangile selon saint Matthieu et ses principaux parallèles* [Rome: Biblical Institute Press, 1978], 143) rightly notes that this text cannot be used "to conclude that Jesus supported the political movement of the Zealots."

37"Anyone who loves his father or mother more than me is not worthy of me; anyone who loves his son or daughter more than me is not worthy of me; **38**and anyone who does not take his cross and follow me is not worthy of me. **39**Whoever finds his life will lose it, and whoever loses his life for my sake will find it.

10:37-39   Human relationships in this age may thus prove life threatening, but even at best they remain fallible and inconsistent. Hence, even what should be the best and closest of human relationships, in the family, ought never stand in the way of serving God (v. 37).[40] "Worthy" here carries more the traditional sense of *deserving* and refers in context to those whom Jesus will accept. Theological syntheses must balance Eph 6.1-4 and 1 Tim 5:8 with teachings like these. Devotion to family is a cardinal Christian duty but must never become absolute to the extent that devotion to God is compromised.

Verse 38 offers a parallel statement about those not worthy of Jesus. The reference to the "cross" surprises us since these are early days in Jesus' ministry, and he has not yet predicted or explained what will happen to him. Yet Jews under Roman rule well understood the practice of carrying a cross en route to crucifixion. At this stage in his ministry, Jesus may be using the phrase "take his cross" as simply implying a willingness to sacrifice one's life, if necessary, for him.

Verse 39 restates the two options of vv. 32-33. In the first half of each clause, finding and losing one's life means *saving and losing one's physical life*. In the second half of each clause, "lose" and "find" refer to eternal death and life. The importance of this verse made it the most frequently quoted saying of Jesus in the New Testament (cf. 16:25; Mark 8:35; Luke 9:24; 17:33; John 12:25). The immediate context of finding or losing one's physical life refers to the prospect of martyrdom, but the principle enunciated here may be applied to many situations in which people seek only prosperity or pleasure rather than less glamorous discipleship. "For my sake" is "a claim which is monstrous if He who makes it is not conscious of being Divine."[41]

40"He who receives you receives me, and he who receives me receives the one who sent me. **41**Anyone who receives a prophet because he is a prophet will receive a prophet's reward, and anyone who receives a righteous man because he is a righteous man will receive a righteous man's reward. **42**And if anyone gives even a cup of cold water to one of these little ones because he is my disciple, I tell you the truth, he will certainly not lose his reward."

---

[40]Luke 14:26 has a parallel saying that puts the issue more starkly but is explained by Matt 10:37 (the Semitic "hate *X* and love *Y*" = "love *Y* more than *X*").

[41]Plummer, *Matthew*, 157.

(c) Receiving God's Messengers (10:40-42). **10:40-42** In closing
this sermon, Jesus describes the proper response to him in yet a third way.
Receiving Jesus is equivalent to receiving God, but not all will meet Jesus
in the flesh. Others must respond to him as they see him in his disciples.
In the context of persecution, the hospitality described here could involve
harboring those wanted by authorities at considerable risk to the hosts.[42]
The true prophets contrast with the false ones of 7:15-23, and, as there,
refer to all who proclaim God's Word. "Righteous" people, as consistently in Matthew, are those who obey God's will by following Jesus (see
comments under 5:17-20). "Little ones" in Matthew also regularly refer
to disciples (see comments under 18:6). It is also possible that each suc-
cessive term highlights a slightly larger group of Christians. "Prophets"
would then be restricted to certain leaders; "the righteous," to a broader
category of relatively mature believers; and the "little ones" would
include all the ordinary, unobtrusive, and even marginalized members of
the community of faith.[43]

Jesus is saying in three roughly equivalent ways that those who receive
his followers, because they accept what those individuals stand for, will
in turn be received by God. "Because he is" is literally *in the name of* and
refers to recognizing the prophet, righteous person, or "little one" for who
he or she is. The "he" in each of these cases (vv. 41a,41b,42a) thus refers
to the disciple and not to the one offering hospitality. The person receiving the disciple is thus becoming a believer. "Receiving" or "not losing"
a reward in v. 42b must therefore imply receiving or not receiving eternal
life, not some specific status in heaven. Offering a cup of cold water, a
very small gesture of help, ties back in with vv. 11-15 and implies the
kind of hospitality that included acceptance of the message as well as the
messenger (v. 14a). Verses 40-42 comprise the only one of the three subsections of vv. 32-42 in which the negative alternative is not given by
way of contrast. The focus in each case is on the right choice; Jesus' missionary discourse closes on an optimistic note in hopes of a positive
response.

---

[42]R. H. Mounce, *Matthew*, GNC (San Francisco: Harper and Row, 1985), 98.
[43]See E. Schweizer, "Matthew's Church," in *The Interpretation of Matthew*, ed. G. Stanton (Philadelphia: Fortress, 1983), 129-55.

—————— *SECTION OUTLINE CONTINUED* ——————

2. Opposition Experienced in Christ's Mission (11:1–12:50)
   a. Implicit Opposition (11:1-30)
      (1) John the Baptist and Jesus (11:1-19)
         (a) John's Doubts about Jesus and Jesus' Reply (11:1-6)
         (b) Jesus' Testimony Concerning John (11:7-15)
         (c) The Crowd's Reaction to John and Jesus (11:16-19)
      (2) Judgment on Unrepentant Cities (11:20-24)
      (3) The Alternative: The Rest Christ Can Provide (11:25-30)
   b. Explicit Opposition (12:1-50)
      (1) Sabbath Controversies and Their Outcome (12:1-21)
         (a) Picking the Grain (12:1-8)
         (b) Healing the Man with the Shriveled Hand (12:9-14)
         (c) Withdrawal from Hostility (12:15-21)
      (2) Exorcism Controversies (12:22-45)
         (a) Jesus' Exorcistic Powers (12:22-37)
         (b) The Sign of Jonah (12:38-42)
         (c) The Return of the Evil Spirit (12:43-45)
      (3) Family Controversy (12:46-50)

2. Opposition Experienced in Christ's Mission (11:1–12:50)

To date Jesus has encountered hostility only briefly (9:34), but it has been pointed and will continue to grow. Opposition is implied throughout chap. 11, with John doubting (vv. 2-3) and Jesus rebuking the crowds (not just the Jewish leaders now but "this generation," v. 16) for improper responses to both John and himself. Then he denounces several Galilean cities even more severely (vv. 20-24). In chap. 12 the opposition becomes explicit. The Pharisees challenge Jesus' Sabbath practices and even begin to plot his death (vv. 1-14). The brief charge of 9:34 is turned into a full-fledged debate about whether Jesus is diabolical or divine (vv. 22-37). Jesus threatens condemnation on the whole generation (vv. 38-45) even more sternly than in 11:20-24. Yet at the end of each of these two chapters, Matthew interrupts the hostilities and denunciations to include Jesus' appeals to the crowds to become true disciples (11:25-30; 12:46-50). Thus we are reminded that the opposition is not yet unrelenting or inevitable.[1]

---

[1]For an excellent and detailed study of these two chapters, to which many of the observations concerning structure are indebted, see D. Verseput, *The Rejection of the Humble Messianic King* (Frankfurt: Peter Lang, 1986).

a. IMPLICIT OPPOSITION (11:1-30). Following an introductory verse
(v. 1), Matthew groups together teaching on the developing relationship
between John and Jesus (vv. 2-19): John's question about Jesus (vv. 2-6),
Jesus' views of John (vv. 7-15), and Jesus' rebuke of "this generation" for
its response to both John and himself (vv. 16-19). Next, vv. 20-24 more
directly threaten judgment upon the unrepentant cities in which Jesus had
worked many of his miracles. By way of contrast, the chapter concludes
with Jesus' offer of rest for the spiritually weary (vv. 25-30).

**[1]After Jesus had finished instructing his twelve disciples, he went on from
there to teach and preach in the towns of Galilee.**

*(1) John the Baptist and Jesus (11:1-19). (a) John's Doubts about
Jesus and Jesus' Reply (11:1-6).* **11:1** Verse 1 could easily be taken as
the conclusion to the previous sermon in chap. 10 or as a separate transitional verse. But it is more closely connected with what follows (by *de*
[but], NIV renders "when" in v. 2) and parallels 8:1 as an introduction to
subsequent material. Jesus' teaching and preaching in Galilee suggests
that he has resumed his relatively popular and successful ministry (as
described in 4:17–9:33). But ominous overtones are quickly heard.[2]

**[2]When John heard in prison what Christ was doing, he sent his disciples
[3]to ask him, "Are you the one who was to come, or should we expect someone
else?"**

11:2-3 John abruptly reappears in Matthew's narrative, now in prison
(cf. the passing reference in 4:12). Matthew's audience apparently knew
something of this episode already and needed no further preparation for
the narrative. Matthew 14:1-12 will explain the incident more fully. Luke
prepares his readers for John's arrest in tidier fashion (Luke 3:19-20).
John is probably imprisoned in Herod Antipas's territory, in the fortress at
Machaerus, east of the Dead Sea and thirteen miles southeast of
Herodium[3]—itself just south of Jerusalem (cf. Josephus, *Ant.* 18.5.2).
Here Matthew notes only John's doubts, which lead him to send his fol-
lowers to question Jesus. He has heard specifically of the works of *the*
Christ (NIV lacks the article).[4] The "works" presumably refer to Jesus'
entire ministry thus far but focus specifically on his miracles as illustrated

---

[2]As the NIV margin explains, "of Galilee" is the (probably correct) interpretation of the
Greek "their"—already distancing Jesus some from what were also *his* towns.

[3]D. C. Allison and W. D. Davies, *A Critical and Exegetical Commentary on the Gospel
according to Saint Matthew*, ICC, vol. 2 (Edinburgh: T & T Clark, 1991), 469.

[4]Contra the NIV, the Greek reads, literally, *the Christ*, still a title rather than a proper
name, and obviously reflects Matthew's perspective rather than John's, since otherwise
John's question would be meaningless.

in chaps. 8–9. These mighty deeds should have reinforced John's confidence in Jesus' messiahship. Why then does one who had such a high view of Jesus (3:11-14) now question him? Almost certainly the main answer has to do with John's languishing in prison. Why would one who had promised to free the prisoners (Luke 4:18) not get John out of jail? Most likely John also wondered why there were no signs of the imminent judgment of the wicked that he had predicted (Matt 3:10). In fact, Jesus' "messiahship" little resembled the political and military program of liberation many Jews anticipated (cf. John 6:15). "The one who *is* to come" [contra NIV "was"] repeats the title John had used for Jesus in Matt 3:11 (*ho erchomenos*).

⁴Jesus replied, "Go back and report to John what you hear and see ⁵The blind receive sight, the lame walk, those who have leprosy are cured, the deaf hear, the dead are raised, and the good news is preached to the poor. ⁶Blessed is the man who does not fall away on account of me."

11:4-5 Jesus' reply simply points again to his works, but he now itemizes them. Matthew has illustrated each of these miracles in chaps. 8–9. Probably Jesus wants to remind John of the messianic significance of some of the specific miracles of healing (recall Isa 29:18-19; 35:5-6; 61:1 LXX). Such works were in fact undermining the evil powers of the universe, even if in surprising ways. Jesus also alludes to his preaching of the good news, as illustrated in chaps. 5–7, particularly to the "poor" (see comments under 5:3). Similar remarks appear in greater detail in his Nazareth manifesto (Luke 4:16-30), in which he also quotes Isaiah (Isa 61:1-2a) but stops just short of the predictions of doom (61:2b), as if to stress that his current ministry does not yet involve judgment. Jesus' preaching has also been disseminated more widely by the mission of the Twelve, which chap. 10 introduced. In his sermons Jesus has emphasized that he is inverting the world's standards of greatness, so it should surprise no one that his concept of messiahship did not involve political or military aspirations.

11:6 In beatitude form Jesus encourages John, and everyone else with similar doubts, to remain faithful to him no matter what may come. "Fall away" is from the key Matthean term *skandalizō*, which in various contexts can be translated *take offense, stumble,* or *cause to sin* and is cognate to our English *be scandalized* (see comments under 5:29-30).⁵ Understandably, many Christians have been embarrassed by John's doubts and have tried to minimize them. But we should recognize that "open and inquiring doubt was taken very seriously" by the early church and that "if faith is not

---

⁵On the offensiveness of Jesus' ministry and the contemporary need to recover some of the offensiveness of the gospel, see esp. C. L. Mitton, "Uncomfortable Words: IX. Stumbling-block Characteristics in Jesus," *ExpTim* 82 (1971): 168-72.

simply assent to a proposition but life with God, then it can live only by increasing and decreasing, in experiences that strengthen or endanger it."[6]

[7]As John's disciples were leaving, Jesus began to speak to the crowd about John: "What did you go out into the desert to see? A reed swayed by the wind? [8]If not, what did you go out to see? A man dressed in fine clothes? No, those who wear fine clothes are in kings' palaces. [9]Then what did you go out to see? A prophet? Yes, I tell you, and more than a prophet. [10]This is the one about whom it is written:

> **" 'I will send my messenger ahead of you,**
>   **who will prepare your way before you.'**

(b) Jesus' Testimony Concerning John (11:7-15).   **11:7-10** John's followers return to their master to report Jesus' words, but their question had apparently been posed in a larger public gathering. If doubts were current about Jesus, then naturally there would be questions about John's role as well, especially now if he could be thought to have changed his views of Jesus. Jesus addresses these questions by reassuring his audience of the legitimacy of John's prophetic ministry. He does so first by posing two rhetorical questions that anticipate a negative reply. The setting of John's wilderness ministry made it obvious that those who went to see him would not be expecting a fragile, weak, or vacillating individual ("a reed swayed by the wind")[7] or one who enjoyed the ease of material comfort ("dressed in fine clothes"). "Fine" (*malakos*) is more specifically "soft, delicate, luxurious"[8] and can even imply effeminacy (1 Cor 6:9). One visited kings' *houses* (more literal than NIV "palaces" and perhaps referring to numerous types of homes owned by royalty) and not the desert to find people dressed like that. Instead, the crowds would have associated John with the role of a prophet, both by the clothing he wore and by the harshness of his message (recall 3:1-10). Moreover, John was not just any prophet but the last in a series of prophets who prepared the way for Messiah and brought the old covenant era to its culmination. John fulfilled Mal 3:1 (here interpreted with the language of Exod 23:20). The forerunner of the Lord (Mal 3:1) was naturally associated with the forerunner of the "day of the Lord," namely, Elijah (Mal 4:5). In v. 14 Jesus will make this equation between John and Elijah explicit.[9]

---

[6]E. Schweizer, *The Good News according to Matthew* (Richmond: John Knox, 1975), 256.

[7]R. G. Bratcher (*A Translator's Guide to the Gospel of Matthew* [New York: UBS, 1981], 126) thinks of a person without strong conviction easily swayed by public opinion.

[8]J. P. Louw and E. A. Nida, eds., *Greek-English Lexicon of the New Testament* (New York: UBS, 1988), 704.

[9]For more detail on this text and the use of Malachi in the New Testament more generally, see C. L. Blomberg, "Elijah, Election and the Use of Malachi in the New Testament," *CTR* 2 (1987): 99-117.

[11]I tell you the truth: Among those born of women there has not risen anyone greater than John the Baptist; yet he who is least in the kingdom of heaven is greater than he. [12]From the days of John the Baptist until now, the kingdom of heaven has been forcefully advancing, and forceful men lay hold of it.

11:11 Thus John climaxed pre-Christian revelation. "Born of women" (v. 11) was simply a Semitic idiom for *human.* Jesus is contrasting all of those who lived prior to the advent of the new covenant with those who will live to see the new age established. Even the least of these will surpass the greatest of the old era (even as the splendor of the new covenant surpasses that of the old covenant; cf. 2 Cor 3:7-18) because of the unique blessings associated with the in-breaking kingdom. These blessings include the once-for-all forgiveness of sins, the greater sense of immediate access to God's presence, and the permanent indwelling of the Spirit.[10] Matthew does not specifically state when the new age begins. Commentators debate whether vv. 11 and 13 place John with the old age or the new age; undoubtedly the best approach identifies the period of Jesus' ministry as transitional. But Matthew apparently sees John as not living to experience the actual inauguration of the "kingdom of heaven," suggesting that the division between the ages must occur after John's death. In view of the central role of Christ's atonement for salvation history, the complex of events including Jesus' death, resurrection, and the sending of the Spirit at Pentecost is the obvious choice for this dividing line. The present aspect of the "kingdom of heaven," somewhat equivalent to the church age, must be in view here since it would be incongruous for Jesus to exclude John from future salvation. The greatness and leastness described must therefore also refer to present benefits of participation in the kingdom, not degrees of reward in heaven.

11:12 Verse 12 forms an amazingly difficult interpretive crux.[11] The difficulties arise because *biazomai* and *biastēs* ("forcefully advancing" and "forceful men") can be taken as either positive or negative terms. The NIV renderings seem implausible. *Biazomai* is most commonly negative and passive, meaning *to suffer violence.*[12] The *de* (*but*) that introduces v. 12 suggests a contrast with v. 11, also making v. 12a more likely negative. *Biastai* in conjunction with *harpazousin* ("lay hold of," but more commonly *attack*) seems likely to be negative too: violent people attack the kingdom. This

---

[10]Because the Greek μικρότερος (NIV "least") is actually a comparative and not a superlative form (lit., *lesser*), it is sometimes translated "the younger" and taken to refer to Jesus as compared with John. But this is not the most natural meaning of forms of "μικρός" ("little"), and the comparative form commonly replaced the superlative in Hellenistic Greek.

[11]For a full survey of the history of interpretation, see P. S. Cameron, *Violence and the Kingdom: The Interpretation of Matthew 11:12* (Frankfurt: Peter Lang, 1984).

[12]See G. Schrenk, "βιάζομαι, βιαστής" in *TDNT* 1:609-14.

combination of translations would then lead the verse to be rendered something like "from the days of John the Baptist until now, the kingdom of heaven suffers violence, and violent people attack it."

This translation fits well with the narrative flow of Matthew. Despite the many blessings of the arriving kingdom, from the early days of John's ministry to the present moment in Jesus' life, God's reign has nevertheless received increasing opposition. John has been arrested by Herod. The Jewish teachers are increasingly opposing Jesus,[13] and people are growing more and more discontent with Jesus' refusal to promote revolution.[14] Luke's apparent parallel (Luke 16:16) is so isolated and in such a different context that it hardly seems germane to an interpretation of Matthew, despite its seemingly more positive sense there.

[13]For all the Prophets and the Law prophesied until John. [14]And if you are willing to accept it, he is the Elijah who was to come. [15]He who has ears, let him hear.

11:13-15 Following the almost parenthetical remarks of v. 12, v. 13 reaffirms that John augurs the end of an era. The "for" that begins v. 13 seems to refer to v. 11 rather than v. 12. The "Prophets and the Law" have pointed forward to the time of John's ministry, but now Jesus is bringing the age of fulfillment. Verse 14 then completes a little chiasmus[15] by spelling out the implications of v. 10. John in fact is, literally, *Elijah, the one who is to come* (contra NIV), i.e., not the literal Elijah of old returning to earth from heaven, which John himself denies being (John 1:21), but one who comes in Elijah's "spirit and power" (Luke 1:17). "If you are willing" shows that Jesus recognizes that his is not the only currently held interpretation of Malachi, but in v. 15 he calls his audience to accept it through careful hearing. This short call reappears frequently in the Gospels and elsewhere in Scripture (e.g., 13:9,43; Luke 14:35; Mark 7:16; Rev 2:7; and cf. Isa 5:4 for possible Old Testament background), again suggesting that Jesus' teaching is not entirely self-evident, particularly to those who only superficially listen and think.

---

[13]Cf. the usage of "violent people" in the Qumran literature to refer to false teachers, as noted especially by B. E. Thiering, "Are the 'Violent Men' False Teachers?" *NovT* 21 (1979): 293-97.

[14]Thus P. W. Barnett ("Who Were the 'Biastai' [Matthew 11:12-13]," *RTR* 36 [1977]: 65-70) sees the violent people as those who came to Jesus to try to force him to bring the kingdom in the wrong way (e.g., John 6:14-15); and W. E. Moore ("Violence to the Kingdom: Josephus and the Syrian Churches," *ExpTim* 100 [1989]: 174-77) even more explicitly equates the violent people with the Zealots.

[15]That is, inverted parallelism, in this instance *ABCB'A':* A and A'—John as Elijah (vv. 10,14); *B* and *B'*—John as the Culmination of the Old Testament era (vv. 11,13); *C*—The Current Attack on the Kingdom (v. 12).

The flow of thought of vv. 7-15 may be summarized in this fashion: despite John's questions, he should not be seen as weak or vacillating. In fact, he is the greatest in a long succession of prophets. But great as he is, something greater is here, namely, Jesus and the kingdom. But these are being attacked rather than universally welcomed. Still, such opposition should not deter would-be disciples, for God's predicted scenario is unfolding according to plan.

[16]"To what can I compare this generation? They are like children sitting in the marketplaces and calling out to others:
[17]" 'We played the flute for you,
    and you did not dance;
we sang a dirge,
    and you did not mourn.'
[18]For John came neither eating nor drinking, and they say, 'He has a demon.' [19]The Son of Man came eating and drinking, and they say, 'Here is a glutton and a drunkard, a friend of tax collectors and "sinners." ' But wisdom is proved right by her actions."

(c) The Crowds' Reaction to John and Jesus (11:16-19). **11:16-19** The initial questions from John's disciples probably reflected a growing skepticism among others in the crowd too. Not only are some beginning to doubt Jesus, but vv. 7-8 suggest some were starting to revise their estimation of John. So Jesus replies to those who would respond to God's messengers this way. Rejection of both John and Jesus is inconsistent and hypocritical, like children playing in the marketplace (their playground in that day) who refuse to play the wedding and funeral games their companions propose. Similarly, Jesus' contemporaries lament John's asceticism and berate Jesus' indulgence. The specific charges of John having a demon and Jesus being a glutton and drunkard have not been previously recorded in Matthew and, in light of what we have read, are clearly false. On the other hand, John was stern, and perhaps his preaching at times seemed like the ravings of a madman. And Jesus is fairly called "a friend of tax collectors and 'sinners.' " Upcoming events, however, will vindicate the wisdom of the behavior of both Jesus and John (v. 19b), even though that behavior often proves countercultural and therefore unpopular.[16] Jesus' little parable (on which, see further under chap. 13) thus teaches three lessons: "(1) The joyful message of forgiveness should be freely celebrated and not dampened by legalistic restrictions (M 11:17a,19a). (2) The solemn message of repentance should not be ignored but taken with seriousness (vv. 17b,18). (3) The truth of both

---

[16]Luke's "children" (Luke 7:35), replacing Matthew's "works," personifies this concept but amounts to the same thing.

of these principles will be demonstrated by those who implement them (v. 19b)."[17]

"Like" in v. 16 implies *it is the case with . . . as with* and does not mean that the people of "this generation" are like the children calling out. It is the case with "this generation" as with the situation described in the story. In fact, "this generation" actually resembles the recalcitrant play-mates who refuse to join in any of the proposed games.[18] "This generation" is puzzling also because it seems to indict all Israel of that time. But it cannot be so taken because Jesus' disciples were Jews too, and large Jewish crowds were still following him with some measure of approval. The third-person language ("they") here in fact seems to distance Jesus' remarks from his present audience. On the other hand, the view that "this generation" refers just to the leaders of Israel seems to be too narrow. The approach that takes it as the leaders speaking in their official capacity on behalf of the whole nation, so that the entire nation comes under God's judgment even as individuals may continue to be saved, introduces subtleties for which there is no textual warrant here. Those who accept or reject Jesus in v. 25 are not described in categories of official leaders versus individuals. Probably Jesus is making a simple generalization from the prevailing reactions of the leaders (cf. Luke 7:29-30), which were starting to spread to others and would eventually turn into a crescendo of opposition among the masses as well (Matt 27:25). His words cannot justify absolute statements about God's rejection of all Jews or of the entire nation of Israel.[19]

We, too, often have our doubts about John and Jesus and cannot accept the full force of the biblical witness to their life-styles. We either prefer grace without moral absolutes or law without the opportunity to live responsibly, free from strangling regulations. Jesus was not "a glutton and a drunkard," but as a friend of tax collectors and sinners he ate and drank with them (9:10-13).[20] Some Christians today give the faith a bad reputation because of immoral excesses, but probably a larger number would never have to worry about being so caricatured because they come nowhere close to imitating Jesus' fellowship with disreputable people. It

---

[17]C. L. Blomberg, *Interpreting the Parables* (Downers Grove: InterVarsity, 1990), 210.

[18]O. Linton, "The Parable of the Children's Game," *NTS* 22 (1976): 159-79.

[19]Cf. J. L. Nolland, *Luke 1-9:20*, WBC (Dallas: Word, 1990), 343. Note also with A. Sand (*Das Evangelium nach Matthäus*, RNT [Regensburg: Pustet, 1986], 243: "In opposition to 'this generation,' the [Christian] community must be as another generation, a generation of the new age which accepts and realizes this new world order."

[20]The view that this drinking did not include alcoholic beverages is untenable by any fair canons of historical research. See N. L. Geisler, "A Christian Perspective on Wine-Drinking," *BibSac* 139 (1982): 46-56, who nevertheless argues for abstinence as an important, strategic choice for Christians to make today.

is also interesting to reflect on the combination of gluttony and drunkenness used here, a pairing that recurs elsewhere in Scripture (cf. Deut 21:20; Prov 23:21). Christians today seldom consider the possibility that the two are equally sinful. We no doubt drastically underestimate the former and somewhat overestimate the latter. And to the extent that Jesus rejects the Zealot option (terrorism as a means of promoting social change) for both leaders and their followers, this parable implicitly condemns both oppressive authority (as John did earlier) and violent revolution (as Jesus does later).

[20]Then Jesus began to denounce the cities in which most of his miracles had been performed, because they did not repent. [21]"Woe to you, Korazin! Woe to you, Bethsaida! If the miracles that were performed in you had been performed in Tyre and Sidon, they would have repented long ago in sackcloth and ashes. [22]But I tell you, it will be more bearable for Tyre and Sidon on the day of judgment than for you. [23]And you, Capernaum, will you be lifted up to the skies? No, you will go down to the depths. If the miracles that were performed in you had been performed in Sodom, it would have remained to this day. [24]But I tell you that it will be more bearable for Sodom on the day of judgment than for you."

(2) Judgment on Unrepentant Cities (11:20-24). **11:20-24** Now the rebukes become more explicit. Jesus employs the common Old Testament form of a woe (cf., e.g., Num 21:29; 1 Sam 4:8; Isa 3:9-11; Jer 13:27; Ezek 24:6-9)—an exclamation of "how greatly one will suffer,"[21] mingling doom with pity. Jesus laments God's coming judgment on the cities in which many of his miracles occurred. As with "this generation" (v. 16), the judgment of "cities" reflects God's response to a general rejection of Jesus, not an absolute condemnation of every individual (as was true also with Sodom; cf. v. 24 and recall 10:15). Matthew has said nothing about Jesus ministering in Korazin or Bethsaida, but 4:23-25 and 11:1 leave plenty of room for such ministry. These two cities were nearby to the north and east of Capernaum.[22] Tyre and Sidon were paradigms of Israel's enemies of old (cf. Isa 23; Ezek 26–28; Amos 1:9-10). Sodom (like Gomorrah) typified the wickedness of Canaan before Israel settled in it. Jesus claims that many in both pairs of towns would have repented had he worked his miracles there. "Sackcloth and ashes" were common public tokens of repentance in antiquity. One who wore sackcloth donned a coarse undergarment, often made of camels' hair. Ashes were sprinkled on one's head (cf. Esth 4:3 and Jonah 3:6-9). Tyre, Sidon, and Sodom

---

[21]Louw and Nida, *Greek-English Lexicon*, 243.

[22]There is some dispute on the location of Bethsaida, since there may have been two separate communities with that name. See *ISBE*, ad loc., for further details on all the cities referred to here.

would have averted destruction by these actions. Hence, these Old Testament towns will be judged less severely (recall comments under 10:15).

But God will deal with Korazin, Bethsaida, and Capernaum more severely because they have received more immediate, dramatic, and straightforward revelation.[23] Capernaum's attitude is even more specifically likened to the arrogance of the king of Babylon's aspirations and its fate to God's subsequent judgment of that ancient despot (Isa 14:12-15).[24] A well-attested textual variant (not noted by the NIV) reads "be thrown down" instead of "go down." The "depths" refer literally to *Hades* (the Greek counterpart of *Sheol*—the shadowy underworld of Old Testament times) but are probably not to be distinguished here from other terms for eternal judgment. "Skies" is more literally *heaven*. A harsher contrast than between Capernaum and Sodom could hardly be imagined. And for a Jew in Jesus' audience, to prefer Sodom would have been outrageous. Little wonder that hostility soon increased.

[25]At that time Jesus said, "I praise you, Father, Lord of heaven and earth, because you have hidden these things from the wise and learned, and revealed them to little children. [26]Yes, Father, for this was your good pleasure.

(3) The Alternative: The Rest Christ Can Provide (11:25-30).[25] **11:25-26** The language of these verses is very Johannine but also very Jewish.[26] "At that time" is a looser connection than the English translation might suggest (cf. 12:1). The original context of vv. 25-30 is therefore unknown, but Matthew includes them here to show that despite the growing opposition to Jesus discipleship remains the only alternative that satisfies the deepest of human longings. In what is apparently a public prayer, Jesus praises God in wording reminiscent of Dan 2:19-23. He again reveals his intimate relationship with God as his Father (see comments under 6:9) but also underlines God's sovereignty as Master of the universe. The increasingly polarized response to Jesus in fact forms part of God's eternal plan. "These things" refers to the overall significance of Jesus' mission.[27] The language of these verses ("hidden," "revealed," "your good pleasure") is incontrovertibly predestinarian in nature, but the

---

[23]Cf. F. D. Bruner (*The Christbook* [Waco: Word, 1987], 425): "*Christian* countries are in special trouble on judgment day, not because Jesus has not really been in their communities but because he has. Jesus' presence, without change, can lead to a damnation deeper than Sodom's."

[24]Cf. again Bruner, *Christbook*, 428: "Capernaum stands for all self-conscious Christianity, for all Christianity smug in its possession of Jesus, in its being the center of Jesus' work."

[25]For a full-length study of this passage, see C. Deutsch, *Hidden Wisdom and the Easy Yoke* (Sheffield: JSOT, 1987).

[26]For relevant background, cf. D. C. Allison, Jr., "Two Notes on a Key Text: Matthew 11:25-30," *JTS* 39 (1988): 477-85.

[27]R. T. France, *The Gospel according to Matthew*, TNTC (Grand Rapids: Eerdmans, 1985), 198.

language of free will appears equally clearly in vv. 20-24, in which people are judged for their rejection of Jesus, and in vv. 28-30, in which Jesus offers salvation to those who will respond more positively. Scripture in fact regularly and without sense of contradiction juxtaposes the themes of divine sovereignty and human responsibility (e.g., Gen 50:19-20; Lev 20:7-8; Jer 29:10-14; Joel 2:32; Phil 2:12-13).[28]

The history of the church is littered with attempts to reject or subordinate one of these two themes to the other, as, classically, in the Calvinist-Arminian debate. Both themes must be affirmed, and affirmed simultaneously, in order to be true to Scripture and to Christian experience. Few believers have ever denied that they freely chose to accept Christ, but neither have they denied that key individuals and circumstances in their lives were influential in that decision in ways they did not manufacture. God has chosen and drawn all who freely come to him.[29]

"Little children" refers to those who respond to God by acknowledging their dependence on him (cf. comments under 18:4). The "wise and learned," as the opposite category of persons, must therefore represent those who feel they have no need for God. Verse 25 thus cannot be used as a proof text for anti-intellectualism. Jesus does not contrast "wise" versus "stupid," but he does declaim a godless intellectualism.[30]

27"All things have been committed to me by my Father. No one knows the Son except the Father, and no one knows the Father except the Son and those to whom the Son chooses to reveal him.

11:27 If vv. 25-26 claim that humility is a prerequisite for receiving God's revelation, v. 27 adds that one cannot come to God without accepting Christ (cf. 1 John 2:23). "All things" are left unspecified but probably carry the sense of *all authority* (cf. 28:18). Clearly Jesus and God have a unique relationship. He is God's Son in a different sense than believers are God's children (John 1:12). *Epiginōskō* means more than *know*, involving the most intimate and fullest acquaintance. The theology is not yet Trinitarian but prepares the way for the references to the Father and Son in the baptismal formula of 28:19.

---

[28]See D. A. Carson, *Divine Sovereignty and Human Responsibility* (Atlanta: John Knox, 1981).

[29]One of the best treatments of predestination from a moderate or centrist Calvinist perspective is M. J. Erickson, *Christian Theology*, vol. 3 (Grand Rapids: Baker, 1985), 907-28; and from a moderate or centrist Arminian view, cf. W. L. Craig, *The Only Wise God* (Grand Rapids: Baker, 1987). In either system election is not a deterrent but an incentive to evangelism; without God's prior activity none could ever hope to be saved, but God saves only through the free human actions of preaching and conversion.

[30]Cf. D. A. Carson, "Matthew," EBC, vol. 8, ed. F. E. Gaebelein [Grand Rapids: Zondervan, 1984], 275: "The contrast is between those who are self-sufficient and deem themselves wise and those who are dependent and love to be taught."

²⁸"Come to me, all you who are weary and burdened, and I will give you rest. ²⁹Take my yoke upon you and learn from me, for I am gentle and humble in heart, and you will find rest for your souls. ³⁰For my yoke is easy and my burden is light."

11:28-30 Jesus now appeals for a response to his revelation. All may come, at least all who hurt and who recognize their spiritual need. The "little children" (v. 25) will accept him and thus demonstrate their election (v. 27). The "wise and learned" (v. 25) are precisely those who reject his call and thus show they were not chosen. The distinction between the two categories of individuals is therefore not intellectual but volitional. "Weary and burdened" reflects the daily labor of carrying a pack on one's back. Tired workers need refreshment and renewal (cf. Jer 6:16); Jesus equates the Christian life with spiritual rest. In describing his provision of this rest, Jesus borrows imagery from the plowing of fields. Like the yoke that couples oxen together, discipleship does not exempt one from work but makes it manageable. Jews commonly spoke of taking on the yoke of the Torah to refer to the acceptance of the stipulations of the law. But, as the Sermon on the Mount has made plain, Jesus calls people not to the law but to himself.

"Learn" echoes the exhortation of rabbinic instruction. No doubt, like many of the Jewish teachers, Jesus is "gentle" (the same word as "meek" in 5:5) and "humble." But unlike them, Christ offers work that is refreshing and *good* (more literal than NIV "easy") because it brings salvation.[31] Christ's yoke is thus "light." None of this implies that Jesus' "greater righteousness," as illustrated in the Sermon on the Mount, is not extremely challenging or demanding. Jesus' requirements are no less stringent than those of the Jewish teachers, but they can be accomplished more readily because of the strength Christ provides through the Holy Spirit.[32] Jesus did not escape the hard life, but he could experience rest and refreshment in its midst. Christians are not promised freedom from illness or calamity, but they may experience God's sustaining grace so that they are not crushed or driven to despair (2 Cor 4:8-9). The rest Jesus offers his disciples enables them to overcome a certain measure of "fear, anxiety, uncertainty, and meaninglessness in the joy and peace of God's very presence in Jesus Christ."[33] By way of contrast, most Jews found the interpretations of the law imposed on them by their leaders increas-

---

[31]BAGD, 886. χρηστός can mean *easy* in the sense of easy to wear. It is derived from a term for *useful* or *suitable* and is linked with concepts of *good, pleasant,* and *kindly.*

[32]Cf. Deutsch (*Wisdom,* 46): "The yoke of Jesus is easy and his burden light precisely because that yoke brings one into fellowship with the gentle and lowly one, with the result that the promised rest is already present."

[33]F. Stagg, "Matthew," in *The Broadman Bible Commentary,* vol. 8, ed. C. J. Allen (Nashville: Broadman, 1969), 145.

ingly burdensome (23:4; cf. Acts 15:10, which uses the identical "yoke" imagery).[34]

The sequence of thought of vv. 25-30 thus progresses as follows. The increasing polarization of response to Jesus in fact reflects God's sovereign choices (vv. 25-26). Jesus is God's unique agent in the outworking of those choices (v. 27). This gives him God's authority to call people to himself (vv. 28-30). The invitation to come to Christ remains for all today, but now as then it requires the recognition that persons cannot come by exalting themselves (recall v. 23) but only by completely depending on and trusting in Christ.

b. EXPLICIT OPPOSITION (12:1-50). Now Jesus' opponents appear directly on the scene. Two Sabbath controversies (vv. 1-8,9-14) lead to Jesus' withdrawal from hostility and to Matthew's characteristic explanation of events in terms of the fulfillment of prophecy (vv. 15-21). An extended controversy regarding Jesus' exorcistic activity then ensues (vv. 22-45). But, as in chap. 11, chap. 12 closes with an alternative to all this hostility, the call to discipleship that makes one a part of the true family of Jesus (vv. 46-50).

¹At that time Jesus went through the grainfields on the Sabbath. His disciples were hungry and began to pick some heads of grain and eat them. ²When the Pharisees saw this, they said to him, "Look! Your disciples are doing what is unlawful on the Sabbath."

(1) Sabbath Controversies and Their Outcome (12:1-21). (a) Picking the Grain (12:1-8). **12:1-2** Matthew continues to organize his material topically. "At that time" in Greek is a very loose temporal connective (cf. 14:1). Matthew 12:1-14 is linked to 11:25-30 by the contrast between the yoke of discipleship and the yoke of the law and by the theme of rest (11:28). In first-century Judaism rest meant, above all, observing the Sabbath—ceasing from all work on Saturday, the seventh day of the week. Sabbath observance was in fact one of the three most important and distinctive badges of Jewish life, along with circumcision and the dietary laws. If coming to Jesus provided rest for the whole of life, then it is not surprising that he should come into conflict with regulations that prevented various kinds of work on one specific day out of seven. At the very least, Jesus shows that he feels free to disregard the

---

[34]A reference to Pharisaism has been disputed here (see M. Maher, "'Take My Yoke Upon You' [Matt. 11.29]," *NTS* 22 [1976]: 97-103); but it was already well-defended by H. D. Betz, "The Logion of the Easy Yoke and of Rest (Matt 11:28-30)," *JBL* 86 (1967): 10-24. The debate continues concerning the nature of first-century Palestinian Judaism more generally. Among recent writers see E. P. Sanders, *Paul and Palestinian Judaism* (Philadelphia: Fortress, 1977). But note the important correctives in S. Westerholm, *Israel's Law and the Church's Faith* (Grand Rapids: Eerdmans, 1988).

oral laws that had grown up around the Sabbath. But his words will suggest more than this (see comments under vv. 3-8), namely, that the Fourth Commandment itself is fulfilled in him and therefore need no longer be observed literally. The apostle Paul will make these conclusions more explicit in Col 2:16-17 and Rom 14:5-6.

The details of the setting here are sparse. The ripening of the grain suggests springtime, perhaps a few weeks after Passover.[35] Matthew does not explain why the group was out traveling on a Sabbath, where they were going, or why they were hungry, merely that Jesus' disciples pluck some grain to satisfy their appetites. As in 9:9-13, the Pharisees criticize their actions, though again it is unclear exactly when and where the ensuing dialogue occurs. Their accusations stem from the oral Torah, which included reaping as one of thirty-nine activities specifically forbidden on the Sabbath (cf. *m. Sabb.* 7:2).[36]

³He answered, "Haven't you read what David did when he and his companions were hungry? ⁴He entered the house of God, and he and his companions ate the consecrated bread—which was not lawful for them to do, but only for the priests. ⁵Or haven't you read in the Law that on the Sabbath the priests in the temple desecrate the day and yet are innocent? ⁶I tell you that one greater than the temple is here. ⁷If you had known what these words mean, 'I desire mercy, not sacrifice,' you would not have condemned the innocent. ⁸For the Son of Man is Lord of the Sabbath."

12:3-8 Jesus does not reply by arguing that the Pharisees have gone beyond the written law with their prescriptions. But he does cite Scripture to justify his actions. He refers first to the episode in which David broke the written law but was held blameless and second to provisions within the law itself to exempt certain people from the various Sabbath laws. The first passage (1 Sam 21:1-6) describes David and his companions when they became hungry after fleeing from Saul. Ahimelech, the priest at Nob, let them eat the sacred showbread, despite the restriction of Lev 24:5-9 that only priests could eat this bread. Jesus' second example appeals to Num 28:9-10, which required priests to work on the Sabbath by offering various sacrifices.

But Jesus was not of Levitical, priestly lineage; nor is there any evidence that his life was in danger or his needs nearly as urgent as David's. Jesus' point is not that analogous circumstances exist to warrant exceptional practices but that "one greater than the temple is here" (v. 6). By implication the point of v. 4 is therefore also that "one greater than David

[35] A. H. M'Neile, *The Gospel according to St. Matthew* (London: Macmillan, 1915), 168.

[36] Though there may be as many as four such laws that were transgressed—reaping, winnowing, threshing, and preparing a meal (R. H. Mounce, *Matthew*, GNC [San Francisco: Harper and Row, 1985], 112).

is here" (cf. 22:41-45).[37] It is not, therefore, the particular situation in which Jesus finds himself that justifies his disciples' behavior but his very nature and authority which can transcend the law and make permissible for his disciples what once was forbidden.[38] Thus the passage displays the same logic as 5:17-48. Verse 8 brings the dialogue to its logical climax. Jesus' sovereign authority will determine how the Sabbath is now fulfilled in the kingdom age.

Matthew's unique additions (vv. 5-7 and the reference to hunger in v. 1), particularly v. 7, with its quotation of Hos 6:6 (on which see comments under 9:13), have suggested to many that Matthew is trying to tone down the radical nature of Jesus' claims as compared with Mark's and Luke's accounts (Mark 2:23-28; Luke 6:1-5). Matthew would then be trying to depict Jesus making a valid exception to the law still within the framework of the law. But if these were his intentions, he would have needed to have removed vv. 6 and 8, and one would have expected him to have retained the phrase "in need" of Mark 2:25. It is better, therefore, to take v. 7 as pointing out a rationale for Jesus' contravening the Sabbath law. His approach is not arbitrary but based on God's priorities of putting compassion above ritual, which Sabbath-keeping can so often hinder.[39]

[9]Going on from that place, he went into their synagogue, [10]and a man with a shriveled hand was there. Looking for a reason to accuse Jesus, they asked him, "Is it lawful to heal on the Sabbath?"

(b) Healing the Man with the Shriveled Hand (12:9-14). **12:9-10** Matthew immediately illustrates this point with a second pronouncement/controversy story about Jesus and the Sabbath, this time involving a local synagogue service. Here the Pharisees themselves take the initiative to stir up controversy by posing the question of whether or not it is "lawful to heal on the Sabbath" (an issue that will become a common source of conflict in Jesus' ministry—cf. Luke 13:14; John 5:7-9). The handicapped man in question has a "shriveled hand," a disability that had probably not occurred recently and that in no way threatened the man's life or health. If

---

[37]Cf. France, *Matthew*, 202-3.

[38]If the neuter (rather than masculine) gender of the "one" in v. 6 is pressed, then we should translate "something greater than the temple is here" (cf. NIV marg.), referring to the new authority, teaching, and/or kingdom Jesus brings, not simply to his person. But such grammatical distinctions are often blurred in Hellenistic Greek.

[39]On whether or not Jesus' logic would have convinced by rabbinic standards, cf. E. Levine, "The Sabbath Controversy according to Matthew," *NTS* 22 (1976): 480-83 (yes); versus D. M. Cohn-Sherbok, "An Analysis of Jesus' Arguments concerning the Plucking of Grain on the Sabbath," *JSNT* 2 (1979): 31-41 (no). Cohn-Sherbok seems more convincing— further evidence that Jesus' point is not simply part of an intramural Jewish debate but challenging the unchanging permanence of the law head-on.

Jesus wished to help the man, he could obviously wait one day until the Sabbath had passed. The situation did not require immediate action. Interestingly, the Pharisees' question presupposes their belief that Jesus could genuinely heal the man.

11He said to them, "If any of you has a sheep and it falls into a pit on the Sabbath, will you not take hold of it and lift it out? 12How much more valuable is a man than a sheep! Therefore it is lawful to do good on the Sabbath."

12:11-12 Jesus replies with a short parable (all but v. 12b is unique to Matthew in this context), which contrasts the value of animals and humans (cf. 6:26 and 10:31). He points out the inconsistency in the oral law, which permits the rescue of an animal from a pit (e.g., *b. Sabb.* 128b) but not the healing of an individual whose life is not possibly in danger (e.g., *m. Yoma* 8:6—contra the Qumran sectarians, who rectified this inconsistency by prohibiting both actions—CD 11:13-14). Yet again Jesus' conclusion does not challenge just the oral law. Instead, Jesus makes the sweeping pronouncement that "it is lawful to do good on the Sabbath." Bonnard calls this principle "disturbing, for, if generalized, it would make all organized church life impossible: there is always some 'good' to undertake in preference to a religious duty."[40] But Jesus is not contrasting some "good" with religious duty. He does not encourage the Jews to stop worshiping. He is contrasting activity with inactivity. There is always some good to do on the Sabbath which makes total cessation of labor no longer appropriate. Of course, human beings need physical rest and need it on a regular basis, but this is different from prescribing one day in seven on which particular activities are banned as morally improper.[41]

13Then he said to the man, "Stretch out your hand." So he stretched it out and it was completely restored, just as sound as the other. 14But the Pharisees went out and plotted how they might kill Jesus.

12:13-14 Thus Jesus heals the man. He commands him to move his hand in such a way as to prove that he is healed (cf. the command to the paralytic in 9:6). Matthew stresses the completeness of his healing, a great "good" indeed (v. 12), and sharply juxtaposes the strongest statement of Pharisaic antagonism to date. "Kill" here has the sense of

---

[40]P. Bonnard, *L'Évangile selon saint Matthieu* (Neûchatel: Delachaux et Niestlé, 1963), 175, quoted by France, 205.

[41]For an excellent popular treatment of the application of the Sabbath commandment in the New Testament age, see W. Barclay, *The Plain Man's Guide to Ethics: Thoughts on the Ten Commandments* (Glasgow: Collins, 1973), 26-48. For scholarly and detailed analysis, see esp. D. A. Carson, ed., *From Sabbath to Lord's Day* (Grand Rapids: Zondervan, 1982).

arrest—initiating the legal proceedings that would culminate in capital punishment.

The New Testament nowhere equates Sunday or Lord's Day observance with Sabbath-keeping, nor does it suggest that the Sabbath is to be treated any differently from other Jewish ceremonial days and rituals simply because of its presence in the Ten Commandments (cf. Col 2:16-17). The early church actually forbade any cessation of labor on the Sabbath, viewing such rest as "Judaizing." For the first three centuries of church history, Gentile Christians rarely had an opportunity to rest anyway, inasmuch as the Roman work week did not provide for a weekly day off. Modern Sabbatarianism is largely the legacy of Puritan legalism. To be sure, contemporary American Christianity desperately needs to recover the centrality of worship and of life in Christian community, but this is an entirely separate issue from Sabbath observance and not helped by injunctions against work or other activities on Sunday (or Saturday). Instead, churches should become far more creative in the days, times, places, and formats they make available for people to gather in fellowship and worship in order to minister more adequately in a culture that is rapidly rescinding the privileges the Western church has enjoyed since Constantine—including Sunday as a guaranteed day off for most workers. As for the Sabbath commands, believers fulfill them when they heed Matt 11:28-30 and rest daily in the Lord (cf. Heb 4:9-11, in which "Sabbath-rest" is equated with becoming a believer). Objectors, ancient and modern, fail to grasp that "freedom from ritual commandment need not lead to moral chaos but within the Kingdom of God imposes a responsibility far greater than any law could demand."[42]

[15]Aware of this, Jesus withdrew from that place. Many followed him, and he healed all their sick, [16]warning them not to tell who he was. [17]This was to fulfill what was spoken through the prophet Isaiah:
[18]"Here is my servant whom I have chosen,
 the one I love, in whom I delight;
 I will put my Spirit on him,
 and he will proclaim justice to the nations.
[19]He will not quarrel or cry out;
 no one will hear his voice in the streets.
[20]A bruised reed he will not break,
 and a smoldering wick he will not snuff out,
 till he leads justice to victory.
[21]In his name the nations will put their hope."

---

[42]Mounce, *Matthew*, 114. For further details on these applications, see esp. C. Blomberg, "The Sabbath as Fulfilled in Christ," in *The Sabbath in Jewish and Christian Traditions*, ed. T. C. Eskenazi, D. Harrington, and W. Shea (New York: Crossroad, 1991), 196-206.

(c) Withdrawal from Hostility (12:15-21). **12:15-21** Jesus' time to die has not yet come, so he leaves this area of greatest danger. Still the crowds follow, more interested in further healings than concerned about the Pharisees' threats (v. 15). Jesus' injunctions to silence, in this context, must stem from his desire to avoid premature arrest and execution (v. 16). Verse 17 views Jesus' withdrawal as the fulfillment of Scripture. In the longest Old Testament quotation in his Gospel, Matthew depicts Jesus as God's suffering servant (Isa 42:1-4), who does not fight back against those who oppose him. The heavenly voice quoted part of this text at Jesus' baptism (3:17); here God reaffirms his choice of and love for that Jesus, whom the Spirit anointed (v. 18). The passage in Isaiah predicts that God's servant will bring justice, but not by force or violence. Verse 19 does not preclude the strong denunciation of evil, as vv. 25-45 will make clear. "No one will hear" means that few will respond adequately, not that the servant will not speak,[43] though indeed Jesus never persists in arguing or trying to convince those who reject him (cf. vv. 38-42). Matthew may also see here a rejection of the overtly revolutionary or Zealot perspectives of his day. Verse 20a affirms Jesus' consummate gentleness (recall 11:29-30). The imagery refers to that which could be damaged by the slightest touch (like a "reed"—recall 11:7). Verses 20b-21 promise that he will ultimately bring justice and victory for Gentile as well as Jewish followers. The "nations" of vv. 18-21 are the *ethnē*—all "peoples" of the world.

In some of the suffering servant passages of Isaiah, the prophet explicitly identifies God's servant as Israel (Isa 44:1; 45:4; 49:3). In other places an individual seems more likely in view (esp. in 52:13–53:12). In Isa 42:1-2 "servant" may signify the nation Israel or the Messiah or the Messiah as the fulfillment of God's plans for Israel (a popular theme in Matthew; see comments under 2:13-15). Jewish interpretation varied, but already in the *Tg. Isa* 42:1, this text was taken as messianic. Matthew's use of Isaiah thus falls squarely within the already established range of interpretive options. The text form is quite different from the LXX, while retaining a few agreements with the LXX as over against the MT.[44]

As part of the first of the suffering servant songs which culminate with chaps. 52–53, Isa 42:1-4 points to what Matthew will have Jesus make increasingly clear: his cross must precede his crown. He comes first to

---

[43]See esp. J. H. Neyrey, "The Thematic Use of Isaiah 42,1-4 in Matthew 12," *Bib* 63 (1982): 461. Neyrey's entire article (457-73) provides a good study of the whole passage and notes connections between the Isaiah quotation and many parts of Matt 12.

[44]For the texts see G. L. Archer and G. C. Chirichigno, *Old Testament Quotations in the New Testament* (Chicago: Moody, 1983), 112-13; for a discussion of the changes, see R. H. Gundry, *Matthew: A Commentary on His Literary and Theological Art* (Grand Rapids: Eerdmans, 1982), 229-30.

suffer before returning in splendor. His disciples must often follow a similar path (16:24). Still, Christians are not called to quietism and inaction in the face of injustice but to patience, prayer, and a prophetic voice that denounces evil. But they await ultimate vindication from God, to whom alone belongs vengeance and the ability fully to right the wrongs of this world (cf. Jas 5:1-11).

(2) Exorcism Controversies (12:22-45). The pattern of 9:32-34 (Jesus' exorcism, the crowd's astonishment, and the Pharisees' accusation) is repeated in vv. 22-24, but this time Jesus responds and at some length (vv. 25-37). Verses 38-42 seem to have shifted the topic, but the Pharisees request a sign presumably to justify Jesus' exorcism, and vv. 43-45 return explicitly to the topic of evil spirits.

22Then they brought him a demon-possessed man who was blind and mute, and Jesus healed him, so that he could both talk and see. 23All the people were astonished and said, "Could this be the Son of David?"

(a) Jesus' Exorcistic Powers (12:22-37). **12:22-23** Like the man in 9:32-33, this demonized individual is unable to speak. In this case he is blind too. Jesus cures both afflictions. Matthew does not specifically label the healing an exorcism, but v. 24 assumes one has occurred. The crowd is characteristically astonished and raises the question of Jesus' identity. On "Son of David," see comments under 1:1; 9:27. But the wording in the Greek suggests more skepticism than before and could fairly be translated, *This man isn't the Son of David, is he?* The increasingly widespread rejection of Christ implied in 11:16-24 is thus illustrated.[45]

24But when the Pharisees heard this, they said, "It is only by Beelzebub, the prince of demons, that this fellow drives out demons."

12:24 The Jewish leaders repeat their earlier charge (see comments on 9:34; for Beelzebub/Beelzeboul see comments on 10:25). Interestingly, this charge persisted as a common view of Jesus among Jews in the early centuries of the Christian era. They did not deny the genuineness of his miracles but ascribed his power to the devil, so that he was branded a sorcerer (e.g., *b. Sanh.* 107b; *b. Sabb.* 104b) and worthy of death (*m. Sanh.* 7:4). On Jesus' exorcisms more generally, see comments on 4:24; 8:28-34.

25Jesus knew their thoughts and said to them, "Every kingdom divided against itself will be ruined, and every city or household divided against itself

---

[45]The Greek construction is an interrogative negated by μή. The NIV ("Could this be the Son of David?") does not make this grammatical feature clear. B. Newman and P. Stine (*A Translator's Handbook on the Gospel of Matthew* [New York: UBS, 1988], 383) note that the question does not necessarily imply an absolute no for an answer, but it certainly introduces a significant measure of uncertainty.

will not stand. [26]If Satan drives out Satan, he is divided against himself. How then can his kingdom stand? [27]And if I drive out demons by Beelzebub, by whom do your people drive them out? So then, they will be your judges. [28]But if I drive out demons by the Spirit of God, then the kingdom of God has come upon you.

12:25-28 On the clause "Jesus knew their thoughts," see under 9:4. Jesus responds with an analogy from civil warfare to the accusation that Satan was empowering him. Internal conflict within a country, town, or even family, if unchecked, will tear it apart (v. 25). "Ruined" is more literally *laid waste*, in the sense of becoming a desert or wilderness. Jesus concludes that because demonization promotes Satan's designs, Satan would not himself seek to cast out demons (v. 26). He would be undermining his own work. Moreover, Jesus is not the only exorcist in the area. Other Jews practiced exorcism as well. Without evaluating this state of affairs, Jesus points out that the logic of the charge against him condemns those making it. If Satan is the one who enables exorcisms, then other Jewish exorcists must also be devilish. Jesus' accusers judge their own "people" (literally, *sons*) by their accusations (v. 27).

If, however, the Pharisees' logic proves faulty, then the question of the true source of these other exorcists' power remains unaddressed. Holy men like Hanina ben Dosa, who were unaffiliated with any particular Jewish sect, could certainly have been "righteous" Jews, in the sense of Matthew's description of Joseph in 1:19, and thus truly empowered by God.[46] The crowds nevertheless perceive Jesus' ability and authority as superior (cf. 9:33b). Jesus himself claims that he exorcises by the power of the Holy Spirit,[47] who descended on him at his baptism, marking the inauguration of God's reign, and who permanently empowers all disciples for ministry in the messianic age.[48] Verse 28 is arguably the single most important teaching of Jesus on realized eschatology—the present aspect of the kingdom (on which see the discussion under 3:2).[49] Debate continues on the meaning of *ephthasen* ("has come"), but some sense of *arrival* seems inescapable here.[50] Matthew also uses the "kingdom of God"

---

[46]On these so-called charismatic holy men, see G. Vermes, *Jesus the Jew* (Philadelphia: Fortress, 1973), 63-68; A. E. Harvey, *Jesus and the Constraints of History* (Philadelphia: Westminster, 1982), 98-119.

[47]Both vv. 27 and 28 begin with first-class conditions. Obviously Jesus cannot believe that he casts out demons both by Beelzebul and by the Spirit. The first condition simply assumes this hypothetical possibility for the sake of argument, to demonstrate its logical corollary.

[48]Apparently a Matthean emphasis, since Luke 11:20 has "finger" of God, a characteristically Semitic anthropomorphism and undoubtedly the more literal translation.

[49]See classically C. H. Dodd, *The Parables of the Kingdom* (New York: Scribner's, 1936).

[50]See G. E. Ladd, *The Presence of the Future* (Grand Rapids: Eerdmans, 1974), 138-45. C. C. Caragounis ("Kingdom of God, Son of Man and Jesus' Self-Understanding," *TynBul* 40 [1989]: 3-23, 223-38), however, argues that the verb refers to the death of Jesus in the very near future.

(rather than "kingdom of heaven") for the first time, probably to parallel the "Spirit of God"[51] in the previous clause.

[29]"Or again, how can anyone enter a strong man's house and carry off his possessions unless he first ties up the strong man? Then he can rob his house. [30]"He who is not with me is against me, and he who does not gather with me scatters. [31]And so I tell you, every sin and blasphemy will be forgiven men, but the blasphemy against the Spirit will not be forgiven. [32]Anyone who speaks a word against the Son of Man will be forgiven, but anyone who speaks against the Holy Spirit will not be forgiven, either in this age or in the age to come.

12:29 Jesus now illustrates the correct interpretation of his exorcisms with an analogy or short parable. One cannot attack a well-protected home without first rendering the guard powerless. So, too, Jesus must first bind Satan before he can plunder (*carry off* or *rob*, from the same verb stem as "lay hold of" in 11:12) his house, i.e., cast out his demons. The exorcisms demonstrate that God in Christ is decisively defeating the devil. As has often been noted, D-Day has come, though not yet V-Day. Satan is in his death throes. His last flurry of activity, to change the metaphor, is like that of a chicken (or perhaps better a snake!) with its head cut off.

12:30-32 Jesus next employs the metaphor ("gathering" and "scattering") of either a shepherd or harvester. Verse 30 must be balanced by Mark 9:40, with both verses interpreted in context.[52] The point here is that Christ leaves no room for neutral ground. If people cannot accept his teaching and work, they are in danger of God's judgment. Forgiveness is possible for all kinds of sins when a person repents (the implied condition in v. 31, as the summaries of John's and Jesus' teaching in 3:2 and 4:17 have made very clear), save for one—blasphemy against the Holy Spirit. "Blasphemy" usually referred to some form of profaning God's name. "Blasphemy against the [Holy] Spirit" is not defined in this context but must refer to what Jesus' accusers are at least in danger of committing. J. F. Walvoord captures the sense concisely: "attributing to Satan what is accomplished by the power of God"[53] (cf. Isa 5:20).

Listeners steeped in the Old Testament would call to mind the laws that labeled particularly defiant sin as blasphemy and seemingly unforgivable (see esp. the sinning *with a high hand* of Num 15:30-31)—the

---

[51]See Carson, "Matthew," 289.

[52]On which, see Bruner (*Christbook*, 461): "Our exclusivity must be in witness to *Christ*, not an exclusivity requiring, necessarily, membership in our branch of the church. These two sets of verses teach Christians to walk the narrow but exciting road of Christ-centeredness and church-openness, to be both deeply evangelical and broadly ecumenical."

[53]J. F. Walvoord, *Matthew: Thy Kingdom Come* (Chicago: Moody, 1974), 89.

flagrant, willful, and persistent rejection of God and his commands.[54] These Pharisees' attitude to Jesus is comparable. Verse 32 repeats the contrast between forgivable and unforgivable sins, this time apparently specifying the worst of the former. The contrast between the Son of Man and the Holy Spirit is not clear. It has been taken as a reference to rejecting Jesus before rather than after Pentecost (when the Spirit came to indwell all believers). But here Jesus is already working miracles by the power of the Spirit, so the contrast seems more likely one between rejecting Jesus when the evidence is ambiguous (recall the very ambiguity of the "Son of Man" title; see comments under 8:20) and rejecting him when his actions clearly demonstrate the Spirit's presence.[55] The end of v. 32 makes it plain that the lack of forgiveness in view here is eternal.

This is not the only place in the New Testament in which an unforgivable sin appears (cf. Heb 6:4-6; 1 John 5:16). Christians have often tried to identify this sin with such things as murder, adultery, or divorce; and individual believers have often wondered if they have committed such a sin. Even if all the details are unclear, we should observe that in this text only Jesus' enemies are in any danger—those who have never professed any allegiance to him and, at least in the pages of Scripture, never do. Instead, they intensify their opposition to the point of crucifying him. Probably blasphemy against the Holy Spirit is nothing more or less than the unrelenting rejection of his advances. Jesus' teaching thus parallels Acts 4:12. If one rejects the Spirit of God in Jesus, there is no one else in all the cosmos who can provide salvation. But we dare never label anyone as having committed this sin. Only God knows human hearts, and we would often make the wrong guess. Moreover, professing believers who fear they have committed the unforgivable sin demonstrate a concern for their spiritual welfare which by definition proves they have not committed it.

Jesus' warning against blaspheming the Holy Spirit should make believers extremely cautious about attributing the actions of other professing Christians to the devil. To be sure, we must test the spirits (1 John 4:1), including those in our own midst, and recognize that Satan can masquerade as an angel of light (2 Cor 11:14). But unambiguous evidence of diabolical empowerment must be present before we level such charges: flagrant doctrinal or moral perversion, unusual hostility to Jesus' name

---

[54]W. C. Kaiser, Jr., *Toward an Old Testament Ethics* (Grand Rapids: Zondervan, 1983), 298.

[55]Cf. Schweizer, *Matthew*, 288: "Lack of faith is forgivable as long as it is merely a response to a report about the Son of Man, but not when the great works of the Spirit, described in verse 28, take place." D. Hill (*The Gospel of Matthew*, NCB [London: Oliphants, 1972], 218) sees the distinction as between an attack on Jesus' person and on the power by which he works.

and the redemptive mission of his followers, and extraordinary behavior not attributable to medical or psychological disorders. Apart from very serious signs such as these, one should tread most cautiously when speaking of Satan's direct influence in Christian circles. One of the most unfortunate violations of this principle is the common charge that certain spiritual gifts prominent in the charismatic movement actually come from the devil, particularly in light of the marvelous growth of this wing of Christianity in many parts of the world that have long seemed impervious to the gospel. Ironically, those making such charges more closely resemble the Pharisees in this text and hence remain more in danger of committing the unforgivable sin themselves than do those they associate with Satan.[56]

33"Make a tree good and its fruit will be good, or make a tree bad and its fruit will be bad, for a tree is recognized by its fruit. 34You brood of vipers, how can you who are evil say anything good? For out of the overflow of the heart the mouth speaks. 35The good man brings good things out of the good stored up in him, and the evil man brings evil things out of the evil stored up in him. 36But I tell you that men will have to give account on the day of judgment for every careless word they have spoken. 37For by your words you will be acquitted, and by your words you will be condemned."

12:33-37 In keeping with v. 30, Jesus now asks his audience to "come clean." A charge like that against him, when completely serious, is only possible if those making it are controlled by Satan and not inspired by God (as these Pharisees would have claimed). Verse 33 repeats the imagery of 7:16-20 (see comments there). In v. 34a Jesus echoes John's charge of 3:7 ("you brood of vipers"), showing that he believes his accusers represent the bad tree with its bad fruit. Verse 35 resembles 6:21. A tree is to its fruit what a person's heart is to his or her speech. A person is either good or evil, and the wicked will not escape condemnation (v. 36). God will judge even "careless" (*idle* or, literally, *workless*[57]) words. What may seem like merely trivial or casual remarks may at times better reflect the true attitudes of one's heart than more carefully chosen words (as precisely in v. 24). But, as in 10:26, all words ultimately reflect one's more fundamental commitments (cf. v. 37 and Jas 3:1-12). On the most important words that acquit and condemn, see under 10:32-33.

---

[56]M. Green (*Matthew for Today* [Dallas: Word, 1989], 126) notes a quite different parallel: "I have known a bishop on one occasion close a church rather than allow an evangelical clergyman to go there." For the only recent, book-length study of this theme, see E. Lowestam, *Spiritus Blasphemia* (Lund: Gleerup, 1968).

[57]Cf. G. B. Caird (*The Language and Imagery of the Bible* [Philadelphia: Westminster, 1980], 22): These are "deedless" words, like "a broken promise" or "an unpaid vow."

³⁸**Then some of the Pharisees and teachers of the law said to him, "Teacher, we want to see a miraculous sign from you."** ³⁹**He answered, "A wicked and adulterous generation asks for a miraculous sign! But none will be given it except the sign of the prophet Jonah.** ⁴⁰**For as Jonah was three days and three nights in the belly of a huge fish, so the Son of Man will be three days and three nights in the heart of the earth.** ⁴¹**The men of Nineveh will stand up at the judgment with this generation and condemn it; for they repented at the preaching of Jonah, and now one greater than Jonah is here.** ⁴²**The Queen of the South will rise at the judgment with this generation and condemn it; for she came from the ends of the earth to listen to Solomon's wisdom, and now one greater than Solomon is here.**

(b) The Sign of Jonah (12:38-42). **12:38** Compare the shorter, similar episode in 16:1-4. The Pharisees' request seems highly incongruous given the "sign" (NIV adds "miraculous") just performed by Jesus. But since the Jewish leaders could attribute exorcisms to the devil, they wanted to see a less ambiguous miracle that could come only from God. One wonders what would have done the trick.

12:39-42 Jesus refuses to play their game. He does not work wonders on demand and especially not for skeptics. Their request reveals their evil intent and lack of faith (as in vv. 34-35). "Adulterous" applies the common Old Testament metaphor for idolatry (see under 5:32). Again Jesus rebukes "this generation" (see under 11:16-19). In this context he is looking ahead to increasing rejection by his contemporaries (see the future tense "will be" with the same expression in v. 45). The only sign Jesus will provide, therefore, is the "sign" that is Jonah.[58] Jonah's languishing in the big fish for three days (Jesus here quotes Jonah 2:1, LXX [1:17 English]) parallels the period of Jesus' death. But since Jesus would remain dead for *only* three days, the "sign" must include his resurrection as well. Indeed, the only sign the Jews do receive that differs from what Jesus has already done or taught involves his death and resurrection. Yet Luke 16:31 makes it plain that even this kind of sign will not convince the hard-hearted. Even the resurrection will not compel belief in the way the Jewish leaders desire. Hence, Mark 8:12 can phrase Jesus' reply simply as, "No sign will be given."[59]

This is Jesus' first unambiguous prediction of his death in Matthew, still not as explicit as it will become, and probably understandable only in retrospect. "Three days and three nights" represents a Semitic idiom for

---

[58]"Of the prophet Jonah" should be read as an appositional genitive. Cf. N. Turner, *Grammatical Insights into the New Testament* (Edinburgh: T & T Clark, 1965), 60.

[59]Cf. J. Swetnam, "No Sign of Jonah," *Bib* 66 (1985): 126-30; cf. V. Mora, *Le signe de Jonas* (Paris: Cerf, 1983), 26.

any portion of three calendar days.[60] So there is no need to see a contradiction with the traditional Holy Week chronology, including a Friday crucifixion and Sunday resurrection, or to propose any alternative chronologies. As in 10:15 and 11:21-24, Jesus brands these Jewish leaders as worse off than certain Gentiles of Old Testament times. But in this case, he compares those rejecting him with those Gentiles who actually repented and heeded God's Word favorably—the Ninevites (see Jonah 3) and the Queen of Sheba (see 1 Kgs 10:1-10).[61] Such Gentiles will join with believers of every time and place on Judgment Day to condemn all who reject Jesus. The fate of Jesus' contemporaries proves all the more tragic and ironic because the Gentiles in Jonah's and Solomon's time believed after hearing God's "lesser" spokesmen, while "this generation" refused to believe even after hearing "one greater" (vv. 41-42).[62] Matthew has now shown Jesus as greater than the priestly cult, prophets like Jonah, and kings like David and Solomon (cf. 12:3-8).

43"When an evil spirit comes out of a man, it goes through arid places seeking rest and does not find it. 44Then it says, 'I will return to the house I left.' When it arrives, it finds the house unoccupied, swept clean and put in order. 45Then it goes and takes with it seven other spirits more wicked than itself, and they go in and live there. And the final condition of that man is worse than the first. That is how it will be with this wicked generation."

(c) The Return of the Evil Spirit (12:43-45). **12:43-45** Jesus now returns to consider the incident that started this whole discussion, the exorcism of v. 22. He wants the man who was liberated, along with everyone else present, to realize that freedom from demon possession is not enough. Ownership by the devil must be replaced with ownership by Christ (cf. Rom 6:15-18). Otherwise one's release is only temporary. Moral reform without Christian commitment always remains inadequate. Jesus likens the situation to a house made ready for new occupants which still stands vacant. Squatters will soon move in. No person can live long without serving someone. Satan will always return to attack that which is left defenseless, and each success leads him to increasingly worse designs, whether, as here, to literal repossession by an even greater number of

---

[60]See Gundry, *Matthew*, 244, for references.

[61]Thus many see the *preaching* of Jonah as the "sign," but the reference to his preaching is not as near in the context to the sign as the reference to his time in the fish's belly. Nor would preaching be as appropriate a sign in this context, since Jesus has been preaching for some time already, and his preaching is not nearly as dramatic as the resurrection. Moreover, v. 40 seems without purpose if it is not intended to describe the sign of Jonah. Cf. further Carson, "Matthew," 295-96.

[62]On the ambiguity of the gender of "one," see under v. 6.

demons (the number seven may indicate completeness of possession) or with the more widespread degeneracy of repeated sin, which characteristically renders humans more insensitive to their guilt (cf. Rom 1:18-32).[63] The "rest" the evil spirit seeks here contrasts sharply and ironically with the rest Christ offers (11:29) and links this controversy with the Sabbath controversies of 12:1-14. The "wicked generation" ties back in with v. 39 and is a uniquely Matthean addition. Matthew will vividly demonstrate the truth of vv. 43-45 by depicting the growing hostility against Jesus throughout the remainder of his narrative.

46While Jesus was still talking to the crowd, his mother and brothers stood outside, wanting to speak to him. 47Someone told him, "Your mother and brothers are standing outside, wanting to speak to you."

(3) Family Controversy (12:46-50). **12:46-47** Verses 46-50 do not provide as clear a break from hostility as did 11:25-30, but still this paragraph shifts gears by closing the chapter with an invitation to discipleship despite the growing rejection of Jesus. Jesus' mother Mary, with his brothers James, Joseph, Simon, and Judas (cf. 13:55),[64] have been wanting to get through the crowd to speak with him. Only now does Jesus learn of their presence. Verse 47 is relatively well attested (though it does not appear in two important early manuscripts, א and B) and was probably omitted by mistake because it ends with the same Greek word as does v. 46 (*lalēsai*, "to speak").

48He replied to him, "Who is my mother, and who are my brothers?" 49Pointing to his disciples, he said, "Here are my mother and my brothers. 50For whoever does the will of my Father in heaven is my brother and sister and mother."

12:48-50 Jesus does not directly address his family but does implicitly rebuke them. They deserve no preferential treatment. Human kinship does not take priority over spiritual kinship, and Jesus is busy ministering to crowds that include his spiritual family. On calling disciples his brothers, cf. Heb 2:11; also cf. Matt 28:10. The "will of God," as throughout Matthew, means obedience to God's commands by following Jesus. Matthew does not say what Mary thought of her unusual son at this point in his career, but the most natural reading of Mark 3:21 would include her

---

[63]"Arid" (literally, *waterless*) places, as not satisfying the demon's search for rest, probably tie in with the sea viewed as the devil's abode (8:23-27) and the choice of the demons in 8:28-34 to take their new hosts (the swine) into the water.

[64]The most natural interpretation of "brothers" is that these are Joseph's and Mary's natural children, younger than Jesus, although they could refer to Joseph's children by some otherwise unknown previous marriage. There is no biblical support for the later doctrine of Mary's perpetual virginity (see comments under 1:18-25).

among those who thought he was "out of his mind." His brothers are singularly unimpressed and in no way yet his supporters (cf. John 7:1-5). Given the strong family ties in ancient Palestine, Jesus' attitude here would have proved as shocking as in 8:22 and 10:37 (on which see comments there).[65] More positively he points to believers as people who should care for each other as if they were family members. Jesus does not call any of his disciples "father," however, not just because Joseph is not present (many think he is by now dead), but, as in 23:9, because Christians have only one "Father . . . in heaven." Paul will later contemplate the extraordinary evangelistic potential of displaying to the world a family-like unity in the church (Eph 3:5-10). The all too common contemporary divisiveness and lack of warm interpersonal relationships in the Christian community seem scandalous in comparison.

---

[65]Particularly in light of a socioanthropological analysis. Cf. D. M. May, "Mark 3:20-35 from the Perspective of Shame/Honor," *BTB* 17 (1987): 83-87.

SECTION OUTLINE CONTINUED

C. Progressive Polarization of Response to Jesus (13:1–16:20)
1. The Polarization Explained: Kingdom Parables (13:1-52)
   a. Speaking to the Crowds (13:1-35)
      (1) The Parable of the Sower (13:1-9)
      (2) Jesus' Purpose for Speaking in Parables (13:10-17)
      (3) The Interpretation of the Parable of the Sower (13:18-23)
      (4) The Parable of the Wheat and the Weeds (13:24-30)
      (5) The Parables of the Mustard Seed and Leaven (13:31-33)
      (6) Summary (13:34-35)
   b. Speaking to the Disciples (13:36-52)
      (1) Interpretation of the Parable of the Wheat and Weeds (13:36-43)
      (2) The Parables of the Hidden Treasure and Pearl of Great Price (13:44-46)
      (3) The Parable of the Dragnet (13:47-50)
      (4) The Parable of the Scribe Trained for the Kingdom (13:51-52)
2. The Polarization Enacted: From Jew to Gentile (13:53–16:20)
   a. Rejection of Jesus and John: Incorrect Christology (13:53–14:12)
      (1) Rejection of Jesus by His Hometown (13:53-58)
      (2) Rejection of John by Herod (14:1-12)
   b. Jesus Is the Bread of Life for Jews and Gentiles (14:13–16:12)
      (1) The Son of God Reveals Himself to Israel (14:13-36)
         (a) Feeding the Five Thousand (14:13-21)
         (b) Walking on Water (14:22-33)
         (c) Healings in Gennesaret (14:34-36)
      (2) The Son of David Turns from Israel to the Gentiles (15:1–16:12)
         (a) Kosher Laws Rescinded (15:1-20)
         (b) The Canaanite Woman's Faith (15:21-28)
         (c) Feeding the Four Thousand (15:29-39)
         (d) The Demand for a Sign (16:1-4)
         (e) Warning against the Jewish Leaders' Influence (16:5-12)
   c. Revelation to Peter of Jesus' Identity: Correct Christology (16:13-20)

C. Progressive Polarization of Response to Jesus (13:1–16:20)

The rising opposition 9:36–12:50 has illustrated leads Jesus increasingly to spend time with those who will respond more positively. Right up to the end he has his supporters, but there is a growing polarization of response to his ministry. Matthew 13:1-52 explains this polarization through a series of parables and indicates Jesus' reaction to it. He will give extended explanations of his more cryptic teaching only to those who are prepared to accept his message and claims. Matthew 13:53–16:20 finds Jesus applying this same principle to more than just his teaching ministry; ultimately he leaves Jewish territory altogether in order to find a more responsive audience among various neighboring Gentiles.

1. The Polarization Explained: Kingdom Parables (13:1-52)

Here begins the third major block of Jesus' teaching. As with the missionary discourse (chap. 10), Matthew combines material from Mark and "Q" with information unique to his Gospel. Like the Sermon on the Mount, this discourse is most naturally viewed as a selection of Jesus' teachings from one particular occasion, which Mark and Luke have abbreviated and redistributed elsewhere in their accounts (cf. v. 53). For the first time, however, Matthew presents an entire sermon comprised of parables. The interpretation of parables has been debated throughout church history. The literature on the topic is enormous.[1] I have elsewhere articulated and defended my views at length;[2] here I can only state my positions.

The most significant question in the history of interpretation has been whether to treat parables as detailed allegories or as simple, down-to-earth stories that make only one main point each. A growing number of scholars are recognizing that neither of these extremes can be justified and are opting for a variety of mediating perspectives. I believe that the parables are limited allegories and that we may usually associate one

---

[1]A detailed history of interpretation and bibliography appears in W. S. Kissinger, *The Parables of Jesus: A History of Interpretation and Bibliography* (Metuchen, N.J.: Scarecrow, 1979). The most seminal study of the modern era of scholarship is A. Jülicher, *Die Gleichnisreden Jesu*, 2 vols. (Freiburg: Mohr, 1899). The standard twentieth-century text is J. Jeremias, *The Parables of Jesus* (Philadelphia: Westminster, 1972). New directions in literary and rhetorical criticism, along with other recent hermeneutical developments, are best illustrated in B. B. Scott, *Hear Then the Parable* (Minneapolis: Fortress, 1989). The best detailed evangelical survey of all the major parables is S. Kistemaker, *The Parables of Jesus* (Grand Rapids: Baker, 1980). H. K. McArthur and R. M. Johnston (*They Also Taught in Parables* [Grand Rapids: Zondervan, 1990]) print and discuss a plethora of rabbinic parallels. D. Wenham (*The Parables of Jesus* [Downers Grove: InterVarsity, 1989]) offers the best popular level exposition.

[2]C. L. Blomberg, *Interpreting the Parables* (Downers Grove: InterVarsity, 1990).

main point with each main character (or groups of characters), almost never more than three per parable. When elements of a parable were "stock metaphors" in ancient Judaism, we may usually assume that Jesus used them in similar fashion—e.g., masters, fathers, and kings for God; servants and sons for God's people or helpers; a harvest for judgment and a feast for the messianic banquet, and so on. But all elements viewed as symbolic must be given interpretations that could have come readily to mind to a first-century Galilean, Jewish peasant audience. If there is doubt about whether a certain detail in a parable is significant, interpreters should err on the side of caution and not read in meaning that may not be present.[3]

The main question for interpreting parables in Matthew involves the role of this chapter in its overall narrative flow. Classic dispensationalism sees Matt 13 as the turning point of Jesus' ministry when he withdrew his offer of the kingdom from Israel. This view requires seeing the rejection of "this generation" in chaps. 11–12 as fairly official or absolute. But positive and negative responses from the Jews in fact continue all the way to the crucifixion. So it is better to think of a series of shifts in reaction to Jesus throughout the Gospel. Parables are not a new form of teaching characteristic of a new phase of ministry at this point in Matthew (cf. 7:24-27; 9:16-17; 11:16-19; 12:29), and Jesus will often continue to address his critics with more straightforward language (15:3-7; 16:2-4; 19:4-9,17-22; and much of chaps. 21–23).[4] Instead, the parables appear here as an important explanation of why the response to Jesus is becoming increasingly polarized and as a prediction of how that polarization will continue to grow. For those whose hearts are already hardened, parables conceal, even as they reveal new truths for those who are more receptive (vv. 12-13). Matthew 21:45 makes clear that the understanding of the parables is not so much cognitive as volitional. Those outside the kingdom "understand the provocative claim of the parables very well, but they are not prepared to accept it . . . Jesus' speaking in parables is not a riddle as such. What is perplexing is the behavior that it calls forth—that man can see salvation personified and nevertheless not come to conversion and belief."[5] Again, "Jesus deliberately concealed the Word in parable lest men against their will should be forced to acknowledge the

---

[3]For studies closest in perspective to my own, see esp. M. Boucher, *The Mysterious Parable* (Washington: CBAA, 1977), and L. Ryken, *How to Read the Bible as Literature* (Grand Rapids: Zondervan, 1984), 139-53, 199-203.

[4]The most thorough (and generally helpful) study of Matt 13 is J. D. Kingsbury, *The Parables of Jesus in Matthew 13* (Richmond: John Knox, 1969).

[5]H. Klauck, *Allegorie und Allegorese in synoptischen Gleichnistexten* (Münster: Aschendorff, 1978), 251.

Kingdom, and yet He allowed them enough light to convict them and to convince them."[6]

The structure of Matt 13 seems to be that of an extended chiasmus (inverted parallelism), even if the more typical subdivisions adopted here best reflect the actual content.[7] The two halves of this outline clearly show the divisions between outsiders and insiders already discussed. The center of a chiasmus highlights its most important teaching. In this case Matthew points to Jesus' allegorical interpretation as the key to understanding his parables.

[1]**That same day Jesus went out of the house and sat by the lake.** [2]**Such large crowds gathered around him that he got into a boat and sat in it, while all the people stood on the shore.** [3]**Then he told them many things in parables, saying: "A farmer went out to sow his seed.** [4]**As he was scattering the seed, some fell along the path, and the birds came and ate it up.** [5]**Some fell on rocky places, where it did not have much soil. It sprang up quickly, because the soil was shallow.** [6]**But when the sun came up, the plants were scorched, and they withered because they had no root.** [7]**Other seed fell among thorns, which grew up and choked the plants.** [8]**Still other seed fell on good soil, where it produced a crop—a hundred, sixty or thirty times what was sown.** [9]**He who has ears, let him hear."**

a. SPEAKING TO THE CROWDS (13:1-35). *(1) The Parable of the Sower (13:1-9).* **13:1-3a** *On that day* (NIV "same" does not appear in Greek) and "house" tie this section closely in with the events of the end of chap. 12. The crowded Galilean lakeside forces Jesus into a boat just offshore, which also serves as his pulpit. He begins teaching via a series of "parables." The Greek *parabolē* translates the Hebrew *māshāl*, which could refer to a wide variety of types of figurative speech.[8] The common

---

[6]T. F. Torrance, "A Study in New Testament Communication," *SJT* 3 (1950): 304-5.

[7]D. Wenham, "The Structure of Matthew XIII," *NTS* 25 (1979): 517-18:

A. sower—parable on those who hear the word of the kingdom
  B. disciples' question and Jesus' answer about the purpose of parables + interpretation of sower
    C. tares—parable of kingdom on good and evil
      D. mustard seed and leaven—pair of parallel kingdom parables
        E. conclusion of crowd section and interpretation of tares
      D'. treasure and pearl—pair of parallel kingdom parables
    C'. dragnet—parable of kingdom on good and evil
  B'. Jesus' question and disciples' answer about understanding parables
A'. scribe—parable on those trained for the kingdom.

[8]Cf. Jeremias, *Parables*, 20: "parable, similitude, allegory, fable, proverb, apocalyptic revelation, riddle, symbol, pseudonym, fictitious person, example, theme, argument, apology, refutation, jest."

element in all of them seems to have been some kind of analogy which could be singularly illustrative or frustratingly perplexing.[9]

13:3b-9 Jesus' first parable describes how the crowds hear and respond to his teaching, including his teaching in these parables. Jesus supplies an interpretation for the parable in vv. 18-23, which would probably have been more self-evident to his original audience than it usually is today, although it was still not entirely transparent (note v. 9, on which see comments under 11:15).[10] The four kinds of soil on which the seed fell reflected the common experience of ancient farmers, who employed broadcast sowing—scattering seeds in all directions by hand as they walked up and down the stony paths that divided their fields.[11] The imagery of sower and soil was standard in Jewish circles (2 Esdr 4:26-32; ʿAbot R. Nat. 8:2). Jesus uses this imagery to illustrate the four types of response people are making to the preaching of God's reign. Once one realizes that Jesus is talking about preaching the word, it is not difficult to see the first three soil samples as involving those in whom that word took no root, who thus never made any profession of faith; those whose initial commitment proved superficial and temporary; and those who, while first appearing like true disciples, demonstrated they could not survive competing demands for their loyalty. The most unusual feature of the parable is the extraordinary crop produced by the seed that fell on good soil. A tenfold to twentyfold yield was often considered superior.

Many readers have wondered how to fit these four categories of individuals into the two categories into which Jesus has already made clear everyone falls (cf. 7:13-27; 10:32-42). The answer is actually fairly straightforward. The first three kinds of soils are all inadequate. None of them stands for people who were ever true believers, despite certain outward appearances. For farmers, only those plants that *bear good fruit* ("produced a crop," v. 8) count for anything. True believers are thus only those who bear proper spiritual fruit (7:16-17). Of the rest Jesus says, "I never knew you" (7:23). What counts is not profession of faith but perseverance in faith. To be sure, all true Christians will persevere, but only by observing who perseveres can we determine who those true Christians

---

[9]See J. W. Sider, "The Meaning of *Parabolē* in the Usage of the Synoptic Evangelists," *Bib* 62 (1981): 460; *idem*, "Proportional Analogy in the Gospel Parables," *NTS* 31 (1985): 1-23.

[10]See esp. P. B. Payne, "The Authenticity of the Parable of the Sower and Its Interpretation," in *Gospel Perspectives*, vol. 1, ed. R. T. France and D. Wenham (Sheffield: JSOT, 1980), 163-207.

[11]A rather fruitless debate has raged over whether sowing preceded plowing in ancient Palestine, thereby making the farmer's "wastage" more intelligible. The best answer seems to be that sometimes it did and sometimes it didn't. See esp. P. B. Payne, "The Order of Sowing and Ploughing in the Parable of the Sower," *NTS* 25 (1978): 123-29.

are. Matthew's climactic focus, however, remains on the astonishing impact of those who are faithful. Jesus provides his followers with an important reminder of God's continued blessings on their work, even as large numbers of people become increasingly hostile to the gospel. He will make this point again in vv. 31-33. For further comments on the parable of the sower, see comments under vv. 18-23.

[10]The disciples came to him and asked, "Why do you speak to the people in parables?"

[11]He replied, "The knowledge of the secrets of the kingdom of heaven has been given to you, but not to them. [12]Whoever has will be given more, and he will have an abundance. Whoever does not have, even what he has will be taken from him.

(2) Jesus' Purpose for Speaking in Parables (13:10-17). **13:10-12** Although it forms part of the section about Jesus' speaking to the crowds, this dialogue occurred in private (Mark 4:10). It probably took place later, though conceivably it could have occurred at this time, with Jesus speaking quietly to the disciples huddled near him while the crowds waited further in the background. Apparently the disciples recognize that something in Jesus' teaching is not fully clear to everyone, hence their question. Matthew includes these verses in the section on preaching to the crowds because they supply Jesus' rationale for speaking to them as he has. Jesus' reply points to the two-pronged purpose of parables—to reveal and to conceal.

As in 11:25-30, divine sovereignty and human responsibility are carefully balanced. Verse 11 introduces an undeniably predestinarian note. Certain privileges are reserved for Jesus' followers that are not available to everyone else.[12] Verse 11a reads more literally, *To you has been given to know the mysteries of the kingdom of heaven. Mysteries* ("secrets") in the New Testament reflects the Aramaic background of *raz* (cf. Dan 2:28; 4:9). The term conveys primarily the sense of a *secret now revealed* but also contains the element of *something inscrutable.*[13] As subsequent parables will clarify (see vv. 31-33), the mysteries here are not related to the establishment of the church or any supposed postponement of the kingdom but to the fact that the kingdom is present yet not with irresistible

---

[12]But cf. R. T. France (*The Gospel according to Matthew*, TNTC [Grand Rapids: Eerdmans, 1985], 223-24): "It does not discuss how one *becomes* a disciple, i.e., how one may move from one side of that division to another. Still less does it say that such a transfer is impossible—after all, presumably the disciples were themselves once 'outside.' What it does make clear is that natural insight is not enough; spiritual enlightenment is given (v. 11). But how and to whom it is *given* is not the theme of these verses."

[13]Cf. R. E. Brown, *The Semitic Background of the Term "Mystery" in the New Testament* (Philadelphia: Fortress, 1968); C. C. Caragounis, *The Ephesian Mysterion* (Lund: Gleerup, 1977).

power.[14] Verse 12 then explains the growing polarization of Jesus' audience as the natural outgrowth of the election described in v. 11. What a person "has" or "does not have" refers to the true insight that leads one to embrace Jesus and his kingdom, except in the final clause of v. 12, "even what he has will be taken from him," which must refer to a more limited insight or openness that has not yet accepted the gospel (or perhaps, as in Luke 8:18, meaning *what he thinks he has*).[15]

> [13]This is why I speak to them in parables:
> "Though seeing, they do not see;
>   though hearing, they do not hear or understand.
> [14]In them is fulfilled the prophecy of Isaiah:
>   "'You will be ever hearing but never understanding;
>   you will be ever seeing but never perceiving.
> [15]For this people's heart has become calloused;
>   they hardly hear with their ears,
>   and they have closed their eyes.
> Otherwise they might see with their eyes,
>   hear with their ears,
>   understand with their hearts
> and turn, and I would heal them.'

13:13-15 Verse 13 introduces a second reason for Jesus' speaking in parables. The Greek of v. 13a reads literally, *For this reason I speak to them in parables, because* (even though the NIV leaves "because" [*hoti*] untranslated).[16] "This reason," then, points forward to the principle of v. 13b involving human response. The hidden aspect of the parables' message is thus both a cause of and a response to people's unwillingness to follow Jesus. "Seeing" and "hearing" are each used in two different senses

---

[14]G. E. Ladd, *The Gospel of the Kingdom* (Grand Rapids: Eerdmans, 1959), 56.

[15]France, *Matthew*, 221: "The laws of capitalist economics (capital breeds income; lack of capital spells ruin) serves as 'parable' of spiritual enlightenment."

[16]Here lies the most famous difference between Matthew's and Mark's versions of this passage. Mark 4:12 uses ἵνα ("in order that") instead of ὅτι, almost certainly to denote purpose. See esp. J. R. Kirkland, "The Earliest Understanding of Jesus' Use of Parables: Mark IV, 10-12 in Context," *NovT* 19 (1977): 1-21. On the resolution of this apparent contradiction, see D. A. Carson ("Matthew," EBC, vol. 8, ed. F. E. Gaebelein [Grand Rapids: Zondervan, 1984], 309): "Matthew has already given Jesus' answer in terms of divine election (v. 11); now he gives the human reason. While this brings him into formal conflict with Mark 4:12, he has already sounded the predestinarian note of Mark 4:12. Here Matthew includes much more material than Mark; and in the ordered structure that results from the inclusion of such new material, verbal parallels are lost in favor of conceptual ones." Contra the common view that Matthew has weakened Mark's purpose clause and turned it into a result clause (as represented most recently in the otherwise excellent survey of the use of Isaiah 6:9-10 in Jewish and early Christian exegesis, by C. A. Evans (*To See and Not Perceive* [Sheffield: JSOT, 1989], 107-13).

here, once for simple sensory perception and then for the kind of insight that leads to acceptance of the gospel and discipleship. "Understanding" is a key word for Matthew in this chapter, especially in vv. 19 and 23, where he adds the term to his sources. The language of v. 13 is taken almost verbatim from Isa 6:9-10, LXX.[17] Jesus declares that the words of Isaiah are now being fulfilled. The word for "fulfill" here (*anapleroō*) is different from before, the only time in the New Testament this verb in used with reference to Scripture. Verse 14a probably means *the prophecy of Isaiah applies to them*[18]—i.e., the pattern of behavior in Isaiah's time is repeating itself and being completed in Jesus' day among those who reject him. "Ever" and "never" are somewhat misleading translations in light of Isa 6:13, which looks forward to the future restoration of at least some of those who are now obdurate. The sense is better rendered *you will surely hear but not understand; you will surely see but not perceive* (cf. Rotherham). Meanwhile v. 15 explains the current plight of those who reject Jesus. God confirms such people in their hard-heartedness in response to their freely chosen disobedience (as in the larger context of God's call to Isaiah to prophesy to rebellious Israel; cf. also the sequence of events in Rom 1:18-32). Jesus sees his preaching in parables, in part at least, as a kind of judgment from God upon unbelieving Israel.

[16]But blessed are your eyes because they see, and your ears because they hear. [17]For I tell you the truth, many prophets and righteous men longed to see what you see but did not see it, and to hear what you hear but did not hear it.

13:16-17   On the other hand, for those whose hearts are open to God's word, the parables provide much illumination. Jesus' followers are indeed privileged because they are living in the age of the fulfillment of the Old Testament promises that even the greatest of God's faithful people of old longed to see (cf. esp. Heb 11:39-40; 1 Pet 1:10-12). The disciples will not grasp everything Jesus says; the contrast with outsiders is relative rather than absolute. But they will be privy to Jesus' explanations to move them on to greater understanding than most in the crowds have (vv. 18-23,36-43). On "blessed" see comments under 5:3.

[18]"Listen then to what the parable of the sower means: [19]When anyone hears the message about the kingdom and does not understand it, the evil one comes and snatches away what was sown in his heart. This is the seed sown along the path. [20]The one who received the seed that fell on rocky places is the man who hears the word and at once receives it with joy. [21]But since he

---

[17]The LXX changes from the MT (imperatives to indicatives) are not that significant since the former are highly ironic.

[18]J. P. Louw and E. A. Nida, eds., *Greek-English Lexicon of the New Testament* (New York: UBS, 1988), 1:161.

has no root, he lasts only a short time. When trouble or persecution comes because of the word, he quickly falls away. [22]The one who received the seed that fell among the thorns is the man who hears the word, but the worries of this life and the deceitfulness of wealth choke it, making it unfruitful. [23]But the one who received the seed that fell on good soil is the man who hears the word and understands it. He produces a crop, yielding a hundred, sixty or thirty times what was sown."

(3) The Interpretation of the Parable of the Sower (13:18-23). **13:18-23** See also comments under vv. 1-9. Whether the people are meant to correspond to the seed or to the soils is more a problem for us than for Aramaic speakers. *Soil sown with seed*, as a whole, is in view in each case.[19] S. Kistemaker concisely captures the three main points of the passage and the three subpoints under the final point: "The Word of God is proclaimed and causes a division among those who hear; God's people receive the Word, understand it, and obediently fulfill it; others fail to listen because of a hardened heart, a basic superficiality, or a vested interest in riches and possessions."[20] The parable provides a sober reminder that even the most enthusiastic outward response to the gospel offers no guarantee that one is a true disciple. Only the tests of time, perseverance under difficult circumstances, the avoidance of the idolatries of wealth and anxiety over earthly concerns (recall 6:25-34), and above all the presence of appropriate fruit (consistent obedience to God's will) can prove a profession genuine.

[24]Jesus told them another parable: "The kingdom of heaven is like a man who sowed good seed in his field. [25]But while everyone was sleeping, his enemy came and sowed weeds among the wheat, and went away. [26]When the wheat sprouted and formed heads, then the weeds also appeared.

[27]"The owner's servants came to him and said, 'Sir, didn't you sow good seed in your field? Where then did the weeds come from?'

[28]" 'An enemy did this,' he replied.

"The servants asked him, 'Do you want us to go and pull them up?'

[29]" 'No,' he answered, 'because while you are pulling the weeds, you may root up the wheat with them. [30]Let both grow together until the harvest. At that time I will tell the harvesters: First collect the weeds and tie them in bundles to be burned; then gather the wheat and bring it into my barn.' "

(4) The Parable of the Wheat and the Weeds (13:24-30). **13:24-30** Jesus is apparently speaking to the crowds again (cf. v. 36). Many are no doubt wondering: *If the kingdom of heaven has arrived, why has it not triumphed more overtly and visibly? If Jesus is its herald, why is response to*

---

[19]See P. B. Payne, "The Seeming Inconsistency of the Interpretation of the Parable of the Sower," *NTS* 26 (1980): 564-68.

[20]Kistemaker, *Parables*, 29.

him not more uniformly positive? What the parable of the sower described in terms of four categories of soil with the same kind of seed in each, the parable of the wheat and weeds speaks of in terms of two different kinds of seed sown by two different individuals, a farmer and his enemy. At the agricultural level, the story is not very realistic, though such sabotage did occasionally occur. But the meaning, of course, remains at the spiritual level. The weeds (*zizania*) are more literally *darnel*, often at first indistinguishable from wheat. Just as the wheat and weeds were often superficially similar in appearance and if sown too close to each other were too intermingled in their root systems to be pulled up separately, so too God's people are sometimes outwardly hard to distinguish from his enemies. They can be too interconnected with them in society for anyone to try to purify the world from evil without hurting those who are good.[21] Nevertheless, in Jesus' society many Zealots, and at times even his disciples (cf. Luke 9:54), were often eager for precisely this to happen. Jesus warns them they must wait for the final judgment.[22]

Jesus' principle here applies in every age to the question of why God allows evil and suffering in the world. His creation can be purged of all evil only through the judgment and re-creation of the universe at the end of the age because evil resides in *every* person. God's delay in bringing the end of the world is thus entirely gracious, giving people more opportunity to repent (2 Pet 3:9). Jesus reserves an interpretation of the specific details of the passage for a more private audience with his disciples (on which see under vv. 36-43). But even without that interpretation, one may discern three stages to the story's plot—the initial obstacles to the kingdom (vv. 27-28a), the inauguration of the kingdom (vv. 28b-30a), and the final consummation of the kingdom (v. 30b). From the actions of the farmer and the fate of the wheat and weeds, one learns that God will permit the righteous and wicked to coexist in this age but that he will eventually separate the wicked, judge them, and destroy them, while gathering the righteous together to be rewarded by enjoying his presence forever.

(5) The Parables of the Mustard Seed and Leaven (13:31-33). Jesus' next two parables prove closely parallel. They are not full-fledged narratives but short analogies or similes. Each presents only one main character and probably teaches only one central truth. Jesus likens the kingdom to a mustard seed or lump of yeast that grows from inauspicious, seemingly

---

[21]"Formed heads" is literally *bore fruit*, the mark of a true disciple, as with the production of the crop in v. 8.

[22]Cf. D. Patte (*The Gospel according to Matthew: A Structural Commentary* [Philadelphia: Fortress, 1987], 194): "One cannot become a disciple—and have the proper vocation—as long as one thinks that one's vocation should be primarily negative, judgmental, a vocation to fight evil."

insignificant beginnings to attain a greater size (the mustard seed) or have more widespread influence (the leaven) than many would ever have suspected. The current manifestation of God's reign within Jesus' small band of disciples seems relatively impotent; one day many will be astonished about how their movement grew and impacted the world.

[31]He told them another parable: "The kingdom of heaven is like a mustard seed, which a man took and planted in his field. [32]Though it is the smallest of all your seeds, yet when it grows, it is the largest of garden plants and becomes a tree, so that the birds of the air come and perch in its branches."

13:31-32 The mustard seed was proverbial for its smallness (*m. Nid.* 5:2). "Your" is not in the Greek but captures the correct sense. Jesus is not speaking in absolute terms as a biologist but in the frame of normal experience in Jewish agriculture. Mustard seeds were the smallest seeds commonly planted in Palestinian fields. "Garden plants" is thus better translated *herbs* or *vegetables*. Mustard plants usually look more like large bushes than like small trees, but they can grow to ten or twelve feet, enabling birds to roost in their branches ("perch" equals *nest* or *live*). Jesus may be alluding to Ezek 17:23 (cf. Dan 4:12), in which the birds of the air nest in the branches of the mighty cedar tree (God's kingdom in Israel). Even large mustard bushes pale in comparison with the lofty cedar; still Jesus may be employing deliberate irony.[23] What may not look like much to the world will in fact fulfill all God's promises.

[33]He told them still another parable: "The kingdom of heaven is like yeast that a woman took and mixed into a large amount of flour until it worked all through the dough."

13:33 So too the tiny amounts of yeast a breadmaker mixes into a large batch of dough cause the whole loaf to rise. "Mixed" is literally *hidden*, but the expression is probably just a graphic description of the baking process and not to be allegorized. Again we see the remarkable pervasiveness of a small agent. "Large amount" reads, literally, three *satas* (variously estimated at twenty to forty-five liters), which could feed well over one hundred people. It is sometimes argued that yeast, often a metaphor in Jewish literature for the spreading influence of evil and used in this way by Jesus in 16:6, must also here refer to the growing opposition against him. But immediate context must always take precedence over background. Yeast can be a positive symbol (e.g., Lev 7:13-14; 23:17) and, with all the parables dealing with the growth of plants and seeds in this chapter having the positive referent of the growth of the kingdom, the parable of the yeast must almost certainly be taken this way too.

---

[23]R. W. Funk, "The Looking-glass Tree Is for the Birds," *Int* 27 (1973): 3-9.

Together the parables of the mustard seed and leaven pair illustrations of typical male and female tasks of Jesus' day and probably reflect his concern to relate well to women as well as men in his audience.[24] Neither parable depicts the culmination of the kingdom so impressively as to justify grandiose dreams of Christianizing the earth, but each does caution against a defeatism or siege mentality when Christian witness seems temporarily ineffective. One day God's causes will triumph.

[34]Jesus spoke all these things to the crowd in parables; he did not say anything to them without using a parable.
[35]So was fulfilled what was spoken through the prophet:
"I will open my mouth in parables,
 I will utter things hidden since the creation of the world."

(6) Summary (13:34-35). **13:34-35** These verses bring to a close the first main section of Jesus' sermon in parables. Verse 34b does not refer to Jesus' teaching beyond this immediate occasion. Matthew uniquely and characteristically sees Old Testament fulfillment at work, this time involving Ps 78:2.[25] As with several of the quotations in the infancy narrative, this "fulfillment" is not an exegesis of the Old Testament text but a typological application. In the original psalm, Asaph was announcing to a new generation God's mighty deeds in Israel's past. "Parable" obviously implies a quite different kind of story here. "Hidden" refers primarily to that which was not yet revealed to one group of individuals despite being well known to everyone else. But the psalmist's language also suggests that he intends to disclose patterns in the events not always recognized even by those for whom the stories were familiar.[26] Still, Asaph's words are clearly intended to reveal and explain God's actions. So even for the crowds in Jesus' audience, the parables are not uniformly concealing (cf. Mark 4:10, in which more than the Twelve are insiders). Some among them can perceive with true spiritual insight and respond appropriately.

[36]Then he left the crowd and went into the house. His disciples came to him and said, "Explain to us the parable of the weeds in the field."

b. SPEAKING TO THE DISCIPLES (13:36-52). *(1) Interpretation of the Parable of the Wheat and Weeds (13:36-43).* **13:36** Jesus now turns to those privileged to receive even more insight. "The house" is apparently the same as in 13:1. The distinction between the crowds and the disciples, however,

---

[24]For even stronger, though clearly overstated conclusions, see E. Waller, "The Parable of the Leaven: A Sectarian Teaching and the Inclusion of Women," *USQR* 35 (1979-80): 99-109.

[25]The first half of the text parallels the LXX verbatim. The second half is closer to the MT.

[26]On which see esp. Carson, "Matthew," 321-23.

is further blurred by the disciples' having to make this request. But at least they had the opportunity to ask and the benefit of Jesus' answer.

37He answered, "The one who sowed the good seed is the Son of Man. 38The field is the world, and the good seed stands for the sons of the kingdom. The weeds are the sons of the evil one, 39and the enemy who sows them is the devil. The harvest is the end of the age, and the harvesters are angels.

13:37-39 Jesus gives his interpretation of the parable of the wheat and weeds. He specifically identifies the farmer with himself (on "Son of Man," see comments under 8:20). This suggests that a similar equation would be legitimate in the parable of the sower. But, derivatively, the farmers in both passages can stand for all who sow God's Word. The other allegorical equations Jesus makes follow naturally. That "the field is the world" warns against applying this parable too quickly to the institutional church. It may be true that in many local churches saved and unsaved people are mixed together, but this in no way justifies the rejection of fair and loving attempts to purify the church (cf. 18:15-20), as classically advocated by Augustine. "Sons of" again appears in the sense of people who belong to something. It is interesting that a third factor is added to the two of vv. 10-17 to account for those who reject Christ. Not only do God's sovereign purposes and people's freely chosen rebellion explain why some refuse to believe, but Satan is also to blame. Yet, as the rest of Scripture clearly indicates, the tempter's activity never jeopardizes God's sovereignty (nothing happens apart from God's permissive will, Rev 9) and never relieves humans of their accountability (we never need succumb to temptation unless we choose to, 1 Cor 10:13). The harvest was a standard metaphor for judgment, and angels regularly figure as God's helpers in Jewish portrayals of Judgment Day.

40"As the weeds are pulled up and burned in the fire, so it will be at the end of the age. 41The Son of Man will send out his angels, and they will weed out of his kingdom everything that causes sin and all who do evil. 42They will throw them into the fiery furnace, where there will be weeping and gnashing of teeth. 43Then the righteous will shine like the sun in the kingdom of their Father. He who has ears, let him hear.

13:40-43 Jesus now shifts the focus from the present situation to future judgment. He interprets some of the same elements of the parable again, but not all (most notably the enemy). And the field now becomes not the world but the kingdom (v. 41).[27] Because "kingdom" does not equal "church," v. 41 does not contradict v. 38. As consistently else-

---

[27]For a detailed comparison of these two interpretations of the parable's imagery (vv. 37-39,40-43), see M. de Goedt, "L'explication de la parabole de l'ivraie (Matt. xiii, 36-43)," *RB* 66 (1959): 32-54.

where, God's kingdom refers to his sovereign rule. This time the focus is more on his control not just over his church but over the cosmos. As the vice-regent of God's sovereignty, Jesus promises painful punishment for those who reject him. These people are described, literally, as *everyone who causes sin and does evil* (v. 41—not two separate categories as the NIV seems to suggest). But he promises radiant glory for the "righteous" (v. 43)—those who do God's will by becoming disciples of Christ. The "fiery furnace" comes from Dan 3:6 but is used in 2 Esdr 7:36 for hell. On the weeping and gnashing of teeth, see comments under 8:12. On verse 43b see comments under v. 9.

(2) The Parables of the Hidden Treasure and Pearl of Great Price (13:44-46). Another pair of short similes or analogies follows (as in vv. 31-33). Again each contains one character and teaches one point, namely, that the kingdom is so valuable that it is worth sacrificing anything to gain it.

⁴⁴"The kingdom of heaven is like treasure hidden in a field. When a man found it, he hid it again, and then in his joy went and sold all he had and bought that field.

⁴⁵"Again, the kingdom of heaven is like a merchant looking for fine pearls. ⁴⁶When he found one of great value, he went away and sold everything he had and bought it.

13:44 Jesus likens one who enters the kingdom to a man who sells everything he owns in order to buy a field containing a treasure that will more than compensate for his sacrifice. One should not worry about the man's ethics in hiding the treasure. We need neither justify his behavior nor imitate it. This is simply part of the story line that helps to make sense of the plot.[28] Jesus frequently tells parables in which unscrupulous characters nevertheless display some virtue from which Christians can learn (cf. esp. Luke 16:1-8; 18:1-8). Similarly, one must not interpret the buying of the treasure as an allegory for the atonement, as if Jesus were the treasure hunter purchasing our redemption.[29] As in a similar rabbinic parable about Israel entering the promised land (*Mek. Beshallach* 2:142f.), the man who finds the treasure is more naturally seen as the person seeking after God's blessings.[30]

---

[28]J. W. Sider ("Interpreting the Hid Treasure," *CSR* 13 [1984]: 371) believes that the rehiding is significant but only in that it reinforces the commitment required to attain the treasure.

[29]As, e.g., in J. A. Gibbs, "Parables of Atonement and Assurance: Matthew 13:44-46," *CTQ* 51 (1987): 19-43.

[30]Cf. F. Stagg ("Matthew," in *The Broadman Bible Commentary*, vol. 8, ed. C. J. Allen, [Nashville: Broadman, 1969], 159), who nevertheless notes that "paradoxically, salvation is free yet costs everything."

13:45-46 Jesus makes the same point by describing a merchant who purchases a costly pearl. Again the man gives up everything to obtain his treasure. Sometimes God calls would-be disciples literally to sell all (19:21), but they must always abandon anything that would stand in the way of wholehearted allegiance to Christ and the priorities of the kingdom. Interestingly, in the parable of the pearl the man is searching for wealth, whereas in the parable of the hidden treasure the man stumbles across it. As with the parables of mustard seed and leaven, Jesus is reaching out to every person in his audience. He calls the spiritual seeker as well as the apathetic atheist.

[47]"Once again, the kingdom of heaven is like a net that was let down into the lake and caught all kinds of fish. [48]When it was full, the fishermen pulled it up on the shore. Then they sat down and collected the good fish in baskets, but threw the bad away. [49]This is how it will be at the end of the age. The angels will come and separate the wicked from the righteous [50]and throw them into the fiery furnace, where there will be weeping and gnashing of teeth.

(3) The Parable of the Dragnet (13:47-50). **13:47-50** This passage closely resembles the parable of the wheat and weeds (vv. 24-30), especially with its interpretation (v. 49) and closing refrain (v. 50). The net was a large seine or dragnet spread out over a considerable area of water. A good catch of fish could require strenuous effort to haul to shore (cf. John 21:6-8). The parable of the dragnet does not focus on the preliminary situation of good and bad existing together, but it nevertheless teaches the three-part message that God will judge all people on the last day, gather together the righteous for further service and safekeeping, and discard as worthless those who are unredeemed. "All kinds" (v. 47) is, more literally, *all races*, a strange way of speaking of fish but a natural way of emphasizing the universality of God's judgment of people.[31]

[51]"Have you understood all these things?" Jesus asked.

"Yes," they replied.

[52]He said to them, "Therefore every teacher of the law who has been instructed about the kingdom of heaven is like the owner of a house who brings out of his storeroom new treasures as well as old."

(4) The Parable of the Scribe Trained for the Kingdom (13:51-52). **13:51-52** Given the disciples' partial lack of understanding (explicit in v. 36 and implicit in vv. 10-23), Jesus now asks if they understand (better) after these last three parables. They claim that they do, but their insights will not always carry over to other situations (cf. 15:16). Jesus

---

[31]Cf. J. D. M. Derrett, 'ΗΣΑΝ ΓΑΡ ἉΛΙΕΙΣ (Mk i.16): Jesus' Fishermen and the Parable of the Net," *NovT* 22 (1980): 125-31.

nevertheless likens the disciples to *scribes* ("teachers of the law") "instructed" (literally, *discipled*—as in 28:19) for the kingdom. Properly trained disciples may be compared with the Jewish teachers of the law in that they too are equipped to instruct others. No special gift or office of "scribe" seems to be in view here. But Matthew may be thinking of Jesus' disciples, like other scribes, as endowed with wisdom, authority, the right understanding of the law, and perhaps some measure of prophetic inspiration.[32] Jesus then elaborates the comparison by picturing a house owner rummaging through his storeroom and finding a variety of old and new items. In light of v. 35, Jesus probably means that as his disciples teach God's will, they will be drawing out the meaning of the Hebrew Scriptures ("things old"), while showing how they are fulfilled and apply in the kingdom age ("things new").[33] As other Jews increasingly reject him, Jesus will focus more and more on the preparation of his disciples as the new locus of God's activity in the world (cf. v. 38).[34]

Parables provide a model for Christian teachers in every era. Storytelling makes lessons much more vivid and enticing than the mere listing of principles. What is more, they can communicate unique insights not easily translated into propositional language. They draw listeners into what might otherwise seem a more threatening conversation, enabling them to consider God's claims they might otherwise reject without further thought. This was classically illustrated already in King David's day, with Nathan's parable of the ewe lamb (2 Sam 12:1-10). Though cognitive understanding is often enhanced, parables do not always bring about the desired response. By forcing people to decide for or against Jesus, parables may be said to drive away those who reject him and in that sense conceal the truth from them. Our preaching ought also to bring people gently and tactfully to a clear point of decision, even as we recognize that there will be diverse responses to the gospel's call to repentance and faith in Jesus. Despite all opposition God still rules, furthering his purposes and hastening the day when his people will be vindicated. Hence, it is worth sacrificing whatever is required to be on his side.

2. The Polarization Enacted: From Jew to Gentile (13:53–16:20)

Here begins the last major section of narrative in Matthew's Gospel before Jesus' journey to the cross. Matthew has been consistently raising

---

[32]D. E. Orton, *The Understanding Scribe: Matthew and the Apocalyptic Ideal* (Sheffield: JSOT, 1989).

[33]Cf. A. Sand, *Das Evangelium nach Matthäus*, RNT (Regensburg: Pustet, 1986), 293; Patte, *Matthew*, 199.

[34]For further perspectives on this parable and its significance for Matthew overall, see O. L. Cope, *Matthew: A Scribe Trained for the Kingdom of Heaven* (Washington D.C.: CBAA, 1976).

the question of Jesus' identity when the crowds marvel at his authority in preaching and healing (chaps. 5–9). People have taken sides, for and against Jesus, in increasingly polarized fashion (chaps. 11–13). But those closest to Jesus (his disciples) have not yet given an explicit, definitive answer about who they think he is. So even as other key Matthean themes continue in this section, most notably the increasing rejection of Jesus by Israel and the surprising openness to him among Gentiles (fulfilling the predictions of 13:1-52 concerning sharper lines of demarcation between insiders and outsiders), these chapters also raise the Christological question more pointedly.

Matthew 13:53–14:12 introduces this section by juxtaposing the people's rejection of Jesus and a ruler's rejection of John, both based on mistaken assessments of who Jesus is. The section thus begins by illustrating the wrong answers to the Christological question. Matthew 14:13-36 presents more of Christ's miracles, especially over nature, which raise the question of his identity as starkly as ever to date. Verse 33 supplies the best answer any of the disciples has yet given. Matthew 15:1–16:12 reflects Jesus' ensuing withdrawal from Israel, both geographically and ideologically, in response to its rejection of him, even as various Gentiles are increasingly accepting him. Matthew 16:5-12 forms an inclusio with 14:13-21, dealing with Jesus' feeding miracles, and suggests that 14:13–16:12 forms the main body of this section. This unit shows Jesus as the true Bread for both Jews (14:13-36) and Gentiles (15:1–16:12). Matthew 16:13-20, finally, brings this section to its conclusion with Peter's climactic confession on behalf of the disciples as they journey toward Caesarea Philippi. This mature understanding of who Jesus is comes only from divine revelation.

Matthew 13:53–16:20 thus divides into three main parts, as Matthew progresses from the rejection of Jesus (13:53–14:12) to the polarization of responses to Jesus (14:13–16:12) to a divinely enabled confession of who he really is (16:13-20).[35] From 13:53 on, the episodes in Matthew's narrative also occur in increasingly chronological sequence and more closely parallel Mark's selection of material, but the events from Jesus' life that both writers have chosen to recount still largely depend on thematic links from one passage to the next.

a. REJECTION OF JESUS AND JOHN: INCORRECT CHRISTOLOGY (13:53–14:12). Jesus is first rejected in his hometown because his kinsfolk cannot believe he is anyone special, not even a prophet. Herod then mistakenly views him as John resurrected. This leads Matthew to narrate the story of John's death.

---

[35]For alternative structures cf. D. W. Gooding, "Structure littéraire de Matthieu, XII, 53 a XVIII, 35," *RB* 85 (1978): 227-52; and J. M. O'Connor, "The Structure of Matthew XIV-XVII," *RB* 82 (1975): 360-84, and the literature there cited.

⁵³When Jesus had finished these parables, he moved on from there. ⁵⁴Coming to his hometown, he began teaching the people in their synagogue, and they were amazed. "Where did this man get this wisdom and these miraculous powers?" they asked. ⁵⁵"Isn't this the carpenter's son? Isn't his mother's name Mary, and aren't his brothers James, Joseph, Simon and Judas? ⁵⁶Aren't all his sisters with us? Where then did this man get all these things?" ⁵⁷And they took offense at him. But Jesus said to them, "Only in his hometown and in his own house is a prophet without honor."

⁵⁸And he did not do many miracles there because of their lack of faith.

(1) Rejection of Jesus by His Hometown (13:53-58). **13:53-57a** As with 8:1 and 11:1, 13:53 rounds off the previous discourse but more closely introduces Jesus' subsequent ministry. Jesus proceeds to Nazareth (v. 54a), which Matthew describes only as his *patris* (either *homeland* or "hometown," but since Jesus is already in Galilee, "hometown" must be the sense). A much fuller account appears in Luke 4:16-30. Luke and Matthew probably record the same event, but Luke has moved his version forward as an introduction to the key themes of Jesus' ministry (as Luke 4:14b-15 itself hints).

Jesus returns to his practice of teaching in the synagogues (cf. 4:23), though this may well be the first time he has spoken in the synagogue in Nazareth. His audience reacts with amazement, as the crowds consistently do elsewhere (e.g., 7:28; 22:33). They recognize Jesus as wise. This is the third and final use of this adjective in Matthew (cf. 11:19; 12:42). Some have seen in these references a distinctively Matthean "Wisdom Christology,"[36] but the data on which this hypothesis is based are rather slim. Matthew may or may not view Jesus as Wisdom personified. In this text the congregation is merely commending him for his astuteness and morality. The Old Testament consistently defines wisdom as beginning with the fear of the Lord (e.g., Prov 1:7). In light of v. 58 and the fixed liturgy of the synagogue service, which would normally have precluded Jesus' interrupting worship to work wonders, the "miraculous powers" of v. 54 probably refer to what Jesus has done elsewhere, reports of which have followed him home. The people's amazement increases because they know the members of his family, who seem ordinary enough. Residents of Nazareth probably also remember Jesus' childhood and young adulthood, which were apparently not particularly distinguished (see comments under introduction to 3:1–4:16).

Verses 54b-56 are even somewhat disparaging, inasmuch as Jesus' upbringing would point out that he had received no formal rabbinic training.[37]

---

[36]See esp. M. J. Suggs, *Wisdom, Christology, and Law in Matthew's Gospel* (Cambridge, Mass.: Harvard University Press, 1970).

[37]Sand, *Matthäus*, 301 (citing Gaechter), notes that the upshot of all these questions is to imply, "Surely he is just one of us."

"Carpenter's son" recalls Joseph's occupation. In light of the wording of the questions about the rest of his family, one would have expected the crowds to ask, "Isn't his father the carpenter?" This, coupled with the lack of reference to Joseph anywhere in the Gospels or Acts following Jesus' infancy, has suggested to many that Joseph may be dead by this time, but no one knows for sure. A "carpenter" could also be a *stone mason*.[38] Mark's account shows that Jesus had practiced Joseph's trade prior to his baptism and public ministry (Mark 6:3).

On the biological and spiritual relation of the rest of Jesus' family to him, see comments under 12:46-50. Though they do not yet support him, James and Jude (the abbreviated form of Judas) will later distinguish themselves as Christian leaders (on James, see Acts 15:1-29) and as writers of inspired epistles. Only here does Matthew indicate that Jesus had an unspecified number of sisters as well.

Yet despite their amazement, Jesus' fellow Nazarenes cannot accept his claims about himself (cf. Luke 4:17-21), and they take particular offense when he reminds them of God's past preference for certain Gentiles over many Israelites (cf. Luke 4:25-30). "Took offense" in v. 57a (or *scandalized*, on which see comments under 5:29-30) may also carry the sense of *refused to believe*.

13:57b-58 Matthew, however, does not itemize all these objections. Instead, he proceeds immediately to Jesus' pronouncement, which explains his role as a prophet and accounts for his rejection. Verse 57b sounds like a popular proverb that was already in circulation.[39] The reaction of Jesus' "own house" is vividly depicted in Mark 3:21. Throughout Christian history many of Jesus' followers have experienced the truth of this teaching: those who have known them best from an early age on are often least willing to accept them as spiritually gifted or empowered. The upshot of Jesus' stay in Nazareth is that he severely curtails his miracle-working ministry there (v. 58), particularly his healings (cf. Mark 6:5).[40] Significantly, "their lack of faith" does not refer to inadequate confidence on the part of his followers but to the rejection of Jesus by unbelievers. On the relationship between faith and miracles, cf. above under 9:34. On refusing to work wonders to satisfy skeptics, see comments under 12:38-42.

---

[38]Louw and Nida, *Greek-English Lexicon* 1:520, define τέκτων as a "builder," who would be "skilled in the use of wood and stone and possibly even metal."

[39]See J. Gnilka, *Das Matthäusevangelium* (Freiburg: Herder, 1986-88), 1:517, for possible sources.

[40]Matthew's "did not . . . because" correctly interprets Mark's "could not." It was not that Jesus was actually impotent in the face of unbelief but that he chose to limit himself in this way.

¹At that time Herod the tetrarch heard the reports about Jesus, ²and he said to his attendants, "This is John the Baptist; he has risen from the dead! That is why miraculous powers are at work in him."

(2) Rejection of John by Herod (14:1-12). **14:1-2** "At that time" links this section to the previous one only very loosely. The connection is more topical. The Nazarenes illustrate one false understanding of Jesus. A second is that of Herod, who thinks that Jesus is John the Baptist resurrected. "The tetrarch" identifies this Herod as Antipas, son of Herod the Great. (On the division of the elder Herod's kingdom, see comments on 2:22.) Antipas governed Galilee and Perea from 4 B.C. to A.D. 39.[41] Matthew last referred to John as in prison in 11:2. Verses 3-4 will explain how John got there. Matthew has already underlined several similarities between John's and Jesus' ministries, so Herod's opinion is understandable. His belief in the possibility of resurrection was undoubtedly based on Pharisaic doctrine but may well have intermingled various superstitious notions as well (cf. Josephus, *J.W.* 1.30.7 on the "ghosts" of Alexander and Aristobulus in Herod's palace). This belief seems to demonstrate the existence of a contemporary rumor that John had been raised.[42] The "miraculous powers" are most likely those to which 13:54,58 refer, where the same word (*dynameis*) has just been used.

³Now Herod had arrested John and bound him and put him in prison because of Herodias, his brother Philip's wife, ⁴for John had been saying to him: "It is not lawful for you to have her." ⁵Herod wanted to kill John, but he was afraid of the people, because they considered him a prophet.

14:3-5 Verses 3-12 interrupt the sequence of events with a flashback to explain how John had been arrested and executed. He had spoken out too bluntly against Herodias when she divorced Antipas's half brother Herod Philip (probably not the same individual as Philip the tetrarch) in order to marry Antipas himself (vv. 3-4), in violation of Lev 18:16. (For further details cf. Josephus, *Ant.* 18.5.2.) Mark paints a more nuanced and detailed picture of Herod, who combines anger with admiration for John. Matthew's Herod is more unrelentingly antagonistic, and his narrative is characteristically more abbreviated. But there is no contradiction between the two accounts.[43] The tension between Matthew and Mark is actually reflected within Matthew's account itself, as Herod's desire to kill John in

---

[41]See H. W. Hoehner, *Herod Antipas* (Cambridge: University Press, 1972), for the fullest discussion of this man and his life.

[42]S. J. Nortjé, "John the Baptist and the Resurrection Traditions in the Gospels," *Neot* 23 (1989): 349-58.

[43]On the problems of harmonizing Josephus and the Gospels, see especially Hoehner, *Herod*, 124-49; on the differences between Matthew and Mark, see pp. 149-65.

v. 5a competes with his distress at the request for John's head in v. 9. But such emotional swings frequently characterize despotic rulers. Mark 6:20 further explains this combination of moods. Herod's recognition of John's holiness inspires a mixture of respect, fear, and disgust, typical among those not committed to God's standards. Only Matthew emphasizes the crowd's view of John as a prophet (v. 5b), which once again ties him closely to Jesus and links this narrative to the previous passage (cf. 13:57). Verse 5b will be repeated almost verbatim in 21:46 to explain the Jewish leaders' reluctance to act against Jesus during the Passover festival.

⁶On Herod's birthday the daughter of Herodias danced for them and pleased Herod so much ⁷that he promised with an oath to give her whatever she asked. ⁸Prompted by her mother, she said, "Give me here on a platter the head of John the Baptist." ⁹The king was distressed, but because of his oaths and his dinner guests, he ordered that her request be granted ¹⁰and had John beheaded in the prison. ¹¹His head was brought in on a platter and given to the girl, who carried it to her mother. ¹²John's disciples came and took his body and buried it. Then they went and told Jesus.

14:6-12   This paragraph describes John's fateful day. Salome, Herodias's daughter by her previous husband Philip, so entertains[44] the crowd at a birthday celebration for Herod that he makes her a rash vow (vv. 6-7). Mark 6:23 spells out the qualification implicit in the offer of "whatever she asked." Herod could not have surrendered more than 50 percent of his power and still continued to reign. Salome apparently has the opportunity to consult with her mother about Herod's offer. The daughter is probably about twelve years old (in v. 11 she is a *korasion*, on which see comments under 9:24) and not free to speak for herself. Herodias, who is more eager than her husband to be rid of John and his preaching, thus asks for his execution and the gruesome proof of it (v. 8).

In a touch of poignant but tragic irony, Herod's reply shows that he is more concerned to save face in front of his guests than to uphold justice and morality (vv. 9-11).[45] "The king" in v. 9 is probably also ironic, as when used of Herod's father in 2:1,3. Matthew calls Antipas "king" precisely at the moment in which he acts least kingly. Herod, of course, probably never expected that his offer would result in such a request, but he nevertheless grants it. Verse 12 will refer to some later time when John's followers heard of his execution and bravely requested his headless corpse. Devout Jews prized a proper burial. John's disciples would have

---

[44]The word "danced" (from ὀρχέομαι) does not in itself imply any sensuality, nor does any appear in this context. But the Herodians were infamous for immorality, so one cannot exclude the idea of erotic dancing here.

[45]Cf. Carson, "Matthew," 339, citing Plumptre: "Like most weak men, Herod feared to be thought weak."

preserved his good reputation. Verse 12 ties Jesus in with John again. John's martyrdom foreshadows Jesus' own passion and crucifixion.[46]

b. JESUS IS THE BREAD OF LIFE FOR JEWS AND GENTILES (14:13–16:12). This section is tied together by two parallel feeding miracles and Jesus' summary reflections on them (14:13-21; 15:32-39; 16:5-12). At first Jesus continues to minister to Jews (14:13-36); then he turns from them to the Gentiles (15:1–16:12). In each section the Christological question continues to be sharply focused.

(1) The Son of God Reveals Himself to Israel (14:13-36). Two major miracles demonstrating Jesus' power over nature are followed by a brief summary of his further healing activity. This section also contains the strongest Christological confession to date by his Jewish disciples (v. 33). For now Jesus is still ministering in Israel, and his Jewish followers acknowledge him as Son of God.

13When Jesus heard what had happened, he withdrew by boat privately to a solitary place. Hearing of this, the crowds followed him on foot from the towns. 14When Jesus landed and saw a large crowd, he had compassion on them and healed their sick.

(a) Feeding the Five Thousand (14:13-21). **14:13-14** "When Jesus heard" chronologically follows 14:1-2, since vv. 3-12 formed a flashback.[47] Jesus withdraws as in 2:22 and 12:15. Geographically distancing himself from hostility will become an increasingly recurrent pattern. Chapters 14–16 are dominated by Jesus' going in and out of the province of Galilee, especially by means of several lake crossings. These crossings will later relate to his alternation of ministry between Jews and Gentiles. Here Jesus escapes whatever danger he perceives from Herod, but he does not elude the crowds. So these are presumably Jews from Galilee who have followed him on shore around the lake. "Privately" may or may not imply without his disciples, but they reappear at least by v. 15. The "solitary place" of v. 13 is the *wilderness* or unpopulated area east of Galilee. On Jesus' compassion and the metaphor of sheep and shepherd, see comments under 9:36. Healings occur as characteristically elsewhere. Interestingly, Matthew substitutes this reference to Jesus' healing (v. 14) for Mark's emphasis on his teaching (Mark 6:34). And he never again refers to Jesus' teaching in the summaries of his ministry with crowds. Perhaps Matthew wants to distinguish the crowds from the Jewish leaders as still the objects of Jesus' beneficence but also to distinguish the crowds from

---

[46]For a detailed list of parallels, see Allison and Davies, *Matthew* 2:476.

[47]Cf. L. Cope, "The Death of John the Baptist in the Gospel of Matthew," *CBQ* 38 (1976): 515-19.

the disciples who are his true followers to be further instructed and illuminated.[48]

[15]As evening approached, the disciples came to him and said, "This is a remote place, and it's already getting late. Send the crowds away, so they can go to the villages and buy themselves some food."
[16]Jesus replied, "They do not need to go away. You give them something to eat."
[17]"We have here only five loaves of bread and two fish," they answered.
[18]"Bring them here to me," he said.

14:15-18 The "remote place" in v. 15 translates *erēmos*, the same word as the "solitary place" in v. 13. The disciples are understandably concerned about the crowd's need to eat. We are not told how far from the villages everyone is, but they could easily be several miles away. Jesus replies as if the disciples have a large store of food available (v. 16). "You" is emphatic (as is the "we" of 15:33; see comments on both pronouns there). The disciples describe the only provisions of which they know (v. 17). The standard Jewish loaf of bread provided a meal for three. Jesus requests the food, and the disciples bring it (v. 18).

[19]And he directed the people to sit down on the grass. Taking the five loaves and the two fish and looking up to heaven, he gave thanks and broke the loaves. Then he gave them to the disciples, and the disciples gave them to the people. [20]They all ate and were satisfied, and the disciples picked up twelve basketfuls of broken pieces that were left over. [21]The number of those who ate was about five thousand men, besides women and children.

14:19-21 The presence of grass in the wilderness suggests a spring date, which John's reference to Passover confirms (John 6:4). As the crowd prepares to eat, Jesus takes the bread and fish, thanks God, and breaks the loaves. Jesus' actions reflect the standard practice of a Jewish head of household at the beginning of an ordinary meal. "Gave thanks" is, literally, *blessed*, in the sense of praising God. Jesus may well have pronounced the common Jewish benediction, "Blessed art Thou, O Lord our God, King of the Universe, who brings forth bread from the earth" (*m. Ber.* 6:1). In the feeding of the four thousand the corresponding word will be a form of *eucharisteō* (15:36), but this too was a common verb for giving thanks. It would be anachronistic to read in a reference to the Lord's Supper or "Eucharist" in the context of either feeding miracle, though conceivably Jesus could have intended these miracles to foreshadow the Lord's table. In retrospect it is of course easy to see why Christians might find eucharistic symbolism here, and Matthew's wording may suggest that he saw some

---

[48]Cf. J. A. Comber, "The Verb *Therapeuō* in Matthew's Gospel," *JBL* 97 (1978): 431-34.

such symbolism too,[49] even though there is no particular parallel between the fish and the wine. But in the original context of Jesus' life, no indication is given that any such symbolism was present. The nature of the miracle itself is not described; apparently no one saw it take place (cf. the water turned into wine at Cana in John 2:1-11). But Jesus provides enough food for well over five thousand people (the women and children could easily have more than quadrupled the size of the crowd),[50] in addition to abundant leftovers. The word for "basketfuls" (*kophinos*) describes a distinctively Jewish basket for carrying kosher food.[51] And the addition of "women and children" may reflect the language of Exod 12:37, along with Matthew's concern to include the marginalized of society.[52]

This miracle is sometimes seen as simply an illustration of Jesus' compassion for human need, but the lack of urgency in the setting hardly merited such a wonder. The disciples' suggestion of v. 15 offered a realistic alternative. Rather, feeding the five thousand—providing bread for Israel in the wilderness—almost certainly was meant to call to people's minds God's supernatural feeding of the Israelites with manna in their wilderness wanderings in Moses' day. Jewish tradition had come to believe that the Messiah would repeat this miracle of abundant provision of food on an even grander scale.[53] The promise of Ps 132:15 and the somewhat similar miracles of 1 Kgs 17:9-16 and 2 Kgs 4:42-44 also provide important background. The collection of twelve baskets (one per apostle?) may well have been intended to call to mind the twelve tribes of Israel. Again we see evidence that Jesus is creating a new Israel out of those who will follow him and foreshadowing the messianic banquet (as also in 22:1-13; 26:29). He must therefore be the Messiah.[54] Applications of this passage must focus on Christology and spiritual sustenance rather than making vague and sometimes false promises about God meeting all our physical needs. John develops precisely this spiritual import of the miracle by placing Jesus' "Bread of Life" discourse, given in the Capernaum synagogue, shortly after his account of the feeding miracle (John 6:26-59).[55]

---

[49]See the list of verbal parallels between 14:13-21 and 26:20-29 as laid out in Allison and Davies, *Matthew*, 2:481.

[50]The counting, or at least an estimate, could have easily been done in light of the arrangements described in Mark 6:40, which would also presumably bring together family units.

[51]S. T. Lachs, *A Rabbinic Commentary on the New Testament: The Gospels of Matthew, Mark, and Luke* (Hoboken, N.J.: KTAV, 1987), 241.

[52]For both of these options see France, *Matthew*, 237.

[53]See P. Borgen, *Bread from Heaven* (Leiden: Brill, 1965).

[54]See esp. E. Stauffer, "Zum apokalyptischen Festmahl in Mc 6,34ff.," *ZNW* 46 (1955): 264-66. Cf. W. L. Lane, *The Gospel according to Mark*, NIC (Grand Rapids: Eerdmans, 1974), 229.

[55]The feeding of the five thousand is in fact the only miracle to appear in all four Gospels, "perhaps because it shows so comprehensively how Jesus is equal to all human need, whether social or spiritual" (F. D. Bruner, *The Churchbook* [Dallas: Word, 1990], 530).

²²Immediately Jesus made the disciples get into the boat and go on ahead of him to the other side, while he dismissed the crowd. ²³After he had dismissed them, he went up on a mountainside by himself to pray. When evening came, he was there alone, ²⁴but the boat was already a considerable distance from land, buffeted by the waves because the wind was against it.

(b) Walking on Water (14:22-33). **14:22-24** John 6:14-15 explains the urgency with which Jesus "dismissed" the disciples and crowds in v. 22 (from Greek *apolyō*, more literally, *sent away*, as in v. 15). This threat of trying to force Jesus to become king, coupled with his original desire to go to a solitary place, accounts for his actions in v. 23 as well. He needs to be alone for prayer. *Kat' idian* ("by himself") links this text with v. 13 (where it is translated "privately"). One ought not pray just during times of crisis (Luke presents Jesus as regularly in prayer—e.g., 5:16; 9:18; 9:28-29; 11:1), but prayer is particularly crucial on such occasions (hence, Matthew and Mark refer to Jesus at prayer only here and in Gethsemane—cf. Matt 26:36-46).

A storm reminiscent of 8:23-27 comes up suddenly, so that the disciples make very little progress on their journey. "Buffeted" is more literally *tormented*, a word that elsewhere can refer to demonic hostility against people (Matt 8:6; Rev 9:5). So, as in 8:29, there may be an occult element at work here. Normally the disciples would have completed the lake crossing easily by now, even if they had waited a little while for Jesus at Bethsaida (cf. Mark 6:45).[56] The "considerable distance" of v. 24 is, literally, *many stadia*. One *stadium* equaled approximately six hundred feet. John says they have rowed twenty-five to thirty stadia (three to four miles), and the lake was approximately four to five miles wide.

²⁵During the fourth watch of the night Jesus went out to them, walking on the lake. ²⁶When the disciples saw him walking on the lake, they were terrified. "It's a ghost," they said, and cried out in fear.

²⁷But Jesus immediately said to them: "Take courage! It is I. Don't be afraid."

14:25-27 Jesus apparently spent considerable time in prayer. Between 3:00 and 6:00 a.m. (the "fourth watch"—dividing 6:00 p.m. through 6:00 a.m. into four three-hour segments), the disciples see him walking across the lake over the waves. The only thing they can deduce is that they are seeing a disembodied spirit of some kind. "Ghost" (*phantasma*) in v. 26 refers to a specter or apparition from the realm of the dead (as in the episode of Saul, Samuel, and the witch of Endor in 1 Sam 28). "Fear" must here mean *terror*. With the night and the storm,

---

[56]Cf. Carson, "Matthew," 343, on the grammar and significance of "while" in v. 22, which is better rendered *until*.

the entire scene certainly created a horrifying spectacle with preternatural overtones. In v. 27 Jesus calls to his disciples to "take courage" (the same verb translated "take heart" in 9:2,22). Cranfield notes: "If it is a result of obedience to Christ's command that the church or the individual Christian is in a situation of danger or distress, then there is no need to fear."[57] "It is I" reads, more literally, *I am*. This is not bad grammar but a conscious echo of the divine name of Yahweh, as in Exod 3:14. Though still somewhat veiled, this is perhaps Jesus' clearest self-revelation of his divinity to date.[58]

> [28]"Lord, if it's you," Peter replied, "tell me to come to you on the water." [29]"Come," he said.
>
> Then Peter got down out of the boat, walked on the water and came toward Jesus. [30]But when he saw the wind, he was afraid and, beginning to sink, cried out, "Lord, save me!"
>
> [31]Immediately Jesus reached out his hand and caught him. "You of little faith," he said, "why did you doubt?"

14:28-31 In this uniquely Matthean section, Peter asks for the power to imitate Jesus' miracle. "If it is you" (v. 28) is a potentially misleading translation for a first-class condition. The logic more closely resembles that of 10:1,8, when Jesus passes his miracle-working authority on to his disciples. *Since it is you, please enable me to do the same thing you are doing* better captures the intent of Peter's request. Matthew surely saw "Lord" in the strongest sense here, as equivalent to Yahweh, whether or not Peter intended it that way. The motive for Peter's request is unstated and apparently irrelevant. Jesus agrees and enables Peter to start walking toward him (v. 29). Before he gets as far as Jesus, however, he begins to "doubt" his ability to continue (v. 31), remarkably due more to the strong winds than to the water below (v. 30).[59] The word "doubt" (from Greek *distazō*) suggests the idea of trying to go in two different directions at once or of serving two different masters simultaneously. Having lost his initial faith, Peter is unable to go on, begins to sink, and must be rescued. His cry echoes the plea of all the disciples in 8:25. In v. 31 Jesus rebukes Peter for wavering, as he did all the disciples in 8:26. Here is the first of five key texts in chaps. 14–18 in which Matthew inserts references to Peter not found in any other Gospel (cf. 15:5; 16:17-19; 17:24-27; 18:21).

---

[57]C. E. B. Cranfield, *The Gospel according to St. Mark*, CGTC (Cambridge: University Press, 1977), 228.

[58]See esp. A. M. Denis, "La marche de Jésus sur les eaux," in *De Jésus aux Évangiles*, ed. I. de la Potterie (Gembloux: Duculot, 1967), 238, 244. Cf. Lane, *Mark*, 237-38.

[59]Cf. G. T. Montague (*Companion God: A Cross-Cultural Commentary on the Gospel of Matthew* [New York: Paulist, 1989], 169-70): Peter sees the wind because he "no longer sees Jesus." His "little faith" is "trust that falters out of fear."

On the significance of all five, see comments under 16:18-19, but it is worth noting here that the climactic focus in this passage rests more with Peter's failure than with his accomplishment.

³²And when they climbed into the boat, the wind died down. ³³Then those who were in the boat worshiped him, saying, "Truly you are the Son of God."

14:32-33   The storm stills and the disciples' reverence and understanding of Jesus reach a new high. Jesus is the very Son of God, exercising prerogatives reserved in the Old Testament for Yahweh himself (cf. Job 9:8 and Ps 77:19). Still, something remains inadequate in this confession, since 16:13-20 will bring the disciples even greater understanding (and failure). This inadequacy is probably related to their ignorance of Jesus' mission of suffering that lies ahead. Thus far their Christology is based solely on Jesus' mighty acts, scarcely the ideal basis for faith (cf. John 20:29). Mark 6:52, while jarringly different from Matthew's conclusion and reflecting Mark's emphasis on the disciples' lack of understanding, is thus not contradictory.[60] Followers of Jesus in fact regularly experience a combination of faith and doubt. For now, however, Matthew wants to focus on the positive side of the disciples' response and on the proper answer to the question of who Jesus is.[61]

³⁴When they had crossed over, they landed at Gennesaret. ³⁵And when the men of that place recognized Jesus, they sent word to all the surrounding country. People brought all their sick to him ³⁶and begged him to let the sick just touch the edge of his cloak, and all who touched him were healed.

(c) Healings in Gennesaret (14:34-36).   **14:34-36**   As in 8:1-17 and 9:18-34, Matthew appends an abbreviated, summary account of Jesus' miracle-working activity to the two preceding, fuller miracle stories. Gennesaret (v. 34) lay on the western shore of Galilee, south of Capernaum, for which the disciples had originally headed (John 6:17). Mark says they had started out for Bethsaida as well, probably as a preliminary stopping point (see comments under vv. 22-24). The storm no doubt blew the boat off course. The crowds bring the "sick," as frequently before (v. 35). The

---

[60]For additional differences between Matthew and Mark, along with possible theological explanations, see C. R. Carlisle, "Jesus' Walking on the Water: A Note on Matthew 14:22-33," *NTS* 31 (1985): 151-55.

[61]Mark may also be consciously suppressing various references to Jesus as "Son of God" throughout his Gospel so as to reserve the uses of that title for key places in the beginning (1:1), middle (9:7), and end (15:29) of his narrative. See J. P. Heil, *Jesus Walking on the Sea* (Rome: Biblical Institute Press, 1981), 75. Heil's study is also the fullest discussion of this miracle overall. On both the feeding of the five thousand and the walking on the water, cf. further C. L. Blomberg, "The Miracles as Parables," in *Gospel Perspectives*, vol. 6, ed. D. Wenham and C. Blomberg (Sheffield: JSOT, 1986), 337-40, 342-45.

specific behavior of the people in v. 36 parallels that of the hemorrhaging woman in 9:20-21, on which see comments there. The different word for "healed" used here (from Greek *diasōzō*) may carry extra emphasis and mean *completely healed* (cf. Weymouth, "restored to perfect health"). By including this paragraph, Matthew highlights the positive response to Jesus by large numbers of Israelites, however superficial or inadequately motivated it may be. The healings en masse demonstrate Jesus' concern to minister to the entire people of God, regardless of their state of ritual purity. The theme of 15:1-20 follows naturally.[62]

(2) The Son of David Turns from Israel to the Gentiles (15:1–16:12). This section begins and ends with controversies between Jesus and the Jewish leaders. As clearly as anywhere to date, Jesus rejects their teaching, especially concerning who is clean and unclean (15:1-20). He rebukes their demand for a sign (16:1-4) and warns his followers against their influence (16:5-12). In between these passages Jesus goes farther away from Israel than he has before, well into Gentile territory, where, in striking contrast with the Jewish leaders, both an individual woman (15:21-28) as well as large crowds (15:29-39) respond enthusiastically and with keen insight.

¹Then some Pharisees and teachers of the law came to Jesus from Jerusalem and asked, ²"Why do your disciples break the tradition of the elders? They don't wash their hands before they eat!"

(a) Kosher Laws Rescinded (15:1-20).[63]   **15:1-2**   Yet another controversy pits Jesus against the religious leaders of Judaism. The new element introduced here is that these leaders come "from Jerusalem." They would presumably present a greater zeal, authority, and implicit threat. Their question refers specifically to the oral laws ("the tradition of the elders,"—i.e., of their forefathers) which had been developed to help explain and apply the Scriptures. The handwashing was more ceremonial than hygienic, though obviously both elements were involved. The entire Mishnaic tractate *Yadim* ("Hands") would later outline various required ritual cleansings. It was inconceivable that the disciples would break these laws if Jesus had not already disregarded them (as confirmed by Luke 11:38), but the Pharisees and scribes still frame their question somewhat respectfully by questioning only his followers' behavior.

³Jesus replied, "And why do you break the command of God for the sake of your tradition? ⁴For God said, 'Honor your father and mother' and 'Anyone

---

[62]D. Hill, *The Gospel of Matthew*, NCB (London: Oliphants, 1972), 249.

[63]See R. P. Booth, *Jesus and the Laws of Purity* (Sheffield: JSOT, 1986), for a book-length traditio-historical and legal analysis of this passage, largely in its Markan form.

who curses his father or mother must be put to death.' [5]But you say that if a man says to his father or mother, 'Whatever help you might otherwise have received from me is a gift devoted to God,' [6]he is not to 'honor his father' with it. Thus you nullify the word of God for the sake of your tradition.

15:3-6 Jesus nevertheless perceives their tone as one of accusation. Avoiding conversational niceties, he employs a standard rabbinic technique and replies directly with a counterquestion (v. 3), which is based on the premise that the oral law actually contravened the written law. He does not address the specific charge concerning hand washing but challenges the validity of the oral Torah more generally. He supports his own accusation by means of an entirely different example from Pharisaic tradition, in which the *Corban* laws (e.g., *m. Ned.* 1:2-4; 9:7) conflicted with obedience to the Fifth Commandment (Exod 20:12; Deut 5:16) and with God's penalty for one form of disobeying that Commandment (Exod 21:17; Lev 20:9), both of which he quotes in v. 4. The *Corban* practice in view was that of pledging money or other material resources to the temple to be paid upon one's death. These funds could therefore not be transferred to anyone else but could still be used for one's own benefit while one was still alive (v. 5).[64] The situation turns ironic in that the Pharisees' laws prevented compassionate help for others in need, including those, like parents, to whom one was most obliged. As Bruner observes, "There is a devotion to God that hurts God because it hurts people."[65] Of course, the Jewish leaders themselves would not accept Jesus' charge as worded in v. 6a.[66] Jesus nevertheless claims that their laws require persons to violate Mosaic commandments. Verse 6b echoes the question of v. 3 in the form of a rebuke. Laws designed to build a fence around the Torah are actually undermining it. "Nullify" means to *invalidate the authority of.* The Greek verb (*akyroō*) originally meant *to break a covenant.*

[7]You hypocrites! Isaiah was right when he prophesied about you:
[8]"'These people honor me with their lips,
but their hearts are far from me.
[9]They worship me in vain;
their teachings are but rules taught by men.'"

15:7-9 The inconsistencies of those who enforce the "tradition of the elders" make them "hypocrites" (on which see comments under 6:2). The

---

[64]See J. A. Fitzmyer, "The Aramaic Qorban Inscription from Jebel Hallet et-Turi and Mk 7:1/Mt 15:5," in *Essays on the Semitic Background of the New Testament* (London: G. Chapman, 1971), 96, for an ancient ossuary inscription found near Jerusalem almost exactly paralleling the wording of v. 5b here.

[65]Bruner, *Churchbook*, 543.

[66]The textual variant noted in the NIV marg. for v. 6 ("father or his mother") is weakly attested and naturally understood as a later addition.

situation Isaiah spoke of regarding his contemporaries is thus being reenacted (Isa 29:13).[67] The temple worship and its ritual are scrupulously
supported but at the expense of a genuine relationship with the living God
that recognizes the priorities of human need and does not erect institu-
tions and rules that inhibit social and interpersonal responsibility. Jesus'
logic here parallels his use of Hos 6:6 in Matt 9:13 and 12:7, in which
sacrifice has replaced mercy.[68] How much church attendance and "Christian" activity preoccupy believers today with things they assume please
God yet without ever really ministering materially or spiritually to the
desperately needy people of our world? How much of our money is tied
up in church buildings or spent only on programs and activities to make
ourselves happy rather than caring for the hurting in our midst and across
the globe? The more affluent sectors of Western Christianity frequently
and frighteningly resemble the religion of the Pharisees as depicted
here.[69] God declares all such religion "vain" or *futile* (v. 9).

**[10]Jesus called the crowd to him and said, "Listen and understand. [11]What
goes into a man's mouth does not make him 'unclean,' but what comes out of
his mouth, that is what makes him 'unclean.'"**

15:10-11 The Jerusalem officials apparently asked their question publicly, with the crowds on the periphery. Jesus now addresses these crowds
more directly. (Verse 12 implies that the Pharisees have either receded to
the background or more probably left altogether, most likely in disgust.)
Returning to the specific question of handwashing, Jesus now goes beyond
simply challenging the oral law to rescinding the entire category of Old
Testament laws concerning ritual purity. The dietary laws were at the
heart of these regulations. Washing one's hands, e.g., prevented the person
from defiling the food and rendering it "unclean." Mark 7:19b ("In saying
this, Jesus declared all foods 'clean'") spells out the radical implications
of Jesus' statement in v. 11, even if these implications were not fully
understood until after the events of Acts 10. Matthew is not toning down
Mark by eliminating this explanation. Mark's conclusion follows logically
even from the words of Christ which Matthew retains.[70] There are no

---

[67]On the form of the quotation and for a comparison with the LXX and MT, see R. T.
France, *Jesus and the Old Testament* (Downers Grove: InterVarsity, 1971), 248-50.

[68]Cf. J. N. Oswalt, *The Book of Isaiah*, vol. 1, NIC (Grand Rapids: Eerdmans, 1986),
532: "To speak of reducing [the fear of the Lord] to a set of do's and don't's is to move one's
faith from the center to the periphery of life."

[69]See esp. the description of the "fortress church" and its antidote in F. Tillapaugh, *The
Church Unleashed* (Ventura: Regal, 1982).

[70]Cf. W. C. Allen (*A Critical and Exegetical Commentary on the Gospel according to
S. Matthew*, ICC [Edinburgh: T & T Clark, 1907], 166): "Christ's saying directly contravened
the Mosaic distinction between clean and unclean meats." For a different interpretation, which
keeps Jesus within the bounds of Pharisaism though on one extreme end of a spectrum, see
A. I. Baumgarten, "Korban and the Pharisaic *Paradosis*," JANES 16-17 (1984-85): 5-17.

unclean foods for Christians or any other practices that render persons ritually pure or impure. More significantly, as in Acts 10, this means that Jesus' followers should not treat any people as unclean, as vv. 21-39 here will shortly demonstrate.

The principle of Matt 5:17 is at work again. The dietary laws remain relevant for believers today only in that they point people to Jesus, who makes the unclean clean. Christians dare not discriminate against anyone on the basis of race, sex, socioeconomic status, or nationality or treat any given individual as inherently inferior to any other. Such behavior in fact illustrates the *moral* sin that still does defile a person, as in the reference in v. 11 to what comes out of one's mouth, revealing the state of one's heart (cf. 12:34). Moral purity, by contrast, will include honor and care for parents and grandparents, including financial support, if necessary and possible, as they grow old (1 Tim 3:4). These responsibilities were recognized even by the pagan world in Jesus' day. Hence, failure in this area exposed Christians as "worse than an unbeliever" (1 Tim 5:8). Matthew 10:37 does not contradict these principles because care for our parents forms part of God's will. We may see that others' needs are provided for without maintaining so much loyalty to them that God's priorities are neglected.

12Then the disciples came to him and asked, "Do you know that the Pharisees were offended when they heard this?"

13He replied, "Every plant that my heavenly Father has not planted will be pulled up by the roots. 14Leave them; they are blind guides. If a blind man leads a blind man, both will fall into a pit."

15Peter said, "Explain the parable to us."

15:12-14 Such radical teaching would inevitably offend Pharisees then as it does today.[71] Again, Matthew uses his favorite verb *skandalizō* ("offended"; see comments on 5:29-30). It is not possible for Christians to avoid all offense; sometimes "*some* people must be hurt [offended] so that *all* people will not be [damaged]."[72] The dietary laws were one of the three major badges of Jewish identity in the first century along with Sabbath-keeping and circumcision. Jesus has now directly challenged two of those three badges (cf. 11:28–12:14). Jesus' reply in v. 13 recalls 13:29. The imagery of v. 13 may have originally come from Isa 60:21. The Pharisees' reaction doesn't surprise Jesus because he knows they are not all truly God's people. Instead, he warns of their coming judgment; but as in the parable of the wheat and weeds, the disciples can leave that to God

---

[71]Cf. E. Schweizer (*The Good News according to Matthew* [Richmond: John Knox, 1975], 327): "It would be hard to frame a sharper attack on Israel's faith in its own election."

[72]Bruner, *Churchbook*, 549.

(v. 14a). The Pharisees will even undermine each other with their teaching, like blind people leading other blind people into "a pit," a kind of ditch or trench likely to cause injury and prove difficult to get out of (cf. 12:11). The imagery is particularly ironic in light of Rom 2:19.[73]

15:15 As in 13:36 the disciples ask Jesus for an explanation concerning the "parable," which will here refer to the short metaphor of v. 11. In Mark the whole group asks the question (Mark 7:17); in Matthew, Peter is their spokesman. This is the second of the five unparalleled references to Peter in Matthew 14–18 (see under 14:28-31), and it casts Peter in an entirely negative light, even if the plural "you" of vv. 16-17 shows that all the disciples were similarly befuddled. Peter's question demonstrates again that cognitive understanding of Jesus' metaphors is not all that is at stake. Even the Pharisees understood Jesus' words enough to be put off (v. 12). The question also further blurs the line of distinction between the disciples and the crowds. One can hardly speak of the crowds clearly rejecting Jesus and the disciples clearly accepting him even at this advanced stage in his ministry. The disciples' obtuseness is heightened because, given the nature of Jesus' reply, they apparently do not pick up even on all of the cognitive level of meaning. Or, perhaps more likely, they do understand Jesus' point but recognize that its implications are so radical that they want to make sure of what Jesus has in mind. This would fit the pattern of chap. 13, where that which is most offensive in the parables ultimately involves claims about Jesus and their implications for discipleship.

16"Are you still so dull?" Jesus asked them. **17**"Don't you see that whatever enters the mouth goes into the stomach and then out of the body? **18**But the things that come out of the mouth come from the heart, and these make a man 'unclean.' **19**For out of the heart come evil thoughts, murder, adultery, sexual immorality, theft, false testimony, slander. **20**These are what make a man 'unclean'; but eating with unwashed hands does not make him 'unclean.'"

15:16-20 In v. 16 Jesus rebukes the disciples for their *lack of understanding* ("so dull"). On understanding cf. under 13:13-15,51 and 15:10. In light of v. 15, it is hard to see how Matthew can be viewed as significantly improving Mark's picture of the disciples. Verses 17-20 clarify and illustrate the distinction between ceremonial and moral cleanness. Ritually impure food harms no one. What the body doesn't use is eliminated

---

[73]The textual variant "guides of the blind" misses the point of Jesus' illustration and likely resulted from an attempt to streamline the awkward but probably original reading "blind guides of the blind," which in turn is more naturally abbreviated in still other textual variants to "blind guides." The NIV avoids the more cumbersome expression in v. 14a, since v. 14b adequately expresses the idea of "guides of the blind."

through the digestive tract (v. 17).[74] Jesus is obviously not talking about ingesting that which does bodily damage, such as the abuse of alcohol or drugs. Morally impure behavior and speech, however, always harms oneself and others and remains an offense to God (v. 18). Jesus' illustrations combine in sequence the Sixth through the Ninth Commandments of the Decalogue (Exod 20:13-16). These are introduced by general sins of the thought life and supplemented by the sins of sexual immorality (*porneia*), naturally associated with adultery, and of *blasphemies* (a better rendering of Greek *blasphemiai* than "slander"), naturally linked with false testimony (v. 19). Verse 20b brings the discussion back full circle to the original charge of v. 2 and makes it plain that God's people no longer need to observe ritual hand washing.

Christians today ought to ponder long on the implications of vv. 17-20. Many churchgoers continue to attend services and activities faithfully, even while indulging, without repentance, in sexual sin on the side, or even while mistreating fellow Christians with unkind or abusive speech.[75] Such people remain defiled in God's eyes rather than those who violate rules of human origin about how Christians should act. Sadly, the latter are often precisely those who are condemned by their more legalistic brothers and sisters in Christ.[76] Like the Pharisees, the defenders of those rules seem always able to find some Scripture they can twist to offer support for their traditions.

²¹Leaving that place, Jesus withdrew to the region of Tyre and Sidon. ²²A Canaanite woman from that vicinity came to him, crying out, "Lord, Son of David, have mercy on me! My daughter is suffering terribly from demon-possession."

(b) The Canaanite Woman's Faith (15:21-28). **15:21-22** Jesus has obviously withdrawn from Israel ideologically in vv. 1-20; now he again withdraws geographically. This time he does not cross to the eastern shore of the Sea of Galilee but heads northward to "Tyre and Sidon," port cities in what today would be parts of Lebanon and Syria. Matthew uses the Old Testament place names, as he does with the word "Canaanite" in v. 22, instead of Mark's "Syrophoenician" (Mark 7:26, NRSV), in order to conjure up their evil connotations from bygone eras. On Tyre and

---

[74]The NIV "goes . . . out of the body" is a euphemistic translation of the Greek εἰς ἀφεδρῶνα ἐκβάλλεται," which might be rendered, more literally, *is cast into the toilet*, which was probably a disposal bucket emptied onto a dungheap.

[75]Cf. A. Plummer (*An Exegetical Commentary on the Gospel according to S. Matthew* [London: E. Stock, 1909], 212): "Rigid scrupulosity about things of little moment may be accompanied with utterly unscrupulous conduct in matters that are vital."

[76]Bruner (*Churchbook*, 541) likens Jesus' action to a very conservative Christian leader today who would choose to allow his followers to dance or drink.

Sidon see comments under 11:22. With the coming of Jesus, these cities receive another opportunity to repent. "Canaanite" was the general term for the pagan inhabitants of the promised land Israel was told to conquer in Joshua's day. On this woman's lips, "Lord" (most recently used by the disciples during the Christophany of 14:28,30) will again call Jesus' divinity to Matthew's readers' minds. "Son of David" (cf. 1:1; 9:27; 12:23) is the distinctively Jewish designation for the Messiah and proves equally striking on this pagan woman's lips. "Have mercy" echoes the cry of the blind men in 9:27 and appeals to Jesus to relieve the plight of this woman's daughter. On demon possession see comments under 4:24; 8:28-34; 9:32-34; and 12:22-45.

23Jesus did not answer a word. So his disciples came to him and urged him, "Send her away, for she keeps crying out after us."
24He answered, "I was sent only to the lost sheep of Israel."

15:23-24 Surprisingly, Jesus breaks his pattern of immediately responding to requests for healing. His silence therefore seems deliberate and dramatic. The closest parallel to date has been the seemingly unintentional delay before Jesus raised Jairus's daughter (9:18-26), a delay that ultimately magnified both the miracle and God's glory. Nevertheless, the woman perseveres, and the disciples request that Jesus heed her cries. "Send away" is ambiguous; it could mean either with or without granting her request. But Jesus' protest in v. 24 makes better sense if the disciples had asked Jesus to do what the woman wanted.[77] This verse is uniquely Matthean and closely parallels 10:6 (see comments there). Perhaps the same solution to the particularist-universalist tension applies here; Jesus must first go to the Jews, and then he will move on to the Gentiles (cf. the use of "first" in Mark 7:27). More relevant to the immediate context, however, since Jesus has actually left Israel already,[78] is the interpretation that takes these words as a test or prompt of some kind designed to draw out the woman into further discussion. Perhaps Jesus is replying according to the stereotypic Jewish understanding of "Son of David" (v. 22) to see just what kind of belief this woman has.[79]

---

[77]Patte, *Matthew*, 221; H. N. Ridderbos, *Matthew*, BSC (Grand Rapids: Zondervan, 1987), 288.

[78]The claim (Allen, *Matthew*, 168) that Jesus is actually on the border of Galilee, with the woman having come out of pagan territory to meet him, so that Matthew does not see a Gentile ministry in view here, seems very unlikely. Verse 21 seems clearly to place Jesus deep in Gentile territory.

[79]Cf. further R. H. Gundry (*Matthew: A Commentary on His Literary and Theological Art* [Grand Rapids: Eerdmans, 1982], 314: "The snubbing of a Gentile casts the faith of that Gentile in all the better light and by this means justifies a mission to the Gentiles now that Jewish officialdom has rejected Jesus."

²⁵The woman came and knelt before him. "Lord, help me!" she said.

²⁶He replied, "It is not right to take the children's bread and toss it to their dogs."

²⁷"Yes, Lord," she said, "but even the dogs eat the crumbs that fall from their masters' table."

²⁸Then Jesus answered, "Woman, you have great faith! Your request is granted." And her daughter was healed from that very hour.

15:25-28 The woman merely repeats her plea for help but also kneels. Whatever her intention, Matthew will see some kind of worship here. Jesus pursues the question of the distinction between Jews and Gentiles (v. 26). Jews frequently insulted Gentiles by calling them "dogs,"— the wild, homeless scavengers that roamed freely in Palestine. But the diminutive form here (*kynarion* rather than *kyōn*) suggests a more affectionate term for domestic pets, particularly since these dogs eat under the children's table.[80] Even at best, Jesus' remarks still strike the modern reader as condescending. Jesus apparently wants to demonstrate and stretch this woman's faith. The "children" must then refer to Israel and the "bread" to the blessings of God on the Jews, particularly through Jesus' healing ministry. The woman disputes none of Jesus' terms but argues that, even granting his viewpoint, he should still help her (v. 27). The Gentiles should receive at least residual blessings from God's favor on the Jews. In fact, the Old Testament from Gen 12:1-3 onwards promised far more than residue. The woman reveals a tenacious faith even as a Gentile (v. 28). Jesus explicitly commends this faith, closely paralleling the narrative of 8:5-13 (as does also his instantaneous healing from a distance). Matthew's distinctives underline her faith by the addition both of her words in v. 22 and of Jesus' praise here. "Your request is granted" more literally reads *let it be done for you as you wish.*

²⁹Jesus left there and went along the Sea of Galilee. Then he went up on a mountainside and sat down. ³⁰Great crowds came to him, bringing the lame, the blind, the crippled, the mute and many others, and laid them at his feet; and he healed them. ³¹The people were amazed when they saw the mute speaking, the crippled made well, the lame walking and the blind seeing. And they praised the God of Israel.

---

[80]See Louw and Nida, *Greek-English Lexicon*, 44. The NIV tips the scales in favor of this interpretation by translating "their dogs" instead of "the dogs" (the Greek article often has the force of a possessive adjective). For a development of this line of interpretation, see J. D. M. Derrett, "Law in the New Testament: The Syro-Phoenician Woman and the Centurion of Capernaum," *NovT* 15 (1973): 161-86. For a development of the alternate interpretation that the dogs are wild ones, see R. A. Harrisville, "The Woman of Canaan: A Chapter in the History of Exegesis," *Int* 20 (1966): 274-87. F. Dufton ("The Syrophoenician Woman and Her Dogs," *ExpTim* 100 [1989]: 417) argues that the discussion begins with wild dogs but shifts to domestic ones! Nothing in the context or diction explicitly supports this view.

(c) Feeding the Four Thousand (15:29-39). **15:29-31** This episode remarkably parallels the feeding of the five thousand (14:13-21) and is therefore regularly labeled a doublet (on which concept see comments under 9:27-31).[81] But this seems unlikely.[82] Given that Jesus had come from the region of Tyre and Sidon and will return to his homeland by boat (Magadan in v. 39 is probably equivalent to Magdala on the western shore of Galilee), Matthew apparently intends us to see Jesus as still in Gentile territory here. Mark 7:31 reinforces this interpretation since Jesus has just been in the Decapolis, east of Galilee. What is more, the end of Matt 15:31 makes most sense as a reference to Gentiles praising Yahweh, specifically as the God "of Israel." (In all other Gospel references to Jews glorifying God, he is called simply "God"; Matt 9:8; Mark 2:12; Luke 5:25-26; 7:16; 13:13; 18:43.) And the word for "basketfuls" in v. 37 is *spyris*, a more Hellenistic term than the *kophinos* of 14:20. So it is better to see Jesus as deliberately repeating for Gentiles what he previously offered to Jews.[83] He is the Bread of life for all the world, even if a more consistent and thoroughgoing ministry to the Gentiles still awaits his resurrection. Pairs of feeding miracles also occurred in the days of Moses and of Elijah/Elisha (Exod 16; Num 11:4-9; 2 Kgs 4:1-7,42-44).

Going up the mountainside and sitting down (v. 29) harks back to 5:1 and may hint at a teaching ministry here too. As with the account of the feeding of the five thousand, Matthew prefaces the miracle story with a description of Jesus' healing, this time more fully itemizing the various categories of illnesses as if to stress that as many kinds of sick people were healed among the Gentiles as among the Jews (vv. 30-31; cf. 11:5). Mark narrates one of these miracles at length, describing the cure of a deaf-mute, and separates this account from the feeding of the four thousand (Mark 7:31-37). Matthew characteristically abbreviates and summarizes, but the crowds of vv. 29-31 and 32-38 need not be identical, so there is no necessary contradiction here.

[32]Jesus called his disciples to him and said, "I have compassion for these people; they have already been with me three days and have nothing to eat. I do not want to send them away hungry, or they may collapse on the way."

[33]His disciples answered, "Where could we get enough bread in this remote place to feed such a crowd?"

---

[81]See esp. R. M. Fowler, *Loaves and Fishes* (Chico, Cal.: Scholars, 1981), who adds the interesting twist of arguing that the feeding of the four thousand is original and the feeding of the five thousand the later creation.

[82]C. L. Blomberg, *The Historical Reliability of the Gospels* (Downers Grove: Inter-Varsity, 1987), 146-48.

[83]Cf. N. A. Beck, "Reclaiming a Biblical Text: The Mark 8:14-21 Discussion about Bread in the Boat," *CBQ* 43 (1981): 52.

³⁴"How many loaves do you have?" Jesus asked.
"Seven," they replied, "and a few small fish."

15:32-34 Jesus' compassion reminds us of 14:14, but now it applies
to the crowd's physical as well as spiritual hunger. They have remained
with him not merely for the better part of one day but for three. Whatever
food supplies may have fed the crowd at first have now been exhausted.
Jesus' charisma has kept the crowds from leaving despite their hunger.
This hunger is now severe enough that the option of 14:15 could prove
dangerous. Verse 33 provides both the interpretive crux and the potential
key to understanding this passage. At first the disciples' question seems to
reflect the height of obtuseness. The solution to their problem is obviously for Jesus to do what he did before and work a miracle. But the
emphatic "we" (a uniquely Matthean touch), corresponding to the
emphatic "you" of 14:16, may explain matters. Previously, Jesus had told
his disciples to solve the problem themselves. They couldn't, so he did.[84]
But he has consistently passed on his miracle-working authority to the
Twelve, including as recently as 14:28-31 (despite the abrupt ending of
Peter's walking on the water). Most likely the disciples think that Jesus'
remarks in v. 32 imply that they should miraculously provide food for the
crowd, and they are not convinced they can do it.[85] This makes their
question much more understandable, though, in any event, Matthew does
not present the disciples in a particularly positive light. In v. 34, as
before, Jesus inquires about their provisions. This time they specify the
number of loaves but not the exact quantity of fish.

³⁵He told the crowd to sit down on the ground. ³⁶Then he took the seven
loaves and the fish, and when he had given thanks, he broke them and gave
them to the disciples, and they in turn to the people. ³⁷They all ate and were
satisfied. Afterward the disciples picked up seven basketfuls of broken pieces
that were left over. ³⁸The number of those who ate was four thousand, besides
women and children. ³⁹After Jesus had sent the crowd away, he got into the
boat and went to the vicinity of Magadan.

15:35-39 The details of the miracle closely parallel those of 14:19-
20, on which see comments there. This time no grass is mentioned (is this
a different site or time of year?). The baskets (v. 37) refer to a larger con-
tainer than was previously used, and the specific word is more appropriate
for Gentiles (see comments under vv. 29-31). There are four thousand
rather than five thousand men, not counting other family members (v. 38).
Seven may be the number of completeness or universal influence. Jesus

---

⁸⁴Cf. Gundry, *Matthew*, 320.
⁸⁵J. Knackstedt, "Die beiden Brotvermehrungen im Evangelium," *NTS* 10 (1963-64):
315-16.

thus offers to the whole world exactly what he first offered to Israel. Many respond positively even as the Jews are increasingly rejecting the gospel (recall v. 31b).[86] Finally, Jesus returns to Israel (v. 39). Mark's "Dalmanutha" is otherwise unknown (Mark 8:10) but probably, like Matthew's "Magadan," is an alternate name for Magdala. Magdala may be the same as *Migdal Nunya* (*fish tower*), a suburb of Tiberias on the west bank of Galilee.[87]

¹The Pharisees and Sadducees came to Jesus and tested him by asking him to show them a sign from heaven.

(d) The Demand for a Sign (16:1-4). **16:1** In 12:38-39 the Pharisees and scribes demanded an unambiguous sign to prove the divine origin of Jesus' exorcisms. As soon as Jesus returns to Jewish territory, the Pharisees and Sadducees confront him with a similar demand. This time they explicitly label the sign as "from heaven," a common Jewish expression (on their desire, cf. 1 Cor 1:22), probably here hoping for a uniquely apocalyptic and triumphal manifestation of Christ's power.[88] As in 3:7 only Matthew mentions the Sadducees, no doubt to underline the hostility implied by this combination of groups, which were otherwise at odds. The reappearance of a form of the verb *peirazō* (*test, tempt*) recalls Satan's more explicit lures in 4:1-11.

²He replied, "When evening comes, you say, 'It will be fair weather, for the sky is red,' ³and in the morning, 'Today it will be stormy, for the sky is red and overcast.' You know how to interpret the appearance of the sky, but you cannot interpret the signs of the times. ⁴A wicked and adulterous generation looks for a miraculous sign, but none will be given it except the sign of Jonah." Jesus then left them and went away.

16:2-4 Virtually all of v. 4 echoes verbatim Jesus' reply to the parallel demand in 12:39, on which see comments there. Whether or not Jesus explained "the sign of Jonah" here, as on that previous occasion, is unknown. Matthew will expect his readers to understand what it means from the earlier passage.

Verses 2-3 present a comparison between the signs of the sky and the signs of the times. As clouds move from west to east, the dawn sunlight will tint them in the west, portending rain as the day progresses. In the evening the same phenomenon suggests that the clouds have almost disappeared,

---

[86]Cf. Ridderbos (*Matthew*, 292): "The disciples were given another lesson that Christ's gift can provide in abundance, even where this might be least expected: in a desolate place and among people who did not belong to God's covenant."

[87]Removing the first syllable of *Migdal Nunya* could give rise to a form (*Dalnunya*) similar to Dalmanutha.

[88]J. Gibson, "Jesus' Refusal to Produce a 'Sign' (Mk 8.11-13)," *JSNT* 38 (1990): 37-66.

bringing good weather instead. We preserve this proverb today with the rhyme: "Red sky at morning, sailors take warning. Red sky at night, sailors delight." If the Jewish leaders can recognize what the weather is likely to be by the appearance of the sky, why can they not recognize the dawning of the kingdom of heaven and the messianic age by what Jesus does and teaches? Jesus has already provided plenty of signs to this end.

There is a textual question regarding the inclusion of vv. 2b-3 that does not yield an easy answer. Many think these words are a later addition to Matthew's text, but probably they should be allowed to stand as original. A few important early manuscripts omit these verses (א, B, f^{13}), but the vast majority includes them. They were more likely left out to harmonize with Mark's similar omission than interpolated from the entirely different context of Luke 12:54-56. It could well be in the largely Alexandrian textual tradition that omitted them that it was recognized that Jesus' illustration was less understandable in the Egyptian climate, in which the same signs of the sky were not always present.[89]

⁵When they went across the lake, the disciples forgot to take bread. ⁶"Be careful," Jesus said to them. "Be on your guard against the yeast of the Pharisees and Sadducees."

(e) Warning against the Jewish Leaders' Influence (16:5-12). **16:5-6** Once again Jesus withdraws from hostility, heading for the eastern shores of the Sea of Galilee. Matthew's incidental remark in v. 5 sets the stage for the disciples' misunderstanding in v. 7 and their subsequent dialogue with Christ. In v. 6 Jesus warns against the spreading evil influence of the teachings of the two groups that had just "tested" him. Mark 8:15 has "Herod" instead of the "Sadducees," but since the latter, unlike the Pharisees, were the group that had made its peace with the Roman Empire and its client rulers, both versions mean approximately the same thing. In a different context, Luke 12:1 has Jesus refer to "the yeast of the Pharisees" as hypocrisy, which should explain why he warned against their teaching here, a point Matt 23 will elaborate in much greater detail. Since the teaching of the Pharisees and Sadducees is grouped together, and since the two sects disagreed on so many specific points of law, their common "yeast" may be their more general rejection of God's will for people to respond to Jesus with discipleship. Hyperconservatism and hyperliberalism in contemporary religion and politics also share the common features of dogmatism and judgmentalism and remain an insidious threat to the true church of Jesus Christ.

---

[89]Cf. B. M. Metzger, *A Textual Commentary on the Greek New Testament* (New York: UBS, 1971), 41. For the opposite conclusion and fuller discussion of evidence for both sides, cf. T. Hirunuma, "Matthew 16:2b-3," in *New Testament Textual Criticism*, ed. E. Epp and G. D. Fee (Oxford: Clarendon, 1981), 35-45.

⁷They discussed this among themselves and said, "It is because we didn't bring any bread."

⁸Aware of their discussion, Jesus asked, "You of little faith, why are you talking among yourselves about having no bread? ⁹Do you still not understand? Don't you remember the five loaves for the five thousand, and how many basketfuls you gathered? ¹⁰Or the seven loaves for the four thousand, and how many basketfuls you gathered? ¹¹How is it you don't understand that I was not talking to you about bread? But be on your guard against the yeast of the Pharisees and Sadducees." ¹²Then they understood that he was not telling them to guard against the yeast used in bread, but against the teaching of the Pharisees and Sadducees.

16:7 Furthering the motif of the disciples' obtuseness, Matthew now presents them as thinking that Jesus is speaking of literal bread. Because they forgot to bring any, they think that Jesus must be warning them against buying food from these groups of Jewish leaders.

16:8-12 The disciples' comment understandably leads to Jesus' rebuke, which Matthew translates with his characteristic term for "little faith" (*oligopistos, -ia*; cf. 6:30; 8:26; 14:31; 17:20). One might have expected Jesus to complain of their little intelligence instead; but if they really recognized him as the Bread of life, based on a mature faith and correct Christology, they would be thinking on a spiritual level concerning the yeast too. So he reminds them of his two feeding miracles, and especially of the superabundance of the leftovers, in order to make them think again on this metaphorical plane. Incidental support appears here as well for viewing those two miracles as distinct. Interestingly, the difference between the words for baskets is preserved in vv. 9-10, confirming our hunch that these terms were significant pointers to the one miracle as for Jews and the other for Gentiles (see comments under 14:13-21; 15:29-39). In v. 11 Jesus then repeats the warning of v. 6, and this time the disciples understand (v. 12a). As in chap. 13, only Matthew inserts these extra references to the disciples' understanding.⁹⁰ There may be an underlying Aramaic play on words in v. 12b, given the similarity between "teaching" (*ʾamîrʾā*) and "yeast" (*hămîrʾā*).⁹¹

c. REVELATION TO PETER OF JESUS' IDENTITY: CORRECT CHRISTOLOGY (16:13-20). These verses are loaded with interpretive conundrums, especially vv. 16-19.⁹² The passage represents the zenith of the disciples'

---

⁹⁰On the form, significance, and authenticity of this dialogue, see E. E. Lemcio, "External Evidence for the Structure and Function of Mark iv. 1-20, vii. 14-23, and viii. 14-12," *JTS* 29 (1978): 323-28.

⁹¹Montague, *Companion God*, 178.

⁹²For the fullest discussion of the interpretive options based on one important cross section of church history, see J. A. Burgess, *A History of the Exegesis of Matthew 16:17-19 from 1781 to 1965* (Ann Arbor: Edwards Brothers, 1966).

understanding to date and brings the second, main section of Matthew's Gospel (4:17–16:20) to its climax. Their triumph will prove short-lived, however, as Matthew's third and final section begins with Jesus' journey to the cross, which the disciples are not prepared to accept.

¹³When Jesus came to the region of Caesarea Philippi, he asked his disciples, "Who do people say the Son of Man is?"
¹⁴They replied, "Some say John the Baptist; others say Elijah; and still others, Jeremiah or one of the prophets."
¹⁵"But what about you?" he asked. "Who do you say I am?"
¹⁶Simon Peter answered, "You are the Christ, the Son of the living God."

16:13 Having crossed the lake, Jesus and his followers head upstream along the Jordan River to its headwaters near Caesarea Philippi, approximately twenty-five miles north of the Sea of Galilee. Formerly known as Paneas, a center of worship for the Greek god Pan, the city recently had been renamed by Philip the tetrarch in honor of himself and Augustus Caesar. Matthew does not tell us why Jesus and the disciples went here, but it is easy to imagine them once again foreshadowing the more extensive Gentile ministry that lies ahead. Matthew, however, focuses solely on the dialogue Jesus initiates with the Twelve. He questions their perception of the crowds' views of his identity, not for his own information but to correct the misconceptions that have arisen.

16:14 All the opinions the disciples report are complimentary and demonstrate that Jesus remains quite popular. The crowds view him as some kind of spokesman for God. The equation with John the Baptist recalls Herod's fears in 14:2 and suggests that others shared these sentiments. Elijah represents the messianic forerunner of Old Testament prophecy (see comments under 11:7-15). Many had obviously not made the link between Elijah and John the Baptist. It would be natural to think of Jesus also as a kind of Jeremiah, a preacher of judgment and repentance who was widely rejected by the leaders of his nation.[93] Some may have even speculated that Jesus was a literally resurrected Jeremiah, in light of certain Jewish expectations to that effect (cf. 2 Esdr 2:16-18 and 2 Macc 15:12-16). Various other prophetic options were no doubt inspired by texts like Deut 18:15-18. But all of these identifications of Christ are inadequate.

16:15-16 Jesus presses the disciples further for *their* response (v. 15). "You" here is emphatic. "I" makes it clear that the "Son of Man" in v. 13 is Jesus. In v. 16 Peter answers as spokesman for the Twelve,

---

[93]See B. T. Dahlberg, "The Typological Use of Jeremiah 1:4-19 in Matthew 16:13-23," *JBL* 94 (1975): 73-80, for further possible typological connections.

who had been addressed collectively. Here is the first time in Matthew that anyone in Jesus' audiences has unambiguously acknowledged him as the "Christ" (*Christos*—Messiah—see under 1:1). Peter immediately adds the title "Son of God" as in 14:33, where all the disciples had acclaimed Jesus with this form of address. Apparently, Peter now has a deeper appreciation for Jesus' unique relationship with the Father.[94] Nevertheless, full-orbed Trinitarian theology will not develop until a later date. Peter also adds the adjective "living," a characteristically Jewish way of referring to God to distinguish him from lifeless idols and also a reminder that only Yahweh has life in himself which he can impart to others. But the disciples' insight has now definitely surpassed that of their Jewish contemporaries.

[17]Jesus replied, "Blessed are you, Simon son of Jonah, for this was not revealed to you by man, but by my Father in heaven. [18]And I tell you that you are Peter, and on this rock I will build my church, and the gates of Hades will not overcome it.

16:17 Verses 17-19 comprise the third uniquely Matthean addition concerning Peter in these central chapters (cf. under 14:28-31; 15:15). Jesus begins with a beatitude (on which see under 5:3), praising Peter's reply. He addresses him by his full Jewish name. *Bariōna* has been frequently translated as "son of Jonah" (as in the NIV), but this would contradict John 1:42 and 21:15 unless Simon is simply seen as a spiritual son of Jonah.[95] It is better, therefore, to recognize that the Greek spelling is a legitimate transliteration and abbreviation of *bar Johanan* ("son of John").[96] Jesus' calling Peter "son of John" nicely balances Peter's address to his Lord as "Son of God." Jesus attributes to Peter's confession insight stemming from divine revelation rather than human deduction. The language does not specify how God revealed himself or require some sudden flash of insight, but it does affirm that God has led Peter to his correct understanding. "Man" is literally *flesh and blood*, a stock Semitic idiom for mortal humanity. On God revealing truth to his elect, cf. comments under 11:25-27.

16:18 Acknowledging Jesus as the Christ illustrates the appropriateness of Simon's nickname, "Peter" (*Petros* = *rock*). This is not the first time Simon has been called Peter (cf. John 1:42), but it is certainly the most famous. Jesus' declaration, "You are Peter," parallels Peter's confession,

[94]Cf. France (*Matthew*, 253): Peter's confession "went beyond a merely nationalistic fervour to an awareness of Jesus' special relationship with God."

[95]As, e.g., in Mounce, *Matthew*, 162.

[96]Cf. Carson, "Matthew," 375.

"You are the Christ," as if to say, "Since you can tell me who I am, I will tell you who you are." The expression "this rock" almost certainly refers to Peter, following immediately after his name, just as the words following "the Christ" in v. 16 applied to Jesus. The play on words in the Greek between Peter's name (*Petros*) and the word "rock" (*petra*) makes sense only if Peter is the rock and if Jesus is about to explain the significance of this identification.[97]

It is often alleged, however, that the "rock" must be Christ or Peter's confession of Christ,[98] especially since the days of Luther and the Protestant Reformation. These alternatives understandably react against traditional Roman Catholic equation of Peter with the first pope and against an elaborate ecclesiology built on this verse. But a legitimate interpretation of vv. 18b-19, as below, predicates nothing of this, so there should be no theological objections to taking Peter as "this rock."[99] A distinction between "Peter" and "this rock" is also often affirmed on the basis of the two different Greek words, but grammar requires this variation because the ending of *petra* ("rock") is feminine and could not be used for a man's name. The underlying Aramaic would have used *kepha* in both instances, in which case the problem disappears altogether.

So what does Jesus promise Peter? He will be the foundation on which Christ will build his "church." Here is the first use of *ekklēsia* in the Gospels. It occurs only three times, all in Matthew, and the other two references are both in 18:17. Many hold that Jesus did not conceive of establishing a church and that these verses are later Matthean insertions. But the nature of Jesus' instruction to his community of followers certainly implied their continued existence in some form,[100] even if there is little of an "institution" yet in view. Moreover, the word *ekklēsia* in Hellenistic Greek often simply meant *an assembly*, as is also true of the underlying Aramaic *qāhāl*—a gathering of people for a particular purpose. In the Old Testament these gatherings normally involved the Israelites at worship, so that precisely such a community surrounding the

---

[97]Cf. France (*Matthew*, 254): "The word-play, and the whole structure of the passage, demands that this verse is every bit as much Jesus' declaration about Peter as v. 16 was Peter's declaration about Jesus."

[98]A full defense of this latter view appears now in C. C. Caragounis, *Peter and the Rock* (Berlin: de Gruyter, 1990).

[99]Interestingly, J. E. Bigane III (*Faith, Christ or Peter: Matthew 16:18 in Sixteenth Century Roman Catholic Exegesis* [Washington: UPA, 1981]) shows that prior to 1560, even in Roman Catholic circles, there was great diversity of interpretation of this verse, which only later hardened to viewing just Peter as the rock as a counterresponse to Luther's protests.

[100]Cf. esp. G. Lohfink, *Jesus and Community* (Philadelphia: Fortress, 1984); more briefly, cf. L. Goppelt, *Theology of the New Testament*, vol. 1 (Grand Rapids: Eerdmans, 1981), 207-22.

Messiah had become a standard Jewish expectation.[101] Jesus, however, implies nothing here of any particular church structure or government; he merely promises that he will establish a gathered community of his followers and help them to grow.[102]

Once Matt 13 is recognized as in no sense an absolute rejection of the Jews as a whole, it is virtually impossible to sustain the view that Jesus is here offering the church as an alternative to the kingdom. Instead, Christ's "church" will comprise *the community of people who submit to God's kingly rule* (recall that *kingdom* equals *kingship—God's rule* or *reign*). The popular view that the church is somehow to separate itself from society, based on the derivation of *ekklēsia* from *ekkaleō* (*to call out*) affords a classic example of what linguists call the etymological fallacy. Words often develop meanings over time that differ from their roots. The only sense in which the word *church* in New Testament times means *those who are called out* is that believers routinely gather together by leaving their separate places of residence or work.[103]

In v. 18b Jesus promises the indestructibility of his church. That the "gates of Hades will not overcome it" proves cryptic because gates are naturally seen as defensive protection, while "overcome" suggests an army on the offense. Is Jesus saying that Hades (Heb. *Sheol—the grave—* probably, as with *hell*, in the sense of *Satan's domain*) cannot conquer the church or that it cannot resist the church's advances? Is Satan on the defense or offense here? The latter seems more likely. In other Jewish literature "gates of Hades" is frequently idiomatic for "powers of death" (based on Isa 38:10).[104] This interpretation fits better into the historical

---

[101]Cf. W. F. Albright and C. S. Mann (*Matthew*, AB [Garden City: Doubleday, 1971], 195): "A Messiah without a Messianic Community would have been unthinkable to any Jew."

[102]On the authenticity of this passage, cf. esp. B. F. Meyer, *The Aims of Jesus* (London: SCM, 1979), 185-97; G. Maier, "The Church in the Gospel of Matthew: Hermeneutical Analysis of the Current Debate," in *Biblical Interpretation and the Church: The Problem of Contextualization*, ed. D. A. Carson (Nashville: Nelson, 1985), 45-63. On the possible parallels between Peter as the foundation of the church and Abraham as the father of the Jewish people, see esp. Allison and Davies, *Matthew* 2:623-24.

[103]For further detail on the New Testament doctrine of the church, see esp. D. A. Carson, ed., *The Church in the Bible and the World* (Grand Rapids: Baker, 1987); and R. L. Saucy, *The Church in God's Program* (Chicago: Moody, 1972). Less baptistic but still extremely helpful are D. Watson, *I Believe in the Church* (Grand Rapids: Eerdmans, 1978), and R. P. Martin, *The Family and the Fellowship* (Grand Rapids: Eerdmans, 1979).

[104]Carson ("Matthew," 370) gives additional references. C. Brown ("The Gates of Hell and the Church," in *Church, Word, and Spirit*, ed. J. E. Bradley and R. A. Muller [Grand Rapids: Eerdmans, 1987], 15-43) creatively argues that the phrase is a prediction of Christ's passion and of the ultimate triumph of his messianic mission. But he fails to account adequately for the role of the church in this verse.

context of the increasing hostility against Jesus and his small band of disciples. The parables of the mustard seed and yeast (13:31-33) have already promised surprisingly large results and a widespread impact, despite inauspicious beginnings. Similarly here Jesus encourages his followers that, irrespective of how Christianity may be attacked in a given place and time, the church universal will never be extinguished. Sects and cults which claim that true Christianity entirely disappeared from the world during certain periods of church history contradict Jesus' teaching here.

¹⁹I will give you the keys of the kingdom of heaven; whatever you bind on earth will be bound in heaven, and whatever you loose on earth will be loosed in heaven." ²⁰Then he warned his disciples not to tell anyone that he was the Christ.

16:19-20 But in what sense is Jesus building his church on Peter? Verse 19a gives the answer. Jesus promises Peter the "keys of the kingdom," apparently to be interpreted by v. 19b as the authority to "bind" and "loose."[105] The metaphor of binding and loosing was variously employed in ancient Judaism but often was used for the interpretation of Torah and for decision making more generally. Many therefore support the GNB's "prohibit" and "permit,"[106] which would fit Jesus' use of these terms in 18:18 in the context of church discipline. But this translation reflects a fairly late, rabbinic usage; more immediate parallels suggest that one should pursue the imagery of keys that close and open, lock and unlock (based on Isa 22:22) and take the binding and loosing as referring to Christians' making entrance to God's kingdom available or unavailable to people through their witness, preaching, and ministry.[107] This entrance to the kingdom will include the forgiveness of sins, tying this text in closely with John 20:23, which displays a very similar structure, and also with Jesus' use of the phrase "keys of knowledge" in Luke 11:52. Illustrations of Peter's privilege may then be found throughout Acts 1–12, in which Peter remains at the forefront of leadership in the early Christian proclamation of the gospel.[108] It is also possible that Jesus envisions the unlocking of the powers of heaven to combat the attacking powers of the underworld.[109]

---

[105]For a survey of the five main interpretations of these expressions, see esp. R. H. Hiers (" 'Binding' and 'Loosing': The Matthean Authorizations," *JBL* 104 [1985]: 233-50), whose own "exorcistic" interpretation seems even less likely than the rest.

[106]See esp. J. D. M. Derrett, "Binding and Loosing," *JBL* 102 (1983): 112-17.

[107]See esp. G. Korting, "Binden oder lösen: Zu Verstockungs- und Befreiungstheologie in Mt 16,19; 18,18.21-35 und Joh 15,1-17; 20,23," *SNTU* 14 (1989): 39-91.

[108]See esp. W. G. Thompson, *Matthew's Advice to a Divided Community* (Rome: Biblical Institute Press, 1970), 192. Contra the GNB rendering, cf. esp. H. W. Basser, "Derrett's 'Binding' Reopened," *JBL* 104 (1985): 297-300.

[109]J. Marcus, "The Gates of Hades and the Keys of the Kingdom (Matt 16:18-19)," *CBQ* 50 (1988): 443-55.

A long and somewhat stalemated debate has centered around the future perfect passive verbs in v. 19. In Classical Greek a reasonable translation of these two verbs ("will be bound" and "will be loosed") would be "will have been bound" or "will have been loosed" (NIV marg.). Jesus would then be stressing how God's sovereign initiative is worked out in the church.[110] But in Hellenistic Greek this construction was often roughly equivalent to a simple future passive (as in the main text of the NIV), in which case Jesus teaches that God has delegated his authority to the church, which he leaves to act on its own initiative to bring people into the kingdom, which entrance he then ratifies.[111] A mediating solution, supported by recent linguistic research, may be best with the translation *will be in a state of boundedness/loosedness.*[112] Jesus' point, then, will simply be that God promises that all who enter the kingdom do so in accordance with God's sovereign will, without specifying one way or the other whose action caused whose response.

In a slightly different context Jesus repeats his promise of binding and loosing for *all* the disciples (18:18). Peter's privilege must therefore be qualified, as consistently elsewhere in Matthew. Peter is the disciples' spokesman, but as their representative and not just their leader. Ephesians 2:20 and Rev 21:14 will refer to all the apostles as the "foundation" of the church. Peter's primacy is more chronological, in the unfolding events of early Christianity, than hierarchical.[113] Commentators often argue that Matthew has the highest view of Peter of any of the Gospel writers and closest to that of early Catholicism. But, as has already been seen, Matthew paints a consistently negative or at least ambiguous portrait of Peter, which may make it more probable that he was trying to temper an already overexalted view of that apostle.[114] These verses do indeed provide the most positive portrait of Peter's understanding anywhere in the Gospels, yet vv. 22-23 will almost immediately modify that picture dramatically. Even in v. 20 Matthew retains Mark's messianic secret motif, all the more jarring in light of his expansion of Peter's confession in the previous verses. Verse 20 makes sense, however, because Peter's view of Jesus as Messiah is still inadequate. Peter is not yet prepared for the road to the

---

[110]See esp. J. R. Mantey, "The Mistranslation of the Perfect Tense in John 20:23, Mt. 16:19, and Mt. 18:18," *JBL* 58 (1939): 243-49; and *idem*, "Evidence That the Perfect Tense in John 20:23 and Matthew 16:19 Is Mistranslated," *JETS* 16 (1973): 129-38.

[111]See esp. H. J. Cadbury, "The Meaning of John 20:23, Matthew 16:19, and Matthew 18:18," *JBL* 58 (1939): 251-54.

[112]S. E. Porter, "Vague Verbs, Periphrastics, and Matt 16:19," *FNT* 1 (1988): 155-73.

[113]Cf. esp. J. D. Kingsbury, "The Figure of Peter in Matthew's Gospel as a Theological Problem," *JBL* 98 (1979): 67-83; J. D. M. Derrett, "'Thou Art the Stone, and upon This Stone . . . ,'" *DownRev* 106 (1988): 276-85.

[114]See esp. A. Stock, "Is Matthew's Presentation of Peter Ironic?" *BTB* 17 (1987): 64-69.

cross, nor does he recognize that Jesus' death must precede the establishment of the church and that Jesus' followers must suffer before God's kingdom will triumph (vv. 24-28).[115] Matthew may well be tempering a theology of glory prevalent in his day with a prevailing theology of the cross and/or trying to push his church into a more egalitarian and less hierarchical structure.[116]

At any rate, there is obviously nothing in these verses of the distinctively Catholic doctrines of the papacy, apostolic succession, or Petrine infallibility or of the Protestant penchant for Christian personality cults. In fact, in Acts, Peter seems to decrease in importance as the church grows (on Peter's life more generally, see comments under 10:2). Instead, Matthew presents the challenging and exciting promise of God's presence with his entire church, as it seeks to witness and minister to the world, in a way that should encourage no one to despair but stimulate all to service. With this passage the largest section of Matthew's Gospel draws to a close (4:16–16:20), and the main body of Jesus' ministry is complete. Matthew has highlighted all facets of Jesus' words and works, save one— the road to the cross. Jesus has transferred his authority to his disciples so they can work wonders and bring people under God's rule. Now they must learn that they too have crosses to bear.

---

[115]Cf. Carson, "Matthew," 375: "Having come to faith, [the disciples] must not go beyond the Master himself in the means and limitations of his self-disclosure. The aim must not be to hide Jesus' identity from Israel or to keep it an esoteric secret but to guarantee (1) that the decisive factors in the conversion of men are not nationalistic fervor and impenitent messianic expectation but faith, obedience, and submission to Jesus; and (2) that the events leading to the cross are not to be short-circuited by premature disclosure."

[116]Cf. esp. E. Schweizer, "Matthew's Church," in *The Interpretation of Matthew*, ed. G. Stanton (Philadelphia: Fortress, 1983), 135-37, 139-41.

───────────── *SECTION OUTLINE* ─────────────

III. THE CLIMAX OF JESUS' MINISTRY (16:21–28:20)
  A. Focus on Coming Death and Resurrection (16:21–18:35)
    1. Implications for Discipleship: Correcting Misunderstandings
      (16:21–17:27)
      a. First Exchange Concerning Christ's Death (16:21-28)
        (1) Jesus' Prediction (16:21)
        (?) Peter's and Jesus' Rebukes (16:22-23)
        (3) Jesus' Further Instruction on Self-Denial (16:24-28)
      b. Foreshadowing Future Glory (17:1-21)
        (1) Jesus' Transfiguration (17:1-9)
        (2) Discussion about Elijah (17:10-13)
        (3) The Faithlessness of the Rest of the Disciples (17:14-21)
      c. Second Exchange Concerning Christ's Death (17:22-27)
        (1) Jesus' Prediction (17:22-23)
        (2) Discussion about the Temple Tax (17:24-27)
    2. Implications for the Church: Humility and Forgiveness (18:1-35)
      a. On Humility (18:1-14)
        (1) The Disciples' Humility (18:1-9)
          (a) Positive Illustration: Childlike Dependence on God
            (18:1-5)
          (b) Negative Illustration: Causing Sin Risks Damnation
            (18:6-9)
        (2) God's Humility (18:10-14)
      b. On Forgiveness (18:15-35)
        (1) Forgiveness Withheld without Repentance (18:15-20)
          (a) The Process of Confrontation (18:15-17)
          (b) The Process of Ratification (18:18-20)
        (2) Unlimited Forgiveness with Repentance (18:21-35)
          (a) Positive Illustration (18:21-22)
          (b) Negative Illustration (18:23-35)

───── **III. THE CLIMAX OF JESUS' MINISTRY (16:21–28:20)** ─────

As in 4:17, "from that time on, Jesus began to" marks a new stage in the Gospel's events. The shift from popular ministry to the road to the cross could hardly be more abrupt. Jesus begins explicitly to predict his suffering, death, and resurrection. All events now build toward that climax. Matthew's alternation of large blocks of narrative and discourse paired together continues, though now narrative will precede discourse.

A. Focus on Coming Death and Resurrection (16:21–18:35)

Matthew 16:21–17:27 finds Jesus dwelling on his coming passion and its implications for discipleship. Much teaching occurs in this section even as it formally remains "narrative." Matthew 18:1-35 presents Christ's fourth "sermon"—the so-called Community Discourse. In the former section Christ corrects the disciples' misunderstandings, related particularly to their triumphalist expectations. In the latter section he presents the positive alternative—nurturing humility and forgiveness.

1. Implications for Discipleship: Correcting Misunderstandings (16:21–17:27)

Matthew 16:21–17:27 falls neatly into three similarly structured parts, with (1) a teaching or revelation from Jesus, (2) a response by Peter, and (3) further teaching by Jesus in light of Peter's response but with implications for all the disciples. The first part contains Jesus' initial passion prediction, Peter's rebuke, and Jesus' further instruction concerning the way of the cross (16:21-28). The second part presents the transfiguration, Peter's misunderstanding, and Jesus' subsequent explanation of it, a pattern that is then reenacted in the faithlessness of the Twelve at the foot of the mountain followed by Jesus' explanation of their inability to exorcise (17:1-21). In the third part Jesus again predicts his suffering, which leads to a dialogue with Peter and a short parable with implications for all the disciples (17:22-27). The two passion predictions thus frame 16:21–17:27 and create an *a b a* structure. The parameters of these subdivisions are also confirmed by the changes of place and time noted in 17:1 and 22.[1]

21From that time on Jesus began to explain to his disciples that he must go to Jerusalem and suffer many things at the hands of the elders, chief priests and teachers of the law, and that he must be killed and on the third day be raised to life.

a. First Exchange Concerning Christ's Death (16:21-28). *(1) Jesus' Prediction (16:21).* **16:21** "From that time on, Jesus began to" matches the introduction to 4:17–16:20. Hints of Jesus' knowledge of his coming fate have appeared previously (9:15; 10:38) but never unambiguously. Here Jesus speaks plainly. Anticipating that he may be killed does not require any supernatural insight (recall 12:14), but more than just common sense must lie behind the prediction of his resurrection. Most of his ministry has taken place in and around Galilee. But now he must go to Judea and to Jerusalem, the capital city of Israel, the heart of the power of

---

[1]Matthew 17:22-23 is more often taken with the preceding section, but cf. L. Sabourin, *L'Évangile selon saint Matthieu et ses principaux parallèles* (Rome: Biblical Institute Press, 1978), 240.

the Jewish authorities, where hostility against him will increase to the point of execution. The triad of leaders presented here reflects the three main groups of politico-religious authorities in Jerusalem. "Elders," who have not been previously mentioned, refer to members of the Sanhedrin who did not belong to some other specific party or profession. The "chief priests" and scribes ("teachers of the law") appeared together in 2:4, also in Jerusalem, foreshadowing this hostility. Jesus does not explain the divine necessity behind the word "must" here, but he will account for it in 20:28. Jesus also looks beyond his death to his resurrection and vindication, though he does not elaborate at this point. "On the third day" uses inclusive reckoning (Friday, Saturday, Sunday). Inasmuch as the rest of the Gospel describes the events that culminate in the crucifixion and resurrection, this verse serves to introduce not only 16:21-28 but all of 16:21–28:20.[2]

22Peter took him aside and began to rebuke him. "Never, Lord!" he said. "This shall never happen to you!"
23Jesus turned and said to Peter, "Get behind me, Satan! You are a stumbling block to me; you do not have in mind the things of God, but the things of men."

(2) Peter's and Jesus' Rebukes (16:22-23). **16:22** This dialogue contrasts sharply with Peter's praiseworthy confession in vv. 16-19. One could scarcely imagine a more complete about-face. Peter has not yet conceived of a suffering Messiah. Only Matthew gives Peter's actual words here, as he underlines the magnitude of his failure. "Never, Lord," is, more literally, *Mercy on you, Lord.* "This shall never happen" could be rendered *No way shall this happen!* Together, Peter's two outbursts prove extraordinarily emphatic.

16:23 Trying to thwart God's plan for Jesus' life is in fact the role of the devil, not of a disciple; hence, Christ's reply. Jesus is not accusing Peter of literal demon possession, but he is dramatically indicating that the perspective Peter represents, however unwittingly, is the same as Satan's. Peter therefore is no longer acting like the foundation block of the church but like a "stumbling block" (Matthew's characteristic *skandalon*—here as *an enticement to sin*).[3] Peter reflects the viewpoint of unredeemed humanity ("the things of men") rather than God's will. "Get behind" means "get away" (GNB), almost *out of my sight!* and uses the identical command (*hypage*) as in Jesus' rebuke of Satan in 4:10.

---

[2] On the meaning and authenticity of Jesus' various passion predictions, see esp. H. F. Bayer, *Jesus' Predictions of Vindication and Resurrection* (Tübingen: Mohr, 1986).

[3] For a development of this contrast, see M. Wilcox, "Peter and the Rock: A Fresh Look at Matthew XVI:17-19," *NTS* 22 (1975-76): 73-88.

²⁴Then Jesus said to his disciples, "If anyone would come after me, he must deny himself and take up his cross and follow me. ²⁵For whoever wants to save his life will lose it, but whoever loses his life for me will find it. ²⁶What good will it be for a man if he gains the whole world, yet forfeits his soul? Or what can a man give in exchange for his soul?

(3) Jesus' Further Instruction on Self-denial (16:24-28).[4] **16:24** As in 16:16, Peter may well have simply verbalized the thoughts and concerns of all of the Twelve. So Jesus reiterates the message of 10:38. "Take up his cross" is again likely metaphorical, referring to submission to God's will wherever it may lead and explained further by the parallel phrase "deny himself." But the more ominous possibility that some disciples might literally be crucified looms larger in the wake of Jesus' prediction in v. 21. Self-denial does not imply self-abuse or lack of self-esteem. As Jesus' disciples believers should have a better self-image than any other people, but it should be based on God's grace and not their merit. Self-denial does, however, mean putting God and his kingdom priorities first. This should have a visible impact on the nature of one's financial commitments and service to church and world and should lead to the rejection of self-centered arrogance and pride.[5] According to Allison and Davies, "Discipleship is a doing of what is right no matter how irksome the privations, no matter how great the danger."[6] The Beatitudes (5:3-12) provide as good a commentary as any on the concept expressed more concisely here.

16:25-26 Verse 25 closely parallels 10:39 so that vv. 24-25 together repeat the same thoughts in sequence as in 10:38-39, on which see comments there. Verse 26a rephrases the rationale for self-denial. The logic of Jesus' command depends wholly on the existence of life beyond the grave, which will make the joys and sorrows of this life pale into insignificance in comparison. Accumulation of all the goods and pleasures of this earth cannot possibly secure eternal life, yet without eternal life all such accumulation will prove futile and damning.[7] Without surrendering one's present life to Christ, one cannot have eternal life with him. Verse 26b forms a rhetorical question, implying the answer "nothing." There is no way to buy, trade, or earn salvation. "Exchange" (*antallagma*), as a

---

[4]Each of vv. 25-28 is linked to the preceding verse by a catchword or phrase, a typically Hebraic connective device: θέλω, τὴν ψυχὴν αὐτοῦ, [απο]δώσει, ὁ υἱὸς ἀνθρώπου. See D. C. Allison and W. D. Davies, *A Critical and Exegetical Commentary on the Gospel according to Saint Matthew*, ICC, vol. 2 (Edinburgh: T & T Clark, 1991), 668.

[5]Cf. further M. P. Green, "The Meaning of Cross-Bearing," *BibSac* 140 (1983): 117-33.

[6]Allison and Davies, *Matthew* 2:681.

[7]On the centrality of these themes in early Christianity, see W. Rebell, "'Sein Leben verlieren' (Mark 8.35 parr.) als Strukturmoment vor- und nachösterlichen Glaubens," *NTS* 35 (1989): 202-18.

typical term for commercial transactions, can refer to a *price*. In contrast, a person acquires salvation only by responding to Christ's death and resurrection with wholehearted discipleship and allegiance to him (again cf. 20:20-28). On "soul" see comments under 10:28.

[27]For the Son of Man is going to come in his Father's glory with his angels, and then he will reward each person according to what he has done. [28]I tell you the truth, some who are standing here will not taste death before they see the Son of Man coming in his kingdom."

16:27-28 Jesus goes on to remind us that glory indeed awaits ahead but only after suffering. Christ will compensate and exalt all believers (and judge unbelievers) when he returns in *his* glory, which exactly represents the radiance of God the Father (Heb 1:3). High Christology again appears here since Jesus functions precisely as the God of Old Testament prophecy (see Zech 14:5). "What he has done" is more literally *his practice* (a singular noun) and refers to an individual life viewed in its entirety. Did one commit oneself to Jesus, or did one serve only oneself (recall 10:32-33)? The language of judgment according to works appeared originally in Ps 62:12 and Prov 24:12. Characteristically, this Old Testament allusion is Matthew's unique insertion. The glory of Jesus' second coming will soon be foreshadowed in his transfiguration (itself a foretaste of his resurrection). Verse 28 remains cryptic but is best taken as just such a reference to Jesus' transfiguration—the very next event described. Second Peter 1:16-18 reinforces this equation of the transfiguration with Christ's coming in glory, while the parallelism between vv. 27a and 28b, each speaking of the "Son of Man coming" further supports this interpretation.[8] Other popular but less probable views of "the Son of Man coming in his kingdom" include taking the clause to refer to the resurrection, the sending of the Spirit at Pentecost, or Christ's coming in judgment to destroy the temple in A.D. 70. Still others think that Jesus mistakenly expected to return while some of the Twelve were still living.[9]

---

[8]See esp. C. E. B. Cranfield, *The Gospel according to Saint Mark*, CGTC (Cambridge: University Press, 1977), 285-88. Others argue that an emphatic proclamation that some would not die before an event only a week away makes no sense. Against this see Cranfield's "Thoughts on New Testament Eschatology," *SJT* 35 (1982): 503: "I would assume that the point of the solemn language about not tasting death is that the persons referred to would have the privilege of seeing in the course of their natural life what others would only see at the final judgment."

[9]For a full history of interpretation, see M. Künzi, *Das Naherwartungslogion Markus 9,1 par: Geschichte seiner Auslegung* (Tübingen: Mohr, 1977); more briefly, cf. J. Brooks, *Mark*, NAC, vol. 23 (Nashville: Broadman, 1991), 138-40; G. R. Beasley-Murray, *Jesus and the Kingdom of God* (Grand Rapids: Eerdmans, 1986), 187-93.

The message that suffering must precede glory remains scandalous even today for many people, including professing Christians. To be sure, God does not call all his followers to suffer equally or in the same way. But those who stress only the availability of physical and material blessings through Christ in this age, or who promise freedom from persecution as a reward for Christian maturity, completely invert Jesus' teaching here and risk finding themselves excluded from his kingdom. Those who have been blessed materially must use their resources generously to help the dispossessed and oppressed of this world, especially when fellow believers suffer. At the same time, we dare not focus on people's physical needs to such an extent that we do not call them to reckon with Judgment Day, the age to come, and the need to follow Jesus to gain eternal life. Otherwise we save people's physical lives only to leave them eternally damned. Self-denial alone accomplishes nothing of everlasting value unless it flows from a saving relationship with Jesus Christ.[10]

¹After six days Jesus took with him Peter, James and John the brother of James, and led them up a high mountain by themselves. ²There he was transfigured before them. His face shone like the sun, and his clothes became as white as the light. ³Just then there appeared before them Moses and Elijah, talking with Jesus.

b. FORESHADOWING FUTURE GLORY (17:1-21). *(1) Jesus' Transfiguration (17:1-9).*[11] **17:1-3** The scene and time now change. "After six days" and "about eight days" (Luke 9:28) both refer to a week later. Matthew's version could preserve an allusion to Moses' receiving the law on Sinai after six days' preparation (Exod 24:16). Jesus takes the three "inner core" disciples (cf. Mark 5:37; Matt 26:37) and leaves the rest farther down the mountainside. They will reappear prominently but ignobly in vv. 14-21. Like the mountain of Jesus' great sermon (chaps. 5–7), this one is unidentified. Mt. Tabor in the middle of Galilee is the traditional site, but it is not that high (about 1,900 ft.), a town remained on top of it in the first century, and v. 22 seems to imply that the disciples had left central Galilee. Modern commentators often suggest Mt. Hermon, northeast of

---

[10]On this necessary balance, see F. D. Bruner, *The Churchbook* (Dallas: Word 1990), 599: "In recent church history the doctrinal concern has been at the heart of the best conservative Christianities; the ethical concern, of the best liberal Christianities. The trick—the gift to be prayed for—is devotion to both doctrine and ethics, to Jesus and his justice, without rejecting either."

[11]See esp. W. L. Liefeld, "Theological Motifs in the Transfiguration Narrative," in *New Dimensions in New Testament Study*, ed. R. N. Longenecker and M. C. Tenney (Grand Rapids: Zondervan, 1974), 162-79; and literature there cited. For a more wide-ranging study, cf. J. A. McGuckin, *The Transfiguration of Christ in Scripture and Tradition* (Lewiston, NY: Mellen, 1986).

Galilee, as an alternative, but it may be too distant and rugged (over 9,200 ft.) for such a climb. Perhaps Mt. Meron, just northwest of the sea of Galilee, the highest mountain completely within Israel itself at nearly 4,000 feet, remains the best suggestion.[12]

Jesus is "transfigured," or, in more common English, *transformed* (from Greek *metamorphoō*; cf. the English *metamorphosis*). His appearance is changed. His skin and clothes shine with dazzling brilliance and whiteness, suggesting glory, sovereignty, and purity. With him appear Moses and Elijah. Their presence may have to do with any or all of the following observations: they were key representatives of the law and prophets, they lived through the two major periods of Old Testament miracles, they were key messianic forerunners whose return was often expected with the advent of the Messiah, and they were often believed never to have died but to have gone directly to God's presence (2 Kgs 2:1-12 makes this clear with reference to Elijah; in the case of Moses the belief is based more on intertestamental literature like the *Assumption of Moses*). Of course, both men, as "Old Testament saints," are still awaiting their final resurrection. Nothing here indicates that they had actual bodies when they appeared; God's servants throughout Old Testament times apparently had some consciousness of his presence even after they died and remained in a disembodied state.[13] Conceivably, the entire transfiguration event could have been a supernaturally staged but subjective vision of some kind for the disciples' benefit (*horama*—"what you have seen" in v. 9—is more commonly translated *vision*), but this interpretation seems much less likely.[14]

[4]Peter said to Jesus, "Lord, it is good for us to be here. If you wish, I will put up three shelters—one for you, one for Moses and one for Elijah."

[5]While he was still speaking, a bright cloud enveloped them, and a voice from the cloud said, "This is my Son, whom I love; with him I am well pleased. Listen to him!"

17:4 Peter interrupts this "Christophany" with a comment that betrays his confusion at what is happening. Matthew does not explain Peter's remarks (cf. Mark 9:6), but the "shelters" (from Greek *skēnē*) will call to mind the wilderness tabernacles of Moses' day and suggest some attempt on Peter's part to make a dwelling place for the three so as to

---

[12]W. L. Liefeld, "Luke," in EBC, vol. 8, ed. F. E. Gaebelein (Grand Rapids: Zondervan, 1984), 929.

[13]See D. Alexander, "The Old Testament View of Life after Death," *Themelios* 11 (1986): 41-46.

[14]Although BAGD, 577, gives "vision" as the first definition for ὅραμα, it immediately adds, following Artemidorus, "something that can actually be seen, in contrast to . . . φάντασμα = a figment of the imagination."

encourage them to stay longer. "It is good for us to be here" will then mean not that it is good that Peter, James, and John can help put up the tents but that it is good that all of the participants can preserve this moment for some length of time. We are not told how the disciples recognized Moses and Elijah.

17:5 God now interrupts Peter with the cloud of his presence and with his heavenly voice. The cloud reminds us of the one that overshadowed Moses on Sinai, leading to his dazzling splendor when he descended from the mountain (Exod 34:29-35, on which cf. also Paul's remarks in 2 Cor 3:7-18), the cloud that enveloped the tabernacle when God's glory filled it (Exod 40:34), and the cloud that followed the Israelites by day throughout their wilderness wanderings (Exod 40:36-38). Second Maccabees 2:8 looks forward to the cloud and glory of the Lord in the days of the Messiah. The heavenly voice repeats verbatim the words of Matt 3:17 from Jesus' baptism. Just as God publicly endorsed Jesus as the royal Messiah and Suffering Servant prior to the beginning of the main stage of his ministry, now at the beginning of the road to the cross he repeats his endorsement even more dramatically, though much less publicly. God's confirmation proves even more crucial because the notion of a suffering Messiah seemed so incongruous. The heavenly voice adds the words, "Listen to him!" Jesus must still be followed and obeyed, even as he heads off to die. The words echo the language of Deut 18:15b on heeding the prophet like Moses who would arise in later days.

6When the disciples heard this, they fell facedown to the ground, terrified. 7But Jesus came and touched them. "Get up," he said. "Don't be afraid." 8When they looked up, they saw no one except Jesus.

9As they were coming down the mountain, Jesus instructed them, "Don't tell anyone what you have seen, until the Son of Man has been raised from the dead."

17:6-8 In light of Jesus' reply in v. 7, the disciples' fear in v. 6 (Greek *ephobēthēsan*) will be more terror than reverence, though this term, like their posture, may suggest an element of worship as well. The disciples' reaction and Jesus' response closely resemble the closing episodes of the two sea rescue miracle stories (8:25-27; 14:26-33) and may have been inspired by Dan 10:18-19. Both reaction and response appear only in Matthew. When the disciples look up again, Moses and Elijah have disappeared. "They saw no one except Jesus" reads more literally, *They did not see anyone but Jesus only*. The word *only* (*monos*) comes at the end of the sentence for emphasis. The disciples must focus on Christ alone. He will prove sufficient for their needs.

17:9 The motif of silence appears for the final time in Matthew, and for the first time Jesus suggests the injunction is not permanent. After the resurrection the disciples must tell others about his transfiguration. Here is the most important interpretive key to the messianic secret motif: Christ's mission can be fully understood only after he has completed his ministry of suffering and has subsequently been vindicated. The glimpse of his glory revealed by his transfiguration, like the glimpses given by his other miracles, which generated commands to silence, may not be allowed to hinder his journey to death. On "Son of Man" see under 8:20.

As suggested by 16:28, the transfiguration foreshadows Jesus' resurrection and his return.[15] If 16:21-28 stressed the need for Jesus' passion, here Matthew provides a balancing reminder of Jesus' coming glory. Three disciples are privileged to come to an advance viewing. Even as we must today avoid the heresies of the so-called health-wealth gospel and of a triumphalist ecclesiology, it is equally important to note that God does give us from time to time foretastes of glory. But we cannot predict when and how he will provide them, we dare not demand them, and for most people they will probably remain the exception rather than the norm. The question, for example, with respect to physical healing should never be "why am I not healed?" but "why am I *ever* healed?" We should be grateful for whatever glimpses of glory God graciously gives. They often provide crucial sustenance for us during hard times, but they will not do away with hard times altogether.

[10]The disciples asked him, "Why then do the teachers of the law say that Elijah must come first?"

[11]Jesus replied, "To be sure, Elijah comes and will restore all things. [12]But I tell you, Elijah has already come, and they did not recognize him, but have done to him everything they wished. In the same way the Son of Man is going to suffer at their hands." [13]Then the disciples understood that he was talking to them about John the Baptist.

(2) Discussion about Elijah (17:10-13). **17:10** Peter's confusion is now followed by general perplexity concerning Elijah. The logic of the disciples' question is uncertain, perhaps because they are again portrayed as somewhat dense. Didn't they remember Jesus' explanation in 11:14? But seeing Elijah has apparently reminded them of the Jewish belief, based on Mal 4:5, that Elijah would come as a messianic precursor. Perhaps the sequence of thought here is: if Jesus is the messianic Son, then why are the scribes ("teachers of the law") still looking for Elijah? Or they may wonder if this appearance of Elijah on the mount of transfiguration fulfills Malachi's prophecy even more directly than the ministry of John the Baptist. In light of Jesus' answer in v. 11, they may also be wanting to know why Malachi speaks of the restoration of all things

---

[15]But cf. Allison and Davies, 2:707 for parallels with Jesus' execution as well.

(Mal 4:6), which has not yet literally occurred. In fact, if we give full logical force to the connective "then" in this verse, the disciples may be asking, If Elijah is to come and restore all things, why can he not prevent the death of the Son of Man (since Jesus' reference to his resurrection in v. 9 obviously implies he must die first)?[16]

17:11-13 By way of reply, Jesus will point out that Elijah, as forerunner, did not come to prevent the Messiah's suffering and death but to foreshadow it.[17] But first Jesus reassures them that Malachi's prophecy was fulfilled in John the Baptist. The restoration he brought must thus have included his ministry of preaching and the widespread repentance to which it led. Full restoration of course awaits Christ's return (Acts 1:6; 3:21), leaving open the question whether there is a yet unfulfilled part of the prophecy regarding Elijah. Revelation 11:3-6, in which one of the "two witnesses" has a miracle-working ministry closely parallel to Elijah's, suggests there may be but is not clear about how literally this text should be taken. The two witnesses could well stand for the entire witnessing community of the people of God in the last days. As for the Jewish leaders, they still look for Elijah because they have rejected John the Baptist (v. 12a). Herod even executed him (v. 12b). And the same fate awaits Christ (v. 12c). In Matthew's distinctive conclusion, based on his previous pattern of pointing out the disciples' insight, we learn that these three finally do understand (v. 13).[18]

[14]When they came to the crowd, a man approached Jesus and knelt before him. [15]"Lord, have mercy on my son," he said. "He has seizures and is suffering greatly. He often falls into the fire or into the water. [16]I brought him to your disciples, but they could not heal him."

(3) The Faithlessness of the Rest of the Disciples (17:14-21). **17:14-16** Jesus, Peter, James, and John reach the point at the foot of the mountain where they had left the other nine. Luke 9:37 notes that they arrived there the day after the transfiguration. Crowds surround the rest of the disciples. One man is particularly distressed over his son's malady, uniquely described in Matthew as *epilepsy* (from Greek *selēniazō*—NIV "has seizures"—not as in KJV "lunatick"). His seizures have put his life in danger of burning (perhaps from the fire that heated his home) or drowning (perhaps in an open courtyard well). But protective measures could have minimized these dangers, suggesting that more than mere ill-

---

[16]Cf. R. H. Gundry, *Matthew: A Commentary on His Literary and Theological Art* (Grand Rapids: Eerdmans, 1982), 346-47.

[17]See H. N. Ridderbos, *Matthew*, BSC (Grand Rapids: Zondervan, 1987), 322.

[18]Cf. further C. L. Blomberg, "Elijah, Election, and the Use of Malachi in the New Testament," *CTR* 2 (1987): 100-108, and the literature there cited.

ness is involved. Verse 18 concurs. Demon possession has caused this illness, and the demons repeatedly try to harm the boy and threaten his life (cf. Mark 9:22), as they characteristically do with people they torment. Jesus has encountered similar problems frequently before; the key distinctive in this passage is his disciples' inability to deal with the problem. Their impotence makes for a jarring return to the real world after the mountaintop experience of the transfiguration. Jesus had given the disciples full authority over demons as long ago as in 10:8. By now they should be performing exorcisms with great confidence.

17"O unbelieving and perverse generation," Jesus replied, "how long shall I stay with you? How long shall I put up with you? Bring the boy here to me." 18Jesus rebuked the demon, and it came out of the boy, and he was healed from that moment.

17:17-18   In his disgust Jesus rebukes the disciples as if they were part and parcel of the whole wicked generation of those who rejected him (cf. 11:16; 12:39,45). Again the line between the disciples and the crowds is blurred. The adjectives "unbelieving" and "perverse" echo Deut 32:5,20 and suggest both faithlessness and immorality. Jesus' exasperation—"How long shall I stay with you? How long shall I put up with you?"—may reflect his normal human emotions but also distances him from *sinful* humanity.[19] He then cures the man's son. As in 9:32 and 12:22, we learn this particular illness was demon induced, hence the exorcism. As in 9:22 and 15:28, the healing is said specifically to be instantaneous and enduring. But Matthew still does not focus on the miracle nearly as much as on the disciples' faithlessness.

19Then the disciples came to Jesus in private and asked, "Why couldn't we drive it out?" 20He replied, "Because you have so little faith. I tell you the truth, if you have faith as small as a mustard seed, you can say to this mountain, 'Move from here to there' and it will move. Nothing will be impossible for you."

17:19-20   As in 13:36 and 15:12, the disciples privately ask for an explanation, this time not of a parable but of their failure. Jesus attributes this failure to their miniscule faith (*oligopistia*, cognate to Matthew's favorite adjective *oligopistos*, "little faith"). As in 13:31-32, Jesus uses the proverbial smallness of the mustard seed to make his point dramatically, but he balances his rebuke with a measure of optimism (not found

---

[19]D. A. Carson ("Matthew," EBC, vol. 8, ed. F. E. Gaebelein [Grand Rapids: Zondervan, 1984], 391): "The rhetorical questions . . . express not only personal disappointment but also Jesus' consciousness of his heavenly origin and destiny."

in the parallel account of Mark 9:28-29) by promising that even just a little more faith than they had could move mountains. "Moving mountains" was also proverbial for overcoming difficulties (cf. 1 Cor 13:2; and *b. B. Bat.* 3b). At the foot of a mountain Jesus' illustration proves particularly apt. "This mountain" most naturally refers to the mount of transfiguration, in the shadow of which they are still standing. But Jesus' words are obviously metaphorical since neither God nor Christ ever rearranged the topography of the land by supernatural intervention. Nor is a miracle necessary to move literal mountains, merely earth-moving equipment.[20] R. T. France observes: "It is important to observe here that it is not the 'amount' of faith which brings the impossible within reach, but the power of God, which is available to even the 'smallest' faith."[21] Moreover, for Matthew, the type of faith required always involves commitment to Jesus and obedience to his commands, which must therefore always include praying, "Thy will be done" (6:10).

"*Nothing* will be impossible for you" must thus be interpreted as *nothing Jesus has given you the authority to do*, such as this exorcism.[22] Obviously, many other things are impossible for believers—based on the limitations of their humanity and of God's will. As v. 22 immediately makes plain, even Jesus' own miracle-working abilities did not permit him to escape the cross despite repeated temptation to do precisely that. See 1 Cor 6:12; Phil 4:12-13 for other important limitations on the permissibility and possibility of Christians doing "all things." Verse 20 nevertheless provides a precious promise we dare not ignore. Much is not accomplished for the kingdom because we simply do not believe God will adequately empower us or else because we undertake various activities in our own strength rather than God's. Yet we must recognize the limitations of this promise, in light of other Scriptures, and not use it to foist a guilt trip on ourselves or others when faith does not eliminate every calamity from our lives.

[17:21] Verse 21 (see NIV marg.) does not appear in several of the oldest and best manuscripts (א, B, Θ, and various Italic, Syriac, Coptic, and Ethiopic manuscripts) and was probably added to harmonize with a later form of Mark 9:29. Even in Mark the original reading most likely referred only to prayer and not to fasting (א, B, it[k], geo[l], and Clement).

---

[20]One thinks, e.g., of the elaborate siege-works erected by the Romans at Masada (ca. A.D. 70) or of the massive land bridges built by Alexander the Great in his various campaigns (ca. 330 B.C.), both of which involved prodigious feats of earth moving in a day without modern equipment.

[21]R. T. France, *The Gospel according to Matthew*, TNTC (Grand Rapids: Eerdmans, 1985), 266.

[22]Cf. Carson, "Matthew," 391.

²²**When they came together in Galilee, he said to them, "The Son of Man is going to be betrayed into the hands of men. ²³They will kill him, and on the third day he will be raised to life." And the disciples were filled with grief.**

c. SECOND EXCHANGE CONCERNING CHRIST'S DEATH (17:22-27). *(1) Jesus' Prediction (17:22-23).* **17:22-23** The scene shifts again. Jesus and the disciples are back in Galilee, apparently near Capernaum (v. 24). Matthew recounts Jesus' second passion prediction as an abbreviated version of 16:21. No distinctively new information emerges, but Jesus phrases this prediction so as to contrast *the* "Son of Man" with other "men." Matthew does describe a new response from the disciples— their grief. "Filled with grief" more literally reads *they grieved exceedingly.* The disciples are no longer overtly fighting the idea of Christ's death, but understandably they are still not liking it.

²⁴**After Jesus and his disciples arrived in Capernaum, the collectors of the two-drachma tax came to Peter and asked, "Doesn't your teacher pay the temple tax?"**
²⁵**"Yes, he does," he replied.**

(2) Discussion about the Temple Tax (17:24-27). **17:24-25a** This section appears only in Matthew and is one of the most difficult in the Gospel to understand, both in terms of the significance of certain details and in light of its location in this context.[23] Jesus and the Twelve return to Capernaum, their home base for the Galilean ministry. Perhaps their arrival at the city toll booth on the edge of town stimulated the tax collectors' question (cf. 9:9). Perhaps Matthew includes this episode because, as a former tax collector himself, he was particularly interested in the dialogue. At any rate, Jesus finds himself again embroiled in controversy. This time the interrogators ask his disciples about his practice, instead of asking him about the disciples' behavior, as in 12:2. The issue at stake is the two-drachma tax, also known as the half-shekel tax. One shekel equaled four drachmas, and a drachma was approximately equivalent to the Roman denarius—the standard wage for a day laborer. Hence, this tax involved two days' wages. All Israelite males over the age of twenty paid this tribute annually for the upkeep of the Jerusalem temple. The practice stemmed from the commands of Exod 30:13 and 38:25-26; later developments are reflected in Josephus (*Ant.* 18.9.1; *J.W.* 7.6.6) and the Mishna (*Seqal.*).

Interestingly, the tax collectors phrase their question as if they expect an affirmative answer. Verse 24b might be less ambiguously rendered,

---

[23]The best survey of background material for this passage is W. Horbury, "The Temple Tax," in *Jesus and the Politics of His Day*, ed. E. Bammel and C. F. D. Moule (Cambridge: University Press, 1984), 265-86.

Your teacher does pay the two-drachma tax, doesn't he? Jesus apparently has done nothing to make anyone doubt his obedience to Jewish law on this issue, but in light of his views on other laws, the question is certainly worth asking. What is more, formally ordained rabbis (which Jesus was not) were already exempt from the tax. Would Jesus, despite his lack of formal training, claim the same privilege? Peter affirms that his master does pay the tax. By singling out Peter, perhaps as the recognizable leader of the Twelve, the tax collectors bring Peter to center stage for the third time in as many passages (cf. 16:22-23; 17:4). Again, Jesus' reply has implications for all disciples. This is also the fourth of Matthew's five unique additions concerning Peter in these middle chapters of his Gospel (cf. 14:28-31; 15:15; 16:17-19). In this instance, however, Peter's role seems quite neutral; little can be deduced about Matthew's reasons for highlighting him here.

When Peter came into the house, Jesus was the first to speak. "What do you think, Simon?" he asked. "From whom do the kings of the earth collect duty and taxes—from their own sons or from others?"
26"From others," Peter answered.
"Then the sons are exempt," Jesus said to him.

17:25b-26 This time Jesus initiates the dialogue with Peter. By means of a metaphor or short parable, he raises the question of whether or not he and his followers should have to pay this tax,[24] even if they have so far chosen to do so. A royal household, and sometimes even all the *citizens* of an empire (this is the other possible sense of "sons"), as over against slaves or conquered people, may not have to pay taxes to earthly kings. So also God's true children should not have to pay tax to him. The New Testament consistently emphasizes all giving to the Lord's work as voluntary, never compulsory, even as it urges believers to great generosity in their giving (see 2 Cor 8–9). The temple tax was a distinctively Jewish levy and must be distinguished from taxes to Rome. Jesus' command here in no way conflicts with his orders in 22:15-22. The temple tax showed solidarity with Israel as over against Rome. Yet even in 22:21 it is not clear whether the motive for paying taxes to Caesar stems from a divine mandate or from a standpoint of expediency—to promote Christianity as law-abiding. Romans 13:1-7 suggests to many that obedience to human authorities, including paying one's taxes, is a divinely ordained command. First Peter 2:12–3:22 seems to imply that such obedience is primarily evangelistic in motive. Each continues to apply in different situations.

---

[24]"Duty" and "taxes" in v. 26 refer more specifically to customs or toll and census tax, respectively.

[27]"But so that we may not offend them, go to the lake and throw out your line. Take the first fish you catch; open its mouth and you will find a four-drachma coin. Take it and give it to them for my tax and yours."

17:27 This verse is perhaps the strangest in Matthew's Gospel. It seems to describe a miracle performed for relatively trivial and self-serving purposes. But in fact all that Matthew records is a command from Jesus to Peter. We do not know what resulted.[25] Given Peter's track record of misunderstanding, it would be rash to hazard a guess. It is possible that v. 27 is even some kind of metaphor, not intended to be taken literally, perhaps implying that Peter should catch fish that can be sold to pay the tax for them both or that he should trust in God, who will supply his children with what they need.[26] Or perhaps we are to understand that, at least at this point in their ministry, Christ and the disciples are virtually penniless, so that they are actually quite needy and otherwise unable to pay the tax.[27] Coins have been found in the mouths of fish from the Sea of Galilee, so yet another reasonable explanation is that Peter did exactly what Christ commanded and that the miracle was one of prescience more than provision. The coin in view here is a *statēr*, equivalent to four drachmas, which would thus pay the two-drachma tax for two people. What *is* clear is that Jesus is reinforcing two of the frequent themes of his teaching: (1) disciples should avoid unnecessarily offending others (15:12-13 has shown that they cannot avoid all offense); (2) ultimately Jesus has freed them from obeying the law, both oral and written, except inasmuch as it is fulfilled and reinterpreted in his person and teaching (cf. under 5:17-20). If God's people are freed from paying the tax for the temple's upkeep, they must be freed from the sacrifices for which the temple existed.

2. Implications for the Church: Humility and Forgiveness (18:1-35)

Matthew 16:24-28 began to unpack for the disciples the implications of Jesus' journeying to the cross. Now in his fourth lengthy discourse in Matthew,[28] Jesus elaborates on the implications for the disciples as a community. Jesus' suffering will demonstrate to what extent he is prepared to humble himself (recall 11:29; 12:19-21; and cf. Phil 2:6-8), which should inspire humility in his disciples (Matt 18:1-9), even as the

---

[25]Contra, e.g., J. F. Walvoord, *Matthew: Thy Kingdom Come* (Chicago: Moody, 1974), 133; W. Hendriksen, *The Gospel of Matthew*, NTC (Grand Rapids: Baker, 1973), 679.

[26]Cf. further C. L. Blomberg, "New Testament Miracles and Higher Criticism: Climbing up the Slippery Slope," *JETS* 27 (1984): 433-34.

[27]See esp. R. Bauckham, "The Coin in the Fish's Mouth," in *Gospel Perspectives*, vol. 6, ed. D. Wenham and C. Blomberg (Sheffield: JSOT, 1986), 219-52.

[28]On the composition of these discourses, cf. under chaps. 5-7; 10; 13. Once again Mark has a shorter version of Matthew's sermon, while Luke scatters parallels throughout his Gospel.

Father humbles himself in seeking to save all his children (vv. 10-14). Jesus' death will also make forgiveness possible for all (26:28) though actualized only in those who repent. So, too, the disciples' approach to forgiving one another should have two sides: forgiveness withheld when there is no repentance (vv. 15-20) and unlimited forgiveness when there is genuine repentance (vv. 21-35).[29]

a. ON HUMILITY (18:1-14). *(1) The Disciples' Humility (18:1-9).* Jesus begins with a positive example of the proper humility his followers should emulate (vv. 1-5). Then he makes the same point negatively by warning against behavior that would cause a person or others to sin (vv. 6-9).

¹At that time the disciples came to Jesus and asked, "Who is the greatest in the kingdom of heaven?"
²He called a little child and had him stand among them. ³And he said: "I tell you the truth, unless you change and become like little children, you will never enter the kingdom of heaven. ⁴Therefore, whoever humbles himself like this child is the greatest in the kingdom of heaven.

(a) Positive Illustration: Childlike Dependence on God (18:1-5).
18:1 "At that time" reads, literally, *at that hour.* It may nevertheless be as general an expression as in 11:25 or 12:1. Still, as Jesus' passion draws ever nearer, events in Matthew seem more strictly chronological and more closely linked. So if not a literal sixty minutes after the previous dialogue, Matthew may at least imply that this next discussion took place very soon afterwards. The question the disciples ask fits in well with frequent Jewish discussions about hierarchy in various walks of life. The disciples' question recalls Jesus' teaching in 5:19 and 11:11. As in those texts, attention is probably centered on the present aspect of the kingdom, on the relationships within the community of followers Jesus is establishing, especially since he has already seemingly indicated that one of the Twelve, Peter, would somehow be greater than the rest (16:17-19). The present tense "is" thus underlines the disciples' concern about status and privilege in the community soon to be set loose on the world rather than any debate about future reward in heaven.[30] Matthew 18:1 may link with 17:24-27 in that

---

[29]On the narrative flow and sequence of sections in this discourse, cf. P. Bonnard, "Composition et signification historique de Matthieu 18," in *De Jésus aux Evangiles,* ed. I. de la Potterie (Gembloux: Duculot, 1967), 130-40. The most detailed modern treatment of the whole chapter is that of W. G. Thompson, *Matthew's Advice to a Divided Community* (Rome: Biblical Institute Press, 1970).

[30]Cf. J. J. Collins, "The Gospel for the Feast of the Guardian Angels (Mt. 18:1-10)," *CBQ* 6 (1944): 423-34; Ridderbos, *Matthew,* 332, thinks that the disciples ask about the future aspect of the kingdom but that Jesus answers by referring to the present aspect.

Jesus has raised the question about the behavior of kings in 17:25, which may have set the disciples thinking about *their* kingdom again. Jesus' singling out of Peter, James, and John to accompany him for the transfiguration (17:1-13) would also have raised questions in the disciples' minds about varying degrees of privilege. Nevertheless, their question seems highly inappropriate in light of Jesus' recent and repeated passion predictions and teaching on self-denial.

18:2-4 Jesus replies by means of an object lesson, almost an enacted parable. Matthew does not say where the disciples were, but apparently there were others nearby, including at least one child. Jesus solemnly declares the disciples must *turn away* ("change"; from Greek *strephō*)[31] from their preoccupation with status and must humble themselves like children. This humility cannot be a subjective attitude (children rarely act humbly) but an objective state (children do depend almost entirely on the adult world for their protection and provision). In first-century thought children were often very little esteemed. Jesus ascribes to them great value, but here his more immediate point is that would-be disciples must share their condition of utter dependence, in this case, on God. Without a recognition of one's fundamental inability to save oneself and without a subsequent complete reliance on God's mercy, no one can enter the kingdom of heaven. Conversely, those who most clearly perceive their helplessness and who respond accordingly are the greatest in the kingdom (again the "is" refers to the present aspect of the kingdom).[32] But Jesus' criterion for greatness is also his criterion for entrance into the kingdom, so it is not clear that Jesus is establishing a true hierarchy even in the kingdom's present form. This text should make us uncomfortable. The disciples' concern was "who is greatest in the kingdom," i.e., which one of us is greatest. Jesus replies, "Unless *you* change, . . . you will never enter the kingdom." All who are confident in their own kingdom standing should take stock. Is our confidence that of a child trusting the goodness of our Father, or is our confidence in ourselves?

5"And whoever welcomes a little child like this in my name welcomes me.

18:5 The disciples must not merely humble themselves; they must welcome all others who humble themselves as believers. In light of the wording of v. 4 ("whoever humbles himself like this child"), the "little child" of v. 5 most naturally refers to any true disciple. F. D. Bruner comments, "Matthew 18:1-4 calls us *to* humility, then v. 5 gives us a major

---

[31]See esp. J. Dupont, "Matthieu 18:3," in *Neotestamentica et Semitica*, ed. E. E. Ellis and M. Wilcox (Edinburgh: T & T Clark, 1969), 50-60.

[32]Cf. A. H. M'Neile, *The Gospel according to St. Matthew* (London: Macmillan, 1915), 260, "He will be the greatest who has the least idea that he is great."

way to *practice* humility."[33] The welcome is in Christ's name. As in 10:40-42, Jesus has in mind people who welcome disciples because they accept their message and thus become disciples themselves.

⁶But if anyone causes one of these little ones who believe in me to sin, it would be better for him to have a large millstone hung around his neck and to be drowned in the depths of the sea.

(b) Negative Illustration: Causing Sin Risks Damnation (18:6-9). **18:6** The NIV keeps vv. 5-6 together as a paragraph, but with the UBSGNT it is better to separate them. Granted v. 6 continues Jesus' teaching about "these little ones" and is therefore transitional, nevertheless the shift to the discussion of those who cause sin creates a stronger thematic link with vv. 7-9 than with vv. 1-5.[34] Matthew's favorite *skandal*-word group introduces v. 6 and links it back with 17:27 ("offend," *skandalisōmen*). But here the sense is "cause to sin," perhaps especially in the sense of *cause to apostatize* rather than *cause offense.* "Who believe in me" demonstrates that the "little ones" still refer to the disciples, though perhaps focusing particularly on those who are most disenfranchised or deemed insignificant.

One who might otherwise cause such a little one to sin ought to long for dramatic, decisive, physical death rather than risk eternal judgment. The "large millstone" (literally, *millstone for a donkey*) referred to the huge stone wheels that were attached to a horizontal bar connected to a donkey's harness. As the animal walked around in circles, the wheel rolled over a raised stone slab (similar in appearance to a large birdbath), crushing the grain underneath. *Pelagei* ("depths") refers to the deepest part of the sea. With this vivid metaphor, Jesus leaves no one in doubt over the certainty of drowning. Jesus' logic proceeds as in 5:21-22. He does not imply that one evil act leads to damnation, but a life-style characterized by causing others to sin is incompatible with true discipleship.

⁷"Woe to the world because of the things that cause people to sin! Such things must come, but woe to the man through whom they come! ⁸If your hand or your foot causes you to sin cut it off and throw it away. It is better for you to enter life maimed or crippled than to have two hands or two feet and be thrown into eternal fire. ⁹And if your eye causes you to sin, gouge it out and throw it away. It is better for you to enter life with one eye than to have two eyes and be thrown into the fire of hell.

---

[33]Bruner, *Churchbook*, 637.

[34]Verse 6 begins with a δέ ("but"), whereas v. 7 proceeds without any transition. On this structure cf. further B. M. Newman and P. C. Stine, *A Translator's Handbook on the Gospel of Matthew* (New York: UBS, 1988), 578.

18:7 On the "woe," see comments under 11:21. Verse 7 recognizes the inevitability of seduction in a fallen world but at the same time affirms the accountability of all offenders. Romans 5:12 reiterates this dual cause. Since the fall all inherit a sinful nature, making sin inevitable in their lives, but all people freely choose to go along with that nature. God in Christ offers a way out of this otherwise hopeless situation, so that those who reject Jesus have only themselves to blame. They cannot escape everlasting punishment. "The man" of v. 7b is probably generic, but Matthew's original audience must surely have thought of Judas in particular, especially after they read the very similar remarks of 26:24. The reference to "the world" in v. 7a shows that temptations to sin come from outside as well as inside the community of professing believers.

18:8-9 Jesus now applies the same principle of taking drastic action to those who would cause *themselves* to sin. These verses mirror the logic of 5:29-30 and reuse much of the identical imagery. There Jesus applied these hyperboles to lust. Here he applies them to any kind of sin.[35] Disciples must radically reject anything that will lead them into evil. A stark contrast thus remains between those who recognize their complete dependence on God, and who therefore welcome other believers in humility and service, and those, including professing believers, who lead themselves and others to sin. In an age when divisions and conflict too often characterize Christian relationships, these verses offer a sober reminder that people whose lives more often than not display a lack of love for Christians with whom they associate may well not be Jesus' disciples at all and thus remain under threat of damnation. Conversely, oppressed and marginalized Christians should find great encouragement here. Faithful dependence on God, regardless of how others treat one, makes a person great in God's eyes.

(2) God's Humility (18:10-14). Jesus proceeds with the well-known parable of the lost sheep. The main plot unfolds exactly as in Luke 15:3-7, but most of the details differ. These two passages probably represent similar teachings of Jesus from two separate settings in his ministry.[36] In Luke Jesus uses the lost sheep to represent unsaved sinners. In Matthew

---

[35]Cf. M. Green (*Matthew for Today* [Dallas: Word, 1989], 172): "Does your hand offend you, the hand raised in anger or grasping at money? Does your foot offend you, the places it takes you to and the Christian service it declines to undertake? Does your eye offend you— the ever-unsatisfied eye of the consumer society? Be single minded! Deal ruthlessly with whatever causes you to stumble in your walk with Christ in the body of his Church."

[36]For more details on this issue using the Lukan parables paralleled elsewhere in the Gospels as a test case, see C. L. Blomberg, "When Is a Parallel Really a Parallel? A Test Case: The Lucan Parables," *WTJ* 46 (1984): 78-103.

he applies the parable to errant disciples, as the distinctive framework of the passage (vv. 10,14) makes plain.

10 "See that you do not look down on one of these little ones. For I tell you that their angels in heaven always see the face of my Father in heaven.

12 "What do you think? If a man owns a hundred sheep, and one of them wanders away, will he not leave the ninety-nine on the hills and go to look for the one that wandered off? 13And if he finds it, I tell you the truth, he is happier about that one sheep than about the ninety-nine that did not wander off. 14In the same way your Father in heaven is not willing that any of these little ones should be lost.

18:10 "Look down on" means *despise*. "These little ones" repeats the expression of v. 6. Here Jesus provides the rationale for the commands of vv. 1-9. We should humble ourselves and never cause others to sin because God never despises his people but rather is always concerned to go to great lengths to preserve them (cf. 1QH 5:20-22). Verse 10b proves somewhat cryptic. It may or may not imply the idea of guardian angels, that each person has an angel watching out for and representing him or her before God. Similar Jewish beliefs were common (e.g., *b. Sabb.* 119b), having developed out of Ps 91:11. Others see a more collective concept here, as with the angels who watch over nations in Dan 10:10-14 or over churches as in one interpretation of Rev 2:1–3:22. Qumran seemed to combine an individual and collective role for angels in the worshiping community (1QSa 2:9-10).[37] Seeing God's face seems to imply access to God (cf. similar expressions in 2 Sam 14:24; 1 Kgs 10:8). At any rate, Heb 1:14 teaches that angels are concerned for believers and serve them. So Jesus' words here are appropriate even if we cannot be sure of all the specific ways in which angels minister to us.

[18:11] Most of the earliest and most reliable manuscripts (e.g., א, B, L*, Θ*, f^1, f^{13}) omit v. 11 (see NIV marg.). It was most likely added by a later scribe to connect the parable more closely with 9:13 and/or inspired by Luke 19:10.

18:12-14 The rhetorical question implies an affirmative response in the Greek: *of course that is the way one would act.* The sheep/shepherd imagery parallels 9:36. Allusions to Ezek 34 seem likely, so that at least implicit Christology is present. Jesus is a good Shepherd (cf. John 10:1-18), even if God is more immediately in view. The ninety-nine refer to faithful followers of Jesus who no longer need to repent because they are not straying from him. The wandering sheep is the believer—"one of

---

[37]See W. D. Davies, *The Setting of the Sermon on the Mount* (Cambridge: University Press, 1964), 226-28 for more details concerning Jewish background texts.

these little ones"—who wanders away from intimate fellowship and consistent obedience. The Greek "one of [them]" (v. 12) employs the same wording as in vv. 5-6,10 and reappears in v. 14, so it is clear that Jesus still has Christians rather than literal young people in mind. Leaving the ninety-nine does not imply they are unprotected; other shepherds would keep watch over them. At the spiritual level, of course, God is able to search for the wanderer even while still protecting those who have not strayed. "If" in v. 13 introduces a third-class condition, which allows for the possibility that the shepherd will not find the sheep. Human freedom permits some people to hide from God, and he will not force them to return against their will. The theme of greater joy over the recaptured stray may seem incongruous but only to those whose hearts are hardened like that of the prodigal's older brother (Luke 15:25-32). The reality of human existence is that greater joy often does follow the recovery of those who had previously caused greater distress. There is enough joy, however, for everybody, and ideally disciples should display a steady constancy in their walk with the Lord, even if it does not elicit as great extremes of emotion. Verse 14 considers the case of the potential apostate but leaves unaddressed questions such as: Can such a person actually be lost for eternity, or is this only temporary loss of fellowship with God? Are these "little ones" simply professing and not genuine followers? The reference to the Father's will does not solve these problems because although God is not "willing" that any should perish (2 Pet 3:9), some do.

The three main points associated with the main characters of the parable apply equally to unbeliever (Luke) and backslidden Christian (Matthew): (1) God takes the initiative to go to great lengths to bring back to himself those who are estranged from him. (2) Reclaiming such people should lead to joyous celebration. (3) The faithfulness of the majority may never excuse us for ignoring anyone who still remains distant from God.[38] Practical applications require a strong emphasis on pastoral care in our churches; workable implementation demands carefully structured and monitored networks of undershepherds, small groups, and ministries of visitation.

b. On Forgiveness (18:15-35). God's constant quest to reclaim all the lost does not imply that everyone will respond positively. Ultimately, he will have to condemn some because of their failure to turn from sin. So it is appropriate for Jesus to raise the question of how believers should treat one another when they sin. Everything hinges on an individual's

---

[38]Cf. further C. L. Blomberg, *Interpreting the Parables* (Downers Grove; InterVarsity, 1990), 179-84. For more historical background, see E. F. F. Bishop, "The Parable of the Lost or Wandering Sheep," *ATR* 44 (1962): 44-57.

response to those who point out his or her sin. Here Jesus deals with the wrong response first; then he elaborates on the right reaction.

15"If your brother sins against you, go and show him his fault, just between the two of you. If he listens to you, you have won your brother over. 16But if he will not listen, take one or two others along, so that 'every matter may be established by the testimony of two or three witnesses.' 17If he refuses to listen to them, tell it to the church; and if he refuses to listen even to the church, treat him as you would a pagan or a tax collector.

(1) Forgiveness Withheld without Repentance (18:15-20). (a) The Process of Confrontation (18:15-17). **18:15** The case Jesus presents involves an individual believer who has been wronged by another Christian ("brother"), presumably in the same community of believers. "Against you" is missing in a few important early manuscripts (א, B, f^1) but was most likely omitted due to "homophony"—parts of different words that sound alike so that part of the text is accidentally omitted.[39] There are times, of course, when it is both appropriate and necessary to correct believers for sins affecting third parties, but this can easily turn into meddling. The illustration here is personal. The offended believer has the responsibility to *convict* or *convince* (from Greek elenchō—"show him his fault") the other person privately.[40] Ideally, the two individuals should resolve the problem without involving anyone else. The source for Jesus' command may lie in Lev 19:17-18. Galatians 6:1 offers a good commentary on the spirit of and rationale for such correction. "Listens" means *responds properly.* How often personal confrontation is the last stage rather than the first in Christian complaints! It frequently seems as if the whole world knows of someone's grievances against us before we are personally approached. Hopefully, following Jesus' guidelines will win over[41] Christian brothers or sisters before anyone else ever has to know about the problem (cf. Jas 5:19-20).

18:16 Not everyone, however, will respond properly to loving, personal confrontation. The second step, if the first step fails, is to involve at least one or two other people in the discussion. In this context these people will almost certainly be fellow believers, though no particular officers of the church are specified. One would presumably look for those likely to prove most helpful. Impeccable integrity would seem to be a pri-

---

[39]Ἁμαρτήσῃ ends with identical sounding two syllables as the next two words, εἰς σέ.

[40]Newman and Stine, *Matthew*, 586, suggest as explanatory translations "take the matter up with him," "speak with him about it," or "explain to him how he has sinned."

[41]From κερδαίνω, often applied by Paul in evangelistic contexts outside the church but by Matthew in penitential contexts within the church. Cf. Bruner, *Churchbook*, 649.

mary prerequisite so that no one's views are misrepresented if the matter does eventually have to come before the whole church. The individual who takes one or two witnesses thus creates a group of two or three witnesses, thereby fulfilling the command of Deut 19:15. Often one person alone is too much of a "co-dependent" to deal adequately with recurrent sins of those closest to him or her. Effective intervention by qualified counselors is increasingly forming a crucial part of Christian life in our sick society. The primary goal, however, is to resolve an individual's conflicts by involving as few other people as possible.

18:17 If step two fails, step three requires a person to bring the complaint before the "church." Here appear the only other references to "church" in the Gospels outside of 16:18. Jesus does not explain how we should air our grievances before the church; after all, he has not yet given any teaching on church structure. Applications should major on flexibility and sensitivity.[42] The main point is that the grievance is made more public. A similar procedure appears at Qumran in 1QS 5:25–6:1, where the emphasis again rests with private resolution if at all possible.[43] Ultimately, if the sinner remains recalcitrant, the entire church community must in some sense be made aware of the offense so that the rebellious individual has nowhere to hide. If even this procedure fails to bring repentance, then as a last resort Jesus commands the entire community to dissociate itself from the individual. Yet even this drastic action remains rehabilitative rather than retributive in design. This dissociation has come to be called "excommunication" or "disfellowshiping," though usually these terms imply a much more institutionalized procedure than can be derived from Jesus' brief comments here.

To treat a person as a "pagan or a tax collector" means to treat him or her as unredeemed and outside the Christian community. Such treatment resembles the Old Testament practice of "cutting" someone "off" from the assembly of Israel (e.g., Gen 17:14; Exod 12:15,19; 30:33,38). But Christian disfellowshiping must have two components to it. Primarily, it means not allowing someone to participate in public, corporate fellowship with the church, even as orthodox Jews shunned the "traitorous" tax collectors or "unclean" Gentiles. But in light of Jesus' consistent compassion for pagans and tax collectors, surely he must also want Christians, individually, to continue to reach out to these people and call them to repentance. Second Thessalonians 3:14-15 makes these twin themes clear, and

---

[42]See esp. J. C. Laney, *A Guide to Church Discipline* (Minneapolis: Bethany, 1985); *idem*, "The Biblical Practice of Church Discipline," *BibSac* 143 (1986): 353-64.

[43]For a comparative study, see F. G. Martínez, "La reprensión fraterna en Qumrán y Mt 18,15-17, *FNT* 2 (1989): 23-40.

if 2 Cor 2:5-11 forms the sequel to 1 Cor 5:1-5,[44] then we may have at least one specific illustration within Scripture itself of how excommunication led to repentance and restoration.[45]

In an age in which churches can be sued for disciplining their members unless procedures have been stated in writing and disseminated and explained to all the congregation, it is imperative to think carefully about how to implement Jesus' instructions. Many churches avoid the problem simply by disobeying Jesus and making no attempt to follow his principles. Application also proves difficult because our society for the most part is not made up of those tightly knit communities whose welcome or rejection had a powerful impact on individuals in the ancient world. Today, church members who are disciplined often leave one congregation for another that accepts them with no questions asked. Only as we re-create intimate community within the local church and networks of accountability among different churches can we hope to apply these verses effectively. But without this application, sin in the church will continue to compromise the unity and testimony of God's people.

[18]"I tell you the truth, whatever you bind on earth will be bound in heaven, and whatever you loose on earth will be loosed in heaven.

[19]"Again, I tell you that if two of you on earth agree about anything you ask for, it will be done for you by my Father in heaven. [20]For where two or three come together in my name, there am I with them."

(b) The Process of Ratification (18:18-20). **18:18** Verse 18 repeats 16:19b almost verbatim, but this time Jesus gives authority to all the disciples, not just Peter. On the imagery and grammar of this verse, see under 16:19. In this context Jesus is almost certainly referring to the procedures of vv. 15-17 involving the withholding or bestowing of forgiveness and fellowship. As in 16:19, "binding" and "loosing" are more likely parallel to John 20:23 than to the rabbinic maxims on permitting or prohibiting certain behavior.[46] Verse 18 also presupposes that the church is acting according to Jesus' guidelines given in vv. 15-17 and is generally seeking and sensitive to God's will. Then the church's loosing and binding—forgiving or refusing to forgive—carries the very authority of God.

18:19-20 Sadly, these verses have often been taken out of context and misused. It ought to be obvious that God regularly does *not* fulfill a promise like that of v. 19 if it is interpreted as his response to any kind of

---

[44]As is convincingly defended by C. Kruse, "The Offender and the Offence in 2 Corinthians 2:5 and 7:12," *EvQ* 60 (1988): 129-39.

[45]Cf. V. C. Pfitzner, "Purified Community—Purified Sinner," *AusBR* 30 (1982): 34-55, who notes that concern for the sinner is more crucial than purification of the community.

[46]See esp. Thompson, *Matthew's Advice*, 202.

request. In this context v. 19 simply restates the theme of v. 18. The word
for any "thing" (*pragma*) is a term frequently limited to judicial matters.
Here Jesus reiterates that actions of Christian discipline, following God's
guidelines, have his endorsement. This remains true even if they come
from a very small fellowship, including but not limited to the "two or
three" gathered in vv. 15-16. "My Father in heaven" links back with
vv. 10-14 and nicely balances "two of you on earth." God is of course
omnipresent, but he is uniquely present in every Christian gathering as
his Spirit indwells believers. In context v. 20 then assures God's blessings
on action properly taken to try to reconcile believers to one another (as in
vv. 15-18).[47] "I am with them" parallels "it will be done for you by my
Father in heaven." Jesus implicitly equates himself with God and promises his continuing spiritual presence in the church after his death. Echoes
of the Immanuel theme of 1:23 (God with us) reverberate.

(2) Unlimited Forgiveness with Repentance (18:21-35). Verses 15-
20 seem harsh to modern ears but probably would not have seemed so in
the first century. Verses 21-35 have lost their force in our age, following
centuries of domestication and familiarity with these texts, but they
would have been shockingly radical when first spoken.

**21Then Peter came to Jesus and asked, "Lord, how many times shall I for-
give my brother when he sins against me? Up to seven times?"**
22Jesus answered, "I tell you, not seven times, but seventy-seven times.

(a) Positive Illustration (18:21-22). **18:21** Here appears the fifth
and last of the uniquely Matthean insertions involving Peter in chaps. 14–
18. As with 14:28-31 and 16:16-19, the account begins positively enough
but ends with Peter still needing significant correction. Peter seems to
have learned the lesson of Jesus' teaching in vv. 10-14 and generously
proposes to forgive fellow disciples seven times. Seven is a common biblical number for completeness and goes well beyond the rabbinic maxim
of forgiving three times (e.g., *b. Yoma* 86b, 87a). "Against me" parallels
"against you" in v. 15. Peter's words likely allude to the sevenfold avenging of Cain; Jesus' reply contrasts starkly with the seventy-sevenfold
avenging of Lamech (Gen 4:24).[48]

18:22 Jesus no doubt stuns Peter with his reply. The famous "seventy
times seven" (NIV marg.) is probably better translated "seventy-seven

---

[47]Cf. E. Schweizer, *The Good News according to Matthew* (Richmond: John Knox,
1975), 374: "It is assumed, of course, just as in 7:7-11, that the community prays according
to God's will, as Jesus taught his disciples to pray in the Lord's Prayer."
[48]Cf. M'Neile, *Matthew*, 268: "The unlimited revenge of primitive man has given place
to the unlimited forgiveness of Christians."

times," based both on the most common rendering of the Greek *hebdomē-kontakis hepta* and on the Genesis allusion noted above. But Jesus' point remains equally dramatic. We dare not keep track of the number of times we grant forgiveness. Jesus takes Peter's number of completeness and multiplies it considerably. Few people ever have to forgive the same person this often, at least not over a short period of time. But Jesus' point is not to withhold forgiveness after the seventy-eighth (or 491st) offense. As with the principles in vv. 15-16, Jesus' advice may work well with unbelievers too, but his primary focus remains on believers. And genuine repentance, which includes changed behavior, must occur, or the principles of vv. 15-18 come into play instead.[49] The subsequent parable (vv. 23-35) will illustrate both the incredible generosity believers should demonstrate in forgiving fellow believers who do beg for mercy and promise to change as well as the severe judgment awaiting those who refuse to forgive or respond properly to forgiveness.[50]

(b) Negative Illustration (18:23-35).　As in vv. 10-14, Jesus uses a parable to explain the rationale for his previous commands. In a nutshell his teaching is this: God eternally and unconditionally forgives those who repent of so immense a debt against him that it is unconscionable for believers to refuse to grant forgiveness to each other for sins that remain trivial in comparison.[51]

23 "Therefore, the kingdom of heaven is like a king who wanted to settle accounts with his servants. 24As he began the settlement, a man who owed him ten thousand talents was brought to him. 25Since he was not able to pay, the master ordered that he and his wife and his children and all that he had be sold to repay the debt.

26 "The servant fell on his knees before him. 'Be patient with me,' he begged, 'and I will pay back everything.' 27The servant's master took pity on him, canceled the debt and let him go.

18:23-27　This parable mirrors the most common form of rabbinic parable—a story involving a king with servants or sons. The king almost

---

[49]But see R. H. Mounce, *Matthew*, GNC (San Francisco: Harper and Row, 1985), 180, for another possible resolution: "Though it may be necessary to exclude the nonrepentant from the believing community, personal forgiveness of the individual should never be withheld."

[50]Cf. further J. D. M. Derrett, "'Where Two or Three Are Convened in My Name . . . ': A Sad Misunderstanding," *ExpTim* 91 (1979-80): 84: "The positive obligation to forgive is not absolute and invariable, since that would destroy discipline." But the individual is obliged to forgive if the offender genuinely repents.

[51]Cf. T. Deidun, "The Parable of the Unmerciful Servant (Mt. 18:23-35)," *BTB* 6 (1976): 219, on the change of heart demanded by the love of God made manifest in Jesus.

always stands for God; the servants, for God's people. Often obedient and disobedient servants provide a contrast between righteous and wicked behavior. Settling accounts is a natural metaphor for judgment. Ten thousand talents would have been an enormous debt, on the borderline of what the ancient mind-set could have conceived (cf. NIV marg.). Estimates in modern currency range from several million to one trillion dollars. The "talent" was the highest known denomination of currency in the ancient Roman Empire, and ten thousand was the highest number for which the Greek language had a particular word (*myrias*; cf. our *myriad*).[52] One might conceive of this first servant as an extremely wealthy governor or satrap, a very powerful official in his own right. Since he is unable to repay his debts, he and his family must be sold, along with all their assets, in order to raise at least some funds for the king. He will obviously recoup nothing anywhere close to the amount owed, but something is better than nothing. Selling people into slavery to pay their debts was extremely common in the ancient world. The man begs for mercy and makes a promise he almost certainly will not be able to keep. To the astonishment of Jesus' original audience, the king pities the man and cancels his debt. Not only will he not sell him into slavery, but he will not require repayment of any kind. Sheer grace is at work here. "Took pity" is the same word for the *compassion* that characterizes Jesus' emotions and behavior in 9:36; 14:14; 15:32; and 20:34.

28"But when that servant went out, he found one of his fellow servants who owed him a hundred denarii. He grabbed him and began to choke him. 'Pay back what you owe me!' he demanded.

29"His fellow servant fell to his knees and begged him, 'Be patient with me, and I will pay you back.'

30"But he refused. Instead, he went off and had the man thrown into prison until he could pay the debt. **31**When the other servants saw what had happened, they were greatly distressed and went and told their master everything that had happened.

18:28-31 The second scene of the parable now ensues. The same scenario is reenacted, only now between the servant just forgiven and a fellow servant of his. The sum owed here is paltry in comparison to the previous sum, even if the NIV margin "a few dollars" is misleadingly small. A hundred denarii represented a hundred days' wages. Still,

---

[52]P. Perkins (*Hearing the Parables* [New York: Paulist, 1981], 124) thinks the number would have reminded a Jewish audience of the fabled riches of the Egyptian and Persian kings—not inconceivable but not within the bounds of their own experience. Cf. also M. C. de Boer, "Ten Thousand Talents? Matthew's Interpretation and Redaction of the Parable of the Unforgiving Servant," *CBQ* 50 (1988): 214-32.

estimates of the value of a talent range from sixty to ten thousand denarii, so that the ratio of one hundred denarii to ten thousand talents could be anywhere from six thousand to one to one million to one. The servant's severity in choking his fellow servant and demanding repayment appears all the more despicable in light of this disparity of debts. In v. 29 the second servant pleads for mercy with almost the exact words the first servant had used with the king. But just as the sums owed sharply contrasted with each other, so also the first servant's response proves entirely opposite to the king's generosity (vv. 30-31). "He refused" is literally *he was not willing*, showing that the servant made a conscious choice to harden his heart. Needless to say, the other servants are outraged and report the matter to the king.

[32]"Then the master called the servant in. 'You wicked servant,' he said, 'I canceled all that debt of yours because you begged me to. [33]Shouldn't you have had mercy on your fellow servant just as I had on you?' [34]In anger his master turned him over to the jailers to be tortured, until he should pay back all he owed.

[35]"This is how my heavenly Father will treat each of you unless you forgive your brother from your heart."

18:32-34 The two original characters reappear on stage for scene three. Furious that his lavish mercy was so spurned, the king vents his rage. He orders the servant to be imprisoned and tortured "until he should pay back all he owed." Since the man has no way of earning this kind of money in jail, the king's orders guarantee a life sentence.

18:35 Jesus' conclusion reminds us of what v. 23 made clear—that the purpose of the story is to communicate a spiritual lesson about the kingdom of heaven. It also points out that, at least on this occasion, Jesus was not trying primarily to conceal truth from the crowds but to clarify it for his disciples. The reference to a "brother" ties Jesus' conclusion in with Peter's original question (v. 21). The following three themes emerge from the main characters and episodes of the parable: God's boundless grace, the absurdity of spurning that grace, and the frightful fate awaiting the unforgiving. The law of end-stress highlights the third of these, but all are important.[53] Carson correctly captures the balance of mercy and judgment reflected here: "Jesus sees no incongruity in the actions of a heavenly Father who forgives so bountifully and punishes so ruthlessly, and

---

[53]Cf. J. Jeremias, *The Parables of Jesus* (Philadelphia: Westminster, 1972), 213: "God has extended to you in the gospel, through the offer of forgiveness, a merciful gift beyond conceiving," but "God will revoke the forgiveness of sin if you do not wholeheartedly share the forgiveness you have experienced." Then "God will . . . see that his sentence is executed rigorously." See also B. B. Scott, "The King's Accounting: Matthew 18:23-34," *JBL* 104 (1985): 429-42.

neither should we. Indeed, it is precisely because he is a God of such compassion and mercy that he cannot possibly accept as his those devoid of compassion and mercy."[54]

The subordinate details of the parable should not be pressed. Verse 34 does not promulgate any doctrine of purgatory. Even when one allegorizes the prison, torturers, and repayment, one winds up with a picture of hell, not purgatory, since this man could almost certainly never repay his debt or escape. Nor is it obvious that the retraction of forgiveness has a clear spiritual analogue. Jesus may be teaching that no true disciple could ever act as this servant did; those who do so show that they have not really received forgiveness. Alternately, he may be indicating that God makes forgiveness available for everyone, but only those who appropriate it by a life of forgiving others show that they have genuinely accepted his pardon.[55] Similar teaching occurs in the Sermon on the Mount (6:14-15), in which Jesus makes clear that those who are lost were never previously saved (7:21-23).[56] Frighteningly, many in Christian circles today seem in danger of this judgment because they refuse to forgive fellow believers, speak kindly to them, cooperate with them, or accept their apologies. Counselors often discover that a client's unwillingness to forgive someone lies deep at the heart of all kinds of personal problems. Jesus declares that if people die without having resolved such problems, they may exclude themselves from eternal life with him.

---

[54]Carson, "Matthew," 407.

[55]Cf. Blomberg, *Parables*, 242.

[56]Cf. Ridderbos, *Matthew*, 346: "Whoever tries to separate man's forgiveness from God's will no longer be able to count on God's mercy. In so doing he not merely forfeits it, like the servant in the parable. Rather he shows that he never had a part in it. God's mercy is not something cut and dried that is received only once. It is a persistent power that pervades all of life. If it does not become manifest as such a power, then it was never received at all."

―――――――――― SECTION OUTLINE CONTINUED ――――――――――

B. The Road to Jerusalem: Impending Judgment on Israel (19:1–25:46)
1. True Discipleship versus Harsher Condemnation for the Jewish
   Leaders (19:1–22:46)
   a. Journeying to Judea (19:1–20:34)
      (1) Further Instructions for Disciples Based on Concerns
          Raised by Outsiders (19:1–20:16)
          (a) Pharisees and Divorce (19:1-12)
          (b) Disciples and Children (19:13-15)
          (c) The Rich Man and Eternal Life (19:16–20:16)
              1) The Controversy (19:16-22)
              2) The Dialogue with the Disciples (19:23-30)
              3) The Parable of the Vineyard Workers (20:1-16)
      (2) Further Focus on Jesus' Passion, with Contrasting
          Responses from His Audience (20:17-34)
          (a) Third Passion Prediction (20:17-19)
          (b) An Inappropriate Response: James and John Seek
              Status (20:20-28)
          (c) An Appropriate Response: Two Blind Men Seek
              Mercy (20:29-34)
   b. Judgment on the Temple in Jerusalem (21:1–22:46)
      (1) Actions of Judgment (21:1-22)
          (a) Entrance into Jerusalem (21:1-11)
          (b) Judgment on the Temple by Purification (21:12-17)
          (c) Judgment on the Temple by Threatened Destruction
              (21:18-22)
      (2) Controversies with the Jewish Leaders (21:23–22:46)
          (a) The Temple Authorities Ask about Jesus' Authority
              (21:23–22:14)
              1) The Controversy (21:23-27)
              2) The Parable of the Two Sons (21:28-32)
              3) The Parable of the Wicked Tenants (21:33-46)
              4) The Parable of the Wedding Banquet (22:1-14)
          (b) The Pharisees and Herodians Ask about Taxes
              (22:15-22)
          (c) The Sadducees Ask about the Resurrection (22:23-33)
          (d) The Lawyer Asks about the Greatest Commandment
              (22:34-40)
          (e) Jesus Asks about the Messiah (22:41-46)

B. The Road to Jerusalem: Impending Judgment on Israel (19:1–25:46)

Now Jesus leaves Galilee for the last time. From 19:1–25:46, Matthew's final combination of narrative (19:1–22:46) and discourse (23:1–25:46), he will be on the road to his fateful destination. He finally will arrive in Jerusalem, where he teaches in the temple and in the environs of the city. From a human perspective these chapters are tied together by the impending sense of Christ's condemnation *by* the Jewish leaders. From a divine perspective Jesus increasingly reveals God's condemnation *of* the Jewish leaders. As hostilities against Jesus continue to mount, Matthew uniquely emphasizes Christ's distinctive teachings for the disciples (esp. in chaps. 19–20) and stresses how Jesus' actions reveal Israel under God's growing wrath (esp. in chaps. 21–22), a theme that will dominate chaps. 23–25.

1. True Discipleship versus Harsher Condemnation for the Jewish Leaders (19:1–22:46)

This section of narrative, which continues until the final major block of Jesus' teaching begins (chaps. 23–25), is tied together geographically by the motif of Jesus' journey to Jerusalem. He leaves Galilee to go to Judea, and to the holy city there, as he has previously prophesied (19:1; 20:17-18,29). He draws near to Jerusalem (21:1), arrives (21:10), stays in the area (21:17), and teaches in the temple (21:23–22:46).[1]

So this section falls neatly in two, both geographically and theologically. In 19:1–20:34 Jesus is literally "on the road," continuing to teach a variety of people, and following up public discourse with private teachings for the disciples to correct their misunderstandings. In 21:1–22:46 Jesus has arrived at Jerusalem and its environs, teaches extensively in the temple, avoids traps set by those who wanted to arrest him, and ultimately condemns the people who have rejected him.

a. JOURNEYING TO JUDEA (19:1–20:34). These two chapters begin and end with explicit references to Jesus on the road, surrounded by great crowds and healing people (19:1-2; 20:29-34). Overall they divide into two main subsections. First come a series of three controversy stories in which different individuals or groups approach Jesus with a specific concern (19:1–20:16): the Pharisees try to trap him in his views on divorce (19:3-12), children are brought to him for blessing (19:13-15), and the rich young man inquires about eternal life (19:16–20:16). In each of these cases, Jesus makes important pronouncements that lead to or stem from

---

[1]See B. M. Newman and P. C. Stine, *A Translator's Handbook on the Gospel of Matthew* (New York: UBS, 1988), 655; E. Schweizer, *The Good News according to Matthew* (Richmond: John Knox, 1975), 401-3.

the disciples' misunderstanding. In the first and third instances, subsequent dialogue directly addresses these misunderstandings. The second subsection (20:17-34) begins with Jesus' third passion prediction (20:17-19) and is followed by inappropriate and appropriate responses. In light of what Jesus must suffer, how dare James and John's mother request status and privilege for her sons (20:20-28). Far more sensitive is the appeal of the two blind men on the Jericho road simply for mercy (20:29-34). In both 19:1–20:16 and 20:17-34 the true nature of discipleship emerges—lowliness and service as over against power and prestige.

[1] When Jesus had finished saying these things, he left Galilee and went into the region of Judea to the other side of the Jordan. [2] Large crowds followed him, and he healed them there.
[3] Some Pharisees came to him to test him. They asked, "Is it lawful for a man to divorce his wife for any and every reason?"

(1) Further Instructions for Disciples Based on Concerns Raised by Outsiders (19:1–20:16). (a) Pharisees and Divorce (19:1-12).[2] **19:1-2** Chapter 19 begins by referring back to Jesus' previous sermon, as after his first three discourses (8:1; 11:1; 13:53). Jesus has already predicted that he must be killed in Jerusalem (16:21); now he deliberately heads there. In Matthew, as in Mark and Luke, this is the first instance we learn of Jesus traveling to Jerusalem during his adult ministry. John has portrayed him going there regularly in conjunction with the major Jewish feasts (John 2:13-25; 5:1-47; 7:1–10:39), as faithful adult Jewish males were supposed to do. The Synoptics' silence does not contradict John. No Gospel claims that Jesus never previously visited Jerusalem, but Matthew, Mark, and Luke choose to concentrate primarily on Jesus' Galilean ministry.[3]

---

[2] For detailed interpretation and application of this passage, see C. L. Blomberg, "Marriage, Divorce, Remarriage and Celibacy: An Exegesis of Matthew 19:3-12," *TrinJ* n.s. 11 (1990): 161-96. A good symposium reflecting four prominent Christian perspectives on divorce and remarriage is W. House, ed., *Divorce and Remarriage* (Downers Grove: Inter-Varsity, 1990). The best detailed studies of these questions, approximating to the three most common of these four views, are W. A. Heth and G. J. Wenham, *Jesus and Divorce* (Nashville: Nelson, 1985); J. Murray, *Divorce* (Philadelphia: OPC, 1953); and W. F. Luck, *Divorce and Remarriage* (San Francisco: Harper and Row, 1987). The closest book-length treatment to my own perspective is now C. S. Keener, . . . *And Marries Another: Divorce and Remarriage in the Teaching of the New Testament* (Peabody: Hendrickson, 1991).

[3] For an excellent defense of the historicity of John's chronology, see J. A. T. Robinson, *The Priority of John* (Oak Brook: Meyer and Stone, 1987), 123-57. For theological motives behind the sequence and selection of events in Mark, see esp. W. L. Lane, *The Gospel according to Mark*, NIC (Grand Rapids: Eerdmans, 1974); for Luke see C. H. Talbert, *Reading Luke* (New York: Crossroad, 1982).

Matthew reserves treatment of Jesus' ministry in Jerusalem for the end of his Gospel, because for him Jerusalem stands for the majority of Jews who have rejected Christ and for the climax of official hostility against Jesus, which leads to his death. Matthew does not want to distract his readers by recalling Jesus' earlier but short-lived popularity in Judea. We are not told how long before his final Passover (probably April A.D. 30) he left Galilee once and for all or how long he spent on the road before arriving in Judea, but one probable reading of John 10–12 is that he never again returned to Galilee after his appearance in Jerusalem in December of (presumably) A.D. 29 for the Hanukkah festival (John 10:22). In that case he would have embarked on the trip described here at least by late fall of 29. "To the other side of the Jordan" probably refers to crossing into Judea from the east. Jesus probably followed a popular route along the east bank of the Jordan river which avoided Samaria. Many commentators thus refer to most of the events of chaps. 19–20 (greatly expanded in Luke 9:51–18:34) as forming Christ's Perean ministry, after the name of the long, narrow province east of the Jordan. But this identification remains speculative at best, since "Perea" never appears by name here or elsewhere in the New Testament.[4] Matthew includes his characteristic references to the crowds following Jesus and to Christ's healing ministry among them.

19:3 For Matthew the topic of divorce follows naturally after a sermon on humility and forgiveness (chap. 18). The Jewish leaders try to trap Jesus, as in 16:1. Their question reflects the intra-Pharisaic debate between the "schools" of Shammai and Hillel concerning the correct interpretation of Deut 24:1. In that passage God apparently permitted divorce for "anything indecent." Shammai, placing the emphasis on "indecent," took this to refer to sexual unfaithfulness; Hillel, placing the emphasis on "anything," allowed divorce even for as trivial an offense as a wife burning her husband's food (*m. Git.* 9:10). The recent Herodias affair (14:3-12), along with Jesus' own teaching in 5:31-32, may also have influenced the Pharisees' question (for further background see under 5:31-32). The wording reflects only a man's perspective, since women were rarely if ever able to divorce in ancient Judaism. Yet although no reciprocal language appears in this context, 5:31 and Mark 10:11-12 show that Jesus' teachings on the topic granted both women and men equal privileges and responsibilities. The specific historical background that

---

[4]There are more complex explanations of the geography implied in Matt 19:1, especially in light of the more awkwardly phrased parallel in Mark 10:1, but they are probably less likely. On the theological versus geographical outline of Luke's central section, see C. L. Blomberg, "Midrash, Chiasmus, and the Outline of Luke's Central Section," in *Gospel Perspectives*, vol. 3, ed. R. T. France and D. Wenham (Sheffield: JSOT, 1983), 217-61.

informed this debate, the particular way in which the question is phrased, and the unscrupulous motives behind the Pharisees' approach all warn us against the notion that Jesus was comprehensively addressing all relevant questions about marriage and divorce. For example, the problem of wife beating would not even be considered, since a man would scarcely divorce a woman for this reason.

4"Haven't you read," he replied, "that at the beginning the Creator 'made them male and female,' 5and said, 'For this reason a man will leave his father and mother and be united to his wife, and the two will become one flesh'? 6So they are no longer two, but one. Therefore what God has joined together, let man not separate."

19:4-6 Jesus goes beyond Deuteronomy and the Pharisees' debate to a creation ordinance. "Haven't you read," as in 12:3,5, challenges his interrogators' understanding of the Scriptures. He quotes the LXX of Gen 1:27 and 2:24 almost verbatim. God originally intended for marriages to be permanent. He created two complementary genders for each other[5] (even if vv. 10-12 will explain that God has not designed every single individual to be married). The marriage covenant has two parts to it. To "leave . . . and be united" means *to transfer one's fundamental allegiance from parents to spouse*. In the biblical world this did not often refer to setting up a separate domicile; extended families regularly lived together. "One flesh" describes the interpersonal intimacy that should characterize the marriage partnership and culminate in sexual relations.[6] Verse 6a makes it clear that this creation ordinance remains in effect even after the fall of the human race, the giving of the law, and the coming of the kingdom with Jesus. Verse 6b puts forward the text made famous by thousands of marriage ceremonies—humans should do nothing to sunder the divinely ordained union of holy matrimony. Without vv. 4-6a one could imagine v. 6b implying that some marriages are not ordained by God; in context this view is indefensible. On the contrary, precisely because God wants *all* marriages to be permanent, we dare not do anything to jeopardize them.

---

[5]F. D. Bruner (*The Churchbook* [Waco: Word, 1990], 670-71), insightfully remarks: "If God had supremely intended *solitary* life, God would have created humans one by one; if God had intended polygamous life, God would have created one man and several women (Chrys., 62:1:382); if God had intended homosexual life, God would have made two men or two women; but that God intended monogamous heterosexual life was shown by God's creation of one man and one woman."

[6]See esp. D. Atkinson, *To Have and to Hold* (Grand Rapids: Eerdmans, 1981), who further elucidates how marriage is best described as a covenant, which tragically can be broken, rather than as an indissoluble, mystical union that remains even after divorce (as traditionally held by Roman Catholics, and, curiously, by some very conservative Protestants).

[7] "Why then," they asked, "did Moses command that a man give his wife a certificate of divorce and send her away?"

[8] Jesus replied, "Moses permitted you to divorce your wives because your hearts were hard. But it was not this way from the beginning. [9] I tell you that anyone who divorces his wife, except for marital unfaithfulness, and marries another woman commits adultery."

19:7   The Pharisees' counterquestion raises the obvious objection: Why did God permit divorce in Old Testament times if he categorically opposed it? Since the Pharisees were trying to trap Jesus, it is natural to assume that they are subtly but deliberately misrepresenting Scripture here. Deuteronomy 24:1-4 granted no permission for divorce but prohibited a woman who had already been divorced and remarried from being remarried to her original husband. Still, it is understandable that such legislation should be seen as presupposing that God did permit divorce under certain circumstances, and Jesus himself has already referred to Deut 24:1 as a command in 5:31. So perhaps the Pharisees' question is less deceitful than many imagine.

19:8   Jesus does not challenge their logic, only the permanence of the Mosaic law. God's provisions for divorce were temporary, based on the calloused rebellion of fallen humanity against God. He did not originally create people to divorce each other, and he therefore does not intend for those whom he re-creates—the community of Jesus' followers—to practice divorce. As in the Sermon on the Mount, Jesus proclaims a higher standard of righteousness for his followers than the law of Moses. This distinction suggests that we must be more lenient with non-Christians who divorce but also that we may not include "hard-heartedness" as a legitimate excuse for Christians divorcing. Strikingly, the word "your" dissociates Jesus from this sin, even while indicting his contemporaries along with the Israelites of Moses' day.

19:9   Here appears the climactic pronouncement and interpretive crux of this passage.[7] Numerous historical, grammatical, and lexical conundrums puzzle Matthew's readers. Why does the clause "except for marital unfaithfulness" not appear in the parallel passage in Mark 10:11-12? Should Mark's version be taken as more original, reflecting an absolute prohibition which Matt 19:9 tones down? Or should Matthew be interpreted in a way that makes his apparent "exception clause" no exception at all? Is Matthew perhaps speaking only of separation or annulment and not divorce? The background of the Shammai-Hillel debate makes the last

---

[7] In addition to Blomberg, "Marriage," see esp. D. A. Carson, "Matthew," in EBC, vol. 8, ed. F. E. Gaebelein (Grand Rapids: Zondervan, 1984), 410-20, for a survey and critique of the various options; and P. F. Lockery, "Divorce and Remarriage in the New Testament," Master's thesis, Fuller Seminary, 1987, for a full-length treatment.

of these suggestions most unlikely. Grammatically, *mē epi* ("except for") has been translated as "even for," or "not considering the case of," but these are highly unlikely renderings of the Greek. The phrase should be taken as a genuine exception.[8] Probably Mark simply takes this exception for granted, since in both the Jewish and Greco-Roman cultures divorce and remarriage were universally permitted and often mandatory following adultery. Matthew merely spells out several parts of Jesus' dialogue more fully for his largely Jewish-Christian audience.

Porneia ("marital unfaithfulness") has been translated a number of different ways but should be taken as referring to adultery or related sexual sins (see commentary on 5:32).[9] The uniqueness of 19:9 lies in its combination of a reference to adultery with permission for the "innocent" party to remarry. Some scholars deny that the exception clause modifies both verbs ("divorces" and "marries another") and argue that even when divorce is permitted, remarriage is always wrong.[10] But a careful grammatical analysis renders this interpretation unlikely.[11] Some also make much of the early church fathers' rejection of all remarriage as counting strongly in favor of their interpretation. But this reading of Christian history overlooks important dissenters in the earliest centuries and does not take adequate account of the growing, unbiblical asceticism, especially in sexual matters, which increasingly pervaded the Greek and Roman church.[12]

Key issues of application continue to divide believers. If Jesus did permit divorce and remarriage in at least the one instance of marital unfaithfulness, are there any other situations in which divorce and remarriage may be permitted? First Corinthians 7:15 indicates at least one, when an unbelieving partner wishes to leave a believing spouse. But how could Paul, even under the inspiration of the Spirit, add a second exception to Jesus' "no divorce" policy if he recognized Jesus' words as comprehensively addressing all possible situations? Yet 1 Corinthians is an equally "occasional" document. Paul's comments about sex and marriage in

---

[8]B. Vawter, "Divorce and the New Testament," *CBQ* 39 (1977): 528-42, abandoning his earlier view to the contrary.

[9]E.g., incest, homosexuality, prostitution, molestation, or indecent exposure. Cf. B. Malina, "Does *Porneia* Mean Fornication?" *NovT* 14 (1972): 10-17; and J. Jensen, "Does *Porneia* Mean Fornication? A Critique of Bruce Malina," *NovT* 20 (1978): 161-84.

[10]W. Heth and D. Wenham, *Jesus and Divorce* (Nashville: Thomas Nelson), 113-20; cf. esp. G. J. Wenham, "The Syntax of Matthew 19.9," *JSNT* 28 (1986): 17-23.

[11]P. H. Wiebe, "Jesus' Divorce Exception," *JETS* 32 (1989): 227-33, though he exaggerates the conclusiveness of the evidence for the opposite position. Cf. S. E. Porter and P. Buchanan, "On the Logical Structure of Matt 19:9," *JETS* 34 (1991): 335-39.

[12]See esp. P. Harrell, *Divorce and Remarriage in the Early Church* (Austin: Sweet, 1967).

1 Cor 7 seem to be addressed to Christians who were too zealously promoting celibacy (scarcely a common problem in the modern world!),[13] so could there be additional legitimate grounds for the dissolution of a marriage?[14] Many who answer affirmatively offer no clear-cut criteria and seem to endorse "divorce on demand." Many who answer negatively continue to treat fellow believers divorced on other grounds as second-class citizens of the kingdom no matter how genuine their repentance.

Perhaps the best approach is to ask what these two exceptions of Jesus and Paul have in common. Both destroy at least one of the two fundamental components of marriage, either the "leaving and cleaving" or the "one flesh" unity. Both leave one party without any other options if attempts at reconciliation are spurned. Both recognize the extreme seriousness of divorce as a last resort and as an admission of defeat. These observations seem to leave the door open for divorce as a final step, as perhaps the lesser of evils, when all else has failed, similar to excommunication for unrepentant sinners. To open this door of course means that some will abuse their freedom and walk through it prematurely. And undue attention to the exception clause of v. 9 risks losing sight of Jesus' overall point that divorce is *never desirable*. Married people should always be seeking ways to improve and enhance relations with spouses rather than wondering how they can get out of the commitments they have made.[15] Those who divorce and/or remarry on any grounds must admit failure, repent of the sins that led to the dissolution of their marriage, and vow to remain faithful to any subsequent relationships. A new marriage is not continuous adultery.[16] At most, the first sex act with a new partner is what violates the previous relationship, but more likely Jesus is using the term "adultery" in a metaphorical sense to refer to the divorce itself (see under 5:32).

[10]The disciples said to him, "If this is the situation between a husband and wife, it is better not to marry."

[11]Jesus replied, "Not everyone can accept this word, but only those to

---

[13]G. D. Fee, *The First Epistle to the Corinthians*, NIC (Grand Rapids: Eerdmans, 1987), 267-357.

[14]One reason for thinking so is the inconsistency of the position that maintains that a divorced person cannot remarry so long as his or her previous spouse has not had sexual relations with any other partner, no matter how closed to reconciliation that individual may be. This leaves the party desiring either reconciliation or remarriage in the strange position of having to hope that his or her previous partner sins by committing adultery, to free the person for a new relationship!

[15]For additional helpful applications to people in various marital statuses, see Bruner, *Churchbook*, 681-87.

[16]C. D. Osburn, "The Present Indicative of Matthew 19:9," *RestQ* 24 (1981): 193-203.

whom it has been given. ¹²For some are eunuchs because they were born that way; others were made that way by men; and others have renounced marriage because of the kingdom of heaven. The one who can accept this should accept it."

19:10-12   Only Matthew includes these verses. Given that Jesus' position proves stricter than Shammai's, even with the exception clause, the disciples think that fulfilling marital obligations may be harder than remaining single. Jesus agrees but only in a very limited way. God has designed some people not to marry, but apparently not too many. "This word" probably refers to the disciples' outburst in v. 10—the nearest possible antecedent[17]—and not to Jesus' teaching in v. 9. No technical language of "gifts" or "calling" appears here, but some special empowerment seems implied, challenging the traditional Roman Catholic view that strength for celibacy is available to anyone for the asking and in fact is mandatory for ordained clergy. Just as God creates a few people without fully functioning sexual organs, and just as men sometimes are castrated (most commonly in biblical days with the officials who superintended a royal harem—cf. Acts 8:27), so also God enables certain individuals to remain celibate even though they could engage in sex if they so chose. *Eunuchs* ("those who have renounced marriage") "because of the kingdom of heaven" voluntarily accept a celibate life-style in order to be better able to devote their whole lives to God's work (cf. 1 Cor 7:25-38).

If many Roman Catholics have overly exalted celibacy as an ideal, most Protestants have drastically undervalued it. Christian singles need much more support from their married friends and their churches, who must value them as equally significant members of the body of Christ. In a society that constantly pressures people into hasty marriages, the church desperately needs to encourage all who sense God leading them to remain single, for however long or short a period of time, to remain faithful to his guidance.[18]

¹³Then little children were brought to Jesus for him to place his hands on them and pray for them. But the disciples rebuked those who brought them. ¹⁴Jesus said, "Let the little children come to me, and do not hinder them, for the kingdom of heaven belongs to such as these." ¹⁵When he had placed his hands on them, he went on from there.

---

[17]Against an important line of interpretation best represented by Q. Quesnell, "'Made Themselves Eunuchs for the Kingdom of Heaven' (Mt. 19,12)," *CBQ* 30 (1968): 342-46.

[18]Cf. further W. A. Heth, "'Unmarried for the Sake of the Kingdom' (Matthew 19:12 in the Early Church)," *GTJ* 8 (1987): 55-88, without endorsing his interpretation of the antecedent of "this word." Cf. also F. Stagg, "Biblical Perspectives on the Single Person," *RevExp* 74 (1977): 5-19.

(b) Disciples and Children (19:13-15). **19:13** This second controversy story strikingly contrasts with the previous one. There the powerful Pharisees were rebuffed; here relatively helpless children are embraced. Whatever time interval has elapsed between dialogues, Matthew is grouping his material topically. A controversy about children follows naturally on a debate about divorce. An unspecified group of people bring some children (*pais* does not necessarily imply "little" children) to Jesus. They request a blessing for these youngsters. Laying on of hands, accompanied by prayer, formed a typical Jewish "blessing"—asking God for his favor to rest on someone (cf. Gen 48:14-15). One rabbinic tradition describes the custom of bringing a thirteen-year-old boy to the elders in Jerusalem at festival time "to bless him and pray for him that he may be worthy to study the Torah and engage in good deeds" (*Sop.* 18:5). But here the disciples are annoyed at a further interruption of their journey, perhaps betraying the generally low esteem in which children were held in antiquity. In a sense it is Jesus' own followers' attitude that threatens to trap him here, even as the Pharisees more consciously had tried to confound him in the previous controversy. Jesus' "little ones" (the disciples) compare unfavorably with real "little ones" (the children).

19:14-15 Jesus rebukes the disciples and uses the children to teach an object lesson about the right way to enter God's kingdom. "Such as these" shows that all children are not automatically saved but rather all those of any age who come to God with a childlike attitude—recognizing their utter dependence on their Heavenly Father (as in 18:3-4). In chap. 18 Jesus was teaching the disciples privately; here he instructs a wider audience. Again he focuses on the present aspect of the kingdom; people enter it as they become his followers. Mention of the "kingdom" further ties this passage back in with the previous one (cf. v. 12). "Do not hinder" (from Greek *mē + kolyō* parallels language found elsewhere in the context of baptism (3:14; cf. Acts 8:36; 10:47; 11:17) and is therefore sometimes seen as justification for infant baptism.[19]

But this interpretation is wholly implausible. Neither water nor babies appear anywhere in this passage, while *mē + kolyō* recur elsewhere in New Testament contexts where there is no possible allusion to baptism (e.g., Luke 6:29; Acts 24:23; 1 Cor 14:39). Jesus does, however, give his blessing before proceeding on his journey. Jesus' special concern for these children suggests that Christians should highly prize their young people. Child evangelism should remain a priority, especially in light of children's particular openness to the gospel. Believers ought to treat their children as special recipients of God's love even prior to their conscious

---

[19]See esp. O. Cullmann, *Baptism in the New Testament* (London: SCM, 1950), 71-80.

commitment to Christ rather than emphasizing their lostness. Ceremonial expressions of the value of our children are also most appropriate, as with infant dedications or with some form of a spoken blessing in conjunction with the distribution of the Lord's Supper, which children should otherwise avoid actually celebrating until making their own professions of faith.[20]

(c) *The Rich Man and Eternal Life (19:16–20:16).* This third consecutive controversy story is structured very much like the first (19:3-12). Jesus begins a dialogue with an "outsider," which culminates in a climactic pronouncement (19:16-22). The disciples raise further questions that Jesus answers (19:23–20:16). In this case, Jesus' reply becomes much lengthier because he includes a parable to illustrate his teaching (20:1-16). The repetition of the refrain of 19:30 in 20:16, and the causal connection ("for") in 20:1 without any pause in Jesus' remarks, shows that 20:1-16 is meant to go with 19:23-30. The contrast between 19:16–20:16 and 19:13-15 emerges plainly. The children turned out to be nearer to the kingdom than most might have suspected; the rich man demonstrates that he is further away than most would have guessed.

16 Now a man came up to Jesus and asked, "Teacher, what good thing must I do to get eternal life?"

17"Why do you ask me about what is good?" Jesus replied. "There is only One who is good. If you want to enter life, obey the commandments."

1) The Controversy (19:16-22). **19:16** Matthew gives few details about this individual. In v. 20 he will tell us that the man is "young" (*neaniskos*, a term that could encompass ages twenty to forty); and in v. 22, that he is rich. Luke calls him a "ruler" (*archōn*—probably a synagogue official—Luke 18:18). Matthew adds the expression "good thing" to clarify that the man was asking about what kind of deeds could earn him eternal life. Along with v. 29, this is the only actual mention of "eternal life" in Matthew. What the rich man calls "eternal life," however, Jesus' calls the "kingdom" (v. 23) and the disciples call being "saved" (v. 25). Rarely do these three terms appear together in the same context in Scripture. In light of the synonyms, eternal life must have both temporal and qualitative aspects to it (cf. Dan 12:2-3). "Teacher," as in 8:19 and 12:38, reflects the inadequate understanding of one who is not a true disciple. Still, there is no indication that this man is trying to trap Jesus. His question may well be genuine, revealing his own sense of some personal inadequacy.

---

[20]For an interdisciplinary symposium on vv. 13-15 and pars., from a variety of newer hermeneutical perspectives, see *Semeia* 29 (1983): *Kingdom and Children.*

19:17 The first part of Jesus' reply proves quite puzzling. Matthew has toned down the awkwardness of Mark 10:18, which seems to have Jesus deny his own goodness, though if Matthew's stress falls on "me," some of this tension remains even here. Jesus apparently is probing the young man to see why he is not satisfied with the obvious Jewish answer to his question, namely, that a person must do the good things that the only good God, Yahweh, has already commanded.[21] Jesus is not admitting his own sinfulness or hinting at his deity. The rich man would have appreciated neither of these points. Rather, he is diverting attention from the young man's inadequate criteria for entering into life and focusing on the standard of divine goodness.[22]

[18]"Which ones?" the man inquired.

Jesus replied, " 'Do not murder, do not commit adultery, do not steal, do not give false testimony, [19]honor your father and mother,' and 'love your neighbor as yourself.' "

19:18-19 The man is not satisfied. Perhaps he knows the rabbinic debates about the weightier matters of the law or about how to sum up the law in a commandment or two. Perhaps he is looking for a loophole to avoid obeying certain less desirable commands. Which ones can save a person? Jesus focuses on the second table of the Decalogue, presenting the Fifth through Ninth Commandments in the order six, seven, eight, nine, five (cf. Exod 20:12-16 and Deut 5:16-20). He appends Lev 19:18, the second half of his own twofold summary of the law, which he will present in 22:37-39. All of these commands focus on external and observable behavior that others can evaluate. The reader wonders if Jesus is setting the man up for the logic of the Sermon on the Mount, if he will teach again how no one can ever truly keep these commandments.

[20]"All these I have kept," the young man said. "What do I still lack?"

[21]Jesus answered, "If you want to be perfect, go, sell your possessions and give to the poor, and you will have treasure in heaven. Then come, follow me."

[22]When the young man heard this, he went away sad, because he had great wealth.

---

[21]On harmonizing the differences between Matthew and Mark, see esp. D. A. Carson, "Redaction Criticism: On the Legitimacy and Illegitimacy of a Literary Tool," in *Scripture and Truth*, ed. D. A. Carson and J. D. Woodbridge (Grand Rapids: Zondervan, 1983), 131-37. For a different approach cf. R. L. Thomas, "The Rich Young Man in Matthew," *GTJ* 3 (1982): 235-60.

[22]A. Plummer, *An Exegetical Commentary on the Gospel according to S. Matthew* (London: E. Stock, 1909), 265.

19:20-22 The young man insists that he has obeyed these laws, but still he senses a lack in his life. Mounce suspects that the man's "uneasiness reveals an instinctive human awareness that legalism falls short of God's intention."[23] Surprisingly, Jesus does not challenge the man's claims though presumably he could have. Jesus does not have to convict this young fellow of overconfidence because he already has admitted to a sense of inadequacy, apparently in some entirely different and yet undisclosed area of his life. Jesus now puts his finger on this area. He gives two commandments and promises two results for obedience to those commands. The young man must sell his possessions and give them to the poor, and then he must follow Jesus in discipleship (v. 21). Together the commands form an invitation literally to "go on the road" with Jesus' itinerant troupe, making a clear break from his former life-style. Almsgiving and discipleship will make the man "perfect" (*teleios*), completely *whole* or *mature* (as in 5:48), and he will receive the promise of eternal life which he requested, described here as "treasure in heaven" (cf. 6:20). Almsgiving was a cardinal virtue in Judaism, but this extreme sacrifice was never commanded. The Babylonian Talmud (*b. Ketub.* 50a) forbade giving up more than 20 percent of one's income, though exceptions did occur in practice (cf. *b. Ta^can* 24a). The two commands to sell all and follow Jesus must be kept together. Giving up all that one possesses, without the love that only a relationship with Jesus can produce, profits nothing (1 Cor 13:3).

The man's response confirms that Jesus has uncovered the facet of this fellow's life that has been haunting him (v. 22). The young man refuses to make such radical financial sacrifice because he has *many possessions* (NIV's "great wealth" is less literal, too exaggerated, and too easily makes most of us think we are poorer than this man). He was, in short, at least in the small middle class of first-century society, which seemed "rich" in the eyes of the vast majority. The man goes away *grieving* (*lypoumenos*; NIV's "sad" is too mild), just as the disciples grieved after Jesus' second passion prediction (17:23). Neither this man nor the Twelve are prepared for Jesus' suffering servanthood and the concomitant self-denial which discipleship demands.

As in the dialogue with the Pharisees on divorce, Jesus tailors his remarks to a specific situation. We may generalize from v. 21 even less than from v. 9, inasmuch as Jesus is addressing just one man in his unique circumstances. In Luke two stories follow closely on the heels of this episode (Luke 18:18-30) that prove Jesus makes different demands of different individuals. Zaccheus gives away only half his income and uses some of the rest to pay back those he had defrauded (Luke 19:1-10). The para-

---

[23]R. H. Mounce, *Matthew*, GNC (San Francisco: Harper and Row, 1985), 186.

ble of the talents encourages God's people not to give money away but to invest it wisely for their Master's use (Luke 19:11-27). But in each of these passages, Jesus commands Christians to use all their possessions, not just some fixed percentage of them, for kingdom priorities. If money stands in the way of a person's committing his or her life to Christ, Jesus will make the identical demands on that individual as he did on this young man. If the obstacle is something else, the demands will vary. But many who have claimed to trust in Christ are still unprepared to serve him with all of their possessions. True Christian stewardship will examine mortgages, credit, giving, insurance, investments, and a whole host of areas of life not often brought under Christ's lordship. Ridderbos's remarks should cause some soul searching: "The man of course did not think that his riches were more than eternal life, but he must have told himself that he did not really have to give up his wealth to gain it."[24] Or, with Gundry, "That Jesus did not command all his followers to sell all their possessions gives comfort only to the kind of people to whom he would issue that command."[25]

[23]**Then Jesus said to his disciples, "I tell you the truth, it is hard for a rich man to enter the kingdom of heaven.** [24]**Again I tell you, it is easier for a camel to go through the eye of a needle than for a rich man to enter the kingdom of God."**

2) The Dialogue with the Disciples (19:23-30). **19:23-24** With a solemn, emphatic introduction ("I tell you the truth"), Jesus laments how hard it is for rich people to surrender to kingdom priorities (v. 23). In his day, as in the early church and as in most parts of our world today, the poor have proved most responsive to the gospel. The well-to-do will more likely think that they don't need Christ or at least not in every area of life. But if he is not "Lord of all," then he is not "Lord at all." Verse 24 restates the prosaic idea of v. 23 in hyperbolic language, perhaps based on a wordplay between the similar-sounding Aramaic words for "camel" (*gamal*) and "acts of benevolence" (*gemiluth*), which rich people ought to be performing.[26] Moreover, the camel was the largest Palestinian animal; the needle's eye, the smallest commonly used opening.[27] The statement may well have been proverbial and recalls the imagery of the narrow door in 7:13-14. There is no solid historical evidence to support the legend that a narrow gate in the Jerusalem wall was called the Needle's Eye, and the

---

[24]H. N. Ridderbos, *Matthew*, BSC (Grand Rapids: Zondervan, 1987), 358.

[25]R. H. Gundry, *Matthew: A Commentary on His Literary and Theological Art* (Grand Rapids: 1982), 388.

[26]J. D. M. Derrett, "A Camel through the Eye of a Needle," *NTS* 32 (1986): 465-70.

[27]Gundry, *Matthew*, 390.

manuscript support for "rope" as a substitute for "needle" is very weak
and very late (59, lectionary 183, and Armenian and Georgian versions).
There is important, incidental evidence in these verses for viewing the
"kingdom of heaven" and the "kingdom of God" as synonymous.

**25When the disciples heard this, they were greatly astonished and asked,
"Who then can be saved?"**
**26Jesus looked at them and said, "With man this is impossible, but with
God all things are possible."**
**27Peter answered him, "We have left everything to follow you! What then
will there be for us?"**

19:25-26 The disciples respond in amazement, perhaps reflecting the
Jewish tradition that equated riches with God's blessing. If those usually
viewed as most blessed by God are so unlikely to make it into the kingdom, who in the world stands a chance (v. 25)? Jesus replies that,
humanly speaking, no one does. But God can and does regenerate hearts,
making it possible to serve him rather than mammon, which is otherwise
everyone's "bottom line" (cf. 6:24).

19:27 Peter now shifts gears. If Jesus' ideals call disciples to abandon
their families and jobs in favor of itinerant ministry, then the Twelve
have proved splendid models. Just what treasure lies in store for them
(v. 27)? Because Jesus does not rebuke Peter, his question may stem more
from confusion than from selfishness. The disciples may think they have
done the right thing but wonder if they too lack something.[28] Still, they
have asked the wrong question. Those who do good because they are
looking for a reward risk forfeiting it (6:1-18; cf. Luke 14:7-14).

**28Jesus said to them, "I tell you the truth, at the renewal of all things,
when the Son of Man sits on his glorious throne, you who have followed me
will also sit on twelve thrones, judging the twelve tribes of Israel. 29And
everyone who has left houses or brothers or sisters or father or mother or
children or fields for my sake will receive a hundred times as much and will
inherit eternal life. 30But many who are first will be last, and many who are
last will be first.**

19:28-30 Jesus nevertheless responds graciously. Verse 28 is Matthew's unique insertion into this dialogue. Christ looks forward to the
"renewal of all things" (*palingenesia*). The word refers to "regeneration"
or "new birth" and was something of a technical term in Stoic thinking (a
prevalent Greco-Roman philosophy of the day) for the dissolution and re-
creation of the cosmos. Here the concept reflects a completely Jewish
background (cf. Isa 65:17; 66:22; and, in the New Testament, 2 Pet 3:10-

---

[28]Cf. Ridderbos, *Matthew*, 360.

13; Rev 21-22).[29] Nothing less than new heavens and a new earth await Christ's followers after he returns in glory. The "Son of Man" imagery here certainly seems to parallel Dan 7:13-14. At that time the disciples will reign with Christ and decisively judge the people of Israel. Both the Twelve and Israel seem respectively to represent believers and lost humanity in general, in light of the broader teaching of 1 Cor 6:2-3 that all Christians will judge the whole world and even angels. So we cannot conclude that the apostles necessarily receive any privilege they do not share with all believers. But the comparison of the Twelve with the twelve tribes of Israel again highlights the theme of the church replacing Israel as the locus of God's saving activity in the new age.

The "hundredfold" compensation (recall 13:8) for everything abandoned, particularly family and home, envisages an eternal family and dwelling place unspeakably more wonderful than anything this earth has to offer (v. 29).[30] But in this future world, many well-to-do, powerful, and influential people, including those from religious circles, like the rich young man of vv. 16-22 and unbelieving Israel of v. 28, will find themselves "last"—judged and excluded from God's presence (v. 30a).[31] On the other hand, all the dispossessed and powerless who have followed Christ will be honored and exalted, especially those who voluntarily adopted or maintained their poverty for the sake of serving Jesus (v. 30b). The sequence of "will receive . . . and will inherit eternal life" (v. 29a) leaves room for what Mark makes explicit—that already now in this age believers have a "hundred times" as many family members and possessions in the body of Christ (Mark 10:30). Here is a graphic picture of what the church should look like (recall under 6:33), especially in sharing material possessions with needy fellow believers. "For my sake" is Matthew's unique addition and again implies a high Christology.

This entire episode should challenge First-World Christians, virtually all of whom are among the wealthiest people in the history of the world, to radical changes in their personal and institutional spending. The solemn warnings of Jas 2:14-17 and 1 John 3:17 demand much more serious

---

[29]On the background and meaning of "new birth" terminology in the NT, see esp. W. D. Mounce, "The Origin of the New Testament Metaphor of Rebirth." Ph.D. diss., Aberdeen University, 1981. Note also the alternative translation, *resurrection*, defended by J. D. M. Derrett, "*Palingenesia* (Matthew 19.28)," *JSNT* 20 (1984): 51-58.

[30]Luke 18:29 includes "wife" as something potentially abandoned. Matthew probably omits this reference to avoid the misconception that divorce for the sake of full-time ministry is permissible.

[31]Bruner (*Churchbook*, 720) likens the "many" of v. 30a to the unfruitful soils in the parable of the sower, the false prophets of 7:22-23, the travelers on the broad road leading to destruction (7:13), and the apostates of 24:5,10-12.

attention, lest many professing Christians tragically find themselves damned on Judgment Day. [32]

3) The Parable of the Vineyard Workers (20:1-16). "Eternal life" in 19:29 has provided some closure with 19:16. Matthew 19:16-30 can thus be seen as a self-contained unit. But 20:1-16 follows without a break to illustrate the principle of 19:30. Jesus' use of a parable to further explicate a dialogue or controversy is characteristic rabbinic practice. This pattern will occur twice again in chaps. 21–23 with parables unique to Matthew (21:28-32; 22:1-14).[33]

¹"For the kingdom of heaven is like a landowner who went out early in the morning to hire men to work in his vineyard. ²He agreed to pay them a denarius for the day and sent them into his vineyard.

³"About the third hour he went out and saw others standing in the marketplace doing nothing. ⁴He told them, 'You also go and work in my vineyard, and I will pay you whatever is right.' ⁵So they went.

"He went out again about the sixth hour and the ninth hour and did the same thing. ⁶About the eleventh hour he went out and found still others standing around. He asked them, 'Why have you been standing here all day long doing nothing?'

⁷'Because no one has hired us,' they answered.

"He said to them, 'You also go and work in my vineyard.'

20:1-7 In vv. 1-2 Jesus pictures harvesttime, during which a farmer will hire a certain number of seasonal workers each day according to his needs. The number of times this man has to look for more workers suggests that the story is not entirely realistic and that Jesus is more interested in communicating spiritual truths. The vineyard often stands for Israel in Jewish thought (see esp. Isa 5:1-7). The denarius was a standard minimum day's wage, so the landowner's promise is entirely fair.

In vv. 3-5a the scene repeats itself three hours into the workday at 9:00 a.m. with others who are "doing nothing." This phrase translates the one word *argos*, which more literally means *without work*. These men are not deliberately avoiding labor (cf. v. 7). With their families they may well go hungry that evening if they do not find work. The marketplace sits at the center of town as the major gathering site for community activities. The employer gives them the same assignment as those he hired at sunup but promises payment merely in terms of what is "right" (*dikaios*—*just* or

---

[32]For an assessment of the significance of the sociological contexts for Jesus' radical claims about material possessions, see D. M. May, "Leaving and Receiving: A Social-Scientific Exegesis of Mark 10:29-31," *PRS* 17 (1990): 141-54.

[33]For a full-length treatment of this parable against its Jewish background, see C. Henser, *Lohnmetaphorik und Arbeitswelt in Mt 20, 1-16* (Freiburg: Universitätsverlag; Göttingen: Vandenhoeck und Ruprecht, 1990).

fair). They would have expected the appropriate fractional percentage of a day's wage, but the farmer never specifies his commitment.

Verses 5b-7 describe how the farmer goes out again at noon and 3:00 p.m., the remaining major divisions of the ancient workday. The employer apparently makes the same vague promise of a fair wage. The workers no doubt have the same expectations as their predecessors. With only one hour of the working day left, at 5:00 p.m. the farmer hires yet one more group of workers. Because Jesus will center attention on this group when the master begins to pay his workers, he stops abbreviating the story here and draws out the dialogue in more detail.

8 "When evening came, the owner of the vineyard said to his foreman, 'Call the workers and pay them their wages, beginning with the last ones hired and going on to the first.'

9 "The workers who were hired about the eleventh hour came and each received a denarius. 10 So when those came who were hired first, they expected to receive more. But each one of them also received a denarius. 11 When they received it, they began to grumble against the landowner. 12 'These men who were hired last worked only one hour,' they said, 'and you have made them equal to us who have borne the burden of the work and the heat of the day.'

20:8-12 Here begins the second major episode of the parable. As the workday ends, the master is no longer hiring but paying. He begins with those last hired in order to send strong shock waves among the rest when they learn of the going wage. This story scarcely models good management-labor practices but does disclose profound truths about the nature of God.[34] The first group of workers is stunned as they receive twelve times what they expected. The other workers naturally begin to anticipate similar increases and, in fact, all but the very first group hired do get more than they expected. But the longer a particular group worked, the smaller the percentage increase they receive, and the first group gets no "bonus" at all. "Those hired first" probably includes all of those hired earlier than 5:00 p.m., but those who worked all twelve hours will air the loudest complaints (v. 12). All but the last group hired protest the man's egalitarianism, as most of us would too. Little seems more unequal than the equal treatment of unequals! The workers' "grumbling" echoes the common complaint of Israel against God in Moses' day (e.g., Exod 16:7-12; Num 14:27; Deut 1:27).

13 "But he answered one of them, 'Friend, I am not being unfair to you. Didn't you agree to work for a denarius? 14 Take your pay and go. I want to give the man who was hired last the same as I gave you. 15 Don't I have the

---

[34] R. H. Stein, *An Introduction to the Parables of Jesus* (Philadelphia: Westminster, 1981), 126.

right to do what I want with my own money? Or are you envious because I am generous?'

   [16] **"So the last will be first, and the first will be last."**

   20:13-16 The three main points associated with the three main characters or groups of characters are now stated *ad seriatim*.[35] First, vv. 13-14a focus on the earlier groups of workers and demonstrate God's fairness or justice with all his people. *Hetaire* ("friend") in v. 13 is a distancing form of address and suggests a mild reproach (cf. 22:12; 26:50). *Ouk adikō* ("I am not being unfair") echoes *ho ean ē dikaios* ("whatever is right") in v. 4. The master reminds his workers of the agreement they made and of his full compliance with that agreement. Second, vv. 14b-15 focus attention on the last group of workers as recipients of God's marvelous grace. If God treats no one unfairly, he also deals with many far more leniently than they deserve. God alone in his sovereignty freely chooses whom he will favor and in what ways. "My own money" is better translated *my things*. "Are you envious because I am generous?" is more literally rendered, *Is your eye evil because I am good?* The "evil eye" was often viewed as a diabolical look that could cast a wicked spell on a person. For related thoughts see 6:23. Third, v. 16 underlines God's ultimate perspective—all true disciples are equal in his eyes. That "the last will be first, and the first will be last" ties the parable back in with 19:30. There the "first" were believers; the "last," unbelievers. Here both "first" and "last" are believers. The terms do not imply unequal reward but reflect the order of payment. But if all are treated equally, then all numerical positions of ranking are interchangeable, and v. 30 applies at the spiritual level too.

   Applications of this parable abound. In its original historical setting, the latecomers to the kingdom were the "tax collectors and sinners." In the larger sweep of salvation history, one may think of Gentiles hearing God's word later than Jews, of people coming to faith during different periods of church history or at different ages in life, of Christians with varying degrees of commitment and faithfulness, and the like. The significance of this parable can scarcely be overestimated. Luke 12:47-48 teaches that there are degrees of punishment in hell; Matt 20:1-16, that there are no degrees of reward in heaven. Neither of these facts is commonly known or understood in Christian circles. To be sure, every individual will have a highly unique experience before God on Judgment Day (see esp. 1 Cor 3:10-15). But no text of Scripture supports the notion that these differences

---

   [35]Cf. C. L. Blomberg, *Interpreting the Parables* (Downers Grove: InterVarsity, 1990), 224-25; A. Sand, *Das Evangelium nach Matthäus*, RNT (Regensburg: Pustet, 1986), 402. R. T. France (*The Gospel according to Matthew*, TNTC [Grand Rapids: Eerdmans, 1985], 289) succinctly captures all of these points: "[God's] generosity transcends human ideas of fairness. No one receives less than they deserve, but some receive far more."

are perpetuated throughout eternity. The very nature of grace and perfection preclude such a concept.[36] The reason we object to equal treatment for all is precisely the objection of the workers in this parable—it doesn't seem fair. But we are fools if we appeal to God for justice rather than grace, for in that case we'd all be damned. Nor will it do to speak of salvation begun by grace but ever after preserved by works. True salvation will of necessity produce good works and submission to Christ's lordship in every area of life, or else it never was salvation to begin with. But all who are truly saved are equally precious in God's sight and equally rewarded with eternal happiness in the company of Christ and all the redeemed. Jesus has now finished his answer to Peter's question of 19:27.

The three controversy stories that unite 19:1–20:16 have come to an end. *Ouk exestin* ("Don't I have the right?") in 20:15 forms an *inclusio* with *ei exestin* ("Is it lawful?") in 19:3. The section that began with questions about what God requires humans to do closes, ironically, with illustrations of what humans try to require God to do. The subsection (19:16–20:16) that began with questions about the least believers need to do closes, encouragingly, with illustrations of the most God will do.

(2) Further Focus on Jesus' Passion, with Contrasting Responses from His Audience (20:17-34). Matthew's section describing Jesus on the road to Jerusalem (19:1–20:34) comes to a close with the healing of two blind men (20:29-34). This healing creates closure with the reference to healing in 19:2. In between we have read exclusively about Jesus' teaching. Matthew 20:17-34, if indeed it is a unified subsection, is loosely structured, but it does seem to be organized by combining Jesus' third passion prediction (vv. 17-19) with contrasting responses to his prediction of suffering. Ironically, even en route to the cross two key disciples, together with their mother, still demand privileges Jesus cannot grant (vv. 20-28). More properly, two blind men beg only for mercy, which Jesus does bestow (vv. 29-34).

[17]Now as Jesus was going up to Jerusalem, he took the twelve disciples aside and said to them, [18]"We are going up to Jerusalem, and the Son of Man will be betrayed to the chief priests and the teachers of the law. They will condemn him to death [19]and will turn him over to the Gentiles to be mocked and flogged and crucified. On the third day he will be raised to life!"

[36]See further C. L. Blomberg, "Degrees of Reward in the Kingdom of Heaven?" forthcoming in *JETS*. Cf. M. Green (*Matthew for Today* [Dallas: Word, 1989], 190-91): "There are no rankings in the Kingdom of God. Nobody can claim deserved membership of the Kingdom. There is no place for personal pride, for contempt or jealousy of others. There is no ground for any to question how this generous God handles the utterly undeserving." For a historical survey of the Reformers' views on this doctrine, held in some part as the remnant of Roman Catholic views on purgatory, see E. Disley, "Degrees of Glory: Protestant Doctrines and the Concept of Rewards Hereafter," *JTS* 42 (1991): 77-105.

(a) Third Passion Prediction (20:17-19). **20:17-19** Jesus appropriately introduces this further announcement of his coming fate by reminding his disciples of their destination. They are going "up" because Jerusalem is situated on Mt. Zion. As with the previous predictions, he reserves his words for the Twelve, which Matthew stresses by adding the phrase *kat' idian (privately;* "aside"). The details closely resemble those of 16:21 and 17:22-23. New information in this prediction includes the specific references to the Gentiles and to the nature of Jesus' torment and execution— mocking, flogging, and crucifixion. Matthew will narrate the fulfillment of these prophecies in 27:27-50. The details match standard Roman procedures, since the empire did not permit Jews to execute their own criminals (John 18:31). For further discussion on the nature of crucifixion, see the commentary on chap. 27. The exalted Son of Man must first become God's Suffering Servant. Few, including the Twelve, are yet ready for this. Worse still, immediately after this prediction of Jesus' suffering his disciples will still be arguing about status and glory.

²⁰**Then the mother of Zebedee's sons came to Jesus with her sons and, kneeling down, asked a favor of him.**

²¹**"What is it you want?" he asked.**

She said, "Grant that one of these two sons of mine may sit at your right and the other at your left in your kingdom."

²²**"You don't know what you are asking," Jesus said to them. "Can you drink the cup I am going to drink?"**

"We can," they answered.

²³**Jesus said to them, "You will indeed drink from my cup, but to sit at my right or left is not for me to grant. These places belong to those for whom they have been prepared by my Father."**

(b) An Inappropriate Response: James and John Seek Status (20:20-28).[37] **20:20-23** In v. 20 Matthew tells how James and John's mother comes to Jesus. Mark mentions only the two brothers (Mark 10:35). Matthew would not likely have introduced their mother into the story if she in fact had not approached Jesus with this request, but even Matthew's account suggests that her sons put her up to it, since Jesus shifts his address from the mother in v. 21 to the sons in v. 22 ("You don't know what you are asking" uses second-person plural pronouns). The pathos of a mother's plea would presumably tug at Jesus' heartstrings all the more, but Mark may legitimately speak of the request as coming from the sons. In v. 21 the mother[38] picks up on the promise of 19:28 and asks for her sons to occupy

---

[37]Luke has a fairly close parallel in 22:24-27 in a different context. This may well be a separate dialogue altogether. If it is not, it is most likely Luke who has relocated it for thematic purposes.

[38]Probably Salome (cf. 27:55-56 with Mark 15:40) and perhaps the sister of Mary, Jesus' mother (John 19:25).

the two highest positions of privilege in Jesus' kingdom. Although she has been traveling on the road with the Twelve and the crowds (cf. 27:55-56), Matthew gives no indication that she was party to the earlier conversation between Jesus and the disciples, so here is further evidence that her sons had to have informed her and were in on the request.

In v. 22 Jesus tells mother and sons that they do not yet understand the nature of his kingdom. He redirects their attention to his coming suffering. "Cup" was a common Old Testament metaphor for suffering, especially that caused by God's wrath (e.g., Ps 75:8; Isa 51:17). Jesus asks if John and James are prepared to experience rejection and persecution for their faith. They may not literally die for their discipleship (James did— Acts 12.2, reasonably strong church tradition suggests that John did not[39]), and they will not experience God's wrath (only Jesus could atone for the world's sins), but they can expect to encounter a variety of hostilities in response to their Christian testimony (recall 10:16-25). Their affirmative reply, that they can "drink the cup," simply shows that they still do not understand (v. 22b). Jesus assures them that they will indeed suffer but that he does not have the authority to grant their request (v. 23). During his incarnation, the Son of God remained functionally subordinate to the Father, despite their equality in essence.[40] All authority will be delegated to Christ after his resurrection (28:18), but for now Jesus has voluntarily relinquished some of that authority (Phil 2:6-8). Jesus' wording leaves open the question of whether or not certain apostles or Christians will have some kind of privileged position within his future rule. Yet it is hard to imagine any hierarchy in light of 20:1-16. Jesus' point may well be that God has chosen no particular individuals for such roles.

24When the ten heard about this, they were indignant with the two brothers. 25Jesus called them together and said, "You know that the rulers of the Gentiles lord it over them, and their high officials exercise authority over them. 26Not so with you. Instead, whoever wants to become great among you must be your servant, 27and whoever wants to be first must be your slave— 28just as the Son of Man did not come to be served, but to serve, and to give his life as a ransom for many."

20:24-28   The other ten disciples react more out of jealousy than out of genuine concern for John and James (v. 24). Hence Jesus has to address the whole group on the concept of servant leadership. In the non-Jewish world, as the Jews became painfully aware under Roman occupation, rule by domination and authoritarianism prevailed (v. 25). Sadly, much of the

---

[39]For a concise survey of the disparate traditions, see D. Guthrie, *New Testament Introduction*, rev. ed. (Downers Grove: InterVarsity, 1990), 269-75.

[40]Cf. esp. C. K. Barrett, "'The Father Is Greater Than I' (Jo. 14,28): Subordinationist Christology in the New Testament," in *Neues Testament und Kirche*, ed. J. Gnilka (Freiburg: Herder, 1974), 140-59.

Jewish world operated in the same way, in its own sphere of influence, but Jesus does not focus on this here. Jesus' followers are to behave in diametrically opposite fashion. Would-be leaders must become "servants" or "slaves" (vv. 26-27). They are exempt from no menial task and lead by example rather than by dictum. Jesus' entire thrust is on enabling and empowering others rather than wielding power for oneself.[41] "Wanting to be first" harks back to the request of v. 21 and to the refrain of 19:30 and 20:16. Since Jesus here compares disciples with other disciples, as in 20:16, and since he parallels "first" in v. 27 with "great" in v. 26 (rather than "greatest"), Jesus probably has mere (!) exaltation in view, not gradations within eternal life.

Jesus himself provides the perfect example of servant leadership (v. 28a; cf. esp. John 13:1-17). Few models are more desperately needed in an age of celebrity Christianity, high-tech evangelism and worship, and widespread abuses of ecclesiastical power for self-aggrandizement or, more insidiously, in the name of "attracting" more people to the gospel— a "gospel" that is thereby badly truncated. D. A. Carson observes: "One of the ironies of language is that a word like 'minister,' which in its roots refers to a helper, one who 'ministers,' has become a badge of honor and power in religion and politics."[42]

Verse 28b alludes to Jesus' impending substitutionary and atoning death. This half verse preserves perhaps the most crucial teaching of Jesus about his self-understanding and conception of his mission, especially since a strong case can be made for the authenticity of this saying even using critical criteria.[43] The word "ransom" (*lytron*) would make a first-century audience think of the price paid to buy a slave's freedom. "Life" is the more correct translation here for *psychē*, which in other contexts sometimes means *soul*. Though it has been disputed, *anti* ("for") means *instead of* or *in the place of.*[44] "Many" refers to all who accept Jesus' offer of forgiveness, made possible by his death, and who commit their lives to him in discipleship. Verse 28 as a whole probably reflects the language of Exod 30:12; Ps 49:7-9, and, most significantly, the suffering servant song of Isa 53:10-12. Jesus declares that he will die and thereby pay the penalty for our sins that we deserved to pay.[45]

---

[41]For a practical study of Christian leadership reflecting these principles, see J. E. Means, *Leadership in Christian Ministry* (Grand Rapids: Baker, 1989).

[42]Carson, "Matthew," 432.

[43]See S. H. T. Page, "The Authenticity of the Ransom Logion (Mark 10:45b)," in *Gospel Perspectives*, vol. 1, ed. R. T. France and D. Wenham (Sheffield: JSOT, 1980): 137-61.

[44]See L. Morris, *The Apostolic Preaching of the Cross* (London: Tyndale, 1955), 26-35.

[45]Cf. further J. R. W. Stott, *The Cross of Christ* (Downers Grove: InterVarsity, 1986); L. Morris, *The Atonement* (Downers Grove: InterVarsity, 1983); M. Hengel, *The Atonement* (London: SCM, 1981).

²⁹As Jesus and his disciples were leaving Jericho, a large crowd followed him. ³⁰Two blind men were sitting by the roadside, and when they heard that Jesus was going by, they shouted, "Lord, Son of David, have mercy on us!"
³¹The crowd rebuked them and told them to be quiet, but they shouted all the louder, "Lord, Son of David, have mercy on us!"

(c) An Appropriate Response: Two Blind Men Seek Mercy (20:29-34) **20:29-31** This passage contrasts sharply with the previous one. For the first time, Matthew specifies where Jesus is on his journey (Jericho), probably to show how near he is to Jerusalem. Jericho lay near the west bank of the Jordan about fifteen miles northeast of the capital city. If the crowds had followed the road through Perea (see under 19:1-2), this is where they would arrive when they crossed back over into Judea.[46] The holy city, where Jesus will meet his death, looms ominously close.

This episode closely resembles 9:27-31, but only a handful of words are exactly parallel. Surely Jesus encountered blind people more than once, and it would be natural for Matthew to tell the story of similar events with similar and even stereotyped language. Nor would it be unusual to find blind men in pairs; they would commonly have sought companionship among others like themselves. But Matthew, as the only Evangelist to refer to both men, may include this notice more to highlight his theme about the testimony of two or three witnesses (Deut 19:15; see further under 9:27-31). As before, the blind men address Jesus as the "Son of David" and plead for mercy. Mark supplies the name of one of the men—Bartimaeus (Mark 10:46).

Verse 31 provides more detail than 9:27. Matthew notes that the crowd rebukes the blind men, much as the disciples rebuked the crowd in 19:13. Perhaps they feel it is inappropriate to interrupt the Son of David this close to Jerusalem. Caring for the handicapped will distract from his "triumphal entry" into the city. Their perspective on power unwittingly parallels the attitude of the sons and wife of Zebedee.[47] But as with Jesus' injunctions to silence regarding his identity (most notably in 9:31) the rebuke simply provokes the men to greater outbursts.

³²Jesus stopped and called them. "What do you want me to do for you?" he asked.
³³"Lord," they answered, "we want our sight."

---

[46]Matthew abbreviates Mark 10:46 by omitting half of Mark's awkward construction. Luke abbreviates by omitting the other half (Luke 18:35). There is no contradiction among the texts nor any need to speak of different sites for Jericho. See further C. L. Blomberg, *The Historical Reliability of the Gospels* (Downers Grove: InterVarsity, 1987), 128-30.
[47]D. Patte, *The Gospel according to Matthew: A Structural Commentary* (Philadelphia: Fortress, 1987), 285.

³⁴**Jesus had compassion on them and touched their eyes. Immediately they received their sight and followed him.**

20:32-34   It is not clear if this is the first time Jesus has heard the blind men's cries or if he has deliberately waited in responding to them. His question tries to draw them out (v. 32), much as he did with James and John's mother in v. 21. Again we sense that Matthew is deliberately comparing and contrasting vv. 20-28 and 29-34. This request proves quite legitimate. The blind men have undoubtedly heard of Jesus' reputation and would dearly love their sight restored (v. 33). Jesus heeds their cries with his characteristic compassion (cf. 9:36; 14:14; 15:32), a uniquely Matthean insertion into this narrative. As typically elsewhere, his healing takes effect at once and leads to some measure of discipleship on the part of the ones cured (v. 34). The two men join the great throngs described in v. 29. Jesus allows them to continue just like those he has more formally called.[48] Matthew 19:1–20:34 has now concluded the way it began—with Jesus on the road, surrounded by great crowds and healing people (cf. 19:2). Matthew is building up to the climactic entry of Jesus into Jerusalem with which chap. 21 begins. Jesus seems to have a great host of followers and admirers, but they will soon turn fickle and abandon him.

   b. JUDGMENT ON THE TEMPLE IN JERUSALEM (21:1–22:46)   Jesus and his entourage arrive at the city which is both his destination and his destiny. All action in these two chapters focuses on the temple in Jerusalem. As they enter the holy city from the Jericho road, they would go through the eastern gate and immediately find themselves confronted by the temple precincts, which in that day comprised approximately a thirteen-acre complex of courts and buildings encompassing about one quarter of the entire walled-in portion of Jerusalem (21:1-11).[49] These were the gates Jewish tradition said the Messiah would enter (based on his arrival at the Mount of Olives—Zech 14:4). Also as anticipated, Jesus goes to the temple to purify it (Mal 3–4), though this takes a quite unexpected form (21:12-17). Although he lodges just outside the city in neighboring Bethany, the only event that occurs outside the temple is the object lesson of the imminent judgment upon that building (21:18-22). The first subsection of chaps. 21–22 is thus united by Jesus' *actions* of judgment of the temple (21:1-22). The second subsection presents his *teachings* in the temple in response to a series of traps laid for him by various Jewish questioners (21:23-45). These controversy stories also focus on judgment against those rejecting him: the chief priests and elders, who ask about

---

[48]On this passage as a "call story," see M. G. Steinhauser, "The Form of the Bartimaeus Narrative (Mark 10:46-52)," *NTS* 32 (1986): 583-95.

[49]For a brief description of the sources, construction, design, and significance of this temple and its predecessors, see S. Westerholm, "Temple," *ISBE*, 4:759-76.

his authority (21:21–22:14); the Pharisees, who inquire about taxes (22:15-22); the Sadducees, concerning the resurrection (22:23-33); and the lawyer, on the greatest commandment (22:34-40). Finally, Jesus turns tables on his interrogators and asks them about the identity of the Messiah (22:41-46).[50] In their inability to answer, they judge themselves.

(1) Actions of Judgment (21:1-22). (a) Entrance into Jerusalem (21:1-11). This account is misnamed the "triumphal" entry. Jesus does appear to be at the zenith of his popularity, even acknowledged as the Messiah, but the crowd shows no appreciation for the suffering and death to which he must soon submit himself. Only five days later, some of these people will clamor for his crucifixion, even if the crowd then is not entirely composed of the same individuals as here. (Probably there will be more Judeans and native Jerusalemites present then than in this procession of mainly Galilean pilgrims just arriving in town for the Passover festival.)

¹As they approached Jerusalem and came to Bethphage on the Mount of Olives, Jesus sent two disciples, ²saying to them, "Go to the village ahead of you, and at once you will find a donkey tied there, with her colt by her. Untie them and bring them to me. ³If anyone says anything to you, tell him that the Lord needs them, and he will send them right away."

21:1-3 Bethphage (v. 1) and Bethany (v. 17) were two small villages just to the east of Jerusalem on or near the slopes of the large hill, known as the Mount of Olives, which dominated the skyline of that side of town. Matthew includes the place names to remind his readers how near Jesus is to Jerusalem and perhaps also to evoke the messianic associations of the Mount of Olives (Zech 14:4; see further under 24:3). Jesus is consciously making preparations to enter Jerusalem after the fashion of Zech 9:9, with echoes of Isa 62:11. Zechariah's prophecy was widely interpreted in rabbinic literature as messianic (e.g., *Gen. Rab.* 98.9; *b. Sanh* 98a, 99a; *Qoh. Rab.* 1.9). As again later with their preparation for the Passover (26:18), it is not clear whether the disciples' rendezvous stems from Jesus' prior arrangements or from his supernatural insight. "The Lord" is, more literally, *their Lord/Master* and also suggests a double entendre. The disciples will act as if they are servants of the donkey's owner. If anyone becomes suspicious of their behavior, their reply need mean nothing more than that the owner has asked them to bring him the animals. But Matthew

---

[50]See J. W. Doeve, "Purification du temple et desséchement du figuier," *NTS* 1 (1954-55): 297-308, for the provocative suggestion that these chapters are structured via scriptural allusions to Ps 118:25-26; Jer 7:11,20,25-26; and Ps 118:22-23. R. E. Winkle ("The Jeremiah Model for Jesus in the Temple," *AUSS* 24 [1986]: 155-72) sees even more references supporting Jesus as following the model of Jeremiah throughout his temple ministry.

undoubtedly sees Jesus as the true Master, not only of the donkeys but of all people's property, which he can rightfully demand at any time.

> **⁴This took place to fulfill what was spoken through the prophet:**
> **⁵"Say to the Daughter of Zion,**
> **'See, your king comes to you,**
> **gentle and riding on a donkey,**
> **on a colt, the foal of a donkey.'"**

21:4-5 Matthew follows his favorite practice of inserting fulfillment citations, though a partial parallel occurs in John 12:14-15 as well. Only Matthew mentions two animals. He is often accused of misinterpreting what in the Old Testament was intended to be synonymous parallelism. But irrespective of the correct reading of Zech 9:9,[51] it would be natural for the mother to come along if her colt had never previously been ridden (Mark 11:2).[52] Verse 5 can easily be taken as implying that Jesus rode only on the young donkey, appropriate symbolism for his purity and holiness. "Daughter of Zion" refers to the people of Jerusalem. The "king" will be the Messiah. But an unarmed, plainly clad civilian riding a donkey contrasts sharply with an armed soldier astride a war horse. This Messiah comes in humility, gentleness, and peace. The crowds recognize the messianic implications but seem not to grasp the full significance of the donkey. The fulfillment quotation generally follows the wording of the LXX but omits the lines "Shout, daughter of Jerusalem" (unnecessary repetition) and "righteous and having salvation" (probably because Jerusalem was not now being saved but judged; salvation will come much later).[53]

> **⁶The disciples went and did as Jesus had instructed them. ⁷They brought the donkey and the colt, placed their cloaks on them, and Jesus sat on them. ⁸A very large crowd spread their cloaks on the road, while others cut branches from the trees and spread them on the road. ⁹The crowds that went ahead of him and those that followed shouted,**
> **"Hosanna to the Son of David!"**
> **"Blessed is he who comes in the name of the Lord!"**
> **"Hosanna in the highest!"**

21:6-9 The plan goes off without a hitch as the two disciples do as they have been told. They place their cloaks on the animals while the crowd paves the road with theirs, adding tree branches to their festive car-

---

[51]On the possibility of at least two interpretive traditions arising out of the Zechariah text, see R. Bartnicki, "Das Zitat von Zach IX, 9-10 und die Tiere im Bericht von Matthäus über dem Einzug Jesu in Jerusalem (Mt XXI, 1-11)," *NovT* 18 (1976): 161-66.

[52]Gundry, *Matthew*, 409; Green, *Matthew*, 200.

[53]L. Sabourin, *L'Évangile selon saint Matthieu et ses principaux parallèles* (Rome: Biblical Institute Press, 1978), 269.

pet. John 12:13 refers specifically to palm branches appropriate for a trip from Jericho, "the City of Palms." John 12:1,12 also enables one to identify this as the Sunday before the Friday Passover on which Jesus will be crucified, hence, the liturgical tradition of referring to this day as Palm Sunday. The whole picture conveys celebration and honor, reminiscent of the victory parades with which triumphant kings and generals in Old Testament and intertestamental times were welcomed (cf. 2 Kgs 9:13; 1 Macc 13:51). The strewing of garments and branches further demonstrates how the crowds have the wrong messianic concept. There will be no victory party when they arrive in Jerusalem. The second "them" in v. 7 has as its nearest antecedent in Greek the "cloaks," of which probably more than one were put on each donkey, so there is little or no justification here for the common accusation that Matthew has created an absurd picture of Jesus straddling two animals.

The crowds acclaim Jesus as Messiah with regal, Davidic terminology. "Son of David" also echoes the blind men's cry in 20:30. "Hosanna" originally meant *God save us* but by the first century was probably just a cry of praise to Yahweh. The "He who comes in the name of the Lord," like the "coming one" of whom John the Baptist spoke (recall under 3:11), refers to the Messiah, and the entire beatitude echoes Ps 118:26. On "hosanna in the highest," see also Ps 148:1.

¹⁰When Jesus entered Jerusalem, the whole city was stirred and asked, "Who is this?"
¹¹The crowds answered, "This is Jesus, the prophet from Nazareth in Galilee."

21:10-11 The whole procession has a powerful impact on the inhabitants of Jerusalem, even though they are used to huge crowds of festival pilgrims. "Stirred" is rather mild for *eseisthē* (used of earthquakes and apocalyptic upheavals; 27:51; Rev 6:13). The NEB's "wild with excitement" and Weymouth's "was thrown into commotion" both capture the sense better. "Who is this?" does not imply that the people have never seen Jesus before or do not know his name, though many in town from outside of Israel may not have encountered him previously. But Matthew is more interested in raising the Christological question again. The predominantly Galilean crowd replies truthfully but inadequately. On Jesus as a "prophet," cf. 13:57 and 16:14; as from obscure Nazareth, cf. 2:23. The crowd betrays no knowledge of Jesus' kingly birthplace in Bethlehem (2:5-6). Nevertheless, their fervor temporarily deters the authorities, who would otherwise have arrested him at once (v. 46). Verses 10b-11 are unique to Matthew. Verse 10b may hark back to 2:3 as an indictment of most in the city (*pasa*, often translated "all," here means *the whole* rather than every single inhabitant). Verse 11 furthers Matthew's heightened interest in Christology.

(b) Judgment on the Temple by Purification (21:12-17).[54]   Mark
notes that a night intervenes before this next event (Mark 11:11-12), but
Matthew characteristically abbreviates his narrative and omits this notice.
Jesus' whole purpose in entering Jerusalem is to go to the temple, so Mat-
thew takes his readers straight there. The scene depicted fulfills Mal 3:1b.
The Lord is suddenly coming to his temple.

**[12]Jesus entered the temple area and drove out all who were buying and
selling there. He overturned the tables of the money changers and the
benches of those selling doves. [13] "It is written," he said to them, "'My house
will be called a house of prayer,' but you are making it a 'den of robbers.'"**

21:12-13   Who could have expected this sight? The Messiah, having
been led in apparent triumph into the city, enters the temple, arousing
expectations of pro-Jewish, nationalist action against Rome. Instead, his
attack threatens the sacrificial, worship center of Judaism itself. Jesus
begins to wreak havoc with the tables and chairs set up for changing various regional currencies into the proper shekels needed to pay the temple
tax or purchase animals for sacrifice. These stalls were probably set up at
least three weeks before Passover to prepare for the throngs.[55] (For the
various customs and regulations, cf. the Mishnaic tractate *Seqalim.*) The
poor who couldn't afford to buy sheep to sacrifice could substitute doves
in their place (Lev 5:7). The Mishnaic document *M. Ker.* 1:7 gives evidence, at least from a later date, that extortionary prices for doves exacer-
bated the plight of the poor.

The rationale for Jesus' seemingly bizarre behavior is in fact scriptural.
As he clears the area of those engaged in these various commercial transactions, Jesus begins to fulfill the prophecy that a day would come when
no "merchant" would remain in the house of the Lord (Zech 14:21, NIV
marg.). Then he explicitly quotes portions of Isa 56:7 and Jer 7:11
(recorded here verbatim from the LXX). As it stands, what was intended
to be a "house of prayer" (Mark 11:17 includes the phrase "for all the
nations")—namely the court of the Gentiles—is so filled with commotion
that neither Jew nor Gentile can easily pray here. "Den of robbers" does
not necessarily mean that all the merchants sold their goods at inflated
prices, but it does suggest at least that Jesus considered many of them
generally corrupt. And if "robbers" (*lēstai*) is given the meaning it most

---

[54]W. W. Watty ("Jesus and the Temple—Cleansing or Cursing?" *ExpTim* 93 [1981-82]:
235-39) rejects entitling this passage the temple "cleansing" and sees it rather as a prefigure-
ment of destruction. One may agree with what Watty affirms while retaining the term "purification," following the prophecy of Mal 3:3. Cf. Carson ("Matthew," 442), who notes that
"the purification would entail destruction and building a new temple (John 2:19-22)."

[55]S. T. Lachs, *A Rabbinic Commentary on the New Testament: The Gospels of Matthew,
Mark, and Luke* (Hoboken, N.J.: KTAV, 1987), 347.

probably has in 26:55 and 27:38,44 (*insurrectionist*), then Jesus may be accusing the leaders of having converted the temple into a "nationalist stronghold."

But Jesus' challenge runs deeper than merely lamenting the replacement of worship with nationalism or decrying unjust business practices. The Jewish scholar, J. Neusner, rightly recognizes that Jesus is in fact threatening the whole sacrificial system.[56] He may well have still held out the possibility of repentance within the Jewish system, even at this late date. But with his crucifixion near and already knowing that most of the leadership would reject his reforms, for all intents and purposes he does here dramatize God's imminent judgment on the temple and nation.[57] In his next object lesson, he will predict this impending demise even more graphically.

[14]The blind and the lame came to him at the temple, and he healed them. [15]But when the chief priests and the teachers of the law saw the wonderful things he did and the children shouting in the temple area, "Hosanna to the Son of David," they were indignant.

[16]"Do you hear what these children are saying?" they asked him.

"Yes," replied Jesus, "have you never read,

"'From the lips of children and infants
you have ordained praise'?"

[17]And he left them and went out of the city to Bethany, where he spent the night.

21:14-17 Except for the concluding sentence, these verses are unique to Matthew and fit his emphases on Jesus' healings and his rejection by the officials. Verse 14 describes an appropriate ministry for God's house, in striking contrast to the commercial system Christ has just condemned. Matthew could easily have quoted Hosea 6:6 again; Jesus illustrates the priority of mercy over sacrifice. He also rejects the laws that seem to have prevented such ritually impure people from being in the temple (based on 2 Sam 5:8; cf. *m. Hag.* 1:1; 1QSa 2:5-22). As in 19:13-15, children prove surprisingly good models as over against the religious leaders who should have understood but remain indignant. Their question for Jesus implies that he should rebuke the children for echoing the crowd's earlier words of praise to him (v. 9), a kind of acclamation the leaders find inappropriate. Jesus' response, again using the introductory rebuke "Have you never

---

[56]J. Neusner, "Money-Changers in the Temple: The Mishnah's Explanation," *NTS* 35 (1989): 287-90.

[57]Both M. D. Hooker ("Traditions about the Temple in the Sayings of Jesus," *BJRL* 70 [1988]: 7-19) and C. A. Evans ("Jesus' Action in the Temple: Cleansing or Portent of Destruction?" *CBQ* 51 [1989]: 237-70) argue, more cautiously, that Jesus intended to cleanse or reform but that after his failure it was a logical step for the Evangelists to interpret Jesus' action as symbolizing impending destruction.

read?" tacitly applauds their acclamation in light of Ps 8:2 (LXX 8:3, which is quoted verbatim). There the children are praising Yahweh, so Jesus again accepts worship that is reserved for God alone.[58] Truly, one greater than the temple is here (12:6). Jesus then leaves the city to spend Monday evening in Bethany. Presumably he is still lodging with Mary, Martha, and Lazarus, as in John 12:1.

This whole episode, combining cleansing and condemnation of the temple, proves more significant than is usually recognized. Even radical scholars often accept it as among the most authentic in the Gospels.[59] It provides the final impetus for Jesus' crucifixion (Mark 11:18). It offers an example of Jesus' genuinely human but sinless anger expressed in righteous indignation against the profaning of that which is holy. We usually get angry when our rights are infringed, and it is difficult to be righteous in indignant self-defense. But, like many of the Old Testament prophets, Jesus provides a good paradigm for speaking out publicly about God's indignation against the flagrant defiance of his standards in the world. Once again it is the "clergy" and the "Bible teachers," not the disreputable people of society, who are Jesus' target for attack. Corruption among the leadership of God's people arouses Jesus' wrath more quickly than anything else. But Christ does more than denounce injustice—he takes action against it. That the temple merchants quickly resumed business as usual is often speculated, but we are not told one way or the other. The point is that Jesus did what was right, irrespective of the duration of its effect.

Contemporary application becomes even more urgent in view of the nature of the religious corruption in this passage—financial profit at the expense of the disenfranchised of society. How many millions of dollars are poured annually into our church buildings and activities and thereby taken away from the poorest and neediest of our world? Instead of always embarking on costly building campaigns, many churches need to consider planting new congregations, meeting in alternate sites, adding additional times of worship, and transferring active members to dying churches to infuse new life in them.

An intriguing parallel to this episode appears in John 2:13-17. The evidence for and against this being the same event transposed to a new context in John is finely balanced.[60] But if the two accounts represent separate events, they form an interesting frame around Jesus' ministry and

---

[58]*Babes and sucklings* ("children and infants") could be old enough to speak, in light of ancient customs of nursing mothers. See R. Alden, *Psalms: Songs of Devotion*, EvBC, vol. 1 (Chicago: Moody, 1974), 25.

[59]See esp. E. P. Sanders, *Jesus and Judaism* (Philadelphia: Fortress, 1985), 61-76; cf. V. Eppstein, "The Historicity of the Gospel Account of the Cleansing of the Temple," *ZNW* 55 (1964): 42-58.

[60]Blomberg, *Historical Reliability*, 170-73.

underline even more the importance of his desire to purify his countrymen's worship. And, as John makes more explicit (John 2:16), the problem of replacing worship with commerce remained a crucial threat to the life of God's people. Even in Matthew, Jesus attacks the "buyers" as well as the "sellers," so that it is not just the merchants' corruption that upsets him.[61] Compare our contemporary services and religious broadcasts in which appeals for money overshadow true piety and devotion, or churches in which business concerns seem to outweigh spiritual planning. Even our leadership is often chosen more for its financial acumen than for Spirit-filled living. In light of v. 13, we ought to have far more prayer meetings than committee meetings.[62]

[18]Early in the morning, as he was on his way back to the city, he was hungry. [19]Seeing a fig tree by the road, he went up to it but found nothing on it except leaves. Then he said to it, "May you never bear fruit again!" Immediately the tree withered.

(c) Judgment on the Temple by Threatened Destruction (21:18-22). **21:18-19** *Prōi* ("early [in the morning]") does not specify which morning is in view. Mark makes it clear this episode happened in two stages, over a two-day period (Mark 11:12-14,20-24). Without contradicting Mark, Matthew improves the style by telling the story all at once and keeping the focus on Jesus entering Jerusalem as the judging Messiah. Thus Matthew abbreviates and combines this flashback to Monday morning (vv. 18-19) with the subsequent events of Tuesday morning (vv. 20-22). Jesus is heading back to Jerusalem, back to the temple. Matthew does not explain why Jesus was hungry. He looks for food on a fig tree in leaf, which has suggested to many that he expected to find fruit, but instead there is none. Yet Mark 11:13 notes that it was not yet the season for figs, so Jesus' subsequent curse must stem from something other than the tree's failure to perform in keeping with its appearance. Apparently the tree did not wither while the disciples were still watching but did within the next twenty-four hours (Mark 11:20). By horticultural standards, this still qualifies as "immediately."[63]

[20]When the disciples saw this, they were amazed. "How did the fig tree wither so quickly?" they asked.
[21]Jesus replied, "I tell you the truth, if you have faith and do not doubt,

---

[61]Cf. France, *Matthew*, 301.

[62]Bruner (*Churchbook*, 754) laments the common reversal of these priorities as "proof that we barely believe in God."

[63]Cf. J. P. Louw and E. A. Nida (*Greek-English Lexicon of the New Testament* [New York: UBS, 1988], 1:644), who emphasize παραχρῆμα as often meaning *suddenly* more than *strict immediacy*.

not only can you do what was done to the fig tree, but also you can say to this mountain, 'Go, throw yourself into the sea,' and it will be done. [22]If you believe, you will receive whatever you ask for in prayer."

21:20-22 The disciples see the tree withered and are astonished. Matthew leaves room for an interval of time before v. 20 but does not specify that this dialogue occurs on the next day. "Quickly" is the same word as "immediately" in v. 19. Both are legitimate translations; perhaps "quickly" should be used in both cases to avoid confusion. In vv. 21-22 Jesus now points out the real meaning of this miracle of destruction. The only other miracle of this nature in the Gospels is the exorcism of the Gadarene demoniacs with their destruction of the swine (8:28-34). As with the loss of the pigs there, the withering of a fig tree shows that God distinguishes between those made in his image (humans) and all other life forms. Jesus uses a vivid object lesson to inculcate the message of the parable of Luke 13:6-9. Unless Israel repents, like the fig tree it will perish.

This enacted parable further teaches Jesus' disciples that adequate faith would enable them to cast even "this mountain" into the sea. The demonstrative adjective "this" is probably significant. As Jesus and company were traveling from Bethany to Jerusalem, they would be facing Mount Zion, the temple mount. Jesus' community will therefore see the overthrow of the temple—physically in A.D. 70 and spiritually with Jesus' death and resurrection in just a few days. Given that the Old Testament described judgment on Israel in terms of the land producing no fig trees (e.g., Mic 7:1-6; Jer 8:13),[64] and given that Mark sandwiches this episode around the temple purification (Mark 11:12-25), it is almost certainly correct to see in this passage a foreshadowing of the destruction of the sacrificial system in Israel.[65]

Matthew thus provides about as dramatic an illustration as one could conceive of God enabling us to do that which seems humanly impossible. This should inspire confidence in his ability to empower us for lesser feats as well. Verses 21-22 partly resemble 17:20, on which see comments there, especially on praying with faith ("if you believe") as presupposing that we leave room for God's will to override ours (6:10). And

---

[64]For a detailed list of symbolic texts in Jewish literature involving fig trees, see M. Trautmann, *Zeichenhafte Handlungen Jesu* (Würzburg: Echter, 1980), 335. On the association of fig trees with the law, cf. M. Wojciechowski, "Marc 11.14 et Tg. Gn. 3.22: les fruits de la loi enlevés à Israel," *NTS* 33 (1987): 287-89.

[65]W. R. Telford, *The Barren Temple and the Withered Fig Tree* (Sheffield: JSOT, 1980), 238-39. Cf. G. Wagner, "Le figuier stérile et la destruction du Temple," *ETR* 62 (1987): 335-42. Sabourin (*Matthieu*, 273) notes that the earliest extant commentary on Mark, by Victor of Antioch, similarly explains this event as an enacted parable of judgment about to fall on Jerusalem (7.6).

despite the generalized, almost proverbial form of v. 22, the close proximity of v. 21 suggests that Jesus still has the temple mount first of all in view. "Whatever you ask for" may well still refer to whatever the disciples request concerning the replacement of the Jewish cult with the new covenant Jesus is inaugurating. And perhaps Jesus further implies, as Harrington phrases it, that "faith and prayer, not temple cult, are now the way to God."[66]

(2) Controversies with the Jewish Leaders (21:23–22:46). Just as 19:1–22:46 began with a series of pronouncement or controversy stories, so now it ends. The first of these controversies is expanded by the addition of three parables, two of which are unique to Matthew. Judgment on the temple and its officials continues, even as the story line furthers the hostility against Jesus and speeds his imminent demise. In each case the questions raised are appropriate for those raising them.

23Jesus entered the temple courts, and, while he was teaching, the chief priests and the elders of the people came to him. "By what authority are you doing these things?" they asked. "And who gave you this authority?"

(a) The Temple Authorities Ask about Jesus' Authority (21:23–22:14). 1) The Controversy (21:23–27). **21:23** Jesus returns to the site of the previous day's debacle. It is interesting that he has gotten away with creating such tumult. Presumably the crowds took a measure of delight in seeing Jesus challenge the religious authorities as he did. Perhaps they even recognized a measure of fulfillment of the prophecies about the purifying mission of the Messiah (recall Mal 3:1–4; cf. *Pss. Sol.* 17:30). But the officials remain outraged and demand to know by what authority Jesus has taken such drastic steps. This question about Jesus' authority appropriately comes from the two groups ("the chief priests and elders") who comprise the temple authorities. The answer of course is simple—he is acting on divine authority—yet if he says this bluntly, he could easily be accused of blasphemy. The leaders' question is no innocent inquiry but a dangerous trap. With their misguided enthusiasm, the crowds may still seem strongly supportive, but these authorities, like the Pharisees (cf. v. 45), more likely want to get rid of him.

24Jesus replied, "I will also ask you one question. If you answer me, I will tell you by what authority I am doing these things. 25John's baptism—where did it come from? Was it from heaven, or from men?"
They discussed it among themselves and said, "If we say, 'From heaven,'

---

[66]W. Harrington, *Mark* (Wilmington: Glazier, 1979), 181. H. Giesen ("Der verdorrte Feigenbaum—eine symbolische Aussage? Zu Mk 11, 12–14. 20f," *BZ* 20 [1976]: 103) describes the miracle as "a symbolic event . . . as an eschatological sign of the inbreaking kingdom of God."

he will ask, 'Then why didn't you believe him?' [26]But if we say, 'From men'—we are afraid of the people, for they all hold that John was a prophet."

[27]So they answered Jesus, "We don't know."

Then he said, "Neither will I tell you by what authority I am doing these things.

21:24-27 Because Jesus recognizes the trap, he refuses to answer directly. Instead, he replies with a counterquestion (recall 19:3-5). He plays their game at their level and so redirects their attention to the question of the source of the authority for John the Baptist's ministry, summed up here as his "baptism." Was John's work human or divine in origin (vv. 24-25a)? In vv. 25b-26 the temple authorities immediately recognize what Jesus is up to. Their private debate about how to reply already indicts them. John the Baptist and Jesus had similar ministries and messages, as Matthew has stressed. The correct answer to the question about John the Baptist's authority, namely, that it came "from heaven," will imply that they should give the same answer to the question about Jesus' authority. The chief priests and elders are not prepared to admit this publicly, but to deny that John was a true prophet leaves them fearing a popular uprising by a crowd electrified with messianic fervor, as has frequently happened in living memory.[67] So the Jewish authorities themselves are trapped and can answer only with a lame expression of ignorance (v. 27a). Jesus therefore replies in kind. He knows the answer to their question, but he will not disclose it as long as they refuse to be honest with him (v. 27b).[68]

2) The Parable of the Two Sons (21:28-32). Jesus continues without interruption and tells a parable. The story implicitly provides the answer to the question of v. 23 which Jesus refused to give more directly. The parable is the first of a series of three; in sequence they depict God's indictment, sentence, and execution of the present Jewish leadership.[69] Commentators often find predictions here of the replacement of Jews with Gentiles in God's plan of salvation, but no such distinction appears in the text. Jesus does not reject Israel as a whole, only the current leadership, which has rejected him.[70] The contrast is not between Jews and Gentiles

---

[67]See R. Horsley, *Bandits, Prophets and Messiahs* (San Francisco: Harper and Row, 1985).

[68]Cf. F. Stagg ("Matthew," in *The Broadman Bible Commentary*, vol. 8, ed. C. J. Allen [Nashville: Broadman, 1969], 201): "Jesus refused to give further answer to their question, not because the question itself was improper but because they were not open to the truth. Jesus had no word for hypocrisy except judgment. If they were not competent to judge John, whose life was completed, how could they judge Jesus?"

[69]Schweizer, *Matthew*, 402.

[70]Cf. A. Ogawa, "Paraboles de l'Israël véritable? Reconsidération critique de Mt. xxi 28-xxii 14," *NovT* 21 (1979): 149.

but rather between those who reject and those who accept Jesus. To date almost everyone in both categories is Jewish, though it will become clear that the two sons, two kinds of tenants, and two groups of guests in these three parables represent any person of any ethnic background who either follows Jesus in discipleship or despises him.

[28]"What do you think? There was a man who had two sons. He went to the first and said, 'Son, go and work today in the vineyard.'
[29] "'I will not,' he answered, but later he changed his mind and went.
[30]"Then the father went to the other son and said the same thing. He answered, 'I will, sir,' but he did not go.
[31]"Which of the two did what his father wanted?"
"The first," they answered.

21:28-31a This passage exhibits the most common structure of Jesus' parables—a story about a master figure with two contrasting subordinates. It closely resembles the parable of the prodigal son, in skeletal form. The father commands his first son to work in the vineyard, just as God had given his chosen nation various laws to follow and tasks to accomplish (v. 28). Like the "tax collectors and prostitutes" (v. 32), a unique combination in Matthew,[71] and like other rebellious people of many kinds, this son at first refused to heed his father's word but later changed his mind (v. 29). The father gives the second son the identical command. This boy promises obedience but then reneges, like the seemingly faithful Jewish leaders who have rejected God's kingdom emissaries, John and Jesus (v. 30; cf. v. 31b). The answer to Jesus' rhetorical question is obvious. The obedient son did his father's bidding despite his initial refusal (v. 31a). Some textual variants reverse the order of the two sons' actions (cf. NASB), and a few change the leaders' answer so that they praise the unfaithful son. But the manuscript evidence is too weak to support this variant (limited to D, old Italic and Syriac versions, and not even noted in the NIV), despite some valiant attempts to make sense of it as the original reading.[72]

Jesus said to them, "I tell you the truth, the tax collectors and the prostitutes are entering the kingdom of God ahead of you. [32]For John came to you to show you the way of righteousness, and you did not believe him, but the tax collectors and the prostitutes did. And even after you saw this, you did not repent and believe him.

21:31b-32 Jesus is still addressing the officials who refuse to accept his divine authority or to acknowledge John's prophetic ministry. So Jesus

---

[71]On which see J. Gibson, "*Hoi Telonai kai hai Pornai,*" *JTS* 32 (1981): 429-33. Jewish prostitutes were hated both for their life-style and for their free association with Romans.

[72]E.g., J. R. Michaels, "The Parable of the Regretful Son," *HTR* 61 (1968): 15-26.

refers to John again. The "way of righteousness" makes clear that the correct answer to Jesus' question about John is that his authority comes from God. The Jewish leaders are being supplanted by the most notorious of sinners because the latter *did* repent and "believe" (a term that links this parable back with vv. 22 and 25). "Ahead of" can mean *instead of* but may also mean *before*, leaving the parable deliberately open-ended. Though time is short, still the leaders have one last chance to change their ways. F. W. Beare objects that no Jew would ever have accepted the charge that he was not working for God,[73] but that is precisely Jesus' point and the shock value of this parable. The three points of the passage, one per character, may thus be summed up as follows: "Like the father sending his sons to work, God commands all people to carry out his will. Like the son who ultimately disobeyed, some promise but do not perform rightly and so are rejected by God. Like the son who ultimately obeyed, some rebel but later submit and so are accepted."[74] Even more concise is this summary: in the kingdom performance takes priority over promise. This remains true in Christian circles today as much as in first-century Israel.

3) The Parable of the Wicked Tenants (21:33-46).   Jesus extends his rebuke of those within Israel who are rejecting him. As in the previous parable, the story describes workers who fail to carry through on their commitments. But this passage goes one step further in predicting the replacement of many within Judaism by another "people" (v. 43)—still not necessarily an explicit reference to Gentiles (note the singular *ethnos* rather than the plural *ethnē*, the normal term for Gentiles) but apparently at least an allusion to the organized community of Jesus' followers, rather than simply, as in the previous parable, individual sinners who turn to God.

33"Listen to another parable: There was a landowner who planted a vineyard. He put a wall around it, dug a winepress in it and built a watchtower. Then he rented the vineyard to some farmers and went away on a journey. 34When the harvest time approached, he sent his servants to the tenants to collect his fruit.

21:33-34   Another vineyard appears. This time the imagery closely parallels Isa 5:1-2, so doubtless Israel is intended (cf. Isa 5:7).[75] The mas-

---

[73]F. W. Beare, *The Gospel according to Matthew* (San Francisco: Harper and Row, 1981), 424.

[74]Blomberg, *Parables*, 188. Cf. *Sipre Deut* 53 for a rabbinic parable with strikingly parallel structure and significance.

[75]The whole structure of the parable, beginning with these scriptural allusions, fits the rabbinic form known as *proem midrash*. See E. E. Ellis, "How the New Testament Uses the Old," in *New Testament Interpretation*, ed. I. H. Marshall (Grand Rapids: Eerdmans, 1977), 205.

ter here is portrayed as a landlord with tenants rather than a father with sons. Both sets of references prove equally appropriate for God and his chosen people. The details of wall, winepress, and watchtower should not be allegorized; they merely underline the care and protection God has lavished on his vineyard, Israel.[76] The farmers will naturally stand for those to whom God has entrusted his nation. The master's departure reflects the common practice of absentee landlords in first-century Palestine and corresponds to the period following God's election of Israel in which he leaves his people to do his will. The time of harvest approaches, and the master wants his due. "Fruit" remains a key term throughout the story (v. 34a, in which "the harvest time" is, more literally, *the time of the fruits,* v. 34b, v 41b, in which NIV translates "crop," and v. 43). And it is a key term elsewhere in Matthew (beginning with the programmatic reference to "fruit in keeping with repentance" in 3:8; cf. also 3:10; 7:16-20; 12:33; 13:8,26; 21:19). The wording in v. 34 may allude to Ps 1:3.

[35]"The tenants seized his servants; they beat one, killed another, and stoned a third. [36]Then he sent other servants to them, more than the first time, and the tenants treated them the same way. [37]Last of all, he sent his son to them. 'They will respect my son,' he said.

21:35-37 The servants' fate recalls the treatment of God's prophets throughout Old Testament history (e.g., Jer 20:1-2; 1 Kgs 18:4; 2 Chr 24:20-21; and cf. Matt 23:34). The farmer hopes that his own kin will gain more respect than did the hired help. The "son" seems to be a veiled self-reference by Jesus. This is probably his first public claim to be the "Son of God" and may well provide the background for Caiaphas's charge in 26:63.[77] By Matthew's time, of course, the reference will no longer be ambiguous and may well play a crucial role in his development of the theme of "Son of God."[78]

[38]"But when the tenants saw the son, they said to each other, 'This is the heir. Come, let's kill him and take his inheritance.' [39]So they took him and threw him out of the vineyard and killed him.

21:38-39 The tenants reason differently than their master. Why hasn't the landlord himself come? Is he perhaps dead and now sending his heir? Do they know this is the man's only son and that there are no other heirs? If they kill him, possession of the vineyard could be even more than "nine-tenths of the law." The action they propose remarkably resembles

---

[76]For a different view that sees a detailed midrash here, see C. A. Evans, "On the Vineyard Parables of Isaiah 5 and Mark 12," *BZ* 28 (1984): 82-86.

[77]France, *Matthew,* 308-9.

[78]See J. D. Kingsbury, "The Parable of the Wicked Husbandmen and the Secret of Jesus' Divine Sonship in Matthew: Some Literary-Critical Observations," *JBL* 105 (1986): 643-55.

that about to be taken against Jesus. Matthew's reversal of the order of the verbs "threw him out" and "killed" in v. 39 is often seen as heightening this parallelism since Jesus was taken outside the city walls and crucified. But the vineyard stands for Israel, and Jesus is not cast out of Israel. Individually, each of the details of this story can be paralleled in first-century Palestinian life.[79] But the unusual combination of events suggests that Jesus' main thrust lies with the spiritual lessons of the story.

40"Therefore, when the owner of the vineyard comes, what will he do to those tenants?"

41"He will bring those wretches to a wretched end," they replied, "and he will rent the vineyard to other tenants, who will give him his share of the crop at harvest time."

21:40-41 The tenants' logic turns out to be fatally flawed, as Jesus' rhetorical question demonstrates. The owner is still alive and well and eager to avenge his son's murder (v. 40). The Jewish leaders again indict themselves (v. 41a), responding in a way that Jesus endorses (Mark 12:9), even while others in the crowd become horrified (Luke 20:16). The landlord will inflict a miserable punishment on those murderous ingrates and will find new tenants for his vineyard who will do as he commands. Verse 41b is Matthew's unique addition and emphasizes a life of righteous obedience.

42Jesus said to them, "Have you never read in the Scriptures:
'The stone the builders rejected
**　has become the capstone;**
the Lord has done this,
**　and it is marvelous in our eyes'?**

21:42 With his by now customary introduction, "Have you never read?" Jesus again reproves the Jewish officials, citing Ps 118:22-23. This passage apparently referred originally to Israel, but later Jewish interpreters tended to see the stone as an individual—Abraham, David, or the Messiah.[80] And if the Messiah (like Abraham and David) can represent Israel, the shift is appropriate. Jesus will again be making a veiled self-reference as the "cornerstone" or "capstone."[81] There is also a wordplay between "stone" (Aram. *eben*) in v. 37 and "son" (Aram. *bēn*) here.[82]

---

[79]See K. Snodgrass, *The Parable of the Wicked Tenants* (Tübingen: Mohr, 1983), 31-40. Snodgrass's work is also the best full-length treatment of the parable overall.

[80]Lane, *Mark*, 420.

[81]As the NIV and margin indicate, there is a problem in determining which of these is the correct translation. Verse 44a fits more naturally the cornerstone (something over which someone can stumble); v. 44b, the capstone (something that can fall on a person).

[82]See M. Black, "The Christological Use of the Old Testament in the New Testament," *NTS* 18 (1971-72): 13.

Israel's leaders' rejection of Jesus does not disprove his messiahship. God specifically predicted that the one whom he would honor would first be rejected. The fate of the son in v. 39 will not be God's last word in the story. The final chapter—Christ's resurrection and exaltation—will indeed be "marvelous in our eyes." Psalm 118:22-23 became a favorite early Christian messianic proof text (cf. Acts 4:11; 1 Pet 2:7). These verses also hark back to the crowd's use of Ps 118:25-26 in v. 9. Matthew has not introduced so many scriptural quotations into one chapter since his infancy narratives (chaps. 1-2), and they continue to pervade the rest of his Gospel. Jesus fulfills prophecy as much in his death as in his birth.

43"Therefore I tell you that the kingdom of God will be taken away from you and given to a people who will produce its fruit. 44He who falls on this stone will be broken to pieces, but he on whom it falls will be crushed."

21:43-44 Verse 43 is unique to Matthew. It emphasizes the transference of leadership in Israel to new individuals. But the use of *ethnos* ("a people"—a collective singular) suggests more than simply the appointment of new leaders; it envisages a new community of disciples who perform the works God commands. Jesus is not so much foreshadowing the shift of God's activity from Jewish to Gentile realms as anticipating the replacement of Israel by the church, which will unite both Jew and Gentile. Those who have rejected Jesus, for whom the cornerstone has become a stumbling stone, will be broken by him. And even if one does not actively oppose Jesus, anything less than genuine discipleship will lead to judgment—the stone will "fall" on and "crush" such a person (allusions to Isa 8:14-15 and possibly Dan 2:34-35). A few manuscripts omit v. 44. Some have argued that a later scribe added it to harmonize Matthew's version with Luke 20:18, but the textual evidence for its inclusion (e.g., ℵ, B, C, f^1, f^{13}, and the Majority Text) is too strong to sustain this view.

45When the chief priests and the Pharisees heard Jesus' parables, they knew he was talking about them. 46They looked for a way to arrest him, but they were afraid of the crowd because the people held that he was a prophet.

21:45-46 The Jewish leaders understand the parable perfectly well at the cognitive level and recognize that the wicked tenants stand for themselves. It is appropriate therefore to follow the procedure we have outlined before in looking for main points associated with the main characters. This time perhaps as many as four appear, though the equation of Jesus with the son, at least in the parable's original context, would have been more subtle. The points may be put like this: "God is patient and longsuffering in waiting for his people to bear the fruit he requires of them, even when they are repeatedly and overtly hostile in their rebellion against him. A day will come when God's patience is exhausted and those who have rejected him will be destroyed. God's purposes will not thereby be thwarted, for he will raise up new leaders who will produce the fruit the original ones failed to provide." Like the son, Jesus will soon be killed, but like the stone, he will subsequently be honored and inflict damage on those who have opposed him.[83]

The leaders respond inappropriately. Instead of worshiping Christ, they intensify their efforts to arrest him. But his popularity with the crowds, however inadequate their perceptions remain, continues to thwart the officials. A riot could lead to Roman military intervention and persecution for all Jews. Verse 45 recalls v. 26 and reminds us that with this parable Jesus is continuing his response to the question about his authority. Jesus wants to make clear that this authority comes "from heaven" (v. 25) but also that he is God's own Son.

4) The Parable of the Wedding Banquet (22:1-14). Again Jesus speaks "in parables" (probably a generalizing plural). His audience has shrunk slightly (Mark 12:12), but his topic has not changed. Here is the third in this series of parables about a master and his subordinates, this time a king and his citizens. As in the parable of the wicked tenants, rebellion and murder intrude, as some of the townspeople kill the king's emissaries. Again the rebellious subordinates are replaced by less antagonistic ones. This third parable brings hostilities to a climax. In 21:28-32 the disobedient son stands for those who reject John and Jesus, but his fate is left open-ended. In 21:33-46 the wicked tenants murder the son, but the master merely evicts them from his property. Now we see God, in the person of the king, destroying those who spurn his advances. The execution of God's sentence against faithless Israel begins to unfold.[84] The somewhat parallel parable in Luke 14:15-24 probably reflects Jesus' use of similar imagery to make slightly different points on a different occasion.[85]

[1]Jesus spoke to them again in parables, saying: [2]"The kingdom of heaven is like a king who prepared a wedding banquet for his son. [3]He sent his servants to those who had been invited to the banquet to tell them to come, but they refused to come.

22:1-3 As in 18:23-35 and regularly in rabbinic parables, the king stands for God. A wedding banquet frequently depicted the fellowship of

---

[83]Blomberg, *Parables*, 249, 251. Cf. M. Hengel, "Das Gleichnis von den Weingärtnern Mc. 12, 1-12 im Lichte der Zenon Papyri und der rabbinischen Gleichnisse," *ZNW* 59 (1968): 1-39. On this fourth point, cf. Schweizer, *Matthew*, 412, who notes that here is the son who says yes to his Father's will *and* does it (contra both sons of the previous parable).

[84]Cf. R. J. Dillon, "Towards a Tradition-history of the Parables of the True Israel (Matthew 21:33-22:14)," *Bib* 47 (1966): 1-42.

[85]Blomberg, *Parables*, 83, 237-39.

the Messiah with his people at the eschatological consummation (recall 8:11; cf. Luke 13:29; Rev 19:9). After 21:37 it is natural to take "son" as a reference to Jesus, but nothing more is made of it in this context. The servants may or may not be meant to stand for God's messengers (as, e.g., the angels; cf. 13:39). The people originally invited to the banquet clearly represent Israel. Their reaction to the king's invitation proves shocking on both the natural and spiritual levels of the story. "They refused" is, more literally, *they were not willing*. The sending of the servants corresponds to the standard Oriental practice of issuing an invitation to an event without specifying the exact time until a later date.[86]

[4]"Then he sent some more servants and said, 'Tell those who have been invited that I have prepared my dinner: My oxen and fattened cattle have been butchered, and everything is ready. Come to the wedding banquet.' [5]"But they paid no attention and went off—one to his field, another to his business. [6]The rest seized his servants, mistreated them and killed them. [7]The king was enraged. He sent his army and destroyed those murderers and burned their city.

22:4-7 The king at first exercises more patience than one would expect of him. He sends his servants yet again to summon those originally invited. He explains how sumptuous the feast will be. He has had all the best food prepared, and now everything is ready. The language of v. 4 echoes Christ's emphasis on the kingdom of God being at hand. *Some* (better than NIV "they"), however, pay no attention to the servants (v. 5). They compound their culpability by adding apathy to rejection. "They paid no attention" is, more literally, *they didn't care*. The ordinary activities of life, both rural and urban, and especially business and money matters, take priority over loyalty to their king. "The rest" do not simply ignore the servants; they prove actively resistant and hostile (v. 6). Their response is just conceivable at the literal level of the story as treason and revolution.[87] But Jesus' point obviously concerns the spiritual level. God's emissaries, as in the parable of the wicked tenants, are mistreated and even killed.

The king's wrath leads to vengeance. The murderers themselves are killed and their city burned. Verse 7 is often viewed as an after-the-fact prophecy of the destruction of Jerusalem by the Romans in A.D. 70. But the imagery actually parallels stereotypic Old Testament and intertestamental descriptions of destruction in war (cf. Judg 1:8; Isa 5:24-25; 1 Macc 5:28; *T. Jud.* 5:1-5) and is not as detailed or accurate (the temple,

---

[86]On the Middle Eastern customs presupposed by the material common to Matthew and Luke, see K. E. Bailey, *Through Peasant Eyes* (Grand Rapids: Eerdmans, 1980), 88-113.

[87]J. D. M. Derrett, *Law in the New Testament* (London: Darton, Longman, and Todd, 1970), 139.

not the entire city, was burned) as one would expect if these words had been penned after the actual fall of Jerusalem.[88] Still, the Roman invasion of Jerusalem may be seen as a partial fulfillment of the principles enunciated here, even if Jesus had Judgment Day more prominently in mind.

8"Then he said to his servants, 'The wedding banquet is ready, but those I invited did not deserve to come. 9Go to the street corners and invite to the banquet anyone you find.' 10So the servants went out into the streets and gathered all the people they could find, both good and bad, and the wedding hall was filled with guests.

22:8-10 The king cannot tolerate an empty banquet hall; he seeks new guests. He now extends his invitation indiscriminately to the riff-raff of society as well as anyone else happening to be on the streets. How all this fits in with the burning of the city in v. 7 is irrelevant, since the focus is on the allegorical level. As in the previous two parables, none of the imagery explicitly extends the offer of the kingdom beyond the people of Israel, but the principle of inviting outcasts makes natural the transition from those rejected within Judaism to the Gentile world. Interestingly, Jesus declares that the originally invited guests are *unworthy* ("did not deserve"), tying in with Matthew's favorite theme of worthiness (cf. 3:8; 10:10-11,13,37-38). One might imagine that the second group of invited guests is equally if not even more unworthy. But the worthiness or unworthiness in view here has to do with one's response to the proclamation of the gospel. These last approached do respond properly, and the kingdom now issues forth in a plentiful community.

11"But when the king came in to see the guests, he noticed a man there who was not wearing wedding clothes. 12'Friend,' he asked, 'how did you get in here without wedding clothes?' The man was speechless.
13"Then the king told the attendants, 'Tie him hand and foot, and throw him outside, into the darkness, where there will be weeping and gnashing of teeth.'
14"For many are invited, but few are chosen."

22:11-13 Still all is not well. One member of the new group of guests appears without proper wedding clothes (v. 11). This episode is often seen as incongruous and as a justification for assuming that vv. 11-14 originally came from a separate parable that Matthew has conflated with vv. 1-10. But nothing in the passage says that this man has not been given time to find proper dress or that he was unable to locate any. Moreover, it

---

[88]Cf. esp. K. H. Rengstorf, "Die Stadt der Mörder (Matt. 22:7)," in *Judentum, Urchristentum, Kirche*, ed. W. Eltester (Berlin: Töpelmann, 1960), 106-29; B. Reicke, "Synoptic Prophecies on the Destruction of Jerusalem," in *Studies in the New Testament and Early Christian Literature*, ed. D. E. Aune (Leiden: Brill, 1972), 123.

is quite possible that the imagery here reflects the custom of a king providing festive dress for those he invites to a banquet.[89] So the king is understandably amazed and he rebukes this man with the distancing form of address, *hetaire* ("friend"), asking him why he has behaved as he has. The man offers no excuse (v. 12). Only imprisonment and punishment—eternal judgment—remain in store for such people (v. 13). At this point Jesus abandons any attempt to retain a meaningful story line at the literal level and speaks purely allegorically (cf. 13:40-42, on which imagery see also comments there).

22:14 Many people hear the summons of the gospel, but only a certain percentage responds properly. In light of the imagery of the parable itself and in view of common Semitic usage, "many" here may well mean *all*. "Few" may thus imply nothing about how many are saved except that the number is noticeably *less than all*. This is interesting use of election terminology. *Klētoi* (literally, *called*) is not to be taken here as irresistible calling, as apparently sometimes in Paul (e.g., Rom 8:29-30) but in the sense of "invited." Those responding properly may be said to have been chosen. The elect are the true community of the people God chooses to save, even as Israel had once been so chosen, but those people must freely respond to the Spirit's work in their lives. The imagery here is in fact more that of corporate than of individual election,[90] but the former cannot exist without the latter. Divine sovereignty and human responsibility are again finely balanced. Neither can be jettisoned at the expense of the other.[91] The man's behavior demonstrates he is not elect. Election does not violate free will nor occur irrespective of the man's conduct.

The upshot of the two episodes of this parable makes the contrast between the originally invited guests and their replacements actually subordinate to the contrast between the two categories of those who are judged (the first group of guests and the man without the wedding garment). The three points that derive from these three characters or groups of characters follow naturally: "God invites many people of different kinds into his Kingdom; overt rejection of God's invitation leads to eventual retribution; and failure to prepare adequately even when apparently accepted by God

---

[89]Despite claims that no first-century evidence attests this otherwise common custom of antiquity, see K. Haacker, "Das hochzeitliche Kleid von Mt. 22,11-13 und ein palästinisches Märchen," *ZDPV* 87 (1971): 95-97. Cf. the plentiful references to other parallels in Gundry, *Matthew*, 439.

[90]See esp. W. W. Klein, *God's New Chosen People* (Grand Rapids: Zondervan, 1990), 67-69.

[91]Cf. A. H. M'Neile, *The Gospel according to St. Matthew* (London: Macmillan, 1915), 317. The "elect" in Jewish thought often are equivalent to the "pious," combining God's sovereignty with human responsibility. Jesus is echoing that use here. Cf. also Mounce, *Matthew*, 212.

proves no less culpable or liable to eternal punishment."[92] Unbelievers today need to know the biblical claim that they face eternal judgment, despite Christians' hesitancy in preaching this message. Professing Christians need to know that they are not exempt from the same danger whenever they replace the true gospel with some substitute of their own designs, for there is no other gospel (Gal 1:6-9).[93]

15Then the Pharisees went out and laid plans to trap him in his words. 16They sent their disciples to him along with the Herodians. "Teacher," they said, "we know you are a man of integrity and that you teach the way of God in accordance with the truth. You aren't swayed by men, because you pay no attention to who they are. 17Tell us then, what is your opinion? Is it right to pay taxes to Caesar or not?"

(b) The Pharisees and Herodians Ask about Taxes (22:15-22). **22:15-17** Here appears the second controversy story of 21:23–22:46. It is the first of four that proceed without interruption, closely following the sequence of questions that formed part of the Passover "haggadah" (service or liturgy): (1) a question regarding a point of law; (2) a question with a note of scoffing; (3) a question by a person of "plain piety"; (4) a question by the father of the family at his own initiative.[94] Jesus is presented with an even more difficult situation than in previous controversies. The Pharisees resented having to pay taxes to Rome as an infringement on Jewish law. The Herodians were a small group of Jews loyal to the various members of Herod's family. They had made their peace with the occupying invaders and saw taxes as an appropriate way to fulfill their responsibilities as good citizens (cf. further the debate in *b. B. Qam.* 113a). The two groups are explicitly trying to "trap" or *snare* Jesus. No matter which side he takes, the other group will be upset. The officials address him with the polite but inadequate title "teacher." Only Matthew adds "you teach the way of God in accordance with the truth." "A man of integrity" more literally reads *you are true.* "You aren't swayed by men, because you pay no attention to who they are" reads, more literally, *It is not a care to you concerning anyone, for you do not look on a person's face.* The NIV captures the correct sense. Jesus never compromises his integrity for the sake of what others might think.

The Pharisees' and Herodians' words are true but designed as flattery to force Jesus to take a public stand on the issue. What does he think about the *tribute* ("taxes," Greek *kēnsos*) to Rome? "Is it right?" equals *Is it*

---

[92]Blomberg, *Parables*, 239. Cf. Sand, *Matthäus*, 439-40.

[93]Cf. further D. C. Sim, "The Man without the Wedding Garment (Matthew 22:11-13)," *HeyJ* 31 (1990): 165-78.

[94]See D. Daube, *The New Testament and Rabbinic Judaism* (London: Athlone, 1956), 158-69.

lawful? and parallels the introduction to the question of 19:3 (as does the reference to *testing* in v. 18, "trap"). This is not the same tax as in 17:24-27 since there Peter was asked about the Jewish temple tax commanded by the Torah. The poll tax for Judea at issue here went to support the foreign, pagan oppressors and had already been attacked by Judas of Galilee in A.D. 6 (Josephus, *Ant.* 18.1.1).

[18] **But Jesus, knowing their evil intent, said, "You hypocrites, why are you trying to trap me?** [19] **Show me the coin used for paying the tax." They brought him a denarius,** [20] **and he asked them, "Whose portrait is this? And whose inscription?"**

22:18-20 Jesus sees through the ruse at once. The Pharisees' and Herodians' insincerity qualifies them for the label "hypocrites," a form of address Jesus will use throughout chap. 23. Jesus asks for the coin used to pay the tax, and they supply a denarius, the day laborer's common wage. Rome is clearly not demanding an exorbitant tribute. He then asks whose name and picture appear on the coin. "Portrait" is, literally, *image* and perhaps highlights imperial ownership of the money. Orthodox Jews would have considered both name and picture as blasphemous, the latter as a violation of the Second Commandment against idolatry and the former because the coin of the emperor Tiberius had inscribed on it the words *Divus et Pontifex Maximus* ("God and High Priest").

[21] **"Caesar's," they replied.**
Then he said to them, "Give to Caesar what is Caesar's, and to God what is God's."
[22] **When they heard this, they were amazed. So they left him and went away.**

22:21 The answer to Jesus' question is obvious. His follow-up statement surprises everyone. In one of the most famous sayings in the Gospels, Jesus avoids the trap by affirming both what the Pharisees and what the Herodians hold dear. God's sovereignty must be acknowledged, but human governments also have a legitimate authority. "Give" means *pay back*—that which is rightfully due. Some commentators have taken Jesus' words as implying "give everything to God" because everything is ultimately his, but this interpretation destroys the delicate balance of Jesus' reply as he seeks to evade both points of the two-pronged attack against him. Reasonable taxation is a legitimate function for all governments, even totalitarian regimes; how much more so with more democratic governments! Christians who avoid paying taxes, or who avoid paying the full amount of their taxes, sin against God even just as surely as in more obviously "moral" arenas.

Verse 21 inspired the Reformation doctrine of differing spheres of authority for government and religion and proved foundational for the

American constitutional separation of church and state. It would be anachronistic, however, to claim that Jesus' words support modern democratic forms of government as opposed to the imperial or monarchichal forms of his day. One can give God his proper due under a monarchy as well as in a democracy, just as authorities, sadly, can usurp prerogatives reserved for God in either system.

A slightly different interpretation of Jesus' words maintains that v. 21 does not divide authority into two distinct spheres but ranks human obligations by recognizing that even government is under God and that it is therefore appropriate to honor it.[95] Yet even as Jesus finds a way to agree with both the Pharisees and the Herodians, though not with all for which each of these groups stands, he even more strongly dissociates himself from the Zealot movement. Jesus was no political revolutionary, though a good case can be made for seeing him radically protesting social injustice in peaceful, nonviolent ways.[96] Obviously this one saying does not provide a comprehensive treatment of the relationship between Christians and government. Other Scriptures reflecting different emphases must obviously be consulted (contrast, e.g., Rom 13:1-7 with Rev 13:1-18).

22:22 The crowd's amazement refers first of all to the way in which Jesus avoided the seemingly foolproof trap set for him. Having failed in their effort, the Pharisees now give way to a new group of antagonists.

[23]That same day the Sadducees, who say there is no resurrection, came to him with a question. [24]"Teacher," they said, "Moses told us that if a man dies without having children, his brother must marry the widow and have children for him. [25]Now there were seven brothers among us. The first one married and died, and since he had no children, he left his wife to his brother. [26]The same thing happened to the second and third brother, right on down to the seventh. [27]Finally, the woman died. [28]Now then, at the resurrection, whose wife will she be of the seven, since all of them were married to her?"

(c) The Sadducees Ask about the Resurrection (22:23-33). **22:23-28** Next appears that Jewish party which rejected the oral Torah and any doctrine not derivable from the five books of Moses (cf. commentary on 3:7).

---

[95]F. V. Filson, *A Commentary on the Gospel according to St. Matthew*, HNTC (New York: Harper, 1960), 235. For a survey of interpretive options, see C. H. Giblin, "'The Things of God' in the Question Concerning Tribute to Caesar (Lk 20:25; Mk 12:17; Mt 22:21)," *CBQ* 33 (1971): 510-27.

[96]See R. J. Cassidy, *Jesus, Politics and Society* (Maryknoll: Orbis, 1978). On the topic of Jesus and politics more generally, cf. also E. Bammel and C. F. D. Moule, eds., *Jesus and the Politics of His Day* (Cambridge: University Press, 1984); M. Hengel, *Was Jesus a Revolutionist?* (Philadelphia: Fortress, 1971); and J. H. Yoder, *The Politics of Jesus* (Grand Rapids: Eerdmans, 1972).

The clearest Old Testament teaching on the resurrection of all people at the end of the age appears in Dan 12:2. There are no unambiguous texts from Genesis through Deuteronomy that put forward this doctrine. But the Sadducees do not couch their question so directly; rather, they try to ridicule the notion of resurrection with a worst-case scenario. Again they address Jesus as "teacher" (see commentary on v. 16). Appealing to the Pentateuchal commandments about levirate marriage (in which a brother is responsible for marrying a deceased brother's widow who has had no offspring in order to try to perpetuate the family line), the Sadducees loosely cite Deut 25:5 and Gen 38:8. They envision an extreme situation in which a woman has gone through seven husbands, all brothers, because she has failed to conceive by any of them (cf. the Mishnaic tractate *Yebamot* for the continuing rabbinic discussion of levirate marriages). The Sadducees could have made their point just as easily with the story of a woman who had had only two husbands, but they want to make the situation look absurd. So they pose the question, Who will be married to whom when the woman and all seven men have new bodies in this supposed resurrection life?

[29]Jesus replied, "You are in error because you do not know the Scriptures or the power of God. [30]At the resurrection people will neither marry nor be given in marriage; they will be like the angels in heaven. [31]But about the resurrection of the dead—have you not read what God said to you, [32] 'I am the God of Abraham, the God of Isaac, and the God of Jacob'? He is not the God of the dead but of the living."
[33]When the crowds heard this, they were astonished at his teaching.

22:29-33 The problem with the question is that the Sadducees are assuming resurrection bodies to be exactly as bodies are now, which includes the capacity for sexual intercourse. Jesus sees two errors in their logic, one regarding their specific question about this woman and the other related to their more fundamental, underlying concerns about resurrection in general. These errors deal, respectively, with their understanding of Torah and of God's power. Concerning the latter, God is able to transform us into creatures who do not engage in sexual relations or procreate. A model for such a being already exists, namely, the angels (cf. the rabbinic tradition in *b. Hag.* 16a, in which, interestingly, demons, in contrast to angels, *are* believed to copulate). Since the Sadducees also do not believe in angels (cf. Acts 23:8), Jesus is probably deliberately inserting this jibe. Lack of sex or marriage does not in any way diminish heavenly bliss. In the life to come, all interpersonal relationships will no doubt far surpass the most intimate and pleasurable of human intercourse as we now know it. Neither jealousy nor exclusivism will mar human interaction in any way.

Regarding the Sadducees' underlying concern about the resurrection not being found in the Pentateuch, Jesus appeals to the implications of Exod 3:6 and its present tense verbs. Whatever we may think of Jesus' interpretation, it obviously impressed his original listeners (v. 33, much as in 7:28-29), who were used to such logic (cf. especially *b. Sanh.* 90b on precisely this issue in which the resurrection is derived from Num 18:28, which speaks of giving the heave offering to "Aaron" in the promised land long after his death).[97] The objection that Jesus' argument proves only the immortality of the soul and not the resurrection of the body ignores the fact that immortality was not an option Jews considered. Either all the body was resurrected or nothing survived. Contemporary objections to Jesus' logic here perhaps reveal an unnecessary rigidity in our modern historical/grammatical hermeneutics rather than any fallacy with Jesus' interpretation.

34Hearing that Jesus had silenced the Sadducees, the Pharisees got together. 35One of them, an expert in the law, tested him with this question: 36"Teacher, which is the greatest commandment in the Law?"

(d) The Lawyer Asks about the Greatest Commandment (22:34-40).
22:34-36 The Pharisees regroup after their defeat in vv. 15-22 to initiate the next round of questioning. Before, they simply sent their disciples; now they come themselves. One, a *nomikos* (*lawyer*, "expert in the Law," avoids reading in anachronistic impressions of the occupation), again tries to trap Jesus. His question seems innocent enough but reflects an intra-Jewish debate on how to rank and/or summarize all of the scriptural commandments and on whether such ranking is in fact possible at all (cf., e.g., *m. Hag.* 1:8; *b. Ber.* 63a; *Mek.* 6). Moreover, given Jesus' radical views on the law, an open-ended question such as this would surely elicit some remark by which Jesus would indict himself.

37Jesus replied: "'Love the Lord your God with all your heart and with all your soul and with all your mind.' 38This is the first and greatest commandment. 39And the second is like it: 'Love your neighbor as yourself.' 40All the Law and the Prophets hang on these two commandments."

22:37-40 This is the first of the controversy stories in which Jesus gives a straight answer to the question, one with which many in his audience

---

[97]For a defense of Jesus' interpretation as displaying the "deepest sensitivity to the context in which Ex. 3.6 originally occurs," namely, as a response of hope in the face of death, see J. G. Janzen, "Resurrection and Hermeneutics: On Exodus 3.6 in Mark 12.26," *JSNT* 23 (1985): 43-58. Alternately, with R. V. G. Tasker (*The Gospel according to St. Matthew: An Introduction and Commentary*, TNTC [London: InterVarsity, 1961], 211) there may be a debate here about the subjective versus objective genitive; i.e., Jesus would be reading the text as referring to the "God to whom Abraham belongs" rather than, more customarily, as the "God whom Abraham worshiped."

would have agreed, and does not rebuke his interrogators either implicitly or explicitly. He quotes Deut 6:5, replacing "strength" with "understanding." Neither form of the text implies a compartmentalization of the human psyche. Rather, both refer to wholehearted devotion to God with every aspect of one's being, from whatever angle one chooses to consider it— emotionally, volitionally, or cognitively. This kind of "love" for God will then result in obedience to all he has commanded (cf. Deut 6:1-3,6-9).

Going beyond the original question, Jesus adds a second commandment that is also foundational—Lev 19:18. "The second is like it" probably means that this commandment is of equal importance.[98] Jewish interpreters had long recognized the preeminent value of each of these laws; Jesus apparently was the first to fuse the two *and* to exalt them above the whole law (though Philo, *Spec. Leg.* 2:15, comes close to doing this).[99] Divine love issues in interpersonal love. "As yourself" is not a call to self-love but does presuppose it. These two commandments are the greatest because all others flow from them; indeed the whole Old Testament "hangs" on them. In other words, all other commandments are summed up and/or contained in these. Verse 40 is unique to Matthew and reminds one of the concerns of 5:17 and 7:12. Matthew omits Jesus' relatively positive interchange with this lawyer following his answer (Mark 12:32-34), in keeping with his unrelenting focus on the hostility against Christ. But the Pharisees could scarcely object to Jesus' reply, even if he elsewhere defines neighbor love much more radically than was customary in Judaism (Luke 10:25-37).[100]

The relationship of all the Old Testament to the double love commandment shows that there is a hierarchy of law that above all requires one's heart attitude to be correct. If this is absent, obedience to commandments degenerates into mere legalism. Combining Jesus' teaching here with his approach to the law, as, e.g., in the Sermon on the Mount, demonstrates that while the principle of love remains constant, applications vary for different circumstances. Nevertheless, Jesus' words also strongly differentiate him from situation ethicists. Love does make specific moral demands, including certain absolutes.[101] What is more, the proper motivation for

---

[98]Cf. esp. B. Gerhardsson, "The Hermeneutic Program in Matthew 22:37-40," in *Jews, Greeks, and Christians,* ed. R. Hammerton-Kelly and R. Scroggs (Leiden: Brill, 1976), 129-50.

[99]Bruner, *Churchbook,* 794, with references to the various partial parallels.

[100]Luke 10:25-28 contains a closely parallel dialogue to the passage here but probably reflects a different controversy on a different occasion in Jesus' ministry.

[101]For balanced views on New Testament ethics more generally, see A. Verhey, *The Great Reversal: Ethics and the New Testament* (Grand Rapids: Eerdmans, 1984); R. E. O. White, *Biblical Ethics* (Exeter: Paternoster, 1979). Moreover, with D. Hill (*The Gospel of Matthew,* NCB [London: Oliphants, 1972], 306): "The summary permits of no fulfillment of the Law, which is not, in its very core, obedience to God and service to one's neighbour."

correct interpersonal relationships always remains a profound sense of gratitude for what God has done for us in Christ. Jesus' twofold answer should warn Christians against emphasizing either piety for God or social concern at the expense of the other.

⁴¹While the Pharisees were gathered together, Jesus asked them, ⁴²"What do you think about the Christ? Whose son is he?"

"The son of David," they replied.

(e) Jesus Asks about the Messiah (22:41-46). **22:41-42** Jesus now turns the tables on his questioners. He has evaded all their traps, which were based fundamentally on their refusal to recognize him as Messiah. This is the topic they really should be talking about. Their problems largely stem from the fact that they are looking for a purely human, nationalistic liberator. Jesus directs his question so as to explore the scriptural nature of messiahship. From whose ancestry is the Messiah to come? The answer, at least for Jesus' immediate audience, would have indisputably been "from the lineage of David" (recall 2 Sam 7:12-14; though cf. Qumran's belief in two Messiahs, one priestly and one kingly—cf., e.g., 1QS 9:11).

⁴³He said to them, "How is it then that David, speaking by the Spirit, calls him 'Lord'? For he says, ⁴⁴ " 'The Lord said to my Lord:

"Sit at my right hand
until I put your enemies
under your feet." '

22:43-44 The Pharisees' answer (v. 42b) sets up Jesus' real question. If the Messiah is merely the human offspring of David, why does David himself speak of him as "Lord"—a master or sovereign above the one who is king of Israel and the highest human authority in the land? Jesus here employs the rabbinic method of setting up an antinomy and then resolving it. He bases his argument on Ps 110:1, assuming with the Judaism of his time the accuracy of the Davidic superscription, and the inspiration of the actual text itself, which would therefore imply its truthfulness. Given these assumptions, the second "Lord" (Heb. *aḏōnāi*, not Yahweh) can only be the Messiah. Again Jesus' reasoning finds pre-Christian Jewish precedent.[102] This "lord" resides at the position of highest privilege and authority, second only to God the Father. He sits next to the Father's throne and rules over all his enemies (Ps 110:4), presumably including those in Jesus' audience!

---

[102]See esp. J. A. Fitzmyer ("The Son of David Tradition and Mt 22:41-46 and Parallels," in *Essays on the Semitic Background of the New Testament* [London: G. Chapman, 1971], 113-26), who also gives a good overall interpretation of the passage, esp. in its Matthean form.

⁴⁵If then David calls him 'Lord,' how can he be his son?" ⁴⁶No one could say a word in reply, and from that day on no one dared to ask him any more questions.

22:45-46   So how can this Christ be merely a human descendant of David? The Pharisees have no answer, nor does anyone else, and no one dares to ask him any further questions. All the traps have failed, and Jesus' listeners have in fact been trapped. Not surprisingly, Ps 110:1-4 becomes the Old Testament passage quoted more than any other in the New Testament. It points to Jesus' messiahship and his exaltation, and the first Christians take their cue from its effectiveness here for use in their later apologetic (see, e.g., Acts 2:34-35; Heb 1:13; 5:6,10; 7:17,21). Modern attempts to dismiss the logic of Jesus' argument by attributing the psalm to someone other than David are the product of post-Enlightenment criticism and, at least in this instance, remain in tension with Christ's teaching.

2. Judgment on the Temple but Also on the Nations (23:1–25:46)

Here appears the final long block of Jesus' teaching. As with three of Matthew's other four sermons of Jesus, much shorter parallels appear in Mark (cf. Mark 12:38-40; 13:1-37); and lengthier ones are scattered about in different contexts in Luke (cf. Luke 11:37-52; 12:35-48; 13:34-35; 17:22-37; 20:45-47; and 21:5-36). The pattern of 21:28–22:14 repeats, with a verdict against Israel (23:1-32), a sentence (23:33-36), and its execution (23:37–24:2). The preceding material (22:41-46, or perhaps all of vv. 15-46) may function as the introductory "trial," and much of chaps.

24–25, by way of application, then warns the church not to fall prey to the same judgment.[1]

The discourse is divided into two potentially separable segments: the public teaching of Jesus in the temple, centering on woes against the Pharisees' and scribes' hypocrisy (chap. 23), and the private teaching for the disciples on the Mount of Olives regarding the destruction of the temple and the end of the age (chaps. 24–25). But several features suggest that Matthew intended chaps. 23–25 to be viewed as a unity. He omits Mark's passage about the widow's mite (Mark 12:41-44), which otherwise more clearly separates the two discourses and changes the topic. He includes the Q material instead, describing Jesus' lament for Jerusalem (23:37-39), as the climax of the "woes," material that clearly provides a bridge to chap. 24. "Your house is left to you desolate" (23:38) anticipates the destruction of the temple, which is explicitly predicted in 24:1-2. Matthew 23:39, with its reference to Christ's return, equally explicitly ties in with the discussion about the sign of Jesus' coming beginning in 24:3. The shift of place and audience between chaps. 23 and 24 parallels the shift that occurred in 13:36, but chap. 13 is nevertheless regularly recognized as a unified discourse. The repeated woes of chap. 23, finally, balance the numerous beatitudes (5:3-12) of the Sermon on the Mount (chaps. 5–7), suggesting that this chapter forms part of Jesus' final discourse in Matthew even as chap. 5 introduced his first major discourse.[2] Still, the "sermon" falls naturally into two parts—judgment just against Israel (chap. 23) and judgment against Israel and all the nations (chaps. 24–25).

a. JUDGMENT AGAINST ISRAEL (23:1-39). Formally three sections appear here: warnings against imitating the Jewish leaders (vv. 1-12), a series of woes decrying their hypocrisy (vv. 13-36), and Jesus' lament and predictions of the resulting coming judgment (vv. 36-39).[3]

[1]Then Jesus said to the crowds and to his disciples: [2]"The teachers of the law and the Pharisees sit in Moses' seat. [3]So you must obey them and do everything they tell you. But do not do what they do, for they do not practice

---

[1]Cf. E. Schweizer, *The Good News according to Matthew* (Richmond: John Knox, 1975), 402; B. M. Newman and P. C. Stine, *A Translator's Handbook on the Gospel of Matthew* (New York: UBS, 1988), 655.

[2]On the unity of chaps. 23–25, see further D. O. Via, Jr., "Ethical Responsibility and Human Wholeness in Matthew 25:31-46," *HTR* 80 (1987): 83-84.

[3]The fullest study of this chapter is D. E. Garland, *The Intention of Matthew 23* (Leiden: Brill, 1979), to which much of the subsequent exposition is indebted, even where it sometimes takes a different direction. On the historical plausibility of Jesus' hypocrisy charges, see S. Mason, "Pharisaic Dominance before 70 CE and the Gospel's Hypocrisy Charge," *HTR* 83 (1990): 363-81.

what they preach. ⁴They tie up heavy loads and put them on men's shoulders, but they themselves are not willing to lift a finger to move them.

(1) Warnings against the Behavior of the Jewish Leaders (23:1-12).[4]
23:1-4 Many of the Jewish leaders may well have left after 22:46. Matthew describes Jesus' audience here as the "crowds" and "disciples." Thus the harsh words against the scribes and Pharisees are probably not so much directly addressed to them as to others—to warn those who still had a chance to repent against following their damning example. Nevertheless, this chapter is often seen as the most anti-Semitic text in all of the Gospels, if not in the entire New Testament. Yet Jesus was a Jew, as were all his followers to date, and not all Jews are condemned in this chapter, not even all the leaders. Even the two groups apostrophized here are probably treated as a whole—not every single member is in view. Jesus does have more positive interaction with certain Pharisees elsewhere, particularly Nicodemus (John 19:39 may imply a favorable outcome to the dialogue of 3:1-15). If it be argued that Matthew betrays no similar qualification, it is probably because he wants to focus here on the Jerusalem authorities who ultimately condemned Christ (23:37a). But v. 37b discloses Jesus' deep emotion and compassion as he empathizes with his countrymen. His previous invective is no harsher than many denunciations found in the Psalms and Prophets (e.g., Ps 58; Jer 23; Isa 5:8-23), and his lament tempers his outburst with a tenderness not always found among other Jewish prophets.[5]

Jesus begins by acknowledging that these leaders are duly authorized officials within Judaism (v. 2). "Moses' seat" referred to an actual chair in the synagogues and stood for the teaching authority of Moses' successors as interpreters of Torah (cf. Deut 17:10).[6] The expression is roughly parallel to our reference to the pulpit as the symbol for preaching or scriptural exposition. Verse 3a, however, seems completely out of keeping with the rest of the passage and therefore has understandably been taken as irony, not to be literally obeyed.[7] France paraphrases, "Of course you may do what they say, if you like, but"; and he speaks of the language as

---

[4]On many plausible (and a few implausible) implications for Matthew's community, cf. B. T. Viviano, "Social World and Community Leadership: The Case of Matthew 23.1-12,34," *JSNT* 39 (1990): 3-21.

[5]A good refutation of the charge of anti-Semitism, along with a defense of the authenticity of Jesus' words here, appears in E. A. Russell, "'Antisemitism' in the Gospel of Matthew," *IBS* 8 (1986): 183-96. Cf. also F. A. Niedner, "Rereading Matthew on Jerusalem and Judaism," *BTB* 19 (1989): 43-47.

[6]See esp. K. G. C. Newport, "A Note on the 'Seat of Moses' (Matthew 23.2)," *AUSS* 28 (1990): 53-58.

[7]See D. A. Carson, "Matthew," EBC, vol. 8, ed. F. E. Gaebelein (Grand Rapids: Zondervan, 1984), 473-74.

tongue-in-cheek.[8] Or perhaps Jesus is implying that people must obey their religious teachers to the extent that their teaching coheres with that of Moses, but no further.[9] This interpretation fits the more positive, recent understanding of the Pharisees' goals in creating a "fence around the Torah"—guidelines to make it easier to know how to obey Moses' law. But Jesus immediately adds that one must avoid imitating much of these leaders' behavior because it is inconsistent with their teaching. The NIV excellently captures the sense of v. 3b—"they do not practice what they preach." The Greek literally reads *they speak and do not do*. This inconsistency is typified by the demands the Pharisees made of others without helping them to perform those duties (v. 4). Similar abuse is recorded in *y. Ber.* 2.3. The demands probably were not originally oppressive but became so after they outlived their original usefulness. Unwillingness to help others may reflect the Pharisaic prejudice against the ordinary *am-ha-aretz* ("people of the land") because they were not as law-abiding. Instead of nurturing and instructing them, the Pharisees ostracized these ordinary folk. For similar sentiments concerning the oral laws, cf. Acts 15:10 and contrast Jesus' "easy burden" in Matt 11:28-30. Obedience that degenerates into legalism becomes equally oppressive in Christian circles today.[10]

[5]"Everything they do is done for men to see: They make their phylacteries wide and the tassels on their garments long; [6]they love the place of honor at banquets and the most important seats in the synagogues; [7]they love to be greeted in the marketplaces and to have men call them 'Rabbi.'

23:5-7 Having warned against imitating the inconsistency between the Pharisees' and scribes' teachings and their practices, Jesus now warns against imitating their performance of good works for human honor or reward. In other words, he pursues the theme of 6:1-18. Here his examples involve dress (v. 5), position (v. 6), and greetings (v. 7).

First, these Jewish leaders paraded their piety by enlarging the length and width of the *tefillin* and *zizith* which they wore. The *tefillin* (Greek *phylakteria*, "phylacteries") were small prayer boxes containing tiny copies of the texts of Exod 13:2-16; Deut 6:4-9; and 11:13-21, which pious men wore on one arm and as a headband. The wearing of these boxes probably developed as an overly literal application of Deut 6:8 and 11:18

---

[8]R. T. France, *The Gospel according to Matthew*, TNTC (Grand Rapids: Eerdmans, 1985), 324.

[9]Cf. A. Plummer, *An Exegetical Commentary on the Gospel according to S. Matthew* (London: E. Stock, 1909), 314; R. H. Gundry, *Matthew: A Commentary on His Literary and Theological Art* (Grand Rapids: Eerdmans, 1982), 455.

[10]Cf. A. H. M'Neile (*The Gospel according to St. Matthew* [London: Macmillan, 1915], 330): "Though they scrupulously observed their own rules, their motive and manner deprived their actions of all value."

and was used as a reminder to prayer and piety. The *zizith*, or fringes on the prayer shawls, were used somewhat like later Catholic rosary beads, fingered and counted in order to keep track of various prayers recited. Jesus himself apparently wore the prayer shawl (recall 9:21), but for many scribes and Pharisees the phylacteries and fringes had become badges of status and opportunities for ostentation.[11]

Second, these leaders enjoyed the honored seats at banquets and in synagogues (a tie-in back with v. 2). One thinks of modern "high church" ceremonialism and "low church" showmanship, both of which often distract from true worship by calling unnecessary attention to the human worship leaders.

Third, they loved to be greeted with titles that underlined their status and prestige. On the specific significance of "Rabbi," see commentary on vv. 8-12.

[8]"But you are not to be called 'Rabbi,' for you have only one Master and you are all brothers. [9]And do not call anyone on earth 'father,' for you have one Father, and he is in heaven. [10]Nor are you to be called 'teacher,' for you have one Teacher, the Christ. [11]The greatest among you will be your servant. [12]For whoever exalts himself will be humbled, and whoever humbles himself will be exalted.

23:8-12 Jesus now shifts from speaking about "them" to "you"—all those among the crowds and disciples (v. 1) who might still truly be or become his followers. He picks up on his observation about greetings from vv. 5-7 and warns specifically against imitating the Jewish leaders in this respect. The three titles he uses as examples of what to avoid are "Rabbi" (v. 8), "father" (v. 9), and "teacher" (v. 10). All commonly referred in Judaism to those who expounded the law. "Rabbi" etymologically meant *my great one*. "Father" was apparently reserved for the patriarchs and revered teachers from the past (cf. the allegedly oldest portion of Mishnaic tradition—the *Pirqe Aboth* or "Sayings of the Fathers"). "Teacher" (*kathēgētēs*) referred especially to a *tutor*.[12] As with many of Jesus' teachings in the Sermon on the Mount, texts elsewhere in the New Testament make it clear that he is not promulgating absolute commands. People are properly called teachers in Acts 13:1; 1 Tim 2:7; and Heb 5:12. Paul will even refer to a spiritual gift that enables some people to be so identified (Eph 4:11; 1 Cor 12:28-29; cf. Jas 3:1). It remains appropriate to call a biological parent one's father, and even one's spiritual parent

---

[11]On the details of these practices and their abuse, cf. esp. J. H. Tigay, "On the Term Phylacteries (Matt 23:5)," *HTR* 72 (1979): 45-53.

[12]B. W. Winter, "The Messiah as the Tutor: The Meaning of καθηγητής" in Matthew 23:10," *TynBul* 42 (1991): 152-57.

may be addressed with this term (1 Cor 4:15; cf. also 1 John 2:13; Acts 22:1). So the point of vv. 8-12 must be that such titles are not to be used to confer privilege or status.

There is thus nothing inherently wrong with the Roman Catholic use of "Father" for priests or with the Protestant "Reverend" for ministers or even with the academic "Doctor" for people with certain degrees. But one wonders how often these titles are used without implying unbiblical ideas about a greater worth or value of the individuals to whom they are assigned. One similarly wonders for how long the recipients of such forms of address can resist an unbiblical pride from all the plaudits. It is probably best to abolish most uses of such titles and look for equalizing terms that show that we are all related as family to one Heavenly Father (God) and one teacher (Christ).[13] The concept of abolishing rank because all are equally instructed and privileged goes back to Jeremiah's own predictions about the nature of the new covenant (Jer 31:33-34).[14] "Brother" or "sister" has a good Christian pedigree and is suggested though not commanded by v. 8, but these terms often sound stilted in the modern world. "Mister" loses the sense of family but proves a reasonable equivalent for the Western male; women are not yet agreed on a corresponding title for themselves. In American Christian circles perhaps the best goal is to strive for the intimacy that simply makes addressing one another on a first-name basis natural.

Verse 11 repeats the language of 20:26 for a larger audience. Verse 12 parallels the thought of 20:27 even if not in the identical language (cf. also Luke 14:11; 18:14). Those who seek merely human reward and honor now in this life will be humiliated before God on Judgment Day. Those who eschew honor and reward now will receive it then.

(2) Woes Decrying the Hypocrisy of the Jewish Leaders (23:13-36). Seven woes, probably a complete number (cf. v. 32), now follow (on the concept of "woe" see comments under 11:20-24). Verses 33-36 may be separable from the seventh woe and seem to provide a conclusion for the whole section. As elsewhere, "hypocrisy" may mean either insincerity or inconsistency, witting or unwitting. Given human nature, most hypocrites probably combine elements of all. On the repeated references to the "teachers of the law and Pharisees," see comments under v. 1. Of several suggestions concerning the structure of the seven woes, probably the best is to see a 2+2+2+1 pattern (three pairs plus a concluding climax).[15]

---

[13]See R. S. Barbour, "Uncomfortable Words. VIII: Status and Titles," *ExpTim* 82 (1970-71): 137-42.

[14]Cf. J. D. M. Derrett, "Mt. 23,8-10 a Midrash on Is. 54,13 and Jer. 31,33-34," *Bib* 62 (1981): 372-86.

[15]Cf. L. Sabourin, *L'Évangile selon saint Matthieu et ses principaux parallèles* (Rome: Biblical Institute Press, 1978), 294-95.

13"Woe to you, teachers of the law and Pharisees, you hypocrites! You shut the kingdom of heaven in men's faces. You yourselves do not enter, nor will you let those enter who are trying to.

15Woe to you, teachers of the law and Pharisees, you hypocrites! You travel over land and sea to win a single convert, and when he becomes one, you make him twice as much a son of hell as you are.

23:13[-14] The first woe decries the ironic state of affairs that those who should be opening the kingdom to people, pointing them to a proper relationship with God, are actually closing the door. They are not in the kingdom themselves because of their wrong attitudes and actions, and therefore others who follow their teaching, seeking after the truth, are instead led astray. Despite an undeniably positive side to Pharisaism in certain circles, in light of v. 4 some elements of legalism, works-righteousness, and merit theology must be in view here.[16] Verses 15-36 elaborate on the scribes' and Pharisees' sins, which in fact run much deeper. Strong external evidence suggests that v. 14 was not part of Matthew's original autograph. It is absent, for example, from ℵ, B, D, L, Θ, f^1, and old Italic, Syriac, and Coptic translations. It was probably added by later copyists to harmonize Matthew's text with Mark 12:40 and Luke 20:47.

23:15 The irony of Jesus' first woe intensifies when one realizes how the Pharisees were actively proselytizing ("convert" equals the Greek *proselytos*)—going to great lengths for every potential new disciple. This probably does not refer to large numbers of new converts but to the earnestness with which "God-fearers" among the Gentiles were encouraged to become full-fledged Jews, accepting the "yoke of the Law," including circumcision.[17] Thus the numbers led astray would increase. The language here is strong ("son of hell") but accurate for any not following the way of the true and living God. Sometimes shock treatment is needed, especially, and perhaps primarily, for wayward religious leaders professing the truth. New converts to any ideology are often easily spurred on to a much greater zeal than can be maintained by those who have been adherents longer and have become more temperate. Strong warnings appear here for those with great evangelistic fervor in any age. Such people had better be preaching the true gospel. Most cults and sects have begun with vigorous proselytizing on the part of those who believed themselves to be representing true Christian teaching.

---

[16]Contra the influential views of E. P. Sanders (*Paul and Palestinian Judaism* [Philadelphia: Fortress, 1977]), see S. Westerholm, *Israel's Law and the Church's Faith* (Grand Rapids: Eerdmans, 1988).

[17]On which see esp. S. McKnight, *A Light among the Gentiles: Jewish Missionary Activity in the Second Temple Period* (Minneapolis: Fortress, 1991).

[16]"Woe to you, blind guides! You say, 'If anyone swears by the temple, it means nothing; but if anyone swears by the gold of the temple, he is bound by his oath.' [17]You blind fools! Which is greater: the gold, or the temple that makes the gold sacred? [18]You also say, 'If anyone swears by the altar, it means nothing; but if anyone swears by the gift on it, he is bound by his oath.' [19]You blind men! Which is greater: the gift, or the altar that makes the gift sacred? [20]Therefore, he who swears by the altar swears by it and by everything on it. [21]And he who swears by the temple swears by it and by the one who dwells in it. [22]And he who swears by heaven swears by God's throne and by the one who sits on it.

23:16-22 Jesus varies his introduction with the epithet "blind guides," on which see under 15:14. The woe regarding Pharisaic casuistry in oath-taking closely parallels the discussion of 5:33-37, on which see comments there.[18] Here Jesus laments the distinctions being made between the temple itself and its gold (vv. 16-17,21), between the altar itself and its gift or sacrifice (vv. 18-20), and between heaven and God himself (v. 22). The first two contrasts are explicitly stated and are different from the examples of the Sermon on the Mount. The third contrast is stated more implicitly and parallels 5:34. The Jews apparently reasoned that, because a lien could not be put on the temple or altar, then oaths invoking those objects were meaningless.[19] Jesus maintains that temple, gold, altar, and gift all point to God and remain equally sacred, so that oaths taken in their name remain equally binding. In the two examples of vv. 16-21, he seems to be making the additional point that what the Jews thought was the lesser item was actually the greater. The irony of their distinctions thus becomes all the more poignant.

[23]"Woe to you, teachers of the law and Pharisees, you hypocrites! You give a tenth of your spices—mint, dill and cummin. But you have neglected the more important matters of the law—justice, mercy and faithfulness. You should have practiced the latter, without neglecting the former. [24]You blind guides! You strain out a gnat but swallow a camel.

23:23-24 Just as the first two woes naturally formed a pair, so also do the third and fourth. In the first two the Pharisees and scribes have misjudged priorities in God's world; in the third and fourth they misjudge priorities in God's Word. Minor matters are overly elevated; major ones are neglected. The former category includes tithing, even down to small herbs ("mint, dill and cummin"; cf. Lev 27:30). In the latter category

___

[18]Cf. also G. T. Montague (*Companion God: A Cross-Cultural Commentary on the Gospel of Matthew* [New York: Paulist, 1989], 255): "Casuistry is always an attempt to find pockets of security against naked surrender to God's demands."
[19]Cf. Gundry, *Matthew*, 463.

appear "justice, mercy, and faithfulness." The first and third of these terms are more commonly translated as "judgment" and "faith." But given the underlying Aramaic speech of Jesus and the reference to the Hebrew Scriptures, the NIV renderings are probably correct. One then thinks of classic Old Testament texts like Mic 6:8 or Zech 7:9-10.[20] The inconsistency in the officials' behavior once again evokes the address "blind guides" (v. 24; cf. v. 16). Jesus likens the Pharisees and scribes to a person upset about a small bug in a soup or drink who nevertheless swallows a huge animal (v. 24). The comparison is obviously metaphorical. It involves an Aramaic wordplay between *gamla* ("camel") and *galma* ("gnat").[21] The last sentence of v. 23 does not imply that Jesus is becoming more conservative with respect to the law or that tithing is mandated of Christians, merely that as long as the Mosaic covenant remains in force (up to the time of Jesus' death and resurrection), all of it must be obeyed but with discernment of its true priorities. Nor does any generalizable distinction between ceremonial and moral law emerge out of this text, although one does recall Matthew's twofold use of Hosea 6:6 (Matt 9:13; 12:7) on the importance of mercy rather than sacrifice.

Christians in many ages have done a remarkable job of majoring on minors and minoring on majors. A scandal of the contemporary church is its unparalleled fragmentation into hundreds of denominations and groupings. Many of these divisions have been over issues nonessential to salvation. True Christians must stand uncompromisingly against all professing believers who promote teaching which, if embraced, would prevent people from being saved (Gal 1–2) but must bend over backwards to get along and cooperate with those who differ on doctrines that do not affect a person's salvation (1 Cor 9:19-23). Otherwise our disunity seriously undermines Christian witness before a watching world. How is an unbeliever to know which group to join? Cross-cultural models like the church in China after the expulsion of Western missions in the early 1950s, in which denominationalism all but disappeared, are important models for us in the West. It is important, however, to insist that churches do all they can to ensure that their members are truly regenerate believers. On the other hand, "justice, mercy and faithfulness," as God's priorities, suggest that evangelical Christians need to devote much greater attention to a compassionate social ethic for the disenfranchised of our world.

---

[20]Cf. H. N. Ridderbos (*Matthew*, BSC [Grand Rapids: Zondervan, 1987], 429): "'Justice' refers to righteous deeds in general; 'mercy' denotes a loving attitude toward one's neighbor; and 'faithfulness' is a sincere and intimate relationship to God."

[21]R. H. Stein, *The Method and Message of Jesus' Teaching* (Philadelphia: Westminster, 1978), 13.

[25]"Woe to you, teachers of the law and Pharisees, you hypocrites! You clean the outside of the cup and dish, but inside they are full of greed and self-indulgence. [26]Blind Pharisee! First clean the inside of the cup and dish, and then the outside also will be clean.

23:25-26 Another inconsistency between minor and major items contrasts ritual cleanliness with impurities of the heart. Jesus' statement here mixes a metaphor with literal language. He is not attacking the ritual practices of washing, as in 15:1-20, since all Jews agreed on the need to cleanse the inside of dishes and utensils. Rather, he is lamenting a concern for matters of ritual purity more generally at the expense of genuine, inner moral purity.[22] "Greed" translates, more literally, as *rapaciousness*. If this term is taken as a hendiadys (two nouns coordinated so as mutually to define each other) with "self-indulgence," one could translate with the GNB "full of what you have gotten by violence and selfishness." Again contemporary parallels prove frightening. Our Christian behavior and church appearance looks exemplary on the outside, particularly on Sundays. But how much do we spend on ourselves, indulging our material and sensual appetites and attacking others without adequate cause? If these problems could be remedied, outward appearances would take care of themselves (v. 26).

[27]"Woe to you, teachers of the law and Pharisees, you hypocrites! You are like whitewashed tombs, which look beautiful on the outside but on the inside are full of dead men's bones and everything unclean. [28]In the same way, on the outside you appear to people as righteous but on the inside you are full of hypocrisy and wickedness.

23:27-28 The sixth woe completes a third pair. It makes the same point as the previous woe, only via the metaphor of beautiful tombstones in cemeteries, so incongruous in view of the death they mask. For other Jews tombs also epitomized ritual impurity. "Wickedness" is, literally, *lawlessness*. These who claim expertise and faithfulness in the law actually contravene it. Compare Paul's rebuke of Ananias in Acts 23:3 (for which v. 5 is probably not a retraction or apology but ironic commentary).[23]

[29]"Woe to you, teachers of the law and Pharisees, you hypocrites! You build tombs for the prophets and decorate the graves of the righteous. [30]And you say, 'If we had lived in the days of our forefathers, we would not have taken part with them in shedding the blood of the prophets.' [31]So you testify against yourselves that you are the descendants of those who murdered the prophets. [32]Fill up, then, the measure of the sin of your forefathers!

---

[22]Cf. esp. H. Maccoby, "The Washing of Cups," *JSNT* 14 (1982): 3-15.

[23]On the variety of possible Old Testament background texts in view here, see especially J. D. M. Derrett, "Receptacles and Tombs (Mt 23,24-30)," *ZNW* 77 (1986): 255-66.

23:29-32 We now reach the climax of the series of woes and return to the theme of the parables of the wicked tenants and wedding banquet (21:33–22:14). Of all the inconsistencies of these Jewish leaders, the one most serious and relevant to the immediate context of Passion Week is their rejection and martyrdom of God's true spokespersons and, above all, of Jesus. Such hostility proves all the more horrific since "this generation" disavows the sins of their forefathers and tries retrospectively to honor them through building and decorating cemetery memorials (vv. 29-30). But they admit they are linked by ancestry to the most wicked in Israel's history, and they exhibit by their current rejection of Jesus their actual spiritual kinship to the rebellious Israelites of old (v. 31). In a bitterly ironic exclamation, Jesus orders them to go ahead and complete their dirty work (v. 32). It should not surprise anyone who understands the behavior of their predecessors. Compare 1 Thess 2:16, probably a conscious echo of this saying of Jesus. The NIV interpolates "sin"; GNB captures the sense, "Go on, then, and finish up what your ancestors started!" Verse 32 alludes to the Jewish view "that the final judgment will come only after men have reached the absolute peak of sinfulness."[24]

[33]"You snakes! You brood of vipers! How will you escape being condemned to hell? [34]Therefore I am sending you prophets and wise men and teachers. Some of them you will kill and crucify; others you will flog in your synagogues and pursue from town to town. [35]And so upon you will come all the righteous blood that has been shed on earth, from the blood of righteous Abel to the blood of Zechariah son of Berekiah, whom you murdered between the temple and the altar. [36]I tell you the truth, all this will come upon this generation.

23:33-36 Jesus' invective continues and reaches its zenith. These particular Jewish leaders are "snakes," like their father the devil (cf. John 8:44). "Brood of vipers" repeats the language of 3:7 and 12:34. The rhetorical question of v. 33b seems to imply there is no escape. "Therefore" equals *for this reason*. As when speaking in parables, Jesus refers to God bringing his true message to intransigent people in a way that simply guarantees they will continue to reject it and increase their hostility (v. 34). On that notion see comments under 13:1-15. "Jesus who sends the prophets does so as one who has the authority and the power to make the Pharisees demonstrate their fundamental wickedness and thus to make them condemn themselves to Gehenna."[25] Here Jesus speaks even more graphically than in his earlier parables and previous references to rejection and hostility (e.g., 10:17-42; 16:24-28; 17:22-23; 20:17-19; 21:33–

---

[24]D. Hill, *The Gospel of Matthew*, NCB (London: Oliphants, 1972), 314.
[25]D. Patte, *The Gospel according to Matthew: A Structural Commentary* (Philadelphia: Fortress, 1987), 328.

22:14). "I am sending" and "you will kill . . . crucify . . . flog . . . pursue" no doubt have his own death and crucifixion in view[26] but focus even more on subsequent hostility against the disciples. These disciples are described in three categories, parallel to those already mentioned in 10:40-42 and 13:52, probably itemizing various kinds of leaders within early Christianity. "This generation" (v. 3b) will therefore climax the generations of rebellion against God, described intermittently but all too commonly throughout Old Testament and intertestamental history. The qualification "this generation" should also warn us against the tragic abuse of this verse by many throughout church history who have not limited Jesus' words to the generation of A.D. 30–70 and have thus condemned Jews of all subsequent eras as well. "On earth" translates "upon the land" and is probably limited to Israel and the places in which its ancestors dwelt.

Thus one arrives at a culmination of God's judgment against the nation as a whole with the destruction of the temple (cf. v. 38; 24:2). On the thought of v. 35, cf. esp. Rev 18:24. "You murdered" shows corporate solidarity of the present rebellious leaders with those of old. "From Abel to Zechariah" suggests the entire sweep of history from the creation of humanity to the time of Christ. Many have assumed that the Zechariah in view here is the murdered prophet of 2 Chr 24:20-21, in which case Berekiah would be a mistaken reference to Jehoiada. Second Chronicles was the last book in the order of the Hebrew canon, so this interpretation creates a nice inclusio with the martyrdom of Abel at the beginning of Genesis. But it is more likely that the historical overview is strictly chronological, with Zechariah being truly the son of Berekiah and the prophet who wrote the second to the last book of the Old Testament (cf. Zech 1:1). There are no independent pre-Christian traditions of his martyrdom, but certain post-Christian Jewish texts seem to hint at it.[27] And there are still other options.[28] Very recently J. M. Ross has made a plausible case for the view that this is an otherwise unknown Zechariah martyred just prior to Jesus' lifetime.[29]

[37]"O Jerusalem, Jerusalem, you who kill the prophets and stone those sent to you, how often I have longed to gather your children together, as a hen gathers her chicks under her wings, but you were not willing. [38]Look, your

---

[26]"You will crucify" is a causative active. The Jews could initiate proceedings that might lead to a crucifixion, but only the Romans could execute a sentence.

[27]See S. H. Blank, "The Death of Zechariah in Rabbinic Literature," *HUCA* 12-13 (1937-38): 327-46.

[28]See R. H. Gundry, *The Use of the Old Testament in St. Matthew's Gospel* (Leiden: Brill, 1967), 86-88; cf. further discussion in C. L. Blomberg, *The Historical Reliability of the Gospels* (Downers Grove: InterVarsity, 1987), 193-95.

[29]J. M. Ross, "Which Zechariah?" *IBS* 9 (1987): 70-73.

house is left to you desolate. [39]For I tell you, you will not see me again until you say, 'Blessed is he who comes in the name of the Lord.'"

(3) Lament for the Coming Destruction of the Temple (23:37–39).
23:37-39 The harsh tone of vv. 1-36 lessens dramatically. Verses 37-39 disclose Jesus' profound sorrow and compassion at the state of events that has brought him to this point of antagonism with the Jewish leaders. These verses play a role in the larger discourse of chaps. 23–25 somewhat comparable to the role of Rom 9:1-5 in the context of Rom 9–11. Jesus, like Paul, demonstrates the extent of his identification with his people despite the harsh words he has for them elsewhere. Jesus' outburst also reminds one of David's tragic lament for Absalom in 2 Sam 18:33 and 19:4. Jesus is a Jew, these are his people, and this is his holy city. To the extent that he is conscious of the divine presence within him, his agony is greatly multiplied. God's chosen people, specially loved and specially blessed, are now spurning and killing his true representatives. How Jesus wishes it had been otherwise!

Still, even during Jesus' ministry, this generation had more opportunity than any other to change the too frequent pattern of Israelite behavior. Even now the whole point of appealing to the crowds with such warnings is that some might still repent. "Jerusalem" is a metonymy (the use of one name or object to refer to a closely related item) for the corrupt leadership of the people. Jesus' words betray great tenderness and employ maternal imagery. God transcends gender and displays attributes that humans often associate with women, as well as those commonly associated with men. Here Jesus wishes he could gather all the recalcitrant "children" of Israel, to love, protect, and nurture them like a mother hen does with her baby chickens. Similar imagery recurs frequently in Jewish literature (e.g., Deut 32:4; Ps 36:7; Ruth 2:12; Isa 31:5).[30] But God never imposes His love by overriding human will. Verse 37b proves crucial and graphic; unbelieving Israel has chosen its own fate. "I have longed" in v. 37a is, more literally, *I wanted*; "you were not willing" in v. 37b is, more literally, *you did not want*.

So God in Christ withdraws from the people, even as Jesus leaves the temple. In 24:1 he leaves their "house" abandoned—devoid of adequate leadership, true godliness, and divine presence (cf. Ezek 10–11). "Desolate" in v. 38 comes from the adjectival form of the word for wilderness (*erēmos*). With the full inauguration of the new covenant at Jesus' death, the temple will no longer play any role in the unfolding plan of salvation history (cf. John 4:23). From then on no special location will be more sacred than any other; God will dwell wherever "two or three come

---

[30]For a full list of references, see I. H. Marshall, *The Gospel of Luke*, NIGTC (Grand Rapids: Eerdmans, 1978), 575.

together" in Christ's name (18:20). Forty years later, in A.D. 70, the temple buildings will literally be destroyed.[31] But Jesus' own departure is most in the foreground here, as the connective "for" beginning v. 39 demonstrates. The departure of Jesus means the departure of God. Jesus will leave and soon be crucified, not to be seen again by these who have rejected him until his second coming. Then they will echo the cries of the Palm Sunday crowd (21:9) and again quote Ps 118:26. Yet this verse leaves Matt 23 ending with a glimmer of hope. Though many have seen this acclamation as merely forced worship, nothing in the context implies that it should not be taken in a more straightforward way. So there may be a hint here of something like Rom 11:25-27, which apparently describes an outpouring of faith in Jesus among Jews at the end of the church age. The people on Palm Sunday acclaimed Christ without understanding; one day they will praise him with understanding.[32]

Would that all Christians displayed this depth of concern for the lost, especially among those closest to them! Would that we made plain with this boldness the eternal jeopardy those without Christ face. Probably only with the former emotion is the latter boldness justifiable. It is equally crucial to stress that the responsibility for their fate rests squarely with the lost, even when we do not always speak out with the boldness we ought (cf. Rom 1:18-32).

b. JUDGMENT AGAINST ISRAEL AND THE NATIONS (24:1–25:46). Jesus' prediction leads the disciples to ask when the destruction of the temple will occur and what will be the signs of his return (vv. 1-3). Jesus' answers to these two questions occupy 24:4-35. Matthew 24:36–25:46 goes on to enjoin watchfulness throughout the entire interim period between Christ's two comings. Together, chaps. 24–25 are often called Jesus' Eschatological (or Olivet) Discourse. The physical judgment of unrepentant Israel is epitomized by the destruction of the temple (24:15-20), but there is a coming judgment of all nations or peoples for which every human must prepare (25:31-46). As with the rest of the large blocks of discourse material in Matthew, there are shorter parallels in Mark (see esp. chap. 13) and longer ones scattered about Luke (see esp. chaps. 12; 17; 21). In at least this instance, however, a strong case can be made for the hypothesis that all three Evangelists drew on one connected discourse source, which was originally fuller than all of the current accounts.[33]

---

[31]For background to the theological significance of this event, see M. N. A. Bockmuehl, "Why Did Jesus Predict the Destruction of the Temple?" *Crux* 25.3 (1989): 11-18.

[32]For a detailed defense of this view, see D. C. Allison, Jr., "Matt. 23:39 = Luke 13:35b As a Conditional Prophecy," *JSNT* 18 (1983): 75-84.

[33]D. Wenham, *The Rediscovery of Jesus' Eschatological Discourse* (Sheffield: JSOT, 1984), who at least raises the question of whether similar procedures might be envisioned elsewhere.

(1) Signs and Times of the Temple's Destruction and of Christ's Return (24:1-35). These verses have yielded numerous interpretations and present all kinds of exegetical conundrums. Carson provides an excellent, brief overview of the major problems and plausible solutions.[34] Space prevents detailed interaction with the alternatives at each stage here. Historically, Christians have held numerous views on eschatology, particularly with reference to the millennium and the rapture, which inevitably have colored their interpretations of this passage.[35] Baptists in particular have commendably tolerated quite a bit of diversity on this topic. A credible outline of this section might well unfold along the following lines: (1) The disciples' introductory question sets the stage for Jesus' teaching (vv. 1-3). (2) Jesus describes preliminary events that do not portend the end (vv. 4-14). (3) The temple will be destroyed during a period of horrible suffering (vv. 15-20), an interim period of "great distress" will ensue (vv. 21-28), and then Christ will return (vv. 29-31). (4) Everything necessary to prepare for this Parousia (Christ's return) will occur within the lifetime of Jesus' disciples (vv. 32-35).[36]

[1]Jesus left the temple and was walking away when his disciples came up to him to call his attention to its buildings. [2]"Do you see all these things?" he asked. "I tell you the truth, not one stone here will be left on another; every one will be thrown down."

[3]As Jesus was sitting on the Mount of Olives, the disciples came to him privately. "Tell us," they said, "when will this happen, and what will be the sign of your coming and of the end of the age?"

(a) Introduction (24:1-3). **24:1-3** As they leave the temple, Jesus' followers continue to marvel at its grandeur (cf. Luke 21:5). Jesus immediately redirects their attention to its transience. He predicts what may have seemed inconceivable at the time—the greatest architectural wonder

---

[34]Carson, "Matthew," 488-95. Representative full-length studies from various perspectives include G. R. Beasley-Murray, *Jesus and the Future* (London: Macmillan, 1954); L. Hartman, *Prophecy Interpreted* (Lund: Gleerup, 1966); V. K. Agbanou, *Le discours eschatologique de Matthieu 24-25* (Paris: Gabalda, 1983); F. W. Burnett, *The Testament of Jesus and Sophia* (Washington: University Press of America, 1981). D. L. Turner ("The Structure and Sequence of Matthew 24:1-21: Interaction with Evangelical Treatments," *GTJ* 10 [1989]: 3-27) nicely surveys four main evangelical approaches to the structure of 24:1-41 and convincingly defends a "traditional preterist-futurist view," which I closely though not exactly follow.

[35]For an introduction to the major perspectives, see esp. R. G. Clouse, ed., *The Meaning of the Millennium: Four Views* (Downers Grove: InterVarsity, 1977); R. R. Reiter et al., *The Rapture: Pre-, Mid-, or Post-Tribulational?* (Grand Rapids: Zondervan, 1984).

[36]Cf. also J. Lambrecht, "The Parousia Discourse: Composition and Content in *Mt.*, XXIV-XXV," in *L'Évangile selon Matthieu*, ed. M. Didier (Gembloux: Duculot, 1972), 309-42; R. Summers, "Matthew 24-25: An Exposition," *RevExp* 59 (1962): 501-11.

in the Middle East will one day be entirely razed. They continue east across the Kidron Valley and climb the slopes of the Mount of Olives, a site already resonant with apocalyptic overtones as the place of the Messiah's coming to judge his enemies (Zech 14:4). Resting on the hillside, and probably looking down on the temple below, the disciples naturally question when such a catastrophe could occur. They ask a second question as well, about the sign that would herald the end of the age and Christ's return, a question likely triggered by 23:39. Jesus will make clear that the destruction of the temple and the end of the age are two separate events, but probably the disciples do not yet recognize this (thus Mark 13:4), scarcely imagining that one could occur without the other. Hence for them the two questions are one and the same.[37]

⁴Jesus answered: "Watch out that no one deceives you. ⁵For many will come in my name, claiming, 'I am the Christ,' and will deceive many. ⁶You will hear of wars and rumors of wars, but see to it that you are not alarmed. Such things must happen, but the end is still to come. ⁷Nation will rise against nation, and kingdom against kingdom. There will be famines and earthquakes in various places. ⁸All these are the beginning of birth pains.

(b) Signs That Do Not Yet Herald the End (24:4-14). **24:4-8** Jesus begins by addressing the second question. Before describing the destruction of the temple itself, he warns against false signs—events that some would claim prove that the end is near even when it is not. Jesus' followers must take care not to be misled by occurrences that will simply be commonplace events of life in the Christian era (v. 4). These events, which are not decisive signs, are common in Jewish apocalyptic literature.[38] Specifically they include: (1) People other than Jesus will claim to be the Messiah (v. 5; vv. 23-28 will repeat this thought, and v. 27 will explain that Christ's return will be universally visible and unmistakable). These false messiahs are not limited to professing Christians. "In my name" means *they aim to usurp Jesus' place* and hence include Jewish pretenders too (most notably bar Kochba in the early second century).[39] But an amazing number of false teachers throughout Christian history and in our own age have fulfilled this prophecy as well. (2) "Wars and rumors

---

[37]Contra J. F. Walvoord (*Matthew: Thy Kingdom Come* [Chicago: Moody, 1974], 182), there are not three questions here. "The sign of your coming and of the end of the age" in Greek reads, more literally, *the sign of your coming and end of the age*. By not repeating the definite article ("the") before "end of the age," Matthew's rendering of Jesus' words is most likely linking the coming of Christ and the end of the age together as one event (Granville Sharp's rule).

[38]See the numerous references in S. T. Lachs, *A Rabbinic Commentary on the New Testament: The Gospels of Matthew, Mark, and Luke* (Hoboken, N.J.: KTAV, 1987), 380.

[39]France, *Matthew*, 337.

of wars" will abound. "Rumors" are, more literally, *unconfirmed reports*, which may or may not be true. Revelation 16:16 and 19:17-19 describe the climactic gathering of God's enemies for the final battle against his people just before the time of Christ's return. But in Rev 19:20–20:3, Jesus physically returns to earth and prevents those armies from inflicting any casualties on his supporters. "Armageddon" may thus not be equated with any ordinary, human war, in which both sides suffer losses without the supernatural intervention of Christ. And no other war prior to this in all of human history has any special claim over against any other war as pointing to the time of Christ's return (v. 6). (3) International hostility and enmity, including but apparently not limited to actual warfare, will also be common (v. 7a). (4) Famines and earthquakes typify natural disasters that will often make people wonder if the end is near, but nothing may be deduced from them (v. 7b). Militarism and war, famine, death, and earthquakes reappear in the seven seals of Rev 6, which depict events prior to the tribulation rather than the decisive eschatological or apocalyptic events themselves. The seals must be broken before the end-time judgments of the scroll to which they are affixed can be read and begun. Like a woman's contractions before her labor and delivery, these preliminary events remind one of the nearness and inevitability of Christ's return. But just as a woman may experience false labor and just as genuine contractions still leave her uncertain about the exact time of delivery, so too the events of vv. 4-8 do not enable us to predict the time of Christ's coming. Birth pangs were in fact a common Jewish metaphor to refer to an indeterminate period of distress leading up to the end of this age (e.g., *1 Enoch* 62:4; *2 Esdr* 4:42; *Tg. Ps* 18:14). Yet in spite of all these disasters and difficulties, Christians must not be alarmed; the end is still to come. Bruner makes the pastoral comment, "In times of crisis, Christians should be the calmest people on the block because they have a dominical *pax.*"[40] (Cf. also Ps 27:3.)

9"Then you will be handed over to be persecuted and put to death, and you will be hated by all nations because of me. 10At that time many will turn away from the faith and will betray and hate each other, 11and many false prophets will appear and deceive many people. 12Because of the increase of wickedness, the love of most will grow cold, 13but he who stands firm to the end will be saved. 14And this gospel of the kingdom will be preached in the whole world as a testimony to all nations, and then the end will come.

24:9-14 Verse 9 begins with the first of several *then*s (Greek *tote*) in this section of the Olivet Discourse. It is not always clear whether "then" means *after, at that time*, or simply *therefore*. Verse 10 has another *tote*,

---

[40]F. D. Bruner, *The Churchbook* (Dallas: Word, 1990), 847.

which the NIV renders "at that time." Probably the meaning in v. 9 is the same; here are the further preliminary signs that do not necessarily prove that the end is coming immediately. Rather, they characterize the entire interadvent period—what we often call the church age. Hence we may continue numbering these items from where we left off under vv. 4-8: (5) Persecution and martyrdom of disciples will proliferate (v. 9). Jesus has already predicted these sufferings in 10:17-25 with a similar generalization (10:22, "all men will hate you") just as here he warns that "you will be hated by all nations." As in 10:22, "all" may mean *all kinds*, though here Jesus' point may be that antagonism against the gospel will emerge among every people group. Such a warning, of course, does not preclude many individuals within each country also embracing the gospel. (6) Apostasy, betrayal, and hatred will run rampant in the church (v. 10). Whereas (5) referred to external hostility, (6) envisions internal strife. "Turn away from the faith" reflects Matthew's favorite *skandalizō* (*to take offense*) and links with v. 9. When persecution increases, some will abandon their faith to save their necks. To the extent that the "gospel" in which they have trusted is only of the "health-wealth" or "prosperity" variety, it will be exceedingly hard to maintain belief under these trying circumstances. Although 7:23 refers to a different category of professing Christians, one may fairly apply its logic here to answer the question about the genuineness of the faith of those who apostatize. (7) False prophets will arise (v. 11; cf. 7:15-22). These are not quite as brazen as those who falsely claim to be Christ himself (v. 5), but their ministries prove equally misguided and damning, as they falsely claim to speak for Christ and his gospel. (8) Spiritual life will deteriorate, perhaps even among true believers, as they tire of fighting the battle against apostasy and persecution (v. 12; cf. Rev 2:4). Perhaps, as with the Ephesian church at the end of the first century, this coldness of love refers more to a lack of good works than to a loss of strong emotion (cf. Rev 2:5).[41] The "increase of wickedness" is, more literally, *lawlessness being fulfilled/ made complete* and echoes 23:32, suggesting a climax of evil (cf. Luke 21:24b with its reference to the "times of the Gentiles" being "fulfilled"). The translation "most," however, is misleading. The Greek reads *the many*, describing merely a large group whose percentage is unspecified. Quite possibly, however, this is a resumptive use of the definite article referring to the "many people" at the end of v. 11, in which case the "love" that will grow cold will be that of those professing Christians who apostatized and not that of true believers who persevered.

---

[41]Cf. Schweizer (*Matthew*, 451): "False doctrine is accordingly not erroneous theology, but an attitude that in practice does not display love." The dichotomy is a false one, but the point is well taken.

Verse 13, by way of contrast, reminds those who do remain loyal of their marvelous inheritance of salvation. Here is the true biblical promise of eternal security or perseverance of the saints, not that all who profess Christ persevere but that those who do persevere demonstrate that they were truly elect. "The end" could refer to Christ's return for those who live that long. For most it will refer to the time of their physical death (as with the martyrs of v. 9). Alternately, "to the end" could be translated *to the uttermost.*[42] In light of v. 9, "saved" here refers to eternal life and not physical protection. Jesus thus offers the sober reminder that for some only the threat of persecution and martyrdom will reveal their true colors (as stressed again throughout the Book of Hebrews).

Separated from the previous eight negative signs that do not herald the end is the promise of yet one more preliminary event: (9) the extensive preaching of the gospel (v. 14). Here is the fulfillment of the Great Commission Jesus will give in 28:18-20. Probably it is separated from the other eight items because it is a more positive development. Jesus does not say that every individual on earth will hear the gospel and certainly not that all who hear will respond appropriately, but he does seem to indicate that the gospel, summed up as the message of the kingdom, will be proclaimed widely throughout the known world (though *oikoumenē* in the first century often referred merely to the Roman Empire), that is, to representative areas and people groups across the globe.

All nine of these preliminary events in fact occurred before A.D. 70,[43] though most if not all have recurred many times since then as well. Various messianic pretenders arose, most notably Theudas (Acts 5:36; Josephus, *Ant.* 20.97-99, 160-72, 188, who describes other false claimants as well). The war of Israel against Rome began in A.D. 66–67 and was preceded by the growing hostility incited by the Zealots. Famine ravaged Judea, as predicted in Acts 11:27-30, datable to ca. A.D. 45–47 by Josephus, *Ant.* 20.51-53. Earthquakes shook Laodicea in A.D. 60–61 and Pompeii in A.D. 62 (cf. also Acts 16:26). Persecution dogged believers' footsteps throughout Acts; internal dissension so tore apart the church at Corinth (1 Cor 1–4) that God even caused some to die (1 Cor 11:30). Numerous New Testament epistles were written primarily to warn against false teachers and perversions of Christianity, most notably Galatians, Colossians, 1 Timothy, 2 Peter, and Jude. Arguably, the concept of "love running cold" most aptly characterized the days of the Neronian persecution of Christians in the midsixties.[44] Paul, finally, with whatever ratio-

---

[42] Agbanou, *Matthieu*, 79; Sabourin, *Matthieu*, 305-6.

[43] See esp. W. G. Thompson, "An Historical Perspective in the Gospel of Matthew," *JBL* 93 (1974): 243-62.

[44] J. Taylor, "'The Love of Many Will Grow Cold': Matt 24:9-13 and the Neronian Persecution," *RB* 96 (1989): 352-57.

nale, could claim that by at least the late fifties, the gospel had gone out to all the *oikoumenē—known world* or *empire* (Rom 10:18).

It is crucial to observe the fulfillment of all these preliminary events prior to A.D. 70. This fulfillment will explain how 24:34 can be true. It demonstrates that everything necessary for Christ's return was accomplished within the first generation of Christianity, so that every subsequent generation has been able to believe that Jesus could come back in their times. It should lead us to reject all views that claim to know for sure that Christ is returning in a given year, decade, or century on the basis of some unique event that has never previously occurred in Christian history (as, e.g., with the reestablishment of the state of Israel or with some future, hypothetical rebuilding of the temple).[45] Moreover, by including the extensive preaching of the gospel (item 9) with the eight negative signs, Jesus offers something of a balance in his presentation of events that must occur before the end. Neither the unrelenting pessimism of traditional dispensationalism nor the unbridled optimism of certain forms of postmillennialism is justified. Instead, the period of time prior to Christ's return will be characterized by a growing polarization between good and evil. God's people will increase in power, witness, and impact in the world, even as persecution and hostility intensify and global conditions deteriorate. Revelation 11:3-13 graphically depicts this polarization, and church history, beginning already in Acts 8:1-4, has frequently demonstrated the truth of Tertullian's slogan that "the blood of the martyrs is the seed of the church."

[15] "So when you see standing in the holy place 'the abomination that causes desolation,' spoken of through the prophet Daniel—let the reader understand— [16] then let those who are in Judea flee to the mountains. [17] Let no one on the roof of his house go down to take anything out of the house. [18] Let no one in the field go back to get his cloak. [19] How dreadful it will be in those days for pregnant women and nursing mothers! [20] Pray that your flight will not take place in winter or on the Sabbath.

(c) The Destruction of the Temple (24:15-20). **24:15-20** Without having answered the second of the disciples' questions ("What will be the sign?"—v. 3), Jesus turns back to the first. When will the destruction of the temple take place? Presumably after these preliminary events that do not actually herald the end. But v. 15 does not begin with "then," merely "when." The only specific advance notice Jesus gives involves an event that will profane the temple, fulfilling the prophecy of Dan 9:27 (cf. Dan

---

[45]Cf. further W. L. Lane, *The Gospel according to Mark*, NIC (Grand Rapids: Eerdmans, 1974), 455-65; C. E. B. Cranfield, *The Gospel according to St. Mark*, CGTC (Cambridge: University Press, 1977), 394-402.

11:31; 12:11). The "abomination that causes desolation" might also be translated as a *desolating sacrilege*. In the days of the Maccabees, the Jews wondered if this prophecy had been fulfilled when Antiochus Epiphanes slaughtered a pig on the temple altar and subsequently destroyed much of the temple precincts, the city of Jerusalem, and thousands of its inhabitants (167 B.C.; cf. 1 Macc 1:54 and 6:7).[46] "Let the reader understand" is a somewhat cryptic aside that Matthew carries over from Mark. Was it there to avoid a direct reference to hostile Roman authorities should the Gospel fall into the wrong hands? Does the "reader" refer to readers of Daniel and call them to discern correctly the meaning or significance of its prophecies? Is the reader the person reading the Gospel aloud to a congregation, who should insert some targumlike explanation at this point? It is hard to be sure.

Jesus does not dwell on any advance warning but on the awfulness of this day. Destruction will arrive so quickly that believers must waste no time in their flight (vv. 16-18). The language of these verses may be inspired by Gen 19:17 on the devastation of Sodom and Gomorrah. The horrors of life in a city under siege are gruesomely enumerated in Deut 28:53-57. Believers must take to the hills in the Judean countryside away from Jerusalem, where it would be harder for invaders to fight and capture them. They must not waste even the short time it would take to go back into their homes to get extra clothing or possessions. They must interrupt whatever they are doing—whether relaxing, as customary on the flat rooftops of their homes, or working, as typically in the fields—and flee with the utmost of haste. They should pray that no one fleeing is pregnant or a nursing mother, since the rigors of travel and hiding, not to mention the unspeakable horrors of treatment should one be captured, would make them suffer greatly (v. 19). So too for all those taking flight if the day turned out to be in the winter, when frequent rains made travel difficult, or on the Sabbath, when the city gates might be shut, stores closed, and various services and forms of transportation unavailable (v. 20). This reference to the Sabbath is found only in Matthew's account. It would be natural for Matthew to include it for his more Jewish audience, but he does not thereby imply, as is often alleged, that he envisions Christians still keeping the Jewish laws.[47] At the beginning of the Roman war with Israel in the late sixties, many Christians did indeed flee Jerusa-

---

[46]For other events that early Jewish and Christian interpreters thought might have fulfilled Dan 9:27, see M'Neile, *Matthew*, 348.

[47]G. N. Stanton ("'Pray That Your Flight May Not Be in Winter or on a Sabbath' [Matthew 24.20]," *JSNT* 37 [1989]: 17-30) surveys the various options for interpreting this verse and concludes that the best approach understands that fleeing on the Sabbath would have antagonized the Jews further and increased persecution of believers.

lem, perhaps recalling Jesus' words. But many headed for Pella, east of the Jordan, not for the Judean hill country.[48]

The imagery of sacrilegious desolation and the temple's destruction calls to mind 2 Thessalonians and particularly the appearance of the "man of lawlessness" in God's temple (2 Thess 2:3-4). Given the repeated patterns of God's activity in history, these parallels should not surprise us. Undoubtedly, much that surrounded the destruction of the temple and the Jewish war in A.D. 70 will be repeated, probably on a larger scale, just prior to Christ's return. But given the thoroughly Jewish nature of all of the details of vv. 15-20, their close correspondence to the actual events of the mid-first century, and the more explicit wording of Luke 21:20-24, there is no reason to take any of Matthew's text here as looking beyond the events that culminated in the destruction of the temple in A.D. 70. The desolation of God's house, briefly predicted in 23:38, is now described with more horrifying detail.

[21]For then there will be great distress, unequaled from the beginning of the world until now—and never to be equaled again. [22]If those days had not been cut short, no one would survive, but for the sake of the elect those days will be shortened.

(d) *The Great Tribulation (24:21-28)*. **24:21-22** Another "then" (*tote*) appears. It does not seem to mean *later* but *at that time* or *beginning immediately*—the NIV does not even break for a paragraph. But the concept of a period of unparalleled distress (based on Dan 12:1) causes problems. If these two verses simply depict the horrors surrounding the war of A.D. 70, it is hard to see how v. 21 could be true.[49] If they point to some end-time sacrilege, just before the Parousia, then it is hard to see how Matthew allows for a gap of at least two thousand years between vv. 20-21. It is probably best, therefore, to understand this period of great distress, or "the great tribulation," as it is more commonly known, as the entire period beginning with the devastation of A.D. 70 and continuing on until Christ's return (cf. "immediately" in v. 29).

Jesus envisages this time as short, but 2 Pet 3:8, quoting Ps 90:4, reminds us that God's perspective on what is a short period of time is not necessarily the same as ours ("a thousand years are like a day"). As with the "abomination that causes desolation" in v. 15, seeing Jesus' reference to the great tribulation as beginning in A.D. 70 does not exclude a later application of this expression to the period of time described in Rev 7-19—the

---

[48]See esp. C. Koester, "The Origin and Significance of the Flight to Pella Tradition," *CBQ* 51 (1989): 90-106.

[49]Despite the efforts, e.g., of Carson ("Matthew," 501) to speak of "never so high a percentage of a great city's population so thoroughly and painfully exterminated and enslaved."

final stages of this entire interadvent period. Revelation 7:14 seems to suggest precisely such an intensification of horrors immediately preceding the end of the age. God's intervention in history plays out in repeated patterns of activity on ever grander or more awful scales. At least in Matthew, however, it would seem that the tribulation Jesus has in mind must refer to the entire church age from A.D. 70 on.[50] Far from this age being a millennium, as in traditional amillennialism, the New Testament era in which we have been living is better characterized as tribulation for believers (though recall the positive side of this period described in v. 14 and the implications noted there).

All this does not mean that life for Christians in this world must remain unrelentingly evil but that in general, due to the opposition of a fallen world to the priorities of God and even despite the powerful inauguration of his kingdom, people will continue to reject the exclusive message of that kingdom. Today believers are increasingly discovering that Christianity's claim to be the only way to salvation elicits irrational hostility by advocates of a pluralism that accepts all views as possible except those that claim to know certain absolute truths. But the millennium and new heavens and earth of Rev 20–22 will put an end to all opposition to the gospel and persecution of believers, more than compensating Christians for previous suffering and injustice. And even before those epochs, the time of distress will be "cut short"—before all believers have been martyred (v. 22). "Survive," more literally, is *be saved*, but this time the physical sense of the term is clear since believers have been promised spiritual preservation. "The elect" (*eklektoi*) are the same group as the "chosen" of 22:14 and therefore must refer to Christians of any race, rather than to literal Israel.

23At that time if anyone says to you, 'Look, here is the Christ!' or, 'There he is!' do not believe it. 24For false Christs and false prophets will appear and perform great signs and miracles to deceive even the elect—if that were possible. 25See, I have told you ahead of time.

26"So if anyone tells you, 'There he is, out in the desert,' do not go out; or, 'Here he is, in the inner rooms,' do not believe it. 27For as lightning that comes from the east is visible even in the west, so will be the coming of the Son of Man. 28Wherever there is a carcass, there the vultures will gather.

24:23-28 *Tote* here can obviously mean "at that time," as in the NIV, but perhaps it has shades more of *therefore* or *so*. The contents of vv. 23-28 do not necessarily follow chronologically after the tribulation but out-

---

[50]Here, with Carson, "Matthew," 495. Cf. H. Hobbs, *An Exposition of the Gospel of Matthew* (Grand Rapids: Baker, 1965), 341: This tribulation "refers to the suffering of the saints in preaching the gospel throughout the period from Jesus' ascension until His return" (though to start with the ascension is probably to start one generation too soon).

line various warnings that follow from the description of the interadvent period in vv. 21-22. Again Jesus warns against being deceived by the kinds of people already mentioned in vv. 5 and 11. He echoes 7:22 in depicting their miracle-working power (v. 24). Believers are not immune to their attacks, but God will protect them from full-fledged apostasy.[51]

Here emerges another indirect testimony to the truth that those who do give up believing demonstrate that they never truly were Christ's followers. But despite Christ's warning (v. 25) believers can be misled in other ways, such as looking for him in some remote or hidden place (v. 26). False messiahs in Israel liked to appear in the wilderness (cf. Josephus, *Ant.* 20.97-99, 167-72), and one common Jewish tradition looked for a Messiah who would be hidden on earth until his manifestation, a tradition possibly in view here with the reference to the "inner rooms."[52] In the twentieth century the Jehovah's Witnesses' belief in a secret, invisible return of Christ in 1914 affords a classic example of what Christ commands us here to avoid. Instead, his actual return will be unmistakable in its nature, universal in its visibility, and cosmic in its scope and effect (v. 27). On the imagery of "lightning," cf. Zech 9:14. Verse 28 then concludes the paragraph by describing metaphorically how all people will be drawn to see Christ upon his return, just as certainly as vultures gather to devour a corpse or animal carcass.[53]

[29]"Immediately after the distress of those days
" 'the sun will be darkened,
   and the moon will not give its light;
the stars will fall from the sky,
   and the heavenly bodies will be shaken.'
[30]"At that time the sign of the Son of Man will appear in the sky, and all the nations of the earth will mourn. They will see the Son of Man coming on the clouds of the sky, with power and great glory. [31]And he will send his angels with a loud trumpet call, and they will gather his elect from the four winds, from one end of the heavens to the other.

(e) Christ's Second Coming (24:29-31). **24:29-31** Jesus now returns to the question of the sign of his coming. He will return "immediately after" the tribulation of the interadvent period. Matthew must be emphasizing this immediacy since he usually deletes this particular

---

[51]"If that were possible" (εἰ δυνατόν) is probably an ellipsis for the protasis of a fourth-class condition (εἰ δυνατόν εἴη) used in an indirect rhetorical question, thus implying that it is not probable that the elect will be deceived.

[52]On which see M. de Jonge, "Jewish Expectations about the 'Messiah' according to the Fourth Gospel," *NTS* 19 (1972-73): 246-70.

[53]Schweizer (*Matthew*, 454-55) limits the birds to the false messiahs and prophets converging like vultures, but he agrees that Jesus' point is that there is no mistaking the presence of the Parousia.

adverb (*euthys, eutheōs*) from his sources.[54] Jesus portrays his return with the typical apocalyptic imagery of cosmic upheaval. He does not intend his language to be taken as a literal, scientific description of events but as a vivid metaphor, much as we speak of earth-shaking developments. From this moment on, the universe can no longer continue as it has been (cf. Rev 6:12-17; 8:12). Jesus' imagery may well also point to the overthrow of the cosmic and demonic powers often associated in paganism with the sun, moon, and stars. Most of v. 29 echoes, without directly quoting (contra the NIV punctuation), texts such as Isa 13:10 and 34:4. At last Jesus mentions the "sign" about which the disciples had asked (v. 30a). Only Matthew makes this reference explicit. But it is not clear whether this sign is the same as the Son of Man appearing in the sky (v. 30b) or some other heavenly ensign or banner (cf. Isa 11:12; 18:3; and 1QM 3:1–4:17), which points to Jesus.[55] Patristic exegesis often thought of the sign as a cross in the sky, but nothing in the text suggests this, even though it is still defended occasionally.[56] It is probably not important to be able to decide among these options, since in any event the sign does not enable anyone to recognize the "signs of the times" until Christ is actually en route to earth. As in v. 15 with the destruction of the temple, Jesus leaves no clues to permit us to know how many years, generations, or centuries after his first coming he will return.

Instead, he focuses on what will accompany his parousia. The *tribes* (*phylai*—NIV "nations") of the world will mourn. The term calls to mind the twelve tribes of Judaism, in which case "the earth" perhaps means *the land*, i.e., of Israel. The mourning clearly alludes to Zech 12:10. Revelation 1:7 uses this text in the same way, while John 19:37 reapplies it to those who mourn the crucifixion. The mourning of the *phylai* may involve repentance or stem from their realization of the coming judgment. In Zechariah the former sense seems more likely. Given that *phylai* more literally means tribes than nations and can easily be seen as referring to Israel, perhaps repentance is in view here too. Then, as in 23:39, we have a hint regarding Israel's future conversion (cf. Rom 9–11).

At this time, Jesus will return in majesty with all authority to judge the world (v. 30b). Clear echoes of Dan 7:13-14 emerge here. The title Son of

---

[54]G. C. Fuller ("The Olivet Discourse: An Apocalyptic Timetable," *WTJ* 28 [1966]: 157-63) equates "immediately" with the concept of "the next significant event in salvation history," but this is an otherwise unparalleled use of the term in the Gospels and thus a much less persuasive interpretation.

[55]See T. F. Glasson, "The Ensign of the Son of Man (Matt. XXIV.30)," *JTS* 15 (1964): 299-300. In other words, the debate involves whether to take the genitive "of the Son" as appositional or objective.

[56]E.g., A. J. B. Higgins, "The Sign of the Son of Man (Matt. XXIV.30)," *NTS* 9 (1962-63): 380-82.

Man in this context must surely refer to a superhuman figure. Jesus' picture contrasts sharply with the suffering and humiliation on the cross, which he knew loomed large in his immediate future even as he spoke. Attempts to take the "coming on the clouds of the sky" as Christ's coming spiritually in judgment against Israel at the time of the destruction of the temple, so that all of vv. 15-35 refer only to first-century events, have to take *parousia* ("coming") in v. 27 in a way that is otherwise entirely unparalleled in the New Testament.[57] It is much more natural, therefore, to understand Christ's coming here to earth, as in Rev 19:11-16, when Jesus brings with him all the company of the redeemed already in heaven to join his faithful people yet on earth and still alive to meet him (cf. Zech 2:6 and Deut 30:4). All this is heralded by an angelic trumpet blast (cf. 1 Cor 15:52; 1 Thess 4:16; and perhaps based originally on Isa 27:13). Walvoord correctly observes that nothing in any of these verses in Matthew describes the rapture (believers being caught up to meet the Lord in the air).[58] Disputes about a pretribulation, midtribulation, or post-tribulation rapture will have to be settled by other texts.

[32]"Now learn this lesson from the fig tree: As soon as its twigs get tender and its leaves come out, you know that summer is near. [33]Even so, when you see all these things, you know that it is near, right at the door. [34]I tell you the truth, this generation will certainly not pass away until all these things have happened. [35]Heaven and earth will pass away, but my words will never pass away.

(f) Concluding Implications (24:32-35). **24:32-35** So what about the perennial desire of disciples for signs to specify when Christ's return is near? Like tender fig tree branches and new leaves that portend the arrival of summer, all the events of Matt 24 point to the nearness of Christ's return (vv. 32-33). But nearness simply implies that nothing more in God's plan of redemption must occur before the end can come.[59] Verse 34 does not imply that Christ will return within the lifetime of his hearers or within some later period of thirty to forty years during which all the

---

[57]As, e.g., in France, *Matthew*, 343-44; contra which see D. Wenham, "'This Generation Will Not Pass . . .': A Study of Jesus' Future Expectation in Mark 13," in *Christ the Lord*, ed. H. H. Rowdon (Leicester: InterVarsity, 1982), 138-41.

[58]Walvoord, *Matthew*, 182.

[59]Cf. C. E. B. Cranfield, "The Parable of the Unjust Judge and the Eschatology of Luke-Acts," *SJT* 16 (1963): 300-01: "The Parousia is near . . . not in the sense that it must necessarily occur within a few months or years, but in the sense that it may occur at any moment and in the sense that, since *the* decisive event of history has already taken place in the ministry, death, resurrection and ascension of Christ, all subsequent history is a kind of epilogue, an interval inserted by God's mercy in order to allow men time for repentance, and, as such an epilogue, necessarily in a real sense short, even though it may last a very long time."

signs occur.[60] Nor is it necessary to follow the NIV margin and translate *genea* as "race," referring to Israel, a much less likely rendering of the Greek than "generation." Rather, "all these things" in v. 34 must refer to "all these things" of v. 33, which show that Christ's return is near and which therefore cannot include Christ's return itself. "All these things" will then refer to everything described in 24:1-26 but will not include the Parousia itself (described in vv. 27-31).[61]

Verse 35 concludes the first half of Jesus' teaching on the Mount of Olives by stressing the certainty of everything that Christ has outlined. His words will endure even longer than the universe itself, which will be destroyed and re-created. As noted under vv. 4-14, the upshot of this chapter is to let the disciples know some more of the details about the temple's destruction, without specifying when it will occur, and to make it plain that from that moment on, the end of the age, signaled by Christ's return, can come at any time.

(2) Commands to Perpetual Vigilance (24:36–25:46). Verse 36 functions as a thesis statement for this entire section and as a topic sentence for its first paragraph, which illustrates the surprise arrival of the end (24:36-42). Next proceeds a collection of parables on watchfulness—the householder and thief (vv. 43-44), the faithful and unfaithful servants (vv. 45-51), the ten bridesmaids (25:1-13), and the talents (25:14-30). The first three parables create an interesting series. In the first Christ's return is completely unexpected; in the second, sooner than expected; in the third, later than expected. Jesus covers all bases; Christians must remain prepared for him to come at any time. The fourth parable then explores more fully what that preparation involves—good stewardship of all God has committed to us. Jesus' discourse culminates with a quasiparabolic picture of final judgment, elaborating the theme of Jesus' return, which each of the preceding parables has depicted more briefly (25:31-46).

36 "No one knows about that day or hour, not even the angels in heaven, nor the Son, but only the Father. 37As it was in the days of Noah, so it will be at the coming of the Son of Man. 38For in the days before the flood, people were eating and drinking, marrying and giving in marriage, up to the day Noah entered the ark; 39and they knew nothing about what would happen until the flood came and took them all away. That is how it will be at the coming of the Son of Man. 40Two men will be in the field; one will be taken and the other left. 41Two women will be grinding with a hand mill; one will be taken and the other left. 42Therefore keep watch, because you do not know on what day your Lord will come.

---

[60]Cf. Carson ("Matthew," 507): "'This generation' can only with the greatest difficulty be made to mean anything other than the generation living when Jesus spoke."

[61]Cf. Ridderbos, *Matthew*, 449.

(a) Introduction and Thesis: No One but God the Father Knows the Time of Christ's Return (24:36-42). **24:36** This verse is one of the most astonishing and significant of all of Jesus' sayings both for eschatology and for Christology. It climaxes the previous discussion and introduces the rest of Jesus' discourse. All these questions about the time of Christ's return are misguided because no one but the Father knows their answers anyway. "Day" and "hour" are regularly used throughout Scripture for "time" in general, not just twenty-four-hour or sixty-minute periods (in Matt cf. 7:22; 10:19; 24:42,44,50; 25:13; 26:45). "Day" especially reflects the Old Testament "Day of the Lord" (cf. esp. throughout Zephaniah) as a stock phrase for the end of the age (cf. Matthew's "day of judgment" in 10:15; 11:22,24; 12:36; and cf. also Rom 10:21; 1 Cor 4:5; 2 Cor 3:14; Eph 6:13). Verses 42-44 will use "day," "time of night" (*watch*), and "hour" interchangeably. "Day" and "hour" appear in synonymous parallelism in v. 50. Hence, Christians who claim they can narrow down the time of Christ's return to a generation or a year or even a few day's period, while still not knowing the literal day or hour, remain singularly ill-informed.[62] Recent pamphlets and popular paperbacks show the tenacity of such contrary views and the havoc they can wreak. We can no doubt expect a new collection of false prophecies littering our Christian bookstores as the intriguing year 2000 approaches.

Verse 36 proves equally significant for Christology. Christ's words disclose his voluntary limitation of the independent exercise of his divine attributes (cf. Phil 2:6-8). Jesus was obviously not bodily omnipresent while he walked on earth. Mark 6:5 describes some restrictions on his omnipotence. Here we have a limitation on his omniscience. Christians who balk at the implications of this verse reflect their own docetism (the early Christian heresy of not accepting the full humanity of Jesus) and lack a full appreciation for the extent of God's condescension in the incarnation and in the various human limitations he took upon himself.[63] The textual variant noted in the NIV margin probably reflects a similar docetism among some early copyists. But the external evidence is strong for the inclusion of this phrase (ℵ, B, D, Θ, *f*[13], old Italic, Syriac, and Coptic versions; and numerous Greek and Latin fathers), and it is far more textually secure in the parallel passage in Mark 13:32.

---

[62]Cf. Carson ("Matthew," 508): "It is ridiculous quibbling divorced from the context to say that though the day and hour remain unknown, we ascertain the year or month."

[63]Cf. Gundry (*Matthew*, 492): "Theologically, we may say that just as Jesus did not exercise his omnipotence except to further the kingdom (cf. his refusal to make stones into bread), so he did not exercise his omniscience except to further the kingdom." Again, "What Jesus could have done because he was divine did not predetermine what he did do as also a man. The incarnation did not destroy divine potencies, but it did limit actualities."

24:37-41 Jesus now illustrates the unexpectedness and unpredictability of his return by comparing it with the arrival of the flood in Noah's day (vv. 37-39). At that time the world's wicked were caught totally by surprise as they went about the ordinary activities of daily life, including festive events, oblivious to their impending destruction. Noah and his seven faithful family members were prepared but still did not know the specific timing of the cataclysm until the last moment (Gen 6–7).[64] Compare the repetition of these two points in 1 Thess 5:1-3 and 4-6, respectively. So also Christ's return will interrupt people in the ordinary activities of life.

Verses 40-41 describe these activities with typical first-century examples—men and women at work at their respective tasks of farming and grinding meal. Some have seen a "secret rapture" in view here (in which believers mysteriously disappear from earth, leaving everyone else to wonder what happened), which often leads to absurd scenarios (e.g., the modern-day notion of cars suddenly without drivers). But the only coming of the Son of Man described so far has been the climactic universal return of Christ in v. 27. The imagery of vv. 38-41 does not suggest anything different. Eating and drinking, marrying and working all represent public activity. These verses simply picture the sudden and unexpected nature of the Parousia.[65] There will be no mystery then; Matthew 25:31-46 will describe the worldwide judgment of humanity that occurs next. In fact, "taken" in vv. 40-41 (though a different verb in the Greek) parallels "took" of v. 39 and suggests that those taken away are taken for eternal judgment (not "raptured"), while those left behind remain with Christ.[66]

24:42 Verse 42 rounds out the paragraph, not as in the NIV beginning a new one, inasmuch as vv. 43-44 form a self-contained parable. Verse 42 highlights the significance that no one knows when Christ will come back; we must be ever vigilant. *Hōra* (*hour*; "day," clearly indicating its figurative sense) links back with the "hour" of v. 36. Jesus' words

---

[64]Some have taken Gen 6:3 as a prediction of the timing of the flood, but probably this verse refers to the shrinking of a typical human lifespan. See J. Sailhamer, "Genesis," in EBC, vol. 2 ed. F. E. Gaebelein (Grand Rapids: Zondervan, 1990), 76-77. Otherwise Noah was given only seven days' notice at some unspecified time following the completion of the ark (7:4).

[65]Cf. F. Stagg ("Matthew," in *The Broadman Bible Commentary*, vol. 8, ed. C. J. Allen [Nashville: Broadman, 1969], 222): "The separation between those *taken* and those *left* will not follow conventional lines such as race or nationality. The lines will run through families and neighbors, separating those who had known ties so close as daily work."

[66]Cf. Walvoord, *Matthew*, 193; R. H. Mounce, *Matthew*, GNC (San Francisco: Harper and Row, 1985), 236.

aptly summarize the thrust of all of 24:36–25:46. Discipleship demands faithful stewardship, not attempts to calculate the timing of the end since such estimates will almost inevitably be mistaken.

⁴³But understand this: If the owner of the house had known at what time of night the thief was coming, he would have kept watch and would not have let his house be broken into. ⁴⁴So you also must be ready, because the Son of Man will come at an hour when you do not expect him.

(b) The Parable of the Householder and Thief (24:43-44). **24:43-44** A parable now illustrates this necessary preparedness. A Christian's vigilance should be like that of a house owner who knew a burglar was coming and thus kept guard at all times of the day or night. This passage creates a shorter parable than most in Matthew thus far. It contains only two main characters and therefore probably makes only two main points: (1) "People must constantly be ready for the possible return of Christ, since (2) he might come at any time and catch some off guard."[67] Like his comparison of God with an unjust judge in Luke 18:1-8, Jesus' point in comparing himself with a thief is limited. He is not depicting himself as a lawbreaker but stressing how unexpected and unpleasant his return will be for those not prepared for it. His imagery apparently proved quite effective since Paul, Peter, and John all reuse it later in the New Testament (1 Thess 5:2; 2 Pet 3:10; and Rev 3:3). It also underlines again the point of v. 36. R. T. France observes: "In view of such plain statements as this, it is astonishing that some Christians can still attempt to work out the date of the parousia!"[68]

⁴⁵"Who then is the faithful and wise servant, whom the master has put in charge of the servants in his household to give them their food at the proper time? ⁴⁶It will be good for that servant whose master finds him doing so when he returns. ⁴⁷I tell you the truth, he will put him in charge of all his possessions.

(c) The Parable of the Faithful and Unfaithful Servants (24:45-51).[69] **24:45-47** Jesus now illustrates his point about preparedness with a more

---

[67]C. L. Blomberg, *Interpreting the Parables* (Downers Grove: InterVarsity, 1990), 278.

[68]France, *Matthew*, 349. M. Green (*Matthew for Today* [Dallas: Word, 1989], 233, 235) labels such speculation "blasphemous" and cites a rabbinic maxim: "He who announces the messianic times based on calculations forfeits his share in the future."

[69]It is disputed whether Luke 12:35-38 and/or Mark 13:33-37 are variant forms of this same parable or separate accounts. Contrast the views of D. Wenham, *The Rediscovery of Jesus' Eschatological Discourse* (Sheffield: JSOT, 1984), 15-49, and C. Blomberg, "When Is a Parallel Really a Parallel? A Test Case: The Lukan Parables," *WTJ* 46 (1984): 83-85. A mediating approach sees purer forms becoming "de-parabolized" over time—see R. Bauckham, "Synoptic Parousia Parables and the Apocalypse," *NTS* 23 (1977): 165-69.

detailed, three-pronged parable. This story varies from the typical parable form in that Jesus envisages two alternative, hypothetical scenarios involving the same character (the servant) rather than an actual contrast between two separate, good and bad characters. But the upshot is the same, though perhaps Jesus makes his point more forcefully this way, provoking his disciples to consider the possibility that they too might go astray. The servant is depicted as an overseer or manager, head over other servants in his master's household. Among other things he will have to see that the rest are properly fed at the proper time (v. 45; cf. 2 Tim 4:1-5). Christians too should be about their Lord's work, honoring him in every area of life. Leaders must serve more than rule. Such people will be "blessed" at the Lord's return (v. 46 is actually a beatitude—"it will be good" renders the Greek *makarios, blessed*). On those persons' rewards (v. 47), see under 25:21,23.

[48]But suppose that servant is wicked and says to himself, 'My master is staying away a long time,' [49]and he then begins to beat his fellow servants and to eat and drink with drunkards. [50]The master of that servant will come on a day when he does not expect him and at an hour he is not aware of. [51]He will cut him to pieces and assign him a place with the hypocrites, where there will be weeping and gnashing of teeth.

24:48-51 The alternative is to imagine the day of reckoning as later than it turns out to be so that one acts irresponsibly and wickedly, thinking that plenty of time still remains for repentance (vv. 48-49). The key word here is *chronizei* (*delays*, "is staying away a long time"). Commentators often claim that Jesus himself could not have said this, that only after the early church recognized the delay of the Parousia could such a saying emerge. But it is not clear that this so-called delay was the problem for early Christianity that it is often alleged to be.[70] What is more, in the historical context of Jesus' life the master's going away for a long time would refer first of all to God's delaying of the Day of the Lord, a problem with which Jews had already been wrestling for several centuries. This Day of the Lord, by Matthew's time understandably reinterpreted as also including Christ's return, will thus catch all unbelievers by surprise and result in judgment for them (v. 50). The picture of the slave caught beating his fellow servants does not portray Christians caught in sin and suddenly damned. Instead, it pictures people who delay coming to terms with God in Christ for too long, so that they suddenly find, whether due to his return or due to their own deaths, that it is too late to repent. God has commanded all individuals to be good stewards of his creation

---

[70]See esp. C. L. Blomberg, *The Historical Reliability of the Gospels* (Downers Grove: InterVarsity, 1987): 33-35.

(Gen 1:26-28) and therefore holds everyone accountable. Those who prove unfaithful stewards can anticipate eternal damnation (v. 51).[71]

The three main points of the parable thus follow: "(1) God rewards and punishes people at the final judgment on the basis of their stewardship of the tasks assigned to them. (2) Faithful stewardship requires perseverance and consistency, for the end could come at any time. (3) Those who postpone their responsibilities and do evil in the meantime may sadly discover that it is too late for them to make amends for their errors."[72]

(d) The Parable of the Ten Bridesmaids (25:1-13). Jesus further illustrates his warning that would-be followers should be prepared for his return at any time with a story in which the master comes back later than expected. The five foolish bridesmaids are not prepared for the long wait. *Chronizontos* (*delaying*, "a long time in coming") links v. 5 with 24:48.

¹"At that time the kingdom of heaven will be like ten virgins who took their lamps and went out to meet the bridegroom. ²Five of them were foolish and five were wise. ³The foolish ones took their lamps but did not take any oil with them. ⁴The wise, however, took oil in jars along with their lamps. ⁵The bridegroom was a long time in coming, and they all became drowsy and fell asleep.

25:1-5 Instead of faithful and unfaithful servants, now we have wise and foolish bridesmaids. *Parthenoi* ("virgins") refers to young women of marriageable age. The word is chosen not to point out their lack of sexual activity but their intimate relation to the bride. The imagery of the parable accurately reflects typical customs of first-century Palestinian wedding festivities.[73] A welcoming processional escorts the newly married couple from the bride's home to a great banquet at the bridegroom's home, some unspecified time after the legal nuptials have been exchanged. Torches light the way in the darkness, so all the bridesmaids have to take enough oil to keep them burning for as long as might be necessary. The two groups of women are described as exactly alike in everything except their preparations. Thus the fact that five fall in each category does not teach that there will be the same number saved as lost. The wait proves longer than all have anticipated, and everyone falls asleep. On the theme of the delay, see under 24:48.

---

[71]On the unusual expression in v. 51, "cut him to pieces," see esp. O. Betz, "The Dichotomized Servant and the End of Judas Iscariot," *RevQ* 5 (1964): 46-47; P. Ellingworth, "Luke 12.46—Is There an Anti-climax Here?" *BT* 31 (1980): 242-43. Probably the term means *cut off*, as in the OT banning of a member from the community of God's people and is not a literal description of some kind of painful, physical punishment.

[72]Blomberg, *Parables*, 193.

[73]See esp. J. Jeremias, *The Parables of Jesus* (Philadelphia: Westminster, 1972), 173-74.

⁶"At midnight the cry rang out: 'Here's the bridegroom! Come out to meet him!'

⁷"Then all the virgins woke up and trimmed their lamps. ⁸The foolish ones said to the wise, 'Give us some of your oil; our lamps are going out.'

⁹"'No,' they replied, 'there may not be enough for both us and you. Instead, go to those who sell oil and buy some for yourselves.'

25:6-9 Finally at 12:00 a.m., perhaps when least expected, the sleepers awaken to a cry that the groom is coming (v. 6). The cry parallels the trumpet blasts of 24:31; 1 Cor 15:52; and 1 Thess 4:16 (which contains both trumpet and shout).[74] At this point the five foolish bridesmaids realize their mistake and beg the others to share their oil with them (vv. 7-8). The five wise young women refuse, since they realize that then all may run out of oil, leaving everyone in the dark (v. 9a). On festive nights such as this, the shops stayed open as long as people might need them, so the girls should go there and purchase extra oil for themselves. Jesus apparently wants to teach that spiritual preparedness may not be transferred from one individual to another. All people are responsible for themselves. But the oil should probably not be allegorized despite frequent and conflicting suggestions that take it to refer to such things as good works, faith, grace, or the Holy Spirit,[75] because none of these can be bought.

¹⁰"But while they were on their way to buy the oil, the bridegroom arrived. The virgins who were ready went in with him to the wedding banquet. And the door was shut.

¹¹"Later the others also came. 'Sir! Sir!' they said. 'Open the door for us!'

¹²"But he replied, 'I tell you the truth, I don't know you.'

¹³"Therefore keep watch, because you do not know the day or the hour.

25:10-13 This extra errand, however, takes too long. The five foolish bridesmaids miss the groom, the processional, and the arrival at the banquet. The door to the groom's home is closed and probably locked to keep out any intruders (v. 10). The five truant girls *finally* (Greek *hysteron*, "later") arrive and beg permission to enter (v. 11). Their cry closely resembles the appeal of 7:21 ("sir, sir" in 25:11 reflects the twice-used *kyrie*). But the bridegroom refuses to let them in.

Thus far all of the parable has seemed reasonably realistic, except perhaps for the unpreparedness of the foolish bridesmaids. But, as always in

---

[74]F. W. Beare, *The Gospel according to Matthew* (San Francisco: Harper and Row, 1981), 484.

[75]As respectively, in K. P. Donfried, "The Allegory of the Ten Virgins (Matt. 25:1-13) as a Summary of Matthean Theology," *JBL* 93 (1974): 423; R. V. G. Tasker, *The Gospel according to St. Matthew: An Introduction and Commentary*, TNTC (London: InterVarsity, 1961), 234; and J. F. Walvoord, "Christ's Olivet Discourse on the End of the Age: The Parable of the Ten Virgins," *BibSac* 129 (1972): 102.

parables, the real point is at the spiritual level, as now becomes clear. An ordinary groom would let the girls enter, but this *lord* refuses admittance and denies even knowing them (v. 12). On this motif of ignorance combined with the closed door, cf. Luke 13:25. The moral of the story proceeds (v. 13) and echoes 24:36,42,50. "Keep watch" means *be prepared* and not necessarily *stay awake*.

The distinctive warning of this parable cautions would-be disciples against refusing to count the cost of persevering in discipleship. The foolish young women resemble the seeds that fell in the shallow soil of 13:5-6,20-21. The language of v. 12, though not as emphatic as that of 7:23, again suggests that this is not a case of true Christians losing their salvation (Jesus does not say "I no longer know you") but of people whom he simply does not recognize because they have never been his.[76] But they may well have professed intimacy with him, just as members of the bridal party usually appear to be close friends of the couple who are marrying. God is frequently pictured as a bridegroom in the Old Testament (e.g., Isa 54:4-6; Ezek 16:7-34; Hos 2:19); Jesus is in some way equating himself with God. On the messianic banquet imagery, cf. under 22:11-14. The three points of the passage may now be summarized: "(1) Like the bridegroom, God may delay his coming longer than people expect. (2) Like the wise bridesmaids, his followers must be prepared for such a delay—discipleship may be more arduous than the novice suspects. (3) Like the foolish bridesmaids, those who do not prepare adequately may discover a point beyond which there is no return—when the end comes it will be too late to undo the damage of neglect."[77]

(e) The Parable of the Talents (25:14-30).[78] In 24:45 the slave was faithful and prudent ("wise"). The ten bridesmaids (25:1-13) illustrated prudence in more detail; the parable of the talents will illustrate faithfulness in more detail.[79] In the parable of the ten bridesmaids, the foolish young women thought the task was easier than it turned out to be; in the parable of the talents, the wicked servant thinks it is harder than it turns out to be. In addition, this passage expands on the nature of the preparedness to which the previous parables were pointing, defining the task with

---

[76]Cf. also H. B. Green (*The Gospel according to Matthew* [Oxford: Clarendon, 1975], 205): "I don't know you" is a rabbinic formula to prevent certain individuals from approaching a person.

[77]Blomberg, *Parables*, 195.

[78]A similar theme and motif reappear in Luke 19:11-27, but again this is probably a separate parable from a different occasion in Jesus' ministry. Cf. Plummer (*Matthew*, 348): "The lesson of the Pounds is that men endowed with the same gifts may make a very different use of them and be very differently requited. The lesson of the Talents is, that men with different gifts may make an equally good (or bad) use of them, and be proportionately requited."

[79]M'Neile, *Matthew*, 359.

which believers are to be occupied until Christ returns, namely, good stewardship for his benefit of all that he has loaned us.

14 "Again, it will be like a man going on a journey, who called his servants and entrusted his property to them. 15To one he gave five talents of money, to another two talents, and to another one talent, each according to his ability. Then he went on his journey. 16The man who had received the five talents went at once and put his money to work and gained five more. 17So also, the one with the two talents gained two more. 18But the man who had received the one talent went off, dug a hole in the ground and hid his master's money.

25:14-18 Jesus illustrates the nature of the kingdom of heaven once again with a story about a master with good and bad servants (v. 14). Again, the master goes away for a while and then returns (vv. 15,19). In this parable the servants are given money to invest wisely. On "talents" see comments under 18:24. The NIV margin suggests somewhat too small a sum. If one talent equaled sixty denarii, a conservative estimate since the denarius was an average minimum daily wage, then at the current (1991) American average five-dollar minimum wage for an eight-hour workday, the talent would be at least equivalent to $2400 (and it might have been much more—see comments under 18:23-35). Not all servants are given the same amount, since each has different capabilities and gifts. F. D. Bruner comments, "In the kingdom of Christ not all are created equal."[80] Nor is everyone expected to perform at the same level of competence, but all are expected to do their best as faithful stewards. The first two servants go to work at once, and each earns a hundred-percent yield on his investments (vv. 16-17). The servant given only one talent makes no investment at all, though he does safeguard the money for his master's return (v. 18; cf. *b. B. Meṣ.* 42a). He has no chance of making any profit but, unlike the others, risks no loss. Yet as the unfolding story will demonstrate, to make no commitments on religious matters is really to make a damning commitment by default.

19 "After a long time the master of those servants returned and settled accounts with them. 20The man who had received the five talents brought the other five. 'Master,' he said, 'you entrusted me with five talents. See, I have gained five more.'
21 "His master replied, 'Well done, good and faithful servant! You have been faithful with a few things; I will put you in charge of many things. Come and share your master's happiness!'

25:19-21 The "long time" of v. 19 matches the "delay" motif of the previous two parables. Later Christian theology would naturally see in

---

[80]Bruner, *Churchbook*, 902.

this interval the delay of the return of Christ, but in the context in which Jesus first uttered these words, his disciples would have thought first of all of the delay of God's coming to bring the Day of the Lord (see under 24:48; 25:5). But at last the time of reckoning does arrive. The first servant displays the results of his work and is praised and rewarded with greater responsibility and with rejoicing in the company of his master. Those who have been good stewards of all the time, material resources, and abilities God has given them (and not just with a tenth of these) can expect commendation, happiness, and eternal life from God. It is not clear if "in charge" in vv. 21 and 23 carries any allegorical freight, but perhaps we can expect eternity to be filled with meaningful activity and responsibility of some kind (we have such at least on Judgment Day—19:28). On the contrast between "few" versus "many" meaning *money* and *things of this world* versus spirituality and heavenly treasures (and with almost the identical wording) cf. Luke 16:10-12.

22"The man with the two talents also came. 'Master,' he said, 'you entrusted me with two talents; see, I have gained two more.'
23"His master replied, 'Well done, good and faithful servant! You have been faithful with a few things; I will put you in charge of many things. Come and share your master's happiness!'

25:22-23 The same pattern repeats with the second servant. The parallel language demonstrates that Jesus makes no distinction between the first two servants regarding the degrees of faithfulness.

24"Then the man who had received the one talent came. 'Master,' he said, 'I knew that you are a hard man, harvesting where you have not sown and gathering where you have not scattered seed. 25So I was afraid and went out and hid your talent in the ground. See, here is what belongs to you.'
26"His master replied, 'You wicked, lazy servant! So you knew that I harvest where I have not sown and gather where I have not scattered seed? 27Well then, you should have put my money on deposit with the bankers, so that when I returned I would have received it back with interest.

25:24-27 In vv. 24-25 the scene changes dramatically. The climax of the parable comes with the arrival of the third servant. This man confesses fearing his boss and believing him to be a severe taskmaster who could not have tolerated the loss of any of his money. *Skleros* ("hard") with reference to persons can also mean "strict, harsh, cruel, merciless."[81] This servant imagines his master as unjust or capricious, likening him to a farmer who harvests fields he did not plant. Such a view of God proliferated among ancient religions and unfortunately recurs far too often among Christians as well. The servant returns the master's money

---

[81]BAGD, 756.

unharmed. But he receives no praise, only fury (vv. 26-27). "Lazy" (*oknēros*) more literally means *shrinking* or *hesitating*. The master does not dispute the servant's characterization of him, but neither need v. 26 be read as agreeing with it. The master's words sound like biting sarcasm. He points out that, even if the servant were right, he should have realized that his inaction proved all the more inconsistent with his premise. Disobedience would surely elicit a severe master's wrath. He should have invested the money as his fellow servants did. His tragic error lay in allowing himself to be paralyzed by his fear.[82]

[28]"'Take the talent from him and give it to the one who has the ten talents. [29]For everyone who has will be given more, and he will have an abundance. Whoever does not have, even what he has will be taken from him. [30]And throw that worthless servant outside, into the darkness, where there will be weeping and gnashing of teeth.'

25:28-30 So instead of being entrusted with greater responsibility and eternal happiness, this servant faces nothing but the prospect of eternal judgment, described by Matthew's recurring refrain of the "weeping and gnashing of teeth" (v. 30; cf. as recently as 24:51). Principles to be learned from both the faithful and faithless servants are then rehearsed. Good stewardship of little things brings greater privilege and responsibility. Poor stewardship leads to losing even what one has. "Has" or "does not have" in the context of v. 29 refers to what a given servant *has or has not accomplished* with the original loans. The principle applies in a preliminary fashion already in this life, though fortunately God displays great grace and gives most people many second chances. The principle will be applied more consistently in a once-for-all fashion on Judgment Day. Giving the one talent to the man who already had ten has no obvious spiritual counterpart and probably is used just to round out a story in which the money of an absentee landlord has to continue to be divided among his servants in some way. It does not suggest a criterion of differentiation among the first two servants, since the second man was equally praised in the identical language used with the first.

The three points of the passage thus approximate to the following: (1) "Like the master, God entrusts all people with a portion of his resources, expecting them to act as good stewards of it. (2) Like the two good servants, God's people will be commended and rewarded when they have faithfully discharged that commission. (3) Like the wicked servant, those who fail to use the gifts God has given them for His service will be punished by separation from God and all things good."[83] This final point

---

[82]Montague, *Companion God*, 279.
[83]Blomberg, *Parables*, 214.

seems appropriate both for those who are overtly hostile to God and his revelation and for those who profess commitment to him but show no evidence in their lives of the reality of their profession.[84]

One need not limit the application of this parable to money matters, but finances probably best illustrate the principles involved. The imagery of investing contrasts with Jesus' earlier command to the rich young ruler to give away all he had to the poor (19:21), though giving money away for kingdom causes is a spiritual investment (cf. Luke 16:1-9). Jesus' imagery does suggest that capital which earns money may create even greater wealth to use for God's glory. But this otherwise valid and important principle can easily prove seductive. Many have vowed to draw the line at a certain standard of living, promising a church or Christian organization all they earn above a fixed level, only to later renege under the lure of other attractive things that extra money can buy. Most Christians never even attempt to draw such a line and find all their income spent on items of no eternal significance or value and gone before they knew they had it. Given the fate of the wicked servant, such behavior proves extremely risky, to say the least.[85] The New Testament never explicitly commands a tithe for Christians, but giving 10 percent of one's income to churches and Christian organizations that give priority to holistic mission, meeting people's spiritual and social needs, is an attainable goal for most. If a majority of Western Christians gave *at least* this amount, and if churches directed it to appropriate ends, much of world poverty could be eradicated and millions more could hear the gospel.

(f) The Sheep and the Goats (25:31-46). The four parables of 24:43–25:30 have all alluded to judgment, even while concentrating more on right living in this life. Finally, Jesus concentrates on that judgment itself, even while alluding to the necessary preparation. The use of a simile in v. 32 ("as a shepherd separates") and a metaphor in v. 33 ("the sheep and goats") has led many to classify this passage as a parable, but from v. 34 on nothing else appears that cannot be taken literally, so it is better not to use this label. Jesus began this discourse by focusing on the temporal judgment against Israel (23:1–24:20); he now ends with an emphasis on the eternal judgment of all the world.[86]

31 "When the Son of Man comes in his glory, and all the angels with him, he will sit on his throne in heavenly glory. 32All the nations will be gathered

---

[84]Ibid., 215.

[85]At the same time, one must not confuse this parable with any doctrine of salvation by works, as the very sensitive study of D. Lyss ("Contre le salut par les oeuvres dans la prédication des talents," *ETR* 64 [1989]: 331-40) stresses.

[86]See S. W. Gray, *The Least of My Brothers: Matthew 25:31-42—A History of Interpretation* (Atlanta: Scholars, 1989), for a detailed history of the interpretation of this text.

before him, and he will separate the people one from another as a shepherd separates the sheep from the goats. [33]He will put the sheep on his right and the goats on his left.

25:31-33 Jesus describes his return in v. 31 with imagery that resembles that of 16:27; 19:28; and 24:30. The picture is one of grandeur, majesty, authority, and judgment. The recipients of judgment are all *ta ethnē* (v. 32a), *the peoples* or *the Gentiles* ("the nations"). Given the use of *ethnē* elsewhere in this discourse, where the Jews apparently are included (24:7,9,14), the first translation seems best. But the shift from the neuter *ethnē* to the masculine *autous* (*them*—"the people") in v. 32b implies that individuals and not just nations or people groups are intended.

So here is a picture of all humanity standing before Christ on Judgment Day.[87] No mention is made of those who died before Christ's return, but it would be natural to view this judgment as the same event as that depicted in 1 Cor 15:51-57 and Rev 20:4, in which all God's people of every era, including those already dead, are resurrected and/or given their new bodies. Of course, those who have died and gone to be with the Lord will already know their eternal destiny; but here the public, universal, even cosmic demonstration of God's justice and mercy is displayed for all to see.[88] It is not clear whether or not the wicked dead are present here; Rev 20:11-15 seems to suggest not.

The separation between "sheep" and "goats" (v. 32) alludes to Ezek 34:17-19. Palestinian shepherds frequently had to separate their flocks this way. Sheep and goats freely intermingled and often looked quite similar in appearance, at least from a distance. We too could probably not guess from superficial knowledge and external appearance who are truly God's people, but he knows. "His right [hand]" (v. 33) refers to a place of honor; the "left" hand, to a place of disgrace (not a third-highest position of honor as in 20:23).

[34]"Then the King will say to those on his right, 'Come, you who are blessed by my Father; take your inheritance, the kingdom prepared for you since the creation of the world. [35]For I was hungry and you gave me something to eat, I was thirsty and you gave me something to drink, I was a stranger and you invited me in, [36]I needed clothes and you clothed me, I was sick and you looked after me, I was in prison and you came to visit me.'

---

[87]Also to be rejected is the view of Calvin, endorsed recently by G. Gay ("The Judgment of the Gentiles in Matthew's Theology," in *Scripture, Tradition, and Interpretation*, ed. W. W. Gasque and W. S. LaSor [Grand Rapids: Eerdmans, 1978], 199-215), in which this is the judgment only of the church, as a *corpus mixtum*.

[88]Cf. Beare, *Matthew*, 493: this judgment is not a trial but merely passing sentence for decisions already made. This understanding similarly dispenses with the claim of Walvoord (*Thy Kingdom Come*, 203) that Jesus' imagery rules out a posttribulation rapture.

25:34-36 Sheep's wool made them more valuable than goats, so naturally Jesus chooses the sheep to represent those individuals who are blessed by God and inherit his kingdom, here envisioned in all its future fullness, though prepared for them from the creation of the world. God intended from the beginning to fashion creatures in community for fellowship with himself. The sheep are blessed because of their good behavior. They cared for Christ, feeding him when he was hungry, giving him drink when thirsty, providing adequate clothing when he was ill-clad (*gymnos*, "needed clothes," frequently translated "naked" but often meaning *only with an undergarment*), showing him hospitality when he was a *foreigner* (*xenos*; "stranger," v. 35), and visiting him when he was sick or imprisoned. Here are three basic human needs, apart from salvation—food, shelter, and companionship.[89]

[37] "Then the righteous will answer him, 'Lord, when did we see you hungry and feed you, or thirsty and give you something to drink? [38]When did we see you a stranger and invite you in, or needing clothes and clothe you? [39]When did we see you sick or in prison and go to visit you?'

25:37-39 Many of the sheep are understandably surprised. No doubt several of these conditions did characterize Christ at various stages of his earthly life, but the vast majority of the "righteous" will not have been present then and there to help him. So how did all this happen? Many interpreters have seen this surprise as indicating that these people were "anonymous Christians"—righteous heathen who did good works but never heard the gospel. But the text never says they were surprised to be saved, merely that they did not understand how they had ministered so directly to Jesus.

[40] "The King will reply, 'I tell you the truth, whatever you did for one of the least of these brothers of mine, you did for me.'

25:40 The King, the Son of Man (cf. vv. 31,34) replies that these people cared for him whenever they performed acts of mercy for "the least of these brothers of mine." Here is a major interpretive crux. Who are these brothers? The majority view throughout church history has taken them to be some or all of Christ's disciples since the word "least" (*elachistōn*) is the superlative form of the adjective "little [ones]" (*mikroi*), which without exception in Matthew refers to the disciples (10:42; 18:6,10,14; cf. also 5:19; 11:11), while "brothers" in this Gospel (and usually in the New Testament more generally) when not referring to

---

[89]Cf. D. Marguerat (*Le jugement dans l'Évangile de Matthieu* [Geneva: Labor et Fides, 1981], 508-9), who speaks of food, shelter, and freedom. But nothing in this passage promises release for those in prison.

literal, biological siblings, always means *spiritual kin* (5:22-24,47; 7:3-5; 12:48-50; 18:15 (2X),21,35; 23:8; 28:10). There may be a theological sense in which all humans are brothers and God's children, though not all are redeemed, but nothing of that appears here or, with this terminology, elsewhere in Matthew. The minority view throughout church history, which is probably a majority view today, especially in churches with a healthy social ethic, is that these "brothers" are any needy people in the world.[90] Thus the passage becomes a strong call to demonstrate "fruit in keeping with repentance" (3:8). Though one need not see any works-righteousness ethic present,[91] many have read the text precisely that way.[92] Yet while there is ample teaching in many parts of Scripture on the need to help all the poor of the world (most notably in Amos, Micah, Luke, and James), it is highly unlikely that this is Jesus' point here.[93] Rather, his thought will closely parallel that of 10:42. The sheep are people whose works demonstrate that they have responded properly to Christ's messengers and therefore to his message, however humble the situation or actions of those involved. That itinerant Christian missionaries regularly suffered in these ways and were in frequent need of such help is classically illustrated with the example of Paul (see esp. 2 Cor 11:23-27) and the teaching of the *Didache* (ca. A.D. 95).

41"Then he will say to those on his left, 'Depart from me, you who are cursed, into the eternal fire prepared for the devil and his angels. 42For I was hungry and you gave me nothing to eat, I was thirsty and you gave me nothing to drink, 43I was a stranger and you did not invite me in, I needed clothes and you did not clothe me, I was sick and in prison and you did not look after me.'

25:41-43 The scenario repeats itself with the goats. These are people doomed to eternal punishment. As the kingdom was prepared, so also the

---

[90]See esp. E. Schweizer, "Matthew's Church," in *The Interpretation of Matthew*, ed. G. Stanton (Philadelphia: Fortress, 1983), 138-39; J. A. Grassi, "'I Was Hungry and You Gave Me To Eat' (Matt. 25:35ff): The Divine Identification Ethic in Matthew," *BTB* 11 (1981): 81-84.

[91]E.g., see Hill, *Matthew*, 330.

[92]E.g., H. B. Green (*Matthew*, 206-7), who takes "the sheep" as the heathen who serve Christ without knowing it.

[93]For recent, more detailed defenses of the majority view, see J. R. Michaels, "Apostolic Hardships and Righteous Gentiles: A Study of Matthew 25:31-46," *JBL* 84 (1965): 27-37; L. Cope, "Matthew XXV.31-46: 'The Sheep and the Goats' Reinterpreted," *NovT* 11 (1969): 32-44; J. M. Court, "Right and Left: The Implications for Matthew 25.31-46," *NTS* 31 (1985): 223-33; G. E. Ladd, "The Parable of the Sheep and the Goats in Recent Interpretation," in *New Dimensions in New Testament Study*, ed. R. N. Longenecker and M. C. Tenney (Grand Rapids: Zondervan, 1974), 191-99.

fire. But it is interesting that the fire was not prepared for the goats but for the rebellious angels. Neither is it prepared "from the creation of the world" (v. 34). These differences support a sublapsarian theology, in which God originally made no provision for lost people or hell in his creative purposes, but once humans and angels freely chose to rebel, then a place of punishment was prepared. No Scripture ever indicates that the fallen angels had any subsequent chance to repent. But people do. So no one need join the demons in this fire. Still, some will opt for hell by rejecting Christ. When they do, they have no one but themselves to blame.

**[44]"They also will answer, 'Lord, when did we see you hungry or thirsty or a stranger or needing clothes or sick or in prison, and did not help you?'
[45]"He will reply, 'I tell you the truth, whatever you did not do for one of the least of these, you did not do for me.'
[46]"Then they will go away to eternal punishment, but the righteous to eternal life."**

25:44-45 The goats ask the same kind of question as the sheep did, and Jesus offers a parallel reply. These people are condemned for sins of omission as well as commission. Improper response to Christian witnesses leads to damnation.

25:46 The closing verse in Jesus' discourse recapitulates both halves of the Judgment Day scene. The parallel between eternal punishment and eternal life makes it difficult to see in the former any kind of annihilationism, even if the word "eternal" can refer to a qualitative rather than quantitative attribute of life and attractive as doctrines of conditional immortality ought to be to anyone with a sensitive heart.[94]

The upshot here, then, as with the culmination of all Scripture in Rev 20–22, is to assert that ultimately there will only be two kinds of people in the world. These will be distinguished on the basis of their response to the gospel and its emissaries, and their eternal destinies will be as distinct as is conceivable. True, everlasting reality is not to be found in this life but in the life to come. Hence, there remains no more pressing priority in this life than to respond properly to Jesus and his messengers by becoming disciples through faith in him. Then we must demonstrate Christ's lordship in our lives through acts of service—to all the needy, yes, but especially to those of the household of faith (cf. Gal 6:10). What is more,

---

[94]Cf. also the warning of P. H. Bligh, "Eternal Fire, Eternal Punishment, Eternal Life (Mt 25:41,46)," *ExpTim* 83 (1971): 9-11: These words are not to be removed as redactional because of a universalist sentimentality, but the context must be preserved. The damned are the religious leaders who oppose Jesus.

picturing Christian witnesses as needy and suffering reminds us of the lot true believers often face.[95] This is graphically seen in the Two-Thirds World today where some estimates suggest that over two hundred million Christians suffer malnourishment daily.

---

[95]Cf. esp. J. R. Donahue, "The 'Parable' of the Sheep and the Goats: A Challenge to Christian Ethics," *TS* 47 (1986): 3-31.

———————— *SECTION OUTLINE CONTINUED* ————————

C. Jesus' Ultimate Destiny (26:1–28:20)
   1. Passion and Crucifixion (26:1–27:66)
     a. Preparation for Jesus' Death (26:1-75)
       (1) Events Preceding Thursday Night (26:1-16)
         (a) Introduction to the Passion Narrative (26:1-2)
         (b) The Jewish Leaders' Plot against Jesus (26:3-5)
         (c) Anointing for Burial (26:6-13)
         (d) Judas Prepares to Betray Jesus (26:14-16)
       (2) Jesus' and the Disciples' Final Hours Together (26:17-46)
         (a) The Last Supper (26:17-30)
         (b) Peter's Denial Predicted (26:31-35)
         (c) Praying in Gethsemane (26:36-46)
       (3) Trial before Jewish Authorities (26:47-75)
         (a) Arrest in Gethsemane (26:47-56)
         (b) Jesus' Trial before the Sanhedrin (26:57-68)
         (c) Peter's "Trial" in the Courtyard (26:69-75)
     b. Sentence and Execution: Good Friday (27:1-66)
       (1) Sentencing Jesus (27:1-31)
         (a) Sentencing by the Jews (27:1-2)
         (b) Judas Sentences and Executes Himself (27:3-10)
         (c) Sentencing by the Romans (27:11-26)
         (d) Mocking by the Soldiers (27:27-31)
       (2) The Execution of Jesus (27:32-66)
         (a) The Crucifixion (27:32-44)
         (b) The Death (27:45-56)
         (c) The Burial (27:57-61)
         (d) The Guard at the Tomb (27:62-66)
   2. Resurrection! (28:1-20)
     a. The Empty Tomb (28:1-10)
     b. The Guards' Report (28:11-15)
     c. The Great Commission (28:16-20)

C. Jesus' Ultimate Destiny (26:1–28:20)

Matthew's Gospel concludes with this final block of narrative.[1] It does not contain any obvious, major literary seams. The events leading to

---

[1]For a detailed bibliography, see D. E. Garland, *One Hundred Years of Study on the Passion Narratives* (Macon: Mercer University Press, 1989). For the fullest treatment of Matthew's distinctive perspectives, see D. Senior, *The Passion of Jesus in the Gospel of Matthew*

Jesus' death follow rapidly one upon another. But differences in content and time of events suggest three subdivisions, one per chapter. Chapter 26 describes the last round of events leading up to and including Jesus' arrest and delivery to the Jewish high court. Chapter 27 narrates proceedings before the Roman tribunal, leading up to and including Jesus' death and burial. All of the events in chap. 26 occurred on Thursday night of "Holy Week" or earlier; all of those in chap. 27, on Friday morning or afternoon. Chapter 28 then jumps to Sunday and the marvelous events surrounding Christ's resurrection and subsequent appearance in Galilee. The break in grammar and topic between chaps. 26–27, however, is not nearly so marked as between chaps. 27–28, so perhaps a twofold division of these three chapters (26–27; 28), with the first section also divided in half at the chapter break, best accounts for all the data.

1. Passion and Crucifixion (26:1–27:66)

a. PREPARATION FOR JESUS' DEATH (26:1-75). This segment includes initial preparations for Jesus' death (by people other than Jesus himself) prior to Thursday night (vv. 1-16), preparation by Jesus himself via the "Last Supper" with his disciples and its sequel in the Garden of Gethsemane (vv. 17-46), and his arrest and trial by the Jewish leaders, including an informal "trial" of Peter (vv. 47-75).

(1) Events Preceding Thursday Night (26:1-16). Verses 1-2 form a heading for the entire passion narrative, as well as for this smaller section. Verses 3-5 then discuss preparations by the Jewish leaders; vv. 6-13, by an unnamed woman in Bethany; and vv. 14-16, by Judas.

[1]When Jesus had finished saying all these things, he said to his disciples, [2]"As you know, the Passover is two days away—and the Son of Man will be handed over to be crucified."

(a) Introduction to the Passion Narrative (26:1-2). **26:1-2** As after Jesus' previous four discourses (8:1; 11:1; 13:53; 19:1), Matthew begins his next block of narrative by relating that Jesus had finished speaking.[2] Here Matthew inserts what could be called Jesus' fourth passion prediction, although v. 2 is more an abbreviation and summary of the previous three (16:21; 17:22-23; 20:17-19). Jesus adds one new element, however, as he specifically announces that his arrest and crucifixion are little more than two days away—the time of the start of the Passover Feast, which

---

(Wilmington: Glazier, 1985). For an overview of the information from all of the Gospels, see E. H. Kiehl, *The Passion of Our Lord* (Grand Rapids: Baker, 1990).

[2]B. M. Newman and P. C. Stine (*A Translator's Handbook on the Gospel of Matthew* [New York: UBS, 1988], 813) suggest that Matthew adds "all" here "perhaps to suggest that Jesus' teaching ministry has now come to an end."

commemorated the Israelites' flight from Egypt in the days of Moses (Exod 12). This chronology fits in with what we have deduced earlier (see comments under 21:1-22). This is still Tuesday. Matthew apparently does not record any events that took place on Wednesday of the last week of Jesus' life. That Passover was an appropriate time for Christ's death will become clear at the Last Supper (see comments on vv. 17-30). Passover fell on 15 Nisan (the twenty-four-hour period from sundown Thursday to sundown Friday). The most likely year in which this date occurred at this time of the week is A.D. 30. The other main option that could fit in with the rest of New Testament chronology is A.D. 33.[3] The next three verses will describe the Jewish leaders' finally getting a chance to fulfill Christ's predictions, but his reminder here emphasizes again that he knows what awaits him and submits willingly.

³Then the chief priests and the elders of the people assembled in the palace of the high priest, whose name was Caiaphas, ⁴and they plotted to arrest Jesus in some sly way and kill him. ⁵"But not during the Feast," they said, "or there may be a riot among the people."

(b) The Jewish Leaders' Plot against Jesus (26:3-5). **26:3-5** "Then" (tote) could be logical or chronological. We don't know for sure when these events took place. Mark 14:1 seems to imply that the plotting had already been underway for some time. Two of the three groups Jesus predicted would be involved in his death (16:21) now assemble to plan his arrest (v. 3). "Palace" (aulē) is the same as "courtyard" in v. 58. Matthew may have any part of Caiaphas's large home in mind, but the regal implications of "palace" make the NIV's translation less appropriate here. Caiaphas was a priest, not a king. The traditional site shown to tourists as Caiaphas's residence, complete with downstairs dungeon, is almost certainly not authentic because it was built on a cemetery, a ritually unclean place not likely to house a Jewish cleric. Caiaphas was installed as "chief" of "chief priests" by Rome in A.D. 18 and would continue to rule until 36. John 11:47-53 elaborates on the type of deliberation presupposed here, though it is not clear if the same occasion is intended. John treats Caiaphas somewhat sympathetically, noting that he was motivated by a concern to save Israel from imperial retribution were Jesus to be viewed as someone who incited the crowds to revolt against Rome. This motive fits in with Matthew's comment on the Jewish leaders' fear that

---

[3] For details incorporating data from all four Gospels, including the question of harmonizing John's chronology of passion week with the Synoptics, see C. L. Blomberg, *The Historical Reliability of the Gospels* (Downers Grove: InterVarsity, 1987), 175-80, and the literature there cited. Cf. now also B. D. Smith, "The Chronology of the Last Supper," *WTJ* 53 (1991): 29-45; and C. I. K. Story, "The Bearing of Old Testament Terminology on the Johannine Chronology of the Final Passover of Jesus," *NovT* 31 (1989): 316-24.

publicly arresting Jesus during the Passover, a week-long series of festivities, might stir up the crowds to riot in protest. Josephus (*J.W.* 1.88) describes a similar tumult in the previous century that made these fears well-grounded. As it turns out, the opportunity presents itself so that the Jewish leaders do arrest Jesus during "the Feast," even as he has just predicted (v. 2). But it is definitely not in public but *by guile* (*dolō*, "in some sly way," v. 4). It is also possible that "not during the Feast" (v. 5) means *apart from the festal crowds*,[4] in which case the leaders may never have intended to delay their scheme any longer. Caiaphas's approach, however, discloses tragic irony. They who would avoid Rome's wrath must instead incur God's. They save their lives but lose their souls (contrast Matt 16:26).

[6] While Jesus was in Bethany in the home of a man known as Simon the Leper, [7] a woman came to him with an alabaster jar of very expensive perfume, which she poured on his head as he was reclining at the table.

(c) Anointing for Burial (26:6-13).[5] **26:6-7** This event actually occurred the previous Saturday night, before "Palm Sunday" (John 12:1-8). Matthew does not contradict John's chronology but thematically places this episode here as another in the series of preparations for Jesus' death.[6] Jesus has been staying in Bethany with the two sisters, Mary and Martha, and their brother, Lazarus. The whole group now proceeds to the home of Simon the Leper (v. 6), presumably a former leper, because he is now living in a house, though just conceivably Jesus and his associates could again be defying traditional social boundaries.[7] The women prepare the meal, and Mary (John 12:3a) breaks open a jar of costly perfume. Mark 14:5 values it at more than a year's wages. She covers Jesus' head (v. 7) and feet (John 12:3b), presumably pouring the liquid over his whole body, just as corpses were to be immersed in sweet-smelling ointments in preparation for burial. The "perfume" is, literally, *myrrh*; the reader may be meant to recall 2:11.

[8] When the disciples saw this, they were indignant. "Why this waste?" they asked. [9] "This perfume could have been sold at a high price and the money given to the poor."

---

[4] See esp. C. Burchard, "Fussnoten zum neutestamentlichen Griechisch," *ZNW* 61 (1970): 157-58.

[5] On this whole pericope, see esp. R. F. Thiemann, "The Unnamed Woman at Bethany," *ThT* 44 (1987): 179-88.

[6] Luke 7:36-50 describes a similar event that actually took place on a different occasion.

[7] Alternately, with A. H. M'Neile (*The Gospel according to St. Matthew* [London: Macmillan, 1915], 374), Simon could be Martha's husband or father, in which case there is no change of venue.

26:8-9   The disciples, particularly Judas, and he at least out of false motives (John 12:4-6), object to what they view as gross waste (v. 8). Surely Mary could have been a better steward of this costly luxury, especially in light of the large number of poor and needy (v. 9). Stagg wonders if Mary and Judas were in fact Jesus' first two followers really to believe that he was going to die but who then expressed their reactions in diametrically opposite ways.[8]

[10]**Aware of this, Jesus said to them, "Why are you bothering this woman? She has done a beautiful thing to me.** [11]**The poor you will always have with you, but you will not always have me.** [12]**When she poured this perfume on my body, she did it to prepare me for burial.** [13]**I tell you the truth, wherever this gospel is preached throughout the world, what she has done will also be told, in memory of her."**

26:10-13   Curiously, Jesus rebukes the disciples for their seemingly laudable objection. He views Mary's act as a once-in-a-lifetime opportunity to demonstrate a special kind of sacrificial love (vv. 10-11). She has created an object lesson for everyone present; Jesus points out the symbolism in her anointing him as preparation for burial (v. 12). There will always be opportunities to help the poor; this may be the last opportunity for Mary to minister to Jesus before his death. "Beautiful thing" in v. 10 literally is *good work*, in keeping with Matthew's positive role for good works. Verse 12 may also point forward to Jesus' execution as a criminal, preventing a later chance for proper burial ceremonies.[9] In fact, Mary's deed will be so praised that Jesus promises it will become a regular part of the story of his life. He thus assumes that the story will indeed be retold. Its inclusion in three of the four Gospels ensured that it was. As in 24:14 Jesus also foreshadows the disciples' obedience to the Great Commission, as they proclaim the gospel "throughout the world" (v. 13).

Sadly this passage has suffered much neglect and abuse. Many people with social consciences find the disciples' objection the same as their own. Those preoccupied with the oppressed and needy of the world often quarrel with any lavish expenditure of monies for church architecture, pageantry, worship, or celebration, however well-intentioned and honoring to Christ they may be. There are in fact times and places for all of this extravagance. So also with M'Neile, "To the few who today spend themselves mainly on worship and meditation (whom Mary again exemplifies in Lk. x.39-42) active 'workers' are warned not to say 'To what purpose is this waste?'"[10] Or with Beare, "The beauty of uncalculating

[8]F. Stagg, "Matthew," in *The Broadman Bible Commentary*, vol. 8, ed. C. J. Allen (Nashville: Broadman, 1969), 231.

[9]R. T. France, *The Gospel according to Matthew*, TNTC (Grand Rapids: Eerdmans, 1985), 363.

generosity is not to be measured by the yardstick of utility."[11] This is an interesting passage indeed after the account of the sheep and the goats in 25:31-46. There helping the (Christian) poor equaled helping Jesus. Here helping Jesus proves better than helping the (unspecified) poor. Varying circumstances make both models possible without contradiction; neither is absolute.

But, far more commonly, well-to-do believers abuse this passage by citing v. 11a as grounds for social inaction. Interestingly, Jesus fairly clearly alludes to Deut 15:11a with these words, which must thus be read in light of the rest of Moses' sentence: "Therefore I command you to be open-handed toward your brothers and toward the poor and needy in your land" (Deut 15:11). Proper teaching from 26:11 must stress that a Christian life-style is generally characterized by that generosity toward the needy. Imitating Mary's "waste" remains the exception rather than the norm. Many Western Christians today have exactly inverted these two and entirely missed the radical demands of this text![12]

[14]Then one of the Twelve—the one called Judas Iscariot—went to the chief priests [15]and asked, "What are you willing to give me if I hand him over to you?" So they counted out for him thirty silver coins. [16]From then on Judas watched for an opportunity to hand him over.

(d) Judas Prepares to Betray Jesus (26:14-16). **26:14-16** Here is the final preparatory event before the actions that can be clearly dated to the Thursday before "Good Friday." Matthew reintroduces Judas as "one of the Twelve" (v. 14), but his readers already know this all too well, so he is probably intending an ironic emphasis. How dare one of this inner band of Jesus' followers actually become his betrayer! On "Iscariot," see comments under 10:4. Judas now goes to those looking for a way to arrest Jesus and offers to provide one for a fee (v. 15). The price is thirty silver coins, the significance of which Matthew will unpack in 27:9-10. If the coin was a shekel, the standard temple currency equivalent to four denarii, then Judas's wage would represent 120 days' earnings. Fulfillment of this plot (v. 16) will come in 26:47-50.

The extent of Judas's treachery can scarcely be exaggerated. The Gospels supply no explanation for his motives.[13] Suggestions have ranged

---

[10]M'Neile, *Matthew*, 375.

[11]F. W. Beare, *The Gospel according to Matthew* (San Francisco: Harper and Row, 1981), 505.

[12]Cf. R. S. Sugirtharajah, "'For You Always Have the Poor with You': An Example of Hermeneutics of Suspicion," *AJT* 4 (1990): 102-7.

[13]For a survey of views, see H. Stein-Schneider, "A la recherche du Judas historique," *ETR* 60 (1985): 403-24. For a plausible account, see D. Roquefort, "Judas: une figure de la perversion," *ETR* 58 (1983): 501-13.

from extremely niggardly ones—a simple desire for a fair sum of money—all the way to rather sympathetic ones—was Judas trying to force Jesus' hand to bring in the kingdom sooner? Perhaps most plausible is an intermediate view, which sees Judas as growing increasingly disenchanted with the type of Messiah Jesus is proving to be, a far cry from the nationalistic, military liberator the Jews hoped would free them from Roman tyranny. Questions about Judas's prior spiritual state remain unanswerable; the Scriptures simply do not tell us. But Matthew may view his defection here as a paradigm of the blasphemy against the Holy Spirit (12:32).

17On the first day of the Feast of Unleavened Bread, the disciples came to Jesus and asked, "Where do you want us to make preparations for you to eat the Passover?"
18He replied, "Go into the city to a certain man and tell him, 'The Teacher says: My appointed time is near. I am going to celebrate the Passover with my disciples at your house.' " 19So the disciples did as Jesus had directed them and prepared the Passover.

(2) Jesus' and the Disciples' Final Hours Together (26:17-46). (a) The Last Supper (26:17-30). **26:17-19** We now arrive at the fateful night itself. Here begins the first day of the Passover, also known as the Feast of Unleavened Bread because nothing with yeast could be eaten or even left in the homes of faithful Jews (v. 17a). We have not actually begun the Passover day itself (which started Thursday at sundown). Technically the Passover was a one-day feast, while the Feast of Unleavened Bread had evolved from a seven- to an eight-day-long festival beginning the day before Passover, but in popular language and thinking the two holidays had coalesced. So this period of afternoon preparations for the evening meal was loosely referred to as the first day of the festival.[14] It was typical for families to celebrate the Passover together, with the head of the (often extended) household, usually the father or grandfather, presiding over the table. Jesus and the Twelve will thus celebrate the meal like a family (recall 12:50). They will need a room in a house spacious enough to accommodate this large group, in the middle of a city teeming with other extended families and groups of families looking for similarly spacious lodging. So careful preparation is needed (v. 17b).

As with finding the donkey in 21:1-3, vv. 18-19 present tantalizing ambiguities. Is this careful planning or supernatural insight on Jesus'

---

[14]See R. H. Gundry (*Matthew: A Commentary on His Literary and Theological Art* [Grand Rapids: Eerdmans, 1982], 524) for abundant references. It is also possible to render the text as "the first day of unleavened *things*" rather than "bread," in which case one does not even need to speak of loose use of language. See A. G. Arnott, " 'The First Day of Unleavened . . . ' Mt 26.17, Mk 14.12, Lk 22.7," *BT* 35 (1984): 235-38.

part—or some of each? Matthew abbreviates the story and refers simply "to a certain man." The Greek reads, literally, *pros ton deina* (*to such-and-such a man*). The additional information of Mark 14:13 could suggest prearranged signals, since men didn't normally carry water jars, and Jesus might want to find a place where the Jewish authorities would not yet discover him. "My time is near" is also ambiguous and susceptible to several interpretations. Whatever others would have thought, Matthew intends his readers to see a reference to the time of Christ's death (cf. v. 45). The Greek word for time (*kairos*) often refers to a decisive moment in the course of history or an individual's life. The disciples follow Christ's instructions exactly, and everything works out as planned. Mark 14:15 describes the place they prepare as a "large upper room."

20 When evening came, Jesus was reclining at the table with the Twelve. 21 And while they were eating, he said, "I tell you the truth, one of you will betray me."

22 They were very sad and began to say to him one after the other, "Surely not I, Lord?"

23 Jesus replied, "The one who has dipped his hand into the bowl with me will betray me. 24 The Son of Man will go just as it is written about him. But woe to that man who betrays the Son of Man! It would be better for him if he had not been born."

25 Then Judas, the one who would betray him, said, "Surely not I, Rabbi?" Jesus answered, "Yes, it is you."

26:20-25 After sundown on Thursday, Jesus and his disciples relax to enjoy the Passover meal. We are not to envisage, with Leonardo da Vinci's famous Renaissance portrait of the last supper, one long rectangular table with people sitting on chairs on either side of it, but rather the *triclinium*. This was a square-cornered, U-shaped combination of three cushions, on which people would recline, lying on their sides with their bodies perpendicular to the cushions and stretched outward away from the center of the room. The food was placed in the middle of the "U," in between the couches. Jesus interrupts the festivities with the horrible prediction of v. 21. He has never previously mentioned betrayal in his passion predictions, and the topic introduces a painfully dissonant note into the conversation, breaking the intimacy of table fellowship and marring the joy of the Passover festivity (though see Matt 20:18). The rest of the Twelve apparently know nothing of the events of vv. 14-16. By speaking to the issue, Jesus makes it clear that he knows full well what Judas is up to. When the events unfold, he will be giving in to them willingly, not tricked by any ruse.

The disciples recognize that Jesus may well have prophetic insight into their own shortcomings. So each one wonders if he himself will somehow succumb and become the perpetrator (v. 22). Yet the question "surely not

I?" is phrased so as hopefully to elicit a negative response. Matthew uses the identical language as in 17:23 (a form of *lypeō* + *sphodra*) to highlight their intense grief. Only Matthew adds the address "Lord," heightening the irony of betrayal.

Jesus replies cryptically. Is v. 23 meant to reveal the identity of the betrayer or simply to restate the truth of v. 21? All the men will dip their bread into the sauce bowl at one time or another during the meal.[15] Verse 24 reaffirms the divine certainty of the coming events and points again to Jesus' fate as scripturally determined, probably alluding to the various suffering servant texts of Isa 42–53. But as in 18:6-7, God's sovereignty does not override human free will or accountability, hence the woe concerning the one who will betray Christ. Had Judas not done the deed, someone else would have, but whoever does it damns himself in the process. (Cf. John 17:12, in which Judas is called the *son of perdition*—"one doomed to destruction.") Some kind of conscious punishment in the life to come is again implied here. Annihilationists cannot say that "it would be better for him if he had not been born," since a person who is totally destroyed simply reverts back to the state of nonexistence as before conception. John 13:26 refers to a slightly different signal that enabled the "beloved disciple" to discern Judas's identity. But 13:27-28 suggests that this conversation took place in hushed tones so that no one else knew or understood except the disciple reclining closest to Jesus.[16]

If this was the case, then perhaps Matthew's v. 25 was also spoken privately. It appears only in this Gospel. Judas cannot call Jesus "Lord," merely "Rabbi." If the dialogue of v. 25 was more audible, then Jesus' words (*sy eipas*) should not be translated as paraphrastically as in the NIV ("Yes, it is you") but rather more literally as, *You said* [it], i.e., *your words, not mine* (cf. NEB "the words are yours"). In this event, Jesus does not reply with an unambiguous affirmative but instead hints that Judas has indicted himself (cf. on 26:64 and 27:11), though Matthew will intend his readers to view Jesus' response as a qualified yes.[17] Presumably, at this point Judas leaves the group (John 13:30). Although Matthew does not

---

[15]S. T. Lachs, *A Rabbinic Commentary on the New Testament: The Gospels of Matthew, Mark, and Luke* (Hoboken, N.J.: KTAV, 1987), 406.

[16]M. Green (*Matthew for Today* [Dallas: Word, 1989], 253) makes the interesting suggestion that "if Jesus was able so to whisper in the ear of Judas, then Judas must have been reclining next to him," in one of the two most favored positions either on Jesus' right or left. "Jesus did everything to show his love for Judas, but in vain."

[17]Cf. W. C. Allen (*A Critical and Exegetical Commentary on the Gospel according to S. Matthew*, ICC [Edinburgh: T & T Clark, 1907], 276): "What was required was just what σὺ εἶπας" expresses, an ambiguous affirmative, suggesting to the traitor himself the certainty that his treachery was known; to others, if they overheard it, a half uncertainty as to what was meant, and leaving opportunity to Judas of withdrawing from his course of treachery before its absolute and final exposure."

explicitly mention his departure, Judas obviously had to leave at some point in order to reappear with the crowds in v. 47. But he does so with full knowledge that Jesus knows what he is plotting. He proceeds anyway.

26 While they were eating, Jesus took bread, gave thanks and broke it, and gave it to his disciples, saying, "Take and eat; this is my body."
27 Then he took the cup, gave thanks and offered it to them, saying, "Drink from it, all of you. 28 This is my blood of the covenant, which is poured out for many for the forgiveness of sins. 29 I tell you, I will not drink of this fruit of the vine from now on until that day when I drink it anew with you in my Father's kingdom."
30 When they had sung a hymn, they went out to the Mount of Olives.

26:26-30 Resuming the Passover celebration, the meal itself begins.[18] Jesus opens with prayer and the breaking of bread (v. 26). A common loaf would be distributed to all. The unleavened bread originally symbolized the haste with which the Israelites departed from Egypt (Exod 12). For additional laws about how to celebrate the feast, see Lev 23:4-8; Num 9:1-14; and Deut 16:1-8. Jesus now invests the bread with new meaning. It foreshadows his body figuratively broken and literally killed in his upcoming death. Jesus' words here have led to massive debates, intra-Christian persecution, and huge theological edifices, the weight of which they cannot bear. The doctrines of transubstantiation (the bread and wine become Christ's actual body and blood) or consubstantiation (Christ is really present "in, with, and under" the elements) make no sense of Jesus' words in their historical context. As Jesus holds up a loaf and declares, "This is my body," no one listening will ever imagine that he is claiming the bread to be the literal extension of his flesh. Moreover, in Aramaic these sentences would have been spoken without a linking verb ("is"), as simply, *this, my body* and *this, my blood*.[19] As frequently elsewhere, Jesus is creating a vivid object lesson. The bread symbolizes (represents, stands for, or points to) his crucifixion in some otherwise unspecified sense.

In vv. 27-28 Jesus turns from the bread to the cup. This is the third of four cups of wine drunk at various stages throughout the evening festivities. It was probably a common cup passed around for all to drink. "Offered" is the same verb as "gave" in v. 27 and does not imply that drinking was optional. Each of the four cups was linked to one line of Exod 6:6-7a. This one tied in with God's promise, "I will redeem you," in v. 6c and hence specifically to his original liberation of the Israelites from

---

[18]On primary sources for the Passover haggadah or liturgy, see G. J. Bahr, "The Seder of Passover and the Eucharistic Words," *NovT* 12 (1970): 181-202.

[19]For the most recent reconstruction of the Aramaic, see M. Casey, "The Original Aramaic Form of Jesus' Interpretation of the Cup," *JTS* 41 (1990): 1-12.

Egypt (*m. Pesaḥ.* 10:6-7). But again Jesus adds new meaning. As they all drink (the "all" refers to all the disciples, not to all of the wine!), he proclaims that the cup stands for his blood about to be shed in his death on the cross. The "blood of the covenant" harks back to Exod 24:8. The use of "cup" rather than "wine" links this passage with 20:22-23 and 26:39. "Fruit of the vine" (v. 29) was a stock phrase used in thanksgiving prayers for the wine (*m. Ber.* 6:1) and therefore does not refer to unfermented beverage, "though it was customary to cut the wine with a double or triple quantity of water."[20]

Here is the inauguration of Jeremiah's new covenant (Jer 31:31-34). "New" does not appear in many of the best manuscripts of Matthew ($\mathfrak{P}^{37}$, א, B, L, Θ, 33, and some Middle Egyptian and Boharic mss.) but does in Luke 22:20, from which it was probably borrowed by later copyists and inserted here. Nevertheless the newness is clear from the Old Testament allusions. Jesus' death will prove redemptive and provide a vicarious atonement. Verse 28 offers a significant parallel to 20:28. The forgiveness of sins "for many," that is, for all who accept Jesus, echoes Isa 53:4,10,12. The covenant language implies the creation of a community, now to be constituted of those who in their eating and drinking identify with the benefits of Jesus' sacrificial death. This "true Israel" stands over against the natural Israel of the old covenant.[21]

Verse 29 anticipates both Jesus' departure and his return. He warns the disciples that he will not again be drinking (or eating or performing any other part of this Passover liturgy) in the immediate future, but he looks forward to rejoining them for the messianic banquet (recall the imagery of 22:1-14, and cf. Rev 19). The kingdom which is now inaugurated will then be consummated in all its fullness. Jesus' words may suggest that he refused to drink the fourth and final cup of this particular meal.

All three Synoptics have accounts of Jesus' Last Supper and so-called "Words of Institution." Interestingly, John's Gospel says nothing about the bread and wine, through he preserves a much fuller account of Jesus' teaching on this last night of his life (John 13–17).[22] But a fourth, closely parallel account does appear in Paul (1 Cor 11:23-26) with distinctive parallels to Luke. The most important of these is the addition of the phrase "do this in remembrance of me." From this command virtually all branches of Christianity have seen grounds for repeating some kind of "Lord's Supper" ("Holy Communion" or "Eucharist") ritual, though they

---

[20]D. A. Carson, "Matthew," in EBC, vol. 8, ed. F. E. Gaebelein (Grand Rapids: Zondervan, 1984), 536.

[21]France, *Matthew*, 369.

[22]Perhaps to avoid encouraging an already overexalted "sacramentalism"? See R. W. Paschal, "Sacramental Symbolism and Physical Imagery in the Gospel of John," *TynBul* 32 (1981): 151-76 for a balanced assessment of the various options.

scarcely agree on many of the other details surrounding its observance. No particular timetable for celebrating the Lord's Supper is commanded here. The early church apparently included it at the culmination of a "love feast" or fellowship meal (cf. Acts 2:42; 20:7-12; Jude 12). One may determine certain principles for correctly observing this ordinance by combining all of the scriptural references,[23] but most church practices go well beyond anything specifically mandated in Holy Writ. This does not mean that all of these practices are wrong, merely that they may not be made normative.[24]

From Matthew's account emerge two key reasons for celebrating the Lord's Supper. One looks backward; the other, forward. First, we commemorate Jesus' redemptive death. Second, we anticipate his return in company with all the redeemed. These two points remain central to all three Synoptic accounts and should form the heart of any theology of this ordinance. Verse 30 rounds off this section by describing the departure of Jesus and the eleven from the upper room, the house, and the city of Jerusalem. But first they sing one or more hymns, probably the closing round of *Hallel* (*praise*) Psalms (Pss 115–18) that formed part of the Passover liturgy.[25] Then the little entourage returns to the Mount of Olives where they heard Jesus preach just two days earlier (24:1).

31Then Jesus told them, "This very night you will all fall away on account of me, for it is written:
"'I will strike the shepherd,
   and the sheep of the flock will be scattered.'
32But after I have risen, I will go ahead of you into Galilee."

(b) Peter's Denial Predicted (26:31-35). **26:31-32** This episode both parallels and contrasts with the prediction of Judas's betrayal. It shows that Judas was not the only one seriously to fail his master. In fact, all twelve will fall away (Greek *skandalisthēsesthe—you will be scandalized*). They will flee (v. 56) and hide (John 20:19), fearing for their own lives and so abandoning Jesus in the time he most needed support. How much like sinful, human nature! But their flight also fulfills Scripture (v. 31; see Zech 13:7). Matthew's Jesus quotes a form of the LXX in which second-person plural imperatives ("strike the shepherd" and "scat-

---

[23]For details on the biblical data, see esp. I. H. Marshall, *Last Supper and Lord's Supper* (Grand Rapids: Eerdmans, 1980). Cf. also J. Jeremias, *The Eucharistic Words of Jesus* (New York: Macmillan, 1955); X. Leon-Dufour, *Sharing the Eucharistic Bread* (New York: Paulist, 1987).

[24]For a brief, historical overview, with excellent suggestions for evangelical ecumenicity, see D. Bridge and D. Phypers, *The Meal That Unites?* (London: Hodder and Stoughton, 1981).

[25]Ὑμνέω in Greek is a verb (*to sing hymns*), not a noun. It does not disclose how many hymns were sung (contra NIV's "a hymn").

ter the sheep") are changed into first-person singular and third-person plural indicatives, respectively ("I will strike the shepherd," and "the sheep . . . will be scattered"). The implied subject of both verbs is God. The action God commands (LXX), even when carried out by others (Matthew), is thus derivatively his action too.[26] Jesus obviously viewed himself as the shepherd and the disciples as his sheep. The meaning in the Old Testament context is not entirely clear. But Zechariah seems to imply that a day would come when God's appointed leader in Israel would be cut off and his people scattered. The Essenes at Qumran saw in this text a picture of the wickedness of a majority of their contemporaries (CD 19:5-9). Later rabbinic interpretations did at times take it to refer to the Messiah.[27] Verse 32 looks ahead to a positive sequel. Jesus had offered Judas no hope when he predicted his betrayal; here he reminds the other eleven of his coming resurrection and return to Galilee, implying that they will again follow him there (as they do in 28:7,16-17).

[33] Peter replied, **"Even if all fall away on account of you, I never will."**

[34] **"I tell you the truth,"** Jesus answered, **"this very night, before the rooster crows, you will disown me three times."**

[35] But Peter declared, **"Even if I have to die with you, I will never disown you." And all the other disciples said the same.**

26:33-35 Peter protests, however, that no matter what the rest do, he will not abandon his master (v. 33). As throughout Matthew (most notably in 14:28-31 and 16:21-23), Peter proves more impulsive than truthful. In fact, Jesus replies, Peter will be even more disloyal than the other ten, by denying even knowing Jesus three times this night before the main cock crow at about 1:30 a.m. (v. 34).[28] Peter repudiates Jesus' notion. He will follow Jesus even to his death if necessary (v. 35). The others also continue to swear their allegiance, but vv. 56,69-75 will demonstrate who is right. The disciples do not even come close to fulfilling their promises.

Peter's impulsive denial of Jesus is obviously not as treacherous as Judas's premeditated betrayal, but Jesus has already said that any who disown him "before men" he will disown before his Heavenly Father (10:33). So the difference between Peter and Judas lies primarily in their subsequent behavior. One may either deny or betray Christ and be forgiven if one genuinely repents. Without repentance (a change of heart followed by right action), both remain equally damning. Contrast the behavior of Peter in 26:75 and Judas in 27:5.

---

[26] See G. L. Archer and G. C. Chirichigno, *Old Testament Quotations in the New Testament: A Complete Survey* (Chicago: Moody, 1983), 163-64, for these and other minor differences.

[27] See references in R. L. Smith, *Micah-Malachi*, WBC (Waco: Word, 1984), 284.

[28] On which, see France, *Matthew*, 371. The first of the two cock-crows to which Mark refers (Mark 14:30) would have occurred earlier.

36 **Then Jesus went with his disciples to a place called Gethsemane, and he said to them, "Sit here while I go over there and pray." 37He took Peter and the two sons of Zebedee along with him, and he began to be sorrowful and troubled. 38Then he said to them, "My soul is overwhelmed with sorrow to the point of death. Stay here and keep watch with me."**

(c) Praying in Gethsemane (26:36-46). **26:36-38** The group proceeds to a garden or wooded area on the western slopes of the hillside known as the Mount of Olives. *Gethsemane* means *oil press* and was an area filled with groves of olive trees, many of them owned by well-to-do Jerusalemites. Jesus leaves the eight at a distance and takes the three "core" disciples (recall 17:1) closer to where he wishes to go and then asks them to "watch" with him. Apparently he means they should stay awake and pray (cf. vv. 40-41). Corporate prayer can often prove more powerful and supportive than personal prayer. Apparently, too, it is already quite late at night. Jesus is *very sorrowful* (*perilypos*, "overwhelmed with sorrow," v. 38) and *distressed* (from *adēmoneō*, "troubled," somewhat too weak a translation). Phillips's "terrible distress and misery" and Weymouth's "crushed with anguish" correctly capture the sense. The language echoes the cries of the psalmist in Pss 42:5-6 and 43:5. Jesus knows of his coming death and the gruesome method of his execution. Spiritually he recognizes the even greater agony involved in bearing the sins of the world. Luke 22:44 describes the extent of his physical suffering in the garden, hence Matthew's "to the point of death." Hebrews 5:7 harks back to this scene, stressing that God did hear Jesus' prayers to be saved from death. He answered them not by sparing Jesus' life but by raising him from the grave. The view that Jesus was praying that he not die prematurely, here in the garden, finds no support in the text.

39 **Going a little farther, he fell with his face to the ground and prayed, "My Father, if it is possible, may this cup be taken from me. Yet not as I will, but as you will."**

26:39 Verse 39 epitomizes Jesus' full humanity and demonstrates the complete extent to which he could be tempted. On the interplay of his divine and human natures in temptation, recall the commentary under 4:1-11. In his sinless, human nature he clearly perceives the horror of his coming execution and very naturally and appropriately asks his Father if there is any way out. Perhaps he has Ps 116:4 in mind.[29] "If it is possible" most likely reflects a first-class condition (which assumes it *is*

---

[29]M. Kiley, "'Lord, Save My Life' (Ps 116:4 as Generative Text for Jesus' Gethsemane Prayer (Mark 14:36a)," *CBQ* 48 (1986): 655-59, though Kiley believes the linkage stems from the early church and not Jesus.

possible; cf. Mark 14:36), as Jesus affirms afresh God's omnipotence. Nevertheless not everything that is possible is part of God's will, and Jesus wants to make it plain that he intends to comply fully with his Father's desire. He will not allow personal preference or ambition to conflict with divine demand.[30] The "cup" again points to his suffering, as he endures God's wrath for the sins of humanity (recall 20:22-23 and 26:27). Thus Matthew simultaneously reveals both Jesus' complete temptability (in his human nature) and his complete obedience. The intensity of the whole episode is portrayed by Christ's posture. To answer the question of how Matthew knew what Jesus prayed, we must assume either that Christ told the disciples, probably during his forty-day postresurrection ministry (Acts 1:3) or that the three (Peter, James, and John) sat close enough to Jesus to hear some of what he uttered before they dozed off.[31]

Here then appears the classic scriptural example of a prayer that God does not answer in the way desired by the one praying, yet without any fault in the person making the request. Here, too, is a key reminder for us. If Christ could plead as boldly as he did, we should feel free also to unload all our deepest desires before God (esp. in light of Ps 37:4). Yet we dare not blame ourselves or others if we do not receive what we ask for when we have asked with right motives (Jas 4:3). If Christ had to guard his own requests with this type of qualification (again harking back to 6:10; cf. Jas 4:15), how dare we ever try to pray for anything without also adding "if it be your will"! A further application emerges from Jesus' sorrow. His depression means "that all depression is not sin . . . in fact, nothing is more *un*helpful than telling people in very sad circumstances not to be depressed."[32]

40 Then he returned to his disciples and found them sleeping. "Could you men not keep watch with me for one hour?" he asked Peter. 41"Watch and pray so that you will not fall into temptation. The spirit is willing, but the body is weak."

26:40-41 Jesus returns to where he left Peter, James, and John and finds them asleep. He has apparently prayed for about an hour and, hence, spoken much more than just v. 39. Incidentally, this passage shows that

---

[30]Thus we need not resort to the suggestion of C. A. Blaising ("Gethsemane: A Prayer of Faith," *JETS* 22 [1979]: 333-43), who sees Jesus requesting and receiving a promise from God that the cup of his wrath not *remain* on him, i.e., a promise of resurrection.

[31]B. Saunderson ("Gethsemane: The Missing Witness," *Bib* 70 [1989]: 224-33) adds the alternative that the enigmatic young man of Mark 14:51-52 may have overheard Jesus pray and later told his followers what he said.

[32]F. D. Bruner, *The Churchbook* (Dallas: Word, 1990), 979-80, who adds that Jesus' depression "teaches important truths to the church: Jesus' true humanity, his free obedience and his real courage."

one hour of prayer was not a long time by Jesus' standards. Contrast, sadly, our meager efforts. A gentle rebuke leads to an exhortation for the disciples to try again to do better. "Men" in v. 40 does not appear in the Greek, simply *you* (pl.). Jesus singles out Peter, though all three have slept. As earlier (see esp. 16:21-23), this supports the view that Matthew is trying to qualify an overexaltation of Peter rather than to pay him special honor. The disciples need spiritual vigilance, which in this case includes physical self-control, to avoid being led into sin, to deny Jesus.[33] The language again echoes the Lord's Prayer. The human spirit has good intentions, but the *flesh* (a better translation than the NIV "body," v. 41) is weak. Perhaps this saying of Jesus is one of the sources which provided Paul with his characteristic use of "flesh." In the context of avoiding "temptation," flesh seems most likely to mean sinful human nature, though, in this case, including frail, physical weakness (a body that wants to sleep) as well. Jesus' proverb is often casually reapplied almost as an excuse for human shortcomings but, in context, is an incentive for disciples to resist temptation. What a contrast the whole scene provides with the disciples' recent boasts (v. 35)!

[42] He went away a second time and prayed, "My Father, if it is not possible for this cup to be taken away unless I drink it, may your will be done." **[43] When he came back, he again found them sleeping, because their eyes were heavy. [44] So he left them and went away once more and prayed the third time, saying the same thing.**

26:42-44 Jesus withdraws and prays a second time. This time he uses the negative adverb with the first-class condition ("if it is *not* possible," v. 42). He has come to believe that it is not within God's will that he avoid the suffering mapped out for him, but he reaffirms his desire to carry out that will irrespective of the cost. Drinking the cup again means undergoing suffering and death. In vv. 43-44 the pattern repeats as Jesus again finds the disciples asleep and retreats for a third round of prayer.

[45] Then he returned to the disciples and said to them, "Are you still sleeping and resting? Look, the hour is near, and the Son of Man is betrayed into the hands of sinners. [46] Rise, let us go! Here comes my betrayer!"

26:45-46 Jesus returns a final time and once again discovers the disciples asleep. This ends the cycle of withdrawals for prayer. His followers' threefold failure perhaps prefigures Peter's threefold denial (vv. 69-75). Jesus now rouses all the disciples with a rhetorical question ("Are you still

---

[33] As in the Lord's Prayer (6:13), some take πειρασμόν ("temptation") here to refer to the eschatological crisis at the end of history, now on the verge of being inaugurated by Christ's death. Cf., e.g., Senior, *Passion*, 82.

sleeping and resting?"—the answer to which is obvious)[34] and alerts them to the arrival of Judas, who is coming to betray him. The sequence of events which will lead from Jesus' arrest to his death is about to begin. On Jesus' "hour," cf. John 2:4; 7:30; 8:20; 12:23; 13:1; 16:4; and 17:1. The decisive moment has come. They must get up and meet the traitor and his henchmen. While Jesus does not seek his own death, neither will he flee from it. Matthew's twofold use of *ēngiken* ("is near" and "here comes") links vv. 45-46 with the repeated references to the near arrival of the kingdom of heaven (3:2; 4:17; 10:7). The verb more literally means *has drawn near* in the sense of *is present.*

The key themes Matthew underlines throughout his passion narrative converge in this conclusion to the account of Gethsemane: God is in control of all these events, however tragic they may seem to others. Jesus is the Son of God who is suffering and dying. His death is humiliating but voluntary, an act of obedience fulfilling God's will.[35]

[47]While he was still speaking, Judas, one of the Twelve, arrived. With him was a large crowd armed with swords and clubs, sent from the chief priests and the elders of the people. [48]Now the betrayer had arranged a signal with them: "The one I kiss is the man; arrest him." [49]Going at once to Jesus, Judas said, "Greetings, Rabbi!" and kissed him.

(3) Trial before Jewish Authorities (26:47-75). (a) Arrest in Gethsemane (26:47-56). **26:47-49** Even as Jesus speaks, Judas arrives. As in v. 14, Matthew calls him "one of the Twelve" to highlight the irony and tragedy of his treachery. He comes with people prepared to fight a dangerous rebel, suggesting that some still fear Jesus will emerge from his "disguise" and take up arms. The "swords," short daggers or knives tied to one's belt,[36] confirm that some Romans soldiers were present, presumably at the request of the Jewish leaders (cf. John 18:12 with its reference to a *cohort,* "detachment of soldiers"). "Clubs" were the more typical Jewish weapon. The rabble was predominantly composed of temple guards and various riff-raff. The groups of Jewish leaders named match v. 3 and, in part, v. 14. In v. 48 Judas is simply called "the betrayer," in light of his infamous act.

Why did anyone have to identify Jesus? Perhaps many in this crowd had not seen him before. Probably he looked very much like one or more of the other Galileans who accompanied him, so that at night he would not stand out in a crowd. Possibly despite the apparent solitude of one corner of

---

[34]Alternately, this portion of v. 45 has been taken as a rather sarcastic command, not to be taken literally and to be punctuated with a period.

[35]D. Hill, *The Gospel of Matthew,* NCB (London: Oliphants, 1972), 332.

[36]R. G. Bratcher, *A Translator's Guide to the Gospel of Matthew* (New York: UBS, 1981), 341, 343.

Gethsemane, the area more generally was teeming with Passover pilgrims who were tenting there. Judas's kiss of friendship, perhaps an unusually elaborate welcome on this occasion, heightens his treachery (v. 49).[37] He acts as if he is giving his master a special honor even as he betrays him. Men in the ancient Middle East customarily greeted one another with kisses on both cheeks, even as they do in various parts of the world today. Judas's word of greeting (*chaire* is roughly equivalent to a hearty *Hello!*) and kiss further suggest that he is coming in peace; with this approach he may be trying to avert any hostile uprising by the rest of the disciples. Once again he does not address Jesus as "Lord" but as "Rabbi" (cf. v. 25 with v. 22), still betraying his distance from Jesus (recall also the use of *didaskalos*, "teacher," in 8:19; 12:38; 19:16; 22:16,36).

50Jesus replied, "Friend, do what you came for." Then the men stepped forward, seized Jesus and arrested him. 51With that, one of Jesus' companions reached for his sword, drew it out and struck the servant of the high priest, cutting off his ear.

26:50a   Jesus' reply is very difficult to translate and appears only in Matthew. "Friend" (*hetaire*) is also a distancing form of address (cf. 20:13; 22:12). The rest of Jesus' words (*eph' ho parei*) read, elliptically, *for which you are here*. Is this a command as in the NIV (i.e., [Do that] *for which you are here*) or a statement (i.e., [I know that] *for which you are here*)? Each of these would again demonstrate Jesus' insight and voluntary acceptance of his destiny. Or do the words form a question, as in the NIV marg. (i.e., [What is the reason] *for which you are here?*), asked not out of ignorance but to highlight the wickedness of Judas's action over against Jesus' innocence? One of the former two options is probably more likely in light of Matthew's emphasis on the themes of Jesus' sovereignty and voluntary submission to his death.[38] A command is more likely than a statement in view of the parallel, less elliptical command in John 13:27b ("what you are about to do, do quickly").

26:50b-51   The guard may thus be seen as complying with Jesus' orders. Interestingly, one of his disciples does turn out to be armed and begins to fight a little. John mentions that this disciple was Peter and that the slave's name was Malchus (John 18:10). Perhaps Peter had interpreted Jesus' previous teaching about swords (Luke 22:36) too literally.[39] Luke adds that Jesus immediately healed the man's ear (22:51).

---

[37]καταφιλέω as a perfective of φιλέω may carry some emphasis. M'Neile, *Matthew*, 394, refers to it as the most terrible instance of Prov 27:6.

[38]The interrogative rendering is also less likely given the introduction of the phrase by a relative pronoun (Beare, *Matthew*, 516).

[39]B. T. Viviano ("The High Priest's Servant's Ear: Mark 14:47," *RB* 96 [1989]: 71-80) believes the attack symbolized the belief that the temple authorities were now disqualified as unworthy of their high office.

[52]"Put your sword back in its place," Jesus said to him, "for all who draw the sword will die by the sword. [53]Do you think I cannot call on my Father, and he will at once put at my disposal more than twelve legions of angels? [54]But how then would the Scriptures be fulfilled that say it must happen in this way?"

26:52-54 All three of these verses are almost entirely unique to Matthew. Jesus clearly renounces any attempt to fight back and defend himself and thus avoid the lot determined for him and prophesied in the Scriptures (v. 54; recall v. 24). He could still call on a heavenly rescue squad, but this would not accomplish his Father's will (v. 53; recall v. 39). Angelic help for Jesus on a much more modest scale has already appeared after previous temptations (4.11; cf. Luke 22:43). At five to six thousand soldiers per legion, twelve legions could literally amount to seventy-two thousand angels. The number underlines the magnitude of the power available to Jesus which he declines to utilize. Compare and contrast the scene of 2 Kgs 6:17.

But Jesus seems to generalize beyond the immediate situation with his words "for all who draw the sword will die by the sword" (v. 52b; cf. Rev 13:10; both references perhaps adapting Jer 15:2). This statement is sometimes interpreted as a call to pacifism, but in fact it is simply an observation that violence breeds violence. Perhaps warfare is sometimes necessary to prevent greater evils done to others but never merely in defense of self or God. Still, the proverbial form as a rationale for Jesus' command suggests it would apply in other situations too. These will have to be settled on a case-by-case basis. Nevertheless, peacemaking activities (which are "blessed," 5:9) repeatedly seem superior to hostility and conflict which simply escalates violence.[40] Certainly there is no justification from this text for actually supporting militarism, as Luther argued.[41] Most balanced of all perhaps is the conclusion of Newman and Stine: "Jesus thereby affirms that it is better to suffer injustice than to use violence as a means of protection or retribution, and this affirmation is underscored by his willingness to walk the route of suffering and death."[42] Recall also 5:39 and comments there.

[55]At that time Jesus said to the crowd, "Am I leading a rebellion, that you have come out with swords and clubs to capture me? Every day I sat in the

---

[40]For a good survey of Christian options regarding warfare, see R. G. Clouse, ed., *War: Four Christian Views* (Downers Grove: InterVarsity, 1981).

[41]As the Lutheran commentator E. Schweizer (*The Good News according to Matthew* [Richmond: John Knox, 1975], 495) correctly recognizes. On 496 he adds: "Matthew's interpolation has turned the story of Jesus' arrest into a fundamental statement about the use of force" and "God's pathway through history, as Scripture teaches and as 'must happen,' is not the conquest of all resistance; it is instead reflected in Jesus' way of the cross."

[42]Newman and Stine, *Matthew*, 848.

temple courts teaching, and you did not arrest me. [56] But this has all taken place that the writings of the prophets might be fulfilled." Then all the disciples deserted him and fled.

26:55-56 Jesus mocks the cowardice of the leaders who come heavily armed. He disclaims any connections with Zealotry or other rebel movements which would require such well-guarded and clandestine measures. His question in v. 55a more literally reads, *As upon a rebel did you come out . . . ?* *Lēstēs* (*rebel*) is often translated "robber," but the NIV rendering (one "leading a rebellion") is better. The two criminals on the cross are also *lēstai* (27:38; unfortunately the NIV reverts to "robbers" there). Jesus reminds the rabble of his repeated presence in the temple and complete vulnerability there. Verse 55b seems to presuppose a longer teaching ministry in the temple than the one or two days of earlier this week, an incidental corroboration of what otherwise is found only in John—repeated accounts of Jesus' teaching in the temple at various festivals throughout his three-year ministry (e.g., John 2:12-22; 7:14–8:59; 10:22-42). Again events follow a scripturally predetermined path (v. 56). No one text is in view here but the "prophets" in general (as in 2:23). Probably the sense is that all of the events leading to Jesus' arrest worked together toward the scripturally prophesied theme that God's servant must suffer (as paradigmatically in Isa 52:13–53:12). The specter of similar arrests, imprisonment, and possible execution frightens the eleven away before they too are taken captive. Their behavior demonstrates how hollow their previous boasts had been (v. 35).

(b) Jesus' Trial before the Sanhedrin (26:57-68). This account is laden with problems. There are numerous apparent illegalities in the officials' procedures. For example, Jews were not to hold trials at night or during festivals. No capital verdict could be reached in one day, and the accused should have been permitted counsel for the defense. The testimony against Jesus was too flimsy to hold up, and the procedure for calling witnesses made a shambles of the law (see esp. the Mishnaic tractate *Sanhedrin*). These numerous irregularities have led to frequent charges of widespread, historical inaccuracies in the Gospel narratives. Centuries of Christian abuse of Jewish people, both verbally and physically, based on the mistaken idea that Jews were the sole or primary perpetrators of Christ's death, aggravate these charges. But it is not clear that all of the laws quoted in the Mishna were in effect prior to A.D. 70, nor that many of them refer to the Sanhedrin as constituted in Jesus' day (as over against the later judiciary body known as the *Beth Din*). In addition, desperate people often break the law or permit exceptions to it in extreme instances (cf. the stoning of Stephen in Acts 7:54-60, which began legally enough but ended with mob action). What is more, Matthew nowhere indicts all of the Jews of his day (see further the comments on 27:25); Jesus' followers

were as Jewish as his opponents. Christians must confess to grave injustices against the Jewish people and gross misinterpretation of the text, but in doing so they dare not rewrite history just because it is potentially embarrassing. One small group of Jewish leaders *was* responsible for sending Jesus on to the Roman authorities. Both Jews *and* Romans were actively involved. But from a theological perspective, *no one person is more to blame than any other*. Jesus bore the sins of every person in the world. God could rightly point the finger at every one of us and legitimately claim that we killed his Son.[43]

[57] Those who had arrested Jesus took him to Caiaphas, the high priest, where the teachers of the law and the elders had assembled. [58] But Peter followed him at a distance, right up to the courtyard of the high priest. He entered and sat down with the guards to see the outcome.

26:57-58 Jesus returns with his captors to Caiaphas's house. John adds that the group first paid a courtesy call to the ex-high priest Annas (John 18:13). The judicial leadership of Israel has gathered. Peter at least starts out more bravely than the rest of the disciples, trailing from a distance, probably trying to make good on his promise of v. 35. On the high priest's home, see comments under v. 3. "Guards" are a particular category of the high priest's servants.

[59] The chief priests and the whole Sanhedrin were looking for false evidence against Jesus so that they could put him to death. [60] But they did not find any, though many false witnesses came forward.
Finally two came forward [61] and declared, "This fellow said, 'I am able to destroy the temple of God and rebuild it in three days.'"

26:59-61 The council makes no pretense of complete objectivity. They are seeking what Matthew calls "false evidence," that is, spurious charges which will make Jesus appear to deserve capital punishment. Still they are keeping up the appearance of legality, so that two or more witnesses must independently agree on their testimony. So the term "false" stems more from a Christian perspective, especially since this term appears here only in Matthew, rather than reflecting a consciously illegal or unethical approach adopted by the Jewish authorities. They were genuinely convinced that

---

[43]A variety of sources pursue the discussion further. H. Cohn (*The Trial and Death of Jesus* [New York: KTAV, 1977]) gives a fanciful but influential revision of history vindicating the Jews. P. Winter (*On the Trial of Jesus* [Berlin: de Gruyter, 1974]) reflects a more sober but still skeptical Jewish treatment. S. G. F. Brandon (*Jesus and the Zealots* [Manchester: University Press, 1967]) thinks Jesus was a Zealot. Best all around, with ample detail, is D. R. Catchpole, *The Trial of Jesus* (Leiden: Brill, 1971). More brief and moderately conservative is A. N. Sherwin-White, "The Trial of Christ," in *Historicity and Chronology in the New Testament* (London: SPCK, 1965), 97-116. Carson ("Matthew," 549-52) gives an excellent overview of the various problems and offers responsible solutions.

Jesus was a blasphemer and worthy of death, so it was just a matter of time before the court could demonstrate it, even if all of the charges were not as seriously investigated as they might otherwise have been. As it turns out, it takes a while to find this testimony, probably surprisingly long from the authorities' standpoint.[44] But, finally, two witnesses do agree, as v. 61 recounts a slightly garbled form of John 2:19 (Jesus did not originally say, "I am able to"). More incidental evidence appears here to support John's account of the temple cleansing as an event at the outset of Jesus' ministry and thus not remembered well. The charge that Jesus claimed he could destroy and rebuild the temple outraged Jewish sensibilities and could easily be interpreted by Rome as a social or political threat. John 2:21 gives the real interpretation of what Jesus actually said. On the "Sanhedrin," recall comments on 5:22 and 10:17. "The whole" court refers to all these who gathered hastily in the middle of the night, who may well have formed a small quorum out of the entire council of seventy.

62 Then the high priest stood up and said to Jesus, "Are you not going to answer? What is this testimony that these men are bringing against you?" 63 But Jesus remained silent.

The high priest said to him, "I charge you under oath by the living God: Tell us if you are the Christ, the Son of God."

64"Yes, it is as you say," Jesus replied. "But I say to all of you: In the future you will see the Son of Man sitting at the right hand of the Mighty One and coming on the clouds of heaven."

26:62-64 As he presides over the court, the high priest demands a reply from the accused, but Jesus refuses to speak (vv. 62-63a). He is not here to defend himself legally any more than he defended himself physically in Gethsemane. He has rather come to suffer, according to God's will. Caiaphas therefore charges him under oath, in the name of "the living God" (on which see comments under 16:16) to answer his question, Is he Messiah or not (v. 63b)? Caiaphas also uses the title "Son of God," but given the common messianic interpretation of this expression (see esp. 2 Sam 7:14; Pss 2:7; 89:26-27; cf. its varied use in 4:3; 8:29; 14:33; 17:5), Christ and Son of God are probably synonymous in his mind.[45]

---

[44]J. F. Walvoord (*Matthew: Thy Kingdom Come* [Chicago: Moody, 1974], 223) remarks that it is strange the high priest had trouble finding witnesses since Jesus had "freely claimed His deity and Messiahship." Precisely the opposite is true. Jesus' most public utterances to Jewish audiences were consistently veiled in their affirmations of his identity. Here is further evidence for this reticence and ambiguity.

[45]On the development of "Son of God," see esp. M. Hengel, *The Son of God* (Philadelphia: Fortress, 1976). J. Marcus ("Mark 14:61: 'Are You the Messiah-Son-of-God?'" *NovT* 31 [1989]: 125-41) takes "Son of God" as qualifying "Messiah" and thus pointing beyond conventional expectation to a more divine figure, though he does not adequately account for the contrast with v. 64b which this interpretation would blur.

With v. 64 we arrive at the Christological climax of the Gospel thus far. Jesus replies with the same words as to Judas in v. 25 (*sy eipas—you said* [it]; "yes, it is as you say"). Mark interprets these words as an affirmative reply ("I am," Mark 14:62); Luke, as *you say that I am* (Luke 22:70; NIV mars this ambiguity with "You are right in saying I am"). Probably again, therefore, Jesus' original Aramaic formed a veiled affirmative, indicting the original speaker. In other words, Jesus is telling Caiaphas, *That is your way of putting it* (cf. RSV, "You have said so," Rieu, "The words are yours").[46] And Caiaphas is correct, up to a point. But Jesus owns none of the nationalistic, anti-Roman associations which the Sanhedrin no doubt still links with "Messiah." So he qualifies his affirmative with a strong adversative (*plēn*) "but" and goes on to quote Dan 7:13 and Ps 110:1. He is the Christ, the Son of God, when those titles are rightly interpreted. But correct interpretation must allow for him also to be the heavenly Son of Man who occupied the most honored position in the universe, next to the very throne of God, second only to his Heavenly Father, and who will return to earth as judge of the cosmos. Jesus then will judge those who now judge him. Obviously, this kind of Messiah is far more than a human revolutionary. Jesus introduces the quotes with the words *from now on you will see* (NIV, less literally, "in the future you will see"), perhaps alluding to his more immediate exaltation (28:18) long before his actual return as judge (25:31).

[65] Then the high priest tore his clothes and said, "He has spoken blasphemy! Why do we need any more witnesses? Look, now you have heard the blasphemy. [66] What do you think?"

"He is worthy of death," they answered.

[67] Then they spit in his face and struck him with their fists. Others slapped him [68] and said, "Prophesy to us, Christ. Who hit you?"

26:65-68 Now the council has clear testimony which they regard as blasphemous. Jesus has equated himself with God or at least associated himself much too closely with him.[47] This is a capital offense. The high priest tears his clothes in the traditional sign of outrage and/or grief (cf. 2 Kgs 18:37; Acts 14:14; and, for a closer parallel involving blasphemy, *m. Sanh.* 7:5). The proceedings need continue no longer.

In vv. 67-68 the authorities' disgust leads them to spit in Jesus' face (a serious insult), physically abuse him (punching and slapping him around), and mock his prophetic reputation. Mark 14:65 adds that "they blindfolded

---

[46]Cf. esp. D. R. Catchpole, "The Answer of Jesus to Caiaphas (Matt. XXVI.64)," *NTS* 17 (1970-71): 213-26, who concludes that the phrase is "affirmative in content, and reluctant or circumlocutory in formulation" (226).

[47]Cf. Gundry, *Matthew*, 546.

him," which explains their charade a little better. Their voices probably dripped with sarcasm as they taunted, "Christ" (Messiah)!

(c) Peter's "Trial" in the Courtyard (26:69-75). If various irregularities make one question the formality of Jesus' trial, this next episode can be referred to as a trial only in a figurative sense. Nevertheless, Matthew's juxtaposition of this passage with the interrogation of Jesus suggests that he wants his readers to compare and contrast the two as parallel in some sense. While Jesus holds up astonishingly well under life-threatening conditions before the most powerful authorities in Judaism, Peter fails miserably under far less threatening conditions in the presence of people of very little status.[48]

[69] Now Peter was sitting out in the courtyard, and a servant girl came to him. "You also were with Jesus of Galilee," she said.
[70] But he denied it before them all. "I don't know what you're talking about," he said.

26:69-70 Peter appears where we left him in v. 58. This episode probably began while Jesus was being questioned indoors. A servant girl claims to recognize Peter as one of Jesus' companions (v. 69). Both gender and occupation underline her powerlessness. But Peter denies the charge (v. 70). He claims not even to know what she is talking about.[49] The verb translated "deny" (from Greek *arneomai*) is the same as the one translated "disown" in v. 34.

[71] Then he went out to the gateway, where another girl saw him and said to the people there, "This fellow was with Jesus of Nazareth."
[72] He denied it again, with an oath: "I don't know the man!"

26:71-72 To avoid the awkwardness of this conversation, Peter retreats to the edge of the crowd. But another woman sees him and makes the same charge (v. 71). This time Peter denies even knowing Jesus. He uses an oath, probably invoking the name of God to solemnize the alleged truth of his statement (v. 72). Contrast Jesus' revealing his true identity following the high priest's oath in vv. 63-64. Peter's sin and guilt are increasing qualitatively as well as quantitatively.

---

[48] On the similarities and differences of these two episodes, cf. further B. Gerhardsson, "Confession and Denial before Men: Observations on Matt. 26:57-27:2," *JSNT* 13 (1981): 46-66.

[49] Cf. L. Sabourin (*L'Évangile selon saint Matthieu et ses principaux parallèles* [Rome: Biblical Institute Press, 1978], 364): "His first denial was obviously more instinctive than deliberate. He may have defended himself less out of fear than to avoid being sent away, since he wanted 'to see the end.' Still, his reply was a lie and as often happens, a lie that led to others, and in the case of Peter it soon involved a false oath and cursing."

73After a little while, those standing there went up to Peter and said, "Surely you are one of them, for your accent gives you away."

74Then he began to call down curses on himself and he swore to them, "I don't know the man!"

Immediately a rooster crowed. 75Then Peter remembered the word Jesus had spoken: "Before the rooster crows, you will disown me three times." And he went outside and wept bitterly.

26:73-75 After some unspecified interval of time, several individuals[50] press charges against Peter more insistently (v. 73). His accent gives him away as a Galilean and not a Judean. Given the number of pilgrims in Jerusalem for Passover, this still scarcely proves his association with Jesus, but Peter is not likely to be thinking along these lines. With v. 74a comes the strongest denial yet. Peter again takes an oath but also "calls down curses." The NIV interprets the object of this verb to be "himself," but it could even be taken to be Jesus. *Katathematizein* comes from the same root as "anathematize"—asking God to punish him (or Christ) if he is lying. Graciously God forbears, but the rooster does immediately crow (v. 74b). Peter recalls Jesus' words of v. 34, recognizes their fulfillment, and breaks down in sobs of sorrow. His repentance may be inferred from his subsequent restoration. Peter will again lead the Twelve in the early chapters of Acts, after the poignant recommissioning scene of John 21:15-19, in which his threefold reinstatement is probably intended to parallel his threefold denial here.

The scenes of Jesus' and Peter's "trials" combine to provide important teaching on the true nature of the Christ, whom we ought to confess, and on the real human failure of his followers to do just that. Such failure, however, need not damage us forever. The marvelous testimonies of the ministries of the apostles in early church history disprove all claims that Christians who have grievously sinned, even if they repent, can never be used as greatly by God as they would have otherwise!

b. SENTENCE AND EXECUTION: GOOD FRIDAY (27:1-66). As noted in the introduction to chaps. 26–28, there is no clear break between chaps. 26–27. Still, the scene shifts to Friday morning and depicts the transfer of Jesus from Jewish to Roman authorities. Similar shifts of time and place separate the events preceding Christ's execution (vv. 1-31) from the crucifixion and burial (vv. 32-66).

(1) Sentencing Jesus (27:1-31). In vv. 1-2 the Jewish authorities formalize their verdict and deliver Jesus to Pilate. Verses 11-26 portray

---

[50]Matthew's plural allows for the diversity of the Gospel accounts in terms of who questioned Peter. Apparently more than three people accused him of being a disciple even if he only denied on three specific occasions. But we can scarcely harmonize with the precision demanded by H. Lindsell, *The Battle for the Bible* (Grand Rapids: Zondervan, 1976), 174-76.

Jesus before the Roman governor, concluding with Pilate's sentence. Verses 27-31 depict the soldiers' mockery prior to the actual crucifixion. In between the first two of these segments appears Judas's suicide (vv. 3-10). Matthew apparently inserted this episode so as to contrast both Jesus and Judas (courage versus cowardice) as well as Peter and Judas (repentance versus despair).

¹Early in the morning, all the chief priests and the elders of the people came to the decision to put Jesus to death. ²They bound him, led him away and handed him over to Pilate, the governor.

(a) Sentencing by the Jews (27:1-2). **27:1-2** It is important to see these two verses as separate from vv. 3-10, contra the NIV section headings. Matthew 27:1-2 is actually linked more closely with the end of chap. 26 than with 27:3, but the verses can stand alone as a short passage reflecting a brief daytime reenactment by the Sanhedrin of the nighttime proceedings (cf. Luke 22:66-71). This hearing may have functioned like a "rubber stamp," but at least it would have brought the proceedings more into conformity with the letter of the law.[51] But the Jews did not have the right to execute capital offenders under Roman law (John 18:31). This claim has been widely challenged but is seemingly corroborated by *y. Sanh.* 1:1,72. So the Jewish leaders take Jesus to the Roman governor early in the morning. Pontius Pilate was the latest in a series of *procurators* or *prefects* of Judea ("governor" in v. 2 is a nontechnical term) appointed directly by Rome under arrangements established after the deposition of Herod Archelaus in A.D. 6. Pilate occupied this office from A.D. 26–36.

The emperor, Tiberius, was scarcely honoring Pilate when he assigned him to this somewhat remote and rebellious territory. Pilate would have found himself in a precarious position. He had to be perceived as loyal to Caesar, while at the same time pacifying the Jews enough so that they would not riot and get him in trouble with Rome. Extrabiblical testimony about Pilate's personality and behavior does not flatter him. He receives low marks for his sensitivity to the Jews and for the meting out of justice and seems simultaneously despotic and insecure (cf. Josephus, *J.W.* 2.9.2-4; Philo, *Leg. ad Gaium* 299-305; Tacitus, *Ann.* 15.44).[52] These two verses also create a certain closure with 26:1-5, with their reference to the same groups of Jewish leaders and their council, even as they introduce a new stage in the proceedings against Jesus.

---

[51]Cf. further Blomberg, *Historical Reliability*, 136-38.

[52]For a summary of information that can be known about Pilate, see A. N. Sherwin-White, "Pilate, Pontius," in *ISBE*, 3:867-69. On the general historicity of the Gospel's portrait of Pilate, see B. C. McGing, "Pontius Pilate and the Sources," *CBQ* 53 (1991): 416-38.

(b) Judas Sentences and Executes Himself (27:3-10). Of the four Evangelists, only Matthew includes this story in his Gospel, though a partial parallel appears in Acts 1:18-19.[53] In addition to contrasting Judas with both Peter and Jesus, Matthew has created a triad of people who shed "innocent blood"—Judas, Pilate, and the Jewish crowds (vv. 4,24-25).[54] This section also fills a conspicuous gap in Mark, who never narrates the fulfillment of Jesus' prediction of this traitor's fate.[55]

³When Judas, who had betrayed him, saw that Jesus was condemned, he was seized with remorse and returned the thirty silver coins to the chief priests and the elders. ⁴"I have sinned," he said, "for I have betrayed innocent blood."

"What is that to us?" they replied. "That's your responsibility." ⁵So Judas threw the money into the temple and left. Then he went away and hanged himself.

27:3-4 Like Peter, Judas has an apparent change of heart after his treacherous behavior. Perhaps he did not expect his betrayal to lead to a crucifixion, thinking either that Jesus would finally mount a revolt and escape arrest or that, if imprisoned, he would not receive so severe a sentence. At any rate, Judas is "seized with remorse" (from Greek *metamelomai*). This verb is much rarer in the New Testament than the typical verb for "repenting" (*metanoeō*) and seems here to refer to a *change of mind* or *feeling of regret*,[56] which falls considerably short of full-fledged repentance (cf. 2 Cor 7:8, in which such remorse precedes repentance; and Heb 7:21, in which it refers to a change of mind and not sorrow for sin), even if in other contexts the semantic ranges of the two words overlap (e.g., Matt 21:29,32). Judas does acknowledge his sin and Jesus' innocence, but he does not demonstrate the mark of genuine repentance—appropriate corrective action. He confesses to the wrong group of people and then simply gives up on life. Judas tries to return the money the Jewish leaders paid him in 26:15, but they have no interest in dealing with the matter further.

27:5 Judas responds in anger and despair. He hurls the money to the floor, probably in the temple treasury room (*korbanas*, v. 6), and goes out and kills himself. Was he inspired by the gruesome model of Ahithophel (2 Sam 17:23)? It is not possible to conclude from Judas's actions that suicide automatically damns a person. There may be reasons why believers

---

[53]On the differences between the two accounts and the possibilities of harmonization, see Blomberg, *Historical Reliability*, 191-92.

[54]A. Plummer, *An Exegetical Commentary on the Gospel according to S. Matthew* (London: E. Stock, 1909), 386.

[55]Sabourin, *Matthieu*, 365.

[56]J. P. Louw and E. A. Nida, eds., *Greek-English Lexicon of the New Testament* (New York: UBS, 1988), 1:319, 373.

would take their lives when they are not fully in control of their senses (e.g., when there is a chemical imbalance in the body), but the Scriptures never commend suicide as do certain non-Christian religions. Suicide is always sinful, in violation of the Sixth Commandment (Exod 20:13), even if it can be forgiven. In Judas's case, however, there is no scriptural warrant for the sentimental notion that he was actually saved. For the Jews, a hanging would have confirmed God's curse (Deut 21:23). By emphasizing Judas's fate, Matthew provides a dire warning to his community about the possible result of apostasy.[57]

6 The chief priests picked up the coins and said, "It is against the law to put this into the treasury, since it is blood money." 7 So they decided to use the money to buy the potter's field as a burial place for foreigners. 8 That is why it has been called the Field of Blood to this day. 9 Then what was spoken by Jeremiah the prophet was fulfilled: "They took the thirty silver coins, the price set on him by the people of Israel, 10 and they used them to buy the potter's field, as the Lord commanded me."

27:6-10 The chief priests remain preoccupied with the letter of the law while oblivious to its spirit. They prove totally insensitive to Judas's desperate state of mind, while still concerned with the finer points of their oral traditions about the use of his money. The word for "treasury" in v. 6 is cognate to *korban*, on which see comments under 15:1-20. From their perspective "blood money" refers to Judas's betrayal of Jesus. For Matthew it will double as an allusion to Judas's death as well. The temple officials refuse to keep the money because it is ritually impure, so they buy a field for use as a cemetery for resident aliens (v. 7). Unclean money buys an unclean place for unclean people! Matthew mentions the potter's field as if it were well-known. An ancient tradition associates it with a site at the east end of the Valley of Hinnom, just south of Jerusalem (cf. Jer 19:7), a natural place for a cemetery (see comments under 5:22). Understandably, a new name became associated with that plot of ground (v. 8). "To this day" refers to the time of writing of the Gospel. Like many Old Testament counterparts, this episode is an etiology—a story told, in part at least, to account for the rise of a particular practice or place name.

Matthew, however, tells the story of Judas's suicide more for the opportunity to cite another fulfillment of Scripture (v. 9a). Verses 9b-10 most closely resemble Zech 11:12-13, with its reference to thirty pieces of silver thrown into the house of the Lord to the potter. But Matthew attributes the citation to Jeremiah. Many commentators thus point to

---

[57] D. P. Senior, *The Passion Narrative according to Matthew* (Leuven: University Press, 1975), 347-52.

Jer 32:6-9, in which Jeremiah buys a field for seventeen shekels of silver. Better still, however, is the interpretation which sees Jer 19:1-13 in Matthew's mind, especially with its references to "the blood of the innocent" (v. 4), the "potter" (vv. 1,11), the renaming of a place in the Valley of Hinnom (v. 6), violence (v. 11), and the judgment and burial by God of the Jewish leaders (v. 11). Matthew is again employing typology and combining allusions to texts in both Jeremiah and Zechariah. As Smith explains of the latter, "Although no strict Messianic view should be seen in the original passage, the quality of leadership is its central theme."[58] The Israelites reject their good leaders (Jeremiah, Zechariah, and Jesus) and therefore suffer under bad ones. What Smith says of the passage in Zechariah applies to Jeremiah as well. Matthew apparently sees references to both passages (and possibly also alludes to Jer 18:2-3) but follows a standard literary convention of his day by referring only to one source (in this case, the more obscure, though probably also the more important one).[59] Compare Mark 1:2, in which Mark conflates quotations from Isa 40:3 and Mal 3:1 (and possibly Exod 23:20) but cites only Isaiah by name. As with most of the references to the Old Testament in the infancy narratives (1:23; 2:15,18,23), the lack of closer parallelism between the scriptural texts and the events narrated testifies to their historicity. Matthew is obviously not falsifying history in order to conform it to passages of Scripture. Rather, he is seeking passages that may in some way illumine the events as they occurred. The NIV loses the force of the staccato barrage of *tim*-words. The last phrase of v. 9 reads, more literally, *the price (timēn) for the one having been priced (tetimēmenou), who they themselves priced (etimēsanto) by the sons of Israel.* For Judas, money meant almost everything.

[11]Meanwhile Jesus stood before the governor, and the governor asked him, "Are you the king of the Jews?"
[12]When he was accused by the chief priests and the elders, he gave no answer. [13]Then Pilate asked him, "Don't you hear the testimony they are bringing against you?" [14]But Jesus made no reply, not even to a single charge—to the great amazement of the governor.

(c) Sentencing by the Romans (27:11-26). **27:11** Matthew resumes the narrative where he left off in v. 2. Pilate asks a different question than Caiaphas did (26:63). Pilate's only concern is whether or not Jesus has broken Roman law, as, e.g., if he were trying to usurp Caesar's authority or aspire to political rule in Israel. So Pilate asks if Jesus is "the king of

---

[58]R. L. Smith, *Micah-Malachi*, WBC (Waco: Word, 1984), 272.

[59]For a detailed study of this passage and Matthew's use of the Old Testament in it, see D. J. Moo, "Tradition and Old Testament in Matt 27:3-10," in *Gospel Perspectives*, vol. 3, ed. R. T. France and D. Wenham (Sheffield: JSOT, 1983), 157-75.

the Jews." Jesus' reply (*sy legeis—you are saying* [it]) echoes his words in 26:25,64 (*sy eipas—you said* [it]), except that he uses the present rather than past tense. This reply should be interpreted as previously, *Your words not mine*, not as in the NIV, "Yes, it is as you say." Here all three Synoptics agree exactly on Jesus' response. Yes, Jesus is the King of the Jews, but not in the way Pilate fears (cf. John 18:36-37). Jesus has committed no crime against Rome. Instead, Pilate, a Gentile, has unwittingly testified to Christ's kingship, even as the Gentile magi did more consciously at the beginning of the Gospel (2:1-12).

27:12-14 Pilate now hears the charges made by the Jewish leaders against Jesus, presumably a summary of the proceedings of 26:60-66. They have subtly changed the accusation to evoke Pilate's question in v. 11, making the charges more serious from a Roman point of view. Pilate is amazed that Jesus refuses to defend himself. The question of v. 13 assumes a positive answer—*You do hear, don't you?* On the motif of Jesus' silence, see under 26:63. The NIV's "not even to a single charge" (v. 14) more literally reads *not even with a word*. Jesus is again fulfilling the prophecy of 12:17-21.

15Now it was the governor's custom at the Feast to release a prisoner chosen by the crowd. **16**At that time they had a notorious prisoner, called Barabbas. **17**So when the crowd had gathered, Pilate asked them, "Which one do you want me to release to you: Barabbas, or Jesus who is called Christ?" **18**For he knew it was out of envy that they had handed Jesus over to him.

27:15-18 Pilate remains unimpressed with the case against Jesus, and he realizes Jesus' popularity with the crowds and the jealousy this has created among their leaders (v. 18). So to be rid of his problem, he tries to pit the crowds against the Jewish authorities. It was a custom at Passover to release one prisoner according to popular demand (though NIV "chosen by the crowd" in v. 15 is an interpretive rendering of the simple dative—*to* or *for the crowd*). Many scholars doubt the historicity of this supposed custom, but indirect evidence in support of it emerges in Josephus, *Ant.* 20.9.3, *b. Pesaḥ.* 91a, and Livy 5.13, although none of these texts proves conclusive.[60] Pilate expects the crowd to opt for Jesus, especially when the only other apparent candidate for release is a man named Barabbas, who was particularly "notorious" (v. 16). *Episēmon* meant *particularly distinguished*, in either a good or bad way.[61] Mark 15:7 gives

---

[60]Cf. R. L. Merritt, "Jesus Barabbas and the Paschal Pardon," *JBL* 104 (1985): 57-68, who notes parallel Babylonian, Assyrian, Greek, and apparently Roman customs at similar festivals. For other possible evidence for this custom, see C. B. Chavel, "The Releasing of a Prisoner on the Eve of Passover in Ancient Jerusalem," *JBL* 60 (1941): 273-78.

[61]So the possibility also exists that the term should be translated "highly admired," i.e., by the more Zealot-minded Jews, as in Bratcher, *Matthew*, 356.

details of his crimes. Remarkable parallels appear between the names of the two prisoners, along with remarkable differences in their character. "Barabbas" means *son of a father* in a simple, human sense. Jesus, on the other hand, was the Heavenly Son of his Heavenly Father, though not yet generally so recognized.

Several important manuscripts and versions (Θ, f^1, 700, Syriac, Armenian, Georgian, Origen), and only in Matthew, add in both vv. 16 and 17 that Barabbas's forename was "Jesus." Although the external evidence for accepting these readings as original is relatively weak, it is hard to imagine anyone creating this potentially embarrassing parallel if it were not true (whether or not Matthew actually wrote it in his autograph). The NIV should at least have given it a marginal reading.[62] Certainly, having both characters named Jesus tightens the parallelism and makes the irony of the crowd's response all the greater.[63] Pilate's question then becomes, *Do you want Jesus Barabbas or Jesus who is called the Christ?* The "Christ" (Messiah) is still a title at this point in history, and Pilate does not think Jesus deserves it.

[19]While Pilate was sitting on the judge's seat, his wife sent him this message: "Don't have anything to do with that innocent man, for I have suffered a great deal today in a dream because of him."

27:19 Another uniquely Matthean detail follows. During the proceedings, as Pilate sits on his judgment seat, apparently at the "Stone Pavement" (*Gabbatha* [John 19:13], which has recently been excavated in Jerusalem), he receives a communiqué from his wife. She has had a dream about Jesus and warns her husband against prosecuting him. Greeks and Romans regularly viewed dreams as an important way in which the gods spoke to people. Quite possibly this dream came from the true and living God even as he spoke to the Gentile magi at the time of Jesus' birth (2:12). The contents of the dream are not disclosed, but apparently it was a nightmare. It at least convinced Pilate's wife of Jesus' innocence. Although scholars have severely exaggerated Matthew's inclinations, there is a sense in which he plays down the Romans' role in Jesus' death and heightens the condemnation of the Jewish leaders as Jesus' true antagonists and the instigators of his death.

[20]But the chief priests and the elders persuaded the crowd to ask for Barabbas and to have Jesus executed.

---

[62]The UBSGNT thinks it original to Matthew with a *C* rating; Nestle-Aland merely puts it in brackets.

[63]Their choice illustrates "the penchant for the people of God to choose violent solutions and leaders rather than Jesus' nonviolent Sermon on the Mount for the resolution of conflicts" (Bruner, *Churchbook*, 1029).

²¹"**Which of the two do you want me to release to you?" asked the gover-**
nor.

"Barabbas," they answered.
²²"**What shall I do, then, with Jesus who is called Christ?" Pilate asked.**
They all answered, "Crucify him!"
²³"**Why? What crime has he committed?" asked Pilate.**
But they shouted all the louder, "Crucify him!"

27:20-23   Pilate, however, is too insecure to uphold the principles of
Roman law or even to follow his wife's intuition. The Jewish leaders stir
up the crowd, perhaps against its natural preference (vv. 20-21). It is
often asked how these masses could so quickly and dramatically turn
against someone they acclaimed as Messiah only five days earlier (21:9-
11). But on Palm Sunday primarily Galilean crowds accompanied Jesus.
Here native Jerusalemites are more evident. And, to the extent that the
crowds did overlap, one must recall their quite different messianic expectations, now almost certainly destroyed by seeing Jesus imprisoned.
Recent events in the Middle East have also reminded us how easily a
small band of religious fanatics can whip up large mobs, using principles
of crowd psychology, to vociferously demand that which they otherwise
would not so staunchly support. Pilate is baffled by the crowd's response
(vv. 22-23). He believes that Jesus has committed no crime. Does the
crowd know something he doesn't? But this is no time for rational discourse, only mass hysteria.[64] The crowd clamors ever more wildly for
Jesus' crucifixion.

²⁴**When Pilate saw that he was getting nowhere, but that instead an uproar**
was starting, he took water and washed his hands in front of the crowd. "I am
innocent of this man's blood," he said. "It is your responsibility!"
²⁵**All the people answered, "Let his blood be on us and on our children!"**
²⁶**Then he released Barabbas to them. But he had Jesus flogged, and**
handed him over to be crucified.

27:24   Verses 24-25 represent another uniquely Matthean insertion.
Both verses at least partially promote Matthew's twofold agenda noted
under v. 19, exonerating the Romans and indicting the Jews. With a dramatic, symbolic gesture, and in order to avoid a riot that could threaten
his job, Pilate refuses to have anything more to do with Jesus' case. He
makes it plain that the famed system of Roman justice with its due process of law has not consented to this man's execution. Yet, despite his
protests of innocence, he does permit a gross miscarriage of justice, so
that Matthew can hardly be accused of whitewashing Pilate. In fact, his

---

[64]Cf. Bruner, *Churchbook*, 1032: "The fewer the reasons, the higher the volume. In any
argument the quieter side is almost always right."

closing words, *you see to it* ("it is your responsibility") closely parallel the Jewish leaders' rebuff of Judas in v. 4. Matthew is portraying Jewish and Roman leaders alike as abdicating their rightful responsibilities.[65]

27:25 The inclusion of the crowd's reply (v. 25) is often seen as the zenith of anti-Semitism in Matthew. Their cry picks up on Pilate's reference to "blood," and they accept responsibility for Jesus' death.[66] This verse has been the subject of much interpretation. Beare claims, "It is appalling for a Christian to think how much suffering has been inflicted upon Jews throughout the ages, partly as a result of this completely fictitious scene."[67] The first part of Beare's lament is sad but true; the second part is utterly false. In fact, it is only when the crowd's cry is interpreted in the context of Jesus' life that it can be defended. If it were the well-thought-out creation of the early church, then it would be absolutely appalling.[68] But as a spontaneous outburst in the frenzy of the moment, it is perfectly intelligible. Clearly the crowd is not condemning their entire race. All of Jesus' followers at this stage were also Jews, and the crowd does not refer to them. What is more, only a small subsection of even the uncommitted masses is involved.[69] "On our children" does not refer to all Jewish people for all eternity but reflects a formula of corporate solidarity and a strong protestation of the crowd's innocence (cf. Lev 20:9-16).[70] In fact, the rhetoric of this verse has been shown to be relatively mild by ancient conventions.[71] Moreover, even though the people's plea asks God to judge them if they are wrong, this does not imply that he will heed their request any more than he did with Peter's self-anathematization in 26:74. The only way to generalize about responsibility for Jesus' death beyond the actual group of people present in this scene is to indict all humanity, as Christians in their more theologically sober moments quickly recognize. Matthew may in fact be drawing a parallel between the crowd and the disciples. Just as one of the Twelve "betrayed innocent

---

[65]So also Stagg, "Matthew," 242.

[66]Cf. R. H. Mounce, *Matthew*, GNC (San Francisco: Harper and Row, 1985), 265: "In the delerium [*sic*] of the moment, a mob determined to crucify one who apparently violated what they held to be sacred would not hesitate to accept full responsibility for what they were about to do."

[67]Beare, *Matthew*, 531.

[68]Cf. Carson, "Matthew," 571.

[69]Cf. esp. J. A. Fitzmyer, "Anti-Semitism and the Cry of 'All the People' (Mt 27:25)," *TS* 26 (1965): 667-71.

[70]See esp. F. Lovsky, "Comment comprend 'Son sang sur nous et nos enfants'?" *ETR* 62 (1987): 343-62; cf. M. Wyschogrod, reviewing R. Kampling, *Das Blut Christi und die Juden* (Münster: Aschendorff, 1984), in *JES* 23 (1986): 682-83.

[71]L. T. Johnson, "The New Testament's Anti-Jewish Slander and the Conventions of Ancient Polemic," *JBL* 108 (1989): 419-44.

blood" (27:4), so now one segment of the uncommitted populace also turns out to accept the blame for "his blood."

Still, popular rejection of Jesus reaches a dramatic climax here. Matthew may well have in mind the motif of 12:45 and 23:36, in which this generation is seen as particularly wicked. If the crowd's "children" most naturally refer to the generation of sons and daughters of those alive here in A.D. 30, then Matthew most likely sees the fulfillment of v. 25 in the destruction of Jerusalem in A.D. 70. But then nothing at all can be deduced about the eternal destiny of subsequent generations of Jews. Matthew 23:39 and 24:30 have already hinted at a future outpouring of repentance within Israel. And, paradoxically, since Jesus' blood is shed for the forgiveness of sins, then the crowd's part in his death ultimately makes available the possibility of their salvation.[72]

27:26 So Pilate releases Barabbas and delivers Jesus to his soldiers, though not before having him flogged. This scourging, itself often fatal, employed a metal-tipped whip known as the *flagellum*, which repeatedly ripped into the naked flesh of the victim's back. This Roman torture further mitigates any charges of the exclusive culpability of the Jews.

[27] **Then the governor's soldiers took Jesus into the Praetorium and gathered the whole company of soldiers around him.** [28] **They stripped him and put a scarlet robe on him,** [29] **and then twisted together a crown of thorns and set it on his head. They put a staff in his right hand and knelt in front of him and mocked him. "Hail, king of the Jews!" they said.** [30] **They spit on him, and took the staff and struck him on the head again and again.** [31] **After they had mocked him, they took off the robe and put his own clothes on him. Then they led him away to crucify him.**

(d) Mocking by the Soldiers (27:27-31). **27:27-31** The fulfillment of 20:19 has begun. Mockery such as depicted here finds parallels in Philo, *Flacc.* 36-39 and Dio Cass., *Hist.* 15.20-21. "The Praetorium" in v. 27 refers to the official residence of the Roman ruler, which also sometimes housed the soldiers' barracks. This could have been located at the Antonium fortress (Pilate's center of activity when in Jerusalem) or Herod's palace (where Antipas of Galilee stayed when visiting). Gathering the whole "company" (literally *cohort*) would involve six hundred men, one tenth of a legion, if the troops were at complete strength. The soldiers mock Jesus' alleged kingship. They clothe him with a loose reddish purple outer garment worn by soldiers and travelers (cf. Mark 15:17)

---

[72]Cf. B. Przybylski, "The Setting of Matthean Anti-Judaism," in *Anti-Judaism in Early Christianity*, vol. 1, ed. P. Richardson and D. Granskou (Waterloo, Ont.: Wilfrid Laurier, 1986), 181-200; T. B. Cargal, "'His Blood Be Upon Us and Upon Our Children': A Matthean Double Entendre?" *NTS* 37 (1991): 101-12; J. P. Heil, "The Blood of Jesus in Matthew: A Narrative-Critical Perspective," *PRS* 18 (1991): 117-24.

and pretend he is a royal warrior (v. 28). They press a garland or wreath of thorns into his head, probably a thorny branch bent into a circle, parodying a crown (v. 29a). They place a reed or rod in his right hand to look like a scepter, and the soldiers then mockingly worship him with feigned adulation as they cry, *Greetings* ("hail"), "king of the Jews," echoing the words of Pilate's question in v. 11 (v. 29b).[73] Then they turn to more direct insults and overt abuse by spitting in his face (recall 26:67) and beating him on the head with the rod (v. 30). The scarlet garment is then removed, his own cloak returned, and he is taken away to the site of the crucifixion (v. 31). It was normal for criminals to be led to the cross naked. The return of Jesus' clothes perhaps reflects a Roman concession to the Jews because of the special shame they attached to appearing naked in public.[74]

(2) The Execution of Jesus (27:32-66). (a) The Crucifixion (27:32-44). Matthew describes very little of Jesus' own experience on the cross, and then not until the last few minutes before his death (vv. 45-66). Instead, Matthew emphasizes how other people experienced the crucifixion: Simon, the soldiers, the passers-by, the Jewish leaders, and the two criminals on the crosses on either side of Christ. In so doing, Matthew stresses the nearly universal rejection of our Lord.[75]

[32]As they were going out, they met a man from Cyrene, named Simon, and they forced him to carry the cross. [33]They came to a place called Golgotha (which means The Place of the Skull). [34]There they offered Jesus wine to drink, mixed with gall; but after tasting it, he refused to drink it.

27:32-34 A convicted criminal was usually expected to carry the horizontal beam for his own cross to the site of his execution, where the vertical beam would already have been put in the ground. But Jesus was apparently too weak and injured from his flogging to go very far along the road (the so-called *Via Dolorosa*—"sorrowful way"; cf. John 19:17). So the soldiers conscript a man by the name of Simon of Cyrene (in Libya), who happens to be coming into town, to help carry the crossbeam (v. 32). Eventually they arrive at Golgotha, which strong, ancient tradition associates with the site that now houses the Church of the Holy Sepulchre, in that day still outside the city walls. The actual appearance of

---

[73]Sabourin (*Matthieu*, 375) refers to this as a coronation parody, including investiture, crowning, homage, and acclamation.

[74]France, *Matthew*, 394.

[75]Cf. Schweizer, *Matthew*, 511-12: "Thus Matthew depicts the crucifixion primarily in terms of mockery." T. L. Donaldson ("The Mockers and the Son of God [Matthew 27.37-44]: Two Characters in Matthew's Story of Jesus," *JSNT* 41 [1991]: 3-18) sees this mockery as the climax of a motif contrasting Jesus' rejection and vindication woven throughout Matthew's Gospel.

Golgotha, however, would have more resembled "Gordon's Calvary," as shown to tourists today. "The Place of the Skull" would refer to the skull-shaped formations in the side of the hill (v. 33). Wine mixed with gall was probably a pain-killing narcotic (*b. Sanh.* 43a), though just possibly a poison. Either way, the potion was probably intended to ease Jesus' misery, though some have seen it as additional torture. But Jesus refuses to decrease his suffering or to lose consciousness of his surroundings (v. 34). Mark 15:23 mentions myrrh instead of gall. Myrrh may be the literal element; and gall, a metaphorical reference to the bitterness of the mixture or a more general term referring to "a substance with an unpleasant taste."[76] Matthew may see a fulfillment of Ps 69:21. The practice itself is perhaps based on Prov 31:6.

[35] When they had crucified him, they divided up his clothes by casting lots. [36] And sitting down, they kept watch over him there. [37] Above his head they placed the written charge against him: THIS IS JESUS, THE KING OF THE JEWS.

27:35-37   So Christ is nailed to the cross (this is what is implied by "crucified" in v. 35)—his feet nailed together at his ankles at the bottom of a vertical pole, his hands nailed at the wrists to either end of the crossbeam. Crucifixion was undoubtedly one of the most gruesome forms of torture and death humans have ever invented. It involved prolonged suffering for up to several days. The final cause of death was usually asphyxiation, since the victim finally became too weak to lift his head far enough off his chest to gasp for air.[77] The soldiers, as usual, cast lots (perhaps variously marked pebbles), just as we might roll dice, for the victim's clothes. Does Matthew see a fulfillment of Ps 22:18, as in John 19:24?[78] It is not clear if Jesus was left totally naked or allowed some kind of covering over his private parts. The soldiers kept watch lest anyone should try to come and forcibly rescue Jesus (v. 36). Also, as was customary, the charge of Jesus' crime was inscribed on a *titulus* (a wooden placard), which was nailed to the top of the cross (v. 37). The

---

[76]BAGD, 883; cf. Louw and Nida, *Greek-English Lexicon*, 103.

[77]On the details of the method, see esp. M. Hengel, *Crucifixion* (Philadelphia: Fortress, 1977); for the theological significance, cf. esp. J. R. W. Stott, *The Cross of Christ* (Downers Grove: InterVarsity, 1986); and L. Morris, *The Cross of Jesus* (Grand Rapids: Eerdmans, 1988). On the issues of sources and redaction, see esp. J. B. Green, *The Death of Jesus: Tradition and Interpretation in the Passion Narrative* (Tübingen: Mohr, 1988).

[78]A few important and/or early manuscripts (Δ, Θ, f^1, f^{13}, Italic, Vulgate, and Syriac) insert material from John 19:24 here, referring to the fulfillment of Ps 22:18. The evidence for its inclusion, however, is very weak. It is surprising the NIV even allows it a marginal reference, given how many other marginal readings are entirely omitted and given that even the UBSGNT itself omits even a mention of this textual variant (itself a somewhat surprising omission).

wording of the charge drips with irony, making it appear as if the Romans believed that Jesus was the King of the Jews. The irony increases when we recognize that, rightly interpreted, the sign proclaimed the truth. John 19:20-22 elaborates on this irony even further.[79]

[38]Two robbers were crucified with him, one on his right and one on his left. [39]Those who passed by hurled insults at him, shaking their heads [40]and saying, "You who are going to destroy the temple and build it in three days, save yourself! Come down from the cross, if you are the Son of God!"

27:38-40 Two *lēstai* ("robbers") are crucified with Jesus (v. 38). Had his cross originally been intended for a third *lēstēs* (v. 16)—Barabbas? In any event, *rebel* or *insurrectionist* is probably a better translation than "robber" (recall comments under 26:55). The nature of their crimes would have more likely involved terrorism and assassination than theft or burglary. Doubtless Matthew saw the parody of Jesus' kingship extended further with the picture of one criminal on each side of Jesus, like a king with his advisors at his right and left hands. Crucifixions were usually held alongside well-traveled roads to remind as many people as possible of the high cost of crime, particularly treason against the empire. The passersby who see Jesus echo the garbled charge against him from the Jewish trial (26:61), perhaps now widely publicized (vv. 39-40). They taunt his apparent impotence. "Hurled insults" is literally *blasphemed*. "Shaking their heads" seems to allude to Ps 22:7. Only Matthew adds, "If you are the Son of God," an exact reproduction of Satan's catcall in 4:3. In this case, however, the first-class condition is more hypothetical, as in 12:27.

Here truly is Jesus' last great temptation, to come down off the cross, and he could have chosen to give in to it. But he would thereby have forfeited his divinely ordained role as the innocent sufferer for the sins of all humanity (cf. 2 Cor 5:21; Rom 3:21-26; Heb 9:26-28). For the sake of our eternal salvation, we praise God that he chose to remain faithful despite this unspeakable and excruciating agony. He thus perfectly illustrated the principle of 16:25 ("whoever wants to save his life will lose it, but whoever loses his life for me will find it"), which applies to all people. It is difficult to study the crucifixion sensitively and sympathetically and not break down in tears. It is almost inconceivable that believers who frequently meditate on Jesus' suffering on their behalf could exalt themselves or quarrel with each other (hence 1 Cor 1:18–2:5 as Paul's response to the problems of 1 Cor 1:10-17). The ground is indeed level at the foot of the cross. That God should send his Son to die for us was the scandal of the Christian message in the first century (1 Cor 1:23) and

---

[79]See esp. G. M. Lee, "The Inscription on the Cross," *PEQ* 100 (1968): 144, for comparison of the Gospel versions of the inscription and the probable literal original.

remains so for many today. But all attempts to remove the doctrine of Jesus' substitutionary atonement from Christianity leave us dead in sin with a religion impotent to save us from eternal damnation.

41In the same way the chief priests, the teachers of the law and the elders mocked him. 42"He saved others," they said, "but he can't save himself! He's the King of Israel! Let him come down now from the cross, and we will believe in him. 43He trusts in God. Let God rescue him now if he wants him, for he said, 'I am the Son of God.'" 44In the same way the robbers who were crucified with him also heaped insults on him.

27:41-44   The Jewish leaders echo the taunts of the crowd (vv. 41-43). They recall Christ's miracles but mockingly lament his inability to repeat them now (vv. 41-42), not understanding that he voluntarily chose not to perform what would have been the most spectacular miracle to date by saving his physical life. Consistent with later Jewish polemic, no one tried to deny that Jesus had previously manifested supernatural power (recall under 12:24). "He's the King of Israel" is obviously sarcastic, as is possibly, though not as clearly, "he trusts in God." Matthew again alludes to Ps 22, this time to v. 8, and possibly also to Wis 2:20. The criminals also join in the mocking, so that torment comes from all sides (v. 44). Luke notes a later change of heart on the part of one of the two criminals (Luke 23:40-43). Matthew, however, does not wish to detract from Jesus' agony. Verse 43 is unique to his Gospel and reflects his emphasis on the Son of God, also alluding to Ps 22:9. Jesus' opponents unwittingly testify to his identity. Precisely because Jesus is the Son of God, he consciously decides not to come down off the cross. Mounce rightly observed, "It was the power of love, not nails, that kept him there."[80]

(b) The Death (27:45-56).   More positive testimony to Jesus' identity emerges from "nature," the Roman centurion and the women. Matthew presents the latter two quite briefly (vv. 54-56); he expounds on the former in more detail (vv. 45-53), noting three unusual events—the preternatural darkness (v. 45), the rending of the temple veil (v. 51a), and the resurrection of the saints (vv. 51b-53).

45From the sixth hour until the ninth hour darkness came over all the land. 46About the ninth hour Jesus cried out in a loud voice, "Eloi, Eloi, lama sabachthani?"—which means, "My God, my God, why have you forsaken me?"

27:45-46   Christ was apparently put on the cross sometime midmorning on Friday.[81] From midday to midafternoon, unusual darkness appears.

---

[80]Mounce, *Matthew*, 268.
[81]See Blomberg, *Historical Reliability*, 179-80.

This is the first of the three remarkable events in "nature" reflecting the cosmic significance of Jesus' death. "Darkness" here obviously symbolizes a great evil, apocalyptic upheavals (recall 24:24; cf. Joel 2:10), and perhaps a new era in salvation history (cf. Exod 10:22). Some have traced this darkness to a great sirocco (wind) storm or to the solar eclipse of A.D. 33, but neither of these events would have created complete darkness, and the latter occurred in a less-likely year (than A.D. 30) for Jesus' crucifixion. It is better to see here a genuinely supernatural event, though, given the coming earthquake, it is not impossible that some kind of natural event was supernaturally timed. While Christ was on the cross, he would utter his famous "seven last words" (or "sayings"). All have particular theological importance (cf. Luke 23:34,42-43; John 19:26-28,30; Luke 23:46).

The only "word" of Christ on the cross which Matthew records, chronologically perhaps the fourth of the seven, is the saying of v. 46. Perhaps because of the power and significance of Jesus' cry, the Aramaic was preserved and then given a translation. Jesus quotes Ps 22:1. The variation in spelling among manuscripts reflects the difference between the Hebrew *Eli* and the Aramaic *Eloi*, both meaning *my God*. All kinds of theological questions are raised here that the text simply does not answer, particularly regarding the relation of Christ's divine and human natures. But the docetic or Gnostic view that Jesus' divine nature actually departed at this time because God could in no way suffer (found as early as mid-second century in the apocryphal Gospel of Peter[82]), has usually been rejected by Christians as heretical. Jesus remains a psychosomatically unified entity all the way to the moment of his death. Yet shortly before he dies, he apparently senses an abrupt loss of the communion with the Father which had proved so intimate and significant throughout his life. Not surprisingly, then, Christian theology developed the belief that at this moment Christ bore the sins of all humanity, spiritually separating him from his Heavenly Father (see references under vv. 38-40 above). The view that Jesus' quotation of Ps 22 anticipates the vindication found in the larger context of the psalm stresses what does not appear in the text at the expense of what does.[83]

---

[82]On which see esp. D. F. Wright, "Apocryphal Gospels: The 'Unknown Gospel' (Papyrus Egerton 2) and the *Gospel of Peter*," in *Gospel Perspectives*, vol. 5, ed. D. Wenham (Sheffield: JSOT, 1985), 207-32, particularly against attempts to rehabilitate this gospel, now most notably illustrated in J. D. Crossan, *The Cross That Spoke* (San Francisco: Harper and Row, 1988).

[83]For further helpful theological reflections on Jesus' abandonment by God in Matthew, see B. Gerhardsson, "Jésus livré et abandonné d'après la passion selon saint Matthieu," *RB* 76 (1969): 206-27.

47When some of those standing there heard this, they said, "He's calling Elijah."
48Immediately one of them ran and got a sponge. He filled it with wine vinegar, put it on a stick, and offered it to Jesus to drink. 49The rest said, "Now leave him alone. Let's see if Elijah comes to save him."
50And when Jesus had cried out again in a loud voice, he gave up his spirit.

27:47-50   Whether the passersby were more cosmopolitan in make-up or whether Jesus' speech was slurred, some mistakenly interpret his words as calling on the prophet Elijah, who would precede the Day of the Lord (Mal 4:5), to come and rescue him (v. 47). For more on Elijah, see comments under 3:1-6; 11:7-14; 17:7-13.[84] One of the crowd either senses his agony or suspects incoherence and again offers a pain killer and/or thirst quencher (v. 48; recall comments under v. 34).[85] Compare John 19:28-30 for more details and the results of this offer. But the rest of the crowd tells the man to stop. They want to see if Elijah will indeed appear (v. 49).[86] Instead, Jesus cries out again and dies (v. 50). Luke 23:46 gives his words—a stunning cry of trust after his sense of divine abandonment. "Gave up his spirit" is simply idiomatic for physical death because Jews believed that one's spirit departed the body after one had stopped breathing. But the text may also be hinting that Jesus in his human nature chooses the moment voluntarily to relinquish his struggle for life. Even in death he is in some kind of control (cf. Luke 23:46).

51At that moment the curtain of the temple was torn in two from top to bottom. The earth shook and the rocks split. 52The tombs broke open and the bodies of many holy people who had died were raised to life. 53They came out of the tombs, and after Jesus' resurrection they went into the holy city and appeared to many people.

27:51-53   Here appear the second and third events from the world of nature which testify to the monumental significance of the crucifixion. One apparently natural event, an earthquake, leads to two somewhat supernatural effects. The temple curtain is split "from top to bottom," perhaps to symbolize God acting from heaven, and the cemeteries disgorge their dead. Yet it is not bones but risen bodies that emerge! Like the preternatural darkness, earthquakes and resurrections resonate with strong

---

[84]Most of the observations of K. Brower ("Elijah in the Markan Passion Narrative," *JSNT* 18 [1983]: 85-101) apply to Matthew's account as well.

[85]On ὄξος, the beverage offered here, see Louw and Nida, *Greek-English Lexicon*, 78: "a cheap, sour wine, evidently a favorite beverage of the poorer people and relatively effective in quenching thirst."

[86]There is a textual variant with part of John 19:34 interpolated here that has been defended as original (e.g., by S. Pennells, "The Spear Thrust [Mt. 27.49b, *v.l.* Jn 19.34]," *JSNT* 19 [1983]: 99-115), but the evidence is too weak to sustain this view.

apocalyptic overtones (cf. esp. Amos 8:9). The latter event is perhaps the most unusual in all of the Gospels and found only in Matthew. All kinds of historical questions remain unanswered about both events, but their significance clearly lies in the theology Matthew wishes to convey. Judgment against the temple has begun (recall chaps. 23–24), and a new age of salvation history has dawned.[87] The temple curtain that was torn was probably the one that separated the court of the Jews from the court of the Gentiles. Ephesians 2:14 seems to recall this rupture when reflecting on the abolition of the barriers between Jew and Gentile in Christ. Garbled accounts of the torn curtain may be reflected in other Jewish sources too (see, e.g., Josephus, *J.W.* 6.5.3-4 and *b. Yoma* 39b), but it is hard to be sure. As an alternative, if the curtain protecting the holy of holies was in view, then Matthew's point could be the new access to God provided by Jesus' atoning death (as in Heb 4:16).[88]

The resurrections illustrate the teaching of 1 Cor 15:20-22. Christ is the firstfruits of the new age, guaranteeing the bodily resurrection of all his people. "Holy people" (often translated *saints*) apparently refer to selected Old Testament believers.[89] This episode further foreshadows 1 Cor 15:23. As the NIV stands, Matthew's account contradicts Paul, inasmuch as the saints actually precede Christ out of the tomb. But the text should probably be punctuated with a period after the "tombs broke open." Then the rest of vv. 52b-53 would read, *And the bodies of many holy people who had died were raised to life, and, having come out of the tombs after Jesus' resurrection, they went into the Holy City* [i.e., Jerusalem]. Contra the NIV rendering of v. 53, there is no "and" in the Greek nor any other reason to pause between "tombs" and "after."[90] If these saints were genuinely resurrected rather than simply revivified or reanimated like Jairus's daughter or Lazarus, then presumably, like Jesus himself, they appeared to others only for a short time and were eventually taken to heaven. But the text refuses to satisfy our curiosity about these points.[91] It is interesting, however, to note Matthew's twofold reference to Jews and Jerusalem as "holy" ("holy people," v. 52; "holy city," v. 53) even after his sweeping condemnation of Israel in chaps. 23-24. Hints again emerge that a remnant in Israel will be preserved.

---

[87]S. Motyer, "The Rending of the Veil: A Markan Pentecost?" *NTS* 33 (1987): 155-57.

[88]For a survey of various other early Christian interpretations, see M. de Jonge, "Matthew 27:51 in Early Christian Exegesis," *HTR* 79 (1986): 67-79.

[89]Christian tradition suggested the pious Jews of Luke 1–2: Zechariah, Simeon, Anna, and Joseph (Bruner, *Churchbook*, 1061).

[90]J. W. Wenham, "When Were the Saints Raised?" *JTS* 32 (1981): 150-52.

[91]For more on the theology of this passage, see esp. D. Senior, "The Death of Jesus and the Resurrection of the Holy Ones (Mt 27:51-53)," *CBQ* 38 (1976): 312-29.

⁵⁴**When the centurion and those with him who were guarding Jesus saw the earthquake and all that had happened, they were terrified, and exclaimed, "Surely he was the Son of God!"**

⁵⁵**Many women were there, watching from a distance. They had followed Jesus from Galilee to care for his needs. ⁵⁶Among them were Mary Magdalene, Mary the mother of James and Joses, and the mother of Zebedee's sons.**

27:54 To add to nature's testimony about the significance of Jesus' death, we now read of the witness of the Roman officer in charge at the cross (cf. the centurion of 8:5-13). The incongruity of his testimony has led to the translation as in the NIV margin. The man may well view Jesus as a typical Greco-Roman "divine man" (a great human hero deified upon his death). Luke 23:47 ("surely this was a righteous man") makes the centurion's original words all the more uncertain. Perhaps the best explanation is that which interprets the confession as meaning, "He was a good man, and quite right in calling God his Father."[92] But Matthew will see further support here for Jesus as the unique Son of God, in some way on a par with deity. Matthew also adds a comment on the great fear of the centurion and his companions. In this context *fear* implies *terror* much more than worship.

27:55-56 Matthew introduces yet one more group of observers. Here is the first indication that anyone who supported Jesus followed him to the cross. The disciples had all fled, though John returned at a later time (John 19:26-27). Many women, however, remained more loyal. Ironically, due to their gender, they would not have been viewed as a public threat and so could safely accompany their Master. These women had cared for him (cf. Luke 8:2-3) and gone with him on his trip to Jerusalem (recall Matt 20:20). They kept a faithful vigil even in the face of the horror of his cross. Matthew again mentions the mother of James and John and adds references to Mary Magdalene and Mary "the mother of James and Joses." Mark calls this latter James "the younger" (*tou mikrou*—literally, *the little* or *the less*, Mark 15:40), probably referring to the less prominent of the two apostles by that name. Apparently these people are still well-known to Matthew's readers. More on Mary Magdalene appears in Luke 8:2. There is no scriptural support for the traditional belief that she was a prostitute or the same woman who anointed Jesus in Luke 7:36-50. John 19:25 refers to a Mary, wife of Clopas, who may be the same as the mother of James and Joses (according to Eusebius, *H.E.* 3.11, Clopas was an uncle of Jesus), and mentions the presence of Jesus' own mother

---

[92]L. Morris, *The Gospel according to St. Luke*, TNTC (Grand Rapids: Eerdmans, 1974), 330, citing A. Plummer, *A Critical and Exegetical Commentary on the Gospel according to St. Luke*, ICC (Edinburgh: T & T Clark, 1896), 539.

as well. John 19:31-37 describes other events that occurred while Jesus' corpse still hung on the cross.

⁵⁷As evening approached, there came a rich man from Arimathea, named Joseph, who had himself become a disciple of Jesus. ⁵⁸Going to Pilate, he asked for Jesus' body, and Pilate ordered that it be given to him. ⁵⁹Joseph took the body, wrapped it in a clean linen cloth, ⁶⁰and placed it in his own new tomb that he had cut out of the rock. He rolled a big stone in front of the entrance to the tomb and went away. ⁶¹Mary Magdalene and the other Mary were sitting there opposite the tomb.

(c) The Burial (27:57-61). **27:57-61** At nightfall (the sun had apparently come back out again at 3:00 p.m.) a rich man named Joseph boldly approaches the Roman governor to ask for permission to give Jesus' body a more decent burial than executed criminals would otherwise have received (vv. 57-58). A burial will also prevent the defilement of the land, in Jewish eyes, which would be caused by leaving the corpse on the cross overnight (Deut 21:22-23). Joseph hailed from Arimathea, a town about twenty-two miles northwest of Jerusalem, which was known to Old Testament readers as Ramathaim, the birthplace of Samuel (1 Sam 1:1). Joseph had become a follower of Jesus, but he had not yet revealed his loyalties in public (John 19:38) because he also belonged to the Sanhedrin (Mark 15:43). Perhaps he had not been present at the previous night's proceedings. Not surprisingly, Matthew omits all this information which might detract from his relatively unrelenting hostility against the Jewish leaders. Pilate graciously grants Joseph's request. Did Pilate recognize Joseph's influential role? Joseph then places the corpse in his own unused tomb, appropriately honoring Jesus' body with the resting place he had originally acquired for his own burial. He wraps the body according to the custom of the times (v. 59). Again John describes the picture in somewhat more detail, mentioning that Nicodemus helped Joseph (John 19:39-42). Joseph's actions call to mind Isa 53:9.

The burial site probably looked something like the "Garden Tomb" tourists still view today, though at a different location. The tomb was not a hole dug in the ground but a cave, with its opening sealed by rolling a large boulder down a slight incline to barricade the entrance (v. 60). It would then require quite a number of strong people to move the stone. The two Marys of v. 56 had apparently followed Joseph and now resume their mourning at the gravesite (v. 61). This verse explains how they know where to go on Sunday morning and should refute all allegations that they went to the wrong tomb!

⁶²The next day, the one after Preparation Day, the chief priests and the Pharisees went to Pilate. ⁶³"Sir," they said, "we remember that while he was still alive that deceiver said, 'After three days I will rise again.' ⁶⁴So give the

order for the tomb to be made secure until the third day. Otherwise, his disciples may come and steal the body and tell the people that he has been raised from the dead. This last deception will be worse than the first."

(d) The Guard at the Tomb (27:62-66).[93]   **27:62-64**   On the next day (Saturday), after "Preparation Day" (*Friday*—the Preparation Day for the Sabbath, not for the Passover), Pilate receives a second request regarding Jesus' burial (v. 62). This time the request comes from the Jewish leaders, who recall Jesus' resurrection prophecies. Had the disciples spread the word Jesus had first told them privately? Of course, the officials do not believe these predictions. They call Jesus a "deceiver." But they do believe that the disciples might come to try to steal the body and then claim a resurrection, throwing the crowds into greater turmoil by "this last deception" than when he previously "deceived" them with his words and works (v. 64). Incidental testimony appears here as well for the almost universal Jewish belief in bodily resurrection. Matthew's unique inclusion of vv. 62-66 underlines his concern to refute the Jewish polemic against Christian claims, which persisted up to his day and which apparently troubled his community (28:15). Such an account of the origins of Christian belief continued for several centuries in Jewish circles (cf., e.g., Justin, *Dial.* 108).

The allegation that Christ's disciples stole his body thus holds the dubious honor of being the oldest alternative to faith in the risen Christ as a response to the fact of the empty tomb, even though it is one of the least plausible alternatives, in view of the subsequent events Matthew narrates. Ironically, had the disciples wanted to steal the body, they could have done so earlier. Had the Jews wanted to make their countercharge (28:13) more credible, they could have claimed that the body had been stolen before the guard arrived. Strong incidental testimony to the truth of the Christian version of the story thus appears here.[94] Against the likelihood that the disciples were in any kind of mood for such bravado, cf. John 20:19. But again it is significant that no early writer—Jew, Greek, or Roman—ever identifies a tomb in which Jesus' body remained. The whole burial scene also stresses the literal, physical death of Christ. The circumstances of his burial make quite silly the theory that he only "swooned" and then recovered in the tomb, despite serious modern attempts to defend this position.[95] Christ's burial also becomes an integral part of the gospel proclamation (cf. 1 Cor 15:4).

---

[93]On which see esp. W. L. Craig, "The Guard at the Tomb," *NTS* 30 (1984): 273-81.

[94]Cf. esp. G. M. Lee, "The Guard at the Tomb," *Theol* 72 (1969): 169-75.

[95]As classically in H. J. Schonfield, *The Passover Plot* (New York: Bantam, 1965).

[65]"Take a guard," Pilate answered. "Go, make the tomb as secure as you know how." [66]So they went and made the tomb secure by putting a seal on the stone and posting the guard.

27:65-66 The words with which Pilate grants his permission are grammatically ambiguous. They could be translated as a command, *have a guard*, making it probable that Pilate was giving the Jews temporary use of a group of Roman soldiers, or as a statement, *you have a guard*, making it more likely that he was telling the Jews to use their own temple police. The evidence is finely balanced between the two views, since the guard ultimately answers to Pilate (28:14) but first reports to the chief priests (v. 11). If the guards are Roman, it is understandable that they would tell the Jews to whom they had been delegated what happened. It seems less likely that Jewish police would be in any danger from Rome for failing to carry out their assignment. If the guard is Roman, then Pilate's ready agreement with both Joseph's and the Jewish leaders' requests probably stems from a sense of guilt and insecurity. He is trying in some small ways to atone for his previous actions but to cause no further offense.

The securing of the tomb would have involved the application to the stone of some kind of substance, perhaps a soft clay, impressed with the Roman imperial stamp. The seal would then be attached to the stone with a large rope or cord. The presence of the soldiers themselves would have been the greater deterrent to a posse trying to roll away the rock and steal the body, but the seal would have been more permanent and made grave robbing an illegal, punishable offense. The guard was presumably to be stationed only for three days (in light of v. 63).

2. Resurrection! (28:1-20)

Here is the climax of Matthew and of the gospel message. As the sequel to the crucifixion, Christ's resurrection and exaltation forms the central event of Christian history and New Testament theology (cf., e.g., Acts 2:22-36; 26:6-8; 1 Cor 15; Eph 1:15–2:10; Col 3:1-4; 1 Thess 4:13-18; Heb 1:1-4; 1 Pet 3:18-22; Rev 5).[96] Without this reversal of the ignominy of the cross, Jesus' death would have atoned for nothing. The resurrection demonstrates Christ's vindication by God, who reestablishes him in heaven as Lord of the cosmos. It is the most spectacular of all the biblical miracles and from a human perspective the most incredible of Christianity's claims. If it is false, Christians are of all people most to be pitied (1 Cor 15:19). If it is true, it guarantees the coming bodily resurrection of

---

[96]For a good study of this theme in the various New Testament writers, see J. F. Jensen, *The Resurrection of Jesus Christ in New Testament Theology* (Philadelphia: Westminster, 1980).

all believers (1 Cor 15:20-28; 2 Cor 5:1-10; 1 John 3:1-3). There is a voluminous literature on topics related to the resurrection, far beyond a simple exegesis of the text of Matthew or of any of the other Gospels, to which the reader is referred for additional discussion.[97]

a. THE EMPTY TOMB (28:1-10). Matthew's key focus in vv. 1-10 (and on into vv. 11-15) centers on the witnesses to the resurrection—the angels, the soldiers, the women, and, more indirectly, the religious leaders.[98]

¹After the Sabbath, at dawn on the first day of the week, Mary Magdalene and the other Mary went to look at the tomb.
²There was a violent earthquake, for an angel of the Lord came down from heaven and, going to the tomb, rolled back the stone and sat on it. ³His appearance was like lightning, and his clothes were white as snow. ⁴The guards were so afraid of him that they shook and became like dead men.

28:1 All four Gospels agree that very early on Sunday morning a group of women headed for the tomb. NIV's "at dawn" is perhaps too specific for what reads more literally "as the first day of the week was dawning" (TCNT). The two Marys are those mentioned in 27:61. Mark 16:1 explains the purpose of their visit: after the Sabbath had passed, they wished to anoint Jesus' body with spices to give him a more appropriate embalming. Perhaps they were hoping to talk the guard into helping them get into the tomb. Instead, the women will become the first witnesses to the resurrection, a fact that seems to guarantee the credibility of the account in a world that usually did not accept women's testimony as legally binding. Were the story fabricated, only male witnesses would have appeared. The role of the women also points to the dawning of a new age of equality among women and men in Christ (Gal 3:28).

28:2-4 This could conceivably be the same earthquake as in 27:51b-52a, if those verses are meant to be taken as concurrent with vv. 52b-53.

---

[97]On philosophical issues, see esp. P. Carnley, *The Structure of Resurrection Belief* (Oxford: Clarendon, 1987). On the theological distinctives of each Evangelist, see G. R. Osborne, *The Resurrection Narratives: A Redactional Study* (Grand Rapids: Baker, 1984). For plausible harmonizations of the four accounts, see J. Wenham, *Easter Enigma* (Grand Rapids: Zondervan, 1984). On the historical credibility of the narratives, see Blomberg, *Historical Reliability*, 100-10, and the literature there cited. For a full-blown apologetic, cf. G. Habermas, *The Resurrection of Jesus* (Grand Rapids: Baker, 1980). The most well-rounded, popular level treatment is still G. E. Ladd, *I Believe in the Resurrection of Jesus* (Grand Rapids: Eerdmans, 1975); at a more scholarly level, cf. M. J. Harris, *Raised Immortal* (Grand Rapids: Eerdmans, 1985); and *idem, From Grave to Glory* (Grand Rapids: Zondervan, 1990). The most thorough liberal study is P. Perkins, *Resurrection* (London: G. Chapman, 1985). Striking Jewish testimony to the credibility of the resurrection appears in P. Lapide, *The Resurrection of Jesus* (Minneapolis: Augsburg, 1983).

[98]S. D. Toussaint, *Behold the King: A Study of Matthew* (Portland: Multnomah, 1980), 315-16.

More likely, however, this is a severe aftershock following that earlier quake. NIV's "violent" is simply *great*. As before, the quake attests to the cosmic significance of the events. It probably preceded the women's arrival, since Matthew seems to link it with the coming of the angel, who is already in place when they get to the tomb (cf. Mark 16:3-4). The angel's sitting (v. 2) perhaps indicates a note of completion or triumph. The earthquake dislodges the rock but was not needed to enable Christ to be raised. Jesus' resurrection had already occurred, notwithstanding the massive stone barrier (v. 6). The resurrection itself is never described anywhere in Scripture, presumably because no one ever saw Jesus leave the tomb. The appearance of the angel in v. 3 matches similar angelic appearances which surrounded Jesus' birth, as do the words "don't be afraid" in v. 5 (cf. esp. 1:20) and combines with chaps. 1–2 to frame the whole Gospel. Mark calls the angel a "young man" (Mark 16:5). Luke adds that a second person/angel was present (Luke 24:4). Neither detail contradicts Matthew. The young man's appearance and garb are appropriately angelic: brilliant, glorious, and pure. The whole scene terrifies the guards and temporarily paralyzes them, so that they cannot intervene. The verb "shook" in v. 4 comes from the same root (*seis-*) as the "earthquake" in v. 2.

⁵The angel said to the women, "Do not be afraid, for I know that you are looking for Jesus, who was crucified. ⁶He is not here; he has risen, just as he said. Come and see the place where he lay. ⁷Then go quickly and tell his disciples: 'He has risen from the dead and is going ahead of you into Galilee. There you will see him.' Now I have told you."

28:5-7 On their arrival, the women are understandably terrified as well though delighted that the question of Mark 16:3 ("who will roll the stone away?") has been resolved. The angel reveals his understanding of their mission. They are looking for a corpse, but no body remains. Jesus is resurrected, not just spiritually alive, so that the tomb is empty. His own predictions have come true (16:21; 17:23; 20:19). Contra the NIV "he has risen," the voice of the verb *ēgerthē* is passive ("he was raised"). No text of Scripture ever speaks of Jesus as raising himself but always as being raised by God.[99] The angel's emphasis, "who was crucified" (v. 5), underlines the reality of Jesus' death. "Come and see the place" verifies that this is the correct tomb and correct location within the tomb, thus stressing that he really is alive. Verse 7 describes the fulfillment of 26:32 and commands the women to tell the Eleven to go to Galilee to see Jesus.

---

[99]John 2:19-20 is the sole possible exception. Jesus does use the active voice to speak of himself as raising the temple, which John interprets in v. 22 to refer to Christ's body. But, interestingly, in that verse, as the interpretation is given, the passive voice reappears.

This does not preclude other earlier resurrection appearances, as described in Luke 24 and John 20, but does prepare the way for his appearance "up north" following the end of the week-long festival of Unleavened Bread, when the Galilean pilgrims would return home.[100] During this appearance, Jesus commissioned his disciples for their future ministry; herein lies Matthew's particular interest.

⁸So the women hurried away from the tomb, afraid yet filled with joy, and ran to tell his disciples. ⁹Suddenly Jesus met them. "Greetings," he said. They came to him, clasped his feet and worshiped him. ¹⁰Then Jesus said to them, "Do not be afraid. Go and tell my brothers to go to Galilee; there they will see me."

28:8-10   The women begin to do as they are told. "Hurried away" translates *went away quickly* and matches the command "go quickly" of v. 7. Their emotions understandably mix fear and joy. Mark 16:8, if the original ending of Mark, refers to a temporary state and presupposes knowledge of subsequent behavior that would include the women's joy and the proclamation of their message. En route to the city, they see Jesus himself, who gives them a cheery greeting (like our *hello*). Their extraordinary response reflects a posture and attitude of utter worship and testifies to the bodily nature of Christ's resurrection. Jesus repeats very closely the words of the angel in vv. 5 and 7. But he now calls the disciples his "brothers," the only such place in the Gospels (but cf. Rom 8:29 and Heb 2:11), disclosing keen psychological insight. Not only does he show himself as still loving and accepting those who had abandoned him, but he even treats them as equals! In other words, they remain laborers with him in the work of the Father.[101] Jesus is neither denying his uniqueness nor deifying the disciples. But he is portraying the church as a brotherhood that manifests more equality than hierarchy, even if some functional differentiation between leaders and followers is clear from other Scriptures (e.g., 1 Pet 5:1-5; Heb 13:17).

¹¹While the women were on their way, some of the guards went into the city and reported to the chief priests everything that had happened. ¹²When the chief priests had met with the elders and devised a plan, they gave the soldiers a large sum of money, ¹³telling them, "You are to say, 'His disciples came during the night and stole him away while we were asleep.' ¹⁴If this report gets to the governor, we will satisfy him and keep you out of trouble." ¹⁵So the soldiers took the money and did as they were instructed. And this story has been widely circulated among the Jews to this very day.

---

[100]See esp. C. F. D. Moule, "The Post-Resurrection Appearances in the Light of Festival Pilgrimages," *NTS* 4 (1957-58): 58-61.

[101]Cf. Ridderbos, *Matthew*, 550.

b. THE GUARDS' REPORT (28:11-15). **28:11-15** We resume the narrative thread of 27:62-66 and 28:4.[102] After the women depart, at least some of the guards are able to move about normally again. They go back into town and first tell the priests what has happened (v. 11). As noted under 27:65, these are probably Roman soldiers, temporarily delegated to do the Jewish leaders' bidding.[103] These leaders decide to bribe the soldiers with a considerable amount of money ("large sum of" in v. 12 translates *enough*) to lie to their superiors. The excuse they are to give is the very one which the guard was designed to prevent in the first place (v. 13). Admitting that they had slept on their watch could have proved fatal. But the priests recognize this danger and promise, euphemistically, to *persuade* Pilate (v. 14, "satisfy") to keep them out of trouble, presumably again with a big enough payoff. Practices that set in motion Jesus' execution—paying Judas with thirty pieces of silver—are simply continuing and escalating. The soldiers accept the proposal, and the lie continues to circulate even in Matthew's time (v. 15; recall comments under 27:64). Bruner notes: "The great enemies of the gospel in this paragraph are (1) a lying leadership, and in their hands, (2) much money."[104]

[16] Then the eleven disciples went to Galilee, to the mountain where Jesus had told them to go.
[17] When they saw him, they worshiped him; but some doubted.

c. THE GREAT COMMISSION (28:16-20).[105] **28:16** We skip ahead a few weeks to the only other event Matthew chooses to include in his Gospel. This short account contains the culmination and combination of all of Matthew's central themes: (1) the move from particularism to universalism in the preaching of the gospel of the kingdom; (2) discipleship and the establishment of the church; (3) Jesus' commands as ultimately incumbent on Christians; and (4) the abiding presence of Jesus as teacher, as divine Son of God, and the risen and sovereign Lord of the universe.

The disciples, minus Judas, are back in Galilee, at least a week after the resurrection (cf. John 20:26 with 21:1) and quite possibly closer to the

---

[102] On the sharp contrast between 27:57-60,62-66; 28:2-4,11-15 and the rest of Matthew 27:55–28:20, see J. P. Heil, "The Narrative Structure of Matthew 27:55–28:20," *JBL* 110 (1991): 419-38.

[103] Ibid., 551.

[104] Bruner, *Churchbook*, 1088.

[105] Much has been written on the form and genre of this passage, but beyond the loose identification of it as a "commissioning narrative," we must admit its relative uniqueness. For representative literature, cf. B. J. Malina, "The Literary Structure and Form of Matt. XXVIII.16-20," *NTS* 17 (1970-71): 87-103; B. J. Hubbard, *The Matthean Redaction of a Primitive Apostolic Commissioning: An Exegesis of Matthew 28:16-20* (Missoula: Scholars, 1974); G. Friedrich, "Die formale Struktur von Mt 28,18-20," *ZTK* 80 (1983): 137-83.

end of the forty-day period of his appearances (cf. Acts 1:3-9). Their climactic commissioning takes place at "the mountain" (or *the hill country*), recalling the setting of the Sermon on the Mount (5:1) and "the mountain" as a place of revelation and communion with God throughout Matthew (cf. 4:8; 14:23; 15:29; 17:1; 24:3; 26:30). They are in "Galilee" because Galilee is home but perhaps also because it is Galilee "of the Gentiles" (4:15). As in his life so also in his resurrection, Jesus anticipates the ministry of the gospel expanding beyond the boundaries of Judaism. The Book of Acts dramatically describes the expansion of this fledgling sect. "Where Jesus had told them to go" apparently refers to more details of the conversation in v. 10 than Matthew recorded there.

28:17 The disciples' response of worship, like that of the women in v. 9, strikes us as appropriate. "But some doubted" raises questions. Is this a different group than those who worshiped? Was a larger gathering than just the Eleven present? What kind of "doubt" does Matthew have in mind? The latter question is more easily answerable. *Distazō* refers more to hesitation than to unbelief.[106] Perhaps, as elsewhere, something about Jesus' appearance makes him hard to recognize at first. Perhaps they fear how he may respond to them. Perhaps their Jewish scruples are still questioning the propriety of full-fledged worship of anyone but Yahweh.[107] Or (most likely?) they may simply continue to exhibit an understandable confusion about how to behave in the presence of a supernaturally manifested, exalted, and holy being. There is no clear evidence that more than the Eleven were present, but the particular grammatical construction *hoi de* ("but some") does seem to imply a change of subject from the previous clause ("they worshiped him").[108] So "they" probably means *some of the Eleven*, while "some" means *the rest of the eleven*. Some of the disciples worshiped Jesus at once; some were less sure how to react.[109]

18 **Then Jesus came to them and said, "All authority in heaven and on earth has been given to me.**
19 **Therefore go and make disciples of all nations, baptizing them in the name of the Father and of the Son and of the Holy Spirit,**
20 **and teaching them to obey everything I have commanded you. And surely I am with you always, to the very end of the age."**

---

[106]See esp. I. P. Ellis, "'But Some Doubted,'" *NTS* 14 (1967-68): 574-80.

[107]Cf. L. G. Parkhurst, "Matthew 28:16-20 Reconsidered," *ExpTim* 90 (1979): 179-80.

[108]K. L. McKay, "The Use of *hoi de* in Matthew 28.17: A Response to K. Grayston," *JSNT* 24 (1985): 71-72; contra K. Grayston, "The Translation of Matthew 28.17," *JSNT* 21 (1984): 105-9.

[109]See esp. P. W. van der Horst, "Once More: The Translation of οἱ δέ in Matthew 28.17," *JSNT* 27 (1986): 27-30.

28:18 Verses 18-20 bring us to the climax and conclusion of Matthew. Jesus is passing the torch to his disciples, even as he promises to be with them forever—spiritually, not physically—to empower them for future mission. Jesus can make the claim of v. 18 only if he is fully God, inasmuch as the whole universe is embraced in the authority delegated to him. And yet he is still in some sense distinct from his Heavenly Father, so that Matthew can use the divine passive in speaking of his having "been given" this authority. Clear allusions to the heavenly Son of Man figure of Dan 7:13-14 appear here. Christ's exaltation, as the result of his resurrection, means that one day "every knee" will bow and "every tongue confess that Jesus Christ is Lord" (Phil 2:9-11), whether or not they do so voluntarily as part of his redeemed people. Because of this authority, Jesus has the right to issue his followers their "marching orders," but he also has the ability to help them carry out those orders.

28:19a The main command of Christ's commission is "make disciples" (*mathēteusate*). Too much and too little have often been made of this observation. Too much is made of it when the disciples' "going" is overly subordinated, so that Jesus' charge is to proselytize merely where one is. Matthew frequently uses "go" as an introductory circumstantial participle that is rightly translated as coordinate to the main verb—here "Go and make" (cf. 2:8; 9:13; 11:4; 17:27; 28:7). Too little is made of it when all attention is centered on the command to "go," as in countless appeals for missionary candidates, so that foreign missions are elevated to a higher status of Christian service than other forms of spiritual activity. To "make disciples *of all nations*" does require many people to leave their homelands, but Jesus' main focus remains on the task of all believers to duplicate themselves wherever they may be. The verb "make disciples" also commands a kind of evangelism that does not stop after someone makes a profession of faith. The truly subordinate participles in v. 19 explain what making disciples involves: "baptizing" them and "teaching" them obedience to all of Jesus' commandments. The first of these will be a once-for-all, decisive initiation into Christian community. The second proves a perennially incomplete, life-long task.

"All nations" translates *panta ta ethnē*. The two main options for interpreting *ethnē* are *Gentiles* (non-Jews) and *peoples* (somewhat equivalent to ethnic groups). The former translation is popular among those who see either Jesus or Matthew as believing that God once-for-all rejected the Jews.[110] We have repeatedly seen evidence that calls this perspective into serious question (see under 10:23; 23:39; 24:30; 27:25). Matthew's most recent uses of *ethnē* (24:9,14; 25:32) seem to include Jews and Gentiles

---

[110]See esp. D. R. A. Hare and D. J. Harrington, "'Make Disciples of All the Gentiles' (Mt 28:19)," *CBQ* 37 (1975): 359-69.

alike as the recipients of evangelism and judgment.[111] God is not turning
his back on Jewish people here. What has changed is that they can no
longer be saved simply by trusting in God under the Mosaic covenant. All
who wish to be in fellowship with God must now come to him through
Jesus.

28:19b Without further qualification, baptism will most naturally
refer to that which John and Jesus have already practiced (see under 3:1-
17; cf. John 3:26; 4:1-3). "Them" (*autous*) shifts to the masculine pronoun from the neuter *peoples* (*ethnē*) and therefore implies a shift from
groups to individuals (as in 25:32). Hence, the missiological debate about
the validity of group conversions cannot be settled by any appeal to this
text. "In [or into] the name" means declaring allegiance to or becoming
associated with the power and authority of Jesus.[112] The singular "name"
followed by the threefold reference to "Father, Son, and Holy Spirit" suggests both unity and plurality in the Godhead. Here is the clearest Trinitarian "formula" anywhere in the Gospels, and it is therefore often
accused of being a very late development and not at all something Jesus
himself could have imagined.[113] But this view misjudges both the speed
of the development of New Testament theology (cf. Jesus as God already
in Acts 3:14-15—unless by circular reasoning this passage is also dismissed as late because of its high Christology),[114] as well as how technical a formula this is. Acts 2:38 demonstrates that other baptismal
formulae were also used in the earliest stages of Christianity. Jesus has
already spoken of God as his Father (Matt 11:27; 24:36), of himself as the
Son (11:27; 16:27; 24:36), and of blasphemy against God's work in himself as against the Spirit (12:28). Mounce states, "That Jesus should
gather together into summary form his own references . . . in his final
charge to the disciples seems quite natural."[115] On the other hand, it is
not inconceivable that Matthew distilled the essence of Jesus' more
detailed parting instructions for the Eleven into concise language using
the terminology developed later in the early church's baptismal services.
As R. E. O. White reflects: "If Jesus commanded the making of disciples
and the baptizing of them 'in my name,' and Matt. expressed Christ's fullest meaning (for disciples 'of all nations') by using the fuller description

---

[111]See esp. J. P. Meier, "Nations and Gentiles in Matthew 28:19?" *CBQ* 39 (1977): 94-
102.

[112]M'Neile (*Matthew*, 436) suggests "to the account of" or "into the possession of."

[113]See esp. J. Schaberg, *The Father, the Son, and the Holy Spirit* (Chico: Scholars,
1982); L. Abramowski, "Die Entstehung der dreigliedrigen Taufformel—ein Versuch," *ZTK*
81 (1984): 417-46.

[114]On which, see esp. R. N. Longenecker, *The Christology of Early Jewish Christianity*
(Naperville: Allenson, 1970).

[115]Mounce, *Matthew*, 277.

current in his own day, who shall say that he seriously misrepresented our Lord's intention?"[116]

28:20a Teaching obedience to all of Jesus' commands forms the heart of disciple making. Evangelism must be holistic. If non-Christians are not hearing the gospel and not being challenged to make a decision for Christ, then the church has disobeyed one part of Jesus' commission. If new converts are not faithfully and lovingly nurtured in the whole counsel of God's revelation, then the church has disobeyed the other part. Key implications for preaching appear here. There must be a balance between evangelistic proclamation and relevant exposition of all parts of God's Word, including the more difficult material best reserved for the mature (cf. 1 Cor 2:1-5 with 2:6-10). So, too, the ministries of the church overall must reflect a healthy balance of "outreach" and "inreach." Individuals who have differing gifts should be encouraged to expend most of their energies developing their strengths, whether evangelizing or nurturing, speaking or serving. Nevertheless, Jesus calls all Christians to be both witnesses and disciplers.

Jesus' words further demonstrate that Christian ethics and morality should first of all focus on Jesus' teaching, even though the Old Testament still remains relevant, as one sees how it is fulfilled in Christ (Matt 5:17-20), and even though the rest of the New Testament remains relevant as further explanation of the significance of Christ and his teachings. But the testimony of the Gospels and the commands Jesus issued (of which more are found in Matthew than in Mark, Luke, or John) must comprise the central core of Christian faith and proclamation.

28:20b Matthew closes his Gospel with Jesus' promise to be spiritually present with his followers until the end of this age, that is, until his return, when he will once again be present bodily (although "the end of the age" might be an idiom roughly equivalent to *forever*). John describes how Jesus had explained this provision in much more detail as the ministry of the Holy Spirit (John 13-17). Acts 2 will describe the decisive moment of the fulfillment of this promise at Pentecost. Matthew chooses to leave his readers here. The disciples represent everyone in the church to which he writes and, derivatively, everyone who professes to follow Christ in any age. The Lord is now risen! He calls his people to become disciple makers, and he promises to be with them irrespective of their successes or failures. Verse 20b forms an inclusio with v. 18, which indicates the central focus of Jesus' closing words. Despite the Great Commission, Matthew wants to end his Gospel centering more on Christ's attributes than on the disciples' task. Verses 18-20 link back with 1:23 to

---

[116]R. E. O. White, *The Biblical Doctrine of Initiation* (Grand Rapids: Eerdmans, 1960), 343-44.

frame the entire Gospel with references to Immanuel—*God with us*. In Jesus, God remains with us for now and eternity! What more do we need to persevere in Christian living? We must go out and obey his commission. But the final word of the Gospel remains Christ-centered. Even when we fail, he remains faithful.[117]

---

[117]On this Christological focus deriving from the framing verses of the commission (vv. 18,20), see esp. D. Hill, "The Conclusion of Matthew's Gospel: Some Literary-Critical Observations," *IBS* 8 (1986): 54-63. On the Christology of vv. 16-20 more generally, see esp. J. D. Kingsbury, "The Composition and Christology of Matt 28:16-20," *JBL* 93 (1974): 573-84.

Selected Subject Index[1]

---

[1]Indexes were prepared by Lanese Dockery.

Person Index

Scripture Index